Studies in Economic History

Series Editor
Tetsuji Okazaki, The University of Tokyo, Tokyo, Japan

Editorial Board Members
Loren Brandt, University of Toronto, Canada
Myung Soo Cha, Yeungnam University, Korea
Nicholas Crafts, University of Warwick, UK
Claude Diebolt, University of Strasbourg, France
Barry Eichengreen, University of California at Berkeley, USA
Stanley Engerman, University of Rochester, USA
Price V. Fishback, University of Arizona, USA
Avner Greif, Stanford University, USA
Tirthanker Roy, London School of Economics and Political Science, UK
Osamu Saito, Hitotsubashi University, Japan
Jochen Streb, University of Mannheim, Germany
Nikolaus Wolf, Humboldt University, Germany

Aims and Scope

This series from Springer provides a platform for works in economic history that truly integrate economics and history. Books on a wide range of related topics are welcomed and encouraged, including those in macro-economic history, financial history, labor history, industrial history, agricultural history, the history of institutions and organizations, spatial economic history, law and economic history, political economic history, historical demography, and environmental history.

Economic history studies have greatly developed over the past several decades through application of economics and econometrics. Particularly in recent years, a variety of new economic theories and sophisticated econometric techniques—including game theory, spatial economics, and generalized method of moment (GMM)—have been introduced for the great benefit of economic historians and the research community.

At the same time, a good economic history study should contribute more than just an application of economics and econometrics to past data. It raises novel research questions, proposes a new view of history, and/or provides rich documentation. This series is intended to integrate data analysis, close examination of archival works, and application of theoretical frameworks to offer new insights and even provide opportunities to rethink theories.

The purview of this new Springer series is truly global, encompassing all nations and areas of the world as well as all eras from ancient times to the present. The editorial board, who are internationally renowned leaders among economic historians, carefully evaluate and judge each manuscript, referring to reports from expert reviewers. The series publishes contributions by university professors and others well established in the academic community, as well as work deemed to be of equivalent merit.

More information about this series at http://www.springer.com/series/13279

Stephan Barisitz

Central Asia and the Silk Road

Economic Rise and Decline over Several Millennia

Springer

Stephan Barisitz
Vienna, Austria

ISSN 2364-1797   ISSN 2364-1800   (electronic)
Studies in Economic History
ISBN 978-3-319-51212-9   ISBN 978-3-319-51213-6   (eBook)
DOI 10.1007/978-3-319-51213-6

Library of Congress Control Number: 2017935008

Printed on acid-free paper

This Springer imprint is published by Springer Nature
The registered company is Springer International Publishing AG
The registered company address is: Gewerbestrasse 11, 6330 Cham, Switzerland

Acknowledgements

I am grateful for numerous comments and suggestions to two anonymous referees, to Andreas Kappeler (Professor emeritus, Institute of Eastern European History, University of Vienna) and Peer Vries (Professor, Institute for Economic and Social History, University of Vienna), Florian Schwarz (Director, Institute of Iranian Studies, Austrian Academy of Sciences), and Olena Lytvyn (Ukrainian State University of Finance and International Trade). The design of the historico-economic maps in this book benefited from the technical expertise of Florian Partl (cartographer, author of the Atlas of the Danubian Countries, technical direction of the Atlas of Eastern and Southeastern Europe), which is much appreciated. Many thanks also go to my employer, the Oesterreichische Nationalbank, and more particularly to Doris Ritzberger-Grünwald (Director, Economic Analysis and Research Department) as well as to Helene Schuberth (Head, Foreign Research Division) for their support. Finally, without the steadfast encouragement from my wife Françoise this book would not have been possible.

Contents

About the Author

Stephan Barisitz is senior economist in the Foreign Research Division of the Oesterreichische Nationalbank (OeNB, Austria's central bank), Vienna, and economic historian. He joined the OeNB in December 1998 and focuses on country research and monitoring of Russia, Ukraine, and other former Soviet republics, notably Central Asian countries, as well as on banking and financial sector analysis. He has written almost a hundred articles, many of them in refereed journals, and is coauthor of a forthcoming study on the New Silk Road. In 2008, Stephan passed his habilitation exam in economic history at the Vienna University of Economics and Business (WU Wien). His habilitation thesis deals with banking transformation in Eastern Europe and Central Asia from communism to capitalism (1980–2006), a book published by Routledge in 2008. He has been lecturer at the Institute for Economic and Social History from 2009 to 2013.

Before coming back to Vienna in 1998, Stephan worked for 3 years as an economist at the OECD in Paris, where, together with a colleague, he was in charge of the Russia-CIS-Bulgaria Desk of the OECD Economics Department. Before that he was from 1992 to 1995 with the Austrian Institute for East and South-East European Studies (OSI), Vienna, responsible for economic research and editing of the institution's publications. Stephan had started out his career as an economist at the Vienna Institute for International Economic Studies (wiiw) back in 1986—i.e., still 3 years before the fall of the Berlin Wall. Stephan had studied economics at the University of Innsbruck, Austria, and, after a research stay at Carleton University, Ottawa, Canada, passed his doctorate in 1986.

List of Tables and Boxes

List of Maps

Central Asia (CA) and the Silk Road (SR): Definitions and Traits

1.1 Motivation and Structure of This Work

Central Asia's manifold geography and peoples and its most colorful economic history—ranging from the incubation of horseback nomadism via the emergence of the Silk Road, the eruption of the largest empire of world history, to large-scale centrally planned development efforts, followed by market-oriented reintegration into the world economy by export-led growth strategies—have fascinated the author. Upon looking into Central Asia's past prior to the European colonial conquest, one soon discovers that the region's economic history is intimately linked to cycles of Silk Road commerce and often even dominated by the latter. The strength of the influence of the Silk Road, running through the heart of the region, on Central Asia's prosperity suggests widening the view to also include systematic investigation of this major traditional network of overland trade routes. This implies that the Silk Road and its ups and downs are seen in this study as the most important—but not the only—determinant of Central Asia's economic fortunes in premodern times. Others, e.g., steppe nomadism, political and religious factors, maritime trade competition, and climate change, also play essential roles and therefore must also be factored in.

The goal of writing a detailed synthetic study on the economic history of Central Asia (CA) and the Silk Road (SR) is justified in the view of the author by the lack of such a publication today and by the need to fill this void, given the economic importance and rising strategic significance of this region. In order to understand contemporary realities and interconnections in this geographic heart of Eurasia—surrounded by economic powerhouses or large promising players like China, India, Iran, Turkey, Russia, and the European Union—it certainly appears important to carefully take stock of the region's economic evolution. What is more, CA cannot but be an integral or pivotal part of any new initiatives or schemes to create a modern "Silk Road" integrating the largest of all continents.

There certainly exist a number of publications dealing with the general history of CA (in various regional definitions) or focusing on the SR (sometimes limited to relatively short periods) or other important phenomena—like the nomadic way of life in Eurasia, the Mongol Empire, Tamerlane, and Chinese or Russian colonialism in the area—in a general historical way. The author, an economist and economic historian, carries out *synthetic* scientific coverage of existing literature—from an *economic* perspective. The focus is on surveying and analyzing a large number of economic and economically relevant noneconomic factors (climatic, technological, military, political, structural, institutional, cultural, religious, social, and other factors) and carefully drawing conclusions.

The field to cover for this effort is vast and stretches back beyond the beginnings of antiquity, because the phenomenon of horseback nomadism and its fundamental impact on C Asian as well as SR history up to the eighteenth century needs to be properly captured and appreciated. The region's premodern history is regarded here as its history up to its penetration and partial conquest by European—in this case Russian—colonialism, which definitely put an end to SR activities (at least if we define them in a traditional sense). The wealth of material the author has consulted and the several millennia of economic history surveyed enable us to arrive at some new conclusions or interpretations on the causes and the periodization of the ups and downs of economic prosperity in CA and along the SR.

Another novelty that demarcates this study from others is the 20 historico-economic maps of the region the author has drafted, which should accompany and facilitate reading. These maps cover successive periods (from the third millennium BCE to the second half of the nineteenth century CE) and include the approx. location of transport and trade routes/the SR network in and beyond CA, depending on the respective era. Three auxiliary maps preceding the above show salient geographic traits, concepts of the regional delimitation of CA, and elements of its resource

© Springer International Publishing AG 2017
S. Barisitz, *Central Asia and the Silk Road*, Studies in Economic History, DOI 10.1007/978-3-319-51213-6_1

endowment. The spatial depiction of the SR network in past centuries may be interesting to compare with the location of current schemes of a "New Silk Road" or "Silk Road Economic Belt" (promoted by China) or "Trans-Eurasian Development Corridors" (promoted by Russia) or other initiatives, as they unfold. But such a comparison is not the task of this work.

The main questions and related issues dealt with in this study are:

- *How did SR trade and business influence the economic prosperity of CA?*
  What were the heydays of the SR and which driving forces contributed to these? Which factors triggered declines of SR activity?
  When did these ups and downs approximately happen and which periods of SR trade can thus be distinguished?
- *What was the contribution of nomadic activity to the C Asian economy?*
  How did nomadic economies and polities function?
  What were the salient traits of the interaction between nomadic pastoralism and sedentary agriculture and crafts in CA?
  What impact did horseback nomads' long-lasting military superiority have on economic relations with settled cultures and the functioning of the SR?
- *What were the economic bases of the Mongol and Tamerlan Empires?*
  How important were SR revenues for these giant states, and how important were other sources, including predatory taxation of subjugated populations?
- *What explains CA's and the SR's long-lasting economic downward trend from the sixteenth century, which ended in a slide into colonialism?*
  In the meantime, was there a temporary regional recovery, and if this was the case, what were the promoting factors?
- *What were the principal differences between China's and Russia's economic policies toward their C Asian colonies in the eighteenth to nineteenth centuries?*

The structure of this work is as follows: Chapter 1 provides information on and discusses definitions and borders of CA, its regional geography, and economic potential. Definitions and salient traits of the SR are also dealt with. As alluded to above, in dealing with premodern CA—the region prior to the penetration of European (Russian) colonialism in the nineteenth century—it appears requisite to accommodate an extensive time frame. As to the choice of starting point of this study, given that a key tenet is to capture and understand the emergence of horseback nomadism in the region and the conditions preceding and conducive to this major civilizational change, it is felt necessary to go back relatively

far in economic history (to about 5000 BCE). In this way the attempt is made to find explanations for momentous developments that already left their imprints on sedentary civilizations and trade routes of early antiquity and continued to do so almost until the break of modernity.

The main part of the study is chronologically structured in three detailed chapters, which reflect major institutional breaks/changes related to C Asian economic/SR development.[1] Chapter 2 analyzes developments up to the establishment and first heyday of the SR in the era of the Han dynasty and the Roman Empire (ca. 5000 BCE to 350 CE), including the emergence of horseback nomadism and warfare. Chapter 3 deals with dynamics leading up to the pinnacle of nomadic power (ca. 350 to 1350 CE), which include the second and third heyday of the SR; the second heyday happened in the period of the Islamic Caliphate and of Tang China, and the third one was organized by the Mongol Empire. Chapter 4 retraces and studies the (first relative, then absolute) economic decline and eventual takeover of C Asian civilizations by outsiders (ca. 1350 to 1885): First the region and its economic artery, the SR, moved from the heart to the periphery of the world economy, and then (after 1750) it headed for colonization by its ever more powerful sedentary neighbors. The how and why of these developments are explained.

Apart from the abovementioned maps, reading is further facilitated by Table 3.1 (on the ups and downs of the SR and reasons for those) and by 14 boxes focusing on salient topics (e.g., aspects of the SR, of nomadism and the nomadic economy, the "gunpowder revolution" and its impact on CA, comparative settler colonialism in the east and west) that cut through or are outside the chronological setup. Chapter 5 finally summarizes major points of the study and draws some conclusions.

1.2   Definitions and Borders of Central Asia

The idea of Central Asia (CA) as a distinct region of the world was introduced by the German geographer Alexander von Humboldt in the mid-nineteenth century. Another geographer, Ferdinand von Richthofen, toward the end of the nineteenth century, defined CA as a large intracontinental area lacking water drainage toward the oceans.[2] This view still makes sense today, since remoteness from the oceans

---

[1] Given available data and sources, any other than a chronological structuring of the study does not seem sufficiently feasible or attractive to the reader.

[2] von Richthofen: Über die zentralasiatischen Seidenstraßen bis zum 2. Jh. n. Chr., in: Verhandlungen der Gesellschaft für Erdkunde zu Berlin 1877, 96–122.

and scarcity of water remain decisive structural and partly limitational elements which mold societal and economic development in the region. As Map 1.1 shows, this clear physical conception of CA includes territories surrounding the world's largest lake, the Caspian Sea, and the extensive lowlands lying east, including the Turanian Plain to the south and the Kazakh Uplands (Saryarka) to the north. Moving further east and south, Turanian Plain and Kazakh Uplands border on a string of mountain ranges running from the Iranian Plateau via the Hindu Kush, Pamir, Karakorum, Tienshan to the Altai Mountains. Crossing the Pamir, Tienshan, and Altai further east, one arrives in vast territories that are generally at a higher elevation, and endorheic/lacking in drainage is drained internally. These territories comprise the Tarim Basin, the Plateau of Tibet, the Dzungarian plain, and the Gobi desert plateau. Accordingly, some geographers call these territories east of Pamir, Tienshan and Altai "High Asia" or "Inner Asia" (Machatschek 1928, 141; Breghel 2003, vii).

Apart from Richthofen's physical geographic definition of CA, there are also politico-cultural definitions. The currently most often used definition limits itself to the joint territory of the five former Soviet republics of Kazakhstan, Kyrgyzstan (the Kyrgyz Republic), Tajikistan, Turkmenistan (Turkmenia), and Uzbekistan, which are independent countries today. They also tend to be jointly called the "Stans" and largely comprise the Turanian Plain, the Kazakh Steppe, and the Tienshan, Pamir, and Altai ranges (Maps 1.1 and 1.2). Particularly in the Soviet period, an even smaller area—namely, the four last mentioned republics—was subsumed under "Middle Asia" (Srednyaya Aziya, the southern half of the abovementioned area) (Stadelbauer 2007, 10).

On the other hand, a larger, also frequently used, definition of CA includes not just the five "Stans" but also the Chinese province of Xinjiang (Tarim Basin, eastern Tienshan, and Dzungaria, bordering the Gobi desert plateau in the east) (Breghel 2003, 2; Hambis (dir) 1977, 4). Given that the territories covered by this larger definition of CA are mostly—if far from exclusively—populated by people of Turkic origin, these areas are sometimes also referred to as "Turkestan," a label that was introduced at the end of the nineteenth century (Geiss 2009, 295).[3] Accordingly, "West Turkestan" (today a less frequently used expression) comprises the abovementioned five former Soviet republics, whereas "East Turkestan" corresponds to Chinese Xinjiang (Lacoste (dir) 1995, 1532; Le Petit Mourre 2003, 1210). This territorial subdivision of the region is identical with that pertaining to western CA and eastern CA (Biarnes 2008, 24).

An even more extensive politico-cultural definition of CA which also surpasses Richthofen's view is to add to the five "Stans" and Xinjiang (as shown in Map 1.1): parts of Siberia, Afghanistan, northern Pakistan, northeastern Iran, the Russian Republics of Tatarstan, Bashkortostan, Russian northern Caucasus, and Kalmykia, the Transcaucasian Republics, Tibet, Qinghai, Mongolia, Chinese Inner Mongolia, and parts of Manchuria (Fragner 2006, 11).

For the purposes of this study, the "medium-sized" definition (Kazakhstan, Kyrgyzstan, Tajikistan, Turkmenistan, Uzbekistan, Xinjiang) is chosen. Depending on historical periods, parts of northeastern Iran, northern Afghanistan, parts of the Chinese province of Gansu (which functions as a corridor, also called Hexi Corridor, between China proper and Xinjiang), and a small slice of southeastern Russia and Siberia (including abovementioned Tatarstan, Bashkortostan, and other territories on the middle and lower reaches of the Volga) may also enter the picture. This territorial frame is chosen for historico-economic reasons, as it is felt that too narrow a focus—e.g., only comprising the "Stans"—would be too exclusively oriented toward the present and the most recent past and would not sufficiently take into account historical relationships as well as an open future. For instance, Silk Road connections were of eminent importance on both sides of the Tienshan and the Karakorum for many centuries. However, taking even more regions on board, along the lines of the abovementioned extensive definition, would move too far away from the vital SR economic network. It would moreover go beyond the capacity of the author and compromise the overall quality of the result. In any case, proceeding from the "medium-sized" definition, the numerous interactions with other regions will be treated in the detail they merit, where necessary.

Taking a second look at CA, one could actually argue in favor of relabeling it "Central Eurasia," given that the region is not unambiguously in the center of Asia but at least partly situated at the continent's northwestern fringes. Adding Europe to Asia and taking the double-continent Eurasia as a term of reference would change the situation. The western part of CA is Europe's direct neighbor; yet the centrality of the eastern part (Xinjiang) to the Asian continent cannot be denied. In any case, we will keep with conventions and not change the label for the above-defined region. Thus, CA occupies a "central position" between the homelands of Europe, Russia, Iran, India, and China (Cummings 2012, 31).

CA at times certainly caught people's imagination and focused minds. From the traditional perspective of surrounding "advanced civilizations," CA has tended to appear in each case as a sprawling unwieldy hinterland, a common residuum, and a partly empty space separating these civilizations as much as connecting them. However,

---

[3] This is so even though the majority of people of Turkic origin live outside Turkestan.

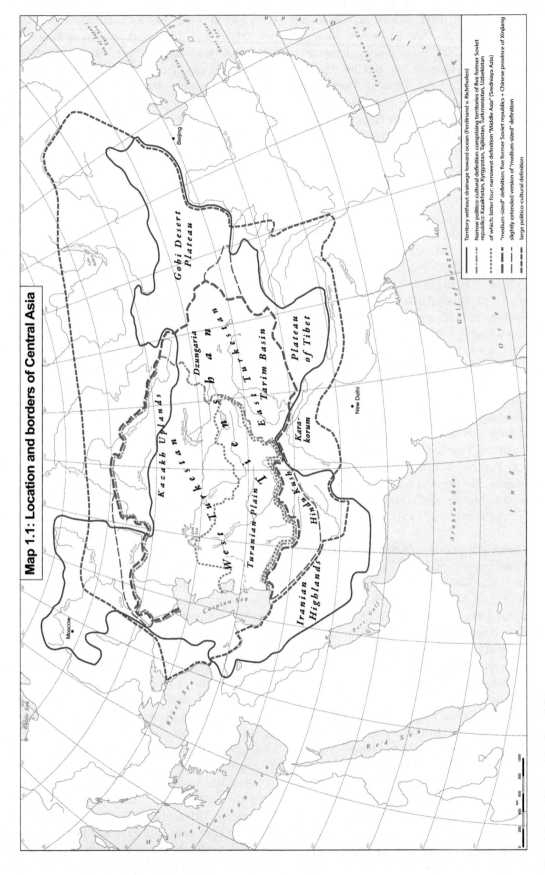

Map 1.1   Location and borders of CA

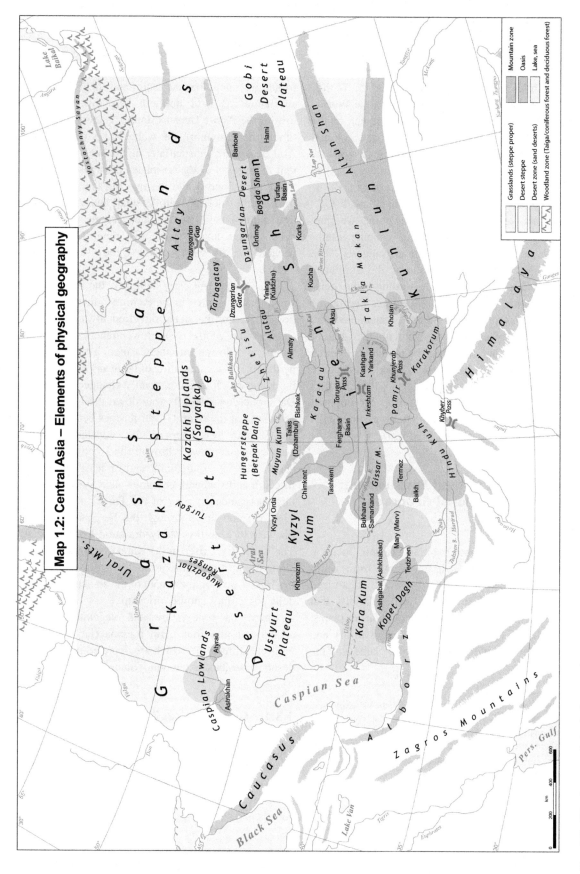

Map 1.2 CA: elements of physical geography

there were also complementary views. The British geographer John Halford Mackinder (1861–1947) referred to the region (not necessarily in line with the above-chosen definition) as the "Heartland" of the "World-Island," the Afro-Eurasian landmass. He produced the simple geopolitical formula: "Who rules the Heartland, commands the World-Island. Who rules the World-Island, commands the World" (Mackinder 1904). This, of course, has to be seen in the context of the "Great Game," the CA-focused colonial rivalry between the British and Russian Empires as well as, in some instances, China, in the nineteenth century (see also below), when the region featured among the last parts of the globe is yet to be carved up by the European colonialists.[4]

Maintaining the colonial-imperial viewpoint, we may consider geopolitics of the steppe as bearing some resemblance to geopolitics of the sea, as Chauprade suggests: "The history of Gengis Khan's empire shows the similarity between steppe and sea imperialism. According to the imperial logic of the grasslands, unlimited pastures permit the development of mass breeding of cattle which feeds an important number of warriors who act with the goal of conquering more land and enlarging the domain of animal husbandry. As it constitutes, like the sea, an extensive space essentially unbridled by natural obstacles, the steppe is indivisible. The steppe calls for hegemony. Thus the imperial logic of the Mongol empire can be compared with that of the British thalassocracy" (Chauprade 2003, 169).

1.3 Central Asian Natural Environment: Synopsis of Regional Geography and Resources[5]

Given its scarcity of water and its intracontinental location cutoff by mountainous barriers to the south from warm humid winds from the Indian Ocean, CA is characterized by an extreme continental climate as well as aridity that increases from north to south and from mountains to plains. The region features a high thermal amplitude with dry and hot summers and cold winters. The aridity explains why the

Central Asian plains naturally feature very few trees. While considerable amounts of precipitation can fall on the mountain slopes, this tends to be highly irregular. All Central Asian rivers are of inland drainage (true to Richthofen's view of the area), except for the Irtysh river and its tributaries, including the Ishim and the Tobol, which drain substantial parts of northern Kazakhstan and Dzungaria toward the Arctic Ocean (Maps 1.1 and 1.2). In prehistoric times (the diluvium), the water levels of the Caspian and Aral Seas were substantially higher than they are today, so that large parts of the Caspian Lowlands and the Turanian plain were flooded and the two big lakes were connected, forming the ancient Aralo-Caspian Sea. A strait of water to the south of the Ustyurt Plateau connected the two lakes. When water levels sank, this connection dried up and became the dry valley of the Uzboy (Machatschek 1928, 145).

Later on, during early antiquity, the Amu Daria river—which has its source in the Pamir Mountains[6] and generally flows in a northwesterly direction toward the Aral Sea—changed the course of its lower reaches, took the Uzboy valley, and flowed into the Caspian. This can be explained by the river's accumulation of large amounts of sediments in its delta, which thus continually changed, so that the Amu Daria one day found its way down the Uzboy valley. This switching of the river's lower reaches between the Aral and the Caspian Seas happened on repeated occasions; most notably, water flowed through the Uzboy in the early thirteenth, the late fourteenth, and at least partly during the fifteenth and sixteenth centuries. The Syr Daria, the second large steppe/desert river of the Turanian plain, rises in the Tienshan and flows through the Ferghana Basin and then likewise in a northwesterly direction toward the Aral Sea. The Tarim river rises in the Karakorum and flows eastward along the northern side of the Tarim Basin to the "wandering" lake Lop Nor (a remnant of the ancient Lop Sea), whose delta sometimes entirely dries up.

Based on topography and vegetation, CA can be subdivided into four main regions (largely running in a west-east direction), which are depicted in Map 1.2: steppe, desert, oases, and mountains (Stadelbauer 2007, 11).

1.3.1 Geographical Zones

The steppe zone lies north of the Caspian Sea, between the Caspian and the Aral Sea, then north of the Aral Sea and the Syr Daria, north of Lake Balkhash, and along the upper reaches of the Irtysh river in northern Dzungaria. The steppe zone is part of the great Eurasian steppe belt stretching more

---

[4] The American journalist and academic Nicholas Spykman (1893–1943) disagreed with Mackinder's geopolitical concept and emphasized that control not of the Heartland, but of the coastlands or, as he called them, the Rimland, was pivotal to global hegemony (Spykman 1942/2007). For a comparison of Mackinder's and Spykman's views, see Barral 2015, 205–209).

[5] While going through this subchapter and its topographic names, which may appear exotic to many, the reader is recommended to pick up an atlas of physical and economic geography and to consult its Central Asia pages or to take a look at the two following maps (Maps 1.2 and 1.3). A minimum degree of familiarity with the geography of CA is a conditio sine qua non for understanding the (economic) history of the region.

---

[6] The uppermost reaches of the Amu Daria are called Piandzh.

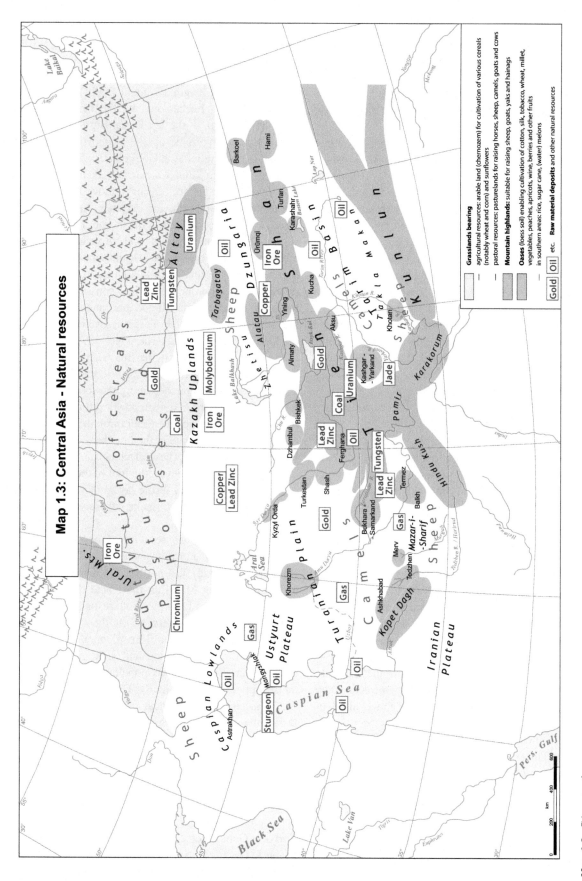

Map 1.3   CA: natural resources

than 8000 km from Manchuria in the east via Outer and Inner Mongolia all the way to southern Ukraine and Hungary in the west. According to Perdue, the steppe consists of three subzones running in an east-west direction (Perdue 2005, 19): the forest steppe in the north, the pure grasslands (steppe proper), and the desert steppe in the south. These three zones witness declining precipitation and vegetation from north to south.

Central Asia hardly touches the forest steppe (which is more common in southern Siberia and adjoins the forests of the taiga), but features extensive grasslands and desert steppes. The grasslands partly boast fertile black earth (chernozem). Very approximately, the 48th or 49th degree latitude separates the steppe proper from the desert steppe (see Chuvin et al. 2008: Histoire de l'Asie centrale…, 31), which implies that the northern parts of the Caspian Lowlands, of the Turgay valley, and of the Kazakh Uplands (Saryarka) are predominantly grasslands (Map 1.2). Extensive regions in the south, including the Ustyurt Plateau and the Hunger steppe (Betpak-Dala, located between the Syr Darya, the Chu river, and Lake Balkhash), make up the desert steppe. The "Kazakh Steppe" (an older name is "Desht-i-Kipchak") is understood to account for most of the C Asian grasslands and even for part of the desert steppe.

The desert zone follows further south. It consists of three large sand deserts: the Kara Kum (Turkish for "black sands"), situated between the Kopet Dagh mountains (at the northeastern fringe of the Iranian Plateau) and the Amu Daria; the Kyzyl Kum ("red sands"), between lower Amu Daria and Syr Daria; and the Taklamakan (literally, "the place where he who goes in does not come out", Waugh 2008, 5), filling out the Tarim Basin. A number of smaller sand deserts border the desert steppe north of the Tienshan.

While the oasis zone is somewhat sandwiched between the desert and the mountains, it is easier to explain by first focusing on the mountain zone. As already pointed out, mountain ranges constitute CA's natural boundaries to the south and also subdivide the region in a south-west north-eastern direction. First proceeding along CA's southern bounds from the west to the east: the Kopet Dagh (from where the Iranian Highlands fall off into the Turanian Lowlands)[7], the Hindu Kush (highest peaks above 5000 m), the Karakorum (highest peaks above 8000 m, blocking or enabling access to the Indian subcontinent), and the Kun Lun (highest peaks above 7000 m, bordering the plateau of Tibet).

As can be seen in Map 1.2, the strings of mountain ranges separating West Turkestan from East Turkestan or western

CA from eastern CA are the Pamirs, the Tienshan (both reaching heights above 7000 m and enclosing various endorheic or drainage-less areas, e.g., the Issyk Koel Lake), the Alatau, the Tarbagatay, and the Altai (above 4000 m). The Tienshan is a far-flung mountain chain boasting a total length of about 2000 km and featuring foothills running further out into the Turanian Plain, e.g., the Karatau, north of the Syr Daria. High-interrupted ridges (e.g., Bogdashan) make up the eastern extremities of the Tienshan, running into the Gobi plateau. While it is difficult to cross the Kun Lun, Karakorum, Pamir, and Tienshan, given their altitudes, it is easier to move from East to West Turkestan further north, for instance, passing through the Dzungarian Gate, between Alatau and Tarbagatay, or traversing the (relatively wide) Dzungarian gap, along the upper reaches of the Irtysh (Machatschek 1928, 156). The Southern Ural Mountains, although located just outside CA, do constitute a border area. The open space between their foothills, including the Mugodzhar range to the south, and the north shore of the Caspian provided a "gateway" (in German: "Völkertor", Hassinger 1931, 104) of potentially uninhibited access to the European continent from the East, which bore far-reaching historic implications.

The oasis zone stretches along the foot of the mountain ranges and along the bed of steppe/desert rivers. These areas receive abundant supply of water through mountain streams, many of which originate in the big glaciers of the Tienshan, Pamir, or Karakorum. These glaciers can function as veritable water towers. Moreover, the foot of the mountain ranges often tends to bear very fertile layers of yellow loess soil— the loess zone— which makes these oases particularly attractive for settlement.

To enumerate some oases north of the Kopet Dagh, Hindu Kush, and Tienschan, from west to east (Map 1.2): Ashgabat (former Ashkhabad), just north of the Kopet Dagh; Tedzhen and Mary (former Merv), at the inland deltas of the rivers Tedzhen/Harirud and Murgab, both rising in the Hindu Kush; Termez-Balkh-Mazar-e Sharif, on the upper Amu Daria; Bukhara, Samarkand, and Karshi, on the Zeravshan and Kashka Daria rivers flowing out of the southern Tienshan; the Ferghana Basin, a large, populous, and very fertile oasis on the upper reaches of the Syr Daria, enclosed by chains of the Tienshan; Tashkent, near the middle course of the Syr Daria (the oasis has the historic name of Shash); followed further down the river by Shimkent and Turkestan (on the southern flanks of the Karatau); heading further east along the northern edge of the Tienshan, Taraz (Dzhambul), on the Talas river; then Bishkek, on the Chu river; Almaty, near the middle course of the Ili river; Yining (Kuldzha), on the upper course of the Ili; Urumqi (southern Dzungaria); and Barkoel (Gobi desert). The Zhetysu or Semirechie (Land of Seven Rivers) is broadly understood to consist of the lower reaches of the Ili valley, including the oasis of Almaty and the

---

[7] The Kopet Dagh's extension to the Caspian Sea is made up by the higher and the lower Balkhan Mountains, between which the Uzboy/Amu Daria at times reached the Caspian.

valleys of other rivers flowing from the Tienshan, Alatau, and Tarbagatay through desert-like terrain into Lake Balkhash.

To add some oases south of the Tienshan/in the Tarim Basin, from west to east: Kashgar, Yarkand, Aqsu, Kucha, and Korla/Karashahr, all located on tributaries of the Tarim river; Turfan, in a depression (the Turfan Basin), 154 m below sea level; and Hami (the Hami Basin). One more oasis in the Tarim Basin should be mentioned: Khotan, equally lying on a tributary of the Tarim river but in the south, at the foothills of the Karakorum and Kun Lun. Amu Daria and Syr Daria are major rivers that cut through the desert and therefore give rise to river oases in the midst of "hostile" terrain: this goes particularly for the large and ancient Khorezm (or Khwarazm) oasis on the lower reaches of Amu Daria, an oasis which throughout history has tended to be somewhat isolated from its neighbors. Kyzylorda on the middle course of the Syr Daria is also worth mentioning. To complete the picture, the lowest reaches of the Volga and Ural rivers likewise cut through desert-like territory, which would argue for including Astrakhan and Atyrau on the fringe of the C Asian belt of oases.

1.3.2 Resources and Economic Potential

Following the chosen definition, Central Asia comprises a territory of 5.64 mn km^2 and a total population of about 90.9 mn (2015, partly projected).[8] This corresponds to a relatively low overall density of population (about 16 inhabitants per km^2), which is understandable due to abovementioned factors of topography and climate.

Water is of paramount importance in the region: Against the background of CA's extremely arid climate, the availability of this resource in mountainous terrain is by far not sufficient to compensate for the scarcity of water in large flat parts of the region. Therefore water is certainly the most important natural resource in need in CA, a treasure whose prudent management would seem pivotal. Water availability and scarcity has been a determinant factor in the development of local civilizations. Given overutilization of water of the Syr Daria and the Amu Daria for purposes of production growth, in just over half a century since 1960, the Aral Sea's surface has shrunk to a tiny fraction of its past size. The Aral Sea as an economic resource may all but vanish in the future. Notwithstanding that calamity (see also below), CA's mountain ranges have been assessed to bear major potential for hydroelectric power generation.

Depending on the amount of precipitation declining from north to south, the steppe zone can boast an abundance of both arable land and pastures. As depicted in Map 1.3, the northern grasslands with their fertile chernozem and maroon-colored earth are well-suited to the cultivation of various cereals (notably wheat, barley, corn) and sunflowers. Extensive pasturelands have provided an excellent ground for raising horses, sheep, camels, goats, and cows. Horses were particularly vital for transportation, communication, and military activity before the industrial revolution and constituted a precious export good. Further south, the fertile loess soil and water supply in numerous oases have helped sustain the flourishing cultivation of silk, cotton, tobacco, wheat, millet, vegetables, peaches, apricots, wine, berries, and other fruits. Near subtropical conditions in some southern areas have even rendered possible the growing of rice, sugar cane, and melons, especially watermelons. The borderlands between oases and sand deserts are conducive to the herding of camels[9] and of high-quality sheep (karakul, famous for their wool and fur). The austere highlands of the Tienshan (e.g., those surrounding the Ferghana Basin), Pamir, and other mountain ranges are suitable for raising sheep, goats, yaks, and hainags (a crossbreed of yak bulls and domesticated cows).

While geologically less hardened sediments in far-flung lowlands as well as mountain rims are likely to contain oil and natural gas deposits, mountain ranges and mountainous areas often store veins of ore. Thus, a large part of the Turanian Plain, especially the eastern shore of the Caspian Sea (including the peninsula of Mangyshlak), bears rich oil deposits; in the Kara Kum desert, lots of natural gas has been found. Primarily, oil is extracted in the Ferghana valley and north and south of the Tienshan range in Dzungaria and the Tarim Basin. Coal is found in large quantities in the Kazakh Uplands (Saryarka) near Karaganda, as well as in the Tienshan. The southern Kazakh Uplands harbors major iron ore deposits. The Tienshan ranges, especially their northern flanks, are "sprinkled" with extraction sites of precious metals and radioactive minerals (gold, copper, lead, zinc, chromium, molybdenum, uranium, tungsten). Gold and copper are also found in the eastern Kazakh Uplands; another place to find gold is the Kyzyl Kum desert. Pamir, Karakorum, and Kun Lun harbor deposits of various kinds of jade (Map 1.3).

CA arguably boasts locational or "geopolitical" resources: CA's location in the heart of Eurasia has made it a vast connecting space between a number of civilizations on the geographic periphery of this double-continent. CA has

---

[8] This is made up of Kazakhstan (2.72 mn km^2, 17.3 mn inhabitants in 2015), Kyrgyzstan (0.2 mn km^2, 5.83 mn inhabitants), Tajikistan (0.14, 8.41), Turkmenistan (0.49, 5.31), Uzbekistan (0.45, 30.7), and Xinjiang/China (1.66, 23.3).

[9] Camels are largely used as pack animals. In the southwest of CA (mostly in present-day Turkmenistan), the one-humped camel (dromedary) predominates, whereas in more northerly or mountainous regions, the two-humped (Bactrian) camel is most widespread (Hambly (ed) 1966/1979, 17).

functioned as an economic, political, and cultural transmission belt between Europe, the Near East and Persia, India, China, and Russia. No other region of the planet is at the crossroads of so many major cultures and states. Furthermore, CA is probably the world region whose (economic) history has been most intensively molded by the interaction between nomadic and sedentary groups as well as by various kinds of intermediary stages between settled farming and nomadic pastoralism (Rasuly-Paleczek 2006, 172; Paul 2012, 25).

The C Asian crossroads have sometimes served as a staging post and runway for large-scale invasions of neighboring civilizations. Far more often, the C Asian crossroads functioned as a base of extensive multidirectional trade and exchange with and between these civilizations—along the overland SR—which was active for almost two millennia (see below). Given the number of cultures and states interacting and the extraordinary mobility of nomadic peoples and polities across the region, CA may be the area featuring the most complicated political history on earth.

Perhaps in some way reflecting these unique locational assets (or alternatively, liabilities), a fair number of C Asian toponyms are full of symbolism, e.g., Khorassan = "land of the rising sun," Tienshan = "heavenly mountains," Khan Tengri (one of the highest peaks of the Tienshan, on the present-day border between Kazakhstan, Kyrgyzstan, and China) = "God of blue sky," Altai = "Golden Mountains," Kun Lun = "cloud of haze,"[10] Muztagh Ata (high peak of the western Kun Lun range) = "father of the ice mountains," Zeravshan = "gold donator," Kara Kum = "black sands" which also means "bad sands," Kara Bogas (gulf on the eastern side of the Caspian Sea) = "Black maw," Aral Sea = "sea of islands," Tengiz Koel (steppe lake in central Kazakhstan) = "lake of the sea," Zhetysu or Semirechie = "the area of seven rivers," Transoxiana or Mavarannahr = "That which is beyond the river (Oxos/Oxus)," Takla Makan = "The place where he who goes in does not come out," Betpak-Dala (desert steppe in south-eastern Kazakhstan) = "hunger steppe" or "plain of misfortune," and Turk (actually a dynastic name) = "strength" or "power."

1.4   Definition and Salient Traits of the Silk Road

The geographer von Richthofen in the 1870s did not only deliver a pertinent geographic definition of CA; he also coined the term "Silk Road" (more precisely its plural, "Seidenstraßen"). Von Richthofen referred to trade routes running through CA and linking east and west (i.e., China,

India, and the Mediterranean world)[11]. He underlined that geographically, there was no such thing as a single SR; the "Silk Roads" constituted a network of transcontinental commercial routes. Henceforth, we follow the usual linguistic usage, also of scholars, and speak of the "Silk Road" while bearing in mind the connotations of the plural expression.

Again as in the case of CA, definitions of the SR vary. Waugh goes beyond trade and uses the term as shorthand for economic and cultural exchange across Eurasia for up to two millennia (2002, 1). Perdue goes beyond two millennia and traces the beginnings of the SR at around 1500 BCE, the period of the emergence of the mobile Andronovo cultures in the C Asian steppe and their trading activities (2003, 491). Rasuly-Paleczek focuses on the network or systemic character of the trade routes connecting various regions of Eurasia (2006, 172). Gumppenberg and Steinbach point to the emergence of the SR as the connection or integration of two old semi-continental trade routes: the first was developed following Alexander the Great's conquests and led from the Mediterranean to the Yaxartes/Syr Daria; the second led in the opposite direction from central China to the Tienshan (2004, 245).

We can thus view the SR (sometimes also called "Great SR") as a network of intercontinental and regional trade routes that provided commercial, cultural, and technological exchange between Europe, CA, India, and China from antiquity until the early Modern Age. The SR embodied trans-Eurasian connectivity. Given high transportation costs, it was mostly low-weight—low bulk—high-value goods, predominantly luxury goods, that were traded along the routes (Cameron and Neal 2003, 32). Chinese silk goods fulfilled these requirements perfectly; moreover they were produced in large quantities and much desired internationally (Mokyr 2003, 369). While the Middle Kingdom initially held a monopoly on silk production, later other trading partners produced the valuable fiber too. At times, Chinese silk even fulfilled functions of a general medium of exchange (de facto money) in the Middle Kingdom itself and along the above network of trade routes across Eurasia, which therefore fully merits its name. Other luxury goods frequently traded on the Silk Road included brocade, embroidery, paper, precious metals, carpets, apparel, glass, horses, and slaves. Over time, and especially in regional markets, some lower-cost bulkier goods also gained importance, like grain, olive oil, other preserved foodstuffs, wax, lumber, textiles, and manufactured goods.

Apart from merchandise trade, there was also intensive cultural exchange: world religions (Buddhism, Christianity, Manichaeism, and notably Islam), scientific and technical knowledge (e.g., production of silk, paper, paper money, gunpowder, printing technology), arts (dances, acrobatics,

---

[10] In von Richthofen's view, the Kun Lun is "the spine of Asia" (Machatschek 1928, 161).

[11] von Richthofen: Über die zentralasiatischen Seidenstraßen...; see also above.

mime, taming, magic, music, painting, architecture), as well as literature spread via the SR. Traders, merchants, diplomats, monks, pilgrims, missionaries, soldiers, refugees, nomads, and urban dwellers were active on the network (Wollenweber and Franke (eds) 2009, 27).

Routes changed over the years according to local conditions; at any given time, any portion of the network might be struck by war, robbers, or natural disaster: the northern routes were intermittently plagued—or protected—by nomadic horsemen; the southern routes were endangered by fearsome deserts and frozen mountain passes (Mayhew 2010, 36).

A typical recurring transaction was the barter of Chinese silk (in demand almost everywhere) for C Asian horses (much needed to bolster the military power of any premodern state) (Boulnois 2009, 48–49). The intellectual interchange of ideas, technologies, and faiths probably created the world's first "information superhighway," as Mayhew put it. He also observed that while the bulk of trade headed west, religious ideas (e.g., Buddhism, Islam) primarily travelled east (2010, 37). But these routes unfortunately also functioned as avenues for the international dissemination of epidemics and pandemics. The most famous of the diseases spread by the SR was the "Black Death," the bubonic plague, which originated in Southeast Asia and is estimated to have killed up to a third of China's and Europe's population in the fourteenth century (see also below).

Connections/exchange between China and Europe has existed at least since the Bronze or Iron Age (see above). Many experts agree that regularity, organization, and transcontinental extension of exchange (from eastern to western Eurasia) make up essential traits of SR trade. In this respect a breakthrough was achieved by China opening up the routes crossing Tienshan and Pamir for official international trade through its military expeditions to CA in the late second century BCE. Thus the two semi-continental routes mentioned above were merged into one (Waugh 2007, 4, 10; Shen 2009, 35; Baipakov et al. 1997, 62). In this sense, the SR existed for almost 2000 years (first century BCE to nineteenth century CE), in an east-west direction extending about 6000–7000 km most of the time. The SR expired upon European (Russian) conquest and colonization of large parts of CA and their transformation into a peripheral component of the modern industrial world economy.

References

Baipakov K, Kumekov B, Pischulina K (1997) Istoria Kazakhstana v srednie veka. Rauan, Almaty

Barral P-E (2015) Les grands théoriciens des relations internationales – 100 auteurs majeurs. Studyrama, Levallois-Perret

Biarnes P (2008) La Route de la soie – Une histoire géopolitique. Ellipses, Paris

Boulnois L (2009) Les Routes de la soie – Aux origines de la mondialisation, Entretien avec Grataloup. Sciences Humaines, Auxerre

Breghel Y (2003) An historical atlas of CA. In: di Cosmo N, Sinor D (eds) Handbook of oriental studies (Handbuch der Orientalistik), Section 8: Central Asian Studies. Brill, Leiden

Cameron R, Neal L (2003) A concise economic history of the world – from Paleolithic times to the present. Oxford University Press, New York

Chauprade A (2003) Géopolitique – constantes et changements dans l'histoire. Ellipses, Paris

Chuvin P, Letolle R, Peyrouse S (2008) Histoire de l'Asie centrale contemporaine. Fayard, Paris

Cummings S (2012) Understanding CA – politics and contested transformations. Routledge, New York

Fragner B (2006) Zentralasienbegriff im historischen Raum. In: Fragner B, Kappeler A (eds) Zentralasien 13.-20. Jahrhundert. Promedia, Wien

Geiss PG (2009) Mittelasien. In: Bohn T, Neutatz D (eds) Studienhandbuch Östliches Europa, Band 2: Geschichte des Russischen Reiches und der Sowjetunion. Böhlau, Wien

von Gumppenberg M-C, Steinbach U (eds) (2004) Zentralasien: Geschichte – Politik – Wirtschaft – Ein Lexikon. C.H. Beck, München

Hambis L (ed) (1977) Asie centrale – Histoire et civilisation. Collège de France, Paris

Hambly G (ed) (1966) Fischer Weltgeschichte: Zentralasien (Band 16). Fischer Taschenbuch Verlag, Frankfurt, unaltered edition 1979

Hassinger H (1931) Geografische Grundlagen der Geschichte. Herder, Freiburg

Lacoste Y (ed) (1995) Dictionnaire de géopolitique. Flammarion, Paris

Machatschek F (1928) Innerasien. In: E. von Seydlitzsche Geographie (Hundert-Jahr-Ausgabe), Handbuch Band 3: Außereuropäische Erdteile, Ferdinand Hirt

Mackinder J (1904) The geographical pivot of history. Geogr J 23 (4):421–437

Mayhew B (2010) Central Asia highlights: history. In: Mayhew B, Bloom G, Clammer P, Kohn M, Noble J (ed) Lonely planet guide: Central Asia, 5th edn. Lonely Planet Publications, Oakland, pp 34–61

Mokyr J (2003) CA. In: Mokyr J (ed) The Oxford encyclopedia of economic history. Oxford University Press, Oxford

Mourre (ed) (2003) Le Petit Mourre – Dictionnaire de l'histoire. Bordas, Paris

Paul J (2012) Neue Fischer Weltgeschichte: Zentralasien (Band 10), S. Fischer Verlag, Frankfurt

Perdue P (2003) Silk road. In: Mokyr J (ed) The Oxford encyclopedia of economic history. Oxford University Press, Oxford

Perdue P (2005) China marches west – the Qing conquest of central Eurasia. Harvard University, Cambridge, MA

Rasuly-Paleczek G (2006) Von 'Wilden Reiterhorden' und 'Barbarischen Eroberern'. In: Steffelbauer I, Hakami K (eds) Vom Alten Orient zum Nahen Osten. Magnus, Essen

von Richthofen F (1877) Über die zentralasiatischen Seidenstraßen bis zum 2. Jh. n. Chr. In: Verhandlungen der Gesellschaft für Erdkunde zu Berlin, 96–122

Shen F (2009) Cultural flow between China and the outside world throughout history. Foreign Language Press, Beijing

Spykman N (1942) America's strategy in world politics – the United States and the balance of power. Harcourt, New York

Stadelbauer J (2007) Zwischen Hochgebirge und Wüste – Der Naturraum Zentralasien. In: Sapper M (ed) Machtmosaik Zentralasien, Osteuropa, September

Waugh D (2002) The Origins of the Silk Road. University of Washington Lecture Series

Waugh D (2007) Richthofen's "Silk Roads": toward the archaeology of a concept. In: The Silk Road, vol 5, no 1, summer

Waugh D (2008) The silk roads and Eurasian geography. University of Washington

Wollenweber B, Franke P (eds) (2009) Entlang der Seidenstraße. Wostok, Berlin

From the Beginnings to the Emergence of the Silk Road (SR)

2.1 Early Development of Eurasian Economic and Political Dualism: Toward Nomadism Versus Settled Existence (ca. 5000 BCE to 550 BCE)

Given major and pioneering civilizational changes, the long period of human economic development preceding antiquity in CA provides a dynamic imprint and bears decisive repercussions for the following millennia. To point to a caveat at the outset: Although the salient lines of the following account are clear, details in the literature, e.g., related to dates, may be saddled with some degree of uncertainty. For the following chapter, the author has primarily drawn from publications of Zhambyl Artykbaev, Karl Baipakov, Bert Fragner, Anatoly Khazanov, Iaroslav Lebedynsky, Hermann Parzinger, Jürgen Paul, and Gabriele Rasuly-Paleczek.

2.1.1 Neolithic Revolution and Aeneolithic Period (Copper Age) in CA

Parts of CA have been inhabited since the Upper Paleolithic period (e.g., evidence of activities of hunters and gatherers at Teshik Tash near Dushanbe, today Tajikistan). During the sixth millennium BCE (6000–5000 BCE), Neolithic economic activities—farming and animal husbandry—and the first permanent settlements emerged in the oases of Northeastern Iran and Southern Turkmenistan. These villages featured houses built with sunbaked mudbricks. Given the oasis type of natural habitat, agricultural activity, particularly the cultivation of wheat and barley, soon gained the upper hand over pastoralism. The wheel had been invented. Cattle were used as draft animals. The Dzheitun culture (northeast of the Kopet Dagh range, area around present-day Ashgabat) directly linked up to early agricultural economies in the Middle East and Western Asia. Neolithic communities also existed in the Tarim Basin (Loulan, near Lake Lop Nor) and in the Turfan oasis. Early farming settlements applied the catchment technique of irrigation, which used simple banks to retain floodwater or channels to divert it (Roudik 2007, 12). Moreover, the seasonal floods of rivers, particularly of their estuaries, tended to produce layers of fertile mud which were often used to grow grain (Linska et al. 2003, 52).[1]

About one millennium later (approx. in the fifth millennium BCE: 5000–4000 BCE), the Neolithic revolution spread to the northern parts of CA. Economic activity soon adapted to these mainly steppe-like surroundings: Following various practices of combining farming and stockbreeding, the latter—based on the gradual domestication of sheep and goats—came to outweigh, but not eliminate, agriculture. Food producing activities probably expanded along the steppe corridor from present Southern Ukraine eastwards. The origin of this cultural transfer over several thousand kilometers may have been the Bug-Dniester culture, which had already reached its apex in the sixth millennium BCE (Parzinger 2009, 834). The Kelteminar culture of cattle raisers established itself in the fourth millennium BCE in the oasis of Khorezm (Khwarazm).

We can therefore detect already in the Neolithic period west-east influences running along the northern steppe belt, as well as connections between Iran and the Near East on the one hand and Southern CA on the other. It is not clear whether any important ties existed in the Neolithic era between the North and the south of CA (separated by desert steppes and sand deserts), except for the Kelteminar culture, which apparently had some intermediary function. Obviously also the introduction of agriculture and animal husbandry in the steppe preceded the emergence of nomadism.

Around the turn of the fourth to the third millennium (at ca. 3000 BCE), sedentary farming civilizations apparently spread from Southern Turkmenistan to Bactria (ancient area of the upper Amu Daria basin), Khorezm and Sogdia/Sogdiana (the historic region between the middle Syr Daria and Amu Daria,

---

[1] These activities recall the Nile flood irrigation practices successfully applied in ancient Egypt.

centered on the valley of the Zerafshan river). The sustained production of surpluses of food favored the development of larger settlements and stimulated regional trade. The introduction and use of copper in CA (documented since around 3500 BCE) seem to have been particularly important for steppe cultures and may have facilitated efforts to domesticate horses. These efforts bore initial success in the first half of the third millennium BCE (from about 3000 BCE to 2500 BCE). The domestication of horses reportedly spread from the west to the east: The Sredny Stog culture (north of the Black Sea, Southern Volga area) was one of the first to adopt it, followed by the Yamnaya culture (southern Don-Volga region, Northern Kazakhstan, Southern Siberia, see Map 2.1). Social differentiation made itself felt, and leading personalities started to stand out from the rest of society (first kurgans/burial mounds in the steppe) (Parzinger 2009, 835).

2.1.2 Bronze Age

2.1.2.1 Southern CA: Proto-urban Oasis Cultures

The Bronze Age took hold in Southern CA around the middle of the third millennium BCE (2500 BCE) and lasted till about 1250 BCE. Proto-urban oasis cultures developed: large settlements, in some places even towns, emerged, applying irrigation techniques beyond the simple catchment of water. Artificial irrigation was introduced through the construction of networks of canals, reservoirs, etc. Farmers adopted the plow and planted field and garden crops. Cattle and pigs were bred. Societal division of labor deepened and separate settlement quarters for weaving and other crafts, trade, worshipping, as well as residential areas emerged. Apart from water, one of the foundations of the proto-urban economy was metals/bronze, which was used as material for the production of tools, weapons, and jewelry. Potters used potters' wheels and kilns. Ceramics were professionally produced, with a tendency toward mass production. Wagons for transportation with two to four wheels proliferated (pulled by cattle). Pronounced differences of welfare started to arise (Linska et al. 2003, 53).

The first apex of settled cultures in CA emerged around 2000 BCE and was named the Oxos civilization (Oxos = Greek term for Amu Daria). As Map 2.1 shows, the oasis cultures included Namazga-tepe, Altyn-tepe (both in Southern Turkmenistan, southeast of today's Ashgabat), Sapalli (in Bactria/Southern Uzbekistan), and Zamanbaba (Sogdiana/lowlands of Zerafshan). Also, oases of the Tarim basin (Qiemo on its southern rim) and Hami and Barkoel were inhabited in this period and featured agropastoral activities. There are indicators of increased demographic growth, which likely triggered first outmigration movements. Relationships to neighboring ancient oriental civilizations (e.g., Babylon, Mesopotamia;

Shang culture/dynasty, Northern China) developed/were sustained.

Since the middle of the second millennium (around 1500 BCE), intensive contacts of the oasis settlements with mobile steppe cultures are documented, particularly with groups of the Andronovo culture (see below), which approached Southern CA from the north. These contacts may or may not have contributed to a temporary decline of sedentary farming activities and populations and their eastward migration. Climate change and increasing aridity from 1500 BCE (see below) may have also played a role. In any case, in the late Bronze Age, the Namazga and Altyn-tepe cultures moved the zones of their intensive development from the foothills of the Kopet Dagh/Southern Turkmenistan toward Margiana/the areas around the inland deltas of Murgab and Tedzhen rivers and to Bactria/the upper Amu Daria basin.

2.1.2.2 Northern CA: Domestication of Horse (Expansive Andronovo Culture)

The Bronze Age in the C Asian steppes lasted roughly from 1800 BCE to 1000 BCE. The domestication of the horse was largely concluded; reins and horse-drawn wheeled chariots were introduced, combined with the use of bows and arrows. Ox-drawn carts were also in use. Horseback riding probably made its first appearances in the region. Bactrian (two-humped) camels were domesticated too. While the horse multiplied man's mobility across the grasslands, the camel enabled people to cross long distances in extremely dry areas like sand deserts and therefore was aptly named "ship of the desert" (Cameron and Neal 2003, 79). Handling horses and camels as well as managing herds of livestock was facilitated by the adoption or invention of bronze (an alloy of copper and tin, substantially harder than copper). Copper and tin ores were extracted in the mineral-rich Kazakh Uplands[2] and processed in settlements on the Syr Daria and in other areas in close vicinity to the steppe belt. Bronze tools, weapons, and objects included horse gear, knives, arrowheads, spears, daggers, axes, mirrors, and decorative fittings. Animal husbandry (particularly sheep, horses, goats, cattle, and pigs) gained further ground, while agriculture still played a role. In the Kazakh steppe, wheat, millet, barley, and rye were grown, mostly in small fields along rivers and near lakes (Litvinsky 1996, 159).

The Indo-Iranian Andronovo culture, which developed in the first half of the second millennium BCE and soon extended from the Pontic steppes (Southern Ukraine) to the

---

[2] Copper mining in the Kazakh Uplands (Saryarka) quickly gained traction and soon reached a peak. Allegedly even dams were built to provide the water needed for large-scale washing of ore (Parzinger 2009, 839).

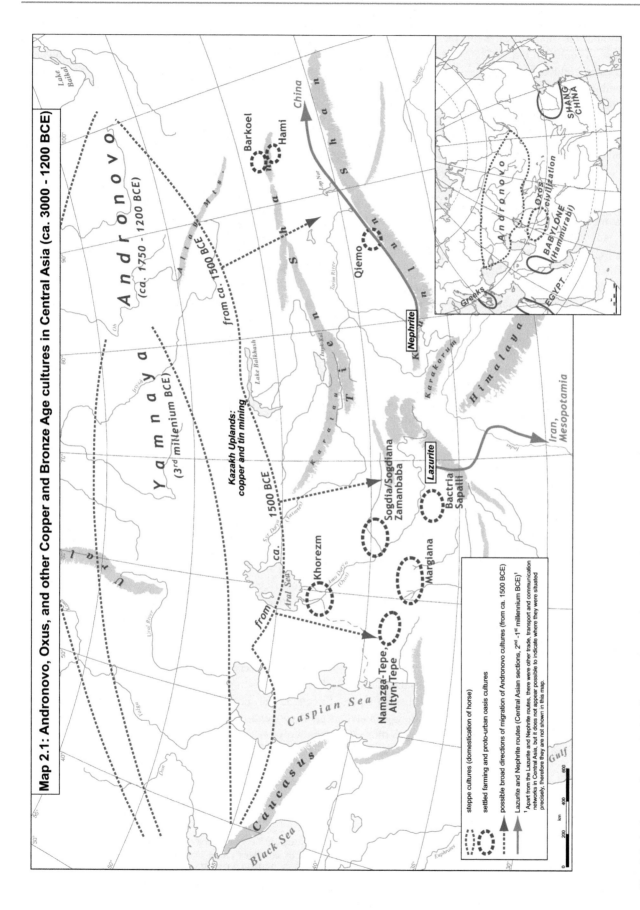

Map 2.1   Andronovo, Oxos, and other Copper and Bronze Age cultures in CA (ca. 3000–1200 BCE)

Yenisey, was the most well known of the "steppe bronze cultures" and the major bearer of the abovementioned innovations. People of the Andronovo culture were not only herdsmen and agriculturalists but also experienced miners and metalworkers. Larger fortified settlements were built in the steppe, protected by walls and ditches. This was accompanied by a hierarchization of settlements, some of which took over functions of central connecting points for widely branching long-distance networks of travel and communication in Eurasia which were established in the course of the second millennium BCE. Social stratification took hold and a warrior-type male elite emerged, with chariots as their symbol. Gradually, housing practices evolved: while solid, rectangular houses with basements initially prevailed, easier-to-build huts then became more popular, followed by lighter abodes (proto-yurts) (Cattani 2007, 37).

Apart from the "push factor" of enhanced mobility through horsemanship, possibly combined with the impact of climate change, the "pull factor" of increasing raw material demand for metallurgy and the search for new copper and tin deposits may have triggered far-reaching migration movements of the steppe dwellers: Around 1500 BCE, Andronovo groups expanded and advanced east and south into Dzungaria, parts of the Tarim Basin, Semirechie, Ferghana, Sogdia, Bactria, Khwarazm, and southern Turkmenistan (Map 2.1); knowledge of bronze metallurgy spread relatively quickly across extensive territories (Parzinger 2009, 836–837). In the southern regions (foothills of Kopet Dagh, Bactria, Sogdia, Tarim Basin), the Andronovo groups encountered the abovementioned developed sedentary cultures that had already mastered bronze technologies.[3] Having descended thus far, the steppe tribes may have incited sedentary cultures in Southern Turkmenistan to relocate, or the steppe tribes may have mingled with the settled civilizations, as a result of which new agricultural centers evolved in the region. In initiating these changes, the Andronovo groups either gradually moved (back) toward a more sedentary way of life and eventually became fully settled or remained in their organizations but often borrowed new elements of the settled culture.

The Andronovo culture was later superseded by the Karasuk culture, which had originated in the Minusinsk basin (upper Yenisey, Siberia), was ethnically mixed (Indo-European and Mongolian), improved the handling of horses, and dominated the C Asian steppes from around 1300 BCE to 1000 BCE.

Apart from the Karasuk culture, the civilizations referred to so far (whether mostly agricultural or stock raising, whether in Northern or Southern CA) were of predominantly Indo-European ethnic origin (and spoke mostly Iranian). Around 1000 BCE, broadly speaking, one could distinguish: Scyths, living in the steppe plains in the north of the region; Massagetes, living in the area of the Aral Sea; Sakas, inhabiting the steppes west of the Tienshan and Pamir as well as the river oases of the Syr Daria and the Amu Daria; Tokharians, living in oases of the Tarim basin and in Turfan; and Cimmerians, living in the Pontic steppes (Southern Ukraine).

2.1.3 Iron Age

2.1.3.1 Southern CA: Urbanized Trade-Oriented Proto-states

From around 1250 BCE, in continuous development from Bronze Age communities, the Iron Age Oxos culture or civilization made its appearance in Southern Turkmenistan (Yaz), Margiana and Bactria (Tillia, Kuchuk)[4]. Iron Age cultures also developed in other oases, including Sogdiana, Ferghana (Chust), Tashkent, Khorezm, and oases of the Tarim basin. Larger towns/cities were established, e.g., Samarkand, Merv, Bactra/Balkh, Khodzhent (Ferghana valley), which sometimes supported populations of tens of thousands and featured impressive fortifications, including citadels and palace-like central edifices (Abazov 2008, Map 4). In some cases, walled towns even possessed second external walls to protect the cities' arable lands and shelters for cattle, which points to the importance security had attained for these settlements.

Efforts at building large dams, dikes, and canals and at expanding and refining irrigation systems constituted a new driver of communal development and tended to lift agricultural productivity substantially. First scientific findings in astronomy and mathematics were applied. Irrigation canal networks advanced in impressive fanlike or comblike shapes, typical for C Asian oases.[5] Various sorts of grain and even rice were cultivated. Given that the infrastructural efforts and ensuing maintenance activities often required direction and coordination of large amounts of labor, "great cooperation,"[6] the consolidation of clans and tribal communities and the strengthening of public authority became a necessity. Local elites and aristocracies gained

---

[3] It was around this time that the "Beauty of Loulan" was buried in Qewrighul near the ancient town of Loulan. This woman's well-preserved remains were wrapped in a shawl of woven sheep's wool and inhumed with a winnowing basket and grains of wheat, thus featuring the interpenetration of economies based on animal husbandry and agriculture in the Tarim Basin about four millennia ago (Millward and Perdue 2004, 33).

[4] Also called "Bactria-Margiana Archaeological Complex" (Paul 2012, 52)

[5] For instance, the emergence of large irrigation works on the lower reaches of the Oxos (Amu Daria) dates from the eighth to seventh centuries BCE (Paul 2012, 91).

[6] Characterized as such in Sellnow et al. (1977, 141)

importance and state-like structures sprang up, usually centered on the largest town(s) of each oasis (Roudik 2007, 13).[7]

For instance, Bactra/Balkh was the capital of Bactria, Merv of Margiana. Various regionally differentiated Indo-Iranian peoples appear to have emerged, e.g., the Sogdians (Sogdiana), who later developed the Ferghana oasis, the Bactrians, and the Khorezmians. Cultural and economic expansion of sedentary, often urbanized systems from the south to the north could be observed, which may recall developments of the Aeneolithic period or the early Bronze Age. In contrast to the Bronze Age though, in the Iron Age, production of food surpluses through sedentary farming and sophisticated irrigation spread further to Ferghana, Tashkent, and Khwarazm.

No region-wide sedentary state emerged but a loose association of small political entities, typically oasis city-states. Irrigation agriculture, crafts, and extensive trade along paths that later became part of the SR network and were strongly linked to Persia constituted the economic pillars of the city-states. First encounters with nomads in the early first millennium BCE were apparently peaceful (see below). Not unlike their Andronovo predecessors, nomadic stock raisers typically arrived from the Eurasian steppes of the north and appropriated the immediate steppe-like environment of the oases as one of their ranges of activity. This particularly goes for the oases of Khwarazm, Sogdia, and Ferghana. There the nomads (mostly Scyths) seem to have at least initially coexisted and even developed symbiotic relationships with peoples living in the urban oasis centers.[8] Nevertheless, hostilities must have soon broken out, and between the eighth- and the sixth-century BCE, a number of cities established fortifications aimed at protecting oases' inhabitants from nomadic attacks as well as probably from dangers coming from neighboring expanding sedentary empires (Empire of the Medes, Persian Empire). Despite the fortifications, the Scyths successfully invaded and looted some of the settlements.

2.1.3.2 Northern CA: Mounted Nomadism, Mobile Pastoralism, and Military Prowess

From around the beginning of the first millennium BCE, the Iron Age reigned in Northern CA (the steppe belt). Ferrous metallurgy contributed to a major breakthrough, which most authors date between about 1000 BCE and 800 BCE: the emergence of mounted nomadism, which led to a further expansion of the steppe dwellers' mobility and the qualitative

strengthening of their military capabilities. Thus, the phenomenon of mounted warrior nomadism (in German: Reiterkriegernomadismus) emerged, which shaped economic and political developments in CA and affected sedentary civilizations at the geographic periphery of Eurasia for almost two and a half millennia. Put slightly differently: mobile steppe tribes and mounted archers left their mark on C Asian and even Eurasian economic history between the Neolithic and the Industrial revolutions. The C Asian steppe belt served, so to say, as the "cradle of mounted nomadism."

According to Kickinger (2006, 58), nomadism constitutes a mobile way of life based on extensive pastoralism focused on cattle. According to Ferret, nomadic pastoralism is defined as a way of life founded on the breeding of livestock whose seasonal movement allows the nomads to optimally exploit available pastures (Ferret 2013, 38).[9] Only at this point was farming either entirely abandoned or reduced to an auxiliary or secondary activity. Nomads thus opted for a strategy of extreme economic specialization (Grataloup 2007, 91; Paul 2012, 523).

The counterpart to the marginalization of agriculture (which remained necessarily connected to a settled existence) was the full mastery of horse breeding; the invention of the bridle, of the saddle, and of pants; and the transition to horseback riding, to mounted archery, and to other equestrian skills. This concentration and innovation extended once again the spatial ranges of pastoral activity and eventually created a decisive edge in warfare for steppe people. Steppe people's huts were first fixed to wheeled platforms and thus turned into covered "wagons" (kibitkas) drawn by oxen, before being replaced by easy to pitch and to strike tentlike yurts (gers). Nomads' extreme specialization in the human division of labor of course implies substantial dependence on outside sources of necessary goods that the pastoralists did not produce themselves (Khazanov 1983/1994, 70, 80).

The emergence of nomadic pastoralism constituted a striking example of human ingenuity and adaptability to the environment. Although there is broad agreement that sedentary cultures conducting farming and animal husbandry preceded nomadic ones and that the transformation was a gradual one (Cattani 2007, 36; Khazanov 1983/1994, 90–92; Lebedynsky 2007, 19; Parzinger 2009, 850),[10] there does not yet appear to

---

[7] This would not be inconsistent with Wittfogel's explanation of the emergence of political rule and urbanization in societies in which mastering water (due to its scarcity or overabundance) is pivotal to survival and economic growth ("hydraulic civilizations") (Wittfogel 1964/1977).

[8] Again, similar to their predecessors, some Scyths opted for eventually settling down in the southern regions.

[9] A more detailed definition of pastoral nomadism, which is not inconsistent with the above two, is given by Khazanov (see Box 2.1).

[10] Parzinger's comparison of the mobility of Paleolithic communities and of pastoral nomads is particularly clear: Hunters and gatherers had to move themselves toward their source of food, whereas nomadic pastoralists moved their source of food to keep it alive and to enable it to grow. Both forms of mobility therefore proceed from utterly different circumstances. Both socioeconomic formations are separated by the domestication of animals, which humanity owes neither to hunters and gatherers nor to nomads but to early farmers (ibid).

be scientific consensus on the causes of the formation of nomadism. Despite this lack of consensus, some factors can be outlined that probably had an impact on its establishment:

- Most importantly: the full domestication of the horse (already achieved in the Bronze Age) and the development of horseback riding.
- Connected with this, technical progress in metallurgy and tool manufacturing (bridle, buckles, other horse gear, referred to above).
- Growth of livestock herds based on improvement of animal husbandry, followed or accompanied by demographic growth of steppe tribes.[11]
- Climate change (lower temperatures and increasing aridity, most pronounced around 1000 BCE) likely cut yields of agriculture in the steppe and may have been the final stimulus (last straw) for pastoralists to abandon/marginalize agriculture once and for all and become nomadic.

Nomadic pastoralists in the first centuries of the first millennium BCE were probably the first humans able to successfully exploit vast unpopulated and unused grasslands and semideserts in Eurasia for purposes of a food-producing economy.[12] From the moment this civilizational innovation had emerged and sedentary agriculture and pastoral nomadism had started to coexist on the territory of CA, shifts between the two ways of life became possible. Such shifts indeed repeatedly happened as parts of adaptive strategies to adjust to the variability of the climatic and political environment. C Asian nomads soon adopted seasonal migration routes, which in the plains typically ran in a north-south direction and in the mountains between lower and higher altitudes. Northern steppe areas would constitute summer pastures; southern locations (sometimes near rivers or oases or on foothills) would be chosen for winter encampments. High mountain pastures (in the summer) would alternate with temporary valley abodes (in the winter). Or nomadization could include "steppe pockets" of oases zones or "nomadic pockets" in settled environments.

Nomads largely made their living from what their animals produced: meat from sheep, goats, cows, and horses; milk from goats, cows, horses, and even camels; butter, curd cheese; a "strong" drink (fermented mare's milk) (kimiz [Turkish], kumys [Russian], or airag [Mongolian]); cloths,

felt boots, and mats from sheep wool; hides and leather from camels and livestock; even fuel could be made out of animal's dung; and tallow could be used for lighting. Usually, nomads' biggest herds consisted of sheep, which could number tens of thousands. According to Khazanov, in the steppe zones of CA, one sheep needs about one hectare of pasture, while in the (steppe-)desert, a sheep needs 3–6 hectares, and in some places even 10—with implications for the spatial organization of economic activities (1983/1994, 51). According to other sources, one hectare of winter pasture in the desert-steppe north of the Caspian Sea could sustain 5–6 sheep or goats or 1–1.5 pieces of cattle. Horses of course needed more pastureland (Paul 2012, 95).

This leads to an essential point: the intensity of economic activity and the resulting density of population in the steppe. As Paul explains it: "Die Bevölkerungsdichte richtete sich dabei nach dem jeweils möglichen Viehbestand. Daher stieß die Bevölkerungsentwicklung in der Steppe an relativ harte Grenzen...." ("The density of population [of the steppe zone] depends on the possible amount of livestock. That is why demographic development in the steppe met relatively strict limits ...") (2012, 26). This chimes with Fragner's assessment above and with Bouvard's description of medieval Kazakhstan: "Loin d'apparaître, dans ces temps-là, comme un "grand vide", l'immense steppe ressemblait davantage à un vaste chaudron où bouillonnaient les existences agitées de peuples et tribus diversement enchevetrés" ("Far from appearing as a "great empty space" in these times, the immense steppe rather resembled a huge cauldron, which bubbled from the agitated existence of various entangled peoples and tribes") (1985, 30).

Nomads also engaged in metallurgy and manufactured some tools for everyday life. Auxiliary agriculture was often limited to the culture of millet, near encampments. Yurts or gers—most nomads' mobile housing—were easy-to-assemble wooden framed tents covered with felt. In some cases, horses, cattle and/or metallurgical products were used as quasi-money (medium of exchange, measure of value/prestige). What nomads could not produce themselves, they procured either from trade with settled people (often via oasis bazaars), through tribute revenue (once nomadic political control had been established over an area) or, if necessary, through raids (razzias). Goods produced by sedentary civilizations most in need by nomads typically were farming products (e.g., grain), textiles (cloth), and manufactured metal products (notwithstanding steppe dwellers' knowledge of metallurgy). Settled populations' demand for nomadic products often focused on horses, meat, milk, and wool (although oasis inhabitants also engaged in limited stockbreeding).

The Scyths soon practiced seasonal migration patterns of up to and beyond 1000 km in what was later Kazakhstan and Dzungaria and advanced from summer pastures in the steppe

---

[11] Given the fragility of steppe and desert-steppe vegetation, growth of herds may have compelled pastoralists to move around more and more, looking for new pastures further and further afield from settlements. This explanatory argument for nomadization has often been put forward by Soviet historians (e.g., Shukow et al. 1956/62, Band 2, 169).

[12] As far as nomadic pastoralists still exist today, they probably remain the only humans capable of making a living from these spacious and harsh lands without having recourse to substantial technical assistance.

belt to winter encampments near the Syr Daria or even in oasis territories of later Xinjiang (Artykbaev 2007, 79,80). The famous "animal art" (French, art animalier; German, Tierstil) was developed by the Scyths and is typical of nomadic horsemen of the Iron Age (Schiltz 1994). The necessity to defend a nomadic clan's or tribe's[13] vital pastures, encampments, and migration routes against interference and appropriations by other mobile groups or by sedentary cultures facilitated the creation of (mobile) nomadic political entities, clanic or tribal associations, which tended to be organized in a strictly hierarchical manner. The symbolic demonstration of the power Scythian princes wielded during their lifetimes is shown in kurgans, where the princes were buried accompanied by rich complements (weapons, gold artifacts, jewelry, wagons, sacrificed servants and horses).[14] These signs of authority however did not prevent the cohesion of nomadic entities from weakening or even evaporating (and, thus, the entities from breaking up) once external pressures or tensions had subsided.

After a period of peaceful coexistence, Scythian tribal organizations—probably banking on their enhanced military capabilities—from the eighth- to the sixth-century BCE launched a number of armed incursions and raids on the oases of Southern CA and beyond into the Middle East and Near East. In the second half of the eighth century, other Scythian groups migrated along the steppe belt from Northern Kazakhstan to Southern Ukraine, where they displaced the nomadic Cimmerians (who moved to the pastures of Anatolia and displaced the Assyrians there) and soon made contact with Hellenic colonists on the northern shore of the Black Sea.

The military superiority that some nomadic cultures achieved over settled ones (or in any case the serious military threat that nomads had come to pose) from around 500 BCE onward may be explained by the extraordinary mobility and skillfulness of mounted pastoralists and the technical know-how of rider-warriors. Practically the entire male population learned to handle horses and use bows and arrows from childhood and therefore could be quickly mobilized as soldiers. Other frequently used arms were long spears, tomahawks, clubs, swords, scimitars, lassos, and daggers. Warriors were often protected by light armors (e.g., ring or scale armors). The nomads were capable of suddenly striking deep into a sedentary state and then retreating ("melting into the steppe") before an infantry-

based army had time to assemble and retaliate or, alternatively, avoiding direct confrontation and enticing sedentary armed forces deep into the steppe, stretching their supply lines and triggering their exhaustion.

Given life in a harsh environment and facing mobile neighbors and potential enemies, entire nomadic tribes, and particularly mounted archers, needed to be constantly alert and prepared for hostilities. In a variation of Olson's words (2000, 7–8)[15], military superiority over sedentary populations at times gave nomadic confederations the choice of gaining revenue via nonmarket avenues either as "roving nomads" (making pillage in various places) or as "stationary nomads" (exacting tribute more or less regularly from clearly defined areas). The degree of exposure to the harsh natural environment, however, was such that a succession of droughts or snowstorms or other calamities could kill large quantities of livestock and thus seriously harm the livelihood of a nomadic society. In the worst case, it could even trigger the (temporary) collapse of the state and thus cause a political vacuum. Nomads' pronounced vulnerability to the elements somewhat tempered but did not eliminate the long-lasting military imbalance.

> **Box 2.1: Nomadism and the Nomadic Economy**
> *Definition, Property rights, and Organization*
> Khazanov (*Nomads and the Outside World*, 16) laid down some in his view essential features of pastoral nomadism:
>
> - Pastoralism is the predominant form of economic activity.
> - Its extensive character connected with the maintenance of herds all year round on a system of free grazing without stables or stocking fodder.[16]
> - Periodic mobility in accordance with the demands of the pastoral economy within the boundaries of specific grazing territories or between these territories (as opposed to continuous migrations).
> - The participation in pastoral mobility of all or the majority of the population.
>
> (continued)

---

[13] A clan is here understood to constitute a community formed by a number of individual families, sometimes linked by common ancestry, while a tribe is regarded as consisting of several clans.

[14] Monumentally large kurgans have been discovered in eastern Kazakhstan and Semirechie as well as in the lower Syr Daria region.

[15] Olson opposes the concept of "roving bandit" and "stationary bandit." Whereas the first engages in occasional plunder, the second, by making his theft a predictable tax that takes only a part of his victims' output, thereby leaves the latter with an incentive to generate income, which over time maximizes the bandit's fruits of theft. This, however, presupposes rational and long-term-oriented human behavior, often unfortunately a heroic assumption.

[16] Or to put in Masanov's words: Whereas the stabling system was based on bringing the fodder to where the cattle were kept, the nomadic system brought the cattle to where the fodder existed (2003, 374).

Box 2.1 (continued)
- Principal orientation of production toward the requirements of subsistence (as opposed to the market production-oriented capitalist ranch).

Khazanov's definition corresponds to full-fledged nomadism, as opposed to semi-nomadism, in which only a part of the population nomadizes, and the rest remains settled. As mentioned above, full-fledged nomadism secured itself a special niche in the division of labor, even if, as Masanov points out (2003, 376), nomads were often skillful in producing numerous tools/objects from their own limited inputs and thus able to achieve a degree of self-sufficiency, at an economic cost. Because fodder was not usually stored either for the winter or for inclement conditions in the summer, there was the danger of mass deaths of animals (these tragic events are known as "dzhuty") in the infrequent cases that deep snow covered the grasslands for too long[17] or that a prolonged drought occurred.[18] Frequent competition, rivalry, and conflict for water and pasturelands in the rough natural conditions of the steppe speak for Toynbee's characterization of nomads as "hardened/stiffened civilizations" in his classification of world civilizations (1976/1979: *Menschheit und Mutter Erde—Die Geschichte der großen Zivilisationen*).

There is consensus among experts that livestock, nomads' most important asset, was generally in private (family/extended family) ownership, whereas pastures and access to water were collectively owned by the clan/tribe. The principal standard of richness or unit of wealth among nomads was the number of livestock or horses owned, which could differ considerably from family to family.[19] Regulations of rights to pastures and migration routes and the defense of these rights against rival nomadic (or sedentary) groups favored the establishment of nomadic political entities which typically contributed to social hierarchization tendencies and to the emergence or strengthening of a nomadic aristocracy. The latter was largely recruited from mounted warriors and/or from wealthier members of the polity.

The tribal chief in many cases was a hereditary leader (patriarch). The tribal chief and, by delegation, the nobility had the right to take important decisions on the appropriation and use of pastures, of water and grazing rights, on preserving order and stability, on migration, and on war and peace. The tribal chief himself was confirmed or elected by gatherings of the nomadic aristocracy. These gatherings or kuriltai (as they were called in Mongol tradition) were event based or organized on an annual basis. They were typically convened for solving common issues of social, economic, or political life. Some clans/tribes prospered, while others floundered, and the prosperous ones tended to absorb the weaker ones. As his group expanded in size and power, the leader's income was based on regular contributions from herders and on special levies, typically about 1% of the herds, in emergencies (Rossabi 2012, 10).

Types of Nomadism and Incentives for Nomadic State Formation

Somewhat at variance with Khazanov's focused definition, Lebedynsky (2007, 22–23), following Russian archeologists, distinguishes between migrational, territorial, and imperial nomadism. Migrational nomadism is nonseasonal and relates to an entire population moving together with its herds, in search of pastures, without a fixed point of reference. The encampments are all provisional. The only assets are the livestock itself, the products of stock raising, of trade and war. This system is rather exceptional and only conceivable in particular circumstances and for a limited time, e.g., when the Huns migrated across CA and conquered parts of Europe. Among the factors that can trigger migrational nomadism are recurring bad weather (e.g., a string of consecutive droughts or severe winters), political changes, population increase, rivalries for pastures, and, particularly, displacement through other (stronger) migrating tribes.[20]

Territorial nomadism is carried out on a precise area, often delimited by natural boundaries, like rivers,

(continued)

---

[17] In this case, hardened snow could turn into ice, and animals would be cut off from food. Among Kazakhs, such periods were known as spells of black ice (gololed, gololeditsa).

[18] This structural weakness had apparently not changed for almost two millennia since the emergence of nomadism.

[19] Thus, e.g., in Kalmyk (Mongol) nomadic tribes of late eighteenth-century Dzungaria (China), a man with 200–300 head of cattle and 400–500 sheep was considered wealthy (upper class), while one with 40–50 cattle and 200–300 sheep was regarded as well-off (middle class) (Miyawaki et al. 2003, 162).

---

[20] This can be likened to a kind of "billiard principle" of a geopolitical chain reaction in the Eurasian grasslands, in which an incoming group A, starting to move for whatever reason, displaces group B, which in turn pushes groups C and D and so on. The whole "chain" of "invader cascades," rebounding across the steppe, may possibly extend thousands of kilometers (Chaliand 1995, 25).

Box 2.1 (continued)

mountains, and borders of ecological zones. Each group (clan or tribe) has its own summer and winter pastures including wells and other access to water between which livestock and people nomadize on a seasonal basis. They do this by following well-defined itineraries of either horizontal (in the plains) or vertical (in the mountains) transhumance.[21] As far as possible, tribes (or clans) tend to separate their respective territories from each other by natural barriers. Neighbors' encroachment on a group's pastures, wells, and routes was a source of conflict (casus belli).[22] In the system of territorial nomadism, winter encampments can become the cores of permanent establishments covering relatively large spaces of 10 km² or more (Paul 2012, 97). They can harbor populations of elderly and poor people, foreign prisoners, slaves, peasants, artisans of various origins, etc. They can become focal points of manufacturing and trade but can also be fortified places and centers of command. Permanent encampments of nomadic leaders and sovereigns may function as "capitals" of nomadic proto-states and states. Territorial nomadism is more commonly practiced than the migrational type and constitutes the economic base of tribal unions and confederations.

Imperial nomadism derives from territorial nomadism and corresponds to a situation where nomadic groups join to form a tribal or steppe confederation and then subdue and extend their authority over (neighboring) nomadic or settled indigenous populations. According to most authors, preparations for conflicts or hostilities with external powers were the most typical cases in which tribal confederations were established.[23] A steppe confederation often consisted of a political hierarchy of the imperial leader and his court, his governors, and their entourages, appointed to oversee tribal leaders and their tribes. In these confederacies, politics was based on personal oaths of allegiance of the freemen to the imperial leader, on the subservience of slaves, and on the following of allied tribesmen and tribeswomen. Subjugated tribes and sedentary cultures often became obliged to pay tribute to the conqueror (Barfield 1989/1992, 5–8; Geiss 2003, 11).

Outright military occupation of sedentary areas was not an indispensable ingredient of imperial nomadic rule; the permanent and credible threat of punitive operations was enough. Some of the nomads settled down in already existing (conquered) towns or created new imperial settlements. The elites often adopted a semi-nomadic life of stockbreeding and exacted tributes and possibly specific services from the subjugated agricultural population. Upon incorporating sedentary areas and witnessing some structural adjustments, the economy of the enlarged nomadic state ("empire") became more diversified.

Whether sedentary areas were included or not: Once a steppe confederation or empire broke apart, larger and smaller tribes or other kinship groups continued to live together only in relatively loose associations. These groups and associations, however, could join a new leading figure anytime, because the reputation of a successful nomadic military commander bore enormous appeal; rank-and-file members of the community hoped that he could provide them with booty and advantageous terms of trade, and therefore these nomads could quickly rally to become his followers. The integration of tribal units into a steppe polity of course did not only proceed on a voluntary basis but was also brought about by the subjugation of unruly or recalcitrant elements. Ruling a steppe empire on a sustained basis moreover implied that the new leader was effectively able to deliver the expected booty, tribute, or good trade relations; otherwise dissatisfaction might quickly spread, undermining the internal stability of the state. Eurasian steppe nomads' high degree of mobility, combined with recurrent fluidity of incentives for state formation, may contribute to explaining the extraordinary spatial dynamics, seemingly bordering on chaos, of C Asian political history.

---

[21] For instance, the nomads of the Pontic (Russian-Ukrainian) steppes passed the winters near the Black Sea or the Sea of Azov and the summers further north in the grasslands. The nomads of the Altay or the Pamir ranges regularly moved between their summer mountain pastures and their wintering grounds on the plain.

[22] As Fragner pointedly remarks, "gemessen an der Lebensführung transhumanter Viehzüchter war die vermeintlich menschenleere Steppe in Wirklichkeit übervölkert" ("given the lifestyle of transhumant cattle breeders, the apparently empty grasslands were actually overcrowded") (Fragner 2006, 15).

[23] But such polities of course could also emerge for other reasons, e.g., to enlarge or optimize mobile livestock production associations (Fragner 2006, 19).

2.1.4 Central Asian Precursor to the Silk Road

One can observe an early blossoming of interregional trade and cultural exchange in and beyond CA at least since Bronze Age steppe cultures had achieved greater mobility. Thus, a kind of Central Asian "forerunner" to the SR emerged around 1500 BCE (see Table 3.1), deriving from two sources and their linkup. On the one hand, traditional trade networks developed that connected oasis centers in the south with each other and with neighboring Iran and Mesopotamia; on the other hand, there were "newly" developed long-range transport and communication networks running along the Eurasian steppe belt from the east to the west and extending from the steppe belt in a north-south direction, crossing the desert zone, reaching the oasis zone, Iran, and Afghanistan. The Andronovo culture, followed by Scythian tribal confederations, developed long-distance trade (partly based on tributary relationships) with sedentary societies and states along the oasis belt and beyond. The steppe tribes sold/ exported horses, livestock products, furs, textiles, bronze and iron bars, and objects; they imported/purchased grain, garments, weapons, manufactured goods, and luxury items.[24]

However, most experts agree that these early exchanges cannot yet be labeled "Silk Road" traffic because the SR is generally seen as a network of transcontinental overland routes of exchange linking east (China) and west (the Mediterranean).[25] While in pre-antiquity, regional trade activities were developing in various parts of Eurasia, not all of these areas already seem to have been reliably linked up with each other (e.g., China and the Tarim Basin on the one hand and Western CA and the Middle East on the other appear to have lacked direct links in those early days).

2.1.5 Encounter and Division of Labor Between Ancient Greeks and Scyths

In the centuries preceding the expansion of the Persian Empire into CA, there was one major and relatively well-documented encounter between (original) C Asians and outside civilizations: From the seventh century BCE, in the far west of the steppe belt, on the northern coast of the Black Sea, close contacts, tensions, hostility, but also extensive

trade and cooperation emerged between Greek colonists and Scythian tribes. While Greeks (particularly Ionians) had crossed the Black Sea and established colonial settlements on the northern coast, including Tyras (on the mouth of the Dniester), Olbia (on the mouth of the Dnepr), Chersonesos, Theodosia (Crimea), Panticapaion, Phanagoria (at the isthmus of Kerch, see Map 4.7), and Tanais (on the mouth of the Don), some Scythian groups had just moved west and displaced the Cimmerians from the Pontic steppes.[26]

Following Herodotes' account, which is corroborated by archeological findings, one can conclude that the Scyths were semi-nomadic in a particular way: there were Scythian farmers and Scythian stockbreeders. The two populations lived clearly separated from each other. The former inhabited territories stretching from the right bank of the Dnepr approximately to the lower Danube; the latter dwelled in lands ranging from the left bank of the Dnepr to the Don and further to the east. The former were largely sedentary, the latter largely nomadic. Scythian sedentariness was also reflected by the establishment of a number of large settlements (towns), fortified by earth walls and bastions, consisting of residential buildings of wood and clay (e.g., Kamianske Horodische/Kamenskoe Gorodische on the lower Dnepr (see Map 4.7), Neapolis near Simferopol on the Crimean peninsula). Concentrated traces of smithies and forges in certain areas within settlements point to the possibility of skilled workers' districts in Scythian towns (Parzinger 2004, 78–81).

The Scythian tribal confederation ruling the Pontic steppes apparently also brought some Greek colonial towns under its sway (e.g., Olbia, near the estuary of the Dnepr, under Scythian control in the second century BCE). Scythian farmers cultivated cereals (wheat, barley, and millet), beans, lentils, onions, and garlic for their own needs as well as for sale to the Greek colonial towns, which functioned as trade intermediaries with Greece (Irmscher et al. 1986, 202). Scythes and sickles were used for harvesting. Scythian stockbreeders' herds consisted largely of horses and cattle, less of sheep and goats. Felt was milled for yurts and hoods, and leather was tanned to produce suits of armor, helmets, trousers, boots, belts, and quivers.

---

[24] Two early trade links emerged at the fringes of CA (Map 2.1): the Lazurite route and the Nephrite route. Already around 2000 BCE, Lazurite (a deep blue mineral which used to be ground into pigment) was mined in the mountains of Badakhshan (northeastern Afghanistan), then sent down the Indus Valley, along the coastline of the Arabian Sea and the Persian Gulf to Iran, Mesopotamia, Anatolia, Syria, and Egypt. Badakhshani Lazurite was also used as a major decorative element in the mask of Tutankhamun's mummy (the famous Egyptian pharaoh who had reigned between about 1332–1323 BCE). From the second millennium BCE, nephrite (a form of jade, from whitish to dark green) was traded from mines in the upper reaches of the Yarkand Daria, near Khotan, to China. In the middle of the first millennium BCE, Lazurite also appeared in the Middle Kingdom (Baipakov et al. 1997, 61).

[25] Geographically, this is a minimum definition. One can easily insist on including in the network parts of the Indian subcontinent and the Black Sea area/Istanbul. For a more detailed discussion of the definition of the SR, see Sect. 1.4 above.

[26] The geopolitical importance of the Pontic steppes in the periods prior to the deployment of artillery is well captured by Karger: "Seit von der östlichen Mittelmeerwelt das Licht der geschriebenen Geschichte auf die pontische Steppe fällt, ist sie ein Durchgangsland für Staemme und Völker gewesen, die das Tor zwischen Ural und Kaspischem Meer von Osten hereinließ." ("Since the eastern Mediterranean world shed the light of written history on the Pontic steppe, the latter has been a transit area for tribes and peoples that the gate between the Urals and the Caspian had let in from the East.") (Karger (ed) 1978, Sowjetunion, 59).

Grain, particularly wheat, was Scythia's main export product to Greece; following the upswing in trade, the Scyths expanded grain cultivation also into territories to the left of the Dnepr, including Crimea. The nomadic aristocracy played an important role in the grain trade and was one of the main beneficiaries. Apart from cereals, other exports to Greece included horses, cattle, sheep, fish, honey, wax, furs, wood, and particularly slaves. Slaves were captured by nomadic raiders in military campaigns[27]. Scythia imported from Greece a number of products, of which wine and metal objects played an important role. The Scythian kings had dependent Greek town mint coins depicting garlands of corn; these coins served as tender in Greek-Scythian trade, which otherwise was dominated by barter. The coins were apparently not used in the confederation's domestic economy (Parzinger 2004, 83–87).[28]

2.2 Central Asia (CA) Under the Sway of Major Empires of Early Antiquity: Achaemenid, Alexander, and Xiongnu (ca. 550 BCE–150 BCE)

In early antiquity, the economic space of CA was ruled or strongly influenced by three major states: two sedentary, the Persian and the Alexander empires (centered in the Middle East and Southeastern Europe), and one nomadic—the Xiongnu Empire (centered in Mongolia). Among primary sources of the following chapter are the publications of Thomas Barfield, Peter Golden, Clive Ponting, Peter Roudik, and Irmgard Sellnow.

2.2.1 Participating in a Giant Sedentary State: Central Asian Oases in the Achaemenid (Persian) Empire (550–330 BCE)

Military expansion incorporated the major oases of Western CA into the Achaemenid Empire. Under King Cyrus II (r. 559–529) Parthia/Khorassan (Northeastern Iran), Margiana, Sogdiana, Bactria, and Khorezm were conquered. Cyrus brought several thousand people to erect fortresses along the southern bank of the upper Syr Daria (in Greek: Yaxartes) to guard newly acquired territory from nomadic incursions. Among the spruced-up or newly built fortress-towns were Maracanda (Samarkand), refounded in 545 BCE, and Cyropolis (Istaravshan), established in 515 BCE. The Persian king in theory ruled like an absolute monarch but left domestic administration to indigenous princes. Cambyses II (r. 529–522) conquered most of the Ferghana basin and expanded from Afghanistan via Gandhara (region in the upper Indus valley, ancient capital: Taxila) to the Indus river and the Punjab. As Map 2.2 shows, the Syr Daria, Aral Sea, and Uzboy (the valley that connected Aral and Caspian seas and was—at the time—fed by the Amu Daria/Oxos) became the northeastern border of the empire.

Extending its reach this far, the empire also incorporated some nomads, particularly Sakas. Yet it continued to face powerful tribes in Northern CA (from west to east: Sarmatians, Sakas, and Massagetes). The Persian kings encountered repeated serious problems with their nomadic neighbors: Cyrus II died in a battle against Massagetes near the Aral Sea; Dareios was not able to defeat evasive Scythian forces in the Pontic steppes.

Dareios I (r. 522–485) divided the empire into 20 satrapies (provinces), headed by satraps (governors appointed by the Persian kings, usually from among relatives, Persian nobles, big landowners or trusted officers) equipped with considerable political, military, and economic authority. The satraps were responsible for maintaining security and order (the local military garrison was assigned to them), collecting taxes and transferring them to the central authorities, and administering justice. Cities were partly self-administered and centers of trade and craftsmanship. The countryside largely consisted of indigenous village communities which were based on subsistence activities and which produced small food surpluses for sale on local markets.

Four Central Asian satrapies were established: Margiana, Bactria, Sogdiana, and Khorezm/Khwarazm. On the other side of the Hindu Kush, Areia, Arachosia, and Gandhara became satrapies. The provinces were saddled with heavy annual tax obligations, also called tribute (Greek: phoros), generally to be paid in silver, grain, and/or livestock. C Asian satrapies are also reported to have paid in lazurite, Indian satrapies in gold. Because land was the prevailing form of wealth, taxes were preferably placed on it. Tax

---

[27] In the context of C Asian, nomadic, and steppe conquerors' practices, it is not always clear how to distinguish "slaves" from "prisoners": Whether they had participated in hostilities or not, people were regularly included in the war booty and captured in order to be sold (Paul 2012, 294).

[28] According to Shen Fuwei, by the seventh century BCE, Scythian tribes had possibly even established a trans-Eurasian link along the full length of the steppe belt. The Scyths may have shuttled on horseback (probably irregularly) all the way between China (the Zhou dynasty) and the Greek colonies and supplied the latter with much-coveted silk. According to the Greek historian Heraclitus, the trade route ran from the Don on the northern shore of the Black Sea to pass the northern shore of the Aral Sea, then turned toward the Syr Daria and Ili rivers to go eastward in the Eurasian steppe to the North of the Tienshan mountains. This route actually later came to be called the "steppe route" (Russian: stepnoy put). These Scyths may have been the first (occasional) long-distance silk traders (Shen Fuwei 2009, 21–23). Silk tissue likely transported along the steppe route was found in graves of the sixth–fifth centuries BCE in southern and western Europe (Baipakov et al. 1997, 61; Kozybaev et al. 2010, 490).

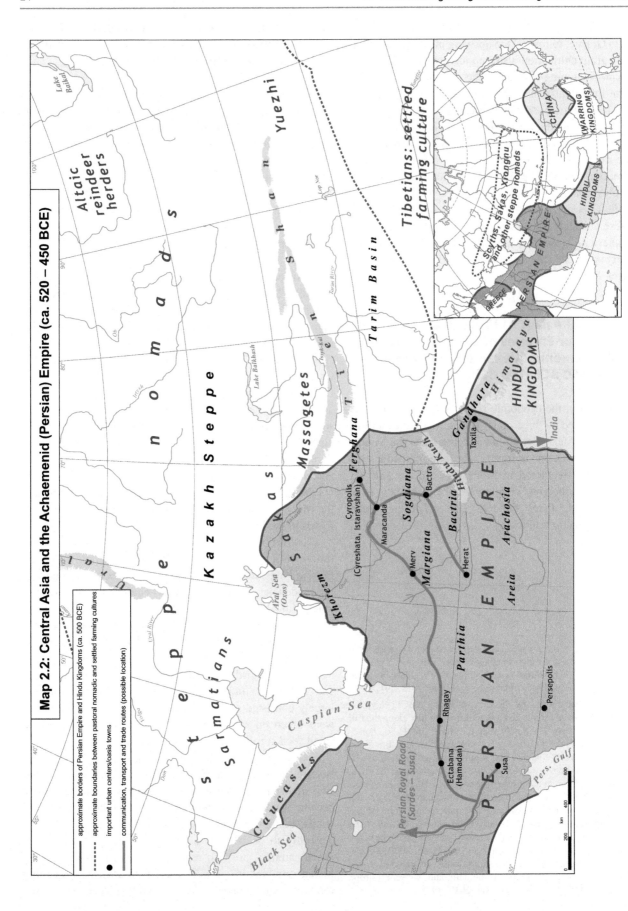

Map 2.2 CA and the Achaemenid (Persian) Empire (ca. 520–450 BCE)

payments in silver and selected official spending in gold (the Achaemenid golden dareikos) reflected—to some degree—a dual currency standard in the empire (Persian bimetallism). The rivers were the king's property. When water was needed for irrigation, a state officer supervised the opening of locks and regulated the amount of water taken by each settlement or tribe. For the opening of locks, a large sum was paid to the officer, who was required to transfer this money to the state coffers (Roudik 2007, 14).

The nomadic Sakas that had been integrated into the Achaemenid Empire were most present in the outlying province of Khorezm, which itself was based on a loose association of settled, semi-nomadic, and nomadic groups. These Sakas in particular were asked to provide cavalry for the military campaigns of the Persian kings. The valley of Zerafshan (Sogdiana) as well as Margiana were areas of intensive trade and exchange. Merv became an important entrepot for caravans. Several domains in these regions, probably benefiting from precious metals mined in the surroundings (see below), started to issue their own coins which apparently supplemented the limited circulation of Persian money (Roudik 2007, 15).

Grandiose palaces and temples were constructed for the new rulers and dignitaries in Susa, Ecbatana, and the new capital Persepolis (Iran). These construction works involved the conscription/forced deployment of artisans and craftsmen from various parts of the empire, including CA, as well as of slaves and prisoners of war from C Asian territories outside the empire. The court's and state's religion was Zoroastrianism[29], but the Achaemenids were tolerant in relation to other religions and did not attempt to force Zoroastrianism on conquered peoples. Royal or crown land (consisting of defeated rulers' extensive domains and properties appropriated by the king or his family) played a role for the royal palace economy as well as for redistribution of land to higher and lower Persian officials. While originally only revocable rights to land may have been transferred, and donations could be canceled, redistributed land soon tended to become a hereditary possession of the beneficiaries, which over time eroded royal authority and central control (Ponting 2001, 145). Redistributed land enhanced the ranks of big landowners. Apart from them, there were numerous small landowners and smallholders (some of whom remained members of village communities (Sellnow et al. 1977, 229).

Given that Achaemenid royal power was understood as absolute rule, there was no clear-cut separation between the palace economy and the state budget. In any case, a substantial share of taxes was used to finance major infrastructural projects which contributed to unifying markets: the construction of long-distance roads, the establishment of the royal postal

system, and the dissemination of Persian irrigation technology throughout large parts of the empire. The Persian Royal Road was primarily used by the army. By the time of Herodotus (ca. 475 BCE), it ran 2860 km from Susa (southeastern Persia) to Sardes (Western Asia Minor). Similar, but probably less sophisticated, roads connected Persia with the ancient cities of Merv, Bukhara, Samarkand (Maracanda), and Herat, and with India (Map 2.2). The royal postal service, installed along the road network, was a new communication system which conveyed official messages with surprising speed because postal stations and relays were established along the connecting routes in regular distances; by having fresh horses and riders ready at each relay, royal couriers could carry messages along the entire distance from Susa to Sardes in 9 days, though normal travelers took about 12 weeks. This combined transport and communication system also stimulated trade. Even early caravanserais were set up along the routes.

Irrigation projects consisted of the state-supervised building of large dams, canals, and particularly subterranean irrigation schemes embodying advanced (for the time) Persian technology. Underground channels (qanats or karez)[30] were drawn from streams in the snow-fed mountains. As Habib explains, wells were dug at particular distances to tap the underground water; the wells were thus connected by the channels, sloping downwards, ultimately to emerge in the open on the lower ground, where the water was used for irrigation. The Persian qanat (karez) system, whose construction was very labor-intensive, had two major advantages: Not only was the water collected from subterranean aquifers without the need for any lifting mechanism, but much of the water, while carried underground, was protected from evaporation as well (Habib 2003, 468; Waugh 2008, 2). With sophisticated hydrotechnical structures in place, new plants, such as peaches, apricots, possibly sugar cane, and oranges, were introduced into newly conquered areas, including C Asian provinces (Mokyr 2003, 369).

Of course not only the setting up of palaces and public buildings but also road construction and the erection of dams and canals—particularly underground channels—were a focus of "great cooperation" in which forced labor tended to be a frequent ingredient. Notwithstanding the empire's various undertakings and expenditures, the generous use of ubiquitous and cheap compulsory labor may have helped the Achaemenid state save a considerable amount of public proceeds which were set aside and accumulated in the royal treasury (particularly in the form of precious metals).

While inclusion into the Achaemenid state strengthened C Asian oases' links with empire-wide and transcontinental

---

[29] Zoroaster/Zarathustra was probably born around 630 BCE in Bactria.

[30] These channels are called qanats in Persia and probably served as models for similar devises called karez in Afghanistan and Xinjiang (see below).

trade of the ancient world, overall economic activity did not flourish as much as it might have. This was because of the limited level of demand, partly stemming from the high taxation and the considerable amount of revenues transferred to the treasury, thus withdrawn from circulation (Sellnow et al. 1977, 229; Ponting 2001, 142). In this sense, Achaemenid monetary policy (carried out by fiscal measures) may have been overly restrictive. A lot of trade was for the elite and mainly in luxury items because the latter were fairly easy to transport, e.g., ivory from India (Litvinsky 1996, 170).

Achaemenid rule provided impulses for urban development of C Asian oases. As Golden points out, Persian-ruled cities were divided into sections: The military-political-administrative core was the kuhandiz/quhandiz (sometimes shortened to kunduz) or "old fortress," "citadel," usually located within the town center. Here, the local rulers (in some cases: governors) resided in a castle along with their entourage and military commanders. The urban treasury, chancellery, a temple for the local cult, and even a prison were within its limits. The town center or inner city was termed shahristan, another Persian word deriving from shahr ("city"). Beyond the outlying suburbs lay agricultural settlements, called rustak/rustaq, surrounding the cities. They produced the melons for which CA was famous, as well as fruits, grapes, vegetables, grains, and other produce. Cloth production, ceramics, glassware, and the manufacture of a host of tools, ranging from cookware to weapons, were also an important part of the C Asian urban economy in Achaemenid times. Towns near rich ore deposits in nearby mountains became both mining and production centers for bronze, iron, gold, and silver manufacturing (Golden 2011, 19).

Strains may have made themselves felt in the Persian economy already from the first half of the fifth century BCE. The persistent burden of heavy taxation and compulsory labor, partly reflecting rising needs of the military, but also high demands of the treasury, were contributing factors. Sizable means were spent on successful military expansion and on protecting exposed areas, e.g., the northeast and its Sogdian traders and businessmen, from nomadic incursions. But sizable means were also spent on unsuccessful campaigns, e.g., in Greece (battles of Marathon in 490 BCE and Salamis in 480 BCE). Dissatisfaction turned into unrest and uprisings, e.g., in Bactria. Repeated dynastic succession struggles did not stabilize the situation. The putting down of the insurgencies escalated requirements for military expenditure and led to destruction, which in turn further increased restlessness and apparently led to a vicious circle. In the early fourth century, first the satrapy of Khorezm, then some nomadic (Saka) and semi-nomadic border areas in the northeast of the empire got rid of Achaemenid rule. The de-facto independence of provinces cut off the Persian treasury from revenues and tended to create obstacles for trade. Increased political instability was accompanied by rising insecurity on the roads.

2.2.2 Cosmopolitism and Economic Expansion: Central Asian Oases in the Empire of Alexander and the Hellenistic States (330 BCE–ca. 150 BCE)

2.2.2.1 Empire of Alexander: First Major European Colonization Effort in CA (330–323 BCE)

Alexander the Great's conquest of CA involved fierce fighting for Sogdiana. Tens of thousands of Sogdians were killed; Samarkand (Maracanda) was completely destroyed. Alexander, however, did not venture as far into CA as the Achaemenids had done: Margiana, Bactria, and Sogdiana as well as parts of the Ferghana basin were included into the empire; as depicted in Map 2.3, the lower stretches of the Oxos (Greek for Amu Daria) including Khwarazm as well as most of the Yaxartes (Syr Daria) remained beyond Alexander's and the Hellenistic states' rule, although the Khwarazmians were loosely dependent on Alexander. In the Kingdom of Khorezm from the end of the fourth to the second century BCE, fortified towns replaced earlier rural settlements, and the irrigation system was extended. Nomadic pressure on the empire's northern border persisted: Alexander's garrisons in Maracanda were repeatedly harassed by Saka incursions. Nevertheless, Greek/Macedonian rule furthered unprecedented urban growth in CA (Roudik 2007, 16).

In order to gain the loyalty of defeated Persians, Alexander posed as the legitimate successor to Dareios III, the last Achaemenid king, for whom he organized a dignified state funeral. Alexander also adopted the elaborate Persian court ceremonial. Moreover, the great Greek/Macedonian leader married Roxane, the daughter of a Sogdian nobleman. He later married Stateira, Dareios III's daughter, who became his second wife. This wedding was staged as the prelude to the mass wedding of Susa in 324 BCE, at which around 9000 Greek/Macedonian soldiers married daughters of influential Persian nobles. Alexander's goal here was to internally stabilize the giant empire which straddled east and west—Asia and Europe—by bringing about an integration of the Greek/Macedonian and Persian elites.

This goal also played a role, as far as Alexander was concerned, in the foundation of about 35 colonial cites in the east of the newly conquered empire, incl. Southern CA, in 330–325 BCE. This happened during Alexander's military campaigns. Some towns were actually newly built, while others were built on pre-existing fortified sites or on sites of former settlements/towns (Roudik 2007, 16). Map 2.3 shows some of the colonial cities: Alexandria Areia = Herat, Alexandroupolis (near Mashhad), Alexandria Margiane = Merv, Alexandria = Kandahar, Alexandria Eschate ("the furthest") = Khodzhent, Alexandria Prophthasia (Zaranj, Region of Sistan, Southwestern Afghanistan/Southeastern Iran). Most of these towns were

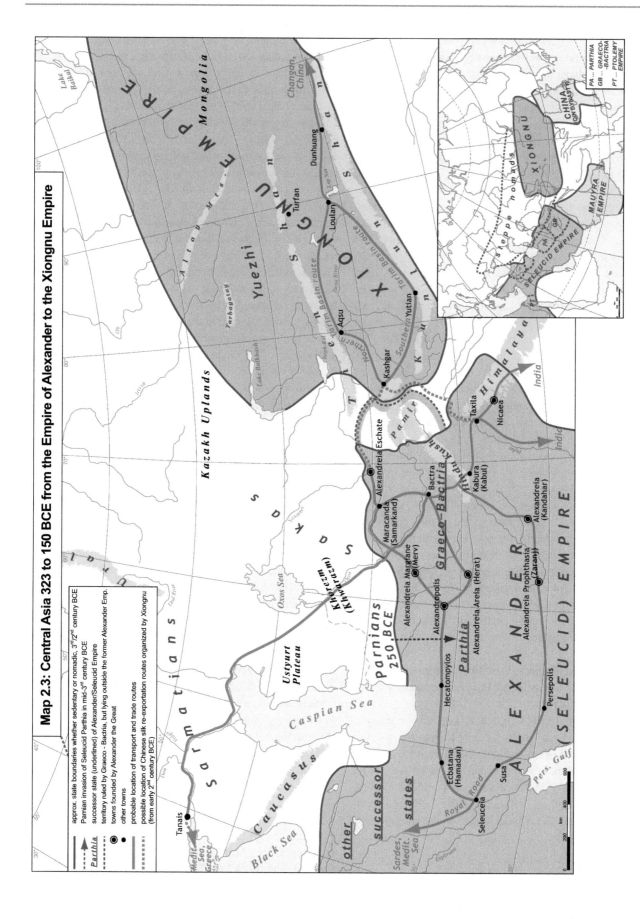

Map 2.3 CA 323 to 150 BCE: from the Empire of Alexander to the Xiongnu Empire

not only strategically important but also lay on long-distance trade routes. Greek/Macedonian settlers (soldiers, craftsmen, traders) as well as mostly Indo-Iranian people from the immediate surroundings moved to these towns.[31] Given their colonial origin, at least initially they did not have much autonomy and were placed under Alexander's/the king's authority. The foundations followed the pattern of the Greek polis, which included a market (agora), a temple, a theater, and a gymnasium. Streets and houses were arranged in a checkerboard-type design. These settlements became centers of Hellenistic culture.

The Achaemenid territorial institution of satrapy (province) was retained. Yet all satraps that had not sworn allegiance to Alexander during the military campaigns were dismissed and replaced by loyalists. Satraps were moreover assisted by centrally appointed financial supervisors. The institution of crown land (basilike chora) also survived and was generously used by Alexander to reward military commanders, relatives, friends, and other dignitaries, as well as to endow newly founded colonial towns. The conversion of the lion's share of the accumulated Persian royal treasury into minted coin money and its expenditure and circulation, in which the Hellenistic towns served as important conduits, gave the economy a major boost and created a currency of Alexander coins which connected Europe and Asia. There is no doubt that the new Hellenistic poleis in CA and the east of the empire contributed to the boom in trade and crafts.

In 323 BCE Alexander died without having settled his succession. Despite some initial success in drawing together different elites and different parts of the empire, centrifugal tendencies remained strong and, over time, gained the upper hand. After a few decades, in the early third century BCE, the empire of Alexander disintegrated or split up into the Diadoch empires of the Antigonids (in Greece), of the Ptolemais (in Egypt and Palestine), of the Seleucids (the lion's share of the remaining territories, including CA), and into some smaller states.

2.2.2.2 Seleucid Empire: Sustained Colonization, Rising International Trade, Prosperity and Inflation

The Seleucids ruled in CA from the late fourth century to 250 BCE. After the turmoil of Alexander's military campaigns, internal peace and external peace were regained for most of the third century BCE. This factor—a "peace dividend"—probably played an important role for the relative economic prosperity witnessed in the Seleucid Empire (Roberts 2002, 218). Although the king attempted to

strengthen his power in the regions with the help of an expanded bureaucracy generally using Greek as its language of communication, in the far-flung empire, the (mostly Greek) satraps were able to sustain a degree of autonomy, not unlike their predecessors in the Achaemenid Empire. The army infantry (Macedonian phalanx) was mixed with cavalry (typically including descendants of C Asian nomads); soldiers were settled as hereditary peasant servicemen in closed armed villages. Similar to the Persian rulers, the Seleucid rulers' main sources of revenue were proceeds from crown lands and the palace economy, taxes in money and in kind, and, where deemed necessary, conscripted labor. Customs duties played a growing fiscal role as trade expanded, benefiting from Seleucid road maintenance and extension in CA and the east.

The Seleucid Empire did not only further develop the road and trade network, it also continued colonization activities; attracted new Greek and, to a lesser degree, local Indo-Iranian settlers; and strengthened colonial cities. Greek viniculture was introduced to CA. While the local artisans and workers in C Asian and eastern towns of the empire mostly worked in family enterprises, the Greek settlers introduced relatively large specialized firms (ergasteries) into the new territories. These firms, employing numerous workers as well as slaves, seem to have been more competitive than the independent indigenous craftsmen. Many of the latter were eventually hired by the ergasteries which thus profited from oriental professional skills. On the other hand, important social and economic cleavages persisted between a privileged, largely Greek/Macedonian urbanized elite, including big landowners, and the rural majority of inhabitants, who were put at a disadvantage (Sellnow et al. 1977, 352–353).

The monetary stimulus originally released by Alexander, the continued inflow of settlers, and the strengthening of Hellenistic cities in CA and the east, as well as political stability, set the stage for a renewed empire-wide economic recovery. This recovery was particularly strong in CA and the east, given the relatively lower initial level of economic development of these territories (compared to Mesopotamia or the eastern Mediterranean). The circulation of money (monetization), which had so far not been highly developed in CA (except for Sogdiana and Margiana), was boosted. In Bactria, the authorities minted gold and silver coins.

International trade running from India through the Seleucid Empire and CA to Greece and Italy expanded. There were three main trade routes between India and the west (Map 2.3): On the northern route, goods were transported from the Punjab across the Hindu Kush (Greek: Paropamisos), often over the Khyber Pass, via Bactra, then along the Oxos (Amu Daria) to the Aral Sea, and from there further to the Black Sea. The first section of the middle route was identical to that of the northern one across the Hindu

---

[31] For instance, Alexander oversaw the resettlement of 20,000 Greeks in the province of Bactria.

Kush to Bactra; then it traversed the Iranian Plateau and descended to the city of Seleucia (in Mesopotamia), before moving on to the Levant. The southern route led from Western India to the Persian Gulf by Sea, then up the Tigris river to the same city of Seleucia (Yang Juping 2009, 16). Among major traded goods were metalwork, cloth, ceramic products (from the empire and from Europe), silk, fragrances, and other precious oriental goods (from India, and via India from further east, probably also China). Indian merchants and craftspeople migrated to the cities of Bactria and spread Buddhism and Brahmanism in CA (Roudik 2007, 17).

The swell of money (due to the conversion of the treasury), however, did not only trigger positive consequences. It corresponded to what we in modern terms might call a sharp relaxation of monetary policy which—with lags typical in this policy field—eventually entailed inflation and instability (Roberts 2002, 219). In the early third century BCE, nomadic tribes attacked CA and destroyed some of its cities. The Seleucids restored the cities as well as trade and surrounded the Margiana oasis with a 240 km long wall. After 250 BCE, new Hellenistic kingdoms emerged in Bactria and Parthia (Northeastern Iran). When the Seleucids strived to compensate these losses in CA by territorial expansion in Greece, they clashed with ascending Rome, which in turn, conquered Greece. Subsequently, the weakened Seleucid rump Empire turned into a kind of buffer state between the new rival powers in the Near East: Rome and the Parthians.

2.2.2.3 Twilight of Hellenism in CA: Early Parthian Empire and Greco-Bactrian Kingdom (250–ca. 150 BCE)

In the middle of the third century BCE, a confederation of Parnian (Indo-Iranian) tribes, horseback-riding nomads excelling in mounted archery, set out from an area they inhabited southwest of the Aral Sea and conquered the Seleucid province of Parthia (Northeastern Iran). The Parnians quickly assimilated to the local Iranian population (while at the same time not entirely abandoning their original lifestyle) and founded the Parthian Empire of the Arsacids, which soon expanded further south (Map 2.3).

The internal organization of the Parthian state was even more decentralized than its predecessors in the region. Arsacid royalty became dependent on a few powerful Persian aristocratic families that typically owned large-scale land holdings and boasted hereditary offices in the kingdom. A considerable part of the rural population—sometimes still organized in village communities—lived and worked on these holdings. In case of war, respective noblemen, together with the subjects on their land, had to contribute to staffing the army. The Hellenistic poleis maintained a special position within the Parthian state. These elements would seem to show some affinity to (much later) feudal institutions in Europe. Salient sources of Parthian state finance were land and poll taxes,

forced labor including slave labor, and levies on trade. The latter gained importance to the extent that international trade expanded, and then eventually, the SR was opened.

The Bactrian satrapy—together with the satrapy of Sogdiana—situated at the northeastern edge of the Seleucid Empire, soon strived for more autonomy from central control. In a situation when the imperial authorities were preoccupied with nomadic pressure and invasion and were politically weakened, in 250 BCE Bactria (incorporating Sogdiana, Margiana, and Areia/the region of Herat) established an independent Hellenistic state, the Greco-Bactrian kingdom. The new state also swiftly struck out south, soon controlled entire present-day Afghanistan, and reached the Arabian Sea and the Indus by 180 BCE (to the detriment of what remained of the Seleucid Empire, Map 2.3). Once Greco-Bactria, which possessed a highly developed urban culture[32], was independent, the kingdom's coin production rose. Like in other states, coins were symbols of sovereignty and prestige, e.g., "King Diodotos coins".[33] At the same time, sufficient monetization greatly facilitated domestic and international trade, particularly for a country that occupied a pivotal position connecting CA and the Middle East on the one hand and India on the other. Probably even more important than trade with India was the flow of culture and religion, as exemplified by the initial flourishing of Greco-Buddhist art.

Pressures of the nomadic Xiongnu (a Turco-Altaic people) from the Eurasian steppe (where they had already established a steppe state centered on the territory of present-day Mongolia) toward the west and southwest[34] eventually pushed other nomads away from their respective C Asian habitats. These other nomads were the Yuezhi (related to the Tokharians of the Tarim Basin, but living further east) as well as Saka tribes of the Turanian Plain. Yuezhi and Sakas subsequently invaded the territory of the Greco-Bactria,[35] first shrinking the size of that kingdom, then, toward the end of the second century BCE, wiping it out altogether (Schiltz 1994, 309). The Parthians took advantage of the partial power vacuum and also expanded into the area.

---

[32] As illustrated by the "Oxos treasure" of sophisticated metal work (British Museum)

[33] They relate to Diodotos, the last Seleucid satrap in Bactria, who declared independence and had himself crowned king of Greco-Bactria (Hambly (ed) 1966/1979, 42). Some Bactrian coins continued to be used (in a deteriorated form) in Sogdiana until the fifth century CE (de la Vaissière 2004, 20).

[34] These possibly deflective movements might have been triggered by the Xiongnu's persistent military confrontation with China (Gernet 1972/1985, vol. 1, 36; see also next chapter).

[35] Corresponds to another example of the "billiard principle" of the Eurasian steppes

2.2.3 East CA in the Xiongnu Empire: Initiation of Transcontinental Silk Trade by the First Major Nomadic State Ruling the Eurasian Steppe (from Around BCE 200)

During the fourth century BCE, tensions between horseback-riding nomadic Xiongnu tribes (possible ancestors of the Huns), mostly inhabiting the territory of present-day Mongolia, and China (Zhou dynasty/Warring States period), grew into open hostility. About a century later, the Xiongnu established their first large tribal confederation under their leader Mao-dun (209–174)[36]. Originally its economic basis consisted almost exclusively of animal husbandry. Hunting played an important secondary role. Farming activities were marginal. In a few years, the Xiongnu subjugated neighboring nomadic tribes and conquered East Turkestan.

The city-states of the sedentary Tokharian (Indo-European) population of the Tarim Basin oases were forced to pay regular tribute (agricultural products and manufactured goods) to and perform labor services for the Xiongnu. With the exception of Dzungaria, that was also populated by nomads, the inhabitants of East Turkestan largely consisted of farmers living in walled towns and cultivating small lots of the Tarim river's alluvial land, as well as exploiting some domesticated animals, and people carrying out craftsmanship and trade (local and further afield). As opposed to Dzungaria, the Xiongnu did not rule the Tarim Basin directly but depended on sedentary imperial agents to exact revenue from local rulers, a practice that was particularly suitable to the nomadic way of life in that it imposed lower administrative costs on the steppe dwellers.

Mao-dun soon went to war against China. At the start of the second century BCE a nomadic confederation of about one million people, relying on its military superiority, confronted and defeated a sedentary empire ruling more than 50 million subjects (Barfield 1989/1992, 49). During the battles and razzias in China, prisoners were captured and deported to Mongolia en masse. In some cases, up to 40,000 prisoners are reported to have been enslaved. Most Chinese prisoners were exploited as slave farmers, typically cultivating millet.[37] The Xiongnu owed their military successes to their improved armament (heavy cavalry, riders wearing armor), to their efficient military organization (decimal subdivision of the army into units of 10,000 horsemen), and to the capabilities of their abovementioned charismatic leader. After the conquests, a

vast area—from Manchuria via Lake Baikal to Lake Balkhash, including East Turkestan and Dzungaria, the Gansu region, and the middle reaches of the Huang-he—was in Xiongnu hands (Map 2.3). An imperial confederacy (imperial nomadism, see above) that employed the principles of tribal organization and indigenous leaders at the local level, the Xiongnu Empire maintained an integrated state structure with an exclusive monopoly of the control of foreign and military affairs.

A quick look at China in these turbulent times: Following the period of the Warring States toward the end of the Zhou dynasty (404–222 BCE), China was reunited by the Qin dynasty (221–207 BCE, first emperor Qin Shihuangdi). The new rulers reformed the country by introducing a uniform writing; replacing territorial princes with a strong and competent civil service; orienting the latter toward Confucian values of loyalty and good governance; standardizing weights, measures, and means of payment; and carrying out large public projects. One of the latter was the erection of the Great Wall by consolidating already existing protective barriers of the old Chinese principalities into a wall of 5000 km, in order to protect the country from recurring attacks by the C Asian "steppe barbarians". Hundreds of thousands of inhabitants participated in this endeavor. From the Zhou dynasty, silk—which had already been produced in China since around 1000 BCE—was used as money.[38] The Han dynasty (206 BCE–220 CE) consolidated Qin Shihuangdi's achievements. Civil servants were paid in silk rolls.

While the modernization of the Chinese Empire was impressive and made it a more difficult target for nomadic attack, it was obviously not yet strong enough to withstand the onslaught of the militarily superior Xiongnu. As Barfield points out, possibly the establishment and the rise of the Xiongnu Empire represented a response to the preceding recovery and consolidation of the Chinese state (Barfield 2001, 235). In any case, Mao-dun obliged the Chinese emperor to pay tribute: Barfield summarizes the arrangements[39] to which the Han dynasty had to agree as a result of its inability to defeat the Xiongnu in the early second century BCE (Barfield 1989/1992, 46; see also Waugh 2002, 4; Freydank et al. 1978, 472). These arrangements constituted the so-called heqin ("Peace and friendship") system:

(a) China made fixed annual payments of silk, wine, grain, and other foodstuffs to the Xiongnu.
(b) The Han gave a princess in marriage to the Shan-yue (the Xiongnu ruler).

---

[36] This appears to be the earliest proven case in history that a tribal confederacy establishes a powerful and extensive state on the Eurasian steppe (Fragner 2007, 35).

[37] According to some calculations, up to 10% of the total Xiongnu population consisted of slaves (Paul 2012, 294).

[38] Under the Zhou, it seems that up to five slaves and one horse were exchanged for one skein of silk (Huyghe and Huyghe 2006, 112).

[39] These arrangements did not fully bring to a halt Xiongnu incursions, devastations and looting in China, though. Tensions with the Han dynasty persisted.

(c) The Xiongnu and China were regarded as coequal states.

(d) The Great Wall constituted the official boundary between the two states.

The large quantities of silk produced in Chinese factories and workshops, provided by the Chinese authorities and shipped into the steppe, did not end up merely decorating yurts and garments, although they were important to enable the Xiongnu ruler to retain his status and secure the loyalty of other nomadic tribes. Some of the extorted silk and other products were traded across the Xiongnu-held lands with their neighbors to the west, all the way to Rome. According to Barfield, Waugh, and de la Vaissière, it is not unreasonable to view this international re-export of Chinese luxury goods that already started in the second century BCE as the real beginning of the SR (Barfield 2001, 235; Waugh 2002, 4; de la Vaissière 2004, 159) (see Table 3.1).

As Map 2.3 shows, this re-export is likely to have taken place via the trade routes running through the north and the south of the Tarim Basin, then across the Tienshan, Pamir, and Karakorum mountains in western and southern directions (to Persia and India). The Xiongnu may have also used a steppe route, which, however, was less stable, and most of which was not under their control. In any case, the trade connections of the Tarim Basin acquired strategic importance.

Box 2.2: Trade Under Conditions of General Nomadic Military Superiority in Eurasia (from about 800 BCE to 1700 CE)

Given conditions of usual nomadic military superiority over sedentary cultures throughout antiquity and the Middle Ages, the settled people tended to be at a disadvantage with respect to terms of acquisition of goods and of trade. Such an imbalance of power would suggest nomadic confederations (e.g., the Xiongnu or their Turko-Mongol successors) generally preferred asymmetric trade relationships. These asymmetric relationships included tributary rents, the extortion of subsidies, if necessary occasional razzias, and "direct appropriation"/confiscations of values instead of reciprocal voluntary exchange. If deemed necessary, nomads might also conquer strategically or economically important sedentary areas (as Mao-dun did in the second century BCE with respect to East Turkestan) despite higher costs of permanent control in this case (imperial nomadism, see above). This does not mean that nomads would not accept reciprocal voluntary exchange ("the free market") if the goods they desired were not attainable otherwise.

In contrast, sedentary states (e.g., China, Parthia, the Kushan Empire, see below), not possessing this military advantage, would generally prefer to conduct mutually

advantageous commercially viable trade, as exemplified in many respects by the first heyday of the SR. Yet in case of a political/military weakness of a trading partner, the sedentary state might also resort to taxing its neighbor or even to conquering areas to assure control of trade routes or pursue other goals (as China did around 100 BCE and in later times in the Tarim Basin). But owing to their military vulnerability vis-à-vis nomadic forces, sedentary states' hold on conquered territories in CA remained tenuous and unstable (up to about 1700). Prices exacted in tribute trade would depend less on economic than on political and military factors.[40]

Given that their lands tended to be spacious, nomadic states would typically use the opportunity to tax transit trade running through their territories (the Mongol Empire and its successor states constitute fitting examples of this practice). If they were lucky in this sense, sat astride transit routes, and were not unduly harassed by nomadic interventions, sedentary states would of course do this too (as demonstrated by the Parthian and the Sassanian Empires for centuries). In both cases, transit taxes also constituted payments for trade protection which could benefit long-distance trade. Sometimes, trade protection services that only militarily superior nomads could offer made accessible or prized open and secured essential but dangerous routes (as happened with a number of branches of the SR under the Pax Mongolica).

2.3 The Great Silk Road: Linking Roman and Chinese Empires (150 BCE–350 CE)

For this chapter, the author has primarily drawn from publications by Thomas Barfield, Shen Fuwei, Andre Gunder Frank, Joel Mokyr, Etienne de la Vaissière, Liu Xinru, and Daniel Waugh.

2.3.1 China, Driven Primarily by Geopolitical Goals, Establishes the Great Silk Road in CA (ca. 150 BCE–ca. 1 CE)

While one might argue that important trade connections and markets emerge spontaneously through mutually beneficial cooperation of interested parties and states, historic reality often witnesses trade creation as a—welcome—by-product of political expansion and conquest. In any case, as will be

---

[40] Perhaps somewhat oversimplifying, Barfield points out that a nomadic leader who failed to establish a lucrative extortion relationship with China was building a political structure on sand (1989, 238).

shown on many occasions below, trade routes and markets can only function once a minimum level of political stability and security is provided.

2.3.1.1 From Tributary Dependence on the Xiongnu to Ruler of the Eastern SR (105 BCE)

The Xiongnu's regular exaction of silk and of other taxes and obligations from the Han dynasty, imposed as a tributary relationship by Mao-dun, constituted a heavy economic burden for China and, of course, gave rise to dissatisfaction in Han ruling circles. Within the framework of the heqin system, and under pressure from recurring nomadic raids and threats, annual Chinese payments of goods and foodstuffs to the Xiongnu at their maximum amounted to 92,000 meters of silk, about 95,000 liters of grain (particularly rice), and 200,000 liters of wine (Barfield 1989/1992, 47). Within the Xiongnu confederation, the Shan-yue retained the exclusive right to conduct foreign (commercial) affairs and used this monopoly power to control nomads' access to China and the redistribution of Chinese goods, trade benefits, and rents to the members of the nomadic imperial court and elite and the leaders of the various tribes. Economic interaction between the two empires took place on three levels:

- Chinese tribute (tax) payments, consisting of silk, wine, grain, and other foodstuffs, to be assigned to various nomadic stakeholders, and furthermore—remaining amounts of silk—to be re-exported, mostly to CA and the west, via routes that later came to be named "Silk Road"
- Booty acquired from (irregular) raids into China, mostly kept by attacking warriors
- Merchandise purchased/bartered by Xiongnu tribesmen for pastoral products on border markets with China[41]

China disguised the true nature of its appeasement policy by devising/simulating an elaborate (reverse) "tributary system" in which large payments to the nomads were described as gifts given to loyal subordinates (barbarians) that were in theory coming to pay homage to the emperor, who represented the Middle Kingdom's superior status. When the system was first regularized, records show that the estimated annual cost of tax payments (subsidies) to China's frontier peoples amounted to one third of the Han

government payroll or 7% of all the empire's revenue (Barfield 2001, 237).

Needless to say, payments from China that funded nomadic states and moreover enabled the bulk shipment of luxury goods via transcontinental trade routes attracted international merchants from CA and elsewhere who often used the nomads' political standing to establish their own profitable relations with the Middle Kingdom. Nomadic elites actively encouraged trade and attempted to attract merchants into their territories because the pastoral economy was not self-sufficient and because the nomads were not adept in marketing and re-exporting large amounts of acquired tribute and in gaining products they coveted through international market relationships. They also wanted to benefit from taxing active overland trade via routes under their control. As Barfield put it, the steppe nomads were not the great long-distance traders, but they acted as patrons for sedentary C Asians who were (2001, 245). In this sense, the impact of nomadic empires on China had global implications because it acted as the catalyst for long-distance foreign trade (Barfield 2011, 169; Brunn et al. 2012, 24).

The Chinese were interested in overcoming the Xiongnu military and economic pressure through forging alliances with states further afield (particularly with the Yuezhi that had been forced to migrate west by the Xiongnu) and through strengthening trade relationships with other states in order to acquire strategically important goods, particularly powerful horses, to be able to confront the Xiongnu cavalry. First, however, China attempted to wean the Tarim Basin (a generally sedentary area, like China itself) and other neighboring regions from the Xiongnu peacefully by means of material incentives (bribery) rather than coercion. The first Chinese diplomatic mission to CA took place in 138–119 BCE under the leadership of the ambassador Zhang Qian; it brought back information on states to the west of China (i.e., Ferghana (called Dayuan by the Chinese), Sogdiana and parts of Bactria, which at that time were just about to be conquered by the Yuezhi).

According to Zhang Qian, most of the inhabitants of Ferghana (Dayuan) were sedentary farmers, but there were also nomads. The approximately 70 cities of the region, most of them walled, contained an aggregate population of several hundreds of thousands. Barley, wheat, rice, lucerne,[42] and wine were cultivated in the Ferghana Basin. The winemaking (inherited from Greek/Hellenistic settlers) was so productive that rich men even managed to store more than 300,000 liters of it.[43] Regarding animal husbandry, the

---

[41] By Han law these markets were restricted to the sale of goods with no military value to the nomads. This type of restriction imposed by a sedentary state on trade with a nomadic power is typical for such a situation and has recurred many times in history (as will be shown below). It might even be compared to the "Western" practice of banning the sale of certain types of weapons and high technology to the hostile "East" during the Cold War.

---

[42] Lucerne served as fodder for horses.

[43] Following Zhang Qian's return, viniculture and some plant species (nuts, carrots) were introduced via CA in central China (Yang Juping 2009, 18; Overseas Chinese Affairs Office (2006), 51).

domestic (Ferghana) horse race was well known: These "blood-sweating heavenly horses," probably ancestors of the Turkmen horse breed Akhal-Teke, were reported to be much larger and stronger than the horses the Chinese and the Xiongnu had; the Ferghana horses were therefore coveted by the Han dynasty (Dmitriev 2009, 47).

In his mission Zhang Qian was accompanied by 300 armed men and a caravan carrying gold and silk goods to pay for expenses and buy influence. While Zhang Qian, who was captured en route by the Xiongnu but managed to escape, brought back lots of valuable information on China's western neighbors, he wasn't successful in gaining allies and strengthening strategic trade relationships. After dispatching numerous other weakly armed missions into CA, which only met limited success and some of which were raided by the Xiongnu, the Chinese decided to boost their defenses and to send large expeditionary forces into the area.

As a defensive measure, the Great Wall was further extended to the eastern edge of the Taklamakan desert. Emperor Han Wudi (141–87 BCE) decided to abandon the heqin policy in favor of the military option. Having included cavalry in their armies (although not yet the "Heavenly Horses"), the Chinese defeated the Xiongnu in a number of battles from 121 to 119 BCE.[44] Although the basin was apparently not entirely occupied, the Ferghana (Dayuan) expedition of 105 BCE achieved its goal: The region's inhabitants (Sogdians and semi-nomadic or nomadic Sakas) that had established the kingdom of Ferghana became vassals of the Chinese Empire and had to pay a heavy tribute in terms of thousands of horses; furthermore the kingdom took the obligation to send a certain number of horses to China on an annual basis (Dmitriev 2009, 47). The Wusuns, a neighboring semi-nomadic people living in the Tienshan and Semirechie, also entered into a tributary relationship with the Middle Kingdom.

Around the same year as the incursion into Ferghana (105 BCE), Parthia and China exchanged embassies and inaugurated official bilateral trade along the caravan route that linked them; with this the Great Silk Road (here also just called Silk Road or SR) came into existence (Table 3.1). At the end of the second century BCE, this major route of trade and communication also passed through Bactria and Sogdiana, which had just been conquered by the nomadic Yuezhi (Kushan Empire, see below) and the Tarim Basin (which was just being subjugated by the Chinese military). From the first half of the first century BCE, China was in control of the trade routes in East Turkestan. Han conquests and control were however facilitated by internal weaknesses that had afflicted the Xiongnu approximately at the same

time: A cattle epidemic had broken out and triggered a famine, and particularistic tendencies had erupted among the tribes constituting the confederation and produced a temporary division of the Xiongnu state into a larger northern part (focused on Northwestern Mongolia) and a smaller southern part (having its center in Southeastern Mongolia, abutting the Great Wall) (Shukow et al. 1956/62, Band 2, 457; Ponting 2001, 250). On the other hand, the high costs the Han had incurred in their campaign of conquest may have signaled to the Chinese that their western expansion had reached its limits.

Soon after taking possession of the Tarim Basin around 100 BCE, the Chinese authorities established the General Protectorate of the western territories (Xiyu duhu), headed by a representative of the emperor (Kauz 2006, 121) (see Maps 2.4 and 2.5). This governor exercised supreme authority in the Tarim Basin and in Turfan, while maintaining the local kingdoms/principalities: About 50 statelets of the region started to pay tribute to the Chinese monarch. The governor's authority was based on the installation of a chain of fixed military-agricultural colonies/garrisons in the region (Millward and Perdue 2004, 35–36). These settlements constituted the tuntian system. Strong military presence remained necessary due to continued sporadic Xiongnu incursions and fighting. The colonies were set up near the watch towers of the Great Wall, then extended to the Jade Gate (Yumen Guan) and from there to Turfan and to the Tarim oases. By instructing the soldiers to farm for themselves during periods of peace, the military achieved a degree of self-sufficiency in a remote area, and transportation costs for shipping food grain from central China were cut.

The Turfan oasis (in the Turfan Basin/Depression) is a key location of the SR (and of East-West Eurasian traffic links until today). As early as the second century BCE (under Xiongnu rule), Turfan was a prosperous oasis with developed agriculture, producing wheat, barley, rice, corn, beans, melons, Hami melons (a kind of muskmelon), sesame, etc. Turfan received most of its water from the snow-capped mountains of the Bogda Shan (an extension of the Tienshan to the north of the oasis, see Sect. 1.3.1), which also possessed large tracts of excellent natural (Alpine) pasturelands, where herds of horses, sheep, cattle, and camels could graze. The earliest identifiable inhabitants of the Turfan area, like those of the Tarim Basin, were probably the Indo-European Yuezhi/Tokharians (see above). In 67 BCE, the oasis was taken over by the Chinese army and the city of Gaochang was constructed there. Turfan became a kind of military-agricultural headquarters of Han dynasty presence in the "Western territories" (Liu 2005; Geng Shimin 1998, 201).

As the tuntian policy shows: while trade motives played an essential role in China's ancient western expansion, geopolitical goals (strengthening of defenses against nomads,

---

[44] However, these victories were achieved at the cost of heavy casualties.

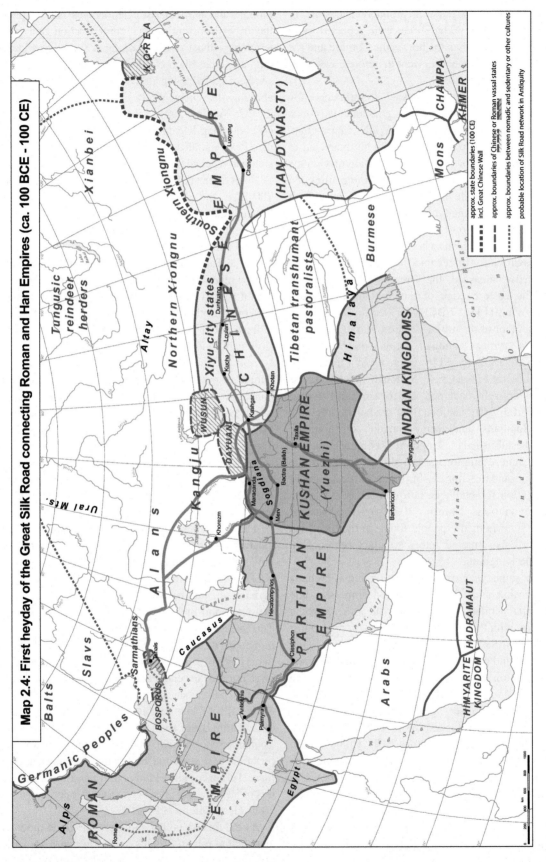

Map 2.4 First heyday of the Great Silk Road connecting Roman and Chinese empires (ca. 100 BCE–100 CE)

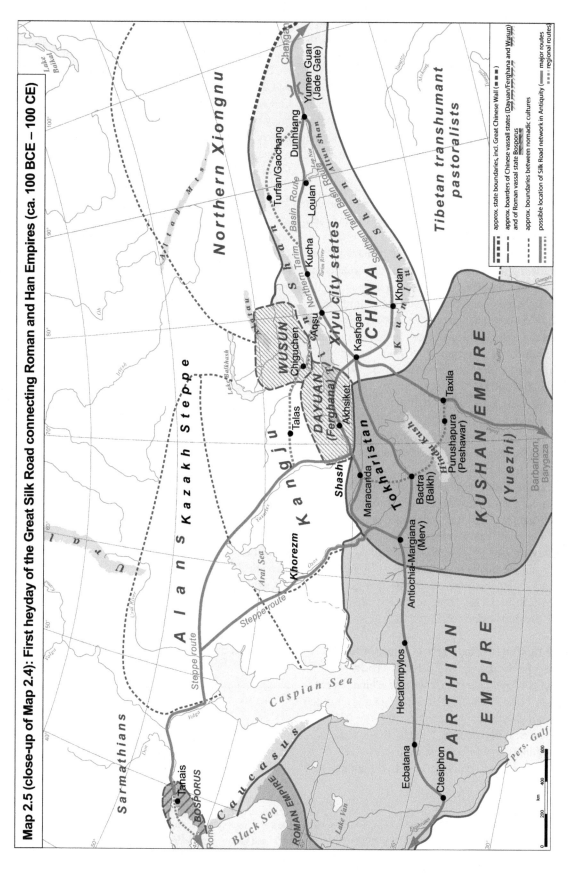

Map 2.5 (Close-up) first heyday of the Great SR connecting ... (ca. 100 BCE–100 CE)

extension of the imperial sphere of power and influence) were in all likelihood pre-eminent, at least in the initial stages of development (not unlike the strategic motives for the Achaemenid Royal Road, for the Hellenistic routes and fortified settlements opening up parts of CA, and for the Roman roads). Beyond the limits of their geopolitical power (Tarim Basin and the tributary regions of Dayuan and Wusun), and notwithstanding partially negative Confucian attitudes about commerce, the Han were interested and actively participated in mutually beneficial market-oriented trade (Roux 1997, 96).

In 54 BCE, the Xiongnu accepted China's peace terms: the Shan-yue agreed to send a hostage to China, pay homage to the emperor, and offer him tribute. Yet China itself continued to pay de-facto tribute (disguised as gifts: silk, gold, rice)—in smaller amounts—to outside nomads to keep the steppe border calm. Under the veneer of diplomatic and pompous language, hostage, homage, and tribute to the emperor in many cases constituted symbolic requirements. The nomadic rulers continued to receive supplies of silk and other goods (including gold and rice) which they could redistribute within the Xiongnu hierarchy or sell/have shipped along the caravan routes (Barfield 1989/1992, 66–67; Perdue 2011, 403).

Once the SR had "opened up" between east and west, caravans increased in size, selective breeding helped to adapt domestic animals—Bactrian camels, horses, and bulls—for carrying goods for longer distances and over higher altitudes. Bazaars and wholesale stores flourished. As Abazov points out, local rulers established clearer norms for issuing their currencies, in order to increase the latter's acceptability inside and outside respective jurisdictions. Local dealers developed rudimentary international currency markets.[45] Merchants nurtured positive relations with and patronage from local rulers by frequently submitting exotic and luxurious presents; this gift-giving tradition may have been one of the origins of regular trade taxation (Abazov 2008, Map 13).[46]

2.3.1.2 The Kushan State, Parthia, and Other C Asian Participants in Early SR Trade

Looking at parts of the nascent SR west of China: as mentioned earlier, the nomadic Yuezhi (related to the Tokharians) and Sakas, under pressure from the Xiongnu, had left their previously inhabited lands and invaded and conquered Sogdiana and Bactria in around 130–125 BCE. The Yuezhi soon settled down in these two regions (both

sides of the upper Oxos[47]/Amu Daria), which thus also received the name "Tokharistan." In the following decades, they took over most of the remaining territory of Greco-Bactria, effectively supplanting this state. In the first century BCE, the Kushan Empire was thus established (see Maps 2.4 and 2.5). The inscriptions on the coins of the first Kushan kings are written in Greek letters, because the Kushan monarchs viewed themselves as successors to the Greco-Bactrian kings; at the same time, some Kushan coins have a square-shaped form struck out in the center, following the Chinese example.[48]

Given their nomadic origins, and their very favorable new geoeconomic location straddling trade routes between east and west (China and Persia) and north and south (Turkestan and India), the Kushans (Yuezhi, Tokharians) were capable of and interested in promoting trade with their neighbors (Whitfield 2007, 206). In particular, their wealth of pack animals gave them the possibility to profit directly from trade with China and, as a transit country, from trade between China, India, and Persia. Chinese control over the routes in the Tarim Basin, well-established connections between Parthia and China, and a successful intermediary role of the Kushans, increasingly benefiting from Sogdian traders, set the stage for growth of transcontinental trade (Roudik 2007, 18).[49]

While the eastern part of the SR was now relatively safe, this could not yet be said of the western part. Relations between the Parthian and the Roman empires, which had both expanded, become neighbors, and started to dispute territories in the Eastern Mediterranean and the Near East, grew increasingly bellicose. The two empires fought intermittent but finally inconclusive wars over a couple of centuries.[50] On repeated occasions, the hostilities could be brought to a temporary halt, e.g., through the diplomatic intervention of the first Roman emperor Augustus (27–14 BCE). Thanks to the peace with Persia that he successfully concluded, the Pax Augusta, the western end of the SR, became secure, too. So, once reliable and functioning links were finally established across Eurasia, trade on the SR from Changan

---

[45] Both of these initiatives resemble in a wider sense attempts to increase what would be later called the convertibility of currencies.

[46] Of course, ad-hoc taxation of trade activities had already existed earlier.

[47] Later also called "Oxus"

[48] Coins of Chinese tradition are round and have a square-shaped hole in the middle. They are cast in bronze and bear an inscription but lack any iconographic design. Traditional Greco-Bactrian/Western coins are also round, but tend to display figurative decoration, and are struck in gold, silver, or bronze (Wang 2009, 94).

[49] This trade was largely organized by sedentary or sedentarized states, in contrast to the earlier-mentioned rise of trade, particularly bulk shipments of silk across the steppe to the West, initiated by nomadic powers (notably the Xiongnu).

[50] These rivals' successors, the Sassanian and the Byzantine empires, continued the contest in the following centuries, with none of the two parties decisively gaining the upper hand.

(the Han Chinese capital), via the Tarim oases, the Kushan Empire, Parthia, Mesopotamia to the Eastern Mediterranean and Europe, actually started to take off in the course of the first century BCE (Shukow et al. 1956/62, Band 2, 458) (Map 2.4).

During the reign of the Parthians (247 BCE–227 CE), Persia remained a decentralized polity. Actually, the Arsacid kings wielded direct authority only over those territories that were situated along the main trade route crossing the country and leading from the Roman Empire to China: running from Ctesiphon/former Seleucia via Hamadan/former Ecbatana and Hecatompylos to Merv (Margiana). The rights of the cities (typically centers of oases), still organized according to Hellenistic principles, were upheld, given that the former constituted welcome royal allies against the powerful land-owning nobility. Moreover, some of these Parthian poleis became focal points of expanding SR trade, which also stimulated activities of craftsmen and traders and boosted royal tax revenue. Apart from overland trade, farming, horticulture, and animal husbandry (particularly horses and sheep) remained important activities. Yet the rising economic disparities between the central SR trade axis of the country and its peripheral regions on both sides of this axis did not favor political stability (Sellnow et al. 1977, 423–424; Irmscher et al. 1986, 215).

Apart from the kingdom of Dayuan (Ferghana) described above, two other small semi-nomadic states, and one nomadic polity, skirted the SR in the north of CA. In the first century BCE, the lands ruled by the predominantly nomadic Wusun (tribal confederation), tributary to the Middle Kingdom, were situated between Lake Balkhash and Lake Issyk Kul (Tienshan). They included the plains of Semirechie, which at that time apparently featured lush grasslands and the mountain pastures of the Tienshan range. The Wusuns were pastoralists and farmers. Their focus was on horse and cattle breeding. The Wusun nomadized relatively short distances: they spent the summer in the mountains and had their wintering places on the banks of the rivers of the lowland.

Wusun agriculture was practiced in the valleys of the Ili and the Chu: stone hoes and bronze sickles were used. First traces of grain cultivation in Semirechie reportedly relate to this time or at least to antiquity (Parzinger 2009, 844). Crafts were developed (e.g., weaving, tanning, forging, and the making of jewels) but not (yet) separated from agriculture. The Chinese estimated the total Wusun population at about 630,000 people. Slaves were used in large numbers, and most of them were owned by the nomadic aristocracy, settled on land, and were used for agricultural activities or crafts. Livestock was considered the most important wealth. Rich noblemen possessed 4000–5000 horses. The Wusun headquarters, Chiguchen, lay on the shores of Lake Issyk

Kul (Poujol 2000, 17) (see also Map 4.7).[51] A side branch of the SR crossing the Tien Shan near the mentioned big mountain lake was controlled by the Wusun, who participated in silk trade and barter.

The Kangju state was a tribal confederation located north and south of the lower Yaxartes (Syr Daria), between the Aral Sea and Lake Balkhash. It included Khorezm as one of its subordinate provinces and reached its peak of power and wealth between the late second century BCE and early first-century CE. Not unlike the Wusun, the Kangju were nomadic pastoralists and sedentary agriculturalists. Their most important economic activity was cattle breeding; they also raised sheep, horses, and goats. Moreover, they were farmers and gardeners on the Yaxartes river banks. To support agriculture, the Kangju built dams, small canals, and reservoirs. They used grain graters and underground storage pits for grain. Among domestic crafts were the processing of stones and bones, forging and pottery, and the making of jewels/jewelry. Hunting and fishing had auxiliary importance (Ministerstvo Sviazi i Informatsii Respubliki Kazakhstan 2010, 298).

The Kangju further developed a partly urban civilization with clay houses, palaces, and fortified walls. The semisedentary tribal aristocracy lived in the centers of the towns and settlements. The headquarters of the ruler of the confederation were in the town of Bitian on the middle reaches of the Yaxartes. During the period of its apex, which coincided with the "opening up" of the SR, the Kangju state had a population of about 600,000 and an army of 120,000. The Kangju were not vassals of China and were repeatedly involved in military hostilities with the Han; they probably tried to gain or strengthen their influence on the international trade routes running through or near their territories. The Kangju traded goods with their C Asian neighbors, with China and Rome; thus they fully participated in SR trade; they even minted their own coins (Roudik 2007, 18). Roman glassware, Chinese silk, lacquerware and mirrors, and carved signet stones from Persia reached Wusun and Kangju territories (Kozybaev et al. 2010, 492–493).

The western neighbors of the Kangju, the Alans, nomadized in the extensive steppes stretching from the Volga to the Aral Sea and from the north shore of the Caspian Sea to the foothills of the Ural Mountains. The Alans seem to have formed a confederation including those tribes that in earlier times had been identified as Sarmatians and Massagetes (Indo-Europeans). The Alans combined

---

[51] The Wusun culture is also reported to have left numerous impressive kurgans (burial mounds). Under the mounds in burial pits, chiefs, warriors, and common people would be laid to rest. Huge tumuli of 100 m in diameter and 18 m in height buried kings and top nobility, whereas tumuli of middle size buried warriors; interred under small mounds were stockbreeders and farmers (Gorod moy rodnoy Almaty, 2004, 29).

typical nomadic pastoralism (mobile animal husbandry) with auxiliary and relatively primitive farming. Warfare and raids were also an integral part of their lives.[52]

Box 2.3: The Great Silk Road, with Particular Focus on Its First Blossoming in the Ancient World (ca. 100 BCE–200 CE)

As mentioned in Sect. 1.4, we can view the Great Silk Road or Silk Road (SR) as a network of intercontinental and regional trade routes that provided commercial, cultural, and technological exchange between Europe, CA, India, and China from antiquity until the early modern age.

Organization and Logistics

The organization of transcontinental trade was highly complex and difficult. It was often thousands of animals, a large number of drovers, and dozens of tons of merchandise that needed to be assembled and moved in caravans. SR merchants would gather safely in numbers, often traveling at night to avoid the heat, in caravans of up to 1000 camels (Roudik 2007, 19). In the middle lay CA, resembling a spacious clearing house that provided its native animals—two-humped Bactrian camels, horses, mules, donkeys, and bulls—to keep the goods flowing in various directions (Mayhew 2010, 37). Selective breeding even helped to gear these animals to carrying goods over longer distances. The Bactrian (two-humped) camel, at home in CA, was particularly important for SR transportation. This animal has the advantage of being better adapted than the (one-humped) dromedary to the extreme variations of temperature typical of the continental climate in the steppe and mountain regions of the interior of Asia. With their winter furs, Bactrian camels were able to cross high mountain passes. Its exceptional endurance and its sensitive feel for underground water sources and nearing deadly sandstorms made the Bactrian camel an indispensable and reliable companion for man on the long and dangerous routes (von Gumppenberg and Steinbach 2004, 248). These beasts of burden were able to transport 200–250 kg of merchandise over distances of 40–50 km (Borgolte 2015, 27).

Caravansareis dotted the routes at about 25 km intervals, the average daily distance traveled, and offered living quarters, stables for animals, supplies of food and forage, and secure storage for valuable cargo; larger city caravanserais were places where goods changed hands, fresh animals were procured, and guides, mercenaries, and resident craftsmen were hired (Roudik 2007, 19). SR trade was usually organized over many sections (relay principle, agents), because it was too unsafe and expensive to equip a caravan for the entire distance. It would take a caravan up to a year to make the whole 6000–7000 km direct trip across Eurasia. Local people, including nomads, acted as caravan guides (caravanbashis) and guards over the most dangerous parts of the journey. Merchants would typically end their trips at a well-known market on the intersection of trade routes, for instance, in Bukhara, Samarkand, or at other thriving oasis towns. Many of the goods were traded or bartered en route and changed their owners a number of times before they reached their final destination. Apart from offering local markets, cities like Merv, Kashgar, or Taxila offered equally vital services, such as brokers to set up contracts and banking houses to set up lines of credit.

Sedentary states, but more importantly nomadic states (given the latter tended to be particularly spacious and militarily powerful, see also below, e.g., Turk Khaganate/Turkic Empire and most prominently the Mongol Empire), provided SR trade protection. On repeated occasions, nomads also created or stimulated SR trade by taxing sedentary cultures/levying tribute through exaction of large amounts of silk and other luxury goods which (apart from being redistributed within the nomadic confederations) generated proceeds via marketing by C Asian and other merchants through SR outlets. As mentioned above, such activities may have even stood at the beginning of large-scale transcontinental silk shipments and therefore may have actually initiated SR trade. In any case, a Eurasian system of overland exchanges emerged, in which nomads and nomadic empires would often act as facilitators and even as aggressive promoters (Barfield 2001, 245).

(continued)

---

[52] For instance, the Alans undertook extensive raiding campaigns in western direction. In the course of the first-century BCE, they were reported to have reached the Danube and to have forced the Roman Empire to take defensive measures (Shukow et al. 1956/62, Band 2, 826).

Box 2.3 (continued)

Products Traded in Large Quantities on the SR in Antiquity (Not Including Re-exports, ca. 50 BCE–200 CE)[53]

The exorbitant transport costs meant that only goods with very high value-to-weight ratios would be carried for profit.

Chinese exports: *silk*, satin, jade, lacquerware, spices, paper, ceramics, iron, steel, leather products

Chinese imports: gold and other precious metals, glass and glassware, cavalry horses, harnesses, bows, elephants' tusks and ivory products, jewelry

Central Asian (Parthian and Kushan) exports: golden peaches, jade, dates, race and cavalry horses, carpets, tapestry, bronze objects, harnesses, bows, particularly from Indian territories—elephants' tusks and ivory products, indigo,[54] spices, sapphires, corals, pearls

Central Asian (Parthian and Kushan) imports: *silk*, gold and other precious metals, lacquerware, particularly to Indian territories—cavalry horses, harnesses, bows.

Roman exports: gold and other precious metals, cut precious stones, amber, pottery, textiles, glass and glassware

Roman imports: *silk*, satin, ivory products, spices, paper, jade, lacquerware, cavalry horses, slaves, jewels, pearls

The balance of SR trade was usually heavily stacked in favor of China (as east-west trade is again in the early twenty-first century!) (Mayhew 2010, 36).

Choice of Routes

The choice of routes depended on the time of year, snowfall, aridity, conditions of passes, regional differences in tax rates, and political and security considerations. The latter, the political factor, turned out to be the most important determinant of the travel itineraries across Eurasia (Wollenweber and Franke 2009, 24). For instance, during later antiquity (from the early third-century CE), the SR "steppe route"[55] seems to have been partly abandoned due to rising instability and insecurity in the area. Since antiquity, shipment by sea has been an alternative not only in times when overland connections were blocked (e.g., see the middleman rivalry between Parthia, which aimed at monopolizing SR transit trade with the Roman Empire, and the Kushan state, which organized alternate seaborne routes). Similar to the relay principle followed by caravans, ships/fleets usually only managed separate sections of the extensive network of maritime traffic (Höllmann 2004, 23).

Who Were the Traders/Merchants?

Depending on the periods and the regions, Sogdians, Chinese, Indians, Arabs, Turks, Uighurs, Bukharans, and, less frequently, Greeks, Jews, and Italians were traveling on the routes and trading in the markets of CA (Boulnois 2008, 22). Practically all of these merchants were sedentary businessmen, not nomads. The Sogdians (sedentary Eastern Iranians originating from Samarkand and other oases of Sogdiana, which never united to a common Sogdian state but consisted of a number of small principalities) participated actively in and soon dominated SR exchanges with China. Already in the Greco-Bactrian kingdom, later in the Kushan Empire, Sogdian merchants grew prominent in Sino-Indian trade. Sogdian business communities (trade colonies) installed themselves in the Tarim Basin (e.g., in Khotan and Loulan), in Gansu (e.g., Dunhuang), and in central China (e.g., Lanzhou, Changan, Luoyang) (Hambis 1977, 46). According to Millward, Sogdians ultimately traded and lived from the Black Sea to Korea (Millward 2013, 25).

As long as the Han dynasty controlled the trade routes of East Turkestan, the Chinese military and civil servants serving there received their salaries in silk, given that the latter was much easier to dispatch from central China than metal coins or grain. Thus, the merchant communities in the "western territories" found important quantities of silk which they could buy relatively cheaply for C Asian or other foreign products. The structure of Sogdian commerce appeared to be made up of a combination of "small merchants touring three or four towns, over a couple of hundred kilometers" and of large commercial companies, often family enterprises. Altogether, an increasing number of foreign merchants flocked to China to buy silk, and the volume of their purchases from the Middle Kingdom is estimated to have exceeded the volume of China's own sales abroad (de la Vaissière 2004, 149, 301; Shen Fuwei 2009, 38).

(continued)

---

[53] Compiled from a survey of a number of publications dealing with SR trade during its first heyday

[54] Indigo = blue dye obtained from various specific plants (Random House Webster's Concise College Dictionary 1999, see also Glossary: some SR textiles, p. 266)

[55] All trade routes that circumvent the Caspian Sea by the north and therefore penetrate the Desht-i-Kipchak are regarded here as "steppe routes".

SR Merchant Capital Accumulation Versus Han Dynasty State Supremacy

Already during antiquity, SR trade gave rise to considerable, if temporary, concentrations of capital. There are reports of SR merchant-millionaires or trader-millionaires. In China, many powerful individuals, including government officials, profited from trade. Throughout the Han period, particularly the Later Han (when tribute paid to the nomads was lower), there were numerous wealthy merchant families who controlled large enterprises. At the elite level of the empire, though, in conformity with Confucian ideology, such enterprises and activities were deemed illegitimate, or at least suspect, and merchants were therefore prohibited from competing in the imperial exams that led to higher government offices. In line with the Confucianist rejection of pronounced inequality and of large independent richness, merchants' wealth was even threatened by arbitrary confiscation (Barfield 2001, 239; Kocka 2013, 25). This, from an economic liberal ideological viewpoint, could be perceived as predatory state behavior.

The abovementioned "islands of private appropriation" were at variance with Han China's bureaucratic economic organization; personal wealth was subordinate to state property. Power and prestige lay not in commerce but in the imperial hierarchy. Given that they were not officially allowed to compete for a civil servant's office, merchants therefore may have had the incentive to "purchase" public offices, often in the fiscal administration, as far as they could get away with it (corruption). Some merchants "invested" in good relations with the authorities by providing credit to members of the state apparatus (Doujon 1990, 43–44).

2.3.2 Apex: A Transcontinental Economic, Cultural, and Technological Artery Linking Four Flourishing Sedentary Empires (ca. 1 CE–200 CE)

2.3.2.1 From the Pivotal Importance of Chinese Silk to the Emergence of an International "Silk Standard"

For centuries, silk, first in the form of a diplomatic gift (or rather: imposed tribute), later as a commercial product, was imported and shipped along the SR mostly by C Asian merchants (de la Vaissière 2004, 301; Tracy 2011, 292). The invention and know-how of silk production were successfully monopolized by China for at least one and a half millennia. Supply of as well as demand for silk was very high, such that silk trade became the backbone of commercial activity on the network of trade routes bearing its name (Fang 2014, 11). In the first- and second-century CE, overland silk trade and international trade more generally between China, Rome, and other countries increased dramatically and reached its apex (Mokyr 2003, 369). Stable regimes in the Roman Mediterranean, Persian Parthian Empire, Kushan Empire, and China under the Han dynasty, as well as relative peace on the nomadic front for most of these 200 years, helped stabilize the routes and uphold favorable conditions for economic activities linking large parts of Eurasia.

To repeat a key finding explained in Sect. 1.4: silk dominated the trade network of the same name because of its lightness[56], low bulk, high value, and immense popularity. Large quantities of silk had originally been exacted from China in tributary payments prior to the Han victory over the Xiongnu, and smaller amounts continued to be levied even after. A probably considerable share of this initial forced silk provision became traded merchandise and provided an initial boost to deliveries on the SR, before the official start of regular and organized international silk trade afforded a second stimulus. With China the only supplier of the good (for the time being), demand was such in the world of antiquity that silk constituted the principal Chinese export for centuries. Silk bolts bore an imperial seal of quality, which enabled their use for large-scale trade. As an in-kind tax or de-facto means of payment, silk was paid to the Chinese state treasury, which used it to remunerate its servicemen and civil servants (including those stationed in oases in the Tarim Basin), to pay for publicly procured goods, and to settle public debt (P.M. History 2011, 55).

Admittedly, since the Han dynasty, the country's chief legal tender or currency unit was the "cash" (qian), a round bronze coin with a square hole in the middle (see above). However, the quantity of this legal tender in circulation had apparently become insufficient to satisfy the needs of economic life, which would imply that China was not adequately monetized by its "cash" at least during parts of the Han era. This could help explain the quasi-currency status silk had attained inside China. Chinese trust in silk as a medium of exchange, a unit of account, and a store of value also had an impact beyond the country and reinforced foreign esteem for the luxurious fabric (Norel 2009, 50). Somewhat like gold, silk became an effective international

---

[56] Silk was easier to transport than metallic coins or bullion, and paper money did not yet exist in the ancient world.

currency, such that one might argue in favor of the existence of a kind of "silk standard" across the Old World or in any case in all regions adjacent to the SR. That said, coins also played a role as money used on the transcontinental network of trade routes, particularly Roman, Chinese, Kushan, and Parthian coins; in this sense, in addition to silk, that was accepted as a general medium of exchange all along the road, the coins' legal tender in the respective empires reflected (varying) degrees of regional monetization of SR trade; beyond that, the SR remained a platform of intensive and often sophisticated barter.

Taking a closer look at Chinese trade and economic activities in CA: Against the backdrop of the Middle Kingdom's strong demand, horses started to be bred commercially in the region, especially in Ferghana. Shule (near Kashgar) at the western end of the Tarim Basin became an important international distribution hub for silk. Agriculture in the Tarim oases under Han rule was apparently stimulated by the tuntian system, but also thanks to rising profits generated by passing trade, which were partly invested into farming. Moreover, agriculture was supported by the upgrading of irrigation technology, possibly intermediated by Sogdian merchants who had established themselves in the Tarim oases (see below) (Hambis 1977, 51). The area from Dunhuang to Turfan grew food grains, mulberries for silk, hemp, and grapes (which were often dried to raisins). In consequence, viticulture along with sericulture reached Turfan by the first or second centuries, the time of the Later Han (Liu 2005).

The temporary weakening of Han China during the time of the usurper Wang Mang (9–23 CE) plus interior disturbances (uprising of the Red Eyebrows) in the Middle Kingdom set the stage for new Xiongnu incursions, which threatened SR trade for some decades. Only after protracted battles with the Han and with other nomads, which lasted to the late first-century CE, did the Xiongnu retreat from the Chinese border areas and turn away in a westerly direction (which recalls the behavior of their ancestors about two and a half centuries earlier). During this phase of Chinese weakness in CA, maritime shipping connections opened up and linked China via ports on the coasts of India and Sri Lanka, step-by-step all the way to Roman-controlled ports in Egypt. From around 75 CE, the oases of the Tarim Basin were again under Chinese control. Regained political stability favored recovery and a renewed flourishing of overland trade until the early third-century CE.

2.3.2.2 The Kushan and Parthian Empires and Beyond: Successful SR Intermediaries

In the course of the first-century CE, the Kushans expanded their rule to Khwarazm/the Aral Sea, Ferghana, Margiana, Southern Afghanistan, Gandhara (the area around Taxila), and the Punjab and incorporated the entire Indus valley, the upper Ganges valley (Northern India), and Gujarat (at the coast of the Arabian Sea); during a period of internal weakness of the Han dynasty in the first half of this century (see above), the Kushan Empire even temporarily extended its authority to the western half of the Tarim Basin, including Kashgar, Yarkand, and Khotan. Kushan administrative models were largely derived from the Iranian Achaemenids and their successors: a kind of satrapy system was set up. There were also quasi-feudal elements, comparable to the Parthian system: the king ruled the empire, and masters of the cities and local leaders of landed estates (nobility) were his vassals. By emitting a uniform standardized currency, the Kushans tried to consolidate state authority and economically integrate their far-flung empire. In this, at least partial success was achieved: the use of coins penetrated the retail trade (Freydank et al. 1978, 254).

Agriculture improved during the Kushan period: wooden plows with iron plowshares were introduced in the first-century CE (apparently, they are still in use in some areas of CA today); more advanced methods of irrigation spread; wide canals (aryks) were extended sometimes over distances of more than 100 km and could be used by large river ships[57]; water-driven machines, including mills for grinding grain into flour, were adopted; many plants were cultivated that are still harvested today, e.g., wheat, millet, barley, lucerne, cotton, wine, vegetables, melons, particularly muskmelons, fruit trees, and mulberry trees; animal husbandry remained important, particularly horse breeding in Ferghana.

This improvement of agriculture, the growth of handicrafts (pottery, metallurgy, glass production, forging, weaving) and mining (extraction of iron, gold, silver, copper, lazurite, nephrite, and rubies)[58] as well as the abovementioned strengthening of the monetary economy/monetization resulted in the growth of trade relations between different regions of CA. Samarkand (Maracanda) lay in the center of caravan trade leading to the remote corners of the sprawling country (domestic trade). Commercial winemakers appeared in Samarkand and Bukhara. Apart from trade between sedentary regions cereals, fruits, handicrafts, and weapons were traded with steppe and mountain nomads in markets situated in the northern border areas and the mountain regions, in exchange for furs, leather, wool, meat and milk products, livestock, and raw materials for weaving.

---

[57] Some of the largest and longest irrigation canals dug in the history of CA date back to the Kushan era.

[58] Chinese sources report that these metals were mined or continued to be mined in the mountains of Ferghana and Tokharistan (Shukow et al. 1956/62, Band 2, 789).

The era of King Kanishka (78–130 CE) and his successors or approximately the last one and a half centuries of the Kushan state (up to about 230 CE) constituted a period of great prosperity and stability. One of the boosting factors doubtlessly was the functioning SR. During this period, large numbers of nomadic livestock breeders (mostly in the northern regions of Kushana), but not all, switched to a settled way of life. After descending southward following the expansion of the Xiongnu Empire and the collapse of the Greco-Bactrian kingdom, the "frontier" between nomadic and sedentary life was somewhat pushed back north again. Not only the administrative division of the state but also the towns and fortified settlements of the Kushan period in some respects recalled Achaemenid traditions. Surrounded by thick clay walls, they contained market places; palaces/citadels typically built on high platforms; public buildings frequently of monumental size; temples of different faiths, e.g., Zoroastrian "Houses of fire"; and Buddhist, Manichaean, and Christian places of worship, convents, workshops, and dwellings. Most new towns were built in Northern India. During Kanishka's reign, the political center of the Kushan state moved from Tokharistan (Kushana/Zerafshan) to Northern India (Purushapura/Peshawar) (Freydank et al. 1978, 254).

While overall tolerant in religious affairs, Kanishka and other Kushan kings adopted a friendly stance toward Buddhism: Relatively soon (from the first-century CE) this religion spread from India on trade paths via the region of Gandhara, which became Buddhist, and the Tarim Basin to central China, and from there on to Japan. Transmission was carried out not only by monks and missionaries, but also by merchants, including Sogdians. The creation of the huge clay buddhas of the cave monastery of Bamian (Hindu Kush, central Afghanistan) has been assessed to date to the prosperous time of Kanishka and his successors. Manichaeism and Nestorian Christianity also spread along the SR, running on and extending from Kushan territory. The impressive Gandharan art (which emerged in the second-century CE) essentially developed from a symbiosis of elements of Greco-Roman, Iranian, and Indo-Buddhist styles, which—partly embodied in tradable artifacts—were transferred via the SR across and beyond Kushana. Thus, it was not only the SR that functioned as a catalyst for the spreading of religion, art, and many other elements of culture, but it was also the sprawling territorial extension of the Kushan Empire at the time that greatly facilitated and probably accelerated cultural dissemination.[59]

Parthia was—like Kushana—a classic transit country and middleman. The Parthian Empire, buttressed by sustained friendly relations with China while remaining in a hostile posture with Rome and a rival posture with the Kushan Empire, tried to draw as much utility as possible from its geoeconomic position. The Parthians greatly profited from transit trade: they collected trade customs duties amounting to 25% of the value of all products passing through their territory. The Parthians tried to prevent the emergence of direct trade or of trade that circumvented their country between Rome and China. Kushan traders were in competition with Parthian traders; both strived to possess the monopoly of transit between east and west. In addition to territorial disputes, commercial disputes and Rome's attempt to break Parthia's stranglehold on SR trade and acquire silk at a lower price contributed to Rome's recurrent warlike relationship with Parthia. The Roman Empire entered into war and concluded peace with the Parthian Empire several times in antiquity but in the end was not successful in achieving its commercial goal. Periods of armed clashes temporarily obstructed movement along the SR and drove up prices for silk and other products.

Notwithstanding these difficulties, the Roman Empire became the largest customer/consumer of Chinese silk. The luxurious gown worn by the Egyptian Queen Cleopatra (51–30 BCE)[60] at her banquet was a dress of Chinese silk. Roman aristocrats, apparently particularly women, coveted extravagant styles and took pride in dressing themselves in silk (Shen Fuwei 2009, 39). Some observers perceived the expensive imports of silk as a reason for widening imbalances in Rome's foreign trade account and for financial difficulties of the state. Despite its high price, the demand for silk became exorbitant (Roman craze for silk). Finally, Emperor Tiberius (14–37 CE) resolved to officially prohibit Roman citizens from wearing silk garments. This desperate measure was aimed at reducing the outflow of gold as payment for silk to Parthia. However, the ban had only limited effect, given that silk had become an entrenched symbol of wealth and high social position (Dmitriev 2009, 47). Writing in the second half of the first-century CE, the Roman author and moralist Pliny complained that silk imports were draining the empire of one hundred million sesterces (= about 8000 kilos or 8 tons) of gold per year.[61]

---

[59] Buddhist art in southern CA, reaching up to Ferghana, Semirechie, and Turfan, refers to the periods from around 100 CE to 700 CE. Buddhist art of East Turkestan is a complicated artistic (cultural) phenomenon to which Indian, Hellenistic-Roman, Tokharian, and

---

Chinese traditions contributed. Across CA, dozens of Buddhist cave monasteries emerged; the long chain of these monuments includes Bamian (Afghanistan), Kara-tepe (Tokharistan/Southern Uzbekistan), Kuchi, Turfan (both: East Turkestan), and, finally, Dunhuang (Gansu) (Litvinsky 1996, 174–175).

[60] The Ptolemaic Kingdom (a Hellenistic state) was incorporated into the Roman Empire in the middle of the first century BCE.

[61] Pliny in the first century complained that the wealth of the empire was being drained wholesale by insatiable female appetite for luxuries from the east (Waugh: The Origins of the Silk Road, 2002, 1).

A possibility was eventually found to circumvent Parthia, even if it was a risky detour. When problems with Parthia appeared insurmountable, the Kushans could redirect caravans from Bactra/Balkh in a southerly direction to the port of Barbaricum on the Indus delta or further south to the port of Barygaza on the coast of Gujarat, from where merchandise could be transported on the sea route (via Aden and the Red Sea) to Alexandria and Rome (Hambly 1966/1979, 59; Overy 2004, 92) (Map 2.4). The importance of any one of the land and sea routes depended on the prevailing political landscape in the Middle East. Maritime east-west trade had already improved in the first century BCE with the discovery of how the monsoon winds would allow direct passage across the Indian Ocean and back, thus avoiding the coastal route with its dangerous reefs and pirates.[62] Another alternative for circumventing Parthia also bore risks: the volatile steppe route (north of the Caspian Sea to the Black Sea). Although there are no records of Roman traders being seen in Changan, nor of Chinese merchants in Rome, an envoy of Emperor Marc Aurel (161–180 CE) is known to have reached one of the Chinese ports in 166 CE (Fang 2014, 20).

The first heyday of the SR apparently also changed the lives of the inhabitants of the semi-nomadic Kangju and Wusun states. Both states lay at or near the northern border of the Kushan Empire and the western border of Chinese-ruled territory and had access to parts of the SR network, particularly to the "steppe route" (Map 2.5). Roman glass and coins, Chinese silk, mirrors, and lacquerware[63] penetrated into these territories (Baipakov et al. 1997, 63).

Irrigated agriculture, mostly in the framework of small communities of stockbreeders and farmers, was practiced in the valleys of the Ili, Chu, and Talas rivers, and on the slopes of the (Dzungarian) Alatau, and thus seems to have spread from more southern-lying oases into Semirechie. In the foothill zones of the In Tienshan, the valleys of the abovementioned rivers and the middle reaches of the Yaxartes (Syr Daria), urban centers existed or emerged, surrounded by walls and towers, e.g., Suyab, Talas, Sairam, and Shash (Tashkent). Among other craftsmen, jewelers, potters, and blacksmiths worked in these settlements; iron, nonferrous metals, gold, and silver were processed (Artykbaev: Istoria Kazakhstana, 98–99). These were probably not only border towns but market places straddling the Northern SR. Thus, signs of urbanization and economic growth in the first two centuries of the Christian era show up not only along the trunk routes of the SR but also in peripheral areas.

As the table in Box 2.3 shows, and as can be expected, during the first heyday of SR trade in ancient times, China specialized in exports of silk, which also included brocade, embroidery, satin, silk yarn, and gauze. In exchange for Chinese silk and paper (the latter was invented in the Middle Kingdom in 105 CE), Rome sent precious metals (e.g., gold), textiles, cut precious stones, and glassware (glass was not manufactured in China until the fifth century). The Chinese appreciated Roman glassware for its colors and glossiness and highly valued Roman craftsmanship. Kushan territories (including Northern India) exported "golden peaches" from Samarkand (Maracanda), jade, exquisite ivory products, spices, and medicinal herbs; "heavenly horses" (race and cavalry horses) continued to come from Ferghana. Parthia (Persia) supplied much appreciated carpets and tapestries, precious metals, dates, and pistachio nuts. Generally, the uniquely self-transporting goods—slaves and horses—were also profitable: slaves were often procured from sedentary cultures, horses from CA.

Box 2.4: Modeling the Silk Road, the Prelude to Globalization?

According to Grataloup (2007, 87–89), the Great Silk Road marks the origins of globalization. The trade routes crossing the Eurasian double continent embody global history. Between Aden and India, and on to Southeast Asia and China, shipping routes have regularly been used at least since antiquity. Thus, on the seaborne Spice Route (Route des épices), pepper, sugar, cinnamon, sandalwood, and other valuable goods were traded. The maritime Spice Route of the south was more than a substitute for the overland SR (Route de la soie) of the north; it was also a complement. These two networks of connection lines between eastern and western civilizations formed the backbone of the ancient world (Haywood 2011, 108). For Grataloup, the present-day triad (North America, Europe, East Asia) embodies an extension of these exchanges of the past, in which transatlantic and transpacific trade have been integrated. In any case, most economic historians argue that only the extension of trade from the "triple continent" Afro-Eurasia to the Americas (and not to forget Australia) really constituted the advancement to "globalized" trade—in the sense of spanning the globe (Osterhammel and Petersson 2003, 26; Fässler 2007, 48–49, see also Box 3.1).

(continued)

---

[62] The first centuries CE witnessed vigorous Indian trade with the Mediterranean world and with China (Ptak 2007, 108).

[63] Lacquerware embodies another Chinese invention: Lacquer is extracted from the natural sap of the lacquer tree and used to produce a highly polished, lustrous surface on wooden objects, including furniture and objects d'art (Griessler 2011, 139–140).

Box 2.4 (continued)

Two well-phrased metaphors put forward by Perdue (2003, 491) sketch salient components of the SR system's structure:

First, think of a large net, composed of many interlocking strings, held up by two or more poles; the poles are the settled agrarian empires: Rome and its successors in the west, China in the east, and India and Persia in the south. These densely populated zones provided the supply and demand forces that power the network. The strings are caravans running along the silk routes. They cross at nodes of exchange: oases scattered along the steppes and deserts.[64]

Perdue's second metaphor invokes the parallels between the vast grasslands and the ocean. Settled empires constitute the mainland with cities on the periphery of the ocean, caravans are ships or convoys, oases are archipelagoes, and nomads are the denizens of the deep—the only people who can live almost entirely off grass and not grain, as Perdue adroitly put it. Trade depended on a precarious balance between these four cultures. Nomads, in exchange for protection fees, ensured that traders could cross the steppe (the ocean) safely. The traders needed access to capital and markets supplied by the peripheral agrarian civilizations. The agrarian oases (islands) supported lodging and restocking points called caravanserais. It was a highly profitable but risky and volatile enterprise.

Khodarkovsky (2002, 29) put forward an apt metaphor similar to Perdue's second (ocean-related) one. Khodarkovsky's metaphor focuses on Russia's viewpoint of its relationship with the nomads, but it could presumably relate to any sedentary neighbor of the Eurasian grasslands: If the steppe was akin to the sea and the Russian towns to ports, the nomads were the seamen, who eventually had to visit the ports to replenish their supplies. Many of the seamen were pirates living off raids against the "ports" or looting the passing ship convoys (caravans); other seamen were guiding and accompanying steppe convoys (caravanbashis) through risky waters. Trade in peace and turning the pirates into guides, merchants, and servicemen was the Russian authorities' principal goal.

2.3.3 Course of the Main Routes of the SR in Antiquity

During its first heyday in the first two centuries CE, the SR network is likely to have connected the following towns/oases (see Maps 2.4 and 2.5):

Luoyang (Chinese capital in the Later Han era)—Changan (Xian)—Yumen Guan ("Jade Gate")—Dunhuang—then (a) northern Tarim Basin route (Loulan—Karashahr—Kucha—Aqsu) or (b) southern route (Shanshan—Khotan—Yarkand)—then both routes reunite in Kashgar[65]—then (a) north across Tienshan (probably via Torugart pass) to Ferghana Basin—Shash (Tashkent)—Maracanda (Samarkand) or (b) south across Pamir (probably via Irkeshtam) to Bactra (Balkh)—then both routes reunite in Merv—then Hecatompylos—Ecbatana (Hamadan)—Ctesiphon (former: Seleucia)—Palmyra—then (a) Antiochia or (b) Tyre (Mediterranean Sea); there are also two routes to the south (India): either from Kashgar across Kashmir (Khunjerab Pass) to Taxila or from Bactra (Balkh) across the Hindu Kush (Khyber Pass) to Taxila, and from there (a) down the Indus to the port of Barbaricum, or (b) branching off from the lower Indus, then running southeast to the port of Barygaza (Gulf of Cambay).

The "steppe route" leading down the Oxus (Amu Daria), via Khwarazm, respectively, down the Yaxartes (Syr Daria), to the northern shore of the Caspian, the lower reaches of Volga and Don (via the town of Tanais), to the Sea of Azov and the Black Sea, had lost some importance in later Roman times but was still at least intermittently in use. One of the reasons for the loss of importance probably was increased insecurity along this route, provoked by the fallout from the long-lasting conflict between Han China and Xiongnu: in various "waves" of migration over three centuries, the Xiongnu, or, as they were later called in the west, the Huns, moved into the Kazakh grasslands and across the Eurasian steppe belt into Europe. As a result of these stormy but protracted and extensive campaigns, apart from the already mentioned Yuezhi, Sakas, and Wusun, some other people living in the steppes further west were harassed, chased away, or incorporated into the emerging Hunnic confederation (e.g., the Sarmatians, Scyths, Alans, Ostrogoths). This turmoil rendered the steppe route much less secure and stable.

---

[64] Abu-Lughod compared the functionality of these oases and "hinterlandless trading enclaves" with that of modern "air terminals, bringing goods and people together from long distances" (1989, 33).

[65] There was also a less frequently used connection across the Tienshan from Aqsu via the Issyk Koel and Talas to the Yaxartes valley (steppe route).

2.3.4 Decline Triggered by Internal Imperial Weaknesses and External Nomadic Pressure (ca. 200 CE–ca. 350 CE)

2.3.4.1 Economic Mismanagement, Political Instability, and Decline of the SR

The fading of the first heyday of the SR and its eventual end was triggered by economic and political troubles in the Chinese and the Roman Empires, followed by the resurgence of military pressure and invasions by Hunnic and other nomadic tribes. Climate change may also have played a role, though a secondary one.[66] Economic mismanagement, excessive tax pressure, and corruption during the Later Han dynasty in the second-century CE gave rise to unrest culminating in the Yellow Turban rebellion of 184 CE. The Han dynasty fell in 220 CE, and China split into three kingdoms. In the course of the third century, Chinese control of Tarim Basin disappeared (Barfield 1989/1992, 92). Independent city-states (mini-kingdoms) reappeared; one of the biggest was the Kingdom of Gaochang in Turfan.

Destabilizing tendencies appear to have befallen the Roman Empire a century later than China. Continuing military expansion had assured the capture of new slaves and territories. By the beginning of the third-century CE, the empire may have become "overextended," stretching from Britain to Northern Mesopotamia and from North Africa to Crimea, which made it increasingly vulnerable to raids from outsiders (most often by Germanic and Celtic tribes). Conquests had grown more costly and came to a halt, stopping the inflow of new resources. On top of persistent or frequent SR trade deficits came rising budget deficits, which were eventually monetized through debasement of coinage/currency, triggering rising inflation (Cameron and Neal 2003, 41–42; Doujon 1990, 58–59).

These internal problems in the large empires at both ends of the SR could not but have repercussions for trade on the transcontinental network itself. The repercussions were soon aggravated by the impact of rising external pressure. After the Xiongnu setback in the first-century CE, and their partial withdrawal from the Chinese borders and movement westward, nomads' strength apparently resurged from around the second century. The Xiongnu/Huns and other tribes intensified the use of metals; the metallic stirrup was invented, which improved the handling of horses; other important inventions were the saber and the composite bow, which put a new effective long-distance weapon into the hands of rider-warriors (Linska et al. 2003, 56). Moreover, climate change—a degree of drying up of the climate

from the fourth- to the fifth-century CE—may have again added a push factor. Around 150 CE, the Northern Xiongnu, weakened from continuous warfare, was partly driven away and partly absorbed by the Xianbei (a probably Mongol-Tunguz nomadic people originating in Manchuria). The Xianbei then created a loosely structured confederation in Mongolia and continuously raided China.

In the early third-century CE, rising pressure from the nomadic tribes of the Hephthalites ("White Huns"), that had migrated southwest from Mongolia and had taken over places previously inhabited by the Kangju and the Wusun, threatened the Kushan Empire.[67] The Hephthalites were pure nomads, and had no towns but encampments of felt kibitkas (covered wagons, tents) near their pastureland. The sedentary Kushan population could not live outside fortified settlements any more. It was this situation of increased fragility and insecurity that the neighboring Sassanian Empire (the successor to Parthia, see below) apparently took advantage of. The Sassanians attacked the Kushan Empire, conquered northwestern core territories (Tokharistan), and thus triggered the collapse of the Kushan state in 230 CE and its partition along the Indus river with the Gupta Empire ruling in India.

Certainly, regional economic disparities between the various Kushan Middle Eastern, C Asian, and South Asian territories had not favored internal cohesion of that polity. As mentioned earlier, the Parthian Empire also suffered from economic disparities, notably between the regions along the SR axis and those further away. The expansion of SR trade since the late first century BCE, while contributing to the accumulation of wealth in Parthia, probably magnified these disparities.[68] It was out of a revolt of one of the local aristocratic ruling families—in the province of Persis, far off the trunk line of the SR—that the new rulers of Persia arose. The first Sassanian king, Ardashir, defeated his Arsacid overlord and rapidly took control of the Parthian Empire (226 CE) and of some areas beyond. The Sassanians strengthened royal central power, declared Zoroastrianism the state religion,[69] established a standing army with armored cavalry at its core, built up a bureaucratic administration, and even returned to a system of satrapies (recalling the old Achaemenid state structure). But the influence of the land-owning nobility, which had challenged central power, remained strong. The Sassanians were not only successful

---

[66] After the climate across Eurasia had reportedly warmed up in the middle of the first millennium BCE, it cooled off again in the second century CE (Vogelsang 2013, 65, 191).

[67] As pointed out by Breghel, in the course of their migration, the Huns had probably destroyed the Kangju confederation (2003, 12).

[68] The burden of the long-lasting warfare with Rome may have added some grievances.

[69] This is the second time Zoroastrianism was declared the state religion in Persia, following a similar act by the Achaemenids.

conquerors of Kushan territories but also asserted their power in the Near East vis-à-vis Rome.

Given the deterioration of the economic and political situations in the sedentary states straddling the SR network (except for the political situation of the Sassanian Empire, which consolidated its power), it is no surprise that transcontinental trade, but also production, supply and demand, deteriorated in the third-century CE. When Chinese military and administrative authority retreated back east from the Tarim Basin, the (mostly Sogdian) merchants followed this retreat and relocated their activities to the Hexi corridor (Gansu province) and central China in order to continue to acquire silk as cheaply as possible. Despite much higher overall costs (predominantly transportation, security, and overhead), the Sogdian merchants created an extended chain of trade communities along the SR between CA and China in order to assure at least a reduced amount of supply to their markets. However, shortages of silk could not be avoided (de la Vaissière 2004, 67, 160). The C Asian economy, especially the manufacturing sectors and commercial services of the transit states (Parthia/Sassanian Empire, Kushan Empire that disappeared) entered into recession. As Gunder Frank emphasizes, there is archeological evidence of the more or less simultaneous decline of a whole string of cities between Kashgar and Bactria and also in Northern India (1992, 30).

2.3.4.2 Simultaneous Fall: Huns Conquer Northern China, most of CA, and Large Parts of Eastern Europe (Fourth-Century CE)

The fourth century saw nomadic military pressure intensifying across Eurasia. As the climate in CA became drier from this century, nomads may have had an additional incentive to abandon their pastures and seek wealth by raiding, plundering, taxing, and conquering their settled neighbors (Mayhew 2010, 40).

Large-scale conquests of territories previously ruled by sedentary states ensued. In 301 CE invading nomads founded the Hunnic-Chinese "16 kingdoms," which took over Northern China and ruled until the middle of the fifth century, while the south of the country was governed by the domestic Jin dynasty.[70] As Map 3.1 shows, at the turn of the fourth to the fifth century, the Hephthalites or "White Huns," having established a nomadic confederacy between the Aral Sea and Tienshan, moved south and conquered Sassanian Central Asian possessions (Bactria, Sogdiana)[71] as well as the northwestern part of the Tarim Basin before they

descended further into Northern India. The recession and the partial desertion of the cities did not strengthen resistance. At about the same time, the Huns took over the rest of the Kazakh steppe and their majority moved west, defeating/integrating the Alans between the Southern Ural mountains, the Don and the Caspian (370 CE), and the Ostrogoths in Ukraine. The Huns set off the "Migration Period" in Europe (375 CE), and arguably even set the stage for the eventual partition and demise of the Roman Empire (476) (Münkler 2005, 91).

In the course of the third- and fourth-century CE, the border between nomadic and sedentary civilization in CA redescended south again. Given heightened insecurity and blockages along the SR, and given the division of post-Han-dynasty China into a northern nomadic-controlled half and a southern half, which remained under domestic Chinese authority, overland trade routes were increasingly replaced by sea routes. On the latter, from the third century, silk—in relatively modest amounts—began to arrive in Rome again (Ptak 2007, 108; Bonavia and Baumer 2002, 18).

SR trade probably reached a low point or was interrupted in the fourth- and fifth-century CE, when three of the major sedentary empires that had participated in the organization of the transcontinental network found themselves in deep crisis or in demise (Rome, Kushan state, China). Therefore, one can speak of an almost simultaneous rise and decline of most of the countries (economies) situated along the SR of antiquity (Gunder Frank 1992, 29). The collapse of the Parthian Empire and its quick "replacement" by the Sassanian state can be seen as an exception because this regime change did not cause or was not linked to a major economic decline.

However, at least up to the late fourth-century CE, the towns of the Tarim Basin, of Kashmir, and of the Indus valley had not been attained by nomadic invasions. These towns upheld strong links with each other, despite the difficult topographic terrain between them. Thanks to Buddhist establishments built up during the Kushan period, the trade routes connecting the Indus valley, Kashmir, and East Turkestan seem to have been still viable after the collapse of the Kushan Empire (about 230 CE), despite the decline or disappearance of the many urban centers that had flourished during the first heyday of the SR.

Buddhist monasteries provided both facilities and guidance for travelers on the trade routes of this "sheltered channel" of exchange. Thus the young Kumarajiva, who became one of the great representatives of Buddhism in China, traveled with his mother between Kucha and Gandhara in the middle of the fourth-century CE (de la Vaissière 2004, 65; Liu Xinru 2010, 84–85). In the fifth century, cotton, indigo, and gold were shipped up the Indus valley via Taxila to East Turkestan and on to China, while silk, tea, and cinnamon found their way through the Tarim Basin to India (Virmani 2012, 21).

---

[70] Not to be confused with the medieval Jin dynasty (1125–1234), led by an elite of Jurchen (people from Manchuria)

[71] These possessions had, a century and a half before, been taken away from the Kushan state.

Accordingly, there appear to be two reasons why SR trade and communications between East Turkestan and India were less affected by the turmoil from the third-century CE. Firstly, invasions of this period largely spared or had less impact on the Tarim Basin, Kashmir, and Northern India. Secondly, Buddhist institutions' efforts to keep civilization functioning and routes of transport and communication intact as far as possible proved successful. The latter activity by the Buddhist clergy in CA would invite comparison with the practical initiatives taken by the Christian church in Europe to save civilizational infrastructure after the downfall of the Roman Empire in early medieval times. Notwithstanding efforts to uphold human settlements, climate change appears responsible for the temporary abandonment of the southern branch of the Tarim Basin SR in the first half of the fifth-century CE, including the desertion of ancient settlements like Loulan and Niya (Waugh 2008, 5; de la Vaissière 2004, 112).

References

Abazov R (2008) The Palgrave concise historical atlas of CA. Palgrave MacMillan, New York

Artykbaev Z (2007) Istoria Kazakhstana. Tsentralno-Aziatskoe knizhnoe izdatelstvo, Kostanay

Baipakov K, Kumekov B, Pischulina K (1997) Istoria Kazakhstana v srednie veka. Rauan, Almaty

Barfield T (1989) The perilous frontier – nomadic empires and China 221 BCE to 1757 CE. Blackwell, Cambridge, MA

Barfield T (2001) Steppe empires, China and the silk route: nomads as a force in international trade and politics. In: Khazanov A, Wink A (eds) Nomads in the sedentary world. Routledge, London

Barfield T (2011) Nomadic pastoralism. In: Bentley (ed) The Oxford handbook of world history. Oxford University Press, Oxford

Bonavia J, Baumer C (2002) The silk road – Xian to Kashgar. Odyssey, Hong Kong

Borgolte M (2015) Kommunikation – Handel, Kunst und Wissenstausch. In: Demel, W u.a. (eds) WBG Weltgeschichte – Eine globale Geschichte von den Anfängen bis ins 21. Band III

Boulnois L (2008) Commerce et conquetes... sur les routes de la Soie. In: Testot L (ed) Histoire globale – Un nouveau regard sur le monde. Sciences Humaines, Auxerre

Bouvard G (1985) Au Kazakhstan soviétique – Chez les conquérants des Terres vierges et les pionniers de l'Espace. Editions du progrès, Moscou

Brunn S, Toops S, Gilbreath R (2012) The Routledge atlas of central Eurasian affairs. Routledge, Abingdon

Cameron R, Neal L (2003) A concise economic history of the world – from Paleolithic times to the present. Oxford University Press, New York

Cattani M (2007) Origine del nomadismo pastorale nelle steppe eurasiatiche. In: Ori dei cavalieri delle steppe – Collezioni dai musei dell'Ucraina

Chaliand G (1995) Les empires nomades—De la Mongolie au Danube (Ve-IVe siècles av. J.C., XVe-XVIe siècles ap. J.C.), Perrin

Dmitriev S (2009) Archéologie du Grand Jeu: Une brève histoire de l'Asie centrale. In: Piatigorsky J., Sapir J. (eds): Le Grand Jeu du XIX siècle – Les enjeux géopolitiques de l'Asie centrale, Autrement

Doujon J-P (1990) Histoire des faits économiques et sociaux – Une analyse par les modes de production. Presses universitaires de Grenoble, Grenoble

Fang Ming (2014) Silk Road. Chinese Red, Beijing. Huangshan Publishing House

Fässler P (2007) Globalisierung – Ein historisches Kompendium. UTB Böhlau, Köln

Ferret C (2013) Le pastoralisme nomade dans les steppes kazakhes. In: Stepanoff C, Ferret C, Lacaze G, Thorez J (eds) Nomadismes d'Asie centrale et septentrionale. Armand Colin, Paris

Fragner B (2006) Zentralasienbegriff im historischen Raum. In: Fragner B, Kappeler A (eds) Zentralasien 13.-20. Jahrhundert. Promedia, Wien

Fragner B (2007) Hochkulturen und Steppenreiche. In: Sapper M. (ed) Machtmosaik Zentralasien, Osteuropa, Sep

Freydank H et al (1978) Erklärendes Wörterbuch zur Kultur und Kunst des Alten Orients, Ägypten, Vorderasien, Indien, Ostasien. Köhler & Amelang, Leipzig

Geiss PG (2003) Pre-tsarist and tsarist CA – communal commitment and political order in change. Routledge-Curzon, London

Geng S (1998) The Uighur Kingdom of Qocho. In: UNESCO: History of civilizations in CA, vol IV

Gernet J (1972/1985) Le monde chinois – 3 volumes, Armand Colin. Volume 1: De l'âge de bronze au Moyen Age (2100 avant J.-C. – Xe siècle après J.-C.). Volume 2: L'époque moderne (Xe siècle – XIXe siècle)

Golden P (2011) CA in world history. Oxford University Press, Oxford

Grataloup C (2007) Géohistoire de la mondialisation – Le temps long du monde. Armand Colin, Paris

Griessler M (2011) China – Eine Annäherung. Holzhausen, Wien

von Gumppenberg M-C, Steinbach U (eds) (2004) Zentralasien: Geschichte – Politik – Wirtschaft – Ein Lexikon. C.H. Beck, München

Gunder Frank A (1992) The centrality of CA: Studies in history. VU University, Amsterdam

Habib I (2003) Science and technology. In: UNESCO: History of civilizations of CA, vol V

Hambis L (ed) (1977) Asie centrale – Histoire et civilisation. Collège de France, Paris

Hambly G (ed) (1966) Fischer Weltgeschichte: Zentralasien (Band 16). Fischer Taschenbuch Verlag, Frankfurt, unaltered edition 1979

Haywood J (2011) The new atlas of world history – global events at a glance. Princeton University Press, Princeton

Höllmann T (2004) Die Seidenstraße. C.H. Beck, München

Huyghe E, Huyghe F-B (2006) La route de la soie ou les empires du mirage. Payot-Rivages, Paris

Irmscher J et al (1986) Einleitung in die klassischen Altertumswissenschaften. VEB Deutscher Verlag der Wissenschaften, Berlin

Karger A (ed) (1978) Fischer Länderkunde. Sowjetunion

Kauz R (2006) China und Zentralasien. In: Fragner B, Kappeler A (eds) Zentralasien 13.-20. Jahrhundert. Promedia, Wien

Khazanov A (1983) Nomads and the outside world. University of Wisconsin, Madison

Khodarkovsky M (2002) Russia's Steppe Frontier: the making of a Colonial empire 1500–1800. Indiana University Press, Bloomington

Kickinger C (2006) Facetten nomadischer Lebensweise. In: Steffelbauer I, Hakami K (eds) Vom Alten Orient zum Nahen Osten. Magnus, Essen

Kozybaev M, Nurpeis K, Romanov Y et al (2010) Tom 1: Kazakhstan ot epokhi paleolita do pozdnego srednevekovia. In: Ministerstvo Obrazovania i Nauki Respubliki Kazakhstan (ed): Istoria Kazakhstana s drevneishikh vremen do nashikh dney v piati tomakh, Atamura

Kocka J (2013) Geschichte des Kapitalismus. C.H. Beck, München

Lebedynsky Y (2007) Les nomades – Les peuples nomades de la steppe des origines aux invasions mongoles (IXe siècle av. J.-C. – XIIIe siècle apr. J.-C.). Errance, Paris

Linska M, Handel A, Rasuly-Paleczek G (2003) Einführung in die Ethnologie Zentralasiens (Vorlesungsskriptum). Universität Wien, Vienna

Litvinsky B (1996) India i tsentralnaya Azia. In: Rossiiskaya Akademia Nauk – Institut Vostokovedenia (ed) Azia – Dialog Tsivilizatsii, Giperion

Liu X (2005) Viticulture and viniculture in the Turfan region. The Silk Road 3(1)

Liu X (2010) The silk road in world history. Oxford University Press, Oxford

Masanov N (2003) Pastoral production. In: Production – Northern areas (Transoxania and the Steppes). In: UNESCO: History of civilizations of CA, vol V

Mayhew B (2010) Central Asia highlights: history. In: Mayhew B, Bloom G, Clammer P, Kohn M, Noble J (ed) Lonely planet guide: Central Asia, 5th edn. Lonely Planet Publications, Oakland, pp 34–61

Millward J (2013) The silk road – a very short introduction. Oxford University Press, Oxford

Millward J, Perdue P (2004) Political and cultural history through the late 19th century. In: Starr F (ed) Xinjiang – China's muslim borderland. Sharpe, Armonk, NY

Ministerstvo Sviazi i Informatsii Respubliki Kazakhstan (2010) Istoria Kazakhstana – Entsiklopedichesky spravochnik. Aruna

Miyawaki J, Cuigin B, Kyzlasov L (2003) The Dzungars and the Torguts (Kalmuks), and the peoples of southern Siberia. In: UNESCO: History of Civilizations of CA, vol V

Mokyr J (2003) CA. In: Mokyr J (ed) The Oxford encyclopedia of economic history. Oxford University Press, Oxford

Münkler H (2005) Imperien – Die Logik der Weltherrschaft – Vom Alten Rom bis zu den Vereinigten Staaten. Rowohlt, Berlin

Norel P (2009) L'histoire économique globale. du Seuil, Paris

Olson M (2000) Power and prosperity – outgrowing communist and capitalist dictatorships. Basic Books, New York

Osterhammel J, Petersson N (2003) Geschichte der Globalisierung – Dimensionen, Prozesse, Epochen. C.H. Beck, München

Overseas Chinese Affairs Office (2006) Connaissances générales en histoire chinoise. Foreign Language Teaching and Research Press, Beijing

Overy R (ed) (2004) The times complete history of the world – the ultimate work of historical reference (6th edn)

Parzinger H (2004) Die Skythen. C.H. Beck, München

Parzinger H (2009) Die frühen Völker Eurasiens – Vom Neolithikum bis zum Mittelalter. C.H. Beck, München

Paul J (2012) Neue Fischer Weltgeschichte: Zentralasien (Band 10), S. Fischer Verlag, Frankfurt

Perdue P (2003) Silk road. In: Mokyr J (ed) The Oxford encyclopedia of economic history. Oxford University Press, Oxford

Perdue P (2011) East Asia and Central Eurasia. In: Bentley (ed) The Oxford handbook of world history. Oxford University Press, Oxford

P.M. History (2011) Von Europa nach China: Große Reiche und rätselhafte Kulturen an der Seidenstraße, no. 2

Ponting G (2001) World history – a new perspective. Pimlico, London

Poujol C (2000) Le Kazakhstan (Que sais-je?). Presses Universitaires de France, Paris

Ptak R (2007) Die maritime Seidenstraße – Küstenräume, Seefahrt und Handel in vorkolonialer Zeit. C.H. Beck, München

Roberts J (2002) The new penguin history of the world. Penguin, London

Rossabi M (2012) The Mongols – a very short introduction. Oxford University Press, Oxford

Roudik P (2007) The history of the C Asian republics. Greenwood Press, Westport

Roux J-P (1997) L'Asie centrale – Histoire et civilisation. Fayard, Paris

Schiltz V (1994) Les scythes et les nomades des steppes – 8e siècle av. JC – 1er siècle ap. JC. Gallimard, Paris

Sellnow I et al (1977) Weltgeschichte bis zur Herausbildung des Feudalismus – Ein Abriss. Akademie Verlag Berlin

Shen F (2009) Cultural flow between China and the outside world throughout history. Foreign Language Press, Beijing

Shukow I et al (eds) (1955–1968) Weltgeschichte in zehn Bänden (Vsemirnaya istoria v desiat tomakh), Bände 2–6 (Band 2 1956/62, Band 3 1957/63, Band 4 1958/64, Band 5 1958/66, Band 6 1959/69), VEB Deutscher Verlag der Wissenschaften

Toynbee A (1976) Menschheit und Mutter Erde – Die Geschichte der großen Zivilisationen (Mankind and mother earth – a narrative history of the world). Claassen, Düsseldorf

Tracy J (2011) Trade across Eurasia to about 1750. In: Bentley (ed) The Oxford handbook of world history. Oxford University Press, Oxford

de la Vaissière E (2004) Histoire des marchands sogdiens. Collège de France, Paris

Virmani S-M (2012) Atlas historique de l'Inde – Du 6e siècle av. J.-C. au 21e siècle. Autrement, Paris

Vogelsang K (2013) Geschichte Chinas. Reclam, Stuttgart

Wang H (2009) Les monnaies de la Route de la soie. In: Whitfield S (ed) La Route de la soie – Un voyage à travers la vie et la mort. Fonds Mercator, Bruxelles

Waugh D (2002) The Origins of the Silk Road. University of Washington Lecture Series

Waugh D (2008) The silk roads and Eurasian geography. University of Washington

Whitfield S (2007) Was there a Silk Road? In: Asian Medicine, no. 3

Wittfogel K (1964) Le despotisme oriental – Etude comparative du pouvoir total. Les Éditions de Minuit, Paris

Wollenweber B, Franke P (eds) (2009) Entlang der Seidenstraße. Wostok, Berlin

Yang J (2009) Alexander the Great and the Emergence of the Silk Road. The Silk Road 6(2)

3.1 From Barbarian Invasions to the Turkic Empire, the First Transcontinental Nomadic State (ca. 350–700 CE)

As mentioned above, economic activity in and transcontinental trade through CA reached low points during the periods of large-scale invasions and migrations of people across Eurasia (fourth and fifth centuries CE). Lack of effective administration in most parts of CA reflected less security and predictability, more uncertainty of the business environment, weighing on all kinds of economic activity. The creation and expansion of the Hephthalite state (largely in the place of the defunct Kushan state) and the stabilization of nomad-dominated Northern China (Northern Wei dynasty) in the late fifth century set a degree of—nomad-supervised—trade activity in motion again. This was followed by more international trade and economic recovery under nomadic oversight once the geopolitical situation had stabilized in the sixth century and the Turkic Empire or Turk Khaganate had emerged and integrated large parts of Eurasia, including most of CA, as can be gleaned from Maps 3.1 and 3.2. The seventh century saw the Tang dynasty's "reconquest" of the Tarim Basin and of territories beyond, as well as the Arab caliphate's takeover of Persia and advance into CA, setting the stage for the reinstatement of the SR as a major network connecting sedentary empires in commercial exchange.

Rafis Abazov, I.M. Shukow, Liu Xinru, Etienne de la Vaissière, and Zhang Yiping are the authors of publications which feature among primary sources of this chapter.

3.1.1 From Instability and Turmoil to the Hephthalite Confederation (ca. 350–550 CE)

From the third century, demographic east-west and north-south movements were vigorous and violent. Mounted archery had reached or was reaching a first degree of perfection thanks to the creation of the stirrup and the saber. In particular, Hunnic peoples were on the move, with consequences: Hephthalites (White Huns) invaded Southern CA and India, and Attila and the tribes he commanded invaded Europe. Due to the weakening or collapse of state power and the spread of chaos, the business climate foundered, merchandise trade dwindled and languished, and irrigation systems in numerous C Asian oases fell into disrepair. Economic and political power splintered in small regions and towns.

The north of China (largely the drainage area of the Yellow river) that had briefly been reunified again in the late third century came under increased nomadic pressure and disintegrated anew in the early fourth century. From the late fourth to the late sixth century, the Tuoba Wei, a Xianbei tribe, ruled Northern China. However, the Tuoba Wei state, which had gained some stability, soon became sinicized (Northern Wei dynasty) and lost its superior military capabilities. Southern China meanwhile remained under the control of changing domestic dynasties. The general circumstances (lack of security) of the time may have had repercussions on technology transfer and the passing on of (formerly well-kept) secrets. In the year 428 CE, Sogdian businessmen taught Chinese tradesmen how to produce high-quality Sogdian-type glass. (Glass had until the fifth century not been manufactured in China.) After China had kept it for about one and a half millennia, the secret of silk making leaked to the Kingdom of Khotan (East Turkestan) in the fifth century (Shukow et al. 1957/1963, Band 3, 140, 142).

In most cases devoid of a central protective power, the oases of Southern CA were small polities, city-states, and often mini-kingdoms, e.g., Khotan. Like in traditional communities, royal power tended to be circumscribed by the council of elders. The kings of some cities had coins minted—and some of these coins, following the Chinese model, had a square struck out in the center. Sometimes, the city-states joined together to form associations under the hegemony of the strongest statelet, which were ruled by assemblies of kings and nobility.

Given that the Sassanian Empire was the only large sedentary state and regime that had survived the Barbarian invasions in CA, Persia—temporarily—became the leading power on a malfunctioning SR. What remained of transcontinental trade continued to be hampered by intermittent wars with Eastern Rome (Byzantium) (see below). Still, the Sassanians minted a stable silver currency, the Sassanian drachma, which was a symbol of dynastic prestige and highly valued also by their trading partners.

As aluded to above, around 400 CE the nomadic confederacy of the Hephthalites (White Huns) conquered Tokharistan from the Sassanian Empire and militarily threatened (what remained of) Persia. In their first attack, they plundered the sedentary population of Sogdiana and Bactria and destroyed infrastructure. In the following decades, the White Huns extended their power to Northern India and took possession of the Indus river valley and the Punjab. Their newly established capital Paykent lay in Sogdiana, southwest of Bukhara (Map 3.1). The White Huns minted silver coins according to former Kushan standards, though the quality was lower due to their lack of experience in commerce (Liu 2010, 85).

Regardless of the turmoil and the difficulties of trade, silk remained very popular in the disintegrating Roman Empire, particularly in Eastern Rome (Byzantium). When Christianity was adopted as a national religion (391), Christians began to wear silk costumes and churches started to use silk fabrics as curtains, which boosted demand. At that time, however, Byzantium (since 395 divided from Rome, capital: Constantinople) was almost completely isolated from China. In the north, Hunnic tribes prohibited people from transiting the area of the Danube, the Black Sea and the Western Eurasian steppe belt. In the east, the Sassanian Empire remained a tough negotiating partner and a major barrier to overcome. Like in the past, intermittent trade arrangements (e.g., in 408–409 CE) were soon followed by military hostilities, which resulted in the interruption of what remained of SR traffic and contributed to weakening both belligerents (Persia and Eastern Rome).

As Rome had done during antiquity, Byzantium in the fourth- and fifth-century CE reluctantly settled for the arrival of the lion's share of silk and other goods from the Orient through Persian hands. Certainly, the coincidence of high Byzantine demand for silk and the scarcity of silk due to widespread political chaos and monopolized supply drove up the price of the coveted fabric. Byzantium's hardship was somewhat alleviated by the switching of some deliveries to the sea route as an alternative (between Southern China and the Mediterranean). Constantinople was eventually able to turn the insecurity in CA to its advantage and achieve a breakthrough in the tedious issue of silk supply (see below).

In the second half of the fifth century, the valleys of the Oxus and the Yaxartes, including Bactria, Transoxiana and Khwarazm, furthermore Zhetysu (Semirechie), the northwestern part of the Tarim Basin, Afghanistan, Gandhara, Punjab, and the valley of the Indus were all controlled by the White Huns.[1] While the capital Paykent featured increasing economic, and particularly trade, activities, many old cities (like Samarkand/Maracanda, Termez) were neglected. Some Hephthalites remained nomadic cattle breeders, while others settled and became involved in agriculture and gardening and produced rice, cereal, and cotton. During this period, land was primarily appropriated by the new tribal elite (Pander 2005, 37; Chvyr 1996, 398).

In the early 480 CE, the Hephthalites achieved major military victories over the Sassanian Empire and forced the latter to pay large tributes, mostly in its appreciated silver currency, the drachma, to the White Hunnic Empire until the first half of the sixth century. As a result, a large part of the Sassanian money supply flowed off into Tokharistan, more precisely Sogdiana. Merchants—primarily Sogdians living near Paykent, but also Khorezmians—gained considerable influence in the Hephthalite state. The White Huns gave Sogdians the opportunity to step up their international trading activities again by selling the extorted Sassanian silver for Chinese and Indian merchandise. Thus, the Sogdian salesmen changed masters (prior to the chaotic two centuries of the Migration Period in Asia, it had been the Kushans). The White Hun capital also came to be known as the city of the merchants, and Sogdiana became a major C Asian hub of population and of consumption (de la Vaissière 2004, 103).

Furthermore, under the oversight of their Hephthalite masters, the Sogdians started to colonize Zhetysu (Semirechie, the "area of seven rivers"). Partly based on remnants of Wusun and Kangju urban settlements, the Sogdians founded towns in the region. Colonization focused on an east-west line in the foothills of the Tienshan, at the level of well-irrigated and rich loess soil, enabling the cultivation of wheat, vines, vegetable gardens, and orchards. The steppe conditions of the plains of Zhetysu favored animal husbandry.

The defeat of the Sassanians by the Hephthalites and tax increases prompted by the tributary burden placed on Persia triggered political instability in the Sassanian Empire: Against the backdrop of weakened royal authority, social tensions between the land-owning aristocracy and the impoverished peasantry contributed to the Mazdakite insurrection (488–529), a mixture of religious movement related to Manichaeism and social-revolutionary uprising harboring demands for a more equitable distribution or even collective

---

[1] Thus, the White Huns controlled a sprawling territory comparable to that of their predecessors, the Kushans.

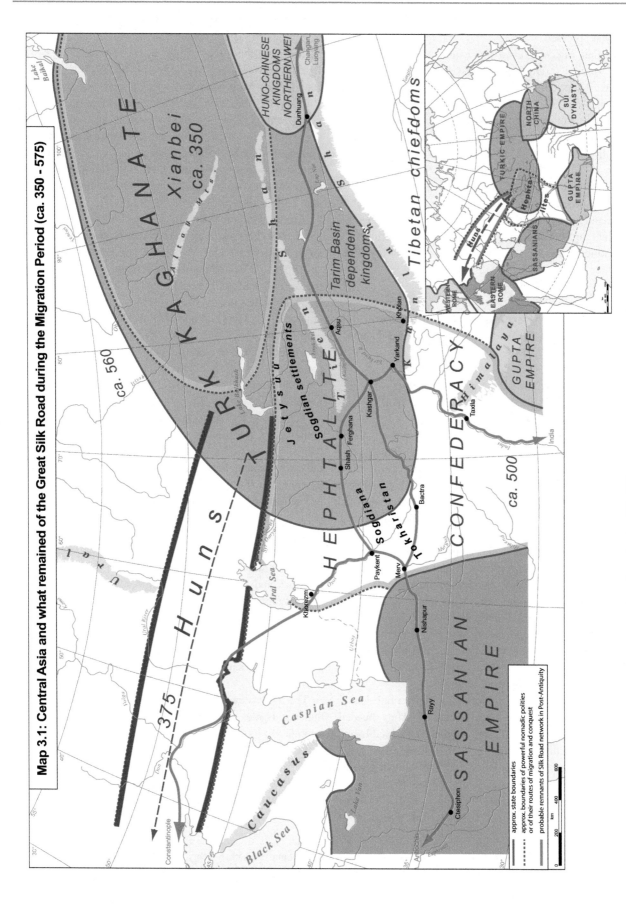

Map 3.1   CA and what remained of the SR during the migration of peoples (ca. 350–575)

ownership of goods. The protracted rebellion was eventually bloodily suppressed.

Sassanian rule stabilized again under Shah Khozrov I (531–579) who strengthened royal power, expanded the central civil service, and reconsolidated the authority of the Zoroastrian church. Khozrov's tax reform followed the model of the Roman Emperor Diocletian. He introduced a land registry and a fixed land tax (depending on classes of soil quality, etc.) instead of variable and arbitrary revenue taxation; he carried out a comprehensive census and determined a new poll tax (graduation according to property size). He also reformed the army by equipping soldiers at public expense and strengthened the network of imperial routes. All in all, the empire developed in the direction of patrimonial-bureaucratic monarchy (Kaemmel 1966, 100; Mirow 2009, 294).

3.1.2 The Turk Khaganate: Spanning from Europe to China and Reanimating Trade (ca. 550–630 CE)

3.1.2.1 The Turkic Empire and Its Sogdian Merchants Resume Transcontinental Tribute Trade with China

It was in the sixth-century CE that Turkic tribes expanded from their heartland in Southern Siberia (Altai Region) and Mongolia to conquer new territories. They were prompted by a combination of factors including rapid population growth, environmental changes (drying up of traditional pastures), pressures from nomadic-ruled China (Xianbei), but also the pull factor of the Huns (after their westward movement) leaving the Kazakh steppes void. In order to expand, the Turks had a technical trump card for warfare: they had developed heavy cavalry equipped with metal armors of their own production (from the iron-rich Altai ranges) (Paul 2012, 177). Finally, the Turks were often led by far-sighted charismatic leaders, who bolstered their military position by allowing various clans and tribes to join their confederacy and enjoy equal rights, although at the same time this could complicate political control.

From around 550 CE, under their supratribal leader Bumin, the Turks went in two directions. They headed southeast, taking the Gobi desert (steppe), and established positions at the Chinese border. In doing this they ousted the Avars (presumedly also an Altaic people), who fled westwards. And the Turks advanced in a southwesterly direction and conquered the lion's share of what is known later as (East and West) Turkestan.[2] The Avars were chased even further west and probably intermediated two important inventions of equestrian warfare from CA to Europe: the stirrup and the saber. Both were first adopted by the Byzantinians (Hambly (ed) 1966/1979, 71).[3] In 552 Bumin founded the Turk Khaganate, which he headed as Kaghan Bumin (552–553). The Khaganate was a large steppe empire going beyond Mongolia and comprising most of CA. Upon expanding into West Turkestan, the Turks had joined the Sassanians under Shah Khozov I in defeating the Hephthalites and wiping out their state (around 565). The Amu Daria (Oxus) became the border between the Sassanian and Turkic empires.

Around 570, under Bumin's successor Mukan (553–572), the Turkic Empire is even recorded to have extended its sway further east into Manchuria and further west to the shore of the Black Sea and the Crimean peninsula. Thus, in the second half of the sixth-century CE, the first trans-Eurasian state directly linking Europe with East Asia had emerged (see Maps 3.2 and 3.3). At the western end of the empire, the Turks took possession of the city of Bosporus (the future Kerch, on the strait connecting the Black Sea and the Sea of Azov) from Byzantium in 576. Diplomatic, political, and economic contacts with the Byzantine Empire were initiated.

The—far-flung, but fragile—Khaganate was an imperial confederacy, a hereditary empire, ruled by the Kaghan, who formally possessed all land. The basis of the Turkic economy was animal husbandry, particularly horse and sheep breeding. In the empire's C Asian parts, there was some specialization on karakul sheep. Camels and cattle were bred in smaller numbers (Baipakov et al. 1997, 9). Upon conquest, the ruler, his court bureaucracy, and the nomadic nobility organized the redistribution of acquired pastures among member tribes; the same goes for the allocation of livestock and slaves taken from the subjugated peoples, as well as of regularly levied tribute. All the territory was divided into districts run by begs or beks (appointed local governors who were usually, but not always, members of the ruler's Ashina clan). The basic level of authority was embodied by tribal leaders running the local affairs of their own people.

The Turks levied taxes on caravan trade and collected duties in border areas. They usually did not interfere in the internal affairs of other nomadic tribes or sedentary regions, including Shash, Ferghana, Transoxiana (Sogdiana), and principalities (kingdoms) in the Tarim Basin; respected their local governments and religious, social, and economic systems; and provided military and diplomatic coverage for

---

[2] They only seem not to have penetrated into the northern fringes of the Kazakh steppe.

[3] According to another theory, Arab-Muslim conquerors introduced metallic stirrups in Southwestern and Western Europe, from where the invention spread east (Rasuly-Paleczek 2006, 185).

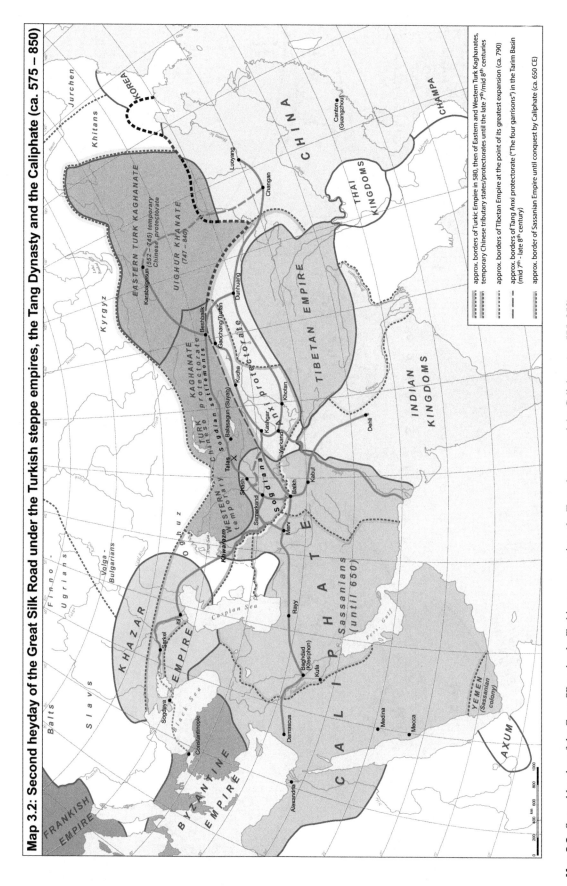

Map 3.2: Second heyday of the Great Silk Road under the Turkish steppe empires, the Tang Dynasty and the Caliphate (ca. 575 – 850)

approx. borders of Turkic Empire in 580, then of Eastern and Western Turk Kaghanates, temporary Chinese tributary states/protectorates until the late 7th/mid 8th centuries

approx. borders of Tibetan Empire at the point of its greatest expansion (ca. 790)

approx. borders of Tang Anxi protectorate ("The four garrisons") in the Tarim Basin (mid 7th - late 8th century)

approx. border of Sassanian Empire until conquest by Caliphate (ca. 650 CE)

Map 3.2 Second heyday of the Great SR under the Turkic steppe empires, the Tang dynasty, and the Caliphate (ca. 575–850)

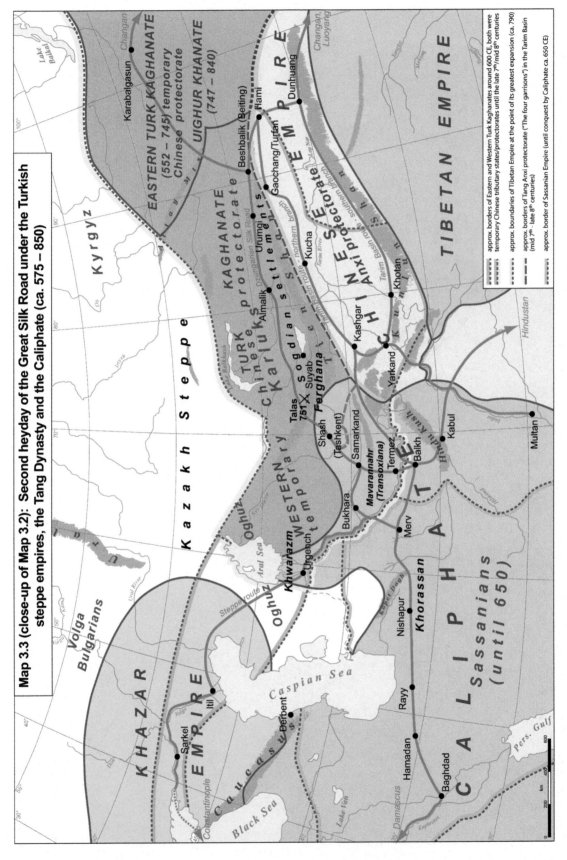

Map 3.3 (Close-up) second heyday of the Great SR under the Turkic steppe empires, the Tang dynasty, and the Caliphate (ca. 575–850)

them. In this sense, for the workers in the towns and the farmers on the fields, peace and security were indispensable—nomadic tribes were able to provide them this. As a quid pro quo, once property and slaves had been confiscated in one-off interventions, the Turks collected tribute, which in most cases constituted fixed dues (Artykbaev 2007, 117).[4]

With the Turkic state now successfully installed at its northern and western borders, China came under concentrated nomadic military pressure. Repeated devastating raids were carried out. Chinese leaders decided that it was prudent to pay large subsidies in silk to gain peace (not unlike their predecessors had done when initially confronted with the Xiongnu). In the early years of the empire, the Turks directly oversaw trade with the Chinese: large amounts of silk were extorted; in exchange, livestock (particularly horses) were delivered, which, in quantity/quality and in market terms, were far from equivalent to the acquired silk. Relatively free border markets also existed in which other livestock (e.g., cattle), hides, and iron were traded for farm produce, manufactures, etc.

As de la Vaissière underlines, the birth of the Turkic Empire gives rise to the large-scale reappearance of silk as a diplomatic gift provided by Northern China to the new Eurasian nomadic power from the 550s (2004, 160). Silk was "big business"; trade soon flourished. In 553, the Turks reportedly brought 50,000 horses to the border; during Mukan's reign, the Northern Chinese court made an annual gift of 100,000 rolls of silk to the Kaghan and was compelled to lavishly entertain hosts of Turkic visitors in the capital (Barfield 1989/1992, 133). Not unlike in periods of the Han era, silk again functioned as a de-facto international currency (Kozybaev et al. 2010, 498).

Meanwhile, the Khaganate had actually acquired silk-making technology through its incorporation of the Kingdom of Khotan, to where the secret of silk production had been smuggled in the fifth century. Yet Chinese output remained incomparably larger, cheaper, and of higher quality. Then, in 555, two Byzantine monks on visit apparently succeeded in hiding eggs of the silk moth and seeds of the mulberry tree in their pilgrim's rods and in smuggling them out of Khotan and the Turk Khaganate to the East Roman Empire (Byzantium). They were acting on the order of Emperor Justin (527–565) and may thus have been carrying out one of the first major acts of economic espionage. A couple of years later, Justin founded the first silk worm breeding and silk manufacturing of Europe in Constantinople (P.M. History 2011, 55). With now at least three sources of production, it became more difficult to keep the secret. Knowledge of silk-making technology spread to

other oases of the Khaganate in the sixth century, to Persia in the late sixth or early seventh century, to Sicily and the Arab caliphate in the seventh, and to the rest of Europe until the tenth century.[5]

Later on, Sogdians, acting as agents for the Turks, probably took over much of the Turko-Chinese trade business. Sogdian businessmen, whose homeland had been incorporated into the Turk Khaganate, were trusted by the Kaghans. A kind of symbiotic relationship, based on mutual benefit, developed between Turks and Sogdians: The Kaghans, thanks to the Sogdians' experience in trading and their connections, were able to dispose of war booty and tribute, particularly silk, in exchange for receiving desired goods; for the Sogdians, the military strength of their protectors guaranteed their safe passage along trade routes, and the Khaganate's political influence assisted them in prizing open new lucrative sources of supply and demand (Khazanov 1983/1994, 256).

Enormous profits seem to have been amassed through the Chinese "ransom," namely, the very large number of silk bolts shipped by the Chinese into the steppe—apparently almost for free. This must have been something like a godsend for the military-commercial Turko-Sogdian elites. The immense flows of silk lasted about 30 years, until the Sui dynasty (masters of a reunited China) put an end to them (de la Vaissière 2004, 189). Afterwards, Chinese silk deliveries to the Turks did not disappear altogether but were reduced and dispersed between Eastern and Western Khaganates and other power centers (see below). All the while, Sogdian traders acted as quasi-monopolists.[6] The lucrative tributary trade system with China was a key institution binding the nomadic empire together. It contributed to generating international trade: The eastern domains of the Turkic state had a principal role in procuring the silk, while the western domains marketed it. Thus, notably Sogdian businessmen became wealthy middlemen linking the economies of China and the west (Gunder Frank 1992, 25; Barfield 2001, 240).

Most of the Turks themselves continued to practice the pastoral way of life in the steppe for an extended period of time.[7] They focused on animal husbandry (main pillar),

---

[4] If one applies Lebedynsky's definition, the Turkic Khaganate appears to fit the classic case of imperial nomadism.

[5] Important silk production centers were, i.a., set up in the Italian cities of Palermo, Lucca, and Venice and in the sixteenth century in Lyons (France). From the seventeenth to the nineteenth century, the silk industry thrived in Krefeld (Germany) (P.M. History 2011, 56).

[6] But this kind of division of labor – cooperation between nomads acquiring booty and exacting tribute, and preferred salesmen disposing of the merchandise and accessing desired products – was nothing new. It was already valid for the Xiongnu and their C Asian commercial agents.

[7] This is in contrast to their Kushan predecessors, most of who settled down relatively quickly after taking possession of Tokharistan.

handicraft, trade, and hunting; moreover, they used economies of towns and oases as necessary complements. Livestock breeding focused on horses (means of transportation and essential for warfare), sheep, and cattle. Mare's milk was an esteemed beverage and used for making alcohol. Sheep were the Turks' main source of food consumption. The quantity of sheep and horses a household possessed was an indication of its wealth. Turks, notably of the Altai region, were renowned as ironsmiths, and iron smelting was a widespread traditional handicraft. The same goes for the making of woodware. Moreover, Turks processed furs and pelts acquired from tribes in Southern Siberia and exchanged them for agricultural produce in oasis markets further south.

As Chinese sources report, the sixth century and the beginning of the seventh century saw the growth of productive forces in the agricultural oases of CA. Strata of the sedentary (often Iranian) population of the Khaganate carried out farming, trade, and craftsmanship, secured the needs of the nomads, and constituted the major class of taxpayers. Irrigation systems were repaired again, and areas of cultivated and irrigated land even expanded. From this period we have the first indications of the cultivation of millet and wheat in Shash (oasis of Tashkent). Weavers, tanners, potters, and glass producers made technical advances (Shukow et al. 1957/1963, Band 3, 140).

As a result of the Turkic expansion into what is today East and West Turkestan, the presence of first nomadic, later partly sedentarized, Turkic-speaking population started to increase throughout CA. Turkic (nomad) newcomers to Southern C Asian oases and towns, e.g., to Sogdiana, only partly and very gradually integrated into the (sedentary) societies. When the Turks eventually started to lead a similar way of life as their fellow (mostly Iranian-speaking) town dwellers, the newcomers however remained connected to military and aristocratic strata of society. The mingling of the Turks' ruling class with the sedentary Iranians, including the Sogdian elite, in many urban centers over the next few centuries produced a remarkable ethnic mix and beautiful artwork in Sogdian cities such as Pendzhikent, Afrosiab (Samarkand), and Varakhsha (near Bukhara) (Mayhew 2010, 40) (see also Map 4.7).

Although in 568 a trade treaty was signed in Constantinople between the Turkic and Byzantine empires, centrifugal political tendencies in the Turk Khaganate and Sassanian opposition to direct Turko-Byzantine trade obstructed relations and reduced the quantity and importance bilateral trade could otherwise have reached. Still, as later embassies to China show, brocades for the Byzantine elite did not have to come via Persia but could be shipped via the steppe route (Tracy 2011, 293).

3.1.2.2 Following Chinese Termination of Large Tribute Payments, the Turkic Empire Splits into Eastern and Western Khaganate

Because of internal disputes and fighting, which had probably also been aggravated by the effect of the Chinese decision to stop major silk deliveries, the Turkic Empire split into two sub-empires, the Eastern and the Western Khaganate in 588. The Eastern Khaganate comprised the approximate territories of Mongolia and the Gobi desert; its center was located in Northern Mongolia. The Western Khaganate united West Turkestan east of the Caspian Sea, south of Lake Balkhash, and north of the Amu Daria, plus most of East Turkestan, and therefore it broadly corresponded to what is today called Turkestan. Its capital lay in Zhetysu.

From the sixth to the eighth centuries, under the protection and encouragement of the (Western) Turks, the Sogdians constructed a large number of agricultural, handicraft, and trade settlements in Zhetysu and Dzungaria, linked by trade routes (Artykbaev 2007, 118; Paul 2012, 170, 172). With this, they actually resumed and extended urban development activities that they had initiated under Hephthalite administration. During early medieval times, many cities flourished in this area. Sogdians and other people circulated intensively between Zhetysu and Gansu, via Gaochang/Turfan, Hami, and Beshbalik. This was probably one of the arteries of trade and exchange between China and the Khaganates (de la Vaissière 2004, 114, 123).

In the sixth and seventh centuries, foreign and transit trade developed primarily with China, but also with India (via Balkh) and Persia (via Merv). Sogdians supplied high-quality Sogdian glass, turquoise, and horses to China in exchange for which they—evidently—imported silk and silk fabrics. Sogdians sold perfume from the west, precious metals (gold, silver, brass) from Persia, and spices, saffron, and sugar (sugarcane) from India. Further, they traded medicinal plants, ammoniac, jewelries, and colored glaze wares. Batches of raw silk and silk fabrics were intermediated to nomadic tribes in the steppe, to Persians and Indians (Zhang 2005, 91). At or beyond the extreme west of the Turkic Empire or of its regional successor, the Khazar state (see also below), goods were exchanged at the edge of the forests of the Upper Volga against Baltic amber, furs, and slaves.

In Samarkand (Sogdiana), not far from the border with Sassanian Persia and with Gupta/Hindu India, precious foreign merchandise was stocked. Sogdian merchants assured the transfer of funds and played the role of bankers. These businessmen also sustained their preference (inherited from their activities in the White Hunnic Empire) for using the reliable Sassanian silver drachma as a general medium of exchange on the international trade routes, apart from the de-facto currency silk. Sassanian silver, beside Chinese silk, continued to circulate widely. In addition to these two means of payment, barter was upheld on a grand scale.

Against this background, it is not surprising that Sogdiana, a kind of federation of city-states, remained quite a prosperous place under Turkic rule. On his route from China via Turkestan to India in around 630 CE, the Buddhist monk and traveler Xuanzang (600–640) wrote that "all inhabitants of Samarkand (were) skilled merchants; when a boy ... (began) to read, he (was) required to study commercial affairs." Xuanzang called Sogdiana the most fertile place on earth, with the whole area looking like a garden (Roudik 2007, 25). Xuanzang also gave a vivid description of Kucha (Tarim Basin, Western Turk Khaganate): "The Kuchi state produces millet, wheat, rice, grapes, pomegranates, pears, peaches and apricots. Gold, copper, iron, lead and tin are mined. They use gold or silver coins as currency.... The climate is mild and the manner of the people is polished" (Geng 1998, 201). The cave temples of Kizil (a Buddhist monastery near Kucha) and Mogao (near Dunhuang, Gansu) reportedly date from around this period. The famous pilgrim also noted that Zhetysu (Semirechie) harbored fields of wheat, millet, and vines; a part of the population of the cities dealt with farming, another part traded.

Xuanzang's report moreover expounds what conspicuous nomadic elite consumption of exacted tribute could consist of. En route, the monk/traveler visited the court of the Western Turk Kaghan or Yabghu at Suyab (near Lake Issyk Koel/Tienshan): Yabghu Tong (618–630) was "covered with a robe of green satin" and bound his loose hair "with a silken band some ten feet in length." The "200 officers" of his entourage were attired in "brocade stuff," and accompanying troops were "clothed in furs and fine-spun hair garments." The Kaghan's tent was "adorned with golden flower ornaments which blind the eye with their glitter." His "officers" were all "clad in shining garments of embroidered silk." Xuanzang was impressed that this "ruler of a wandering horde" had a "certain dignified arrangement about his surroundings" (Golden 2011, 40). Thus one gets a concrete idea of where the part of the extorted silk and luxury actually went that was not swiftly channeled west through the "pipeline" of the SR.

The most important Sogdian cultural contribution to the Turkic realm probably was the script. The Sogdian alphabet was used almost from the beginning of Khaganate history, followed by Uighur history, to write texts in Turkic. Possibly one can also attribute to the Sogdians the diffusion in the Tarim Basin of improved irrigation systems, including those of the karez (qanat) type (Hambis (dir) 1977, 46). Where evaporation of water risked to be too high, e.g., in the Turfan depression, the canals were laid underground. As a result, under the combined impact of heat and humidity, the vegetation sprouted up in the Turfan area and an exceptionally rich agriculture sometimes produced two harvests per year. Production was so abundant that it did not only meet the needs of a dense and demanding oasis population but also permitted the sale of surplus produce to nomads, China, and elsewhere (Roux 1997, 167).

Most of the religions persecuted in neighboring Sassanian Persia found refuge in the Western Khaganate: Judaism[8]; Nestorian, Jacobite, and Armenian Christianity; and Manichaeism. Greater religious tolerance, and a degree of indifference, on the part of the Turkic authorities could have been due to their nomadic origins and their old shamanist customs.[9] Needless to say, Sogdians also contributed to the diffusion of numerous religious ideas, notably those of Buddhism, Nestorianism, and Manichaeism.

Other countries on the SR were also recovering economically: Under the Sui dynasty China reunited in 581 and regained political and economic stability.[10] Megaprojects were tackled: The Great Wall was repaired, and the national road network was extended. The Imperial Canal was built which connects the country's two major rivers, the Huanghe and Yangzijiang. A strong imperial cavalry was established, military colonies were set up at China's northern borders, and, as mentioned above, shipments of silk to the steppe were curtailed.

The situation of the Sassanian Empire improved once the drain of resources to the Hephthalites had been stopped and their military pressure had disappeared. It seems that the Persians also gained access to silk production technology (Abazov 2008, Map 10). Moreover, irrigated fields recovered and expanded also south of the Amu Daria, glass production grew, and craftwork flourished. In the tradition of Parthia, the Sassanian Empire remained a pivotal intermediary in east-west long-distance trade. Persian silk fabrics were soon appreciated in the west. However, hostile relations with Byzantium hardly improved, and competition with the Western Turk Khaganate did not ease; rather it grew more intense.

In continuity from their predecessors, the Sassanian Shahs' goal was to prevent direct contact between Sogdian (eastern) merchants and Greek (western) merchants. In Turko-Sassanian trade agreements, the Persians attempted

---

[8] Prior to leaving the Sassanian Empire, the main Jewish community had lived for centuries in Merv. Between the late fifth and the early seventh centuries, many Jews moved from Merv to Tokharistan and Khorezm (Roudik 2007, 36).

[9] Perhaps owing to the traditional weight of nature in nomads' life, and because of nomads' mobility and frequent contacts with other cultures, rigid and intolerant conceptions of religion did not seem to play a large role in the nomadic world (Schmieder 2015, 199–200).

[10] In the late sixth and early seventh century, the climate also seems to have warmed up again (Vogelsang 2013, 66).

to fix precise locations for carrying out trade in the big border towns near the Amu Daria boundary. The Shah limited the granting of trade permits to Sogdian salesmen and even tried to rein in their traveling on Sassanian territory. In this sense, Merv became the main and well-guarded Sassanian market, warehouse, and meeting place for Persian and Sogdian merchants (de la Vaissière 2004, 207–208). Such restrictions, the Sassanians hoped, would help them protect their transit trade position, maximize their trade profits, and avoid dissipation to competitors. In 575, Persia even conquered Yemen and thus attempted to control alternative maritime trade connections with India (and China).

As alluded to above, in the second half of the sixth century, Byzantium had set up its own silk production, initiated by a superb intelligence coup. Constantinople soon supplied most of the Mediterranean with silk fabrics. This reduced Byzantium's dependence on (Persian-intermediated) Chinese silk, but Byzantium and Europe still harbored substantial demand for the luxurious fabric made in China because of the huge quantities, the high quality,[11] and the attractive and changing variety of silk goods produced by the Middle Kingdom (Nolte 2005, 19).

3.1.3   Tang China and the Arab Caliphate Set the Stage for the Second Heyday of SR Trade (630–Late Seventh Century)

3.1.3.1   Chinese Rule Spreads Along the SR Over Most of Turkestan

After the end of the Sui dynasty (618 CE), the Tang dynasty, originating in the northwest of China, skilled in military affairs, and placing strong emphasis on martial virtues, established its authority over the country. Tang emperors conducted administrative, military, and economic reforms. For instance, agrarian reforms provided a more equitable distribution of land for peasants. Tea was introduced as a crop. A transition took place from a feudal-aristocratic elite (promoted by preceding nomadic dynasties, including the Northern Wei) to a homogeneous bureaucratic elite, recruited through Confucian state exams. The dense network of roads, canals, and postal stations was improved. Around the beginning of the seventh century, the country started to manufacture world-renowned porcelains (but products were not immediately exported in large quantities).[12] Engraving

printing is considered to have emerged in China no later than in the seventh century. This technology spread via the Hexi corridor to East Turkestan and gradually traveled west of the Tienshan and into Arab-controlled areas (Zhang 2005, 155).

A particularly bad winter in 626–627 CE helped bring down the powerful Eastern Turk Khaganate. That year was one of great hardship on the steppe because heavy snows and ice had killed many sheep and horses, which produced a human famine (He and Guo 2008, 67). Moreover, it also appears that Sogdian advisors were trying to apply the concept of regular taxation to the nomadic imperial confederacy. When the pastoral disaster struck the steppe, these officials continued to implement the concept and to levy stable amounts. Thus, there was discontent in large parts of the Sogdo-Turkic society and administration, and a revolt soon broke out. The Tang dynasty quickly took advantage of the disturbances, and in 630 CE, the Chinese army occupied the Eastern Turkic state, which collapsed and was turned into a Tang protectorate. Numerous Turkic nomads were forced to settle in Northern China, and many were engaged in agricultural activities. After the downfall of the Eastern Turkic regime, the Tang dynasty kept the tribal system of the Turks partially intact; the emperor incorporated the Turkic tribal structure into the imperial administration. Nomadic leaders became Tang officials; given their know-how, many were appointed to high ranks in the Chinese military. This proved to be a successful policy in that Turkic troops under the Tang banner made a decisive contribution to expanding China's borders deep into CA (Barfield 1989/ 1992, 145).

In 640 CE the oases of Hami und Turfan were brought under Chinese control again. Turfan (Gaochang) was an oasis in which Buddhism had firmly installed itself and in which the cultivation of grape wine had developed and flourished. Gaochang wines became famous in China. Gaochang was also known for its millet, wheat, sericulture, and many varieties of fruit. The Tang history of Turfan added a new item, cotton: native to India, cotton reached Turfan as a cultivated crop, which soon gained a strong foothold (Liu 2005, 2).

In 645 CE the Tang armies conquered the Tarim Basin, which was placed under the Anxi protectorate ("Protectorate General to Pacify the West," "The Four Garrisons") (Maps 3.2 and 3.3). Once the Chinese military and civil service were reinstalled in the region, Sogdian merchants in China followed and purchased parts of their silk remuneration from the garrisoned soldiers and officials, in exchange for a varied supply of foreign exotic products.[13] In this way, the Sogdians controlled silk deliveries to the west. In the same

---

[11] It seems that the long filament technology (important for making fine textiles) practiced in China did not appear in other silk-producing countries before the mid-eighth century (Liu 2010, 101).

[12] Porcelain embodies fine and translucid ceramics, produced by the burning of kaolin – fireproof white earthenware – at high temperature (about 1200 °C) (Boucheron 2012, 50).

---

[13] Thus silk continued to serve, or served again, as quasi-money in China.

period, the merchants supplied horses to the imperial Chinese stables (Norel 2009, 50). This reopened the way for large-scale trade of silk of commercial, not tributary, origin. Their key position in the Tarim Basin SR business once again afforded the Sogdians handsome profits. Following Turfan's example, other oases in the region also established or expanded viniculture and took up regular deliveries of grapes, raisins, and wine to the Chinese court.

At the same time, Buddhism exerted a strong influence on life in the Tarim Basin and Gansu. Monasteries sustained their important role not only for religious life but also for infrastructure and the economy. Secular sciences, including medicine, mathematics, astronomy, geography, history, as well as poetry, music, and painting were taught in the monasteries. Fields, gardens, male and female slaves, and cattle were at the disposal of these institutions. Parts of their lands were given out in rent. Some monasteries even fulfilled certain banking functions by carrying out moneylending activities. Fragments of medical works in the Dunhuang monastery library were kept not only in Sanskrit, but in Tokharian, Sogdian, and Uighur languages. Some aristocratic rulers (of principalities) mixed secular and religious functions. In Khotan, Kucha, and some other principalities, Buddhism became state religion. The government structure of the Kingdom of Khotan even seems to have evolved in the direction of theocracy (under Tang surveillance). In East Turkestan, Buddhism and its culture probably attained the peak of their influence in the fifth to eighth centuries (Litvinsky 1996, 192).

Around 659, Chinese troops invaded Dzungaria and Zhetysu; indeed the Turkic detachments under the Tang defeated the Western Turks on their own turf. For a short period also Ferghana and at least parts of Transoxiana (Sogdiana) were occupied. In the late seventh century, the Tang dynasty had expanded its influence and set up protectorates over a number of oases in these areas (Samarkand/Kang, Bukhara/An, Tashkent/Shi, and others). The Middle Kingdom was even able to impose new leaders on the Western Turk Khaganate, which was not eliminated but became a tributary state. After some tribal uprisings further west that were not fully brought under control, the western state largely turned into a nominal political entity under increasingly relaxed Tang suzerainty which lasted, at least formally, until the mid-eighth century. Under Sino-Turkic oversight, Sogdiana and Zhetysu were fragmented in numerous small principalities, which remained prosperous, obviously benefiting from SR trade. And silk came to be used as a domestic means of payment also in West Turkestan: The Turkic general Kursul, operating in Sogdiana, payed his troops in bolts of silk (Poujol 2000, 22; de la Vaissière 2004, 244).

In the meantime, China's military capabilities in land combat slowly faded, given the gradual sidelining of Turkic

officials, including military officials, in favor of professional Chinese bureaucrats recruited by the Confucian imperial examination system. After the secret of silk production had escaped and the country no longer retained the silk monopoly, foreign silk textiles started arriving in the Middle Kingdom via the SR in reverse direction. However, these deliveries were (still) no match for the large Chinese exports of the coveted luxury product (Liu 2010, 89).

3.1.3.2 Expansion of Caliphate into CA Opens Up Huge Integrated Economic and Trading Space

Several factors likely contributed to Islam's and the Arab caliphate's strength of conquest: first, Islam's call for social justice, regardless of race, color, social background, tribal origin, or language; second, Islam's enforcement of law and order; third, Muslims' support for trade; and fourth, in the military sphere [the Arabs' effective combination of voluntary armies and professional units, of Bedouin nomadic military strength and sedentary standing armies, and of cavalry and infantry (Abazov 2008, Map 15; Rodinson 1966/2007, 57–59; Liu 2010, 93)]. It also appears important to point out that Islam is not a nomadic religion, nor did it originate with nomads: Muhammed, a businessman, escaped from the city of Mecca to the city of Medina (agricultural oases); then he triumphantly returned to Mecca, establishing that city as the center of the Islamic state. Notwithstanding Bedouin tribes and their valuable military contribution, the Islamic civilization is an essentially urban one (Burlot 1995, 85).

Back to CA: The Sassanians' intensified warfare against Byzantium since the late sixth century (including their unsuccessful and costly siege of Constantinople in 626) ultimately exhausted the military power and economic resources of Persia. After conquering Syria (638–640), the Arabs destroyed the Sassanian Empire and incorporated Persia into the caliphate in 640–650 (of which Khorassan in 650). Merv was taken in 651, Balkh in 652, and Kabul in 664. The Arabs conducted raids into CA/the Western Turk Khaganate. They aimed to destroy, plunder, and weaken prosperous Sogdiana (Transoxiana) in 673. For instance, irrigation systems were ruined. During this attack, the Arabs took 30,000 prisoners and a large booty of precious goods. Initially, the occupation of CA was viewed by the caliphate exclusively as a source of loot and quick income (Roudik 2007, 27–28).

The Arabs confiscated property from the locals, taking their houses for the occupying soldiers and Islamic clergy (ulama). The entire population of conquered areas was subjected to new taxes. The most draconic were ad hoc land taxes and personal levies imposed on those who did not convert to Islam. On the other hand, the new authorities soon granted some—limited—religious tolerance. Jews and

Christians who had been living there long before the conquest were allowed to continue in their former faiths as dhimmis—i.e., followers of recognized monotheistic religions. Dhimmis were obliged to pay jizya—the special poll tax for non-Islamic subjects of the caliph.[14] At the same time, the burden imposed on the faithful of non-recognized religions (e.g., Zoroastrianism, Buddhism, Manichaeism) was so heavy that it entailed the progressive eviction of these religions from the territory ruled by the caliphate, including Persia, Afghanistan, etc.

Once lands had been militarily secured und sufficiently pillaged, it seems, reconstruction was ordered: All localities were instructed to organize themselves and supply their own food and tools to rebuild roads and city walls and repair irrigation canals. In CA, like in Iran, Arab governors were appointed, who were accompanied by scribes and their chancelleries. The new Muslim authorities resettled Arab families in conquered towns and villages (under reconstruction). Under Caliph Osman (644–656), the ruler started giving out confiscated land in the form of iqta—conditional possession for service (which recalls the European feudal practice of granting beneficia to loyal comrades-in-arms and followers) (Geiss 1979, 231).[15]

There is broad agreement that the establishment and expansion of the Islamic caliphate—after a limited period of turmoil—contributed to stimulating the economy and trade on the SR (Abazov 2008, Map 21; Feldbauer and Liedl 2008, 17–18; Leipold 2001, 14). This argument gains even more plausibility if it is seen in conjunction with the economic impact of the extension of Chinese control over most of CA. Furthermore, it seems that the restrictive trade regime of the Sassanian Empire disappeared with the latter's rule and that it was not replaced by protectionist policies on the part of the just established Islamic authorities (de la Vaissière 2004, 253).

The new authorities' principal tolerance/respect for local administrative structures and customary law provided favorable conditions for economic activities. A huge economic space had been created with some essential standardized measures and weights, payment, and trade regulations, with functioning administrative and judicial structures.

Merchants had rights to file complaints in courts or to go all the way to official dignitaries if they felt unfairly treated. Hence the economic success of the Islamic polity including its C Asian territories during Umayyad rule (661–750) seems logical. According to Rodinson (1966/2007: Islam and Capitalism, 60), the merchants of the Muslim Empire conformed to Max Weber's criteria for capitalistic activity; they seized opportunities for profit and calculated their outlays, their encashments, and profits in money terms. And the de-facto practice of lending with interest was carried out extensively (e.g., revenue sharing arrangements or other commercial transactions developed as a widespread substitute), despite the Koran's ban of ryba (usury) (Leipold 2001, 22).

In the early centuries of the caliphate, it is probable that agricultural output in Iran and Islamic-ruled CA, after a short period of destruction and stagnation, developed favorably. The new authorities attempted to continue or improve local/regional agricultural traditions, represented by sedentary peasants, farm laborers, and slaves. Overland roads and irrigation systems were extended and modernized, and water wheels moved by animals as well as watermills were developed. The cultivation of some basic food plants and crops grew in CA. This goes for rice, millet, spinach, sugar cane, and cotton. The latter two became leading export products of the caliphate (Mokyr 2003, 369; Feldbauer and Liedl 2008, 17–18).

With the conquest of Syria, which had belonged to Byzantium, the Arabs had probably acquired the know-how of silk production. Islamic rulers soon presided over the emergence of a state-supervised luxury textile industry that had an important impact on Eurasian silk trade. The tiraz system was created for that purpose.[16] Some tiraz factories were government-run, and some weren't, but in any case, producers needed a license; the license system gave the authorities control over the quality of products from various regions. The tiraz factories mostly employed serf craftsmen and slaves. New Islamic sources would start to compete with and erode Constantinople's regional market position (besides the traditional Chinese presence) and would soon supply Christian Europe with silk yarn and textiles in quantity (Töpfer et al. 1985, 190; Liu 2010, 99–101).

A number of large cities expanded, with new twin towns developing just beside the old cores, e.g., Rayy, Isfahan, Nishapur, Merv, and later Bukhara and Samarkand. Nevertheless, disparities between cities centrally located within regions and those at the periphery may have increased: While the size and the prosperity of provincial centers grew, the importance of many smaller rural towns appears to have shrunk (Burlot 1995, 85; Feldbauer and Liedl 2008,

---

[14] In some cases, however, discontent arose among local peoples who had converted to Islam but were still forced to pay the jizya (poll tax) to the Arab treasury (Soucek 2000, 63).

[15] Compare Ponting's quite broad view of the emergence of feudalism: "In new empires, the initial rulers had to solve three linked problems – how to reward their followers, how to control the newly conquered areas, and how to maintain an army. The solutions adopted were nearly always the same – the grant of conquered land to individuals within the elite so that they could use it to support a given number of soldiers to be provided to the ruler when required. This system is called "feudalism" in European history but it is merely one form of a phenomenon that was common across Eurasia for seven millennia." (Ponting 2001, 145).

---

[16] Tiraz is a Persian word for embroidery.

88). Literacy spread widely in urban settlements. Technically, the networks of Muslim merchants were sophisticated and reflected the existence of commercial rationality which Muhammed had shared himself (Norel 2009, 62). While some Sogdian businessmen were active on former Sassanian territories after their Arab conquest up to the Amu Daria, nothing would allow us to infer more than a limited Sogdian presence on the sections of the SR beyond Merv crossing Persia into Mesopotamia (de la Vaissière 2004, 253).

Trade growth was facilitated by the establishment of well-functioning currency exchanges and of rudimentary banking and insurance systems. Although land ownership remained an important base of local power, merchants advanced to higher positions almost throughout the caliphate, which fits in well with the widespread upswing of trade that happened from the seventh century. Once the Umayyads had created a huge integrated market stretching from North Africa to the Amu Daria and once China had extended its control over CA along the SR all the way to Sogdiana (Transoxiana), it became easier for merchants to cover long distances safely, to avoid political obstacles, and to rein in price arbitrage through middlemen (Mirow 2009, 288). Silk remained the de-facto currency of the SR, also following the latter's revival in the seventh century. No legal tender attained comparable acceptance.

3.1.3.3 Emergence of the Khazar Empire: A Pivotal Intermediary at the Nexus of Europe and Asia

The Khazars were originally a nomadic Turkic people whose existence is attested from the sixth century. After migrating from the East and arriving in the area of the lower Ural, lower Volga, lower Don rivers, at the shore of the Black Sea, and in the plains of the Northern Caucasus, the Khazars were initially subjects of the Turkic and then Western Turkic empires. They achieved their independence after the invasion of the Eastern Turk Khaganate by the Tang (630 CE). In the 630s, the Khazars founded their own Khaganate (state). Their expansion put them into contact with the Byzantine Empire and with Arab conquerors in the Caucasus (see Maps 3.2 and 3.3). Khazars soon turned from a pastoral nomadic to a semi-nomadic lifestyle (Kozak 2007, 303). Some even completely settled down. Livestock breeding, farming, horticulture, fishing, and hunting were important activities in Khazaria. Crop agriculture was practiced along the banks of rivers and in the northern forest-steppe zone, while pastoral nomadism held sway elsewhere. Farming took up very little of the wide open grasslands. Crops were transported both by river and by cart. The Khazars used skiffs for sailing along the Volga. Besides livestock, the Khazars possessed many domesticated camels, which would typically be employed to transport goods (Brook 2006, 63).

The Khazars controlled intermediary trade with products coming from the far north of Eastern Europe (e.g., furs and ivory of walruses and narwhals, for which the key connection was from the Tundra via the Kama river) and running along the Volga to the Caspian Sea or via the Don to the Black Sea (Nolte 1991, 16). The early Khazar era even witnessed the foundation of Sogdaya—obviously a Sogdian establishment—on the shore of Crimea. After the signing of a trade treaty with the Byzantine Empire in Constantinople less than a century earlier (see above), Sogdaya seems to have represented another attempt by the Sogdians to generate sustainable trade relations between the regions of Sogdiana, CA, and the lower Volga on the one hand and Byzantium on the other. Sogdian merchants probably organized trade along the "steppe route" from China via the Turkic heartlands in CA to Khazaria and Byzantium. For this trade linking Asia and Europe, the Khorezmians served as indispensable intermediaries (Maps 3.2 and 3.3). Thus, Khazar commerce included the barter of furs, pelts, and other products from the north against silver objects from Transoxiana or Persia (after the latter's takeover by Arab conquerors) (de la Vaissière 2004, 222, 228).

Evidently, customs duties on merchandise and transportation constituted important sources of revenue for the Khazar authorities. The Kaghan required traders to pay customs duties and tithes on merchandise transported by both land and water routes. As centers of commerce located on strategic points along river courses (particularly of Volga and Don), Khazar urban settlements are described as numerous and prosperous (Brook 2006, 19, 73). With Turkic and Chinese control of West Turkestan waning in the eighth century (i.a., due to migration and nomadic raids coming from the east, Muslim attacks from the south), the "steppe route" temporarily lost reliability and importance. However, the Kama, Volga, Don, and Black Sea routes remained intact, which contributed to the well-being of the Khazar Empire in the following centuries.

3.2 Second Apex of Great Silk Road in the Era of the Caliphate and of the Tang Dynasty (Late Seventh to Late Ninth Century)

For the following chapter, the author has primarily drawn from publications by Rafis Abazov, Thomas Barfield, O.G. Bolshakov, Joseph Burlot, Clive Ponting, Peter Roudik, Svat Soucek, Etienne de la Vaissière, and Zhang Yiping.

3.2.1 Breakthrough to New Climax of SR Trade (Around 675–750)

3.2.1.1 The Two Largest Empires of the World Meet in CA in the Late Seventh Century

Under the Umayyad caliphate (661–750), the Arab commander Qutaiba ibn Muslim conquered Transoxiana, Khorezm, and Ferghana in the first two decades of the eighth century: Bukhara in 709, Samarkand in 710, Khiva (in Khwarazm) in 712, and the Ferghana Basin in 713. Thus, Western Turk/Chinese control of the SR was weakened.[17] The caliphate's initial brutal conquering measures were replicated north of the Amu Daria. Paykent and Pendzhikent (one in the lower, the other in the upper Zerafshan valley) as well as a number of other big cities and smaller oases were destroyed by the Arabs. Shash (Tashkent) was conquered in 750. The conquerors generally treated traders in a better way than other parts of the population: For instance, in 722, the Islamic armies captured the insurgent population of Khodzhent (Ferghana). The nobility and the merchants were separated in two distinct categories, and "only" the first was put to death (de la Vaissière: *Histoire des marchands sogdiens....*, 145). As Roudik reports, the peace treaty imposed on the Sogdians established an annual monetary tribute and a one-off obligation to provide 300,000 healthy male slaves or soldiers (which must have corresponded to a major part of the Transoxianan population!) for the Arab armed forces (2007, 28).

In 713, the Arabs established tight control over farm land in Mavarannahr (or the "Land Beyond the River"), as Transoxiana was now called and subordinated local leaders to the Arab emir (governor, prince). The new Muslim military-administrative elite confiscated or purchased landed property and palaces belonging to dikhans (local hereditary landowners, provincial nobility). Part of the land thus became property of the Arabs, typically of the Arab aristocracy, and the farmers had to pay rent as well as 10% of their harvest to the new elite. Other estates remained in the ownership of the dikhans who submitted to the new authorities and successively converted to Islam. The first mosque was built in Bukhara in 712; subsequently, all other religions were driven out of the city, except for Nestorian Christianity which survived until the fourteenth century and for Bukharan Judaism which is still present today. A specific feature of C Asian Islam is that the most influential orders (fraternities or brotherhoods) of Sufism—a mystical movement that emphasizes the development of a personal spirituality and an internal comprehension of divinity—originated in Khorassan and Mavarannahr. Sufi scholars and spiritual leaders later played an important role in spreading the Muslim faith among the nomads of the Eurasian steppe (Roudik 2007, 29; Fragner 2008, 44).

The caliphate's expansion and encroachment on C Asian territories under (relaxed) Chinese suzerainty probably contributed to the Tang's effort to reallocate a considerable part of the imperial budget in order to reinforce Chinese positions in Turkestani areas they still (formally) ruled. In the first half of the eighth century, 20% of the Tang state's receipts in silk cloth were assigned to the control of the western regions. In these conditions, considerable quantities of "administrative silk" flowed into the Tarim Basin and beyond the Tienshan as salaries and expenses of Chinese soldiers and clerks stationed in the cities en route from Dunhuang to Suyab (de la Vaissière 2004, 159). Sogdian merchants thus continued to sell coveted products from CA and further west to the Tang servicemen in exchange for silk received as salaries, until the 750s when Chinese definitely lost control over West Turkestan.

Overall, after the Han era, the period of the Tang dynasty was the second great epoch of overland silk flows through CA to the west. Large-scale SR trade flourished and reached unprecedented levels during the Tang era between the seventh and tenth centuries (Table 3.1). With the political consolidation of both the Middle Kingdom and the caliphate in the late seventh and the early eighth centuries, the trade network is estimated to have reached the peak of its activity in this period (Perdue 2003, 493; Waugh 2002, 1; Zhang 2005, 778; Schottenhammer 2015, 38; Andrea 2014, 122). Tricontinental commerce of this era stretched from the Atlantic (Morocco) to the Pacific (China) and included the Khazar Empire as well as the Baltic Sea region (Schmieder 2013, 105).

From Western and C Asia, China adopted walnuts, pomegranates, figs, and almonds (Töpfer et al. 1985, 149). Changan, the Chinese capital at the end of the SR, welcomed Sogdians, Persians, Arabs, Turks, and Indians, as well as Japanese, Koreans, and Malays, and became one of the most cosmopolitan cities in the world. It featured Nestorian churches; Buddhist, Manichaean, and Zoroastrian temples; and Muslim mosques. In the mid-eighth century, Changan is said to have grown to almost 2 million inhabitants (Wild 1992, 7; Roberts 2002, 440). Under emperor Xuanzong (712–756), China was tolerant in religious matters and remarkably open toward foreign influences. The Tang era (618–906) was also particularly rich in east-west cultural and scientific contacts (doctors, botanists, astronomers, mathematicians) (Boulnois 2009, 53). The first Chinese state-backed paper

---

[17] China's grip on West Turkestan may also have grown weaker because meanwhile unrest had broken out in the Eastern Turk Khaganate, over which the Tang lost suzerainty in the late seventh century (see below).

Table 3.1 Ups and downs of the Silk Road and its predecessors (from around 1500 BCE to the nineteenth-century CE)

Period[a]	Overland trade development in CA
1500–500 BCE	"Bronze Age/Iron Age forerunner" to the SR Andronovo horseback civilization, Lazurite, Nephrite route
500–200 BCE	Imperial trade networks: Achaemenid and Alexander empires
200–105 BCE	*"Ancient precursor" to the SR* Re-export of Chinese luxury goods through Xiongnu Empire (tribute trade): Military edge of nomadic power, marketing of extorted goods further west
105 BCE–200 CE	***First heyday of Silk Road*** Han dynasty–Kushan state–Parthian Empire–Roman Empire: Political stability and simultaneous flourishing of all four SR empires, transcontinental demand for Chinese silk
of which: 10–75 CE	Temporary weakness: Interior disturbances in China (uprising of the Red Eyebrows)
200–480 CE	SR decline: economic mismanagement and political instability/demise of Han dynasty and Roman and Kushan empires; technical advances and resurgence of nomadic military pressure, climate change, Hunnic invasions, migration of peoples
480–630 CE	Political re-stabilization, re-establishment of tribute trade: Hephthalite confederacy, Turk Khaganate
630–675	Tang Empire conquers most of Turkestan, Arab caliphate creates huge integrated economic and trading space; Khazar Empire at nexus of Europe and Asia
675–875	***Second heyday of Silk Road*** Tang dynasty–caliphate–Khazaria: Political consolidation of new SR empires
of which: 750–800	Temporary weakness: SR trade obstructed by Arab–Chinese war (Battle of Talas) and conflict with Tibet, hostilities between Khazaria and caliphate
875–925	SR decline: Political unrest in China, disintegration of caliphate, renewed pressure from Eurasian steppe
925–1000	*Post-caliphate temporary recovery of SR:* Political re-stabilization, Samanid Empire as east-west trade hub, "Islamic renaissance"
1000–1245	Repeated invasions of Turko-Mongol dynasties from the Eurasian grasslands (partly triggered by increasing aridity) disrupt and re-structure SR activities: Karakhanids, Khitan-Liao, Seljukids, Kipchaks (Polovtsy), Karakhitay (Western Liao) et al.
1245–1345	***Third heyday of the Silk Road*** Mongol Empire (Empire of the Great Khan/Yuan dynasty, Chagatay Khanate, Il-khanate, Khanate of the Golden Horde): SR security upheld (and trade initially subsidized) on a bi-continental politically integrated playing field; Pax Mongolica
of which: 1280–1300	Temporary weakness: Internal Mongol hostilities, interruption of trade boom
1335–1350	SR decline: Political instability (e.g., Red Turban rebellion in China), Mongol disintegration, "Black Death" spreads along the SR
1350–1500	Fragile post-Mongol recovery of the SR: Political re-stabilization, religious unification of CA: Empire of Tamerlane, Timurids, Uzbek Khanate, Golden Horde et al.
from the early 1500s	Pressure from European seaborne competition (maritime route to the Orient) on overland trade through CA
1575–1625	*"Mercantilist" renaissance of SR trade* Simultaneous rule of strong political leaders who carried out economic reforms and largely maintained peace: Khanate of Bukhara, Chagatay Khanate, Mughal India, Kazakhs, Muscovite Russia, Safavid Persia
1625–1775	SR again on the decline: Political destabilization, increasing warfare and raids, unraveling of economic reforms, maritime competition intensifies, religious dogmatism spreads
1775–1825	*"Last glimmer" of the SR* Lease of life for what remained of traditional trade in landlocked, newly isolated C Asian space difficult to access for modern European shipping technologies: "The Khanates" (Bukhara, Khiva, Khoqand), Kazakhs, parts of Russia and China; Pax Sinica
after 1825	Demise of (traditional) SR: Renewed outbreak of turmoil in CA, followed by European colonial conquest (Pax Russica) and inclusion as a raw material appendage into (modern) capitalist world economy

[a]Approximate indications

money was issued back in 650.[18] As mentioned earlier, printing—from wood blocks—was invented before 700.

Also after the Arab conquest of Mavarannahr (Sogdiana), the wealth of merchants of Bukhara and Ferghana was linked to the marketing of Chinese products. Targeted export production, e.g., of Chinese ceramics, gathered momentum (Schmieder 2013, 105–106). In order to guarantee peaceful trade along the SR and strengthen the supervision over the western regions (Turkestan), the Tang dynasty established courier stations along the main roads from Changan to major cities east and west of the Tienshan. The courier stations provided food and shelter for traveling merchants and messengers. The Tang also set up a registration system: all travelers had to register their names, ages, and belongings, and they were issued a road pass, without which they were not allowed to travel. The traders had to pay a certain levy for the privilege of the pass (Zhang 2005, 77). Many Muslim merchants were present in the trading towns of China and other regions (Schottenhammer 2015, 38).

Craftsmen, farmers, and herders became increasingly involved in the commercial production of goods to be sold in large bazaars in Balasagun (near Lake Issyk Koel, up to the mid-eighth century under Sino-Turkic control), Samarkand (up to the early eighth century under Tang suzerainty), Merv, Herat, and Baghdad. Samarkand was known for the production of glass, which was traded along the SR to China. The urban settlements of Zhetysu received a new impulse of development due to the expansion of transit trade through the region. Khotan was widely known for its beautiful jades.[19] The variety of commodities traded increased, although most of them remained luxury items: nephrite jade, precious stones, and jewelry, Central Asian glass, race and cavalry horses, Persian silver, Chinese silk, particularly silk fabrics, lacquerworks, tea, textiles, carpets, ironware, weapons, bullion, spices, salt, medicinal materials, and slaves (high demand for experienced domestic workers, concubines, and craftsmen in the markets of China, Central Asia, and the Middle East). Many terracotta warriors made in the Tang dynasty style of tricolored porcelains were popular to be buried with the Arab rich and powerful (Abazov 2008, Map 21; Zhang 2005, 95).

3.2.1.2 Reinserting Transcontinental Tribute Trade: From the Eastern Turkic State to the Uighur Khaganate

Thanks to military action, in the late seventh century, the Eastern Turk Khaganate—that had been under Chinese protection—became independent again under commander Kutlug (Khan Elterish, 682–691). After numerous raids on China that had brought large numbers of captives[20] and wealth to the Turks, the latter received a new marriage proposal and gifts of silk from the Tang court. Military pressure was upheld on China, and the Middle Kingdom around 710 agreed to a generous subsidy treaty and started to pay tribute again to the Eastern Turkic state. The raids were about insisting that the Tang pay a "subsidy" in the form of silk which the Turks could trade to the west (Ponting 2001, 322). This was done, i.a., by enforcing a biased rate of exchange of 4–5 bolts of silk per horse, whereas on the steppe a horse was rarely valued at more than one piece of silk (Barfield 1989/1992, 152).

In 745 however, weakened by internecine conflicts, the Eastern Turk Khaganate fell victim to the expansion of the neighboring nomadic Uighurs; thus, the Eastern Turkic state was replaced by the Uighur Khanate (an imperial confederacy). Living in close connection with China, which was itself increasingly beset by internal unrest and tensions with the caliphate and other neighbors, the Uighurs continued the practice of bartering nomadic products, mostly their horses, at a forced rate of exchange, for silk and other Chinese goods. The Uighurs thus gained political influence in the Middle Kingdom which they used to support the existing Tang government as long as it honored the subsidy agreement of the time (Der Große Ploetz 2008, 781).

Even more than the Turks before them, the Uighurs benefited from considerable silk tribute payments. The rate of exchange (silk—horse) was advantageous for the Uighurs and increased first to 25 then to 40 pieces of silk per horse in the Uighur era. Thus, eventually the Tang was reported to have bought 7500 horses for 300,000 bolts of silk a year (de la Vaissière 2004, 278). In the case of a Chinese refusal to honor the deal, the Uighurs threatened to cancel the alliance and withdraw their military support. While their predecessors had decided against erecting a permanent city in the steppe, the Uighurs assessed that they had accumulated too much wealth not to establish a fixed fortified capital. They needed a place to store the silk and other goods they had collected, receive traders, and hold court in a way that would centralize their rule as middlemen in the lucrative re-export of silk (Barfield 1989/1992, 157). Probably to an even greater degree than within its Turkic

---

[18] As Cameron and Neal pointed out, the Chinese had already experienced several cycles of inflation and monetary collapse before the West discovered paper money (2003, 82).

[19] There was a great variety of Khotan jades – some crystal white, some emerald green, some black, and some yellow (Zhang 2005, 120).

[20] One such raid in 698 allegedly yielded 80,000–90,000 slaves (Paul 2012, 295).

predecessor state, sedentary Sogdians formed a pivotal elite of advisors, a group of de-facto ministers, actively overseeing Uighur involvement in long-distance trade and assuming administrative responsibilities in the running of a true city on the steppe. The Sogdian civil servants introduced the Sogdian alphabet to the Uighurs (Perdue 2003, 493).

The Uighur capital Karabalgasun was set up with the assistance of Sogdians and Chinese soon after the khanate was founded; the city was deep in the heart of nomad country on the Orkhon river (Northern Mongolia), near where Genghis Khan would later establish Karakorum. Given the definite fixed settlement that they had chosen, one can conclude that the Uighurs had become at least semisedentary. As Barfield explains, Karabalgasun's raison d'être was international trade. The authorities kept written records, and maintained agricultural communities on the grasslands. The intensive farming that grew up around the city was a secondary phenomenon, serving the needs of a place founded and maintained by the long-distance caravan business (Barfield 1989/1992, 157).

3.2.1.3 New Institutional-Economic Structures Created in Islamic CA

The Islamic conquerors, the Muslim regional rulers, and the spread of the religion itself introduced new institutional-economic structures to CA which have had a major impact on socioeconomic development of the region until today. These institutions facilitated interregional communication, determined binding rules, i.a., for economic transactions, and thus contributed to establishing mutual trust between economic subjects (Pernau 2011, 111). Some important elements are described in the following.

The *mahalla* corresponds to a community structure, whether social (extended family), administrative (the smallest unit recognized by the state), spatial, or architectural (neighborhood community) (Poujol 2001, 194–195). These community structures can embody kinship and loyalty networks, residential connections and a comprehensive system of social control (producing a kind of local public self-government). Mahallas may be led by elected local elders who represent the interests of residential administrative districts vis-à-vis state tax collectors, water attendants, etc. Urban mahallas have border walls and entrance gates which are closed in the evening. The street, instead of separating inhabitants, functions as a focus of social life. Some mahallas are organized according to occupational groups (e.g., tanners' quarter, goldsmiths' quarter, etc.) or religious distinctions (Muslims, non-Muslims; Sunnis, Shiites) (Petric 2002, 10).

The spread of *Sharia* ("legal system," Islamic law) was often accompanied by the establishment of elements of patrimonial statehood (standing army, regular taxation, removable civil servants). Typically, the Islamic ruler appointed, paid, and removed *qadis* and muftis as judges and scholars of law in order to deal with issues of criminal, civil, and family law. The qadi controls the Mukhtasib (market inspector), a civil servant in charge of verifying the conformity of weights and measures in markets and bazaars and of punishing dishonest transactions. The Abbasid caliphs reserved for themselves the jurisdiction of appeals, comprising the abuse tribunal (Mazalim), responsible for correcting injustices, in particular such committed by civil servants. Islamic law also acknowledged Adat, customary law. In the Islamic state, the arbitrary power of the ruler was usually circumscribed or at least partly reined in by the ulama (religious scholars) (Burlot 1995, 68–69; Gumppenberg and Steinbach (eds) 2004, 229–231).

The Islamic public domain (in CA) stemmed from confiscations and acquisitions which followed the conquest. Two kinds of such property can be distinguished: Those that the caliph and his palace exploited directly via appointed stewards recruited from central offices and those that the supreme ruler granted to private persons or groups for exploitation for their own benefit (Burlot 1995, 72). The *iqta* system (theoretically) corresponded to the bestowal/assignment of state land for a limited time in order to appropriate tax revenue as a quid pro quo for military service. The recipient of the iqta was called iqtadar. In practice, newly annexed territories were often divided up under the ruling elite of the conquerors; the latter—equipped with hierarchically graded titles—exercised power in lieu of the central authority in territories assigned to them (Rasuly-Paleczek 2006, 190).

Waqf was property owned by Muslim religious institutions, e.g., land owned by mosques, cemeteries, hospitals, and schools. Waqf property did not merely include agricultural land but also water mills, workshops, stores, and even quarrying rights for mines. Waqf property tended to be bequeathed by rulers and faithful. It generally enjoyed tax exemptions and was inalienable and thus constituted a strong economic basis for religious power. In some respects, waqf land could be compared to European monasterial and church land (Ma 2003, 188; Sellnow et al. 1977, 424).

Given that in Arab CA in most cases agricultural land ownership was separated from exploitation, tenant farming (typically sharecropping) dominated. Irrespective of whether the owner was a Muslim or a non-Muslim, land was subject to the *kharaj* (land tax). Craft and trade activities were subject to a sales tax. Muslims additionally paid the alm levy; non-Muslims were charged the jizya (poll tax) (Ott and Schäfer (eds) 1984: Wirtschaftsploetz, 468).

Until the end of the seventh century, the old Byzantine and Sassanian coins remained in circulation in the center and the east of the caliphate. Then, based on their access to the gold produced in Western Africa and transported across the Sahara, the Islamic authorities started to produce their own currency: The Muslim mints issued golden (dinars), silver (dirhams), and bronze coins inscribed in Arabic on both sides, which did not immediately replace or supplant local money in circulation, though. Moreover, the *dinar* (from denarius) imitated the respective Byzantine gold coins, and the *dirham* (from drachma) rivaled the Sassanian silver money, which had been particularly highly esteemed in CA and China (Davidovich and Dani 1998, 391; Ponting 2001, 355). This bimetallism gave rise to the presence of money changers (djahbadh) across the empire, who often became real businessmen, sometimes bankers. Apart from Chinese silk, which continued to function as money, the currencies of the Islamic world started to dominate Eurasian trade (Burlot 1995, 79).

With the expansion and increasing economic integration of the caliphate, Muslim businessmen either introduced or adopted and perfected a number of institutions and rules for accessing capital, for generating business partnerships, for reducing risks, and for enabling interregional cashless payments. The specialized banker did not (yet) exist in the caliphate. Instead, the functions of banker and wholesale businessman were connected with each other. Although usury was banned, Islamic merchants devised numerous credit instruments such as letters of credit and promissory notes to facilitate their trade. They also developed the accounting techniques to keep track of these transactions. Given distances and dangers on SR territory, the transfer of funds constituted an important challenge. In the eighth century, the bill of exchange (lettre de change) emerged, an instrument providing for a third party to pay a sum due to a person. Deferred transfer (or "shakk," from where "check" is apparently derived) was another technique adopted (Burlot 1995, 81; Ponting 2001, 358).

3.2.2 SR Trade Obstructed by Hostilities, but Arabs Transmit Key Chinese Know-How (Paper, Compass) Westward (ca. 750–800)

3.2.2.1 Battle of Talas and An Lushan Rebellion Set Stage for Chinese Withdrawal from West Turkestan and for Arab Acquisition of Key Know-How

The Battle of Talas in 751 and the An Lushan rebellion (755–763) profoundly changed the political framework of business in CA and altered SR trade itself. The major military conflict that took place near the town of Talas (modern Taraz/Dzhambul) between the ruling Eurasian powers of Tang China and the Arab caliphate ended in the defeat of the Chinese forces. The revolt a few years later, led by the Turko-Sogdian military leader An Lushan, triggered unrest in large parts of China and destabilized Tang rule. The

dynasty reached out for its militarily superior Uighur allies, who then intervened and crushed the rebellion. The two capitals of the Tang era, Changan and Luoyang, were brutally cleansed of rebels. There was a high price for this help: The Uighurs demanded and received the right to loot the captured cities. In 765 the Tang had to pay the Uighurs a special subsidy of 100,000 pieces of silk to make them leave the capitals. Under the guise of gift-giving and trade, Chinese tributary payments to the Uighur Empire were ratcheted up. A kind of asymmetric alliance emerged between the two players: China fulfilled lavish and increasing Uighur demands for payment of subsidies, in exchange for which the nomads occasionally intervened to prop up Tang authority in the Middle Kingdom (Barfield 1989/1992, 151–153; Golden 2011, 44).[21]

At the Battle of Talas, the Arabs had gained lots of booty and a large number of prisoners, among who were skilled silk weavers, papermakers, and gold- and silversmiths. The weavers were sent to the caliph's textile workshops in Kufa (Iraq). Mulberry trees soon spread as a commercial crop all the way from CA to North Africa and Southern Spain. The papermakers were installed in Samarkand to establish a paper industry which subsequently played a major role in the development of book production in the Muslim world (Bolshakov 1998, 31). Thus, Samarkand became the Islamic world's leading center of paper production, before yielding that place to Baghdad, then to Damascus, which later became the prime paper supplier of the Christian world (via Spain and Italy) until the era of the crusades. Not before the beginning of the second millennium CE were papyrus and parchment gradually replaced by paper in Europe (Boulnois 2009, 52).

The Chinese eventually (around 760) had to retreat to their military bases in the Tarim Basin including Kashgar; the Western Turk Khaganate collapsed. In 766, the Khaganate of the Karluks (Turkic nomads from the northern foothills of the Tienshan and Zhetysu), established two decades earlier, became independent. The Oghuz (also nomadic tribes of Turkic origin) living in the steppes around the lower reaches of the Syr Daria and near the Aral Sea also attained independence. Despite their victory over the Tang, the Arab conquerors were unable (or unwilling) to move beyond the southern fringes of the Zhetysu area; furthermore they did not venture into the Eurasian steppe, though they remained in CA (Abazov 2008, Map 15).

Around 750, for obvious reasons, the price of silk doubled from 14 to 28 dirhams between Dunhuang and Samarkand. In the aftermath of the Battle of Talas, SR trade, without grinding to a halt, became segmented. The only silk available immediately was produced locally (Gumppenberg and

---

[21] Thus, it could be argued that China had turned into a giant de-facto Uighur protectorate.

Steinbach (eds) 2004, 248; de la Vaissière 2004, 161, 243). It is improbable that the Sogdians were able to reconstitute their commercial links and supply lines before the end of the eighth century. However, since the secret had slipped out of China back in the sixth century, the general know-how (though not all the finesses) of silk production had already spread across large parts of Eurasia. Regardless of their military collision in the mid-eighth century, China and the caliphate coexisted on friendly terms for most of the time (Zhang 2005, 94; Schottenhammer 2015, 37–38).

Notwithstanding the victory of the Islamic armies at Talas, turmoil and instability did not even spare the C Asian provinces of the caliphate. A series of uprisings inflamed the region between the 750s and the early 800s. As a consequence, a large number of Buddhist, Manichean, and Zoroastrian clergy moved to lands further east unconquered by the Arabs. Buddhist communities expanded their influence in East Turkestan and Tibet, where Buddhism even achieved the status of official religion in 787.[22] Rebellions in Khorassan were put down by the caliphal governors, who reorganized the spheres of tax assessment and water use, where things had apparently gotten out of hand. Thus, governor Sulayman al-Tusi (783–787) lowered the level of the kharaj (land tax), which had been raised under the previous governor al-Musayab. The new governor also put an end to misuse of water by the newly installed elite, which had seized extra shares of the precious resource in the Merv oasis in order to direct it to their fields; the use of water in other areas was also subjected to stricter regulation (Bolshakov 1998, 38).

But the frequent tensions and conflicts with the locals had weakened the caliphate, and, eventually, the Islamic rulers agreed to include the local nobility in the highest positions of C Asian (provincial) governments. In Mavarannahr (Transoxiana), a large number of C Asians, including many people in the traditional urban elite, began accepting Islam and benefited from the strong and comprehensive education system (Abazov 2008, Map 16). Gradually, Arabic became the language of government, law, science, and art in Muslim CA. Given the more difficult trade and economic exchange with China in the aftermath of the Battle of Talas, the oasis economies of West Turkestan, including those of Khorassan, Khwarazm, Mavarannahr, and Bactria, somewhat reoriented their commercial relations toward the rest of the caliphate. Despite recurrent instability, trade west of the Tienshan expanded. As Roudik put it, eventually local C Asian lords became tax and rent collectors for the Arabs—in exchange for de-facto political autonomy/independence (2007, 32).

3.2.2.2 Tibet Conquers Part of the SR, While Khazaria and the Caliphate Are at War

During a phase of Tang weakness, Tibet in 770–780 conquered most of the Tarim Basin (particularly the south) and of Gansu from China and attempted to gain control of the SR. Markets in Dunhuang reverted to a pure barter economy; money largely disappeared. Commercial exchange of a Sogdian type went through a very difficult period in the second half of the eighth century. Large-scale overland trade regressed for a least one or two generations (de la Vaissière 2004, 277). The Tibetans had allied themselves with the Arabs and were able to hold sway over some parts of the SR for almost a century. However, Caliph Harun-al-Rashid (768–809) in the early ninth century switched his preferences in favor of China. Near the other end of the SR, the Khazars had been involved in wars against the Arabs during almost the entire eighth century. The Arabs were eventually able to take Derbent (on the western shore of the Caspian), which controlled north-south routes toward Transcaucasia and Iran. Around 750, the Khazar capital was transferred from the Northern Caucasus to Itil (or Atil) on the Volga delta, where a sedentary center of their semi-nomadic state was erected (Maps 3.2 and 3.3) (Dmitriev 2009, 45–47).

Due to the strong influence of the Arab-Muslim civilization, for example, through colonization and settlement activities in the oases of Western CA from the early eighth to the late ninth century, the influence of mounted warrior nomads and of the nomadic way of life in these sedentary centers was temporarily driven back. The only exception was the militarily extremely valiant Turkic slave soldiers that had been acquired in the northern steppe regions. These (former) steppe dwellers were to support the armed forces of the caliphate in its center Baghdad as well as in Mavarannahr and other regions but in some cases created eventually independent powers (see below). On the other hand, the Chinese withdrawal from West Turkestan (following the Battle of Talas) indirectly strengthened the influence of the nomadic civilizations to the north of the oases (e.g., the Uighurs of Mongolia, the Karluks of Semirechie, and the Oghuz of the steppes near the Aral Sea). In any case, some regions like Ferghana and partly also Khorezm seem to have featured a striking picture of symbiosis of nomad and sedentary cultural components (Chvyr 1996, 404).

From the middle of the eighth century, when the Tang dynasty gradually lost control of Turkestan and SR connections became more tenuous, the importance of sea travel increased again (Fang 2014, 27–28).[23] In this respect

---

[22] The Tibetan state had been established and consolidated by a few strong monarchs already in the seventh century, who had militarily unified a number of tribes on the plateau of Tibet and conquered some adjacent regions, also at the fringe of China.

[23] According to Vogelsang, the weakening of the Tang Dynasty also coincided with a worsening of the climate which became drier and colder (2013, 66, 274).

there appears to have been a substitution effect of the overland route in favor of the maritime route, in terms of volume as well as of value. Southern China, notably Canton (Guangzhou), soon welcomed a considerable number of Persian and Arab merchants, who formed trading "colonies" (Ptak 2007, 146; Höllmann 2004, 24). From the ninth century, direct sea trips from the Persian Gulf to China became regular undertakings (Biarnes 2008, 30).

3.2.3 Under Uighur Initiative, Eastern SR Trade Resumes, If on a More Modest Level (ca. 800–875)

From around 800 CE, the Uighurs and the Tang regained authority over some northern parts of the Tarim Basin, Dzungaria, and Zhetysu (Semirechie). They thus (again) oversaw the Northern SR, running north of the Tienshan, circumventing Tibetan positions, and upholding trade with the Arabs. The northern or Dzungarian route had two branches: one ran from the Tang capital Changan via Dunhuang, Hami, Turfan, or Beshbalik (Beiting), Urumqi, Kuldzha (Yining), Almalik, Balasagun, Talas, Shash/Tashkent, to Samarkand; the other started in the Uighur capital Karabalgasun, then joined the first route at Beshbalik and continued via Almalik, Balasagun, to Samarkand. Of course, there was also a direct connection (running about 2000 km across the Gobi desert) between the two capitals, Changan and Karabalgasun (Maps 3.2 and 3.3).

According to de la Vaissière, the traditional trade axis (through the Tarim Basin) continued to be shunned in favor of the longer Dzungarian route due to Tibetan depredations (2004, 277). In the first quarter of the ninth century, the Uighurs militarily controlled the steppe north of the Tienshan all the way to Shash; for instance, in 821 their army was present in Usrushana (near Khodzhent, lower Ferghana valley). The Uighurs established (or resuscitated) a courier system along these trade routes (probably modeled on the preceding Tang system). Once security was re-established, the northern road was used to deliver diverse commodities: silk, linen, precious stones and silver, medicines and dyestuffs, horses, falcons, ostriches, and slaves (de la Vaissière 2004, 281; Gorod moy rodnoy Almaty 2004, 39).

The Karluks (in Zhetysu) become vassals of (tributary to) the Uighurs. During the early medieval era, numerous cities, including the Karluks' capital Koyalyk (Antonovka, near present-day Taldyqorgan, Karatal valley, see Map 4.7), were reported to have flourished along the SR in Zhetysu. In the ninth century, the Karluk Khaganate (766–940) featured a mixed economy with predominant nomadic pastoralism; sheep breeding was the most important economic activity, followed by breeding of horses, goats, cows, bulls, and camels. The nomadic and semi-nomadic stockbreeding tribes adjoined the sedentary tribes of farmers, who mostly cultivated millet. The steppe and the town supplemented each other (Baipakov et al. 1997, 10, 18; Gorod moy rodnoy Almaty 2004, 35).

The Arab traveler Tamim ibn Bahr, who visited Karabalgasun in the 830s, described it as a large walled town with 12 iron gates, "populous and thickly crowded with markets and various trades" (Barfield 1989/1992, 157). The Kaghan's palace had its own wall, as did the city center, which contained temples and administrative offices. As Golden describes, the busy market streets were filled with merchants hawking their goods and services such as ceramics and stone carving. Sellers of the same products were usually grouped together on the same streets, as was typical of many medieval towns of sedentary countries. There were high towers to watch for potential invaders coming from the surrounding grasslands. Nomadic traditions, however, persisted. The Uighur Kaghan had a tent made of gold which topped his palace and could be seen from far away. The tent had room for a hundred people. The surrounding countryside featured intensive cultivation (Golden 2011, 45).

Thus, while Mongolia and the Eurasian steppe did not constitute centers of industrial production, they did function as centers of value accumulation. As Barfield aptly illustrated, Uighur and other nomadic empires acted as giant trade pumps, drawing surplus goods from China and rechanneling them to international markets, pumping commodities into the SR network (2001, 240). In the framework of the Uighur Khanate, the Sogdians remained important caravan merchants and businessmen in the first half of the ninth century. There was also cultural transfer: The Uighurs (after the Turks) adopted the Sogdian alphabetic script to draw up their official records; the Uighurs further developed a sophisticated legal system which included the ability to sue for damages on breach of contract—an essential provision for trade and business (Ponting 2001, 341).[24]

In de la Vaissière's view, the huge quantities of silk that the Uighurs managed to exact made them the richest nomads yet to have appeared in Mongolia. As mentioned above, the Uighurs soon received up to 40 pieces of silk for every horse brought to China. The Chinese sources are full of complaints on what they saw as pure racketeering (de la Vaissière 2004, 279). The nomads had a vested interest in preserving the status quo. At its height, the volume of silk annually extorted from China reached half a million bolts. Payments for horses attained record levels of 50 pieces of silk per horse. Tamim ibn Bahr was also witness to this flow of wealth. As Barfield

---

[24] The caliphate had provided for its own rules to satisfy this requirement.

elegantly put it, Karabalgasun was the flower of a plant that had its roots in Changan (1989, 158). To the additional annoyance of the Chinese authorities, the nomads often let Sogdian merchants travel under their diplomatic protection to trade during tributary visits; these C Asians also received protection in the Chinese capital where they enjoyed extra-territorial status and became the most prosperous group of foreign money lenders in the Middle Kingdom (Barfield 2001, 241).

Around the same time that the Uighurs had asserted their control over the Northern SR (through Dzungaria), the Caliph Harun-al-Rashid switched back his support from Tibet to China. According to Shen Fuwei, during the Tang dynasty, porcelain products had become the most popular household utensils used for eating, drinking, cooking, or storing water and other items. Exports of Chinese porcelain ("chinaware" or "china") began to gain importance at the end of the eighth century. Although porcelain production was not monopolized, state-owned enterprises predominated in the manufacture of this valuable product for the imperial court and for export activity. The caliphate became a prime customer. Chinese porcelain first created a sensation in the court of Harun-al-Rashid, when 20 pieces of exquisite impe-rial chinaware (such as plates, cups, mugs, wine flagons) were offered, in tribute to the supreme ruler, by Ali Ibn'isa, his provincial governor of Khorassan (Shen 2009, 162–163; Schottenhammer 2015, 50). The Muslims' surprise was comparable to what the Chinese may have felt when they first had a glance at Roman glassware; this sensation could have contributed to the caliph's decision to rearrange his diplomatic preferences (see above).

More generally, Eurasian overland trade in the Tang Caliphate era featured silk, silk fabrics, garments, lacquer-ware, porcelain, ceramics, and arms (as contraband) moving west and, on the other hand, leather, horses, and slaves going east. Slaves (of C Asian Turkic or Eastern European Slavic origin) were captured in razzias typically carried out beyond the borders of the Islamic world. Incense, perfumes, woolens, and carpets came from Arabia and Persia. Cotton textiles, cashmere wool, rice, spices, and dyestuff (indigo) came from Northern India. The east (China) continued to produce trade surpluses which gave rise to persistent east-ward flows of precious metals (gold, silver, copper) in money form or in bullion (Norel 2009, 51).

Increasing sedentariness probably gradually eroded the military power of the Uighurs. Internal disputes over succes-sion resulted in civil unrest after 832, and the strength of the Khanate was further undermined by natural disasters/an unusually severe winter (Waugh 2008). After recurring war-fare, in 840 Kyrgyz tribes took advantage of the situation, captured and looted Karabalgasun, and destroyed the Uighur Empire. The nomadic Kyrgyz were a powerful Turko-Mongol tribal union centered in the uppermost Yenisey

region. The Uighur elite fled to the Chinese borderlands and subsequently formed a series of small states in a number of oases of East Turkestan and beyond. There the Uighurs assumed the leadership of the kingdoms of Ganzhou, also called "Yellow Uighurs" (Hexi corridor/Gansu, 840–1030) and of the Kingdom of Qocho (which originally comprised the rich oases of Turfan and Beshbalik/Beiting, then also included Karashahr and Kucha, Urumqi and Hami 840–1209) (Geng 1998, 200). The approximate position of these new Uighur statelets can be seen in Map 3.5. Mean-while, due to lacking support from the caliphate, Tibetan power in the Tarim Basin receded.

In the abovementioned oases, the ruling layer of semi-nomadic Uighurs Turkicized the local mostly Tokharian (originally Indo-European) populations linguistically and merged with them culturally. The Uighurs began to settle in oasis towns and to take up urban and agricultural pursuits. Like their mentors, the Sogdians, they soon developed a rich commercial culture as SR traders. The Sogdians themselves did not have any powerful and committed protector any more. As mentioned earlier, the former Uighur capital Karabalgasun had been a trading center based on the projec-tion of nomadic power. It could not renew itself unless the Kyrgyz (as new masters) re-established the old extractive network, which they did not. The ruins of Karabalgasun gradually reverted to sheep pasture (Barfield 1989/1992, 165).

From the mid-ninth century, the Uighur trading states of Qocho and Ganzhou gave the Uighurs new—if more mod-est—bases to carry on their role as middlemen on the SR; it was them, not the Kyrgyz, who continued to send envoys to Changan offering horses and jade for silk; although they had lost their military power to extort huge subsidies, they maintained important positions in international trade and were generally bent on securing friendly relations with China (Gunder Frank 1992, 32; Krieger 2003, 260). Yet the collapse of the Uighur Khanate had deprived the Tang Empire of a mighty nomadic military ally and certainly reduced transcontinental tribute trade, including silk turnover.

The Kingdom of Qocho became an amalgam of indige-nous settled people professing one or the other of the three religions, Buddhism, Manichaeism, and Nestorian Christian-ity, and of immigrants from the steppe that mostly adopted Buddhism or Manichaeism. Under the influence of the rela-tively advanced economic system of the natives that practiced farming of an irrigated oasis type, the Uighurs gradually gave up their semi-nomadic life and turned to a settled, urban, or agricultural existence (Geng 1998, 202).

This created the foundations for a remarkable civilization consisting of the Uighur ruling aristocracy, their scribes, and civil servants, Tokharian notables, the multiconfessional clergy, craftsmen, merchants, traders, peasants, and slaves.

In the countryside, the landlords possessed extensive farmlands and water resources, with a class of poor tenant farmers beneath them. Buddhist and Manichaean monasteries also owned large tracts of farming land bearing many dependent households. The cotton plant spread throughout the oases of Qocho, particularly in Turfan, and cotton became an export hit to China. Wheat and other cereals were cultivated, and grapes remained the reputation of Turfan (Roux 1997, 33). Later the Uighurs won renown for excelling in the fabrication of vases and of utensils of gold, silver, copper, and iron. The relatively peaceful Kingdom of Qocho also impressed through longevity: It survived right up to and even past its own conquest by Genghis Khan in the early thirteenth century (Soucek 2000, 81; Hambis (dir) 1977, 148).

3.2.4 Central Asian Economy Consolidates in Decentralizing Caliphate: Western SR Regains Prosperity (ca. 800–875)

3.2.4.1 Arab Central Asia's Cultural, Economic, and Trade Development

In ninth-century CA, Arabs continued to occupy high posts in the Islamic military, whereas Persians (Iranians) and Tajiks (Eastern Iranians, see below) gained the upper hand in the civil administration. From around 830, the caliph possessed a bodyguard of Turkic mercenaries and slaves. Because they typically descended from Eurasian steppe warrior nomads, the Turks tended to have an excellent military reputation. Many Turkic slave soldiers soon moved up in the military hierarchy and some reached the top ranks. With the evolution of the post of vizier (chief treasurer, minister, sometimes head of civil administration) under the caliphate, genuine state budgets began to be drawn up for the first time. Various departments consisted of well-staffed offices of civil servants who engaged in correspondence with the provinces and prepared estimates and accounts. A powerful stratum of officialdom, the Irano-Islamic class of secretaries (Arabic kuttab, Persian dabiran) was established. One of their tasks was to master the complex system of the kharaj (land tax), which in its more developed form took account not only of the quality of the land but of the types of crops sown and harvested. Cadasters were reviewed and brought up to date (Bolshakov 1998, 34).

In the first century of Abbasid rule of the caliphate (from 750),[25] Muslim possessions in the Near and Middle East as well as CA grew more united economically, which supported long-distance trade (Ott and Schäfer (eds) 1984:

Wirtschaftsploetz, 468). Under the Abbasids additional state-supervised workshops (tiraz) emerged in CA. These workshops did not only produce textiles (including carpets, curtains, pillows, silk robes) but various types of goods. Slave trade continued to flourish along the frontiers of the caliphate (including in CA).

Autonomist tendencies within the caliphate gathered momentum in the ninth century. One of the strongest families that came to rule Islamic CA were the Tahirides (820–873), a local Iranian dynasty in the province of Khorassan (south of the Amu Daria) under Abbasid suzerainty. To strengthen their region and rule, the Tahirides lowered taxes, built fortresses along the northern borders to protect their lands from incursions of nomadic tribes, organized the building of new canals, opened schools, and propagated Islam, which they saw as a pillar of their rule. The Samanids (from 819), another local dynasty subordinated to the caliph, ruled Mavarannahr (Transoxiana) and Ferghana. Their provincial capital was Bukhara. Under Samanid governors, public order, stability, and property rights were strictly upheld, and qadis (Islamic judges) were highly esteemed (Roudik 2007, 32; Hambly (ed) 1966/1979, 83).

In some regions of the caliphate, e.g., Tabaristan (south of the Caspian Sea), (golden) dinars were used as a medium of exchange. In others, for instance, Mavarannahr, (silver) dirhams were the preferred means of payment. The so-called Bukhar Khudah dirhams were modeled on the former Sassanian silver drachm. Late Sassanian drachms were probably still to be found in the markets of Mavarannahr in the eighth century. Notwithstanding frequent tax payments from Bukhara in silk and silk articles,[26] the tribute received by the caliphate from various cities and districts of Mavarannahr was in most cases calculated in terms of (silver) dirhams (Davidovich and Dani 1998, 392–393).

Once unrest and instability, that had punctured the second half of the eighth century, had passed, agriculture took an upward trend in Islamic CA. Cotton, rice, fruit, wheat, and other cereals were the main products grown in the region. Apart from cotton, the cultivation of rice became particularly widespread (Shukow et al. 1957/1963, Band 3, 539; Anderle et al. (ed) 1973, 346). The latter was extended to all regions of the caliphate that were hot and humid, including Khorassan. Pulses, vegetables, flax (for its oil), and hemp were also cultivated in considerable quantities in CA. The economic importance of sericulture grew. Samarkand was well known for the abundance and quality of its cereals, and Bukhara for that of its fruits. The rich and powerful tended to

---

[25] The Islamic Abbasid dynasty (750–1258) followed that of the Umayyads (661–750).

[26] This is reminiscent of the old Chinese practice of paying bolts of silk as in-kind tax to the state treasury (see Sect. 2.3.2.1).

consume hens and pigeons generously and to complement this food with very spicy or very sweet (pastry) dishes. Olive oil was practically reserved for the better off. In contrast, most people had to content themselves with a rather frugal diet based on rice pancakes or mashed cereals rounded off with vegetables and some fruits (dates, figs) (Burlot 1995, 74).

In the ninth century, raw silk was soon available in CA in such quantities that imports from China started to decrease and that regular exports to Europe became possible. Khorassan is described by Muslim geographers of the time as a region with fertile land, green plains, abundant sheep, delicious fruit, and a wide variety of foodstuffs—in contrast to its appearance a couple of centuries later. This was probably due to the focused implementation of irrigation and land improvement, which in the early centuries of Arab-Islamic rule set the stage for a remarkable blossoming of agriculture in Eastern Iran and allowed extensive food exports (Feldbauer and Liedl 2008, 16, 33).

As far as farming is concerned, the region of Balkh (Tokharistan) was considered unique in CA: As Kasai and Natsagdorj explain, all kinds of fruit (including citrus fruit and grapes), cereals such as wheat, rice and barley, walnuts, almonds, and vegetables were grown there (1998, 381). Tokharistan had the reputation of being the granary of Muslim CA—a far cry from what it became later. The dry melons of Merv (Margiana) were also well known and exported. Sistan (Southwestern Afghanistan) was noted for its meat, fruit, and saffron. Khwarazm, celebrated for its hospitable people, was also known for its cuisine. The region south of the Aral Sea boasted an abundance of fish oil, frozen fish, nuts, honey, raisins, sesame, milk products (mainly a kind of cheese called rabbin), meat, dried plums, and a famous variety of watermelon, which was placed in ice-filled lead containers and exported as far as the supreme ruler's court in Baghdad. Some Khorezmian staple foods were shipped abroad in large quantities—which presupposes farming and fish production carried sometimes to the brink of monoculture—in conditions and phenomena that were not to last (Kasai and Natsagdorj 1998, 381; Rodinson 1966/2007, 64).

The modernization of infrastructure and the upswing of farming were matched by the development of C Asian business and manufacturing in the first centuries of Islamic rule. Business techniques already known in other regions were adopted and complemented by innovations. Traditional textile, glass, and ceramic production lines witnessed an enlargement of their range of goods on offer and of their output volumes. Arms workshops experienced production booms, paper, and sugar factories multiplied throughout the Muslim world from CA to Spain. Cities like Merv, Urgench, Bukhara, and Samarkand became centers of craftsmanship, manufacturing, and trade in the ninth century (Feldbauer and Liedl 2008, 31).

The mass production and sale of textiles took off during the Islamic period. What is more, textiles became the leading industry of Islamic CA (Mokyr 2003, 369).[27] Khorassan became a flourishing place of silk, wool, and cotton textile manufacture. Nishapur's products included white cloth, various kinds of turbans, scarfs, silk undershirts, and other types of cloth which were shipped as far as Iraq (Mesopotamia) and Egypt. Moreover, with its bazaars of shoemakers, drapers, craftsmen, etc., Nishapur was well known as a regional commercial center. Ceramic art reached a degree of perfection and embellished mosques and private homes in Khorassan. Not only Bukhara, also some cities in Khorassan, sent silk products (like white robes) as in-kind tax payments to the court of Harun al-Rashid in Baghdad (Kasai and Natsagdorj 1998, 385–386).

Bukhara itself became famous for its textiles. The city produced various kinds of silk cloth and had renowned weaving factories. The types of cloth known as Bukhari, which were heavy and strong, were bought by Arabs in large numbers. Carpets, rugs, bed covers, mats, and prayer rugs were shipped from Bukhara to other regions, especially to Mesopotamia. Apart from a wide range of cotton and silk goods, the region of Samarkand produced luxurious brocades that were sold in long-distance trade. Samarkand was also a traditional focus of expertise in glass production, and—since the Battle of Talas—a first-rank center of paper manufacture. Finally, Samarkand in the ninth century became an important slave market in CA and focused on the supply of Turkic slaves, which were much in demand, particularly as bodyguards and servicemen (Soucek 2000, 72). Neither did the cotton- and silk-processing industry in Herat and Merv only satisfy domestic (regional) demand. As could be expected, the lion's share of the luxury output of these two towns went to the various countries visited by C Asian caravans. In Khorezm, sable and squirrel furs, goat skins, carpets, bedclothes, silk, silk caps, and cotton robes were produced in large numbers, and the surplus was sold outside the region (Kasai and Natsagdorj 1998, 386).

A large proportion of trade in the Muslim Middle Ages was transit trade (i.e., across and beyond the caliphate). Not surprisingly, Muslim traders (mostly Arabs and Persians) soon took over the bulk of trade on the SR. Jews also started to play an important role, while Sogdian merchants had lost prominence—particularly after the collapse of the Uighur Empire. Islamic institutions, like Buddhist ones before them, established themselves on the major trade routes. Islamic patrons built caravanserais. The Muslim traders' main commercial focus was exchange with the other prosperous and

---

[27] The know-how of the Chinese silk weavers captured in Talas certainly made its contribution to refining the Muslims' silk processing and textile production capabilities.

developed areas of Eurasia—China, India, and Europe (Ott and Schäfer (eds) 1984: Wirtschaftsploetz, 468; Liu 2010, 106). In intermediating trade between east and west, Muslim merchants greatly facilitated the diffusion of technology. Not only the art of making paper, also other elements of Chinese technology, including the magnetic compass, probably reached Europe by way of the Arabs. Trade along the SR was gradually transformed from being primarily one of luxuries to also including major staple cargoes. Given rising domestic production and competition as well as sophistication in various regions of the caliphate and beyond, trade in one luxury product declined—raw silk from China (Ponting 2001, 357).

The Abbasid capital Baghdad became the economic, business, and cultural center of the Islamic world and, thus, on a global scale, only comparable to Changan, the other major capital of the SR. In the cities along the caravan routes, the traders and merchants started to take leading positions economically but not politically. A commercial-capitalist sector emerged, dominated by small and medium traders who formed partnerships for specific ventures (Ott and Schäfer (eds) 1984: Wirtschaftsploetz, 468). Business was largely conducted on credit with payment not due before 60 days. Although dinars and dirhams were legal tender, the money actually used in many cases corresponded to sealed boxes authenticated either by the authorities or by merchants or bankers (Ponting 2001, 358).

However, much of the trade did not involve cash but, as referred to above, promissory notes, orders to pay (checks), and bills of exchange. As pointed out by Rodinson (1966/2007, 68), Goiten has shown how a mainly commercial bourgeoisie took shape in the Muslim world from the second century onward (718–815), imposing the values bound up with these activities during the third century (815–912). And yet this bourgeoisie never achieved political power as a class. Somewhat at variance with the situation in China, Arab businessmen were indeed often respected in their polities. However, and this deviates less from the Chinese experience, Arab businessmen did not attain substantial political power (Kocka 2013, 31).

The caravanserais, situated on the routes and more frequently in the towns, were the places where trade was carried out. The merchants were obliged to call on them in order to pay their taxes. The premises of the caravanserais generally resembled each other: one sole entrance gate and multistory buildings arranged around a square courtyard; these buildings provided for accommodation of the animals or for storing merchandise on the first floor and for rooms for the merchants on the second floor (Burlot 1995, 82).

Once the Arabs and the Khazars in the early ninth century had ceased to be at war with each other, C Asian trade caravans were able to move unhindered (via Khwarazm and the steppe route) to Eastern Europe, the Volga, the Don, and the Kama. C Asians purchased Scandinavian Viking swords, amber, furs, leather, honey, and slaves from Khazars and Eastern Slavs (Russians). Timber—in short supply in the caliphate—remained a much-demanded product needed, e.g., for shipbuilding, in sugar production, and to produce charcoal (Ponting 2001, 357). East European (Russian) timber soon became a Khazar re-export hit to the caliphate. For their part, C Asian traders sold cotton and silk cloths, carpets, silver products, dried fruit, etc. Silk fabrics and luxury items from Bukhara and Merv were exported to Syria and Byzantium. As Feldbauer and Liedl point out, trade profits and revenues from commercial capital, which contributed to urban prosperity in many parts of the caliphate, were mostly reinvested in new trade, commercial activities, and financial transactions, sometimes also in conspicuous consumption; they were more rarely reinvested in industrial production. This type of investor behavior was nothing exceptional at the time (Feldbauer and Liedl 2008, 38).

The impact of the collapse of the Uighur Khanate in 840 and of the further weakening of the Tang dynasty in the second half of the ninth century was also felt on the Silk Routes of West Turkestan and in the Islamic world. From the middle of the century, caravan trade in Iran and Mavarannahr (Transoxiana) declined. This decline was however also triggered by the armed conflict between two regional successor dynasties to the Abbasids, the Samanids (mentioned above, centered in Mavarannahr), and the Buyids (having their stronghold in Western Iran) which culminated in the conquest of the trading center of Rayy (near Teheran) by the Buyids. This warfare, that broke out inside the caliphate, temporarily blocked trade and revealed weakening Islamic state power, which gave rise to (regional) insecurity and uncertainty, dampening economic activities in CA (Feldbauer and Liedl 2008, 30).

According to Feldbauer and Liedl, it would not appear justified to assign a secondary role to agriculture within the caliphal economy. Farming, mostly carried out by sedentary peasants, tenant farmers, small landowners, agricultural workers, day laborers, slaves, and partly also by semisedentary nomads, obviously constituted the central activity that provided for the Islamic economy's resource base. The tax system and public finances also primarily focused on agriculture. This is not to underestimate the dependence of the caliphate's (and its successor states') economic and financial power on long-distance, transit and regional trade. Although government revenues were mostly derived from taxing farmers, large trading cities and even some regions rapidly declined as a result of the blockade or rerouting of trade connections—triggered, e.g., by war-related or politically caused turmoil or unrest, economic policy decisions, a modified range of goods on offer, abrupt adjustments of demand, or by overpowering competition (Feldbauer and Liedl 2008, 30).

The first centuries of Islamic CA were marked by intensive urbanization, particularly in Mavarannahr (Bolshakov 1998, 40; Guseinov 2004, 137). As mentioned earlier, the kuhandiz or kunduz (citadel) and the shahristan (town center) constituted the oldest parts of the C Asian city. The shahristan, which had already existed before the Arab conquest, contained public buildings and the dwellings of the nobility, to which a mosque was added, and was surrounded by walls. Now, rabadas—trade and industrial suburbs and craftsmen's residences—were installed or enlarged. Economic life of the city, including bazaars and warehouses, was concentrated in these rabadas.

As Shukow et al. underline, no urban self-government existed in C Asian towns; in this respect, the latter does not differ from towns across the Near and Middle East. Self-government only existed in the framework of professional organizations (e.g., craftsmen's and traders' corporations), of clergy's associations, and of town districts/neighborhood communities (e.g., mahallas), which had elected elders. Tradesmen of professional branches united in corporations, which somewhat resembled European medieval guilds. The tradesmen often lived in the same parts of a town where they also had their workshops and stores. Within the corporations, the masters (Ustad), the journeymen (Khalif), and the apprentices (Shagird) were separately organized (Shukow et al. 1957/1963, Band 3, 540).

Given their pivotal location near the crossroads of the Muslim and Chinese empires, Bukhara and Samarkand had greatly profited from technology transfer and investment following the Battle of Talas; once SR trade with China/the Uighur Empire recovered in the early ninth century, the two cities were the first to gain. After all, Samarkand was at the end of the northern or Dzungarian Silk Route (see Map 3.2), which bypassed the mostly Tibetan-occupied Tarim Basin and whose security Uighur forces guaranteed. In the ninth century, Bukhara's urban growth (one could even argue: urban sprawl) seems to have been quite impressive. The surface of the town is reported to have multiplied from the eighth to the ninth century. And Samarkand was probably not far behind these dynamics (de la Vaissière 2004, 267). Mokyr concludes that economic prosperity enabled urban population growth in CA during this time, as improved agriculture and flourishing trade meant that the cities could support larger populations (Mokyr 2003, 370).

The ninth century was also a time of blossoming spiritual and material culture in the region. For instance, influences of Persian literature and Greek science and philosophy were absorbed. Apart from their capacity to assimilate, make use of, and transfer technology acquired from other cultures (e.g., paper, silk, magnetic compass, gold, and silversmiths' arts), Arabs and C Asians are known for numerous original achievements. One of the most well known of the latter is the discovery of the algorithm, the mathematical process behind addition and multiplication. Algorithm stems from a deformation of its discoverer's name, Al-Khorezmi or Al-Khwarizmi (latinized as Algorismi). CA's most famous mathematician (approx. 787–850) further had the merit of adopting Indian numerals, which the western world renamed Arab, after also having adopted them. The title of his mathematical work, Al-Jabr, became known in Europe as algebra (Laruelle 2008, 18). Without sliding into a pretense of economic determinism: the engineering demands for building and maintaining irrigation canals necessary for the growing cities of CA had encouraged original work in mathematics (Mokyr 2003, 370). Al-Khwarizmi's research facilitated the building of such canals and the architectural expansion of C Asian cities.

The development of architecture and graphic art reached a high level in ninth-century CA. The technology of the construction of vaults and domes was improved in this period. The caravanserai Kyrk-kys in Termez (Bactria, eighth to ninth century) is an example. Its ground plan corresponded to a square building with thick towers at the corners; from the outside it resembled a fortress; its interior was made up of a complex system of vaults and cupola rooms that were connected with each other by corridors. In the realm of applied arts, ceramics, combined first with monochrome and later polychrome glazing, developed in an impressive way. The designs and the realization of ceramics of Samarkand were particularly beautiful (Shukow et al. 1957/1963, Band 3, 541–543).

Judaism developed relatively freely in the territories under the caliph, and there was a large Jewish colony in Baghdad as well as a colony in Bukhara. Jewish merchants had family members or agents scattered throughout the Islamic world from Spain to CA. Quite soon after the Arab conquest of Mavarannahr/Transoxiana, Jewish merchants were tempted by the routes of the east and soon became important traders in luxury products (jewelry, fabrics, sugar, spices, gold, slaves). Ibn Khurradadhbeh (died in 847) reports of the famous Radhanite Jews that originated in Mesopotamia and crisscrossed the caliphate as long-distance traders (Nizami 1998b, 368; Burlot 1995, 80). The ninth century also witnessed the emergence of the Persian written language Dari or Farsi (literally: courtly language), which resembled the two related colloquial languages, Tajik and New Persian. The Tajik language may have originally been spoken by the (sedentary) inhabitants of the oases of Merv, Bukhara, and some other towns of the vicinity (Shukow et al. 1957/1963, Band 3, 144, 543).

3.2.4.2 Second Heyday of the Khazar Empire and the Western SR in the Ninth Century

Around the beginning of the ninth century—at approximately the same time that the Uighurs and the Chinese re-established SR trade on the Dzungarian route—the wars between Khazaria and the caliphate ended, and the Khazars entered a period of stability, procuring them a degree of prosperity. Subsequently, Khazaria, often allied to Byzantium, ruled the Pontic steppes until the end of the century. The economic basis of the Khazar state was developed farming and stock breeding. Khan Joseph wrote: "Our lands are rich and fertile, every landed estate has a garden and a vineyard." (Kozak 2007, 304). It seems that the semi-nomadic Khazars were becoming increasingly sedentary.

The cities of Khazaria were described as large and prosperous. During its prime, the capital Itil on the mouth of the Volga (near present-day Astrakhan) probably had around 10,000 inhabitants. In 833, the Khazars requested engineers of the Byzantine Emperor Theophile to construct a new fortified capital. This third capital was named Sarkel and was situated on the Don's lower reaches (today Belaya Vezha).[28] State building and internal cohesion also appeared to demand a unifying idea or religion. Until then, the Khazars had venerated Tengri as their supreme deity along with other Shaman gods. As Baumer explains, the choice between "available" monotheistic faiths was largely made according to political criteria. Adopting orthodox Christianity carried the risk of exposing Khazaria too deeply to the influence of Byzantium, and choosing Catholic Christianity would have been an obvious provocation to Byzantium. Islam as the religion of the Khazars' long-time adversaries to the south seems to have been excluded from the start. Therefore, the remaining option was Judaism. This choice was not strange, for many Jews lived on Khazar territory (i.a., in Crimea), and Jewish merchants, the Radhanites (see above), were involved in transcontinental trade on the steppe routes (Baumer 2014, 215).

In 838, under the reign of Bek Bulan, the Khazar Khaganate adopted the Mosaic faith as official religion. (Actually, only the Khazar nobility may have converted; most of the rank-and-file probably continued to adhere to shamanism.) Besides Sogdaya (today Sudak, on the Crimean peninsula), which had come under Byzantine jurisdiction in the eighth century, Matarka (later: Tmutarakan, see Map 4.7), a port on the Taman peninsula, played an increasingly important role in trade across the Black Sea. The Khazars had built Matarka on the ruins of Greek Phanagoria (Asian side of the Strait of Kerch, see above) (Dmitriev 2009, 47; Grousset 1965/2008, 236).

Khazar suzerainty over various Eastern Slavic, Turkic, and Finno-Ugrian populations living in present-day Southern Russia and Ukraine was probably most pronounced in the ninth century. More favorable external political and trade conditions (see above) also contributed to an upswing in Khazaria's international and transit trade, such that the Khaganate could soon be described as a "turntable" (plaque tournante) of SR trade (de la Vaissière 2004: Histoire des marchands..., 181). The "steppe route" from (Arab) Mavarannahr via (Arab) Khwarazm to Itil, Sarkel, and the Black Sea was intact again and regained popularity (see Maps 3.2 and 3.3). Byzantine, Arab, Chinese, and Jewish traders crowded in Itil and Sarkel.

While Rome, Antioch, and Byzantium remained the great silk repositories of the Mediterranean world, and Byzantium turned into an increasingly prominent producer of the desired material, a certain amount of raw as well as processed silk traveled the steppe route from CA via Khazaria to Europe (Nizami 1998b, 368). The Jewish Radhanites were among the traders who crossed Khazaria when venturing to and returning from China, India, and other parts of Asia. Thus, in the ninth century, the Radhanites regularly brought spices via CA and Khazaria to the Byzantine Empire and even the Frankish Empire (Schmieder 2013, 106). In the second half of the ninth century, the Khwarazmian merchants appear to have taken over control of trade on the steppe route from the Sogdians, whose position had been undermined by the collapse of the state of their Uighur protectors (de la Vaissière 2004, 265).

Another factor intervened in the second half of the ninth century, and weakened the Khazars' trading stance: The Varangians (Scandinavian Vikings) conquered parts of central Russia and established control of some of the large rivers, portages, and places of transhipment and trade connections between Northern Europe and the Baltic Sea on the one hand and the Black and Caspian seas, Byzantium, and the caliphate on the other. The Varangians decisively contributed to the foundation of the Kievan Rus, which soon shrugged off Khazar suzerainty and entered into trade competition with the Khazars, so that the latter were eventually forced to share some of their trade rents with the rulers of the Rus. Traders from the Rus also transited Khazar territory: They used Tmutarakan for exchanges with Byzantium. Their ships traveled along the Volga until they reached the Caspian Sea, where they traded with Iranian coastal ports. But the Rus also developed direct trade with the Khazars: The Rus' merchants brought beaver furs, black fox skins, sword blades, and other items and received, e.g., silver coins, especially Arab dirhams, which remained popular across Eurasia because of their renowned high purity (Brook 2006, 78–79).[29]

---

[28] However, Roux has some reservations as to the size and importance of Khazar cities: He points out that most of them were actually market towns, improved encampments, even if many of the improvements had been brought about by Byzantine engineers. Probably, large numbers of Khazar urban dwellers only spent the winter in towns (Roux 2000, 93).

[29] When the demand exceeded the supply for these coins, due to a decline in the availability of coins from north African and Mesopotamian mints, the Khazars started to mint their own silver coins, beginning around the early 820s. The Khazar dirhams (imperfectly) imitated the designs and inscriptions on Islamic dirhams. For trading purposes in Europe, only the weight of the silver mattered, not what the inscriptions on the coins read, so the fact that these were not always perfect imitations was irrelevant (Brook 2006, 79).

3.2.5 Some of the Most Important SR Products Traded in the Tang-Caliphate Era

As mentioned above, while luxury products still dominated SR trade in this period, major staple cargoes also started to play a role.

Main articles of SR exports (according to various surveyed publications, may partly also include re-exports):

Tang China (including Tarim Basin, later: Uighur Kingdoms): silk, silk cloth, textiles, ceramics, porcelain, jades, precious stones, jewelry, tea, lacquerware, ironware, spices, medicinal materials, terracotta statues, arms

Turk Khaganate (West Turkestan, later: Karakhanid Khanate): race and cavalry horses, livestock, cotton, silk, silk fabrics, carpets, walnuts, pomegranates, dried fruits, silver products, slaves

Caliphate (later: Samanid Empire): carpets, paper, glass, cotton, rice, slaves, fruits, incense, perfumes, woolen and silken fabrics and textiles

India (Indian kingdoms): cotton textiles, cashmere wool, spices, indigo (dyestuff), ivory products, pearls, corals

Khazaria: leather, horses, furs, hides, grain, ivory of walruses and narwhals, slaves, sheep, oxen

3.2.6 Approximate SR Network in the Tang-Caliphate Era

During the second climax of the SR from the late seventh to the first half of the eighth century, the trade network included the following routes (east-west), as indicated in the Maps 3.2 and 3.3: Changan–Gansu–northern and southern branches of Tarim Basin routes–Kashgar–then (a) either south (probably via Irkeshtam) (Termez–Balkh (from there Indian junction: Kabul–Taxila–Delhi)–Merv–Rayy–Baghdad) or (b) north (probably via Torugart Pass) (Ferghana–Samarkand–Khwarazm–Itil (mouth of Volga)–Sarkel–Sea of Azov ("steppe route")).

In the second half of the eighth century, SR traffic was affected by temporary blockages due to warfare (Khazar-Arab), occupation (most of Tarim Basin by Tibet), and insurgencies (of regional nature in the caliphate and China). Therefore, east-west overland connections were at times limited to Silk Routes on Islamic territory (e.g., Samarkand–Baghdad, Samarkand–Urgench, or Samarkand–Kabul–Delhi) and, partly cut off from the latter, remaining trade routes on Chinese territory. This corresponds to a period of segmentation of the SR, when maritime connections, namely, from the Persian Gulf to Southern China/Canton (Guangzhou), gathered momentum.

In the ninth century, blockages (e.g., Tibetan occupation) weakened or were circumvented, and warfare (Khazaria-caliphate) was discontinued. SR connections were rerouted/re-established: the Northern/Dzungarian SR (north of Tienshan) gained prominence: Changan–Gansu–Hami–Beshbalik (Beiting)–Almalik–Balasagun–Shash (Tashkent)–Samarkand. From Changan and Beshbalik, there were also long-distance trade routes to Karabalgasun (the Uighur capital in Mongolia). The temporarily interrupted steppe route (Samarkand–Khiva–Itil–Sarkel–Black Sea) was restored.

3.2.7 China Turns Inward, the Caliphate Disintegrates, and Military Pressure from the Eurasian Steppe Intensifies, Destabilizing the SR

In the mid-ninth century, the Tibetan Empire and its remaining hold on some southern parts of the Tarim Basin collapsed. But this did not provide a major respite for SR trade, at least as far as China was concerned. Swelling corruption in the central administration, increasing power of separatist provincial governors, and intensifying tax pressure on the rural population gave rise to domestic unrest, which undermined the Tang dynasty's authority and contributed to its gradual decline. Notwithstanding the emergence of the small Uighur trading states of Qocho and Ganzhou interested in upholding SR trade, the Middle Kingdom suffered losses of output and was less able to support extravagant foreign imports. Trade on the SR decreased (Töpfer et al. 1985, 149; Bonavia and Baumer 2002, 28).

Following the disturbances triggered by the Huang Chao insurrection of 875–884, China effectively lost access to the Central Asian trade routes. The Tang dynasty ended in the early tenth century (906). The country's demographic, economic, and political center moved south, especially to the lower Yangzi valley and the Southeastern Chinese coast. Intensive rice cultivation expanded throughout the south (Maddison 1998, 27; Der Große Ploetz 2008, 681). Simultaneously, powerful nomadic forces re-emerged in Mongolia and started to encroach on territory of Northern China.

As witnessed by the conflict between Buyids and Samanids, the vast Abbasid caliphate (that had already lost control over Maghreb Africa) was subject to increasing particularism. The Islamic Empire's political unity gradually eroded from the mid-ninth century. According to Guseinov, Islamic rulers' wholesale/indiscriminate distribution of iqtas contributed to the eventual falling apart of the caliphate (Guseinov 2004, 80).[30] Moreover, pressures also evolved

---

[30] This might recall the piecemeal feudal transformation of the Holy Roman Empire (German: Heiliges Römisches Reich), partly through concessions of the central authorities, from a kingdom (under Otto I in the tenth century) to a decentralized confederation (under Charles IV in the fourteenth century).

from the outside: in the course of the ninth century, nomadic incursions, typically from the Eurasian steppes, became more frequent. This made more construction of fortifications necessary. For instance, a wall was built around the Bukhara oasis in the early decades of the ninth century (Bolshakov 1998, 38). Around 840, the Samanids took Ispidzab (north of Shash/Tashkent) and built walls around it to protect its inhabitants' crops from nomadic raids. Yet Ispidzab was not merely a military and agrarian outpost but lay on the Northern SR; the town contained many bazaars and caravanserais, and brisk trade with the nomads was also conducted here. Despite abovementioned precautions, later in the ninth century, Bukhara fell to nomadic Turcomans. Although it was taken back subsequently, a period of instability began (Roudik 2007, 34).

Toward the end of the ninth century, at the northwestern end of the SR, the partly sedentarized Khazar Empire that had probably lost some of its military strength, was shaken by a wave of invasions of Turkic nomads from the Kazakh grasslands: The Oghuz of the Aral steppes displaced the Pechenegs of the region of Emba and Ural rivers. The Pechenegs, set in motion, crossed the Volga around 890, entered and pillaged Khazar territory, and destroyed stone fortresses and surrounding towns. For a while the Pechenegs settled between Don and Dnepr, practically in the heart of (what had until then been) Khazaria (Grousset 1965/2008, 237; Dmitriev 2009, 47). Needless to say, all these upheavals disrupted economic activities. Incidentally, Western Europe had just gone through the breakup of the Carolingian Empire and faced repeated attacks and incursions by Vikings and Sarecens (Arab raiders).

3.3   Central Asia Passing from the Sway of Sedentary to Nomadic Dynasties (Late Ninth to Early Thirteenth Century)

Publications by Karl Baipakov, Thomas Barfield, O.G. Bolshakov, Joseph Burlot, Peter Feldbauer, Anatoly Khazanov, N.N. Negmatov, Peter Perdue, Clive Ponting, Gabriele Rasuly-Paleczek, Peter Roudik, Jean-Paul Roux, I.M. Shukow, Svat Soucek, Etienne de la Vaissière, Liu Xinru, and Zhang Yiping feature among the primary sources of this chapter.

3.3.1   Notwithstanding Weaker SR Exchange, Central Asian Intellectual and Cultural Achievements in the Early Second Millennium Boast World Renown

The large-scale overland trade across Eurasia that had flourished between the seventh and ninth centuries declined

toward the end of the ninth century and then may have temporarily recovered in the tenth, before receding again in the eleventh and twelfth centuries. The rising number of states straddling and borders crossing transcontinental trade routes in this period certainly did not facilitate overland trade (Perdue 2003, 493). Since the eleventh century, economic difficulties and crises are reported to have become more numerous in various regions of the Islamic world (Feldbauer and Liedl 2008, 22). At the same time, thanks to improvements in navigation at both ends of the SR (in Arabia as well as in China), long maritime hauls became easier in the ninth and tenth centuries and started to supplant Eurasian overland shipping (Boulnois 2009, 48).

During the Song dynasty (960–1279), China increasingly oriented itself toward the sea. Since 1119, the Chinese had navigated with the help of a compass; in the same century, they sailed all the way to the Persian Gulf. The Middle Kingdom also advanced on other technical fronts—a breakthrough was achieved in typography toward the middle of the eleventh century: the technique of interchangeable typesets was invented, which marked the beginning of a modern printing technology. China had invented gunpowder no later than during the Tang dynasty. Afterwards, with gradual improvements of technical know-how, gunpowder could start to be used for military purposes. Paper money (also invented in the Tang era) became a widely used economic instrument in Song times, while Europeans still handled gold and silver to conduct transactions (Zhang 2005, 143, 153–156). Thus, CA and China from the tenth to the thirteen century in many respects developed independently from each other—but not in all respects. Notwithstanding its impressive accomplishments, China remained militarily inferior to the Eurasian steppe nomads, which had significant consequences (see below).

Somewhat astonishingly, despite less intensive long-distance trade, and despite the fact that political regimes tended to change more often and that instability and warfare were not infrequent in the three and a half centuries from the decline of the caliphate to the Mongol invasion, this was an era of great intellectual activity and cultural ascendency in CA. As Abazov notes, well-educated C Asian professionals and scholars played key roles in the intellectual development also of many parts of the Middle East and South Asia (2008, Map 21). Considerable contributions were made in the realms of mathematics, algebra, astronomy, chemistry, medicine, geography, history, philology, and classical literature. Patronage on the part of the Samanids and the relative political stability of the Samanid era contributed to the expansion of C Asian scholarly activity.[31] Scientific works

---

[31] For more on the Samanid era, see below.

were written in Arabic and, since the end of the tenth century, in Dari (Persian) languages.

Here is a brief overview in chronological order of some of the most important C Asian scholars and intellectuals of the time (Soucek 2000, 85; Roudik 2007, 34):

- *Rudaki* (Abdullah Rudaki, mid-ninth century–941, Pendzhikent, Mavarannahr, was employed at the Samanid court): first great poet of the Persian tongue after the Muslim conquest of Transoxiana, considered father of Tajik poetry.
- *Al-Farabi* (Abu Nasr Muhammad al-Farabi, 870–950, lived in Otrar, then Shash/Tashkent, Samarkand, Bukhara, Baghdad, Persia): philosopher, scientist-encyclopedian, mathematician, physician, composer, musician, linguist, poet, humanist. Famous for his scholastic theories, neo-Platonic, one of the greatest philosophers of the Orient and follower of Aristoteles. Al-Farabi developed a classification of sciences and elaborated a doctrine of the everlastingness of matter.
- *Firdawsi* (Abul-Kasim Mansur Firdawsi, 932–1020, Khorassan): one of the greatest epic poets of Persian and Tajik literature.
- *Ibn Sina/Avicenna* (Abu Ali Husain ibn Sina, 980–1037, lived in Mavarannahr, then Khorezm, then Persia): philosopher, natural scientist, physician, mathematician, poet, and original thinker. Ibn Sina was the greatest scholar of the Islamic Middle Ages—in an age when religious orthodoxy was asserting itself, he endeavored to revive interest in the study of nature. A supporter of rationalism, in physics he continued the traditions of Aristoteles, and in logics and epistemology, Ibn Sina developed further the materialist teachings of al-Farabi. Ibn Sina attained world fame with two works in Arabic language: in the domain of philosophy by the "Kitab ash-Shifa" ("Book of Healing," encyclopedia in 18 volumes) and in medicine by the "Kitab al-Kanun fi't-Tib" ("The Canon of Medicine"). The latter magnum opus became one of the most widely used medical textbooks of the Middle Ages in Islam and Christianity. Ibn Sina's teachings influenced Middle Eastern and Western European medicine up to the seventeenth century.
- *Al-Biruni* (Abu-Raikhon al-Biruni, 973–1048, Urgench/Khwarazm, served under Ghaznavids, also visited India): natural scientist, mathematician, physicist, astronomer, philologist, botanist, mineralogist, geologist, geographer, historian, and ethnographer. He was one of the greatest medieval erudite encyclopedians. Al-Biruni, who knew 500 years before Copernicus that the earth circled the sun and who estimated the distance between the earth and the moon to within 20 km, was mankind's foremost astronomer of his age. His two major works are "The Chronology of Ancient Nations" and "History of India."

- *Yusuf Balasaguni* (Yusuf Khas-Khodzhi Balasaguni, 1018–1080, Balasagun/Semirechie, was employed at the Karakhanid court): poet, author of one of the first C Asian poems in Turkic language "Kutadgu Bilig" ("Knowledge Provides Happiness," philosophical work).
- *Al-Kashgari* (Mahmud al-Kashgari, eleventh century, Kashgar, Baghdad): author of "Divan lugat-at Tuerk"—a Turkic-Arab dictionary, also containing a map of CA with place names, published in East Turkestan in 1071.
- *Al-Ghazali* (Abu Hamid Al-Ghazali, 1059–1111, lived in Tus/Khorassan, studied in Nishapur, moved to court of the Seljuk vizier in Isfahan, then to Baghdad): philosopher and theologist. Insisting on the obligation to carry out ritual practices and assessing that theological knowledge should be completed by love of God, he solidly reconciled Sufism (Islamic mysticism) and religious orthodoxy. His major work "Resuscitation of Religious Science" is regarded as authoritative by Islamic orthodoxy.
- *Yasavi* (Khodzha Ahmed Yasavi, 1103–1166, Yasy (Turkestan)/middle reaches of Syr Daria, Bukhara): preacher of Islam, great Sufi master, founded the mystical brotherhood of Yasaviyya. Author of collection of poems "Divan-i-Hikmet" ("Book on Wisdom") in Turkic language.

The extraordinary intellectual flowering (particularly of mathematics and astronomy) in this particular place and time may have partly emerged out of a synthesis between the local well-developed expertise in irrigation and the reacquired mathematics of ancient Greece and India (Negmatov 1998, 88). This cultural peak doubtlessly constituted a foundation for subsequent mathematical advances in Asia and Europe. Given that religious interpretations and rules probably started to become more rigid as of the eleventh century, the frequent political changes on the ground (including nomadic takeovers), while ushering in temporary insecurity, may have also constrained or delayed deteriorations of the political environment for the development of science and philosophy. In any case, the European Renaissance would be directly influenced by this largely Arab-Persian contribution to the Muslim medieval civilization (Poujol 2008, 40).[32]

---

[32] Starr even argues that during this "Age of Enlightenment," "CA was the intellectual hub of the world. India, China, the Middle East, and Europe all boasted rich traditions in the realm of ideas, but during the four or five centuries around AD 1000 it was CA, the one world region that touched all these other centers, that surged to the fore. It bridged time and geography, in the process becoming the great link between antiquity and the modern world" (Starr 2013, 4).

3.3.2 The Post-Caliphate Era: CA Dominated by Traditional Sedentary and Sedentarized States (Late Ninth–Tenth Centuries)

With the political disintegration of the caliphate (the Abbasid caliph remained in Baghdad but practically lost all secular power beyond Iraq), the most important empires ruling CA (and the Pontic steppes) were the Samanids, Uighurs, and the Khazars. Yet the demise of the caliphate did not mean that the successor states stagnated economically; it depended to a great degree on the economic policy followed by these states (Anderle et al. (ed) 1973, 346). The Samanids had started out under Abbasid suzerainty in 819 before becoming independent in 875. They ruled Mavarannahr (Transoxiana) and adjacent territories until 999. The Uighurs, that had been expelled from Mongolia by the Kyrgyz, had migrated to Xinjiang/East Turkestan, where they founded the Kingdom of Qocho (ca. 840–1218), and to the province of Gansu, where they created the state of the Yellow Uighurs (ca. 840–1030). The Khazar state (ca. 635–1016) came under increasing pressure from nomadic (Pechenegs, Oghuz) and sedentary (Rus) neighbors. Apart from the above three Central Asian states, nomadic powers or confederations existed or had been formed in the region by the Karluks, the Oghuz, the Kimeks, and the Kipchaks (or Cumans/Polovtsy).

3.3.2.1 The Samanids (819/875–999): Bureaucratic State Presides Over "Islamic Renaissance"

"Big Government" Boosts Security with Turkic Military Slaves and Promotes SR Recovery

The Samanid Empire was culturally and economically the predominant C Asian state of this period. Its territory comprised Mavarannahr (Transoxiana), Khorassan, Afghanistan, and Khwarazm; Ferghana was initially ruled by the Samanids but eventually lost to the Karakhanids (Map 3.4). The Samanids were an indigenous Persian-Tajik dynasty in whose realm Arab and Persian were spoken and Sunni Islam had asserted itself.

Ismail Samani (892–907), one of the first Samanid rulers, paid particular attention to building redoubtable armed forces: As one of the first Islamic rulers—apart from the caliph himself—he resorted to massive recruitment of Turkic ghulams (slave soldiers) into his cavalry units. Thus, the Samanid (sedentary) regime's military capability was buttressed in the face of possible nomadic attacks (Abazov 2008, Map 17). As Soucek points out, the ghulams were preferred by the rulers not only for their prowess and hardiness, stemming from harsh earlier life in the steppes, and for their technical skills as mounted archers, but also for their apparent loyalty, which was allegedly unadulterated by

other allegiances (2000, 72). For all these qualities, the Turkic warriors were able to ascend to very high state positions, not only in the Samanid Empire. And in some cases, initial loyalty to the ruling dynasty was eventually sacrificed (e.g., in the case of Sebüktegin, see below).

In continuation of civil service traditions of the caliphate, the Samanids developed a strong, hierarchical, and bureaucratic monarchy. The head of state was the emir (prince), who (theoretically) had absolute power. The central government, appointed by the emir, consisted of ten divans (councils of the ruler, chancelleries, departments/ministries) responsible for overseeing particular areas—e.g., finance, postal service, emir's guards, trade, foreign affairs. District and city chiefs (called hakims) were equally appointed by the emir (Roudik 2007, 33).

Like in the caliphate itself, under the rule of the Samanids in the tenth century, the large fund of public domains quickly shrank: Property was conditionally bestowed (iqta) upon military and civilian staff and favorites or was assigned to Islamic religious endowments or institutions (waqf) for permanent use. In exchange for service to the state, the iqta holders had the right to collect the kharaj and other taxes for their own benefit from the peasants that worked on the land that the former had received. Higher-ranking Turkic warriors were also equipped with iqta lands. While these lands formally remained in public ownership and could not be bequeathed, in practice iqta holders already in the tenth century tried to turn their iqtas from temporary conditional to hereditary possessions (somewhat in analogy to the evolution of the fief in feudal Europe). Generally, big landowners' properties grew at the expense of state land (Anderle et al. (ed) 1973, 346).

As regards coinage and the circulation of money, Ismail Samani adopted the Sassanian practice of issuing prestigious silver coins and for this purpose resorted to the mines of Shash (Tashkent) which were exploited to their exhaustion. The consequence was a sharp one-off increase in the circulation of silver coins. But this was apparently not sufficient to cover the market's or the authorities' needs; copper coins were soon issued in markedly increased numbers under the Samanids (compared to the Arabs) (Davidovich and Dani 1998, 397).

While the Samanids put up an effective administration, at the same time they also appear to have run a relatively "big government" for the conditions of their time. The dynasty spent generously on the building of military fortresses, mosques, palaces, caravanserais, and various public buildings. Samanid patronage assisted in the flourishing of sciences, literature, architecture, arts, and poetry. Bukhara was the capital of the empire as well as the spiritual and intellectual hub of Islamic CA. Samarkand was a key cultural and business metropolis. According to Roudik, the blend of Islam with Iranian culture, then dominant in

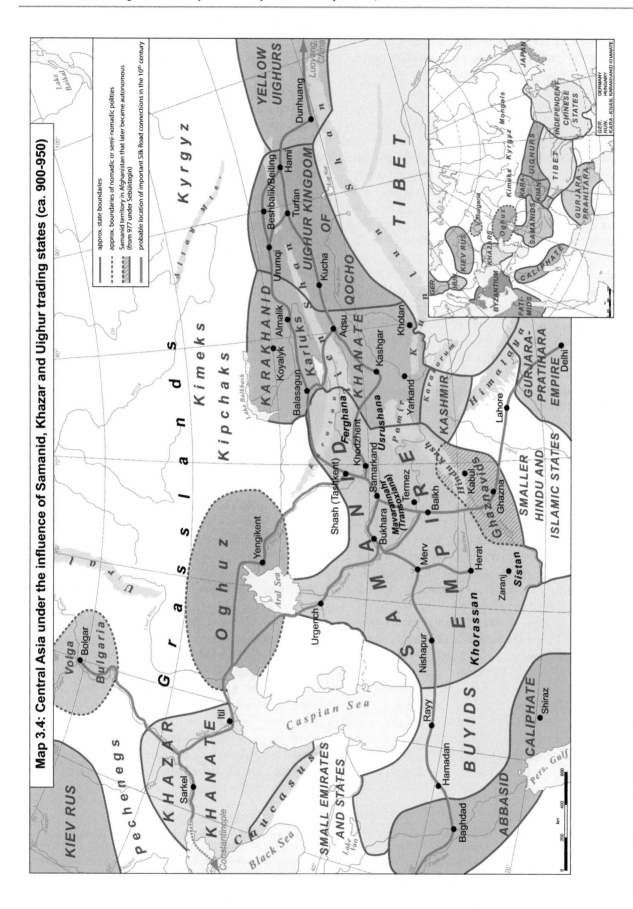

Map 3.4 CA under the influence of the Samanid, Khazar, and Uighur trading states (ca. 900–950)

Mavarannahr, made Bukhara and Samarkand the birthplaces of the "Islamic renaissance" in the tenth to twelfth centuries (see also below). But the Samanids did not insist on the prevalence of religious life over economic interests (Roudik 2007, 29–32).

The political stabilization of Mavarannahr and Khorassan under Samanid rule for almost a century contributed to significant economic growth and prosperity.[33] The upswing of agriculture in the tenth century in CA likely was also owed to specific economic policy measures favoring farming activity: The Samanids lowered rents and taxes levied on the peasants; under their rule, improvements to irrigation systems helped to increase agricultural production. New canals, dams, water mills (asyas), and other hydrotechnical structures were built, and the main canal, which brought water to Samarkand, was lined with lead; this canal reportedly provided drinking water to Samarkand until the Mongol invasion in 1220. A large stone dam and water reservoir in Bast Tagh mountain range (foothills of the Tienshan, north of Samarkand) was set up, new canals were dug from Hari Rud and Helmand rivers (Roudik 2007, 33; Negmatov 1998, 82).[34]

Of course road tolls, duties, professional and trade taxes, as well as urban consumption levies contributed to Samanid state revenue. Compared to the tax intake from the peasantry and from farming production, respective public proceeds from nonagricultural activities were smaller though (Feldbauer and Liedl 2008, 65). The most widespread form of land use was the sharecropping system, under which the land was divided into small plots and let out to tenants who, in exchange, delivered a specified proportion of the harvest. Despite the upswing of agriculture, large numbers of peasants remained almost or entirely landless, living on a precarious subsistence basis; their situation may have contributed to some of the outbreaks of unrest in the period (Negmatov 1998, 81).

As Negmatov explains in detail, in the irrigated lands of Ferghana, Shash, Usrushana (south of Ferghana), Khuttal, Chaganyan (the latter two regions in Northern Tokharistan), Khorassan, Gharchistan, and Sistan (the latter two regions in Southern Afghanistan), the peasants cultivated wheat, barley, rice, millet, oilseeds, and other crops. Cotton was a very important crop in a number of regions (Zerafshan and Ferghana valleys, Merv oasis, and others). In the C Asian oases, horticulture was also highly developed (apricots, peaches, apples, pears, cherries, quinces, plums,

pomegranates, figs, almonds, walnuts), as was the cultivation of vegetables and melons. The melons of Bukhara and Merv were particularly well known and regarded as the best in the world at that time. Another trump card of the oases was viticulture (with dozens of varieties of grapes, the Herat grape being especially celebrated). Sources of the tenth century reportedly register more than a hundred sorts of wine in CA. Date palms were grown in Sistan and sugar cane in the province of Balkh (Negmatov 1998, 82; Shukow et al. 1957/1963, Band 3, 539).

Given this state of affairs, it may not be surprising that geographers of the ninth and tenth centuries are reported to have made numerous enthusiastic accounts of the fertility of the oases and their "unbroken carpets of greenery." The most fertile lands were considered to be located in the area of Balkh[35] and the region (along the Hari Rud and Murgab rivers) connecting Herat and Merv—apparently in a sad contrast to today, when this area exhibits quite modest fertility (Negmatov 1998, 82). Many landowners invested sizable shares of their profits in caravan trade. Accordingly, the provincial nobility and iqta holders had some common stakes with SR merchants.

Mining—not only of silver—prospered in the Samanid era. Negmatov again provides a number of examples: the Ferghana Basin (where many minerals were extracted: iron, tin, silver, mercury, copper, lead, tar, asbestos, turquoise, sal ammoniac, and, apparently, petroleum), the upper Zerafshan valley (iron, gold, silver, and vitriol), Badakhshan and Shughnan (in the Pamir Highlands/rubies, lapis lazuli, silver), Tokharistan (lead, sulfur, a.o.), and Shash (rich gold and silver mines which were partly exhausted during Samanid rule, see above). The mining sector employed free men as well as serfs and slaves (Negmatov 1998, 82–83).

Regarding crafts, one of the main developments took place in textiles—again, in continuation of a takeoff recorded in caliphal times. The manufacture of fabrics flourished in the settlements of Zandana (near Bukhara), Wadhar (near Samarkand), and Darzangi (in the Surkhandarya valley/Tokharistan). These centers produced fine cotton fabrics, and their articles were widely known beyond Mavarannahr. Woolen cloth and garments were manufactured in many places, including towns near the edge of the grasslands: For instance, in Urgench, Arbinjan (between Samarkand and Bukhara), Dzhizak (northeast of Samarkand), and Shash (see Map 4.7). These places, notably

---

[33] Thus, as Feldbauer and Liedl point out, agrarian prosperity and political stability were probably linked under the Samanids (2009, 21).

[34] Together with increased spending for farming infrastructure, the reduction of the tax pressure on farmers may have stimulated output and therefore, possibly, total tax revenue (a Samanid Laffer effect?).

[35] This is obviously in continuation of Balkh's exceptional position in C Asian farming in the era of the caliphate (see Sect. 3.3.2.4.1). The Balkh oasis moreover featured intensive processing of farm produce: For instance, one river alone – the Balkh river – is said to have provided the motive power for 70 water mills.

Shash, were centers of leatherworking, producing leather goods and other items for which there was a market among the nomads (including the Oghuz, see also below). In the towns of Ferghana and Usrushana, and in Khodzhent, armor, weapons, farming tools, and metal dishes were manufactured. The output of ceramics flourished; potters made exquisite and high-quality glazed wares decorated with a variety of adornments (Negmatov 1998, 83–84).

The overall favorable environment stimulated the expansion of regional and international trade. Nomads, including those living in the steppes to the north of the Samanids, were not only interested in leather goods but also purchased grain, bread, dried fruits, cloth, weapons, and utensils, in exchange for which the steppe dwellers supplied livestock, wool, dried skins, and slaves to the markets of Shash, Mavarannahr, and Khorassan. Although the caliphate had politically collapsed, by the tenth century efficient Islamic trading networks extended across large parts of Eurasia as well as North Africa and upheld trade with China, India, the Caucasus, and Eastern Europe (Liu 2010, 104) (Table 3.1).

As Rasuly-Paleczek points out, Samanid overland trade largely recovered/expanded in a northwesterly direction (toward Khazaria, the Rus, and even beyond, to Northwestern Europe) (2006, 177). And according to de la Vaissière, it was via Khorezmian traders that Samanid merchants in the early 900s supplied a large quantity of furs (sable, squirrel, ermine, fox, beaver, hare), goat hides, falcons, Slavic slaves, sheep, and oxen of Eastern European provenance to the caliph of Baghdad (de la Vaissière 2004, 265, 270). In trade with Khazaria and the Rus, the city of Urgench (Khorezm) played the main role; furs were stored and slaves were lodged there. Trade with the Rus princedoms was carried out through the transshipment points of the cities of Itil (lower Volga, Khazaria) and Bulgar (middle Volga), to which rice, dried fruits, cotton, woolen and silken fabrics, and silver dirhams were delivered (Map 3.4). From the Rus in return came furs, skins, wax, honey, amber, cattle, Slavic and other slaves (de la Vaissière 2004: Histoire des marchands sogdiens, 265). No doubt that Khorezm gained prosperity by intermediating such trade (Mankovskaya 1982, 41).[36]

Another route that remained important, although less so than previously, was the trunk route of the "Great Silk Road"—from China via Persia to the Near East. This trunk route now crossed at least four additional borders, as compared to the situation before the demise of the caliphate and the Tang empires. Since the ninth century, Turkic slaves had

been regularly transported from the Transoxianan slave markets across Khorassan and Iran to Mesopotamia and the Islamic heartlands (Shukow et al. 1957/1963, Band 3, 541).[37]

While silk remained a major subject of trade along the SR, and an international de-facto currency, the latter can also be said (with some qualifications) for Byzantine golden solidi and for Samanid silver dirhams, as can be inferred from their appearance in large numbers in European markets (Baipakov et al. 1997, 72–73; see also above). From the tenth century, Song dynasty coins were also used in CA, although China no longer exercised any political hegemony over the region in a comparable way to previous times. The discovery of a certain quantity of Song currency implies that commercial flows of some importance existed, at least from about the mid-tenth to the mid-eleventh century (Hambis (dir) 1977, 50–51).

From Peak of Medieval Urban Civilization of the Orient to Decline and Collapse of the Empire

Urban development was one of the most noteworthy Samanid achievements. In the later ninth and tenth centuries, the cities and towns of Khorassan and Transoxiana, e.g., Nishapur, Merv, Balkh, Bukhara, Samarkand, and Khodzhent, experienced a period of expansion and blossom. Moreover, in the regions of Shash and Ilaq (the valleys of the rivers Chirchik and Angren, tributaries of the Syr Daria), something like an urban sprawl took place under the Samanids (Negmatov 1998, 77, 140).

Bazaars—connected to regional and long-distance trade—played an important role in the unfolding of this dynamism. In Muslim CA, the bazaar was not only a shopping and industrial center, it was also a place where credit and financial deals were made. The evolution of the bazaar appears to have been a speciality of the commerce-friendly traditional Islamic society. The relatively minor importance of international trade fairs, in comparison to Western Europe, probably resulted from the excellent infrastructure which the bazaar provided for commercial activities. Braudel qualified the business life in the bazaars and the quarters reserved for foreigners as "permanent fairs" which rendered European-style trade fairs superfluous (Burlot 1995, 85; Feldbauer and Liedl 2008, 99).

As mentioned above, Bukhara was the intellectual and religious heart of CA and possessed a rich library known by the name of Siwan al-hikma (Storehouse of Wisdom) allegedly containing the rarest and best works of scholarship. Bukhara also benefited from its renown as a traditional center of textiles, particularly of silk textiles. Samarkand,

---

[36] The large number of Samanid silver dirhams found in regions as far away as northern Russia and the Baltics may be evidence of intensifying trading links with the ancient Rus and its western neighbors (Negmatov 1998, 85).

[37] As Fragner points out, slave trade was a very profitable economic activity for Samanid merchants (2008, 40).

in turn, was the Muslim world's first metropolis of paper production (highly valued in Europe) and glass fabrication (highly prized in China) and continued to function in the tenth century as a key slave market. Samarkand thus constituted the economic center of the Samanid Empire and, more widely, of CA. Bukhara was called the "Dome of Islam," and Samarkand became known as the "Mirror of the World," the "Garden of the Soul," or the "Center of the Universe" (Roudik 2007, 33). Irrigation and urbanization lifted Bukhara's population to about 300,000 in the tenth century, which is bigger than it was during most of the Soviet era (about a millennium later!). Bukhara also became the largest and most important center of Jewish population in CA. However, Samarkand grew to reach an even larger number of inhabitants (possibly around 500,000) in the Samanid era (Roudik 2007, 34; Burlot 1995, 87).

The oasis and city of Shash (Tashkent) probably achieved an economic "breakthrough" under the Samanids: The fertile valley, irrigated by the Syr Daria and about 50 canals, and the extraction of mineral resources turned the oasis into an exporter of food, cattle, horses, precious metals, and stones. City walls and other fortifications were erected/reinforced under Samanid rule. Tashkent was a frequently visited rest area and trade center for caravans on their way from China before continuing to Samarkand and Bukhara (Roudik 2007, 60). Overall, in Mokyr's assessment, the Samanid dynasty had turned core regions of CA into the most intellectually creative and economically prosperous area of the Islamic world (Mokyr 2003, 370).

The establishment of the Ghaznavid Emirate in what is now Afghanistan in the last quarter of the tenth century represented the culmination of a process that had begun in the Samanid Empire whereby the military foundations of the state (related to the iqta system) had been transferred from a reliance on indigenous Iranian and assimilated Arab landed classes to a substantial dependence on what originally were Turkic slave troops (Bosworth 1998, 95). Thus, outstanding Turkic army commanders were able to accumulate considerable power.

Sebüktegin, a commander of Oghuz origin, assumed the military authority over a Samanid province before establishing himself in 977—against the will of the central authorities—as the autonomous regional ruler of the town Ghazna and adjacent territories (Eastern Afghanistan) (Map 3.4). Thus, the state of Ghazna was created. Sebüktegin reformed the iqta system in Ghazna, ensuring that his soldiers and followers were equipped with adequate territorial revenue assignments for their material support. Sebüktegin also insisted on control of the reallocation process by the divan (state chancellery, consultative body of the ruler) in Ghazna (instead of by the Samanid authorities in Bukhara). The tradition of Ghaznavid winter plunder raids from the mountain rim of Eastern Afghanistan down to the Indian plains was already initiated in this period.

The above-described armed separatism only added to internal strife at the court that had weakened the Samanid dynasty in the second half of the tenth century and eventually opened the door for two new Turkic powers to divide up the empire (Mayhew 2010, 42). The Samanid state collapsed in 999 when it was attacked by the Karakhanids (a Turkic tribal confederation, originating in the Altai area, that had already conquered Semirechie, parts of East Turkestan and Ferghana) and the Ghaznavids. The empire was split up along the Amu Daria (Map 3.5): The Karakhanids took territories north and east (largely Mavarannahr), while the Ghaznavids (already in Afghanistan) incorporated lands south and west of the river (principally Khorassan and most of Khorezm) into their polity (Rasuly-Paleczek 2006, 178; Krieger 2003, 261).

3.3.2.2 The Kingdom of Qocho and the Yellow Uighurs (from Around 840): Maintaining Trade Links with China

The Uighurs of Qocho (focused on Turfan and other oases of Eastern Xinjiang) and the Yellow Uighurs of Ganzhou (centered on the province of Gansu) straddled SR caravan routes connecting China with CA, India, and the west (Map 3.4). Both soon controlled their respective sections of the trade links. During the Later Tang dynasty (923–936), official diplomatic and trade relations were revived and the Uighurs again became important foreign trade partners of the Middle Kingdom: the Uighurs mostly shipped horses, pastoral and farming products, textiles, jade and other precious materials east and acquired primarily silk in return (Gunder Frank 1992: The Centrality of CA, 32). The modest recovery of overland trade on the eastern part of the SR happened at approximately the same time as the temporary upswing of SR trade in the Samanid Empire and the western part of Eurasia. The two occurrences may have positively influenced each other. In any case, the Uighurs of Qocho were successful in maintaining good relations with various Chinese dynasties right up to the Mongol conquest.

A relatively warm climate and a sufficient water supply (through the karez system) from the Tienshan (Bogdashan) allowed Qocho to grow double crops of grain and a generous selection of fruits and vegetables. Cotton had been cultivated in the region since the seventh century; cotton cloth remained among the prime Uighur exports to the Middle Kingdom. Grapes, as in the past, were a local speciality, and according to some sources, the Qocho administration even collected wine as an in-kind levy. In 982, the Song envoy Wang Yande visited Qocho. In his account he, e.g., pointed out that the area produced five cereal grains, cotton, and brocaded cloth and that the Uighur upper classes retained some traditional nomadic habits like riding, archery, and eating horse meat. The kingdom was still dominated by Buddhists and Manichaeans, while tolerating Christians.

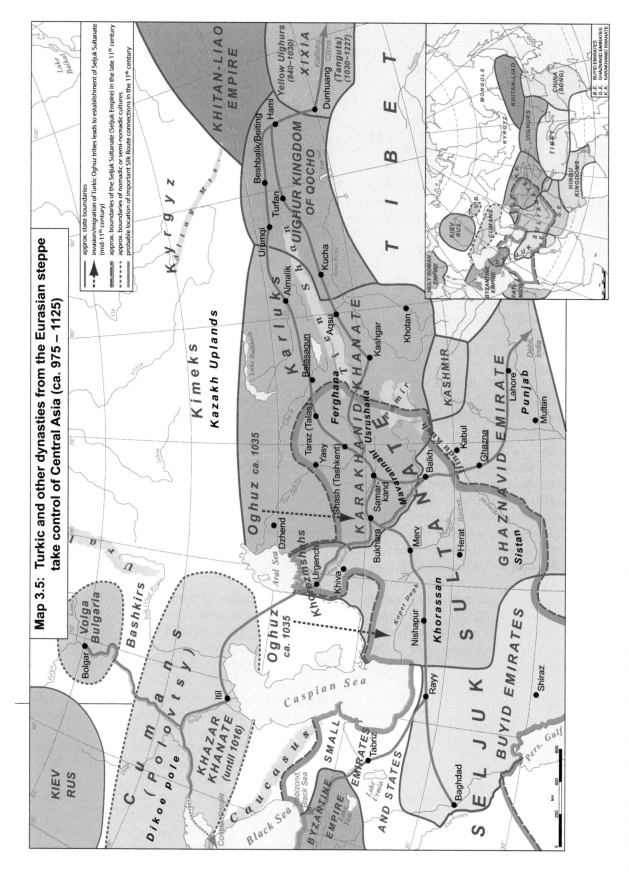

Map 3.5 Turkic and other dynasties from the Eurasian steppe take control of CA (ca. 975–1125)

Rich Uighur patrons paid for the creation of the famous frescoes at Bezeklik (Turfan area) and Kizil (Kucha area) (Millward and Perdue 2004, 41). Everyday life continued to be influenced by Chinese culture. Men reportedly wore garments and hairdress in the Tang style, and women were dressed in long gowns with Tang floral patterns in the Transoxianan style (Geng 1998, 203–205).

3.3.2.3 The Khazars, the Kievan Rus, and Volga Bulgaria (Late Ninth–Mid-eleventh Centuries)

The Khazar Khanate remained a focus of international commerce also in the first half of the tenth century. Commerce with CA is reported to have peaked in the middle of the century[38] and to have sharply slumped toward 1015, approximately when Khazaria ceased to exist (de la Vaissière 2004, 264). The conversion of the Volga Bulgars (another Turkic people)[39] to Islam in the early tenth century in all likelihood delivered a boost to the recovery of trade between the Volga Basin and CA. The Volga Bulgars had founded a largely sedentary kingdom on the middle reaches of the Volga, which played a role as a trade turntable between the Baltics and the Orient (Kappeler 2001, 29). The kingdom's capital was Bolgar, situated at the confluence of Kama and Volga.

Against the backdrop of continuous Khazar-Rus rivalry for dominance of the trade routes and for direct access to the Black Sea, Constantinople, and Caspian Sea, the Rus prince Sviatoslav concluded a military treaty with the Oghuz principality and in 965 launched a war against Khazaria. Sarkel and Itil were soon captured and looted (967), and Khazars were forced to retreat to the Northern Caucasian plain. There a Khazar rump state that could no longer control trade on the lower Don and the lower Volga continued to exist until the early eleventh century. Yet, as O'Rourke points out, in destroying the (semi-nomadic) Khazars, Sviatoslav had removed a powerful buffer between Kiev and the steppe nomads. The Pontic steppes and the southern part of the Rus, including the territory of Kiev, were now exposed to attack by powerful nomadic confederations: first the Pechenegs, then the Kipchaks/Cumans, and finally the Mongols (O'Rourke 2007, 24).

Although the Kievan Rus had taken possession of the Khazar port of Tmutarakan (Matarka) in the Strait of Kerch, the Pechenegs in the late tenth century seriously obstructed Kiev's transit trade along Don and Dnepr and, moreover, controlled the lower stretches of a number of other rivers traversing the Pontic steppes in north-south direction (including the Southern Bug and the Dnestr). Thus, the Rus' access to the Black Sea and Byzantium remained, to some degree, bolted by nomadic military supremacy in the Pontic steppes, also called "Dikoe pole" (Wild Field) by medieval Rus chroniclers (Marchand 2014, 12). Gardizi gave superb descriptions of the Pechenegs with their immense herds, their "barbarian" richness of vases and precious belts, their war trumpets shaped like animal heads, and their profusion of arms (cited in Roux 2000, 131). Finally, in 1036 the Pechenegs were fatally defeated by Yaroslav the Wise—and their place was taken in the mid-eleventh century by the Kipchaks (in Byzantium and Western Europe called Cumans, in Russia named Polovtsy), which were militarily even more dangerous for the Rus (Karger (ed) 1978, 59; Kozak 2007, 305).

After trade between CA and Europe had strongly declined in the early eleventh century, it recovered again but remained relatively weak, given persisting lack of security on the Pontic steppes. In view of these difficulties, the Kievan Rus—which had been founded more or less as a trading state straddling strategic routes crossing Eastern Europe and linking commercially oriented settlements like enclaves isolated in immense woodlands—started to rely more on developing its domestic economy, particularly agriculture, forestry, and crafts. Trading activities were partly redirected toward the Baltics and Northern Europe and to Central Europe (e.g., Cracow and Prague). Novgorod in the Northern Rus gained economic prominence (Tröbst 2009, 70).

3.3.2.4 Nomadic and Semi-nomadic Communities in the Eurasian Steppe Belt

Oghuz principality (ninth–mid-eleventh centuries): During the ninth and tenth centuries, nomadic Turkic Oghuz tribes formed a principality on the lower reaches of the Syr Daria, in the Aral Sea region, and in the Caspian Lowlands. Its capital, Yengikent, "new settlement," lay on the path of major caravan routes which linked towns on the upper reaches of the Syr Daria with areas around the lower Volga (Map 3.4). The Oghuz adopted Islam in the mid-tenth century. In the course of that century, they also displaced the Pechenegs further west.

The ruler of the principality bore the title of Yabghu (which recalls the title of the leaders of the Western Turk Khaganate, see above). The Yabghu's authority was hereditary. The Oghuz polity featured a relatively simple administrative structure. Officials, including tax collectors, collected

---

[38] As de la Vaissière specifies, the volume of commerce on the steppe route (from Mavarannahr via Khwarazm to Khazaria) approximately doubled or even tripled from the ninth to the tenth century (2004, 264).

[39] In the sixth century, the Turkic Bulgars had still lived in the Pontic steppes. Approximately at the time the Khazar state was established (in the seventh century), the Bulgars left the Eurasian grasslands and migrated in two directions: one group of tribes moved northeast up the Volga to the Volga-Kama Basin, where they settled and soon became Muslims (Volga Bulgarians); another group moved southwest, crossed the lower Danube, settled in what was later called Bulgaria, and subsequently adopted Christianity and a Southern-Slavic language (Danube-Bulgarians).

tribute from the nomadic and settled populations. The intermediate rung of the social ladder was occupied by the Beg or Bek (tribal or clan chief, head of district), whose power was also transmitted on a hereditary basis. As might be expected, the Oghuz economy was based on extensive animal husbandry; farming and crafts were secondary activities. Like the other Eurasian steppe peoples described in this subchapter (Karluks, Kimeks, and Kipchaks, see below), the Oghuz bred sheep, goats, horses, oxen, cows, and camels. Sheep played a particularly important part in their economy. The Oghuz hunted furry animals such as the fox, marten, beaver, sable, and ermine and even went after tigers and snow leopards. The fur and hides of wild animals and the products of livestock were sold or exchanged at points (markets) near the settled lands in the south (i.e., bordering the Samanid Empire). For horses, livestock, pelts, wool, etc., the Oghuz purchased grain, handicrafts, a.o., articles (see also subchapter on Samanid Empire above) (Agayanov 1998, 68).

Like most of their nomadic neighbors, the Oghuz engaged in auxiliary agriculture. Semisedentary and settled groups mainly sowed millet, although Al-Idrisi reports that they also cultivated wheat, barley, and even rice (!). Moreover they are reported to have tended vegetable gardens and even vineyards. Still, farming must have scarcely sufficed to cover their own needs. The Oghuz used the skins and hides of domestic animals to produce various types of footwear, apparel, vessels, quivers, bow covers, and horses' harnesses. Among household crafts, the manufacture of weapons such as bows, arrows, and spears held a key place. According to Al-Idrisi, the Oghuz as well as other steppe neighbors were skilled in ironworking and possessed know-how in the making of beautiful, sophisticated ornaments from gold and silver (which may recall the animal art of the Scyths) (Agayanov 1998, 71–72).

Far from merely trading with their neighbors, the Oghuz repeatedly conducted campaigns, raids, and razzias against regions like Khwarazm, Mavarannahr, Khorassan, and Volga Bulgaria. As outlined above, the Oghuz formed a coalition with the Rus against Khazaria. While the Oghuz were attracted by the rich Don, Dnepr, and Black Sea steppes and by the international trading routes hitherto controlled by the Khazars, the Oghuz were not to be the major beneficiaries of the demise of the Khazar Khaganate.

Toward the beginning of eleventh century, apparently increasing oppression by officials and the attempted introduction of a statewide system of regular taxation (undue centralization?)[40] triggered unrest and rebellion among the bulk of the nomadic populace. The Oghuz polity started to decline. The long struggle against the rebellion and the splitting off of some important Oghuz tribes and their migration southward in search of new territories weakened power and authority of what remained of the principality. In the first half of the eleventh century, the Oghuz state foundered under the assault of the Kipchaks (see below), who invaded the Aral Sea and the Northern Caspian region from the east (Agayanov 1998, 68–69; Roux 2000, 179).

Since the tenth century, the Oghuz tribes nomadizing on or near the Ustyurt Plateau (Transcaspian steppe), which constituted the southwestern fringe of the principality, have been described as "Turcomans" or "Turkmens." Given that they seem to have been continually embroiled in internal feuds and warfare, the Turkmens never succeeded in uniting to a nomadic confederation or achieving statehood (Linska et al. 2003, 70).

Karluk Khaganate (766–940): The rural and urban cultural mix of the Karluk nomadic state continued to evolve in Semirechie and adjacent areas. In the Ili valley, urban culture made further advances: Towns expanded territorially in the tenth century, on account of the rabadas and SR trade, which suggests or confirms a revival of the northern or Dzungarian route to China. Archeological materials give an impression of the expansion of urban crafts, particularly pottery and glassblowing, smithery, metal processing, and jewelry production. In the formation of the Karakhanid state (see below), the major role was played by tribes of the Karluk confederacy (Baipakov et al. 1997, 40, 45; Gorod moy rodnoy Almaty 2004, 40).

The Kimek principality (end of the ninth–beginning of eleventh century), also ethnically Turkic, emerged in the Kazakh grasslands north of Lake Balkhash (Kozybaev et al. 2010, 497). The state was ruled by a Kaghan and divided into a number of domains (districts). The rulers of the latter were the descendants of hereditary tribal chiefs and had their lands bestowed upon them by the Kaghan in return for military service. Like the supreme ruler, most rulers of domains also had fortress-residences which were typically located in elevated positions in the steppe. Animal husbandry and hunting dominated the Kimek economy. Wintering places and encampments (qystau), which point to semi-nomadic activity, were located in the middle and lower reaches of the Syr Daria valley. The principality gradually began to decline when particularism started to pervade the system of domains. The domains' increasing autonomy eroded the authority of the Kaghans, so that the state became unable to withstand the pressure of neighboring nomadic peoples. From the beginning of the eleventh century, the Kimek polity constituted a de-facto appendage of the Kipchak state (Agayanov 1998; Oskolkov and Oskolkova 2004, 15).

---

[40] Bureaucratic and inflexible state intervention does not seem to be appreciated and may be a dangerous undertaking in a nomadic society. See also the serious repercussions mentioned above of the rigid attempts by Sogdian advisors to introduce regular taxation in the Eastern Turk Khaganate in the late 620s.

Kipchak tribal confederation (beginning of eleventh–beginning of thirteenth century): The Kipchaks originally constituted a western branch of the Kimek tribal confederation and nomadized in the central part of the Kazakh grasslands. As Kimek power waned (see above), the Kipchaks established their own state and soon ruled over most of the Kazakh steppe, incorporating lands of their former masters. The Kipchaks' principal activity was nomadic pastoralism; there were some pockets of settled people in the southern parts of the confederation. For a still unknown reason—possibly because they perceived and were willing and capable of exploiting weaknesses of their neighbors—the Kipchaks in the first half of the eleventh century spread to the lower Syr Daria, the Aral, and Caspian plains, thus conquered Oghuz territory, and then extended their power further west. The Kipchaks soon replaced the Pechenegs in carrying out armed raids (forays) into the areas of sedentary people living on the Volga and on Rus lands (Oskolkov and Oskolkova 2004, 16).

The Bashkirs, which inhabited approximately the same area as today (the Southern Ural mountains and their western foothills between Kama and Yaik/Ural river), originally spoke a Finno-Ugric language but were turkicized and adopted Islam from the tenth century. The Bashkirs were no "pure" nomads, although their majority practiced nomadic and semi-nomadic pastoralism; in the north and on the heights of the Ural range, some tribes were forest dwellers, hunters, and fishermen; on the foothills some Bashkirs also farmed. The Bashkirs were organized in clans and tribes, but in contrast to their steppe neighbors, by the early second millennium, they had not yet achieved centralized statehood (Kappeler 2001, 43).

3.3.3 Post-Caliphate Muslim Faith: Expansion Throughout CA and Increasing Dogmatization

In the tenth and eleventh centuries, Islam gained many new believers in CA. Islam (though not as a monolithic faith) was already represented by the successor dynasties to the caliphate, e.g., the Samanids, Buyids, Fatimids, etc., and was soon also adopted by Turco-nomadic invaders coming from the north. Conversion began in the major urban centers and by the eleventh century had advanced far even in the remote countryside. By the end of the tenth century, the majority of the Karluk and Oghuz peoples were Muslims (and parts of these peoples were to found the Karakhanid and Seljuq empires, respectively). The Karakhanids encouraged the diffusion of Islam from Mavarannahr into the Tarim Basin and toward the Eurasian steppes. Sufi preachers, including dervish missionaries,

played an important role in spreading the faith among the nomadic peoples (Nizami 1998b, 368).

While Islam was successfully spreading through CA and beyond, its face was evolving. Back in the ninth century, against the background of the centrifugal political tendencies that had seized the caliphate, more religious unity was strived for. Early that century the teachings of the "Mutazilites" (literally: those that separate themselves) were declared state dogma. This branch of Islam emphasized the postulate of individually responsible and free human action, which implied a modified view of God. An important opposing theological direction was the movement of Sunnis, which put forth the fundamental argument that reason accomplishes itself in faith. This dogma helped secure the dominance of divine rules (freedom of will in the sense of the wise submission of the will and mind of the faithful under the workings of the Almighty) (Leipold 2001, 15, 18).

From the late ninth century, Sunni Islam gained the upper hand. It promised a more convincing theological foundation for conserving unity within the Muslim congregation. But neither were the Shiites adherents of rational theology. Thus, Islamic law does not distinguish between sacral and secular law and, in the latter area, between public, private, and criminal norms. Like all other sacral law systems, Muslim law embodies a dogmatic claim to be absolutely true, because divine, law. It is therefore to serve as an eternally valid and to be obeyed system of rules. This affirmed dogmatic claim to truth may be an important cause for the increasing rigidity of the legal system in many Islamic countries from the tenth (or eleventh) century and for consequences of this rigidity for social and economic developments. While specifically commerce- or economy-related rules of the Koran or of Sharia do not appear to be directed against private initiative or business activities, as Leipold discerns, the problem may rather be seen to reside in the integral character of the Islamic system of rules: unity of religion, state, law, economy, education, and science (Leipold 2001, 34).

Thus it would not appear easy to disagree with Max Weber's thesis which identifies the religiously shaped structure of administration, law, and jurisdiction in Islamic countries and polities as a prime obstacle to their development as industrial capitalist market economies (Leipold 2001, 30). The Greek and Indian cultural inputs were soon rejected in the name of religious purity. As Burlot wrote, the doors to the fruits of personal effort (idjtihad) slowly closed, and the intellectual atmosphere in many areas stiffened (1995, 94). Names to which important scientific achievements can be credited became fewer and fewer in the world of Islam after the twelfth century (Habib 2003, 461).

3.3.4 Turkic and Other Dynasties from the Eurasian Steppes Take Control of CA (Mid-tenth–Mid-twelfth Centuries)

From the late tenth century, empires gained importance in CA that were ruled by Turkic nomads from the Eurasian steppes. These Turkic nomads either descended directly from the north and conquered oasis territories or were former slave soldiers that had boasted impressive military carriers in sedentary Islamic states (like in the Samanid Empire) and subsequently established empires of their own. A warming of the climate and further increasing aridity in CA in the early second millennium CE may have constituted an indirect triggering factor of Turkic migrations and state formations in oasis zones. Under changed ecological conditions, demographic pressures in the nomadic societies of the Eurasian steppes became more urgent. Nomads were forced to look for new pastures, and given the balance of military power in CA, it was not difficult for the steppe dwellers to move south and penetrate the sedentary societies.

After sedentary civilization had advanced north into the steppe belt in the era of the caliphate, and after the Samanids largely upheld the status quo, invasions and the creation of new nomadic empires in CA over one or two centuries pushed the border of nomadic civilization down south again. Large parts of the defeated and conquered sedentary population had no other choice but to change to a nomadic way of life or, if they had been nomads previously, to re-nomadize. The repeated influx of Turkic pastoral nomads and their herds (depending on the sequence of invasions) from beyond the Syr Daria was to have a substantial impact on the pattern of land use and agriculture in Mavarannahr and other oasis regions. Neglect of well-established irrigation and soil conservation methods in some areas favored the expansion of deserts and steppes. In this connection, the increase of nomadic pastoral activity can be a cause as well as a consequence of the mentioned deterioration of farming conditions. Loss of fertile land was often linked to disruptions of the important traditional symbiosis between peasants and nomads, which may have had political, demographic, or ecological reasons (Rasuly-Paleczek 2006, 189; Feldbauer and Liedl 2008, 109).

From around the eleventh century, Turkic and later Mongol invasions and military campaigns disturbed SR traffic, which—despite some efforts to re-establish stability—did not regain its past intensity and security until the mid-thirteenth century under Mongol hegemony (Norel 2009, 51). Businessmen and commercial enterprises who during early Islam had benefited from high social esteem and autonomy, often lost prestige and influence in the wake of the military takeovers and/or the militarization of a number of Islamic states (Rodinson 1966/2007, 88; Feldbauer and Liedl 2008, 26).

3.3.4.1 The Karakhanids (942–1089/1210): Continued Stability Under Hybrid of Nomadic Appanage and Islamic Iqta System

The Karakhanids stem from a group of Turkic-speaking tribes belonging to the Karluk confederacy. In the mid-tenth century, this group adopted Islam[41] and created the Karakhanid state on the territory of Zhetysu (Semirechie) and parts of East Turkestan. This nomadic state held sway over Turko-nomadic tribes as well as over settled people of old farming districts and towns. The territory of the Karakhanid Khanate initially consisted of Semirechie, Western Dzungaria, and the western part of Tarim Basin (Aqsu, Kashgar, Yarkand); later, Shash and Ferghana were added; in 999 the former Samanid territory north of the Amu Daria (mostly Mavarannahr) was incorporated (Maps 3.4 and 3.5).

With the conquest, the Turko-*nomadic military aristocracy* assumed (economic) power in Mavarannahr. In the wake of the invasion, many Turkic nomads from Semirechie and East Turkestan migrated south of the Syr Daria.[42] The Karakhanids eliminated the previous Samanid bureaucratic governmental system and extended their type of governance over all their conquered territories. The head of the Karakhanid state was the Karakhan (the Black Khan) or Tamgach Khan (the Khan of the Khans). All lands were declared to be the leader's property. The state was divided into many small units with unstable borders. These administrative units—appanages—were distributed among members of the ruling clan and high-ranking representatives of the nomadic nobility. Rulers of these small units were autonomous and were often allowed to coin their own money (Roudik 2007, 35). Balasagun was chosen as capital of the state. The Tamgach Khan lived not in the town but in his nearby army encampment (orda) (Davidovich 1998, 122–123).

The process of settlement of nomads was complex and consisted at least of two waves: The first wave corresponded to the sedentarization of poor or impoverished nomads, compelled by the circumstances. Given the concentration of the best newly-gained pastures and sources of water in the hands of the nomadic aristocracy, a part of the migrating population soon lost livestock. Eventually, many nomads, particularly from the poorest strata of nomadic society, started to plow the fields and became sedentary. The settled inhabitants cultivated millet and other cultures but did not totally break with cattle breeding. In settling down, these

---

[41] More precisely, Turkic chieftains decided to adopt the new religion and to carry out wholesale conversions of their tribes (Soucek 2000, 75).

[42] There had already been Turkic populations in former Transoxiana before the ninth century, but these had been very small in numbers.

nomads of Turkic origin mingled with the indigenous sedentary/urban population of Iranian stock and thus made a contribution to the piecemeal Turkization of Mavarannahr (Baipakov et al. 1997, 22; Linska et al. 2003, 63).

As mentioned above, the early eleventh century saw a redistribution of the conquered land in favor of the Karakhanid military aristocracy; this goes particularly for remaining state land, only waqf estates were not touched. Islam being the state religion, the Karakhanids turned iqta into the dominating form of landed property. Indeed, it would appear that iqta, which had existed under the (sedentary) Samanids, became more widespread in CA under the (nomadic) Karakhanids (Khazanov 1983/1994, 261). Moreover, in many respects, iqta now turned from a temporary revocable assignment into a hereditary fief, something like the medieval European feodum. Heritability increased the iqtadars' material interest in agriculture and farming revenue. The iqta land owners of the nomadic aristocracy typically drew product rents from their properties. For the time being, most of the nobles continued to live in the steppe. More than a century passed before they would definitely move to the towns. This corresponded to the second wave of settlement of nomads (Hoffmann 2011, 156).

The acquisition of the dikhans' estates by the military aristocracy and the transformation of this property into iqta land gradually led to the near-total disappearance of the dikhans (pre-Islamic local hereditary land owners, see above). The iqta became the specific form of rule of the nomadic nobility over the sedentary peasantry. Iqta lands often comprised estates in the agrarian oases as well as in the steppes. The Karakhanids also endowed waqfs for the benefit of their descendants, a long-term effective means of preserving property amid all the political upheavals of the time (Khazanov 1983/1994, 260–261; Davidovich 1998, 140).

The heyday of the Karakhanid state may have been reached under Ibrahim Tamgach Khan, who ruled in the middle of the eleventh century. Less distracted by intermittent wars, he concerned himself with internal order in the country, the security of its inhabitants, respect for property, commerce, and money circulation. Ibrahim saw to the flourishing of towns and made sure that once redistribution of assets had happened, nomads no longer encroached on the rights of the settled population and did nothing to offend farmers and city dwellers. Public control of market prices existed—at least for some products (e.g., meat). Ibrahim's financial and fiscal policies approached those that had been conducted by Arab governors and Samanid emirs in previous periods (Davidovich 1998, 128–129).

While Ibrahim did not set up a centralized patrimonial state, he did manage to reduce considerably the number of appanages and to streamline the rights of appanage holders. He also established the Karakhan's monopoly over the state's coinage. During his rule, a single system of coinage with different denominations was valid throughout Karakhanid territory. This contributed to the stability of the legal and institutional framework of the economy. Substantial tax revenue flowing into the coffers of the central government allowed sizable infrastructure expenditures which underpinned urban building activity. Ibrahim for example built a hospital in Samarkand where the authorities not only cared for the sick but also gave shelter to the poor. For the benefit of the caravan trade, his son built caravanserais on the roads between Bukhara, Samarkand, and Khodzhent (Davidovich 1998, 130).

Prosperity from Samanid times appears to have continued under Karakhanid rule also in Ferghana. For instance, Ahsiket, located in the north of the basin and on an intersection of the SR, was an economic and political center of Ferghana in the ninth and tenth centuries. The city had a mint and was irrigated by a multitude of bricked canals; a unique system of underground water pipes fed public baths and residential buildings. Archeologists found water-lifting engines or water pumps known as chigir that tapped water from mountain streams. Beyond the production of coins, the city remained a major metallurgical center, exporting high-quality ironware, especially swords. The blacksmiths of Ahsiket acquired the secret of making Damascus steel and created marvelous swords as subtle in design as they were sharp (Saidov et al. 2011, 15–16).

Tashkent (Shash) was famous for its pottery, bowls, sandals, fabrics, and carpets under Karakhanid rule, as Roudik observes (2007, 61). This period also featured new towns springing up and old ones, like Ispidzhab (Sairam), expanding on the middle course of the Syr Daria (see Map 4.7). Almost every town had its bazaar and caravanserai. Materials produced in extensive quantities such as ceramics and glass provide a fair idea of the development of urban crafts. Attractive pottery became cheaper and more easily affordable for the bulk of the urban population as a result of certain technical innovations and the standardization of forms; what is more, these urban articles started to reach remote mountain areas, which would point to some positive developments in the material standard of living of C Asians (Davidovich 1998, 140–141).

Furthermore, in the (former) Karakhanid "heartland," new urban and farming cultures appeared in Northeastern Zhetysu (Semirechie). In this area, in the eleventh to the twelfth centuries, already about 70 urban settlements (gorodishche) were counted, while back in the ninth to the tenth centuries, it had only been about 12 such settlements. In the eleventh to twelfth centuries, the settled population of Northeastern Semirechie consisted of about 35,000–45,000 inhabitants, whereas around two centuries earlier, the corresponding number had been but 1200–1300, which implies that it had multiplied by 20 to 30 times. This is largely explained by the settlement of nomads and semi-nomads (Baipakov et al. 1997, 41).

In the midst of relative prosperity, the khanate was hit by a "silver coin crisis" (Davidovich and Dani 1998, 399), whose general feature was the gradual debasing of silver dirhams with alloys (even involving various copper or non-precious metal alloys). At the same time, the circulation of gold coins was activated even in regions where they had previously played no significant role as money. While in the first and early second decade of the eleventh century, silver dirhams (inherited from the Samanids) were still of a high standard, from around the middle of the eleventh century, some of the mints of the Karakhanid state issued dirhams consisting of an alloy of copper and lead. The minting of silver coins continued until the last quarter of the eleventh century. Eventually, dirhams were almost entirely coined out of copper; only the surface was covered by a thin layer of silver (Davidovich and Dani 1998, 399–400). The cause of the silver crisis seems to have been connected to the using up of C Asian silver reserves: After the large-scale extraction of silver for minting purposes in the Samanid era, the Karakhanids apparently had to contend with a shortage of that precious metal, which they attempted to alleviate by using other metals to support the circulation of money (Baipakov et al. 1997, 47).

In the later eleventh century, the unity of the Karakhanid dynasty was fractured by emerging internal disputes and warfare, and the dynasty was eventually forced to accept the Seljuk's overlordship. After the crushing defeat of the combined Karakhanid-Seljuk armies in 1141, the power over the Karakhanid state fell to the Karakhitays/the Western Liao.

3.3.4.2 The Ghaznavids (977–1187): Moving Toward Oriental Despotism

The Ghaznavids were also Turks, with their roots among the nomads of the Eurasian grasslands, and they had recently converted to Islam. But the Ghaznavids came to power as former slave soldiers of the Samanids (as referred to above). As Bosworth underlines, the Ghaznavids display the phenomenon of the rapid transformation of a line of "barbarian," originally Turkic, slaves into monarchs within the Islamic tradition (Bosworth 1998, 110). After eliminating the Samanid Empire—with the help of the Karakhanids—Mahmud Ghaznavi (who reigned 998–1030), the son of Sebüktegin, in 1000 CE was in complete control of the whole of Afghanistan and the former Samanid territories south of the Amu Daria, including Khorassan and most of Khorezm. Due to frequent military campaigns in India, Mahmud simultaneously held sway over Northwestern Indian territories. Thus the Ghaznavid Empire had emerged, ruled by Sultan Mahmud; as Map 3.5 shows, the Amu Daria was fixed as the boundary between the Ghaznavid and

Karakhanid empires (Shukow et al. 1957/1963, Band 3, 546).

Mahmud's annual Indian campaigns constituted expeditions into Punjab, Hindustan (the upper and middle Ganges plains), Sind (on the lower reaches of the Indus), and Gujarat (Western India). Bosworth gives some examples: In 1004 the Southern Punjab was attacked and an immense booty, including 120 elephants, was taken. An expedition in the winter of 1018–1019 to Northern India captured rich booty, gaining 55,000 slaves, 350 elephants, and much more. The culmination of Mahmud's Indian campaigns was an attack in 1025–1026 on the southwestern coast of the Kathiawar peninsula (Gujarat), where temples endowed with fabulous riches were ransacked. The immense haul gained from the despoiled temples was said to total over 10 million dinars and brought back to Ghazna. The forays deep into South Asia caught the imagination of the Islamic world. Lavish gifts were sent to Baghdad and the caliph bestowed on the sultan—his reputation as "hammer of the infidels" now much inflated—further honorific titles (Bosworth 1998, 103–104).

The regular campaigns in India made up a pillar of the Ghaznavid state: The military incursions were essentially plunder raids, entailing no or few contractual relationships with those subjected to attacks, no subsidy treaties, and practically no quid pro quo (like protection) for the exacted "tribute." In Olson's terminology, these plunder raids would fit into the category of roving banditry. In some cases, attempts were made to impose military aristocracies over foreign populations. The aim of the raids was to exact loot from the Indian princes in the shape of gold, elephants, slaves, and—quite often—troop contingents for the Ghaznavid army. Given that the core of the empire's military support was Turkic, the sultan and his commanders needed to stay geared to the wants and aspirations of these troops and, above all, to act as successful war leaders and organizers of plunder. This underlines the pivotal importance of pillage in upholding the fabric of this C Asian state (Bosworth 1998, 108–110).

Only in Northern Punjab, particularly in Lahore, was an attempt made to set up a civil administration, with the goal of turning this region into something like a regular province of the empire for fiscal purposes. This try was unsuccessful because of the unpacified state of the region and the ruler's inability to control unruly military elements and ghazis (fighters for the faith) (Bosworth 1998, 105).

Yet, for the administration and financing of their empire, the Ghaznavids early on recognized the need for the services of their Iranian subjects, above all as civil servants. The central bureaucracy was composed of separate divans for the vizier (the head of civil administration), the secretary for the army, the heads of intelligence and of the postal service, and the chief steward of the budget. According to Bosworth,

Ghaznavid financial demands generally overrode other considerations. The vizier and the chief steward were under continuous pressure to enhance the flow of revenue and to locate or trace new sources of taxation. Failure here meant dismissal or worse. The vizier also needed to uphold supervision of provincial governors and officials, who might have been tempted, possibly through distance from the capital, to withhold proceeds and to rebel. Tax pressure (the kharaj and a panoply of local levies and dues) and the Ghaznavid tax collectors presumably weighed heavily on the mass of the settled population (peasants, traders, and artisans). But the sufferings of the populace were even worse when the soldiers of the army were dished out unregulated assignments of revenue (barats) which they then collected personally (perhaps comparable to uncontrolled iqtas, bordering on stationary looting) (Bosworth 1998, 111–112).

Farming was concentrated in the oases and essentially small-scale and aimed at subsistence within the rural area concerned or at supplying regional centers like Herat, Merv, and Nishapur. Bosworth only refers to a few highly specialized foodstuffs like truffles or the edible earth of Khorassan that were exported abroad, e.g., to Egypt (1998, 116). Most irrigation in the Iranian highlands and parts of Afghanistan came from subterranean qanats (karez), requiring repeated injections of capital for construction and maintenance which only the wealthier landowners could provide. The sultans themselves were responsible for hydrotechnical structures in the region of Ghazna. The (still) lush pastures of the upper Amu Daria valley and its tributaries (Tokharistan) were famed for horse breeding (Bosworth 1998, 116).

Industrial production comprised small-scale activity of craftsmen and artisans and was mainly destined for local consumption. It was only from Khorassan, where virtually all the towns produced textiles or carpets, that certain celebrated local fabrics, such as the silk brocades of Nishapur, the white cottons of Herat, and the gold-threaded mulham cloth of Merv, were shipped outside the province (Bosworth 1998, 116). These indications seem to show that average income levels, market output, and international trade were less developed in the Ghaznavid than, e.g., in the Samanid era. All in all, Ghaznavid rule appears to correspond to that of a despotic power state, with more arbitrary practices and less respect for rules than its predecessors.

3.3.4.3 The Khitan-Liao and the Xixia Empires (Early Tenth–Early Thirteenth Centuries): Tribute Extractors from Song China

The Khitans were a nomadic people of Mongol origin, probably distant descendants of the Xianbei. The Khitans had defeated the Kyrgyz state in Mongolia in 917 (that, in turn, had previously destroyed the Uighur Empire in 840).[43] Following the collapse of the Tang, in a few decades, the Khitan erected a sprawling polity encompassing all of Mongolia, Manchuria, lower Amur, and Pacific territories as well as parts of Northern China, including Beijing. The ruling elite and parts of the Khitan rank and file soon adopted Chinese customs in some aspects of their culture, if less so in their military practices. The nomadic conquerors, having chosen their residence in Northern China, officially adopted the Chinese language and the Buddhist religion and called themselves Liao dynasty. Historians have identified them as the Khitan-Liao dynasty or Empire (946–1125). In China, the Khitans' name survived as "Khitay," which Marco Polo introduced to medieval Europe, who in turn called China "Cathay." In Russian, the name "Kitay" for the Middle Kingdom has survived until today. The Khitans also changed rapidly from being a purely pastoral nomadic people to one with farming, fortified towns, iron foundries, and weaving factories, most or all adopted from the Chinese (Roux 2000, 140; Ponting 2001, 380).

In about 1030, the Tanguts, a pastoral people related to the Tibetans and stemming from the Ordos Plateau (an elevated steppe plain surrounded by the giant horseshoe bend of the Huanghe/Yellow River and the Great Wall), defeated the Yellow Uighurs. The Tanguts also conquered key SR trading cities and in 1038 established the Xixia Empire (1038–1227), which, like its predecessor, the state of the Yellow Uighurs, straddled the Hexi corridor (Gansu). Like the Khitans, the Tanguts had nomadic and sedentary people under their sway and became at least superficially sinicized.

Given domestic Chinese political weaknesses and lasting military hostilities with the Khitan-Liao and the Xixia, which included numerous raids and razzias of these forces inside China, the Song dynasty (960–1279) concluded peace treaties with both border empires, in which China was obliged to make regular tribute payments to both. In the treaty of Chanyuan (1004), the Song promised to pay annually 200,000 bolts of silk and 100,000 ounces of silver to the Liao; in a treaty revision of 1042, the tribute amounts were adjusted upwards (to 300,000 bolts of silk and 200,000 ounces of silver). The treaty signed with the Tanguts provided for annual shipments of 135,000 bolts of silk, 72,000 ounces of silver, and 30,000 pounds of tea (Connaissances generales en histoire chinoise 2006, 119; Ponting 2001, 380).

The Khitan-Liao, but even more so the Xixia, controlled what remained of overland trade with CA and

---

[43] The Kyrgyz migrated back to their earlier homelands in southern Siberia (Altay/Sayan region), but also moved to the Tienshan, where they became mountain nomads and practiced transhumance.

further west (Paul 2012, 175). The Xixia also enriched themselves by smuggling Chinese salt. Shiba states that most of the silver paid by the Song to the Liao returned to China to settle regular market trade surpluses that prevailed with both of the border empires (Findlay and O'Rourke 2007, 102). This, however, would not exclude the possibility of surpluses of tributary silk being channeled on to the SR and marketed further west (following traditional nomad practices going back to the Xiongnu and the Turks).

Notwithstanding recurrent political turbulences, and despite the drain of tribute payments to the nomads, the period was an economic heyday for China, as mentioned earlier. Yet, the Song dynasty's Achilles heel appears to have been defense: Not measuring up to new nomadic invaders—the Jurchen that had just wiped out the Khitan-Liao Empire in 1125—the Song emperors were forced not only to pay tribute to new overlords but in addition to cede large parts of central China in 1142 (including the entire Huanghe basin) to the Jurchen, which founded the Jin dynasty, which, in turn, swiftly became sinicized.

3.3.4.4 The Seljukids (1038–1194): Sprawling Empire Supports SR Trade but Breaks Up Due to Domestic Structural Flaws

The Seljuk Empire was named after Seljuk ibn Dudak, a tribal chief of the Oghuz, and his descendants. According to Khazanov, it was a chain reaction of events and the unexpected weakness of Middle Eastern states that led to the creation of the Seljuk Empire (1983/1994, 264). Political instability in the Oghuz state (in the lower Syr Daria and the Aral region) may have contributed to the splitting off of some tribes and their migration southward in search of new territories. The southward movement brought the Oghuz (including Turkmen) tribes into Ghaznavid Khorassan in 1035, where their herds devastated the agriculture of many oases: the nomads took livestock from peasants and laid waste to fields. Their depredations also disrupted long-distance commerce. The Seljuk campaigns of conquest triggered a temporary economic decline of the conquered areas. And the Ghaznavid sultan's no longer state-of-the-art, ponderous, conventional-type Islamic army was defeated in May 1040 by some 16,000 Turkmen mounted warrior nomads (Bosworth 1998, 109).

Through superior military power and successful diplomacy, Seljuk and his descendants by the mid-eleventh century had acquired possession or suzerainty over vast lands in CA and the Middle East (Iran, Iraq, Anatolia, Azerbaijan, Khorassan, Margiana, Khwarazm, Mavarannahr, Bactria, Ferghana) including many towns on the SR (Map 3.5). The Battle of Manzikert (Eastern Anatolia) in 1071 even brought the Seljuk Sultanate's victory over the Byzantine Empire and opened the gate to Turkic penetration of Asia Minor (Soucek 2000, 95).[44]

The Seljuks followed the conquering nomad practice of senior members of the ruling family sharing out governorships and administrative territories. Thus, in 1066, various districts in CA were awarded as appanages to Seljuk princes, e.g., Khwarazm, Balkh/Bactria, Merv/Margiana, etc. As usual, conquest altered the composition of ruling classes and led to redistribution of available land. The new (Oghuz) Turkic nomadic aristocracy put pressure on what remained of the old, settled, primarily Iranian nobility. But there was also some redistribution from the Karakhanid and Ghaznavid nomadic aristocracy that had taken possession of land about half a century earlier. Sedentary peasants remained the basic dependent and exploited class (Khazanov 1983/1994, 264, 267).

The new rulers established Merv as the capital of their sprawling empire, which was governed from the central great divan, the sultans' executive organ, presided over by the great vizier. The Seljuks relied on the services of local Khorassanian secretaries and officials (just as the Karakhanids and Ghaznavids had had recourse to the former bureaucratic staff of the Samanids). These civil servants did the actual running of the extensive lands their new rulers controlled (Sevim and Bosworth 1998, 153). After the destructions that had accompanied the conquests and as far as temporary political stability allowed, the Seljuk dynasty attempted to shape the relationship between tax revenues and agricultural income in a favorable way through carrying out investment projects in agricultural and irrigation technologies. Probably as a result, farming did recover under the Seljuks (Feldbauer and Liedl 2008, 110–111).

The new rulers even presided over a degree of urban renewal and, given the size of the empire, a stimulation of overland trade. Merv benefitted from its new role as center of public administration and service activities. Lying on the trunk line of the SR network, the city also flourished as a center of trade, industry, and culture. Moreover, in the twelfth century, a specific institution existed in Merv, the Dviekush, where technical procedures of silk production could be learned. Agriculture in Margiana thrived (Soucek 2000, 96; Liu 2010, 107).

Financing infrastructural development, but first and foremost the large Seljuk armed forces, which had conquered a far-flung empire in a short time, was onerous. The armed forces consisted of two basic elements: first, a professional, highly-disciplined standing army, essentially made up of ghulams, well equipped with cavalry, and supported by a generous system of iqtas, and second: contingents of free

---

[44] Almost four centuries later (in 1453), descendants of the Seljuks put an end to Byzantium and gave birth to the Ottoman state.

troops (mercenaries) of the Seljuks' original supporters, the Oghuz and Turkmen warrior nomads (Sevim and Bosworth 1998, 160; Ducellier et al. 2012, 194).

The eventual downfall of Seljuk power was the result of an explosion of discontent particularly among Oghuz/Turkmen nomads that had moved to the Iranian Plateau, the upper Amu Daria Basin, and other southern oasis regions. As Sevim and Bosworth noted, the sultans had always felt certain obligations toward these kinsfolk of theirs, who had contributed to bringing the Seljuks to power in the first place (1998, 166). The authorities therefore made special administrative arrangements for the Oghuz immigrants in the regions where they had become particularly numerous: special shihnas (chiefs) were appointed to act as channels of communication between the nomads, the local sedentary population, and the Seljuk state, whose more and more prevailing Perso-Islamic ethos had become largely alien to the Turkmens (Amitai 2001, 155). Thus, one could argue that the Seljuk authorities were attempting to establish or secure a nomadic state of the second type, as defined by Khazanov (see below).

While the burden of substantial taxation fell on sedentaries and nomads alike, the nomads remained in a relatively privileged position. Still, the Oghuz in the upper Amu Daria regions of Khuttalan and Balkh eventually rebelled against the tax demands and the heavy-handed collecting methods employed. Punitive expeditions of the authorities were to no avail, and victorious Oghuz bands swept through Khorassan, attacking and plundering several towns and reserving particular violence for members of the Seljuk administration and representatives of religious institutions closely linked to the state. The bands brought renewed destruction (e.g., wrecking of mosques and madrasas (schools, high institutions of learning in the Islamic world) and vandalizing of important libraries in Nishapur). In the mid-twelfth century, the Seljuks—weakened by internecine strife—were defeated by yet another originally Eurasian steppe tribe, the Karakhitay (Sevim and Bosworth 1998, 166, 174).

3.3.4.5 The Polovtsy/Kipchaks Vis-à-Vis the Rus (Mid-eleventh to Early Thirteenth Centuries)

The Kipchak nomadic confederation was primarily a steppe state that, after conquering Oghuz territories between the Aral and Caspian seas, in the mid-eleventh century incorporated previous Pecheneg territories on the Pontic grasslands. Thus, a powerful nomadic polity of considerable size (stretching from the Aral Sea basin to the Carpathians) emerged. The extensive steppe belt ruled by the Kipchaks was soon called Desht-i-Kipchak (Kipchak prairies, Cummings 2012, 21). The confederation of the Polovtsy (as the Kipchaks were called in Eastern Europe) retained its mostly pastoral basis, in which the nomadic population of whatever origin paid taxes based on the size of their herds;

they paid far less than the conquered settled people on the fringes of the Southern Rus (Oskolkov and Oskolkova 2004, 16; Ponting 2001, 441).

Within their state the Polovtsy typically nomadized large distances in a north-south direction. Baipakov, Kumekov, and Pischulina give some examples: some communities spent the winter in Ustyurt and Mangyshlak and in the summer went to the plains of the rivers Emba, Sagyza, and Yaik (Ural) (Caspian Lowlands). Or from the northern shore of the Caspian Sea, other groups nomadized in the summer to the valleys of the Volga and the smaller and bigger Uzen (just east of the lower Volga) (Baipakov et al. 1997, 26). But among the Polovtsy, there were also farmers and craftsmen and increasing numbers of Muslims. The central Kipchak encampments were situated on the lower Volga, approx. where the Khazars had established their capital Itil.

Commerce with the Volga Bulgars and beyond them with the principalities of the Northern Rus was carried out on the river ("Great Volga route"/"Veliky volzhsky put"). Over-land routes served as connections (west) to Kiev and Central Europe and (southeast) to Khorezm. Maritime trade with Byzantium and Anatolia (the Seljuk Sultanate of Rum) mostly proceeded through the port of Sudak/Sogdaya (on the Crimean coast and under Byzantine jurisdiction). The trade (transit) taxes levied on merchandise constituted a considerable part of the confederation's revenue (though it must have been a smaller share than it had been in Khazaria, which had entertained less persistently tense relations with its neighbors). Among Russian and Volga Bulgarian merchandise that transited the Kipchak steppe were furs (most frequently), bows and arrows, other weapons, tree bark, amber, tanned hides, honey, nuts, livestock, and slaves (Oskolkov and Oskolkova 2004, 16; Roux 2000, 182).

Given the Polovtsy's threatening military stance, the Kiev Rus, whose trading and settlement interests clashed with the Kipchak confederation, took recourse to various strategies to master the situation. As O'Rourke observes, these strategies resembled the methods used by China in dealing with its nomadic neighbors, if on a smaller scale: warfare, bribes, subsidies, alliances, and royal marriages were all applied to foster links with nomadic societies of the steppe and make relations easier to manage. Despite sizable costs, these strategies seem to have broadly worked until the Mongol invasions of the thirteenth century (O'Rourke 2007, 24).

Around the middle of the eleventh century—approximately at the same time as the Polovtsy expanded west from the Volga to the Danube and took possession of what was later called Southern Ukraine and Moldavia—the Kiev Rus had attained a first peak of its development. Later, the Rus was more and more affected by particular interests of individual constituent principalities; these centrifugal tendencies were temporarily interrupted by the Great Prince Vladimir Monomach (1113–1125), who once again re-established the "Unity of the Rus." In the south, the Crusades (of Western Christianity) eroded Constantinople's hegemony in the Eastern Mediterranean. The Northern Italian cities (particularly Venice and Genoa), which had around the turn of the millennium established commercial bases in large parts of the Mediterranean and on the shores of the Black Sea, now aggressively entered trade intermediation between the Orient and the west (Karger (ed) 1978, 62–63).

These developments were also a blow to the commercial intermediary position of the Rus which remained under military pressure from the Kipchak steppe. Neither the great prince of Kiev nor the emperor of Byzantium had the means at their disposal to effectively contain the Polovtsy. Persisting Kipchak incursions into the Eastern Slavic principalities were major recurrent topics of the old Russian chronicles. The annals of Kiev registered no less than 50 major raids into Rus territories between 1061 and 1210, not counting smaller razzias. The steppe enemy, so the sources recorded, even attacked armed peasants carrying out their daily work on the fields, burnt down their villages, and took away their wives and children to slavery (Roux 2000, 182; Karger (ed) 1978, 62–63).

Persistent warlike conflicts culminated in the de-facto evacuation of some border territories in the middle reaches of the Dnepr, which roughly corresponds to the center of what later became Ukraine. The term "ukraina" (Ukraine) signifies "borderlands." As Kappeler explains, since the Middle Ages this term has stood for the region on the fringes of the grasslands which separate the world of the settled farmers (Rus) from that of the nomadic pastoralists. "Borderlands" toward the steppe also meant—from the viewpoint of the settled population—defense against invasions of warrior nomads, as well as continuous interaction with the world of mounted archers and of Islam (Kappeler 2003, 15).

3.3.5 Reshuffling of Power on the Eve of the Mongol Invasion (Mid-twelfth–Early Thirteenth Century)

3.3.5.1 The Karakhitay (Western Liao Empire, 1130–1218): Strong SR Orientation, Heavy Taxation of Settled Cultures

The Jurchen, a Tunguz people from Manchuria, were enlisted as allies by the Song against the Khitan-Liao. In the early twelfth century, the Jurchen defeated the Khitan-Liao Empire, broke its rule over Northern China, and founded the Jin dynasty (see also above).[45] The expansion of the Jurchen triggered new migration movements in CA:

Some groups of the defeated Mongol Khitan reportedly reverted back to pure nomadism and moved west. In 1130 they arrived in Beiting/Beshbalik, turned the Kingdom of Qocho into a vassal state, and over time mixed with Turkic-speaking local population. The Khitan now called themselves Karakhitay (Black Khitan), in 1137 beat the Karakhanids, and in 1141 defeated the Seljuks and conquered Mavarannahr. In the 1130s, the Karakhitay state—also called Western Liao Empire—was proclaimed. Greater mobility, together with superior maneuvering of mounted archers, and high discipline, had carried the day for the Karakhitay. In the mid-twelfth century, their leader and conqueror Yelue Dashi ruled East Turkestan and large parts of West Turkestan north of the Amu Daria (Krieger 2003, 260; Soucek 2000, 99).

While they were essentially (resuscitated and partly Turkicized) Mongol nomads, at least the Karakhitay elite spoke Chinese, the court used Chinese script, and the conquerors' dominant religion was Buddhism. Western Liao copper coins were minted on a Chinese pattern and carried Chinese characters. The Liao replaced the Karakhan and established their capital in Balasagun (the former Karakhanid capital). As Sinor remarked, an alien culture was thus superimposed on the local population, the vast majority of which was Muslim, speaking a Turkic or Iranian language (1998, 239).

Perhaps due to this Chinese background, unlike the Karakhanids, the new conquerors did not dole out appanages to their princes. At the same time, neither did Yelue Dashi set up a centralized bureaucratic state in the region. On the contrary, Karakhitay governance of its subjugated lands remained indirect (at arm's length) to the extreme (Millward and Perdue 2004, 43). The ruler of the empire was called gurkhan—a composite of the conventional term khan and adjective guer (universal), a term that would reappear in the Mongol Empire. While the south of the new state (on both sides of the Tienshan) consisted of (at least partly) sedentary polities obliged to pay tribute, the north (Semirechie and Dzungaria), which belonged to the Eurasian steppe belt, became the actual Karakhitay nomadic territory, where the new rulers pastured most of their herds (Khazanov 1983/1994, 258).[46]

The Western Liao, whose territory accommodated all major branches of the SR, whether they ran through the northern steppes to the Black Sea and Constantinople, through the southern oases to Baghdad and the Levant, or across the mountains to Punjab and India, incurred

---

[45] "Jin" means "gold" in Chinese, from which the word "China" is derived (Der Große Ploetz 2008, 676).

[46] Semirechie (Zhetysu) actually also featured several dozen agricultural and trade settlements (some of which had been founded by the Sogdians centuries ago). These do not appear to have been substantially damaged by the Karakhitay nomadic presence.

considerable expenditures to protect these routes and facilitate what remained of transcontinental trade. The Liao also added a long-distance postal system, the Yam—another precursor to an (albeit much larger) Mongol institution (Burbank and Cooper 2010, 97). Local rulers enjoyed almost complete autonomy as long as they recognized the overlordship of the gurkhan and paid their dues and tributes. For instance, the Khwarazm shah (head of a locally ruling Turkic family) was forced to pay an annual tribute of 3000 golden dinars to the Karakhitay authorities. As long as the prescribed tribute arrived punctually in Balasagun, the Liao suzerains were little disposed to interfere in Khorezmian, Uighur, or Karakhanid affairs. In vivid contrast to some of their Muslim vassals, the gurkhans followed a policy of religious tolerance, yet again a feature characteristic of the Mongol era (Sinor 1998, 239–240).

Even though the Liao authorities made few adjustments at the local level, local elites chafed against the oppressive tributes imposed on them. By the end of the twelfth century, unrest broke out throughout the Tarim Basin, Semirechie, and Mavarannahr. In Qocho in 1209, the Uighurs revolted, and their ruler pledged loyalty to the approaching Genghis Khan (Millward and Perdue 2004, 44).

3.3.5.2 The Ghurids (ca. 1175–1206)/The Emerging Sultanate of Delhi

Back in the mid-twelfth century, the Afghan province of Ghur, a rugged mountain region on both sides of the Hari Rud river, to the east of Herat, featured only scattered population pockets, some of whom were protected by elevated fortresses and towers. The regional advance of Islam, its cultural institutions, and the conversion of Ghur took a considerable time. Missionary activity came from Ghaznavid Khorassan. In the second half of the twelfth century, Ghurid armies ousted the Ghaznavids from their core possessions in Afghanistan (Ghazna) and Northern India (Lahore). From 1175, having overthrown Mahmud's successors, Muhammad Ghori expanded his power in India. At the beginning of the thirteenth century, the Ghurid state extended almost 3000 km from Herat in Afghanistan via Delhi (Hindustan) to Lakhnawti (Bengal, Eastern India) and stretched from the borders of Tibet and Kashmir all the way down the Indus river to the coast of Arabian Sea (Nizami 1998a, 177–184).

The decisive cause for this success, as in so many cases in CA, was military superiority: First, the Ghurids had iron and horses in abundance[47]; second, the Ghurid sultans disposed of a nucleus of Ghurid and Khalji warriors from the mountainous core of the empire; third, this fierce—but small—

force was supplemented by the acquisition of Turkic military slaves. As Nizami explains, with all these forces, the sultans were able to make headway in Northern India against the vigorous resistance of the Rajput[48] and the armies of the Indian princes (Nizami 1998a, 188).

Ghurid political authority, initially organized on a patriarchal basis with strong tribal traditions in an almost inaccessible mountain region, acquired some of the features of a state and briefly turned into one of the major empires in the Islamic Middle Ages. The Ghazna region had for two centuries followed the traditions of a Turco-Iranian monarchy. And Hindustan featured a decentralized feudal-like system of government. Thus, the sprawling Ghurid Empire united some quite heterogeneous cultural traditions. The vizier was the head of the civil Ghurid administration. The qadi al-qudat (supreme judge) led the judiciary, with numerous lower-ranking qadis, including a qadi for the army (Nizami 1998a, 186–188).

The Ghurids devastated Ghazna, but in India their role was more constructive. Contrary to the Ghaznavids, the Ghurids did not regularly loot India through plunder raids but ruled the region on an iqta basis: After the conquest of Punjab and Hindustan, the institution of iqta (conditional possession for service, revenue assignment) was successfully introduced in India and helped the integration of feudal units into a centrally organized state structure. In the wake of the Ghurid invasions, Islam spread from its foothold in the extreme northwest of South Asia into much wider regions. Intellectual and scholarly links between India and CA also intensified during this period. According to Nizami, while Ghurid power in its own Afghan homelands eventually waned, the state's Indian territories flourished and paved the way for the emergence of the Delhi Sultanate. In 1206, Qutbuddin Aibak, a Ghurid general who had risen from slave status, broke loose from his hierarchy and established the Sultanate of Delhi. This was to be the most powerful state in Northern India until 1526, when Babur's invasion replaced it with the Mughal Empire (Nizami 1998a, 185–190; Overy (ed) 2004, 146).

3.3.5.3 The Khorezm Shahs (1097–1221): Heyday for the Local Oasis Economy

Although it constituted a major SR intersection, its remote location (on three sides surrounded by desert steppe and on the fourth by an inland sea) probably rendered it easier for Khorezm to remain independent or at least autonomous for extended periods of time. In the eleventh and twelfth centuries—initially under Ghaznavid, then Seljuk, then

---

[47] The Ghurids controlled iron deposits in the mountain ranges of Afghanistan and were skillful in processing the metal (Paul 2012, 177).

[48] The Rajput were originally a warrior people that from the seventh century dominated regions in Northwestern India, which today make up the state of Rajasthan (Le petit Mourre 2003, 958).

Karakhitay suzerainty—Khorezm experienced an economic and cultural upturn. The Khorezmian economy was dominated by highly developed farming, which had unfolded on the basis of an extensive irrigation network featuring canals, ditches, dams, water mills, and other installations. Khwarazm's cultivated zone stretched out far from the Amu Daria to the west and to the east. Here wheat, barley, millet, rice, cotton, fruit, wine, and melons were harvested. The towns of the region also witnessed dynamic craftsmanship and industrial activities. In the eleventh and twelfth centuries, Khorezm remained an important trading hub for shipments to and from the Volga area, the Kievan Rus, Transoxiana, China, and Iran. Dried fruit, grain, rice, carpets, silver, saddles, leather products, and fabrics were Khwarazm's prime export articles (Shukow et al. 1957/1963, Band 3, 548).

At the beginning of the eleventh century, Urgench, the capital of Khwarazm (under Ghaznavid rule), was one of the most beautiful and best laid-out cities in the Orient and an important cultural center. Excellent scholars of the oriental countries, including Ibn Sina/Avicenna and Al-Biruni, temporarily lived at the court of the Khwarazm shah. The fragmentation of the Seljuk Empire and the relaxed suzerainty of the Western Liao (Khorezm being the westernmost corner of their polity) finally allowed the Khwarazm shahs to shake off foreign domination. In turn, these rulers themselves put together a powerful and sprawling—if short-lived—empire in the late twelfth and early thirteenth century. In order to pursue their conquests successfully and strengthen their authority over the lands that they had conquered, the Khwarazm shahs drew many neighboring nomadic Kipchaks (Polovtsy) into their army of 300,000 soldiers and arranged marriages with Kipchak chiefs. In little time the shahs subjugated Margiana, Samarkand, most of Mavarannahr, Khorassan, and large parts of Western Persia. Although conquered regions paid tribute, the far-flung empire actually was hardly more than a conglomeration of quickly amassed provinces and lacked a real backbone of an organized state (Khazanov 1983/1994, 214; Knobloch 1999, 40).

In any case, the region of Khwarazm continued to flourish agriculturally. The geographer and traveler Yaqut, writing just before the Mongol razing of Khwarazm, remarked that when he had been in Urgench in 1219, he had never seen a richer or more attractive town in the world, and he found the Khorezmian countryside extraordinarily fertile, filled with settlements which had markets and an abundance of food. Soviet excavations there seem to show a wide extension of cultivation based on irrigation canals during the twelfth century (Sevim and Bosworth 1998, 175). The shah undertook the rebuilding of parts of Samarkand, including the city wall, the citadel, and other government buildings.

Prior to the Mongol conquest, there was a sizable Jewish community (estimates vary from 5000 to 50,000) in Samarkand, still the largest city of CA, as well as in Bukhara. Jews were largely occupied in trade and commerce as well as in medicine (Roudik 2007, 35–37). While the economy certainly flourished in parts of the state of the Khwarazm shahs, the persistent need for money and resources to uphold military control and defense capabilities led to much hardship and disaffection, certainly outside the region of Khwarazm itself (Sevim and Bosworth 1998, 175). Such was, of course, nothing unique to this heterogeneous empire.

3.3.6 The Subdued SR in the Period Between the Demise of the Caliphate and the Mongol Expansion

While the breakup of the caliphate and of Tang China had contributed to the decline of the SR, its temporary recovery in the tenth century was favored by C Asian (mostly Samanid, but also Uighur, Khazar, and other states') economic policies that supported stability, growth, prosperity, and (international) trade. But this positive constellation or coincidence soon gave way to a sequence of Turkic and Mongol invasions from the late tenth century, an increase of the number of economic crises in various regions of the Islamic world, a decline of security of trade in the Pontic steppes (Dikoe pole/Wild Field), and China's politically and technologically driven reorientation toward overseas trade.

Most previously existing SR connections were still used, while the links from Mavarannahr (Transoxiana) northwest via Khorezm (south of Aral Sea) to the Volga and from Mavarannahr southwest via Merv, Nishapur, Hamadan to Baghdad appear to have accounted for the lion's share of traffic. Connections through East Turkestan/Xinjiang (north via Almalik, Beshbalik/Beiting, Hami, or south via Aqsu, Qocho, Hami) to China also worked, but less intensively. The same goes for the routes to India (typically Bukhara or Samarkand–Balkh–Ghazna–Lahore–Delhi), which were non-operative during Ghaznavid plunder raids. Weaker traffic also characterized the "steppe route" from Shash (Tashkent) via Otrar and Yengikent (northeast of Aral Sea) to the Volga.

3.4 From Large-Scale Devastation to the Third Climax of the Great Silk Road: CA in the Mongol Empire (Early Thirteenth to Mid-fourteenth Centuries)

For the following subchapter, the author has primarily drawn from publications by Rafis Abazov, Janet Abu-Lughod, Karl Baipakov, Thomas Barfield, Gerard Chaliand, E.A. Davidovich, A.H. Dani, Ronald Findlay, Charles

Halperin, Peter Jackson, Andreas Kappeler, Ralph Kauz, Anatoly Khazanov, Karenina Kollmar-Paulenz, B.E. Kumekov, Chantal Lemercier-Quelquejay, Jim Masselos, Timothy May, David Morgan, Kevin O'Rourke, K.A. Pischulina, Morris Rossabi, Jean-Paul Roux, and Shen Fuwei.

3.4.1 Wide-Range Destruction and Empire Building (1206–1240s)

3.4.1.1 The Mongol State and Its Military Technology Under Genghis Khan

The Mongols are linguistically related to the Turkic and Tunguz peoples, within the great family of Altaic languages (which also include Japanese and Korean). The Mongol tribes typically nomadized along the breadth of the Eurasian steppe in Mongolia, which also included some hilly and mountainous terrain, in a north-south direction. The summer camps in the north were typically called "yailaq" and winter camps in the south "qishlaq" (Masson-Smith 2003, 3).

As Khazanov points out, there seem to be foundations for the suggestion that the balance between productivity of pastures, number of livestock, and population size was upset among the Mongols in the late twelfth century. Extended dry spells combined with a renewed sharp decline of temperatures in the twelfth century may have led to a worsening of grazing conditions, giving rise to something akin to demographic pressure and overpopulation in the area (Khazanov 1983/1994, 235; see also Vogelsang 2013, 66, 348). Thus an ecological crisis may have triggered a demographic one, which is likely to have intensified competition of nomadic groups for pastures—a possibility pointed out in a more general framework by Schwarz (2004, 188). Moreover, transcontinental trade, which was highly valued by the Mongols, had already declined for one to two centuries (Roux 1993, 455).

At the top of the traditional Mongol tribal structure was the tribal chief, the khan, who might also preside over a tribal confederation. Nomadic military aristocracy, the princes (noyons), ruled over tribal fractions or clans or possibly over entire tribes. The largest part of the nomadic society was made up of the class of free men and women. All free men were available as warriors (noekers). Finally, the class of collective (non-private) serfs and slaves comprised members of defeated tribes, prisoners of war and their descendants, assigned to regimes of forced labor. At the beginning of the thirteenth century, shamanism was the dominating religion among the Mongols (Lemercier-Quelquejay 1970, 16–17).

After some decades of internal rivalries and warfare against the background of a precarious economic situation on the Mongol steppe, a united nomadic state was established in 1206. That year, the meeting of the tribal chiefs, the kuriltay, proclaimed Temuejin, a lesser nobleman and tribal leader in Eastern Mongolia, Genghis Khan or supreme leader of the Mongols. Occupying the position of Great Khan, Genghis towered over all Mongol tribal khans and princes. Genghis is said to have adhered to a universalistic vision which some historians ascribe to an ideology claiming a mandate from heaven to rule the world (Soucek 2000, 105). In a nutshell, Genghisid messianism could be captured in the formula: "One sun in the sky, one sovereign on earth" (Lemercier-Quelquejay 1970, 67).

Genghis Khan deliberately broke down tribal barriers: The structure of the united Mongol military as well as of the state was reorganized, based on the decimal system. Not tribes and clans but tumens (or tümens, units of ten thousand), units of a thousand, units of a hundred, and units of ten warriors,[49] and their commanders became the basic components of the polity. The tumens and other decimal units had the duty to supply the respective number of fighting men for the army (these are to be regarded as approximate numbers).[50] All senior leaders were made imperial appointees. The essence of this centralizing reform was that noyons (noblemen) no longer held positions within tribal hierarchies but as leaders of tumens or other units, or they received responsibilities at the imperial court. In any case, they became servants of the supreme leader. Noyons of tumen and of units of a thousand exercised the right of disposal over pastures. Noyons' titles to their tumens tended to become hereditary, but the supreme leader could revoke these rights in case of wrongdoings or negligence.

Actually, a tumen or the corresponding region (area of nomadization) did not only consist of about 10,000 men but of perhaps around 40,000 people with 600,000 animals (Turnbull 2008, 72). Once the assignment of an individual or a family to a unit was decided, this individual or family was not allowed to change to another unit. Genghis Khan's military-political system thus broke up the upper segments of the traditional tribal society and political organization of Mongol nomads and partially reshuffled their subdivisions, thus combating the threat of tribalist or clan-based

---

[49] In German called Zehntausendschaften, Tausendschaften, Hundertschaften, Zehnergruppen.

[50] Genghis Khan had not invented the decimal system of structuring the armed forces; it had a long tradition in the steppe empires, starting with the Xiongnu. For example, it was also applied by the Khitan, which ruled northern China as the Liao dynasty. Genghis Khan's innovation was to extend this principle of military organization to the entire society and state (Masselos (ed) 2010, 32).

separatism (Khazanov 1983/1994, 239).[51] Warriors were (supposed to be) united by common ideals and their loyalty to the leader. Later on, in the midst of military expansion (see below), the need to effectively govern an already sprawling empire led to the foundation of its capital in 1220, the city of Karakorum in the center of Mongolia (in the Orkhon river basin).[52]

The Mongols' victories and long-lasting military supremacy over their adversaries, particularly of the sedentary world, were achieved through a mixture of technological and institutional superiority of warfare and better training of soldiers. Thanks to their brilliant horsemanship, Genghis Khan's cavalry armies were extremely mobile, possessed devastating striking power, and were able to mount bewildering flank attacks and encirclements (Overy (ed) 2004, 143).[53] The Mongols' composite bow had a range of about 75 meters, which gave them a distinct advantage over all their rivals whose bows had a range of about 40–50 m. Soldiers (and society) were subject to ruthless and iron discipline. Boys were trained on horseback from a very young age. Genghis and his sons' and successors' bold strategies and charismatic leadership also played a role (Rossabi 2012, 12).

Moreover, the Mongols quickly learned effective techniques of warfare from other peoples, e.g., they upgraded their siegecraft through recruitment of Chinese engineers and experts. Meanwhile, other nomads could only raid around walled fortifications. It was from Chinese examples that the Mongols apparently also acquired the capability to use gunpowder in siege warfare. Genghis Khan's military possessed battering rams and catapults capable of shooting projectiles of up to 70 kg, pots of burning liquid, explosives, and incendiary materials. The Mongols' intelligence and spy networks worked well. Last but not least: Because Mongol women could, with little effort, assume men's herding duties, most of the men could be mobilized for warfare; women thus played a crucial and

possibly decisive indirect role in the military successes (Rossabi 2012, 11–12; Chaliand 1995, 135).

The Mongol invaders accepted total submission. Mongol peace conditions essentially corresponded to the request of unconditional surrender of the enemy. Unconditional surrender assured inhabitants their life but not their property. Storming was fatal: in this case most or all able-bodied men were put to the sword, and their families were enslaved. Craftsmen, doctors, artists, and scholars passed into the ownership of the khans or noyons, who had them deported to their workshops where these enslaved specialists were put to work (Töpfer et al. 1985, 191). Unlike the Turkic tribes, the Mongols—at least initially—were not interested in settling in cities and did not perceive urban centers as potential sources of long-term revenue or economic value added. As opposed to pastures, they did not value farmlands and irrigation systems; thus, in many instances, agricultural lands and infrastructure were systematically destroyed to make place for grasslands. However, over time, Mongol attitudes to dependent sedentary areas evolved and the latter came to be seen as useful adjuncts to the steppe polity.

3.4.1.2 Mongol Conquests and Colossal Damages and Losses in Central Asia

The Mongols' first "wave" of military expansion was carried out under the reigns of Genghis Khan (1206–1227) and his son Ögöday Khan (1229–1241). Given the Mongols' military superiority over practically all the civilizations and states they encountered throughout most of the thirteenth and the first decades of the fourteenth century, the Mongols' request of unconditional surrender left rulers and communities with two possibilities: either give up without a fight and face possible large-scale enslavement or face destruction, slaughter, and possible annihilation. A third possibility of somehow saving oneself and holding one's ground without surrendering only applied in exceptional cases where events were shaped by nonmilitary factors.

The Mongols first sought and quickly gained or reaffirmed control over Siberian territories to the north of Mongolia inhabited by neighboring forest dwellers. These latter typically constituted small nomadic tribes of reindeer herders and caribou hunters. The goal was, among other things, to exact furs and other forest products. In 1207, Kyrgyz begs (local rulers)[54] in the Altay, Sayan and Tienshan ranges submitted to Genghis Khan. Similarly, because the Uighur king of Qocho submitted his declaration of allegiance in time (1209), his realm (including Urumqi, Beshbalik, Kucha, and the Turfan area) was

---

[51] Genghis Khan's breaking up of tribalist structures may bear a distant resemblance to the restructuring of French territorial administration into a large number of départements after the revolution of 1789. These départements were (theoretically) only arranged according to geographic features (were named after rivers, mountain chains, peninsulas, etc.) and to a functionalist logic (every inhabitant of a département should be able to reach its territorial capital (chef-lieu), carry out business there for a couple of hours, and return again in a horse-drawn carriage within one day). The départements were to put an end to traditional historical regions, a legacy of feudalism. However, in the framework of the décentralisation since 1982, French regions reappeared (as amalgamations of départements).

[52] More precisely, the city was founded on the location of Genghis' principal encampment (from the early 1200s).

[53] As Barfield put it, the Mongols developed a Blitzkrieg approach to warfare, which is still studied by modern military strategists (Barfield 1989/1992, 202).

---

[54] These were the descendants of the Kyrgyz that had defeated the Uighur state in Mongolia in 840 and themselves had been overwhelmed by the Khitans in 917.

relatively well treated and preserved its original boundaries (Geng 1998, 203) (see Map 3.7). What is more, large numbers of educated Uighurs entered Genghis Khan's services as civil servants and provided administrative expertise which the initially illiterate Mongol nomads lacked. With the assistance of Uighur scholars, the Sogdo-Uighur-Mongol script was developed and used for imperial communication.

In contrast to the behavior of his neighbors, the Jurchen (Jin) ruler in Northern China did not submit to Genghis but responded militarily and fought the Mongols. As a consequence, the region was subjected to a series of destructive campaigns over a period of 25 years (Rossabi 2012, 64). Beijing was conquered and sacked with great loss of life and partially destroyed in 1215. Manchuria bowed to Genghis Khan a year later. The Karakhitay Empire (including Balasagun, Zhetysu, Dzungaria, and the Western Tarim Basin), which had until 1209 held suzerainty over the Uighurs, accepted Mongol overlordship almost without opposition in 1218.

At this time, the other important C Asian power apart from Mongolia was the state of the Khorezm shahs which had just expanded and become a territorially large empire a few years before (see Sect. 3.3.5.3). The even swifter Mongol expansion was certainly a challenge for the Khorezm shah Muhammad. His troops attacked and massacred a Mongol trade caravan sent by Genghis Khan; moreover, the shah's soldiers killed the envoy dispatched to protest the assault. The Mongol leader regarded this behavior as a heinous crime that demanded punishment and as a casus belli. As the event had happened in 1218 in Otrar, it was called the Otrar incident, which triggered (or served as pretext for) the large-scale devastation of Western CA (1219–1223).

In 1219, Otrar was leveled. In 1220, the famous cities of Mavarannahr and Khwarazm—at that time under the Khorezm shah's rule—Bukhara, Samarkand, Termez, and Urgench all fell with great loss of life (Barfield 1989/1992, 201). The conquest of Bukhara ended in the slaughter of nearly half of the civilian population and the enslavement of most of the rest. Then the city was burnt to the ground. The downfall of Samarkand is reported to have featured a reduction in the number of its inhabitants from 400,000 to 100,000. After prolonged resistance, almost the entire population of Urgench, the capital of Khwarazm, was massacred. Moreover, the sophisticated network of irrigation dams supporting the oasis was destroyed, triggering an environmental catastrophe for the area. Dzhent, on the lower reaches of the Syr Daria, was also destroyed. Khodzhent, the western gateway to Ferghana, resisted bitterly and was razed. Many other towns in the Ferghana Basin (e.g., Andijan) and the Zerafshan valley were savagely pillaged or burnt. After the demolition of Tashkent, the site of the town reportedly remained empty until the following century (Roudik 2007, 33, 41).

In 1221 the Mongols overran Khorassan and Afghanistan, ruining Merv, Nishapur, Balkh, Herat, Kabul, Bamian, and

Ghazna. According to Rashid al-Din, historian and minister of the Il-Khan Ghazan (see below), the Mongols under Genghis Khan had methodically devastated Khorassan and Afghanistan (Grousset 1946/1991, 294). Margiana's impressive irrigation system was thoroughly wrecked. Cities like Herat, that surrendered but then rebelled, were put to the sword. Most of the towns mentioned at the beginning of this paragraph were wiped out with such ferocity that some never fully recovered (Abazov 2008, Map 22). But not only towns but also villages were disposed of. Entire regions, particularly sedentary agricultural ones, were depopulated. Generally, West Turkestan as well as Khorassan had to endure something that must have approximated genocide (Morgan 2007, 65). By 1222 the Mongols had reached the banks of the Indus and by 1223 they took control of the Kazakh steppe. Thus the subjugation of entire CA had been accomplished—amounting to a veritable cataclysm for the oases in the western part of the region (West Turkestan), while the eastern part (East Turkestan) had suffered much less.[55]

The Mongol conquest entailed the expansion of wastelands as well as of the steppe in various places, as will be shown in more detail below; the limit of sedentary civilization was pushed back south again (Burlot 1995, 172). At least in the first years following the conquest, agriculture was intentionally disrupted or decayed through negligence or because farmers had fled, been deported, or lost their lives. Many abandoned fields and fallow lands were turned into pastures for the benefit of Mongol herds.

A separate force rounded the Caspian Sea and in 1223 defeated a united Polovtsy-Rus army in the battle on the river Kalka (Pontic steppes, Eastern Ukraine). Thus, the confederation of the Kipchaks was shattered and the Rus weakened, but the Mongols turned back again for the time being. Soon they destroyed the rebelling Xixia state (1227) and conquered what remained of Northern China (1234). A large number of towns in Northern China were partly or totally razed, enormous damages inflicted on agriculture, and many people enslaved. Part of the economy was "pastoralized" to provide pastures to horses and other livestock. Tibet was occupied in the late 1240s. The principalities of the Rus were

---

[55] Apart from the argument of severe or exemplary punishment for crimes of murder of diplomats and of insubmission, Grousset put forward another argument that might explain the extent of atrocities and terrorist annihilation that was inflicted on Western CA by the Mongol military (1965/2008, pp. 291 and 305): « S'il (Gengis Khan) detruisit dans l'Iran oriental la brillante civilization urbaine qui avait produit un Firdousi et un Avicenne, c'est qu'il entendait ménager aux marches du sud-ouest une sorte de no man's land, de steppe artificielle, qui servit de glacis à son empire ». ("If he (Genghis Khan) destroyed the brilliant Eastern Iranian civilization that had produced a Firdawsi and an Avicenna, the reason was that he meant to arrange a kind of no man's land in the southwestern periphery, an artificial steppe that would serve as a glacis for his empire.")

conquered in 1237–1240, partly in winter campaigns featuring Mongol cavalry armies moving up frozen rivers at great speed—the only successful winter invasion of Russia in history (Maddison 1998, 29; Overy (ed) 2004, 143).

The Volga Bulgarian state was eliminated and the area incorporated into the empire in 1237. In the winter of 1237–1238, Riazan, Kolomna, Moscow, Vladimir, Suzdal, Yaroslavl, and Tver were conquered and looted. In the winter of 1239–1240, parts of the territory of today's Ukraine were severely afflicted, Kiev was conquered, plundered, und burnt down. It appears that the population of the Southern Rus (that lived near the steppe frontier, including Kiev) bore the brunt of the destruction and loss of life. Here, within striking distance of the grasslands, even small towns and villages were wiped out: Around a third of all settlements in the Southern Rus disappeared for good (Emeliantseva et al. 2001/2008, 234).[56]

The Crimea and the town of Sudak/Sogdaya (that had already suffered a destructive incursion in 1223) were definitely annexed. On the other hand, some Northern and Northwestern Rus principalities were spared ravages: The prince of Novgorod, Alexander Nevsky, voluntarily submitted. Incursions affected Poland (destruction of Lublin, Sandomir, Krakow), Silesia (Mongol victory in battle of Legnica/Liegnitz in 1241), Moravia (ravaging of Olomouc, Brno/Bruenn), Hungary (victory in battle of Mohi in 1241), Bosnia, Serbia, Valachia, and Danube-Bulgaria (information provided by Lytvyn). But these successful Central European campaigns did not have further strategic consequences.[57]

With few exceptions, those areas that accepted the new situation (in CA (the Uighur oases including Turfan, Tarim Basin, Kazakh steppe, Zhetysu (Semirechie), and Dzungaria), outside CA (Manchuria, Tibet, Novgorod, and Northern Russia)) avoided destructive campaigns and

retained their leaders and a degree of autonomy. Those areas, however, which rejected Mongol peace terms (unconditional surrender) or reneged on previous agreements (in CA (the oases of the Ferghana Basin, Shash, Mavarannahr (Transoxiana), Khorezm, Bactria (Northern Afghanistan), Merv, Khorassan), outside CA (Jin China, the Tangut Kingdom (Xixia), the Cuman confederation (Pontic steppes), most principalities of the Rus)) became the scenes of numerous attacks and strikes that eliminated much of their population and productive capacity (Barfield 1989/1992, 200).

As a result of the Mongol onslaught, according to Abazov, Western CA is estimated to have lost between 2 and 4 million mostly sedentary people out of a total population of between 10 and 16 million. That would correspond to between 12.5% and 40% of its population, possibly around a quarter. Many cities and areas took 30 to 50 years to recover; some never fully recovered. In China, a drop in population from over 100 million in the Song and Jin eras to around 85 million in the 1290s has to be explained. Even in what is today European Russia and Ukraine, the Mongol campaigns' trail of destruction was horrifying, and losses of life exceeded 10% of the population (in Ukraine it may have reached 20%) (Abazov 2008, Map 22; Morgan 2007, 72; Vernadsky 1953, 333–390). All in all, across Eurasia, the establishment of the Mongol Empire certainly cost many millions of human lives.

Ibn Battuta, the famous Moroccan Muslim traveler, visited Mavarannahr in the second quarter of the fourteenth century (about a hundred years after the inception of Mongol rule) and was appalled by the decay of urban life: While Termez had been reconstructed, Samarkand was still partly in ruins, and Merv and Balkh still bore extensive traces of destruction (Hambly (ed) 1966/1979, 140). Yet due their importance for SR trade, a number of cities were soon rebuilt, at least in their commercial and industrial cores, under Mongol rule. Among these towns feature Bukhara, Samarkand, Termez, Herat, Nishapur, Urgench, and Andijan.

Agriculture, particularly the intensive cultivation in oases, was profoundly disrupted or destroyed. Craftsmen and artisans—often excluded from the mass killings—were initially deported to carry out forced labor in Mongolia (e.g., in the capital Karakorum) or in areas adjacent to the conquerors' heartland or new adopted homelands.[58] Later they were exploited in their own regions and assigned to

---

[56] Its vicinity to the Eurasian steppe was a major drawback for Kiev and contributed to its loss of primacy among the cities of the Rus.

[57] This is because Khan Batu, the commander, was forced to retreat due to internal Mongol political reasons (death of Ögöday Khan, the successor to Genghis, therefore election of new Great Khan). A comparable process happened in 1260 (see below), when the Mongols lost their first major battle to foreign armed forces (the Egyptian Mamluks) in Ayn Jalut (east of Jerusalem) but not because the overall balance of forces was not in favor of the Mongols but due to some disorganization in connection with the unforeseen retreat of the commander, the Khan Hülegü following the death of Great Khan Möngke. The commander halted the campaign and began to travel back to his native land to join the kuriltay, which would elect the new Great Khan. This confirms that at least in the first decades of their empire building, the Mongols' military supremacy over their neighbors and adversaries was such that retreats and setbacks, as far as they happened, were due to nonmilitary reasons. At the same time, this reveals that – as in other nomadic polities – badly regulated succession procedures (lack of a regular, orderly system for succession to the Great Khan) constituted a weak point of Mongol rule that could severely harm imperial interests.

[58] For instance, Northern Chinese technicians, mainly metalsmiths and carpenters, were conscripted from tradesmen's families and accompanied a contingent of Chinese siege engineers during the Mongol invasion of Iran and Iraq (1258) (Allsen 2009, 136). Or captured Persian weavers from Herat were relocated to the north of Turfan in the Uighur area (de la Vaissière 2013, 74). Or Transylvanian miners were moved to Dzungaria, where they were ordered to prospect for gold (Borgolte 2015, 43). In most cases, the redeployments seem to have been long term or permanent.

manufacturing workshops belonging to Mongol dignitaries. Such workshops (karkhaneh) were erected in most conquered lands. A khan's train would include hundreds or even thousands of camels laden, e.g., with gold brocades or other precious fabrics or textiles for regular allocation to regional military commanders or noyons who stabilized their authority by rewarding subordinates in this way (Kauz 2009, 310–311; Allsen 2009, 140).

As Kauz highlights, enormous treasures of art and culture were also lost, most particularly books. There are reports dating from after the turn of the millennium, e.g., by Ibn Sina (Avicenna), on libraries in the cities of Transoxiana and Khorassan, which subsequently had been preserved by the Karakhanids and Seljukids. Apparently, nothing is left of these libraries (Kauz 2011, 130).

3.4.1.3 Institution Building in the New Empire

Genghis Khan and his successors proclaimed liberty of thought and freedom of worship for everyone. They did this despite the fact that the Mongols had their own religion, shamanism, an animistic faith with strong elements of ancestor worship. Mongol leaders embraced or, at least, were indifferent to ethnic diversity. With the important exception of Temuejin's own family and dynasty, origins were not the key for reaching a high social position in Mongol society but performance and merit. This contributed to the multicultural face of the imperial administration. As trade was important to the Mongols, Genghis Khan promoted the free and unencumbered circulation of merchandise throughout his empire and, as far as possible, beyond. He and Ögöday relaunched transcontinental Eurasian long-distance SR trade.

Genghis Khan proclaimed a code of laws, the Yassa (The Great Law), probably at the kuriltay of 1206, though perhaps supplemented later (Morgan 2007, 84). This codification was based on Mongol nomadic customary rules (Yosun), complemented by decrees of the Great Khan; it was further strongly influenced by biligs (maxims) attributed to Genghis. The Yassa contained rules of public law, e.g., committing Genghisids as supreme rulers. Moreover, it contained rules of civil and military administration, of international, criminal, and commercial law. It also dealt with religious beliefs, court ceremonial, social life, and general conduct. Criminal and commercial law were of exemplary severity. In times of peace, robbery or theft were punishable by death (Lemercier-Quelquejay 1970, 49). These sanctions, which certainly appear draconian to us today, were applied, i.a., to protect commerce and prevent intertribal vendettas in times of radical adjustment (Chaliand 1995, 128).

The Yassa was not valid for the entire population, only for nomads. In principle, sedentary inhabitants could keep their traditions and laws, if the latter were not fundamentally in contradiction to the Yassa. All social classes were equal before the law. The "iron fist" of the Yassa probably

enforced a degree of authoritarian social discipline. With the expansion of the empire, it eventually became the most authoritative handbook of Mongol jurisprudence (Chaliand 1995, 128; Masselos (ed) 2010, 38).

Once the empire had reached continental dimensions, Ögöday Khan in 1234 set up a public postal and messenger system, the Yam, which was aimed at providing swift and efficient long-distance communication. It appears that this relay system remained unrivaled for efficiency until the coming of the telegraph (Man 2014, 287). The purposes served by the Yam network[59] were various: (a) to facilitate the travels of envoys and notables going to and from the Mongol courts, (b) to speedily dispatch imperial orders from one part of the empire to another, (c) to transmit and receive intelligence as quickly as possible (very useful in the preparation of military campaigns), (d) to transport goods on public order, and (e) to assist merchants and their trading activities (Morgan 2007, 90).

The structure of the system was based on the erection of postal stations at stages equivalent to a day's journey. According to Marco Polo, this meant about every 40–48 km (around 56–64 km in sparsely populated areas). Other sources (e.g., Rashid al-Din) quote similar figures. But urgent messages/express couriers could go very much faster (320–480 km per day) (Morgan 2007, 91; Kollmar-Paulenz 2011, 42). Each postal station had stocks of fresh horses and fodder for the use of messengers and authorized travelers, a relay of riders, officials, including postmasters, supervisors, assigned road and bridge officers, and other staff. Travelers wishing to use the services of the Mongol imperial post required proper authorization in the form of a "paiza" (which can be roughly translated as "passport"). Paizas consisted of tablets which were hung around the traveler's neck. These tablets were made of different materials: wood, bronze, silver, and gold. The more valuable the material, the more importance was to be attached to the bearer or his/her message. Authorized travelers could change and commandeer horses, food, and services in the relay stations. Travelers benefiting from the services of the Yam would need 5–6 months (including times of rest) to reach Karakorum, the imperial capital (see below), from Europe or the Near East (Masselos (ed) 2010, 38; Roux 1993, 462).

Responsibility for maintenance of the Yam system resided with the Mongol military. Ideally, each postal station was assigned to army units corresponding to two tumens (basic military-administrative units). The army typically

---

[59] Public postal and messenger systems had, of course, existed in other sprawling empires before. ancient Persia (550–330 BCE) had already created one. As mentioned above, the name "Yam" was derived from the communication system of the Western Liao Empire/the Karakhitays (1130–1218), an immediate predecessor to Mongol rule in CA.

ordered the local (settled and nomadic) population to provide the necessary horses, food, and water supplies and cover the costs of the stations (Chaliand 1995, 167). At least theoretically, this was done on a regular rather than an arbitrary basis. Yet in times of corruption, the Yam system was often abused, which turned the postal stations into a heavy burden for the local population. As Barfield notes, the unauthorized use of horses was a recurrent complaint at court (1989: The Perilous Frontier . . .., 206).

The system was upheld by Ögöday's successors; also once the Mongol state had split into four de-facto independent components (ulus, pl. uluses), its empire-wide Yam infrastructure remained intact and seems to have worked, though with occasional interruptions caused by intra-Mongol military hostilities.[60] By and large, the Yam's relatively efficient functioning impressed foreign travelers like Marco Polo and Ibn Battuta. In Morgan's assessment, the imperial mail was probably the most effective Mongol public institution after the army (2007, 93).

Newly conquered territories in CA and elsewhere were first ruled by a Mongol military governor, the Tammachi (plural: Tammachin). After some time (pacification and securing of territory), the military governor was replaced by a civil governor, or Mongol chief civil official, the darughachi (plural: darughachin), also known as baskak (Turkic, initially in the conquered Rus), Daruga (later in the Rus), and Shana (Persia) (Masselos (ed) 2010, 37). As resident representatives of the Great Khan, the darughachin were often placed in cities and oversaw indigenous governing bodies in sedentary areas (e.g., Rus principalities from the 1240s, the Kingdom of Korea from the latter 1250s). The prime duty of darughachin, accompanied by bichigchin (scribes), pertained to the collection of tribute and taxes, i.e., making sure that the proper amount of revenue was forthcoming. Prior to the establishment of a formal taxation system, the Mongols had typically plundered their sedentary subjects (May 2012, 164, 169).

The darughachi supervised local governments, collected taxes or monitored and verified tax collection, and sent revenues to the khan; moreover, the imperial governors recruited soldiers for the Mongol army and allocated corvée (forced labor) obligations, including the staffing of Yam stations and, where necessary, resolved local disputes. Darughachin thus linked local (indigenous) power structures and administrations through their offices with the Great Khan's central establishment (May 2012, 166). To gain oversight over their new taxpayers and the latter's activities

and wealth, as well as over potential recruits for the army and possible laborers for other purposes, the Mongol authorities carried out censuses (a technique borrowed from the Chinese) in all newly conquered territories. At least in principle, the incidence of exaction was determined by reference to the census returns. In Northern Chinese and C Asian territories, the Mongol census was already carried out in 1235–1236, in the Rus principalities in 1245 (Morgan 2007, 91; Rossabi 2012, 44, 86).

To collect taxes, the Mongols originally did not rely on local civil bureaucracies; they opted for "tax farming": The new authorities allowed businessmen, often C Asian Muslims, who became members of quasi-governmental trading partnerships or corporations (ortagh[61]), to exact revenue from conquered territories. Given that these fiscal contractors were bound by few rules and that their primary interest was to maximize profits over a rather short term, the exploitation of the affected populace could be merciless and even unbearable, triggering unrest and instability (Barfield 1989/1992, 204; Rossabi 2012, 45).

A considerable number of Mongol nobles (noyons) and populations under their command moved to conquered lands outside Mongolia. Here the new authorities in some cases equipped the noblemen with appanages as grants for their military service. In other cases the aristocracy simply took possession of lands cultivated by sedentary farmers, then either got rid of the farmers and transformed the lands to pastures or cruelly exploited the agriculturalists (Baipakov et al. 1997, 98). Meanwhile, in the first decades after the conquest, the circulation of money sharply contracted in most affected regions, and in some areas it entirely ceased. Thus, the second quarter of thirteenth century is marked by a drop in the number of mints in CA, by irregular issues of coins and by monetary circulation crises. Samarkand, for instance, entered its "moneyless decades," as Davidovich and Dani put it. Commerce within cities and throughout the region (the volume of which certainly fell) largely reverted to barter (Davidovich and Dani 1998, 404).

The traditional Mongol (nomadic) tax system consisted of alba (tribute) and qubchur (or qubchigur, levy). Qubchur constituted a one percent levy on herds and wool which was paid to the khan (ruler). Both were regular taxes, paid in-kind, but could also be collected spontaneously. With the incorporation of settled areas into the empire, the nomadic population of whatever origin continued to pay taxes based on the size of their herds or flocks. However, they paid comparatively far less than the subjugated sedentary population. Following an unstable transition period, the Mongol authorities started to systematically levy taxes on agriculture, crafts, and commerce. Taxes were first mostly

---

[60] There are estimates according to which after the split of the empire, the Great Khanate (the largest sub-empire consisting of Mongolia, Manchuria, China, and Tibet) accounted for more than 10,000 Yam stations and more than 200,000 postal horses (Roux 1993, 463).

[61] From Turkish ortaq, "partner".

paid in-kind; later monetary payments gained momentum. Ögöday Khan decreed that the qubchur corresponded to one hundredth of a breeder's livestock and to one tenth of a farmer's harvest. Ögöday also established an (agricultural) property tax, depending on the quality of the soil, and a sales tax on luxury products, amounting to one thirtieth of their value (Kollmar-Paulenz 2011, 41; Roux 1993, 276).

Although taxation became more regular over time, there was still room for ad hoc exactions, arbitrariness, and even confiscatory taxation. In general, Mongol taxes were paid on top of already existing indigenous dues, as far as pre-Mongol structures were left in place. This exacerbated the tax burden on settled people. For instance, the Islamic kharaj (or land tax) continued to be levied in C Asian oases. The new authorities moreover ordered the jizya[62] to be paid by all sedentary inhabitants, whether Muslim or not. Severe punishment for tax dodgers promoted punctual payment: Who fell into arrears could be stripped of his/her personal liberty and transferred to the slave market without much ado. However, religious institutions, Christian, Muslim, and other clergy, were exempted form tax obligations (Roudik 2007, 38; Scheck 1977, 49–50).

The abovementioned C Asian merchants that were members of quasi-governmental trading partnerships typically had business know-how in SR trade and exchange of goods produced in China and CA for products coming from outside the empire and coveted by the Mongol nomadic aristocracy. The latter exacted silk, grain, silver, as well as weapons of war produced by captured craftsmen in conquered settled areas but lacked sufficient marketing capabilities. As the nomadic nobility not only wanted to enjoy silk and other valuable extorted goods, but profit from them as well, the C Asians could arrange the lucrative sale or exchange of respective products. The ortaghs may have been instrumental in realizing these trading ventures and generating the SR profits since these enterprises were Mongol-C Asian partnerships protected by the authorities and having access to government finance (Barfield 2001, 246).

Already during the 12 years of Ögöday Khan's rule (1229–1241), a multicultural imperial civil service developed. Members of the small administrative elite tended to be representatives of ethnicities that had already made contact with literacy and public administration, e.g., Uighurs, Arabs, Iranians, and Chinese. Particularly, with the conquest of the Uighur Kingdom and the Western Liao Empire, the Mongols could use the administrative skills of these peoples who had much in common with the conquerors as regards their (original) nomadic way of life: As Bira points out, the Uighurs and the Karakhitay were the intermediaries who transmitted the acquisitions of Islamic and Chinese civilizations to the Mongols. As alluded to above, Sogdo-Uighur was adopted for the writing of Mongol and was used in imperial correspondence (Bira 1998, 253). To avoid a "feudalization" of the administrative apparatus and to prevent high-level bureaucrats from gaining too close relationships with their subjects, civil servants were often stationed far away from their native lands. Therefore, one frequently found Chinese administrators in Iran while Arabs, Iranians, and C Asians, including Turks, would hold posts in China. Ögöday Khan also attempted to standardize weights and measures (Lemercier-Quelquejay 1970, 50; Mokyr 2003, 371).

Ögöday had a splendid court in Karakorum, which was linked to the west and southwest via trade routes on the Eurasian steppe and others descending to Transoxiana and was continuously supplied from China via a north-south road. As a long-distance trade hub and imperial capital, Karakorum was a cosmopolitan city where Christians, Muslims, Buddhists, and people such as Hungarians, Alans, Russians, Georgians, Armenians, and, of course, Chinese and C Asians mingled (Bira 1998, 258). The Mongol court had become truly multicultural, multiethnic, and multireligious.[63] Although the imperial administration generally worked in a flexible and efficient manner, it was precisely this flexibility that rendered it susceptible to corruption, which, in addition to heavy taxation, contributed to the exploitation of subject populations (Masselos (ed) 2010, 38).

Box 3.1: The Giant Mongol Empire: A Driving Force of Early Globalization?

The Mongol Empire: the largest state of world history, more extensive than the British Empire or the USSR!

(continued)

---

[62] The poll tax established during the Arab/Islamic conquest, to be paid by non-Muslim subjects of the caliph (see Sect. 3.3.1.3.2).

[63] To mention some facts reported by Rossabi: Ögöday Khan's subjects built two mosques, Buddhist and Daoist temples, and a Nestorian Christian church within the city. Mostly, captured craftsmen and artisans from China, CA, Iran, and Europe fashioned essential as well as luxury products in many large and small workshops. Areas for the production of glass, gems, precious stones, and bone carving, as well as furnaces for the smelting of metals, especially bronzes, have been excavated. Notwithstanding Karakorum's glory at the time, Wilhelm von Roebroeck, the Franciscan monk-traveler who had visited Karakorum in the middle of the century, proved somewhat prescient in recognizing that the Mongol capital was not ideally situated as hub of a great empire. The city and its neighboring regions could not provide basic provisions for its increasing population. Roebroeck writes that 400 carts of provisions arrived daily from China to supply the city – a costly and inefficient system. While Karakorum did possess, to some degree, a central geopolitical location in the swiftly expanding Mongol state, the city had little arable land in its surroundings, was not near a vital source of raw materials (known at the time), and did not lie on a major SR artery: In terms of logistics it was poorly situated (Rossabi 2012, 46–47).

Box 3.1 (continued)

A look at the size of the Mongol Empire at the time of its maximum territorial and demographic extension (ca. 1290–1330): After Kubilay Khan had conquered Southern China and established suzerainty over most of Vietnam and Burma—while the Mongols had not yet lost control of any other major conquered territories (e.g., in Eastern Europe)—the empire was the largest state in world history. It stretched from the East China Sea to the Carpathians, from the Arctic Ocean to the Mediterranean and the Persian Gulf, from the Baltic Sea to the South China Sea, and "from Crimea to Korea" (Map 3.6). According to Masselos (2010, 34), the entire imperial territory came to about 36.3 mn km², which corresponds to about one quarter of the global land mass and considerably exceeds the territory of the British Empire of 1914 (30.0 mn km²) or that of the Soviet Union of 1990 (22.4 mn km²). It is estimated that during the climax of the Mongol Empire, almost half of the world's population lived under its rule (Geiss 1979, 235).

Tricontinental Afro-Eurasian trade at the Mongol hour—early globalization?

There is not yet consensus among researchers when globalization started. According to Fässler (2007, 46–48), there are a number of viewpoints, e.g.:

10000 BCE: Neolithic revolutions: From this time, these profound changes took place in various parts of Eurasia (author who views this point as the beginning of globalization: K. Anthony Appiah).

5000 BCE: Early world systems: Spreading of farming societies across Eurasia and North Africa, incipient stages of urbanization and hierarchical societies (authors: Andre Gunder Frank, Barry Gills, William McNeill).

1250 CE: Pax Mongolica: First direct and uninterrupted relations between Europe and South and East Asia; sprawling long-distance trade networks across Eurasia and large parts of Africa (authors: Janet Abu-Lughod, Christian Grataloup, Ronald Findlay, Kevin O'Rourke).

1500 CE: European discoveries: Discovery of the globe and incipient European colonialism, early capitalist world system (authors: Immanuel Wallerstein, Jürgen Osterhammel, Rolf Walter).

Currently, most economic historians seem inclined to share the view that modern globalization began in the early sixteenth century, not earlier. Salient arguments in favor of this view are that the circumference of the globe was first discovered and explored in that period (Columbus 1492, Magellan, 1521); the early capitalist system started to quickly expand around the globe in the early sixteenth century; the same goes for the launching of global networks of political, religious, cultural, and economic actors, most notably for the first emergence of global entrepreneurial or business players. Anglo-Saxon researchers appear to prefer the term "archaic globalization" for advances of integration prior to 1500. Of course, as pointed out below, this early phase of globalization unfortunately already included the horrific spread of the bubonic plague along the trade routes infesting large parts of the world: from Burma via the Eurasian steppe to Western Europe and even Greenland and from the Eastern Mediterranean to Morocco on the one hand and Yemen on the other (Fässler 2007, 48–49, 58–59; Walter 2006, 75).

3.4.2 From Predatory Economic Policy to Reforms, Transcontinental Trade Boom, and Centralized Imperial Heyday (1240s–1280s)

3.4.2.1 Division of Mongol Empire into Semi-independent Uluses (Sub-empires)

In accordance with nomadic tribal traditions, the state was divided among descendants of Genghis Khan.[64] It is more precise to say that the Mongol Empire was split into Genghisid uluses—politico-territorial sub-empires, giant appanages, state-like confederations, whose original meaning was not territorial but military-logistical (like tumen).

The four uluses were (as shown in Maps 3.6 and 3.7):

– *The empire of the Great Khan or Great Khanate*: the core of the empire, consisting of Mongolia, Southern Central Siberia, parts of the Far East, Manchuria, Northern China including Gansu, the Eastern corner of Xinjiang (the oases of Hami and Barkoel), Tibet; conquest of Southern China (Song Empire) in 1279; under suzerainty of Great Khanate: Korea (from 1259), Annam, Champa, Northern Burma.
– *The Ulus Chagatay or Chagatay Khanate*: upper Ob and Irtysh river valleys in Western Siberia, Dzungaria, Zhetysu (Semirechie), oases of Ferghana Basin, Shash (Tashkent), Mavarannahr, and Eastern Bactria, oases of

---

[64] The major traits of this division had already been fixed by Genghis before his death (1227).

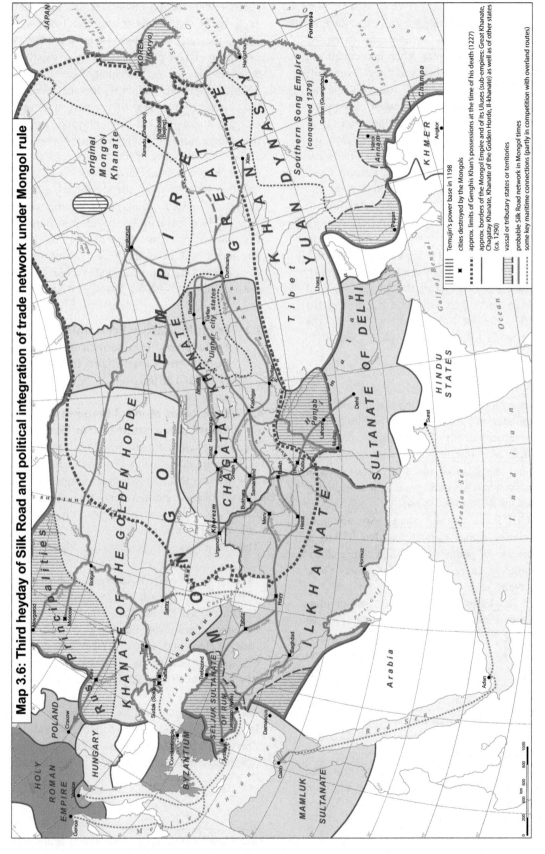

Map 3.6 Third heyday of SR and political integration of trade network under Mongol rule

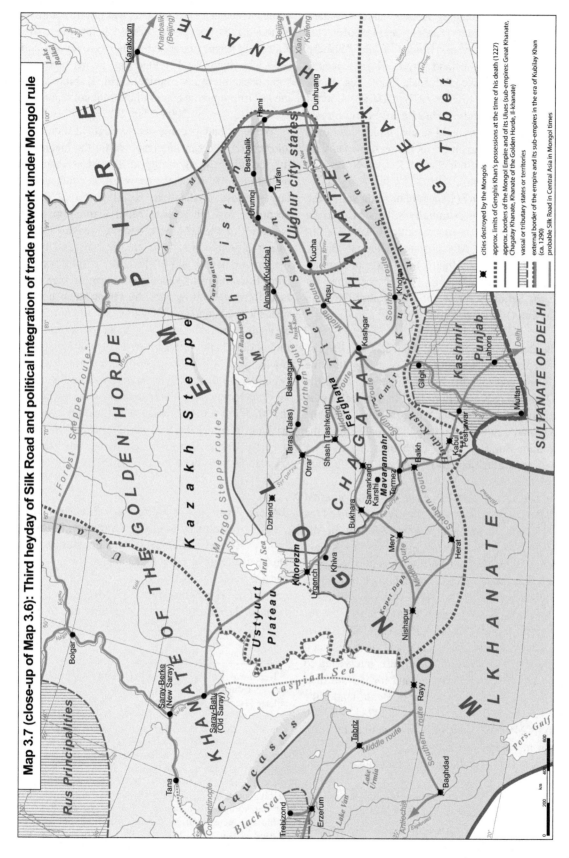

Map 3.7 (Close-up) third heyday of SR and political integration of trade network under Mongol rule

Tarim Basin (Kashgar, Yarkand, Khotan, etc.) and Turfan, Central Afghanistan (including Kabul); under tributary control of Chagatay Khanate (Kashmir and Punjab).

- *Ulus Jöchi or Khanate of the Golden Horde*: Western Siberia west of upper Ob and Irtysh, Kazakh steppe north and west of Lake Balkhash, Aral Sea Basin (Khwarazm and lower reaches of Syr Daria), Ustyurt Plateau, Caspian Lowlands, Volga Basin, Pontic Steppe all the way to Carpathians and Danube; under suzerainty of Ulus Jöchi: Rus principalities (including Kiev, Halych-Volynia, Smolensk, Vladimir-Suzdal, Riazan, Novgorod, Pskov) (from around 1240).

- *Ulus Hülegü or Il-Khanate* (at the middle of the thirteenth century, this sub-empire essentially still needed to be conquered): Khorassan (territory south of Amu Daria), Western and Southern Afghanistan (including Balkh, Herat, and Kandahar), Iran, Iraq (Mesopotamia), Transcaucasia, Eastern Anatolia; under suzerainty of Ulus Hülegü: Seljuk Sultanate of Rum (latter Ottoman state, Asia Minor), Eastern Syria.

The ulus borders, while somewhat fluid, changed surprisingly little over (roughly) a century. At least formally, the sub-empires were held together by the imperial leader, the Great Khan, residing in Karakorum (later in Khanbalik near Beijing), the Mongol military, the Yassa (Mongol law), the Yam (imperial mail), and the official policy goal to keep the SR open for trans-Eurasian trade. Each ulus had its own administrative apparatus and was further divided into tumens.

Ögöday Khan (1229–1241) consolidated the internal structure of the empire and was clearly recognized as supreme leader by all Mongol princes. Already in the period of Ögöday Khan, advisors—particularly his Khitan chief minister in China, Yelue Chucai—started to convince the authorities that taxing settled populations brings more profits than replacing them with herds of livestock, especially if the territory (like Northern China) is unsuitable for animal husbandry (Soucek 2000, 115). Thus the further devastation of the Chinese countryside and its conversion to grazing territory was halted. Ögöday also intervened to put an end to the seizures of farming land for pasture in C Asian oases and ordered the rebuilding of Herat. Under the regency of Töregene (Ögöday's wife, 1242–1246) and Güyük Khan (1246–1248), there was a period of drift, and corruption increased (see below).

Möngke Khan (1251–1259) tightened the reins again, cut corruption, and carried out some fiscal and monetary reforms. During the time of Möngke's reign, the individual sub-empires had gained power, and the Great Khan, who was still regarded as supreme Mongol leader, had to carefully balance different imperial interests.

Kubilay Khan (1260–1294) became Great Khan without being elected at a kuriltay. This was highly controversial and although the empire had reached it maximum size during Kubilay's reign, his actual authority over the entire giant state was much weaker than that of his predecessors and soon became largely nominal. Still, Kubilay was probably the last true supreme leader of the Mongol domain (Chaliand 1995, 141; Abazov 2008, Map 24).

While it had become increasingly difficult to manage and broker divergent interests within the bicontinental polity, the ruling Mongol elite in the Great Khanate began to have trouble resisting the draw of the sophisticated sedentary Chinese civilization. Kubilay started to rule more according to Chinese than Mongol traditions. Against the backdrop of the relative economic weakness of Mongolia (the traditional core of the empire), in 1264 the capital of the Great Khanate and of the entire empire was transferred from Karakorum to Khanbalik (meaning city of the khan, near Beijing).[65] However, the Great Khan had a summer residence, Shangdu or Xanadu, set up north of Beijing. Shangdu retained some elements of a nomadic steppe metropolis (Wild 1992, 8). In 1271, the Great Khan, complying with Chinese tradition, had himself proclaimed "emperor" and adopted the dynasty name "Yuan." Eventually the Mongols also resuscitated, if in a limited version, the tradition of Confucian examinations for candidates wishing to serve in the imperial civil service of the Yuan dynasty. These changes happened in the face of much opposition from the nomadic aristocracy.

3.4.2.2 From In-Kind Arbitrary Exaction to More Regular but Heavy Taxation: Piecemeal Remonetization of the Economy

During the reign of Möngke Khan, the Mongol fiscal system became more standardized, and the arbitrariness that had reigned in tax matters until the mid-thirteenth century was reduced. These reforms were primarily due to the influence

---

[65] This move, Kubilay's rapprochement to Chinese sedentary culture, and centrifugal tendencies elsewhere in the empire triggered or reflected serious tensions among the Genghisids and the imperial nomadic nobility which lasted for decades and undermined the cohesion of the common state. The Mongol capital Karakorum, metropolis of administration and trade, far away from more densely populated areas, had been dependent on large and continuous outside supplies to maintain itself. The move to Beijing had been preceded by a conflict in which Kubilay demonstrated that he who controlled the source of supply, controlled Karakorum: "It had been the custom to bring food for Karakorum on wagons from Khitay. Kubilay Khan banned this traffic and there occurred a great dearth and famine in the region" (Rashid al-Din 1971, 253; Barfield 1989/1992, 218). Karakorum's isolation and structural fragility was nothing new and recalled that of Karabalgasun, the former Uighur nomad capital.

of Yelue Chucai, the Khitan minister and imperial adviser in China (already in Ögöday's times), and of Mahmud Yalavach, a Khorezmian merchant and imperial adviser in CA. From 1252, the Mongol tax system was based on the qubchur (or qubchigur), which remained a 1%-of-livestock levy for nomads but was redefined as a poll tax for settled inhabitants. The sedentary qubchur was usually based on the means of the household (indicated by the census), was paid in cash, could be differentiated between farmers and town dwellers, and could be levied regularly or when needed (Khazanov 1983/1994, 241; Bira 1998, 258). In addition, another tax known as qalan was imposed. The qalan was often paid in-kind rather than in cash and was a general term for occasional exactions imposed on the sedentary population and typically including some kind of corvée (forced labor, in some cases also military assignments). Such exactions would tend to emerge unexpectedly and arbitrarily, and this would go far to explain the qalan's particular unpopularity (Morgan 2007, 88).

A third Mongol tax was the tamgha (sales tax, customs fee, or protection charge), a levy usually imposed at a rate of 5–10% on all commercial transactions and paid by merchants. Thus, the levy was not only applicable to luxury goods, as its precursor had been under Ögöday Khan. It also concerned some kinds of services, prostitution, for example. The tamgha testifies to the importance attached by the Mongol authorities to (international) trade. An official stamped[66] the merchandise, showing that it had been paid. The tamgha actually facilitated trade across the giant empire as it allowed merchants to pay substantially lower rates than in the pre-Mongol era when customs and tolls were payable at the borders of every realm/principality they passed through. Perhaps the most onerous tax was that paid in-kind to the Yam: Nomads and villages near a postal station were obligated to pay a levy in horses and supplies to maintain the station and Yam services in their area; extortions became unbearable in times of administrative wrongdoing (corruption) and abuse of this vital infrastructure (Kollmar-Paulenz 2011, 41; May 2012, 170).

The clergy, whether Muslim, Christian, or other, was largely exempted from taxation. In China this exemption included the Confucian scholarly class, and in the Russian principalities it allowed the Orthodox Church to amass considerable wealth over time (Martinez 2009, 98). As opposed to merchants, who were privileged—peasants were generally subject to very heavy tax pressure. As Morgan explains, exploitation of peasants was generally limited only by the consideration that it was sensible to leave them sufficient means to permit their survival until the next year, so that a

further year's taxes could be collected (2007: The Mongols, 89).[67] The multitude of taxes and variations of the latter reflects a Mongol fiscal system of the thirteenth and fourteenth centuries that was certainly onerous but also pragmatic. Especially from 1270 onwards, many duties came to be paid in cash (Roux 1993, 464; Akhmedov 1998, 266).

A united Mongol imperial currency was not created. Instead, various local currencies continued to circulate (as far as they had not evaporated following the invasion), and different types of Mongol monetary units and coinage were issued under Möngke Khan, in addition to paper money, that had been resuscitated in China during Ögöday's rule in 1236. In practice, though, silver continued to be a preferred means of exchange in many regions. Once the empire had split up, each Ulus (already from the 1260s) started to strike its own coins. Thus, in the Chagatay Khanate, coinage was minted in many large towns, e.g., in Almalik (where the Mongol rulers had their camps), Bukhara, Samarkand, Otrar, Taraz, Kashgar, Osh, Uzgend, and Khodzhent (Akhmedov 1998, 266).

3.4.2.3 Trade-Led Economic Recovery and Pax Mongolica (from 1250s)

Once warfare, destructions, expropriations, and menaces of the latter were largely over, once security of SR trade was established on a vast politically integrated playing field, and once confiscatory taxation had given way to more reasonable fiscal regimes and currency systems had stabilized, a process of economic recovery finally got underway in many regions of the empire—including CA—around the mid-1200s. Thanks also to initial government subsidization of overland SR trade—ortaghs (trading partnerships) were initially given special access to the horse relay system and infrastructure of the Mongol imperial post (Barfield 2001, 246)—rapid trade-driven economic growth set off (Table 3.1).

Of course, high early growth rates should not surprise, given the low level of departure. CA also profited from the removal of trade barriers and the primacy of a single legal order. In around 1250 the era of the Pax Mongolica commenced, which lasted for about a century and allowed for safe travel "from Crimea to Korea" (Mokyr 2003, 371). If merchants used the Yam system, they benefited from a guarantee for their merchandise. If these goods were looted, the population living near the location of the crime had to fully compensate the traders. Apparently never before had the security of travelers and their belongings been so much assured in Eurasia as during this well-policed era (de la Vaissière 2013, 73; Grataloup 2007, 103).

---

[66] There is an interesting resemblance between "tamgha" and the French word "timbre" (stamp).

[67] In Olson's terms, the adoption of this stance by the authorities would correspond to a move from roving to stationary bandit.

Trade was important in all Mongol uluses because of the nomadic nobility's demand for extravagant goods and because the Mongols' politically important and often growing settlements in the steppe needed regular supplies of food and many other products.[68] Moreover, foreign (particularly European) demand for goods from China and other regions under Mongol rule quickly grew. The new security of the trade routes, the absence of customs and other economic borders, and the initial in-kind subsidization of trade triggered a substantial decline of prices over a vast trading space (Masselos (ed) 2010, 43). Cities and villages were repopulated. Despite previous devastations, some producing and trading towns in CA (e.g., Bukhara, Samarkand, Herat, Urgench) and other regions (e.g., in Iran, Tabriz, Isfahan) grew again into new urban commercial centers (Kauz 2009, 311).

The third quarter of the thirteenth century was marked by the regular minting of golden dinars in the empire. Möngke Khan ordered the annual collection of the qubchur (as standard per capita tax of sedentary inhabitants) in these golden dinars. Dinars, that of course had a long tradition in CA going back to the caliphate, thus made their reappearance among the population, and the qubchur was recalculated in them (by weight) (Davidovich and Dani 1998, 405). Silver was partly and temporarily trumped by gold. The successors to Genghis Khan attempted to create a handicraft sector in the sub-empires, but, as explained earlier, this was at the cost of the conquered. From a purely economic viewpoint, the enslavement, transfer, and forced labor of craftsmen and artisans at best corresponded to a zero-sum game; human capital was uprooted here, relocated and concentrated there, not necessarily bearing any net productive effect. Shortly after coming into direct contact with Europe, the Mongols and their commercial associates began selling to Europeans. In all likelihood, the Mongol assortments also included surplus luxury produced by slave workers in factories owned by the nomadic nobility. Mongol-supplied Chinese silk could be bought in Italy by 1257. Not long after, Italian merchants arrived in the Great Khanate (Masson-Smith 2003, 4).

Apart from the imposition of a new stratum of rulers, the structure of society in most C Asian lands did not change much in the Mongol era, although perhaps it became more accentuated: According to Kauz, the dominant strata consisted of the nomadic elite, big landowners, the (often multinational) bureaucracy, merchants/businessmen, and, to some degree, the clergy; the exploited strata were mostly peasants/agriculturalists, partly also craftsmen, and rank-and-file nomads (2009, 310).

3.4.2.4 Empire of the Great Khan: Distribution of Appanages to Nomadic Conquerors—Sinicization of Regime

Already toward the end of Ögöday Khan's reign (following the census in Northern China), Chinese lands were distributed as appanages (shih-yi, literally: "territories for feeding") to important members of the Mongol elite. Not unlike iqtadars, appanage holders had the right to collect taxes from conferred territories in exchange for service to the state. Also, appanages frequently became hereditary. However, this Far Eastern analogy to the Near and Middle Eastern iqta tended to apply to quite large territories and districts. While possibly not as destructive as tax farmers in other parts of the empire, appanage holders' often arbitrary exactions were not conducive to a revival of China's economic life, and their practices were later brought under government control (Khazanov 1983/1994, 246; Barfield 1989/1992, 204).

Kubilay Khan was more open than his predecessors to the Chinese philosophy and ethics of Confucianism and regarded himself as a Chinese emperor (of the Yuan dynasty) as much as a khan of the steppe.[69] From 1275 to 1292, Marco Polo is reported to have served in Kubilay's still cosmopolitan, but increasingly sinicized, administration. Kubilay favored and promoted the use of Chinese state-backed paper money (chao), initially with some success (Roux 1993, 402).

The first emperor of the Yuan dynasty also substantially expanded the Great Khanate and the entire empire: after his predecessor Möngke Khan had conquered Korea (1259), Kubilay crushed the Song dynasty (1279) and annexed Southern China, uniting the entire country under Mongol rule. The conquest was carried out with the assistance of Chinese infantry—more suitable than cavalry for fighting in the hilly and subtropical South. Kubilay banned arbitrary pillage, and the armed forces did not commit comparable atrocities to what had been done half a century before. After the Mongol takeover of Southern China, many Song institutions were preserved (Maddison 1998, 29). Moreover, from China, military expeditions were launched in the 1270s to the 1290s to Japan and Java (unsuccessfully) and to Indochina (partly successfully). Parts of Vietnam and Burma became tributary states under Mongol suzerainty.

---

[68] Although the Mongols eventually decided to wind down Karakorum, they still established a number of important settlements in the steppe, including Old Saray and New Saray (on the Volga) and Sultania (Southern Azerbaijan, Iranian Plateau).

[69] In this respect, one could possibly, in a reverse sense, compare Kubilay to the first successful Tang emperors of the middle of the seventh century that had conquered the steppe and incorporated some nomadic military and administrative elements into the Chinese state.

3.4.2.5 Ulus Chagatay: Ambitious, but Fragile Reconstruction, Growing Economic Disparities

This sub-empire covered the lion's share of CA and boasted a geographically central position within the Mongol Empire. Travelers wishing to cross Eurasia overland in an east-west or west-east direction, could hardly avoid setting foot on the Ulus Chagatay or Chagatay Khanate.[70] The Mongols directly ruling this ulus set up their capital in Almalik (Kuldzha/Yining) in the Ili valley, which was relatively centrally situated between the core lands they ruled (West and East Turkestan, Dzungaria, and Semirechie, see Map 3.7). The Chagatay Khanate consisted of two distinct economic areas: the band of southern oases stretching from Bukhara via Ferghana and Kashgar to Turfan; and the predominantly nomadic grasslands and desert steppes in the north: Dzungaria, Zhetysu,[71] and the Eastern Kazakh steppe. Thus, the south of the sub-empire was mostly inhabited by settled Iranians, surrounded by a half-settled Turco-Iranian population; the north was dominated by Turkic nomads (Weiers 2004, 133). Particularly the inhabitants of the north were now joined by the Mongol elite.

The Chagatayid Khans, ruling from their encampment in Almalik, clung to their nomadic ways and chose to nomadize in the north. Exaction of booty and tribute from the partly ruined towns of Mavarannahr and form largely intact Kashgaria (the Tarim Basin) brought the nomadic aristocracy material benefits but was obviously only a short-term solution, as sustained benefits required reconstruction and a more business-friendly environment. The central authorities in Karakorum intervened, and Ögöday Khan appointed mostly Muslim businessmen as civil governors (darughachi) of the khanate's settled areas; e.g., the Khwarazmian merchant Mahmud Yalavach held authority in Mavarannahr. Yalavach had the irrigation networks along the Amu and Syr Daria rivers repaired, and he ordered the reconstruction of Bukhara and Samarkand and of other cities. As Rossabi points out, by the mid-1230s, agriculture and commerce revived, and Yalavach began to impose regular taxes (2012, 89). His tax reform inspired and became a model for empire-wide tax policies outlined above (May 2012, 169).

After Yalavach's transfer to China (around 1240), the Great Khan appointed Mahmud's son, Masud Beg, an expert on administrative and financial matters, as his successor. The new appointee continued the valuable economic policies initiated by his father. Around the middle of the thirteenth century, the economy of Southern CA started to flourish again, supported by the revival of SR trade once the Mongols had conquered most of Eastern Europe by the 1240s and obstacles for trade connections to the west via the Black Sea had been removed. Samarkand—although not yet entirely built up again—took over the role of a major C Asian trade hub. The Mongols established new silk workshops and factories in the Tarim Basin and other areas to increase the volume of silk production and develop new marketable silk products. Chinese weavers were dispatched to Samarkand to collaborate with local Muslim weavers. Yet recovery was repeatedly interrupted by military tensions and even hostilities at the contentious Amu Daria border with the Ulus Hülegü that had been established in 1250s (see below) (Masson-Smith 2003, 3; Weiers 2004, 134).

Nonetheless, with the revival of the economy and with taxes providing a steady stream of revenues for the khanate, demand for money rose. Masud Beg reformed the coinage in the 1270s. After Möngke's golden dinar had apparently stabilized the monetary situation and re-established trust, high-standard silver dirhams were re-issued not only in Transoxiana but in 15 Chagatayid mints (including in Almalik, Almaty, Otrar, Taraz) and circulated throughout the ulus. Chagatayid silver dirhams did not only serve in regional, but also in transcontinental trade. The minting of silver dirhams was followed by that of copper "felsy," which soon claimed a firm place in retail monetary circulation (Baipakov et al. 1997, 141, 155). In Soucek's assessment, about half a century after the Mongol devastations, Mavarannahr's settled population, whether urban or agricultural, had recovered some of the florescence of its Islamic civilization (2000, 117).

3.4.2.6 Ulus Jöchi/Khanate of the Golden Horde: Strategic Location at the Crossroads of Europe and Asia—Exploitation of Rus Principalities

Genghis Khan's grandson Batu (1227–1256) was the first ruler of the Ulus Jöchi.[72] In the wake of his successful battles of conquest in Eastern Europe, Batu in 1243 established the Mongol Khanate of the Golden Horde and founded its capital Saray near the mouth of the Volga (near present-day Astrakhan).[73] The Khanate of the Golden Horde was beneficially situated in the western part of Eurasia, and it straddled

---

[70] This should have important implications in later decades (see below).

[71] As will be explained below, the initial Mongol onslaught did not wipe out sedentary civilization in Semirechie, but what was left eroded and all but disappeared in the following decades.

[72] Jöchi was the oldest son of Genghis Khan and commander of the first Mongol invasion of Eastern Europe, which took place in the 1220s.

[73] The word "horde" was transmitted to western languages via Russian from Mongol "orda" ("army camp," "khan's court"), and the expression "golden horde" possibly derives from Batu's (the ruler's) gleaming golden-topped tent camp. "Sarai" means "palace" in Mongolian or "big house" in Persian (Shen 2009, 137; Weiers 2004, 118). The resemblance between "Saray" and the Turkish "Serail" is noteworthy.

the major steppe routes connecting Europe with CA, China, India, and Iran. Furthermore, Saray lay at the hub of these connections, where the Eurasian steppe east-west caravan route running from China to the Black Sea intersected with the north-south Volga route leading from the Baltic Sea via the Caspian to Iran or, alternatively, via Khorezm and the Amu Daria to India (see Maps 3.6 and 3.7).[74]

As in other conquered territories, soon after the Mongols had occupied the princedoms of the Rus and had killed many of the powerful princes, they sent civil governors and resident representatives of the khan, called darughachin (or baskak, later in the Rus also called: darughy), accompanied by Mongol military detachments, into important towns and cities of the former Rus. The rulers of the various principalities were henceforth obliged to seek their appointment from the khan and had to travel to Saray to receive their certificates. In 1245 the new authorities conducted a general census of the population (carried out by particular authorized officials, in Russian: "chislenniki") and established a tributary tax system (Shukow et al. 1957/ 1963, Band 3, 691; Morgan 2007, 95, 126).

Although initially private tax collectors (tax farmers) were employed who sought to exact as much revenue as they could, it was eventually determined that this policy antagonized the population. The darughachi then started to use Rus government officials to collect taxes. The Orthodox Church was freed from liability to tax (Rossabi 2012, 87). The baskaks' main responsibilities were the regular exaction and transfer of tribute (in Russian: "vykhod" or "dan"), the drafting of local men into the army, occasionally the requisition and allocation of forced labor, and the maintenance of local order, i.e., the crushing of opposition to Mongol rule (Halperin 1985, 34, 77).

The Mongols' initial large-scale exaction of forced labor certainly affected the Eastern European economy. The new rulers aimed at getting hold of Russian armorers and craftsmen for building fortresses. These experts were enslaved and many of them concentrated in workshops of newly founded towns of the Golden Horde. The deportation of many of the Rus' artisans amounted to an involuntary Russian "brain drain" (one might also say "brain theft"), which in the second half of the thirteenth century led to a regressive development and even to loss of knowledge of specific techniques in a number of trades for which the Rus had previously been well known. This goes for the goldsmith's trade; the production of enamel, of glass jewelry, and of polychrome ceramics; the application of niello and filigree know-how; and other expertise. Some of these skills were no longer present in the Rus principalities for at

least a century—but they were, of course, present in Saray. Industrial trades, metallurgy in particular, suffered a spectacular decline in the former Rus in the thirteenth century and did not really recover until about 200 year later. On the other hand, Russian agriculture, forestry, and fur trapping were soon encouraged by the Mongols (Shukow et al. 1957/ 1963, Band 3, 690; Lemercier-Quelquejay 1970, 100; Halperin 1985, 76).

By supporting commerce, the Golden Horde obtained silk, porcelain, spices, glass, cotton cloth, and other goods and in exchange exported its own manufactured products, including nasij or gold brocades,[75] ceramics, as well as wheat, furs, slaves, etc. Among many other products, precious Asian silk reached European markets via the lower Volga, and coveted pelts and furs went in the other direction (Rossabi 2012, 88; Pickhan 2009, 124). In Europe, the Golden Horde traded, e.g., with Sweden, the Hanseatic League (German: Hanse), Poland, Hungary, Byzantium, and particularly with Italian city-states. The Rus principalities found themselves at the northwestern periphery of the new empire. The prince of Novgorod, Alexander Nevsky (1220–1263), had decided to cooperate closely with the Mongols and successfully fought back military attacks by the Swedes (1240) and the Teutonic knights ("Battle on the Ice" of Lake Peipus, 1242).

Novgorod became an important outer link toward Northwestern Europe (Map 3.6). As the city needed to pay tribute to the Golden Horde in silver, and silver could not (yet) be found in Russia, the principality sent furs and other forest products to Western Europe for silver and woolen cloth, which were then paid/traded east. At times, furs and pelts were also accepted as tribute by the khans, though (Findlay and O'Rourke 2007, 106). According to Shen Fuwei, Novgorod turned into an east-west trading center, featuring caravans from China and CA exchanging their goods, intermediated by Russian traders, with those of the Hanseatic League (2009, 138). Halperin adds that the authorities provided tax exemptions to Hanseatic merchants entering the Mongol Empire through Novgorod and passing through Suzdal (perhaps on their way to Saray). While Novgorod was the entrepot for nearly all Baltic trade entering and leaving the Rus principalities, the city's intimate trade connections with the Orient are attested by archeological finds of silks and glazed pottery from the Muslim East and Damascus swords (Halperin 1985, 80–81).

Mongol rule over the Rus principalities soon turned into a classic system of "indirect rule" ("at arm's length"— corresponding to the first type of nomadic statehood

---

[74] This is obviously a geoeconomic parallel to the location and function of Itil, the capital of the former Khazar Empire.

[75] Actually, these were gold-threaded silk brocades that the Mongol nobility cherished and often bestowed on guests as a symbol of honor (May 2012, 111, 115).

according to Khazanov—see below).[76] Russians and other sedentary inhabitants of the former Rus now hardly lived in or closely near the steppe any more but mostly in the (northern) woodlands. Indirect rule allowed the Eastern Slavs to keep their religious and cultural identity. Also, the inner sociopolitical order of the principalities was not touched. The Orthodox Church kept its privileges (including its tax-exempt status) and its properties. Moreover, Russian traders already in the second half of the thirteenth century received privileges which allowed them to travel freely; plus: these traders benefited from the new regime's provision of security on the roads—security that had previously been all but undeliverable (Pickhan 2009, 123).

Like their Chagatayid counterparts, the Khans of the Golden Horde, while establishing a capital of their Ulus, continued to nomadize. In spring, for instance, Khan Batu and his entourage proceeded from the ruler's winter encampment in or near Saray up the Volga to reach his summer stay in the area of the former Volga Bulgarian state (the Volga-Kama Basin); in the fall they returned south. The former capital of that state, Bolgar, became an important settlement of the new rulers and the central mint of the khanate (Grousset 1965/2008, 469). The Volga-Kama Basin as well as the Northern Caucasus plains emerged as the granaries of the Golden Horde; Saray and other cities in the south received vital wheat supplies but also timber and slaves shipped via the Volga. The Volga also became the transportation route for luxury furs from the northern forests—sable, lynx, and ermine—another parallel to the Khazar era. One of the most precious goods the Mongols possessed in the Eurasian grasslands, respectively, the Desht-i-Kipchak, were huge herds of horses. Large numbers of these horses were regularly exported to the Delhi Sultanate (India), which sorely needed them to uphold its rule on the subcontinent (Jackson 2005, 307; Hambly (ed) 1966/1979, 133).

Golden Horde Khan Batu was succeeded by Khan Berke (1257–1267), who established a new capital of the ulus, New Saray. This settlement, near present-day Volgograd, was even more centrally located than (Old) Saray. In particular, New Saray was nearer to the khanate's important Black Sea ports (see below), and to Kiev, Moscow and Bulgar, without being at a disadvantage in its eastern connections. Under Khan Berke, the authorities' policy of building towns as trading and manufacturing centers was stepped up. Implanted in territories primarily inhabited or used by nomads (the steppe belt as well as the lower and middle reaches of the Volga up to the Volga-Kama basin), these new settlements were equipped with fortresses and a core of artisans' workshops (many of which produced weapons),

as well as an infrastructure of bazaars and caravanserais. In the immediate surroundings, some farming activities were added to enable a minimum of local self-sufficiency (Khazanov 1983/1994, 242).

These Golden Horde steppe towns became a focus of syncretic culture of originally forcefully settled indigenous people, of businessmen and administrators from CA and other corners of the empire, and of the nomadic elite itself.[77] Including town-like settlements, there were reportedly over 100 towns on the territory of the khanate; about 20 of them were large centers and possessed mintage rights. Among the urban centers were Old Saray, New Saray, and Astrakhan on the lower Volga, Soldaya (Sudak, former Sogdaya) and Kaffa (former Theodosia) on the Crimea, Tana (Azov, at the mouth of the Don), and Urgench.[78] These towns soon became flourishing centers of international trade. In contrast, towns and cities in the Rus took longer to recover (Khazanov 1983/1994, 242).

After the European crusades had contributed to weakening Byzantium in the early thirteenth century, the commercially very advanced Italian city-states of Genoa and Venice attained easier access to the Eastern Mediterranean and the Black Sea. This advancement of the two city-states has also been called "commercial revolution," which is seen to have embodied the expansion of trade across Southern Europe, the establishment of new branch offices, and the invention of new forms of capital investment (Lopez, cited by Reichert 2015, 65). Here one could add that advances in business techniques and connections had probably also been achieved to a comparable degree by the Hanseatic League in the North Sea and the Baltics. In any case, perspectives for international trade changed qualitatively once the Mongol Empire had conquered the Pontic steppes and Crimea and had thus in fact opened up overland access for European traders via the SR to Central, Southern, and Eastern Asia and for Asian traders in the opposite direction. Soldaya, which was a thriving port at the time of the visit of the Franciscan monk-traveler Roebroeck in 1253, soon faced stiff competition from nearby Black Sea ports, which all rivaled for expanding business (Jackson 2005, 296).

From the mid-1260s, the khan gave licenses to European countries, notably Italian city-states, which allowed them to found trading colonies (including consulates, warehouses, and other infrastructure) on the northern shore of the Black Sea. The colonies remained under the special protection of the khan, who received large tribute payments from the

---

[76] Indirect rule is also in line with Lebedynsky's definition of imperial nomadism (see Box 2.1).

[77] Here, Khazaria's urbanization was probably another predecessor.

[78] This implies that despite the Mongol's partial razing of Urgench and their devastation of Khwarazm's sophisticated irrigation system in 1221, the city and its infrastructure were reconstructed relatively quickly.

Italians. Initially, both Venice and Genoa were successful; Venice acquired a trading establishment in Tana (Azov), while Genoa created a colony at Kaffa (Grousset 1965/2008, 481). The Venetians however had repeated disputes with the Mongol authorities, and the Genoese eventually gained the upper hand in the intra-Italian commercial rivalry. Venice and particularly Genoa were well-placed to be the middlemen between a growing and increasingly prosperous Western Europe[79] on the one hand, and the Islamic world, China and India on the other, under the conditions of the Pax Mongolica (Findlay and O'Rourke 2007, 94).

Once again, Chinese silks and porcelains became much more accessible in Europe. Already in 1257, silk of "Cathay" was sold by Genoese merchants at the fairs of Champagne. Supplies of raw silk and cotton, but also pepper and other spices were in growing demand in European industries. These imports were paid for not only in silver from new mines opened e.g. in Central Europe, but also with woolen and linen cloth of Flanders and Florence, with velvets or velours, fabrics of various provenance, with jewelry, perfumes, weapons and an increasing variety of other manufactured products (Findlay and O'Rourke 2007, 94).

But Mongol exports from Kaffa, Tana and Soldaya also consisted of goods coming from less faraway places, like furs, leather, wood, amber, salt, wax, grain, wine, fish (particularly sturgeon), caviar,[80] livestock, horses and slaves. As underlined by Jackson, the bulk of export activity from the ports actually comprised furs and slaves. Italian merchants had been involved in Pontic slave traffic as early as 1246, when pope Innocent IV made an effort to secure the release of Christian slaves—Eastern Slavs, Greeks, Bulgarians and Vlachs—whom the merchants were selling to Muslim powers (Jackson 2005, 307). Direct trade relations between the Rus principalities and the Genoese ports on the Crimea (via rivers, portages and overland) were also encouraged by the Mongol authorities. This trade was apparently quite profitable for Novgorod (Lemercier-Quelquejay 1970, 100).

By and large, the wealth of the Italian trading colonies was based on their location at the western end of the transcontinental caravan route and at the eastern end of the maritime trade by Italian ships. Despite occasional disputes and even military confrontations with the khan's authorities, the Italian merchants were able to generate and, moreover, repatriate much capital from profits earned through SR trade. This capital accumulation outside the military and political

reach of the Mongols may have contributed to the development of early capitalism in Europe.[81]

3.4.2.7 Ulus Hülegü/Il-Khanate: Conquest and Ravaging of Middle East, New Nomadic Mass Immigration

Hülegü (Möngke Khan's brother) in the late 1240s and the 1250s conquered the bulk of the Iranian Highlands, Eastern Syria, Mesopotamia, Western and Southern Afghanistan and Baluchistan. Once again, Mongol military operations inflicted great destruction and loss of life. Like Western CA, Iran may have lost about a quarter of its population of a total of 5–10 million. In 1258, Baghdad was partly or totally razed and is said to have lost up to 800,000 people (Kauz 2009, 309). The Abbasid caliphate was wiped out and the last caliph executed. The extent of bloodletting may appear somewhat surprising, given that the Mongols had in the meantime at least partly modified their ways vis-à-vis sedentary people (see Ögöday's change of stance toward settled populations, his ban on further seizures of farmland for pastures, and Möngke's fiscal and monetary reforms). In any case, the reconstruction of Baghdad seems to have gone ahead relatively quickly. When the Polo brothers reportedly arrived in Baghdad in the early 1270s on their trip to China, the city had somehow recovered from the Mongol invasion and apparently even restored a semblance of its former glory or prosperity. Within a decade or two, travelers appear to have again referred to Baghdad as a great commercial center (Rossabi 2012, 57; Zhang 2005, 140).

Hülegü assumed the title of Il-Khan (or "subordinate khan" to the Great Khan). Apart from the abovementioned conquered territories, Eastern Khorassan including Nishapur that had already been conquered by Genghis Khan, Eastern Anatolia, and Transcaucasia that had been acquired by Ögöday and his successor were incorporated into the Il-Khanate.[82] Hülegü Khan's (1255–1265) defeat in the

---

[79] From the late twelfth century, Western Europe was experiencing a boom in cloth and textile production, spearheaded by Flemish towns.

[80] According to Martinez, the sturgeon and caviar were most likely procured from the Caspian Sea, where Marco Polo had noted the presence of Genoese shipping (2009, 104).

[81] Compare Norel's considerations (2009, 176): « Il s'agit de l'idée (developée par Frank et Hobson) d'un capital marchand actif depuis très longtemps d'abord dans l'islam et en Asie puis, par contagion ou stimulation, en Europe même. Il n'y a aucune raison a priori pour que ce capital marchand n'apparaisse pas partout où le commerce lointain exerce ses effets et n'est pas reprimé ou pillé par le pouvoir politique. Et ce commerce lointain oriental commence clairement à toucher l'Europe durant le siècle mongol, voire avant ». ("It's about the idea (developed by Frank and Hobson) of commercial capital which was active already for a very long time in the Muslim countries and in Asia, and later, via contagion or stimulation, in Europe itself. There is no a priori reason why such capital wouldn't appear in all places where long-distance trade has its impact and isn't suppressed or pillaged by the political authority. This long-distance oriental trade clearly started to touch Europe during the Mongol century or even before.")

[82] Great Khan Möngke's decision to integrate Transcaucasia and southern Azerbaijan into the Il-Khanate gave rise to long-lasting tensions with the Golden Horde, which itself had coveted these two regions.

battle of Ayn Jalut in 1260 against the Egyptian Mamluks (one of the rare Mongol military defeats, on the reasons see above) rendered direct Mongol access to the Eastern Mediterranean more difficult and sometimes fragile. Mongol-European SR trade connections through Aleppo and Antiochia were tenuous and sometimes interrupted.[83] Given its favored location in the grasslands of Southern Azerbaijan as well as on a crossroads of important trade routes leading to the southern shore of the Black Sea (Trebizond) and to the Eastern Mediterranean (Antiochia, Lajazzo), Taebriz was chosen as capital of the Ulus Hülegü (Map 3.6).

In the long run, the Mongol invasion had a grave impact on agriculture on the Iranian Plateau. This region largely lacks great rivers and even contains some deserts (Dasht-i-Kavir, Lut). Therefore, farming is, or was until very recently, dependent on the elaborate qanat (karez) system of irrigation—a system of underground water channels that brings the water, often over many kilometers, to where it is needed.[84] Some of these channels were destroyed during the Mongol invasions, and without effective irrigation much of the land would soon revert to desert. Moreover, qanats, even if not actually destroyed, may swiftly cease to operate if they are not continually maintained. As Morgan explains: If peasants were killed in large numbers, or fled from their land and stayed away, or were expelled, arable land could suffer irreparable damage simply through neglect of the qanats. Stripped of their farming hinterland, some cities would soon lack adequate or cheap food supplies and other support, and therefore would probably not be rebuilt to anything approaching their previous size, or in any case would be more costly to reconstruct (Morgan 2007, 70–71).

The Iranian settled economy—and its qanats—had suffered other harmful nomadic invasions earlier, e.g., the Seljuk conquest. The two major factors that set the Mongol invasion apart from others were, first, the extent of the bloodshed (mentioned above), and, second, the dimension of the influx of nomads from the Eurasian steppe. The Mongols sponsored a great nomadic migration wave into the Middle East: In the second half of the thirteenth century, possibly more than 100,000 Mongol or Turkic families and their camps, or according to other sources around 170,000 men, and 680,000 women and children, accompanied by herds of up to 17 million sheep, moved to take possessions in the south. One fifth to one quarter of the nomadic migrants

and their herds were eventually stationed in Anatolia; the rest remained in Iran (Amitai 2001, 152; Wink 2001, 224).

There can be no doubt that the Mongol conquest of Iran led to a sharp and partly irremediable decline in irrigation and agriculture, a substantial transformation of fields into pastures, and the desertification of certain lands. Despite later recovery, numerous villages and towns were never rebuilt (Kauz 2009, 310). Comparable to what the Mongols did in China, Hülegü and his successors established direct rule while preserving part of the bureaucratic apparatus in the Il-Khanate.

In the late 1250s and the 1260s—after and in contrast to Möngke Khan's fiscal reforms—the Il-Khanate authorities imposed irregular and capricious levies on the population. Once more in analogy to early appanage policy/practices in China: As a result of the redistribution of properties carried out by the new authorities, the Mongol and Turkic nobility acquired a lot of what was left of cultivated lands. They often heavily exploited the peasants on these lands and employed arbitrary and violent methods in the process. And the landlords usually did not break away from their own nomadic way of life (Rossabi 2012, 78, 80; Khazanov 1983/1994, 252). Nevertheless, many Turko-Mongol newcomers found themselves under the influence and draw of the ancient Iranian host civilization. The political infighting from Hülegü's death in 1265 until Ghazan Khan's accession in 1295 put off economic stabilization for an extended period.

3.4.3 Internal Mongol Warfare and Interruption of Trade Boom (1280s–1300s)

After the empire was conquered, two opposing ideologies with respect to the management of the economy emerged or resurfaced in the high ranks of the Genghisids (Artykbaev 2007, 139; Rossabi 2012, 121):

– Adherents of old Mongol traditions and values of steppe existence remained enemies of settled life, farming, and towns and were inclined to the merciless exploitation of oases. One might label them "traditionalists."
– Proponents of the second ideology, that had arisen in the context of continuous contact with sedentary civilization, accepted long-term coexistence with settled and town life. These proponents favored the adoption of at least some elements of sedentary institutions. They were in favor of the re-establishment of productive forces, which was regarded as indispensable for the good functioning of tax collection. They might be called "integrationists."

---

[83] This recalls the (inconclusive) clashes, i.a., for control of the SR in approximately the same area between the Roman and Parthian empires more than a millennium earlier and between the Byzantine and Sassanian empires more than half a millennium earlier.

[84] Some qanats date back to the Achaemenid Empire (for more explanation on the qanat/karez system, see Sect. 2.2.1).

Both currents supported the exaction of tribute and looked favorably on (mutually advantageous) trade and merchants' activities. In the long term, proponents of the first ideology were threatened by a stationary and possibly increasingly marginal existence, while adherents of the second tended to be attracted by foreign sophisticated cultures and risked being eventually assimilated by these civilizations.

Against this background, inner-Mongol disputes and conflicts were triggered by Kubilay's policies of Sinicization in the Great Khanate. These policies, clearly along the lines of the abovementioned "integrationist" (second) ideology and conducted by the supreme leader of the empire, gave rise to discontent in other factions of the elite. Moreover, Kubilay's military campaigns and conquests in Southern China and East and Southeast Asia were accompanied by a degree of negligence vis-à-vis the traditional core regions of the empire (Krieger 2003, 266). Kaidu, grandson of Ögöday, became a fierce "traditionalist"[85] and Kubilay's most dangerous rival: As a power base, Kaidu chose Dzungaria and Semirechie (in the north of the Chagatay Khanate), which, notwithstanding some settled areas in Semirechie, were dominated by the nomadic way of life. Open tensions, skirmishes, and warfare broke out around 1270 between the forces of Kaidu, who enlisted the support of some other Mongol princes, and those of the Great Khan. The pretext was a dispute over grazing and camping rights in East Turkestan, where the border between the two khanates ran through (Rossabi 2012, 89).

A three decades' cycle of Mongol internecine wars followed. From the 1280s Kaidu, who had become ruler of the Chagatay Khanate, temporarily severed overland SR connections between China on the one hand and Iran and Eastern Europe on the other (Hambly (ed) 1966/1979, 120; Krieger 2003, 266). In the 1290s, repeated incursions from the Chagatay Khanate and intermittent loose Chagatay rule over Punjab[86] rounded off the separation of the eastern part from the western part of the empire. Under Kaidu's rule the Ulus Chagatay possibly became something like a transasiatic north-south bolt aimed at controlling Eurasian east-west overland trade. This made it vital for Kubilay to keep open the sea route between the Great Khanate and the Il-Khanate. This maritime SR, also called Spice Route (see above), was upheld by Chinese merchant ships during the Yuan dynasty. Marco Polo was compelled to use this route when he accompanied a Yuan princess to Iran in the late 1280s (Shen 2009, 156, 158; Hambly (ed) 1966/1979, 120).

Continuing hostilities from the 1270s to the first years of the new century partly destroyed the irrigation infrastructure of the Turfan region and of some Tarim oases (which had not been harmed during the Mongol conquest). Troops of the Great Khan invaded Kaidu's territories and inflicted major losses on Dzungaria and Zhetysu (i.a., on the latter's sedentary areas). The population of the oases of East Turkestan and Zhetysu was also decimated by famines. As Rossabi aptly put it, given that Kubilay had the resources of China at his command, the wars did not decisively harm his rule. In contrast, the Chagatay Khanate did not have the same means and was indeed detrimentally affected by the wars (Rossabi 2012, 89).

Simultaneously, the Chagatay Khanate fought over territory with the Il-Khans, creating further difficulties for itself. This warfare in the south was also protracted and harmed the agriculture that sustained the towns and SR trade (Rossabi 2012, 90). Since it lay near the Amu Daria border, Transoxiana was directly touched. Il-Khanid armies plundered Bukhara on repeated occasions; in 1273 the city that had just recovered from the Mongol invasion was burned to the ground and then remained uninhabited for 7 years (Weiers 2004, 134). Finally, as alluded to earlier, the Golden Horde and the Il-Khanate were also at loggerheads over territories and occasionally battled each other. Military hostilities between the two uluses even led to a temporary alliance of the Golden Horde with an adversarial foreign power, the Mamluk Sultanate of Egypt.

A few years after Kaidu's death (in 1301), peace was restored and the blockage of the SR removed. Approximately at the same time, relations between the Golden Horde and the Il-Khanate also improved (see below). According to Soucek, Kaidu's death signified the final apportionment and restabilization of the Mongol Empire, however, now consisting of four de-facto independent constituent parts (2000, 112). In terms of internal policies and in some cases even in terms of external military alliances, each ulus undoubtedly went its own way. They were still held together by common trade interests and by the general aim (as a rule) to keep the SR open (Arp 2007/2008, 134).

As mentioned earlier, the Mongol conquest and the accompanying massive migration of Turko-Mongol nomads transformed some sedentary and farming territories in CA, e.g., in Khorassan and parts of the Iranian Highlands, into pasturelands or even wastelands. And not only was the frontier between nomadic and settled civilization pushed

---

[85] This did not prevent Kaidu, once he had become the ruler of the Chagatay Khanate, from giving Governor Masud Beg the green light to continue business-friendly policies of reconstruction of Mavarannahr and other southern oases of the ulus.

[86] Yet the Mongols' lack of success in venturing further into India was partly due to their dislike of the subcontinent's subtropical and tropical climate and partly to the surprisingly strong military response from the Delhi Sultanate that had been established approximately at the same time as the Mongol Empire and whose core consisted of (former) Afghan slave soldiers and a robust cavalry largely consisting of horses imported from the Eurasian steppes, notably from the Khanate of the Golden Horde. Thus, one could infer that Mongols' trade interests were so strong that they at times trumped their overriding strategic interests.

south again; some of the islands of sedentary culture that had emerged within the Eurasian steppe over the previous centuries vanished. This is the case, for instance, for Zhetysu/Semirechie.

The re-nomadization of Semirechie is probably due to three major events: first, the original Mongol conquest (in 1219); second, the moving of a large number of nomads into this territory favorable for animal husbandry (in the following decades); and third, the devastation of Semirechie by the army of the Great Khan in the war with Kaidu (in the 1280s and 1290s). The Mongol takeover of Semirechie (as part of the incorporation of the Western Liao state) did not immediately bring the large-scale destruction of towns, but it opened the door to large-scale nomadic immigration into the "Land of Seven Rivers," which, in the view of herders, featured good pastures. Toward the middle of the thirteenth century, up to 200,000 nomads (the overwhelming majority of them pastoralists) may have converged in Zhetysu, which, as explained above, Kaidu had chosen as his power base (Baipakov et al. 1997, 100).

Given the attractiveness and sheer suitability of the terrain, the newcomers were not interested in exploiting towns and farms from a distance, like it happened in the much larger southern oases of Mavarannahr, Kashgar, and others. It is easy to grasp that the exercise of their economic activity in their chosen new homeland required extensive grazing territories, which entailed the elimination of gardens and irrigation systems and the trampling of herds on cultivated fields. The rising regional concentration of the new nomadic inhabitants triggered the piecemeal wiping out of formerly thriving urban and agricultural civilization (Khazanov 1983/1994, 79; Artykbaev 2007, 100, 139).

Wilhelm von Roebroeck, who passed through the Ili valley about 30 years after the conquest, confirmed that a large number of towns in that valley had been partially or totally ruined by the Mongols in order to make place for grazing terrain. Immediately after the invasion, the towns Koyalyk and Ilibalyk continued to exist in the Karatal and Ili valleys (see Map 4.7), and there were also some urban settlements in the Talas and Chu valleys. But around the middle of the thirteenth century, a general decline of farming and urban life was perceptible. The elimination of the farming hinterland of towns (forcing town dwellers to look for more expensive food further afield) combined with methods of predatory taxation and exploitation of the settled population gradually eroded/removed the economic and social basis of urban structure in Semirechie (Baipakov et al. 1997, 100).

In the valley of the Talas, around ten towns and settlements continued to function. Most of them were situated in the upper reaches of the river where the mining of silver and lead continued, an activity that seems to have had some value added for the new masters. In contrast,

neglect could be observed in the Chu valley; the towns slowly became deserted. According to the findings of archeological research, sedentary life in the lower Ili valley and its surroundings finally stopped toward the end of the thirteenth century in Almaty and other towns. The devastations inflicted by the invasion of Kubilay's forces in the war with Kaidu may have delivered the coup de grâce to settled and urban life in Zhetysu (Baipakov et al. 1997, 143–144; Hambly (ed) 1966/1979, 142–145).

Written sources of the fourteenth to fifteenth centuries witness the Ilibalyk area to have been void of towns or buildings and the region to have reverted to all but pure nomadic pastoralism. Many of the well-known cities of pre-Mongol Southeastern Kazakhstan—Taraz (Talas), Almaty, Koyalyk, Ilibalyk, and other settlements—were practically wiped off the map (Baipakov et al. 1997, 99). Still, major trade routes continued to run through the region. This goes particularly for the SR (and its caravanserais) passing north of the Tienshan and connecting the towns of Balasagun, Almalik, and Beshbalik, and very likely Southern Semirechie was also crossed by the Yam with its well-developed infrastructure, supervised by the relevant tumen administrations. As Soucek explains, Semirechie and Dzungaria had become a kind of typical Mongol homeland, to the extent of acquiring a new name—Moghulistan ("Land of the Mongols" in Persian) (2000, 120). Moghulistan soon emerged as the core of a new political sub-entity of the Chagatay Khanate.

The late thirteenth and the early fourteenth centuries saw a gradual Turkization of the ruling strata of the Mongol nomadic aristocracy as well as of rank-and-file soldiers that had remained in the steppe regions of the conquered sub-empires (outside Mongolia proper). As mentioned earlier, those Mongols that had relocated to China or Iran soon found themselves under the influence and attraction of these large and ancient sedentary civilizations. The gradual cultural assimilation of the Mongols, notwithstanding their ruling positions, was probably due to their small numbers compared to the nomadic or sedentary populations they encountered. A specific process that contributed to Turkization was that Turks who had joined Mongol armies as junior partners under Mongol commanders often began asserting themselves and eventually gained prominent posts in military and government administration (Abazov 2008, Map 23).[87]

Many members of Turko-Mongol ruling elites as well as ordinary tribesmen began converting to Islam in the Khanate of the Golden Horde, the Il-Khanate, and the Chagatay Khanate. The conversions started in the 1260s in the Golden

---

[87] This is no new phenomenon and recalls the ascension of Turkic slave soldiers in the caliphate and under the Samanids.

Horde, when Khan Berke converted to the Muslim faith, spread to the Il-Khanate, where Ghazan Khan adopted Islam in 1295, and to the Chagatay Khanate, with Khan Tarmashirin converting another generation later, in 1330 (Fragner 2008, 48). This may have been due to the influence of Sufism, a mystical movement of Islam that in its popular form frequently appealed to the steppe nomads (see above). The Golden Horde was even declared an Islamic state in 1313, and the Sharia replaced the Yassa as the supreme legal norm (Morgan 2007, 127).

In the Golden Horde, Mongols and Turkic troops started to assimilate with indigenous inhabitants of the Desht-i-Kipchak and the Pontic steppes (the Polovtsy), but also with those of the Volga-Kama Basin (the Volga Bulgarians), to turn into a Turko-Mongol people that was soon called "Tatars." Tatars were Muslims that spoke a Turkic language and whose leaders were often in the ruling strata of the khanate. From this time, Russians and Tatars were separated not only by cultures and languages but also by monotheistic religions and political ranks (Hambly (ed) 1966/1979, 133).[88] In the Chagatay Khanate, Islam, already strong in Transoxiana, was adopted as the state religion in preference to Buddhism which was still widespread in East Turkestan. The Mongols' assimilation to the Turkic population of the Chagatay Khanate was accompanied by their adoption of the Turkic language and the Persian script. Eventually, an original Chagatay-Turkic literature developed.

Khan Tarmashirin's conversion to Islam probably alienated the Shamanist nomads of the Issyk Koel and the Ili area and the Buddhist and Christian inhabitants of the Tarim Basin. The nomads rebelled against him and shifted their allegiance to a new khan in the east. Soon, there were two lines of Chagatayid khans: One line of Islamic Western Chagatayids principally in Transoxiana and Bactria (Northern Afghanistan) and another branch of Shamanist khans ruling over Semirechie, Dzungaria, and East Turkestan including the former Uighuristan (the Turfan area). This second subregion of the sub-empire now came to be called "Moghulistan" (Starr (ed) 2004, 46). The split of the Chagatay Khanate also reflected the resurgence of differences between Mongol "integrationists" and "traditionalists."

3.4.4   Economic Reforms, New Transcontinental Trade Boom, and Decentralized Imperial Heyday (1300s–1340s)

There may be three main reasons for the split of the empire into de-facto independent uluses and for further splits afterwards:

- *Absence of an orderly and undisputed succession procedure*
  The Mongol Empire shared this costly defect with many other nomadic states, which is why few of these polities outlasted their founders. While the Mongols did not escape this logic, for at least two more generations, sufficient discipline and cohesion assured the giant state's survival (Soucek 2000, 107).
- *Geopolitical and power policy clashes between different Genghisid lines*
  These include various occasions of disputes and conflicts between Mongol "traditionalists" (adherents of old Mongol traditions and values of steppe existence) and "integrationists" (who favored the adoption of at least some elements of sedentary institutions).
- *Immense size of empire featuring extreme cultural, religious, and economic diversity*
  This extraordinary diversity that went with the sheer size of the state (probably encompassing up to half of humanity) was bound to lead to centrifugal tendencies (regionalism). Moreover, the heterogeneous mass of peoples and economies was ruled by an extremely small number of members of the power-holding ethnicity.[89] Logistical costs of holding the bicontinental empire together were high despite superb military and infrastructural capacities.

The Mongols' numerical weakness probably accelerated their gradual transformation from political and cultural outsiders to regional insiders. Once half-sedentarized, converted to the regionally dominating religion, and entered the process of assimilation, the Mongols became primarily interested in the fate of the ulus/sub-empire or principality in which they lived and less drawn by overriding imperial nomadic/Mongol concerns. They may even have become culturally estranged from their fellow kin in other parts of Eurasia. Eastern and Western Mongols also drifted apart on account of religious differences: In the Great Khanate, Mongols were inclined toward Buddhism, whereas in the

---

[88] Today's Tatars of the autonomous Republic of Tatarstan in the Russian Federation and the descendants of the Tatars of Crimea (most of whom had been deported to CA in World War II on the orders of Stalin) can be traced back to these Islamized Turko-Mongols.

[89] It is estimated that at Kubilay Khan's time, the Mongols represented less than one percent of the population of the empire (Lemercier-Quelquejay 1970, 56).

other sub-empires they mostly adopted Islam[90] (Kollmar-Paulenz 2011, 45; Lemercier-Quelquejay 1970, 56).

However, as long as the uluses/khanates still had the power and the will to control and protect transcontinental caravan trade, which played such an important role for the prosperity of the empire and its ruling elites, the various parts were held together by common economic interests, as Hambly convincingly argues (ed. 1966/1979, 121). While imperial unity had evaporated from the 1260s, the four now independent Mongol realms managed to maintain a degree of economic cooperation for another three quarters of a century, despite sporadic and sometimes prolonged hostilities. The chief raison d'être of C Asian imperialism was control of the Eurasian SR. Even as the empire splintered, trade and craftsmanship generally continued to thrive. This was underlined by an (albeit short-lived) peace and cooperation treaty, concluded in 1307 by all four Mongol sub-empires and aimed at protecting long-distance trade (Paul 2012, 299).

3.4.4.1 Great Khanate: Further Expansion, Infrastructure Development, and Crisis of Paper Money Circulation

The Mongols in China soon appreciated the utility of a bureaucratic process for collecting taxes in such a huge and sophisticated economy, and they re-established the recruitment of civil servants via the examination system in 1315. The appanage system had already been streamlined and arbitrary practices reined in. Strenuous efforts went to refurbishing the infrastructure, in particular transport and irrigation projects. For instance, the Imperial Canal linking Beijing (Khanbalik) and Hangzhou was restored and widened, e.g., to enable larger deliveries of food from the south to supply the imperial capital. While the paper money system originally proved effective, the treasury seems to have eventually succumbed to the temptation to print more and more bills, which reduced their value and provoked an inflationary situation. This may have been a harbinger of a tendency toward economic decline and crisis which would gradually set in (Maddison 1998, 23; Roux 1993, 402).

3.4.4.2 Chagatay Khanate: Partial Sedentarization of Nomads as Ruling Class—Renewed Monetary Reforms Support Trade

The Chagatayid Khan Kebek (1318–1326) moved, along with many members of the nomadic elite, from (nomadic) Semirechie to (sedentary) Mavarannahr, where he and his court settled in the valley of the Kashka Daria. There he had two palaces built, around which the town of Karshi (meaning "palace" in Mongolian and Turkic) grew up later. Instead of having a darughachi administer, he exerted direct rule over the region himself and attempted to create a strong central power in the khanate. In accordance with Mongol tradition, he divided his polity (or resuscitated its division) into tumens (military-administrative districts). The holdings of many local landowners were converted to tumens, and the landowners themselves became hereditary governors (Ashrafyan 1998, 319).

Kebek Khan contributed to the recovery and reconstruction of C Asian cities, particularly in Mavarannahr. Among the towns he had restored was also ancient Balkh (Bactria), "which, from the time of Genghis Khan was deserted and turned into a tangle of reeds" (Akhmedov 1998, 265). He carried out tax and monetary reforms to stimulate the regional economy and trade and to curb abuses and corruption; in doing this, he attempted to follow the example of the reforms of Ghazan Khan in the Ulus Hülegü (see below). The minting of silver coins was reorganized and standardized (1321). The new monetary unit became known as the silver kebek dinar, or "kebek" or "koepek," a term that survives in the Russian word "kopek" (one-hundredth of a ruble). One kebek dinar equaled six dirhams[91] (Akhmedov 1998, 265).

As mentioned earlier, the Chagatayid Khanate effectively split in two some years after Khan Tarmashirin's (1328–1334) adoption of Islam, and the areas more strongly oriented toward nomadism and shamanism in the north (Semirechie and Dzungaria), together with the Tarim Basin and the Turfan area, broke away to form the principality of "Moghulistan." While most inhabitants of the Tarim Basin and of Turfan were sedentary, in the first half of the fourteenth century, the majority of them were not Muslims (many were Buddhists and Christian Nestorians) and opposed Islamic rule. Moghulistan was a kind a hybrid economy, consisting of a predominantly pastoral nomadic north and an agricultural-urban south. Interestingly, despite the labelling of Moghulistan as more "traditionalist" and of Transoxiana as more "integrationist," in both cases did important parts of the nomadic aristocracy settle in the respective southern oases (e.g., whether Samarkand or Kashgar) and become the ruling class (begs or noblemen) of the sedentary population. For instance, the aristocracy of the Dughlat tribe became the dominating landowners in many oases of East Turkestan (Starr (ed) 2004, 47).

---

[90] With the temporary exception of the principality of Moghulistan, which broke away from the Chagatay Khanate – but this only underlines the rupture between eastern and western Mongols.

[91] Silver money was, i.a., issued in the mints of Otrar (which worked regularly until the end of the 1360s) and of Taraz, Ispidzhab, and Sygnak (Baipakov et al. 1997, 155).

3.4.4.3 Khanate of the Golden Horde: Recovery Spreads to Russia, Heyday of SR Trade via Italian Colonies, Important Mongol Legacy

At the end of the thirteenth century, the Mongol (Tatar) authorities decided to change their way of collecting taxes from the Rus principalities: The collection of the "vykhod" or "dan" (tribute, yield) was passed from the hands of the baskak (darughachin) into the hands of the Rus princes (Shukow et al. 1957/1963, Band 3, 694). Once a minimum level of trust was achieved, this was obviously an easier way for the Tatars to benefit from the extensive taxes that continued to be levied and to be passed on to the Khan; however, by doing this, the Tatars also lost some amount of operational control.[92] In 1332, the collection of taxes from all Russian principalities was delegated to the prince of Moscow, who was recognized as grand prince of Russia (Ledonne 2008, 17).[93]

Around 1300 the metropolitan of the Orthodox Church transferred his seat from half-ruined Kiev to Vladimir, from where his successor moved to aspiring Moscow in 1328. According to Halperin, there are indications that in the first half of the fourteenth century, nonelite segments of the population of the Russian principalities consumed some internationally traded goods and that several cities undertook important construction projects for cathedrals and other public edifices (1985, 81). Apparently, even small towns and some rural areas were able to pay taxes in silver, which points to exposure to overland trade. Oriental goods such as silk, glass, beads, cowrie shells, and boxwood combs have been dug up at village sites in many places of the Russian countryside. This suggests that even the Russian peasant during the Mongol era did in fact have some ties with international markets. By the early fourteenth century, Golden Horde territories reportedly featured about 140 towns (Findlay and O'Rourke 2007, 106; Rossabi 2012, 87).

Under the reign of Khan Uzbek (1313–1340), the Golden Horde may have reached its second economic heyday. Khan Uzbek[94] fostered trade, which had been relaunched again after the period of internecine Mongol warfare affecting the

Chagatay Khanate had passed. With a rising inflow of revenues, he patronized the arts and built new cities which were quickly populated with officials, merchants, and artisans (Rossabi 2012, 88). Craft industries (particularly metallurgy, ceramics, textiles, and leather processing) as well as commerce were promoted (Jehel (ed) 2007, 267).

As Roux explains, New Saray was quite a large settlement at its apex; conservative archeologists estimate its population in the first half of the fourteenth century at around 100,000. For this period we have a detailed description of the Golden Horde capital coming from Al Umari who evokes Saray's lavish markets, baths, and madrasas and the splendor and magnificence of the Khan's court. Ibn Battuta, who visited Khan Uzbek's court between 1332 and 1334, was impressed by New Saray's 13 large mosques, the city's overcrowded bazaars, and the cosmopolitan mix of peoples "composed of Mongols, . . .Kipchaks, Cherkesses, Russians, Byzantinians, and Muslims of Egypt, Iraq and Syria," where "every nationality lives in its own quarter and has its bazaar" (Roux 1993, 479). Apart from craftsmanship, metal production and processing boomed: eight big furnaces were operated. Certainly, massive deportations and forced resettlement had contributed to the upswing at the start, but apparently soon, as Roux points out, living conditions for artisans improved, or they were freed from slave-like exploitation. Moreover the presence of a great court attracted many skilled workers from the outside who organized themselves into guild-like professional corporations resembling those of the Muslim world (ibid).

It was in this period (at some point in the 1330s) that Francesco Balducci Pegolotti, an employee of the Florentine banking house of the Bardi, wrote and published the commercial handbook "Pratica della Mercatura" that also referred to parts of the SR network running through the territory of the Ulus Jöchi, namely, the "steppe route" (Crimea–Saray–Urgench and further east). Moreover, a remarkable example of multilingualism accompanying Mongol or Tatar rule also appeared in the 1330s: The Biblioteca Marciana of Venice keeps a trilingual encyclopedia that probably originated in Crimea and that contains mostly commercial and religious texts—texts in (Vulgar)

---

[92] Of course this change also opened some (limited) possibilities for the princes to manipulate and embezzle tribute payments (Halperin 1985, 85).

[93] Why was Moscow chosen and not, e.g., the richer principality of Novgorod or the more powerful (at the time) principality of Tver? While there may be a number of political and other reasons, one can certainly add that Moscow at that time was a relatively small polity and therefore could not quickly turn into a danger for the Khan; Moscow was centrally located in the former Rus (not at the northwestern periphery), and Moscow was relatively easily accessible from New Saray via the Volga and its tributaries.

[94] The name "Uzbek" was not only famous in the fourteenth century but was to play an important role from the fifteenth century onwards. Abul

Khair Khan, a Genghisid-Jöchid tribal chief from the later line of the khans of Sibir (a regional successor state to the Golden Horde situated in Western Siberia/Northern Kazakhstan) succeeded in rallying a number of tribes formerly subject to the Golden Horde. Probably in memory of one of the most important leaders of the Golden Horde, Khan Uzbek, the tribal confederation gathering around Abul Khair adopted the name "Uzbek." This confederation soon started to expand militarily in a southerly direction (Fragner 2008, 54).

Latin, Persian, and in Cuman (or Kipchak)[95]; therefore the work was called *Codex Cumanicus*. The encyclopedia also includes a selection of idiomatic expressions in German which could be helpful for merchants and businessmen in typical situations on the steppe or at sea (Schmieder 2013, 110–111). As alluded to above, during the course of the history of the Golden Horde, apart from certain temporary fluctuations, the export of slaves was of considerable importance. Within time, Christian slaves were probably greatly outnumbered by Turkic and other slaves, who were soon featured among the Italian trading colonies' most frequent and valuable deliveries to Western Europe (Jackson 2005, 307).

The Genoese colony Kaffa, complete with a bazaar, seems to have sustained its wealth in Khan Uzbek's time: Ibn Battuta counted 200 ships in its port. During the three decades following 1315, transit trade in luxury products (primarily silk and spices) from the Far East had (once again) become a prime focus of trade in the Italian Black Sea ports. However, silk reached these ports not only from the Far East but also from CA, e.g., from (reconstructed) Merv (Jackson 2005, 307). In this period products from India, including spices such as pepper, ginger, and saffron, as well as cotton, linen, and pearls, featured prominently too. Given metallurgy's boom in some cities of the Golden Horde, it is not hard to understand that Italian traders also increased shipments of iron, tin, and copper via their ports to Saray. Overall, one could argue that by about 1320 trips to India and China were no longer an adventure but had become a routine experience for Italian, particularly Genoese businessmen (Jackson 2005, 301–302). This would underline the interpretation that European SR trade had reached its second and major Mongol heyday (namely, during the first half of the fourteenth century), notwithstanding the fact that the empire had already split up politically.[96]

Under Jani Bek (1342–1357) the Golden Horde's economic prosperity and political strength gradually started to slip. In 1345, the SR was blocked by renewed disturbances (this time: civil war) in the Chagatay Khanate; therefore Genoese merchants could no longer access China overland. Then, from 1346, disputes between the Italians and the Tatar authorities degenerated into warfare, obstructing regional trade (Abu-Lughod 1989, 169; Contamine et al. 1997, 295). But much worse was to come a year later (see below). Meanwhile, just north of Bolgar (the Golden Horde's principal mint and the former capital of conquered Volga Bulgaria), the Tatars had established Kazan near the confluence of Volga and Kama. Kazan became a major trade entrepot on Europe's longest river; it collected significant revenues from both riverine and overland trade between the Russian principalities and central regions of the khanate. Muslim merchants dominated trade along the main Volga river routes, but Russians gained influence (Perdue 2005, 79). As it grew, Muscovy became an expanding market for Tatar horses, which were typically bred in the grasslands east of the Volga and many of which were traded on the Moscow markets (Pickhan 2009, 124).

Over time, but particularly in the early fourteenth century, the Great principality of Moscow adopted Mongol/Tatar political, military and economic institutions on a considerable scale. As Perdue points out, these included the dual administrative structure, dividing authority between the chief military commander (Kipchak, bekalribek; Russian, tysiatsky) and the chief controller of the treasury (Kipchak, vizier; Russian dvorsky) (2005, 76). In the military sphere, Mongol/Tatar organization (their extensive use of cavalry), weapons, strategy, and tactics provided models for Russian principalities. Indigenous warriors adopted light armor and learnt from the Tatars how to use new weapons such as metal powder cans (which corresponded to a Mongol use of gun powder but not yet to firepower). The well-known Mongol strategies of feigned retreat or of scorched earth would repeatedly and effectively be applied by Russia in history (Shen 2009, 138; Chaliand 1995, 176).

In the sphere of civil administration, know-how was acquired in fiscal, tax, customs, monetary, and postal

---

[95] Cuman or Kipchak is a Turkic language spoken by the Cumans or Kipchak or Polovtsy, as they were called by the Russians (see above). The Kipchak nomadized in the lands north of the Black and Caspian seas from the late eleventh century and continued to inhabit parts of the area under Mongol rule.

[96] This commercial opportunity-oriented trade interaction between Mongols and Genoa (or Northern Italian city-states) recalls another type of SR interaction, namely, that of the extortionary trade-creating type between the Xiongnu (or Turks, Uighurs, or other nomads) and China, as analyzed by Barfield (see above). Although the types of interaction were quite different in nature, in both cases a degree of mutual dependence between the nomads and their sedentary counterparts or clients tended to emerge over time. Menzel elaborates on the extent of complementarity reached in relations between the Golden Horde and its partner Genoa (even if, in some instances, he simplifies): "The Mongols were a major land power, Genoa a sea power. The Mongols had recourse to cavalry, the Genoese to a galley fleet. The Mongols were innovators in mounted archery, the Genoese in the maritime and commercial sectors. The Mongols were a purely

---

military power, the Genoese a trading power. The Mongols practiced continental expansion, the Genoese carried out maritime expansion safeguarded by port colonies, contractual ports, concessions, and trading posts. The Mongols conquered half of the world, Genoa only possessed a small territory along the Ligurian coast from Monaco to Porto Venere. The Mongols' economic basis was the exaction of tribute from subjugated peoples; Genoa's economic basis was profit realized in middleman trade. Both powers complemented one another, both cooperated, and both participated in the other's strength." Therefore, Menzel concludes, "it is not surprising that both powers' rise and decline displayed a remarkable degree of synchronicity" (2015, 152–153).

matters, as the absorption of Turko-Mongol terminology into the Russian language witnessed (e.g., kazna, treasury; dengi (Kazakh: tenge), money; Khan Kebek (or Koepek), kopek/one hundredth of a ruble; karaul, guard; yamschik, coachman; yamskoy, coach; tovar, commodity/product; kurgan, barrow/tumulus) (e.g., see Karger (ed) 1978, 67; Perdue 2005, 76). Last but not least, some habits of dressing and drinking were passed on: The rulers of Russia wore oriental boots (bashmak, shoe), round caps (kolpak), and gowns (kaftan). The Chinese habit of drinking tea (cha in Chinese) seems to have been passed on, possibly by the Mongols, to the Russians and to other peoples (chay in Mongol, Russian, Persian, Turkic, and Hindi) (Shen 2009, 138–139).

The intensive trade relations of a number or Russian principalities show clearly that the Mongol invasion did not cut off the medieval Rus from the west. As Pickhan underlines, Hanseatic merchants and Western European businessmen came to Eastern Europe not least because the former Rus was included in trans-Eurasian trading activities due to the Pax Mongolica (2009, 123). Overall, Kappeler arrives at a balanced assessment: While the negative consequences of the "Tatar yoke" (including the initial brain drain and structural regression in some areas) are undeniable, the integration into the administratively, militarily, and commercially highly developed Mongol Empire also brought advantages (2000: Russische Geschichte, 18). Russian cities and regions benefited from deepened exposure to and participation in international trade networks (Findlay and O'Rourke 2007, 106; Rossabi 2012, 120).

3.4.4.4 Il-Khanate: From Unsuccessful Introduction of Paper Money to Successful Tax and Governance Reforms

The last quarter of the thirteenth century saw increasing fiscal woes due to maladministration in the Ulus Hülegü. These fiscal woes and revenue problems may have been one of the reasons why Gaykhatu Khan (1291–1295) introduced paper money as legal tender in the khanate in 1294. He strove to follow the example of China that had stepped up the use of paper money under Great Khan Kubilay, with initially favorable results. In Iran, the newly printed pieces of paper were also called "chao." But for the Iranian merchants, not familiar with centuries of Chinese experience with paper script, it probably appeared as something bizarrely new, bearing the imperial stamp of authority but devoid of any material value like precious metals. Businessmen in the bazaars rejected the "chao" despite or probably because of the authorities' efforts to force its adoption by requiring merchants to turn in their precious metals in return for receiving paper currency. Many merchants did not trust the authorities and perceived this policy as a thinly veiled attempt to confiscate truly valuable gold and silver for worthless paper. The Persian experiment proved a disaster and provoked unrest in the bazaars and

popular riots. The court was soon compelled to abandon the attempt (Ott and Schäfer (eds) 1984: Wirtschaftsploetz, 468; Roux 1993, 403; Rossabi 2012, 83).

After decades of disruptions and instability, Ghazan Khan (1295–1304) and Rashid al-Din, his renowned minister, finally managed to improve the business climate and stabilize the Il-Khanate's economy. The new ruler carried out urgently needed tax reforms and tried to introduce a degree of rule of law in the sub-empire. According to Rashid al-Din, who was also the court's historian, Ghazan Khan made a speech to the Mongol nobility in which he justified his proposal to reform the rudimentary fiscal administration of the khanate: "I am not protecting the Persian peasantry; if it is expedient, let me pillage them all …; let us rob them together; but if you expect to collect provisions and food in the future…I will be harsh with you; and you must consider: if you commit extortion against the peasants, take their oxen and seed, and cause their crops to be consumed—what will you do in the future?…" (Morgan 2007, 146).

Ghazan first launched a campaign against corruption. He reined in the number of taxes and levies and prescribed methods and rates of taxation, thereby reducing rates and rendering payments more regular. Capricious and oppressive taxation was abolished (at least officially). Differing from Mongol "traditionalists" who favored nomadic pastoralism at the cost of sedentary agriculture, Ghazan aimed at improving the lot of Iranian peasants (raiyyat). Under his orders the land tax (kharaj) was stabilized and cut, the rights of tax collectors were curbed, and the renovation or rebuilding of irrigation works was finally set about. Incentives were provided to encourage the recultivation of land that had fallen out of use. Ghazan also reduced or abolished levies on trade and crafts and seems to have still managed to raise overall tax revenue (Morgan 2007, 147; Jackson 2005, 292; Roux 1993, 432).[97]

Further measures to improve administration and promote trade comprised the reorganization and strengthening of the khanate's Yam system and the standardization of coinage and of weights and measures. The activities and payment of qadis (Islamic judges) were regulated. The Mongol authorities increasingly entrusted day-to-day administration to Persian civil servants instead of frequently intervening in an ad hoc manner. How far all these reforms were actually implemented is difficult to determine, though. In any case, some nomads (not many) were persuaded to settle (Rossabi 2012, 83; Khazanov 1983/1994, 252). Again in analogy to

---

[97] Thus he was apparently right to expect that by bringing order into a partly chaotic and dysfunctional tax system, the reduction of tax rates and tax pressure can even raise overall tax revenue. While the scale of described policy problems may be hardly comparable, the essence of the problems and notably the expectations connected to tax reforms and reductions are not unfamiliar in modern economies (e.g., see what is known as the Laffer Curve – Laffer 2004).

its experience in China, the ruling class had increasing difficulties in resisting the draw of the sophisticated host culture, in this case Persian and Arab sedentary civilization (Amitai 2001, 153; Rossabi 2012, 80).

Despite tax reforms and improvements, an appropriate way to pay the army had not yet been found since new Mongol conquests had ceased to function as a source of income. In another move which adjusted ruling practices to regional traditions, in 1303 Ghazan Khan issued a yarlyk (decree) on the resuscitation of the iqta system for the financing of the khanate's military. Apart from a small amount of grain, which iqtadars had to place in the state's coffers as an in-kind levy, they could largely keep taxes received from their iqta properties. Iqta in the Il-Khanate tended to comprise large allotments, frequently whole farming districts, which were given to subdivisions of nomads that constituted separate military units. Iqtadar's activities were monitored by the bureaucracy (Khazanov 1983/1994, 253; Feldbauer and Liedl 2008, 57).

As Amitai concludes, the consensus is that Ghazan Khan's reforms enjoyed some success, at least in stabilizing the economy of the Il-Khanate (2001, 153). Petrushevsky assesses that there was evidence of a "revival of agriculture," and finds that "in comparison with the previous system of pure club-law and unrestricted pillage, the new regime was an improvement from the point of view of the raiyyat" (i.e., the peasantry) (1968, 495; cited in Morgan 2007, 147). The Il-Khan's territories also harbored workshops for different kinds of raw silk, e.g., in Merv and Gurgan (just south of the Caspian Sea). Production was boosted, and silk from these regions had been reaching Italy and Europe via the sea or the overland route since the late twelfth century (Jackson 2005, 300). Ghazan's brother Oeljeitue (1304–1316) largely continued previous policies, although without new major initiatives. Both brothers promoted cultural development in Persia (architecture, painting, literature, and science).

Box 3.2: Eurasia at the Height of Long-Range SR Trade: Major Players, Products, and Travelers
What did the major players—China, CA, Persia, India, Russia,[98] and Western Europe—trade on the Mongol SR?

Although mostly luxury items, bearing a high ratio of value to bulk and weight, such as silk, horses, spices, furs, gems, and slaves continued to be traded over long distances, there were quite extensive regional markets for lower-cost bulkier goods like grain, olive oil, other preserved foodstuffs, ferrous metals, wax, and lumber.[99]

Chinese silk was still very important, but no longer overwhelmingly so, since in the half-millennium or so preceding Mongol rule, silk production had spread throughout Eurasia. Other exports: porcelain, ceramics, tea, medicine, etc. China imported spices from Southeast Asia (mostly pepper, ginger, cinnamon, rhubarb from the Moluccas and East Indies) and re-exported them west.[100]

CA (Turkestan; in Mongol times divided up between the Golden Horde, the Chagatay Khanate, and the Il-Khanate) remained strong in the provision of high-quality horses, slaves, weapons (e.g., iron swords, bows), precious stones, jade, glass, nasij (gold brocades), preserved foodstuffs (e.g., edible oils, sugar, wine, dried fruit, salted fish, and caviar).

Persia excelled in selling its carpets. Other exports: saddlery, armors, bronze, enamel, etc.

India (the Delhi Sultanate and Hindu states in the south): With the introduction of the spinning wheel, the Indian textile industry received a fillip. India boosted exports of manufactured cotton, silk, and other textiles and garments in large amounts, which may however have encountered European competition, at least in some Mongol markets. Other exports: spices, rubies, pearls, aromatic roots, ivory products, corals, etc. (Chawla 2006, 150; Abu-Lughod 1989, 285).

Russia (the former Rus) continued to deliver furs, pelts, leather, slaves, grain, wood, ferrous metals, and wax.

Western European exports of fine cloth, fabrics, other textiles, and garments (mostly coming from the highly specialized regions of Northern Italy and Flanders) were increasingly in demand everywhere (Findlay and O'Rourke 2007, 94). Other exports: glassware, metalware, weapons, wood, grain, wine, silver, etc. Despite Western European progress in the production and export of manufactures, European

(continued)

---

[98] Whether Russia (or more precisely the Russian principalities) was really a "major player" in SR trade during the Mongol era is debatable, taking into account that Russia was not even independent at that time. But neither were China and Persia. Moreover, given Muscovy's and the czardom's increasingly active involvement in the region in the following centuries, it appears advisable to include Russia here too.

[99] The information below comes from a number of surveyed publications dealing with SR trade in the Mongol era.

[100] In this context of early globalization, e.g., Venetian and Vietnamese traders would meet in Beijing (Töpfer et al. 1985, 189).

Box 3.2 (continued)

trade with its partners in the east remained in deficit, which continued to be covered largely by shipments or "payments" in silver.

According to Findlay and O'Rourke, a compelling witness to the international integration achieved by the Pax Mongolica comes in the form of price data cited by Lopez (1987, 353): Chinese silk is reported to have sold in Italy during this period for no more than three times its purchase price in China (2007, 108). Also, the cheapness of so many commodities in the Great Khanate (partly because of extortionary workshops?) seems to have amply compensated traders for their troubles (Jackson 2005, 313). Although the launching of domestic paper money in the Il-Khanate was not successful, the Yuan dynasty's paper currency did play a role in

Eurasian trade, as did coinage issued by the various regional ulus authorities (Chawla 2006, 152).

Who were the great travelers? How long did crossing Eurasia take?

There were tens, hundreds, or probably thousands of courageous travelers who hit the overland routes from Rome or Paris via CA to Karakorum or Beijing—or in the other direction. During the previous heyday of Eurasian trade and exchanges, the Tang Caliphate era, the number of voyagers, as judged by travel accounts, while larger than during antiquity, was far smaller than in the Mongol era (Roux 1993, 465; Rossabi 2012, 122).

Some famous Silk Route travelers and envoys in the Mongol era

Francesco Balducci Pegolotti, an employee of the Florentine banking house of the Bardi, at some point in

(continued)

Name of traveler	Profession and provenance	Purpose of trip	Route and destination	Period of time
Giovanni de Piano Carpine	Priest, Peruggia, Italy	Establishment of contact Pope – Mongol khan	Lyon – Kiev – Saray – Otrar – Balasagun – Karakorum	1245-47 (Lyon – Kiev: 7 months, Kiev- Saray – Karakorum: 5 mths)
Wilhelm von Roebroeck	Franciscan monk, Flanders	Establishment of contact French king Louis IX – Möngke Khan	Rome – Constantinople – Kaffa – Saray – Balasagun – Karakorum – Kazakh steppe – Saray – Transcaucasia – eastern Mediterranean	1253-55 (Kaffa – Karakorum: 7 months, Karakorum – Saray: 2½ months)
Rabban Bar Sauma	Nestorian Uighur monk, Xinjiang	Establishment of contact Mongols – European courts	Khanbalik – Khotan – Kashgar – Talas – Khorassan - Constantinople – Rome – Genoa – Paris	1266-88
Marco Polo	Merchant, Venice	Trade and exploration, Establishment of contact Venice – Kubilay Khan	Ayas (Lajazzo) – Baghdad – Hormuz – Balkh – Samarkand – Kashgar – Khotan – Dunhuang – Shangdu (Xanadu) – Khanbalik (Beijing) – Quanzhou (Zaiton) – Strait of Malacca – Hormuz – Taebriz – Trebizond – Constantinople – Venice	1271-95 (Ayas – Khanbalik: 3 years)
Ibn Battuta	Muslim legal scholar, geographer and explorer, Morocco	Exploration of the Muslim world and beyond	Marrakesh – Cairo – Mecca – Baghdad – Antiochia – Constantinople – Astrakhan – New Saray – Samarkand – Balkh – Multan – Delhi – Strait of Malacca – Quanzhou (Zaiton)	1325-46

Box 3.2 (continued)

the 1330s wrote and published the commercial handbook "Pratica della Mercatura," in which he observed that the whole east-west journey was still a long one: Under the Pax Mongolica, it took around 8–10 months to reach China from Crimea (Findlay and O'Rourke 2007, 107; Roux 1993, 462). Yet this was somewhat quicker than the year it had approximately taken travelers to cross Eurasia in antiquity and the early Middle Ages (see above). The pace of the commercial travels as described by Pegolotti approached that of Piano Carpine and Roebroek: about 30–35 km per day (Masson-Smith 2003, 4). This is less than the 40–60 km per day Yam messengers would cover on average, according to Marco Polo (see above).

Compared to the east-west maritime route, the overland route was generally shorter and quicker, unless it was blocked. Maritime transportation had to contend with storms (monsoons) and pirates that were numerous on the Malabar coast (Western India), near Ceylon, in the Strait of Malacca and the East Indies. Therefore, the seaborne route from one end of Eurasia to the other could take twice as long as the overland one (Roux 1993, 461; Jackson 2005, 311).

3.4.5 Some Characteristics, Advantages, and Shortcomings of Mongol "Silk Road Policy"

– *Creation of a giant well-policed and quasi-borderless economic space as well as workshops with enslaved artisans made goods cheaper*

The economic backbone of the Mongol Empire was the SR (defined in Sect. 1.4. as a network of intercontinental trade routes that provided commercial, cultural, and technological exchange). According to the Florentine businessman Francesco Balducci Pegolotti, as late as in the 1330s, the land route from Crimea to Beijing was "perfectly safe, whether by day or by night" (Rossabi 1990, 356). The chief contribution to facilitating trade and exchange across Eurasia by an administration supplying security, peace, and "law and order" was the elimination of intermediaries and the reduction in protection rent (tributes, tolls, etc.). Moreover, the unification of a gigantic territory made transportation costs easier to calculate (Abu-Lughod 1989, 182). This may contribute to explaining why—contrary to practices in pre-Mongol eras, when merchants would typically make rather short trips, for example, from one SR trading center to the next—a larger number of

businessmen now endeavored to cover the whole route, from coast to coast (Roux 1993, 455). Indeed, under Mongol oversight, trans-Eurasian connectivity had arguably reached its apex.

Yet wide-ranging security and transcontinental political unity were not the only reasons why many goods were cheaper in the Mongol era than in earlier periods. Notwithstanding unification under the banner of a trade-friendly empire, competition was not eliminated, neither among merchants and their companies nor among constituent territories. Soon after the Mongol uluses or sub-empires were created, they started to compete or rival with each other in many areas,[101] also with regard to attracting SR traffic to "their" routes or sections of the network. In doing this, the respective authorities had additional caravanserais, campsites, and storehouses built, routes improved, and patrols stepped up. Such was infrastructural competition, e.g., between the Ulus Jöchi and the Ulus Hülegü with respect to routes of access to Europe: the "steppe route" of the north leading to the Black Sea versus the "Middle Eastern route" of the south reaching the Eastern Mediterranean. Moreover, the nobility had established a system (or systems) of workshops employing enslaved craftsmen and artisans. On top of this, products of these workshops might be sold by quasi-governmental trading partnerships which initially enjoyed privileged conditions of use of the Mongol horse relay system (see below). All these possibilities guaranteed the elite access to cheap products of often high quality and ready marketability.

– *Pivotal provision of trade capital and credit for long-distance SR trade*

As Abu-Lughod explains, for long-distance trade across Eurasia, large amounts of initial trade capital were required to purchase the merchandise that was to be shipped for later sale. During the long trip, this capital was "tied up" in goods that might or might not reach their destinations (Abu-Lughod 1989, 16). Yet if successful, these "trade investments" were very profitable: Documents examined by Lopez suggest that a return of 100% on the initial stake was not improbable and in some cases this return could reach up to 500%. On the other hand, such gains have to be set against the fact that the capital might be under risk of total loss for years (Jackson 2005, 313).

Given vagaries of such dimensions, as Abu-Lughod continues, in the Middle East and CA elaborate techniques were developed for pooling capital or for apportioning profit on the basis of formulas dividing between the merchant advancing the goods, the financier

---

[101] Rivalry at times even included, as described above, military hostilities.

putting up the funds to buy the goods, and the partner who accompanied the goods to the point of sale. The elaborate systems for long-distance shipping existing in the twelfth and thirteenth centuries in Genoa and Venice, which may have drawn from techniques already used by Arabs to conduct their shipping trade, were certainly refined through business experience with the Mongol Empire. Notwithstanding lack of trust in paper money in Persia, bankers and trade credit (essentially enforcible promises to pay later and in some other place) appear to have been developed in many places of the empire before they became critical to business in most of Europe (Abu-Lughod 1989, 16–17).

– *However, sizable and sustainable capital accumulation did not materialize within the empire but outside it.*

While "law and order" had been achieved, which facilitated or favored (short-term) trading activities, the Mongol authorities had not established "rule of law" in a modern sense, which would have accommodated or been conducive to (long-term) investment activities. Long-distance trade did give rise to considerable temporary concentrations of capital, but in most cases these were not durable. While they encouraged and initially even subsidized trade from which they then collected generous revenues and benefited directly, the Mongol authorities were also prone to ad-hoc and partly unpredictable interventions in the economy, including changes in taxation, forced enrollment of people in labor schemes, and, of course, confiscation of goods and property.

Even if in later periods of Mongol rule such random government interference did not happen as often any more, the continuing possibility rendered capital accumulation inside the limits of Mongol jurisdiction very risky—unless the investor was very well connected or member of the political elite. Thus, as mentioned above, sizable investment and production were achieved in workshops owned by the nomadic aristocracy. Capital accumulation in the Mongol steppe cities and metropolises was impressive (e.g., Karakorum, Old Saray, New Saray, Shangdu/Xanadu), as witnessed by a number of foreign visitors. However, unfortunately, this investment was ephemeral, eventually all but wiped out by wars. More generally, given that economic wealth was attached to political power, the former was particularly exposed to the danger of bloody and materially destructive conflicts. As regards the interconnection of political and economic power in medieval times, the Mongol Empire was by no means an exception to the rule.

Therefore, it should not be surprising that, despite the large amount of SR trade capital accumulated under the

Pax Mongolica, no incipient capitalist takeoff or proto-industrialization emerged in the sphere of Mongol power. However, SR trade capital <u>was</u> successfully accumulated over the long term—outside the empire, namely, in places like the commercially and economically advanced Northern Italian states of Genoa and Venice, where it indeed contributed to the initial rise of capitalism (Kauz 2009, 311; Norel 2009, 176).[102] While constantly in competition, the Genoese soon dominated trade on the northern branch of the SR (via Tana and Saray), while the Venetians specialized in the southern branch (via the Eastern Mediterranean).

– *Still, evolution from extortionate taxation, forced production, and from initial subsidization of SR trade toward more market-oriented practices*

Before making taxation more predictable and rule-based, the Mongols initially depended on tax farming: they allowed foreigners, often C Asian Muslims who were members of trading enterprises, to exact revenue from conquered territories (Barfield 1989/1992, 204). After sending on proceeds to the Mongol authorities (khans), these "tax farmers" kept the balances for themselves. They therefore often had a short-term interest in exploiting assigned territories. These merchants could then use the resources thus gained to engage in SR trade. In many cases, the Mongols had actually created quasi-governmental trading partnerships, called "ortaghs" or "orthogs," which constituted a system of corporations of Mongol businessmen or aristocrats with international merchants. Enjoying official patronage and access to government finance, the ortaghs soon had a prominent role in SR trade (Boyle (ed) 1968, 509; May 2012, 119).[103]

The C Asian traders themselves and in particular the Mongol elite (the nomadic nobility) exacted goods through predatory taxation and the management of forced labor workshops or manufactures (karkhanahs) for the production of valuable and marketable products (silk, etc.). The ortagh merchants, also called "tujar-i amin" (trustworthy merchants) then sold these goods on the SR and, in exchange, purchased commodities the Mongols

---

[102] In this sense, Gunder Frank argues that even if military superiority was the case for CA, the latter never rose to become a core economic region because it was never the core of sustained capital accumulation (Gunder Frank 1992, 2).

[103] "Ortagh" is Turko-Persian for "partner" (Kollmar-Paulenz 2011, 40).

desired (Masson-Smith 2003, 3).[104] Many tudchar-i amin also had experience in maritime transportation, which was helpful when overland routes were blocked (for whatever reasons). If they lacked sufficient funds to carry out procurement or purchase assignments, the ortagh merchants in some cases received large amounts of money from high-level officials or from the khan himself. Moreover, the rulers sometimes offered the merchants artificially elevated prices for delivering desired goods to their traveling camps or on other occasions reimbursed the traders for losses incurred due to political unrest (Jackson 2005, 293; Kauz 2009, 310; Allsen 2009, 144–145).

Possibly to kick-start or boost ortagh business, Ögöday Khan (1229–1241) initially granted the trading corporations special access to the horse relay system of the imperial post (Yam) and even exempted them from most state obligations (Barfield 2001, 246). The ortaghs were permitted to use postal stations as long as they did not impede military and administrative traffic. Merchants using the Yam system benefited from a guarantee on their merchandise, which, if pillaged, was to be entirely replaced by inhabitants living closest to the location of the crime. However, abuse soon spread and started to weigh on the Yam infrastructure. Töregene and Güyük Khan do not seem to have done much to rein in the problems. Thus, the number of ortaghs multiplied in the 1240s with a resulting increase in Yam traffic as the corporations generously claimed paizas, took advantage of various services, and strained facilities (May 2012, 119–120). In this period, many merchants also moved into the imperial bureaucracy through purchasing offices, which, of course, reinforced corruption. Thus, the generally privileged position of merchants and traders in the Mongol Empire seemed to have attained caricatural dimensions.

While Möngke Khan (1251–1259) put an end to many of the ortaghs' privileges, including their tax-exempt status and restrained corrupt practices, international trade remained a priority for the Mongols throughout their rule. As May points out, the trading corporations themselves were not eliminated but simply reined in from damaging the interests and institutions of the state. The degree to which the ortaghs continued to constitute part of Mongol economic life is

indicated by the fact that it was only after the defeat of the Yuan dynasty in 1368 that the ortagh system more or less collapsed in China (May 2012, 121–125).

Overall, we can detect a tendency of Mongol economic practices moving from a predatory and exploitative to a more regulated and civilized nature. This is witnessed by the broad transition from tax farming to more rule-based taxation, from the trading corporations' privileged and even improper use of state infrastructures to a situation more resembling a level playing field, and from workshops using forced slave labor to enterprises employing and attracting hired specialists. Of course, aside from this broad evolution, many instances of recurrent extortionary behavior and uncertainty persisted.

– *Trade network functioning at its apex but boom relatively narrowly focused*

In the century of Mongol rule in Eurasia, SR trade is reported to have flourished as never before (Masson-Smith 2003, 3; Pernau 2011, 114). This is easy to understand, given the Mongol authorities' strategic priority accorded to transcontinental overland trade, their favorable treatment of merchants, the giant and all-but-seamless trading space created, Pax Mongolica security delivered, and the (initial) subsidization of overland trade via quasi-governmental trading corporations (ortagh), their privileged tax treatment, and access to the imperial postal and messenger network (Yam). With quantitative data unfortunately insufficient or lacking, it is difficult to make a judgment, but available literature appears to confirm that the overall structure of SR trade did not change much in the Mongol era, compared to earlier periods; however, some trading partners—notably those outside the sphere of Mongol control, namely, Western Europe and India—seem to have witnessed some specialization and technological development of their product ranges: Trade in manufactured goods, particularly textiles and garments, gained importance.

CA on the other hand, having had to bear the brunt of destruction (notably West Turkestan) during the Mongol conquests, does not appear to have been particularly successful in refining its merchandise on offer. While the Mongol authorities certainly initiated the swift re-establishment of trade arteries and transferred and concentrated human capital and material resources in workshops producing competitive goods, this constituted a rather focused economic recovery, a targeted effort, which was probably no longer accompanied by the richness of activities and product spectrum the region had possessed prior to Mongol rule. Also, while (transit) trade through CA expanded, the all-but-seamless space implied that the region itself had lost customs dues as a traditional source of revenue and enrichment. China (at least Northern China that had been similarly afflicted by

---

[104] For instance, extorted (tax-farmed or slave-produced) goods may have flowed directly from China or Eastern Europe to sustain Karakorum or Saray, and from there some of these goods (a surplus) possibly flowed on via the SR, to be sold by ortaghs at the limits of the empire (e.g., in Italian Black Sea ports). Agent-host-principal relationships along the lines of Muslim tax farmers exacting resources from China and selling them under Mongol oversight in the thirteenth century are nothing really new and recall, e.g., activities of Sogdian businessmen in China on Turkic assignment in the sixth or seventh centuries or the kind of protection-money relationship that existed between Uighurs and Chinese in the ninth century (outlined above).

the Mongol onslaught as CA) does not seem to have made further major advances in its specialization either.

3.4.6   The Extensive SR Network in Mongol Times

With practically all Eurasian trade brought under Mongol control and with international trade promotion constituting a raison d'être of imperial rule and serving as a "glue" holding the disparate parts of the empire together, the SR network had attained previously unheard-of dimensions (Masson-Smith 2003, 3). Due to the establishment of Karakorum in Mongolia as the imperial capital in 1220, and due to the only tenuous access gained to the Eastern Mediterranean in view of the stubborn geopolitical conflict with the Mamluk Sultanate (Egypt) from the 1250s, the northerly branches of the SR attained greater importance than in previous heydays of Eurasian trade (Jackson 2005, 298).

The difficulty of access to the Eastern Mediterranean as well as the temporary blockage of trade due to internal Mongol hostilities and internecine warfare in the Chagatay Khanate (from around 1280 to 1305) indirectly boosted seaborne trade circumventing these obstacles. This goes for maritime trade (the Spice Route) largely controlled by ships of the Great Khanate and running from China via the Strait of Malacca to the Persian Gulf (Il-Khanate), and it goes for maritime trade running from India via Aden and the Red Sea, Suez, and Alexandria. This latter route around the Arab peninsula escaped Mongol control though and actually benefited the rival Mamluk Sultanate. Therefore, the Mongols tried—unsuccessfully—to thwart and redirect Red Sea traffic to the Persian Gulf (Roux 1993, 461).

As Maps 3.6 and 3.7 show, the far northern route, the "Mongol steppe route," was probably the quickest trans-Eurasian route—leading from Saray straight through the Kipchak or Kazakh steppe north of the Caspian Sea, of the Aral Sea, and of Lake Balkhash via the uppermost course of the Irtysh river and the Black Irtysh and crossing the Altai mountains, to Karakorum, then on to Beijing (Marks 2002/ 2006, 50).[105] Intermittently, there even existed a route fur- ther north—one could call it the "forest-steppe route"— running from Karakorum along the upper Yenisey, the upper Ob, crossing the Ural mountains, and reaching

Kazan and Bolgar on the middle Volga. This route mostly went through the West Siberian forest steppe, along or near the southern fringes of the taiga, just north of the limits of what we regard as CA (Stier et al. (ed) 1991, 73; O'Brien (ed) 2010, 104). Both the Mongol steppe and the forest-steppe routes however lost importance soon after the transfer of the imperial capital from Karakorum to Beijing (Khanbalik) in 1257.

The northern, possibly "classic," route of the time had the following stations: Kaffa (Crimea) or Tana (mouth of the Don)–Saray–Urgench–Otrar (after crossing the Kyzyl Kum)– Balassagun–Almalik–Beshbalik–Hami–Suzhou (Gansu).[106] From New Saray, turnoffs either ran across the forest steppe to Kiev, then on to Lviv and Cracow (Poland), or one could move up the Volga to Bolgar, Kazan, and further to Moscow. From Almalik it was possible to reach Karakorum or Mongolia by crossing Dzungaria and the Altai.

The middle route (see Maps 3.6 and 3.7) took the following course: Trebizond (Southern Black Sea coast)–Erzurum (Eastern Anatolia)–Taebriz–Rayy–Nishapur–Merv–Bukhara– Samarkand–Khodzhent–Kashgar (after crossing the Ferghana Basin and the Alay mountains probably via Irkeshtam)– Kucha–Turfan–Gansu. The oasis of Shash (Tashkent) provided a kind of link between the northern (Otrar) and the middle (Khodzhent) routes. A weaker, but still existing, connection ran south of the Tarim Basin: Kashgar–Khotan–Lob Nor–Gansu. Like in the past, there was a turnoff to India: Kashgar or Yarkand–Gilgit (after crossing the Khunjerab Pass)–Multan (Punjab). Under Mongol rule, most SR traffic reached Europe via the Black Sea (e.g., Crimea and Trebizond) and Constantinople, not the Levant.

Finally, the southern route, partly taking ancient trails, partly including some stages of the middle route, ran here: Ayas (Layazzo) or Antiochia (northeastern corner of Mediterranean)–Erzurum–Taebriz–Rayy–Nishapur–Herat– Balkh–Samarkand–Tashkent (where it linked up to the other routes). The southern route also had some important variations: There was a relatively secure[107] but topographi- cally more difficult connection from the ports of Antalya or Alanya on the southern coast of Asia Minor to Erzurum; there was a less secure but easier to ride connection (that had already existed in Antiquity) running from Antiochia via Baghdad to Rayy. A direct connection from Bactria to Kashgaria ran from Balkh via the Pamir (the uppermost

---

[105] As shown in the table below ("Some famous Silk Route travelers and envoys in the Mongol era"), it reportedly took Wilhelm von Roebroeck only 2½ months to cover the distance from Karakorum to Saray (about 4500–5000 km), which is very fast (60–65 km on average per day without pause) and more than twice as fast as it had previously taken the Franciscan monk, coming from Kaffa, to cover the distance from Saray to Karakorum (in reverse sense).

---

[106] This was also the route suggested by Pegolotti (who himself had collected information about it and described it in detail but had never undertaken the trip personally) (Waugh 2007, 4). The western section of this route was also called "the Route of the Three Seas" ("la route des trois mers"), skirting the shores of the Black, the Caspian, and the Aral seas (Jehel (ed) 2007, 267).

[107] This connection was relatively secure because it was more or less outside the range of hostilities with the Mamluk Sultanate.

reaches of the Amu Daria/the Piandzh river) to Kashgar. Finally, the principal connection between CA and India continued to lead from Balkh via Kabul, the Khyber Pass to Peshawar, Lahore (Punjab), and Delhi.

As Abu-Lughod explains, the simultaneous operation of two different overland routes across CA (a southern and a northern one—notwithstanding various branchings) and of two different maritime routes circumventing CA (via the Persian Gulf and the Red Sea)[108] meant that any blockages at specific synapses of the circulatory system could be bypassed. This prevented the emergence of monopoly protection rents of guarders of individual routes; therefore, goods and people would "get through" despite localized disturbances (Abu-Lughod 1989, 359). For instance, Marco Polo, accompanying a Yuan princess on a trip from China to Persia (1292–1295), had to circumvent the Chagatay Khanate which had intermittently blocked overland trade and which had become a stage of Mongol internecine warfare. Furthermore, the Venetians attempted on repeated occasions to get around obstacles on the steppe route or temporary blockages of the southern route (via the Levant) by approaching Alexandria and aiming for the Red Sea route to India and further east (Exenberger 2009, 231; The Times (ed) 1982, 58).

Box 3.3: Inventions/Innovations Transferred and Cultural Practices Diffused via the SR in the Mongol Era

Generally, trans-Eurasian flows of information continued to prove far more influential in the east-west direction than in the west-east direction. However, once Europeans had acquired useful information, they tended to make use of it swiftly and effectively.

Paper money or paper currency was promoted by the authorities of the Great Khanate, which also tried to introduce it as tender in SR trade—with partial success: SR merchants wishing to trade directly with China needed to accept paper money (chao) in exchange for their goods, before exchanging this paper money for other desired Chinese products. Paper money always needed public trust, a reliable political framework, and at least a minimum of economic stability. Strong bureaucratic state traditions had certainly bolstered the standing of chao in China, where it had already been known and accepted by the public in the Tang era. From the eleventh century (the

Song era), chao was printed by engraving blocks (printing plates). Under the Yuan dynasty, the seal of the Great Khan was printed on paper produced from the mulberry tree. This seal authenticated the bills. The experience and confidence the Chinese had accumulated with paper currency was not attained in the Il-Khanate. Introduced in times of political maladministration and economic disarray in this sub-empire (1294), paper money—also here called chao—was not accepted by merchants and bazaars, threatened to even further destabilize the situation, and was therefore repealed (see above) (Roux 1993, 403). Still, the Mongol authorities may be credited with sustaining and at least attempting to spread the institution of state-backed paper currency (the concept of using a currency other than gold or silver but officially backing it with these precious metals)—an institution that to Europeans of the time apparently seemed bizarre or at least curious.[109]

Engraving printing (the use of wooden-block printing plates) was transmitted westward along the SR under Mongol rule. In the fourteenth century, Europeans began to use engraving blocks. In the mid-fifteenth century, they adopted interchangeable typesets. In 1466 the first European printing shops were set up in Italy (Höllmann 2004, 109; Zhang 2005, 155).

Glassmaking: The development of Western European glass production and glassworks and particularly the upswing in Venetian production since the thirteenth century largely happened thanks to technology transfer from the Islamic/Mongol east to the Christian west. This technology transfer partly proceeded in contractually stipulated channels (Feldbauer and Liedl 2008, 35).[110]

Use of coal as fuel: Marco Polo was the first Westerner to observe the use of coal (utilization of black stones as fuel) in the Middle Kingdom. Later, Ibn Battuta also transmitted information about the use of coal in China (Zhang 2005, 143).

Gunpowder and firearms: Gunpowder was invented in the ninth century (Tang dynasty). The transmission of gunpowder production technology can probably be

(continued)

---

[108] Yet, as mentioned above, the Red Sea route was not controlled by the Mongols.

[109] Roux relates the profound amazement expressed by European travelers Wilhelm von Roebroek and Marco Polo as well as Ibn Battuta when they discovered or reported the use of paper money in the Great Khanate (Roux 1993, 403).

[110] Apparently, the old Roman tradition of glassmaking had fallen into oblivion or had been superseded by C Asian production technology.

Box 3.3 (continued)

ascribed to the Mongols—together with Arabs or C Asians: with its campaigns in the thirteenth century, the Mongol military brought gunpowder to C and Western Asia. The Mongols used, e.g., metal powder cans or makeshift bombs, even rudimentary rockets, but not yet proper firearms. Around the same time, Arab or C Asian merchants possibly conveyed via the SR from the Great Khanate the technology of making gunpowder and fireworks. The Europeans, in turn, appropriated Chinese explosive powder to create new weaponry: in the early fourteenth century, respective knowledge was speedily further developed, and Europeans soon used firearms in wars against Muslim powers (Lemercier-Quelquejay 1970, 98; Höllmann 2004, 113; Stearns 2009, 55).

Glazed painted ceramics: In Persia, the Mongols became acquainted with glazed ceramics, painted in cobalt—a technique that Chinese ceramics factories (workshops) subsequently developed to the refinement of the famous blue-and-white wares which became the epitome of Chinese porcelain or "china."[111]

The abacus, invented in China and believed to have first become widely used during the Yuan dynasty, constituted a major improvement over the previous "calculating sticks" in efficiency and portability. As Shen Fuwei points out, the abacus reached Russia and Poland in the fourteenth century (2009, 139).

Playing cards made their first appearance in the Occident due to Mongol intermediation (Stearns 2009, 55). The first global reference to card games dates from the ninth century during the Tang dynasty.

Drinking tea: Along the SR, the Chinese habit of drinking tea ("cha" is Chinese for "tea") may have been spread, possibly by the Mongols, to many lands: After all, "chay" is Mongol, Persian, Russian, Turkic, and Hindi for "tea" (Shen 2009, 139).

Distilled alcohol, in particular spirituous liquor (araki): Likely first produced by West Asians in Yuan service, araki quickly spread from China throughout Central, North, and South Asia (Allsen 2009, 150).

3.4.7 Political Instability, Disintegration, and Black Death (1330s–1368)

3.4.7.1 The Eurasian Steppe and Longevity of Mongol Dynasties

The cumulative effect of the gradual weakening of the common identity of the uluses and the erosion of common structures of Mongol rule contributed to putting the four sub-empires on different political and economic trajectories. Regional bipolarity opposing nomadic and sedentary regions of the (former) empire gained weight over time: As mentioned earlier, the Mongols controlled large sedentary civilizations in the Great Khanate (China) and the Il-Khanate (Iran, Iraq), as opposed to only partly sedentary populations on the territories of the Golden Horde and the Chagatay Khanate. In Persia and China, the Mongol dynasties lasted under a century, while in Russia the Khanate of the Golden Horde lasted for more than 200 years, and the Crimean khans (descendants of the Golden Horde) reigned Southern Ukraine until the late eighteenth century (although under the protection of the Ottoman Empire). Likewise, the Chagatay Khans survived (as rulers of Moghulistan) until the early sixteenth century.

According to Chaliand, it appears that those Mongol states survived longer that controlled swathes of the Eurasian grasslands and whose ruling nomads were able to uphold their military prowess through continuing steppe life (1995, 143). In contrast, the polities where Mongols began to assimilate to Chinese and Persian ways and where warriors turned into farmers or urban dwellers soon got rid of their former nomadic rulers. Morgan confirms the above view: The Mongols of the Golden Horde probably survived because they had kept their distance from the conquered sedentary populations to a far greater extent than was possible in China or Persia (2007, 181). The same can be said, with some qualifications, for the Mongols of the Chagatay Khanate. In this sense and for "technological" reasons of sustained military supremacy, "traditionalist" rule proved more durable than "integrationist" rule. Clearly, Mongol rule lasted longer in CA than it did in most other regions. While its incidence across Eurasia is not yet as well researched as its impact on Europe, the terrible calamity of the plague (see below) probably contributed to physically weakening the capability of the Mongols to hold sway over their lands and may have distracted them from their common economic interest of supporting transcontinental trade.

3.4.7.2 The "Black Death": A Second Demographic Catastrophe and an Adverse Sign of Early Globalization

Most scholars believe that the Great Plague or "Black Death" originated in Southeastern China and was brought to CA, the Middle East, Europe, and North Africa by

---

[111] For once, this points to technology transfer in the opposite (west-east) direction; and it points to the swift adaptation by Chinese suppliers to demands in faraway places in the Mongol era: The porcelain manufacturing center at Jingdezhen (Jiangsu region) resorted to importing cobalt from the other end of Mongol Eurasia (Eastern Europe) to achieve the color tones most appreciated by the Iranian market (Allsen 2009, 140).

mounted servicemen and by traders traveling the SR. Reports are that the bubonic plague, as it is more precisely called, broke out around 1331 in the province of Yunnan, where it may have arrived from Burma; both territories at that time were under the control of the Great Khanate. The highly infectious disease was triggered by a bacterium (bacillus) which affected mostly rodents (e.g., rats) and was transmitted to humans by fleas (Walter 2006, 74). Mongol armies may have spread the epidemic from Yunnan to various other parts of China; the Black Death is estimated to have killed more Chinese than the initial Mongol invasion, namely, a quarter to a third of the entire population.

Tombstones in a Nestorian Christian graveyard on the shores of Lake Issyk Koel indicate that the plague struck this settlement along the caravan route in 1338–1339. Merchants no doubt carried it to oasis towns and bazaars of trading cities along the northern and southern branches of the SR, which thus "malfunctioned" as highways for infection with the plague (May 2012, 201, 208). It seems that the transportation of furs and bales of cloth favored particularly rapid flea-borne contagion. The Kipchak steppe was reached in 1345. Towns like Astrakhan and Saray (in the north) and Taebriz and Aleppo (in the south) all suffered.

On the northern route, the plague reached Kaffa in 1346 during a siege of the Genoese port by the Tatars of Golden Horde Khan Jani Bek. Following a financial and political dispute which degenerated into a military confrontation, the Mongols famously catapulted plague-riddled corpses or heads of their dead soldiers over the city walls of Kaffa, in what Mayhew regards as one of the world's first examples of biological warfare—an act deemed to have accelerated the transmission of the Black Death to Europe (2010, 46). The Genoese population of Kaffa fled by boat to the Mediterranean coast, spreading the disease to Italy and Western and Central Europe. However, from the shore of the Black Sea, the plague also reached Kiev and then advanced further north. From Aleppo, the infectious illness reached Damascus, Cairo, and Aden (Black 2006, 72–73).

On the whole, the bubonic plague is estimated to have killed about 75 million people, roughly one third of this number in China, around one third in Europe, and one third in other regions, notably CA, the Near and Middle East, India, and North Africa. The pandemic typically recurred in waves of diminishing intensity.[112] As mentioned above, the overall Chinese death toll was estimated at between a quarter and a third of the population; in Europe, the Middle East, and North Africa, the situation appears to have been largely similar (Walter 2006, 77; Findlay and O'Rourke 2007, 111; Stearns 2009, 53).

As parts of CA constituted pivotal SR transit territory, devastating effects of depopulation focused on these trade arteries. After they had recovered from the bloody Mongol invasion more than a century before, trading centers were asked to pay another gruesome human toll: in many cases, up to half of their inhabitants may have fallen victim to the Black Death. The chaos and anarchy created by the cataclysm temporarily halted international trade and effectively cut off the Mongol khanates from one another (Findlay and O'Rourke 2007, 111; Chua 2007, 122).[113] The prosperity of the Golden Horde and the Italian trading towns on the Black Sea collapsed. Due to the recurrence of the plague, populations in many places did not recover until the fifteenth century.

The quick spreading of the disease along the SR (in hardly more than a decade from one end to the other) was largely a consequence of increased mobility. Thus, as Osterhammel and Petersson put it, mounted archery and microbes for the first time created a "Eurasian interrelationship of calamities" (2003, 32). In terms of human casualties—but of course not in terms of material destruction—the Black Death may have matched the traumatic impact of the Mongol wars in CA, which means that the two catastrophes combined must have cost the region at least 40% of its population.[114]

3.4.7.3 Mongol Disintegration: End of Pax Mongolica—Collapse or Shrinkage of SR Trade

The final decades of the Yuan dynasty in China were characterized by misrule, peasant discontent, and famines. Toghon Temuer (1333–1368), the last ruler of the Great Khanate, entertained an oversized and lavish court indulging in wasteful expenditures, despite the quick spreading of the bubonic plague. Eventually the deplorable state of affairs came to a head, and the uprising of the Red Turbans erupted. Based in the south, Ming-controlled forces advanced and in 1368 seized Beijing/Khanbalik. The Yuan court had already decamped for Mongolia (Barfield 1989/1992, 224). After China's experiences with the Mongols, the new Han-Chinese ruling dynasty chose to turn away from the steppe and to foster maritime trade and exploration. Tariff and non-tariff barriers went up again on the overland SR to

---

[112] Thus Schamiloglu estimates that the plague afflicted the Khanate of the Golden Horde in 1345–46, 1364, 1374, and 1396 (May 2012, 209).

[113] The Il-khan regime in Khorassan, Persia and Mesopotamia had already ceased to exist in 1335 and Mongol rule there was swiftly weakening (see below).

[114] However, this does not mean that CA had at least 40% less inhabitants in 1360 than it had had one and a half centuries before, because partly strong demographic growth and possibly some net-immigration had occurred in between.

the Middle Kingdom, and what was left of trade after the ravages of the Black Death declined further (Wild 1992, 9).

The middle of the fourteenth century witnessed an aggravation of disturbances and internecine wars in the <u>Chagatay Khanate</u>; the ulus split into Mavarannahr and Moghulistan (1346, see above). The first ruler of Moghulistan, Tughluq Temuer (1347–1363), as well as some of his successors, repeatedly invaded Transoxiana and looted Samarkand and Bukhara. For this reason, the Irano-Turkic Muslims of the southwest often tended to label their Turko-Mongol neighbors of the northeast as well as their land as "chete" (Turkic for a band of robbers or robbery in general) (Weiers 2004, 136; Hambly (ed) 1966/1979, 145). The <u>Khanate of the Golden Horde</u>, deprived of revenue and weakened by the plague-induced collapse or interruption of SR trade as well as by rising internal rivalries and political instability, could no longer effectively resist Central European powers' military encroachment and conquests in Eastern Europe. Poland conquered Lviv/Lemberg in 1349, and Lithuania took control of Kiev in 1365 (Stanziani 2012, 96; Westermann (ed) 1997, Map: Der Aufstieg Litauens und seine Union mit Polen (1386), 71).

Political drift and infighting in the <u>Il-Khanate</u> following Ghazan Khan's death (1304) gradually eroded his reforms and achievements: Thus the tax system—already a mixture of nomadic and Iranian/Abbasid methods—became increasingly complex and degenerated. The tax burden, the lion's share of which was shouldered by the sedentary population, once again became inordinately heavy (Kauz 2009, 310). Assuming the throne at the age of ten, Abu Said, the last of the Il-Khans (1316–1335), was ill-prepared to rule, and his reign turned out to be chaotic. Abu Said's death led to convulsions that, against the backdrop of the ravaging impact of Black Death, extinguished Mongol rule there in the mid-century (Rossabi 2012, 116; Soucek 2000, 121).

The Sarbadar insurrection created great unrest in Khorassan and adjacent regions and probably contributed to the collapse of Mongol rule. With its varied composition—it included craftsmen, the urban poor, farmers, and small landowners—it was principally a revolt of the settled population against fiscal burdens, yet religious and messianic concepts also played a role (Ashrafyan 1998, 322). The duty to billet officials (nuzul)—which meant the obligation to take into one's house military personnel, officers, and their staff, and to feed and entertain them—had been abolished by Ghazan Khan, but during the reign of Abu Said, the duty resurfaced (Nizami 1998b, 374).

As Nizami explains, the immediate trigger for the revolt of the Sarbadars was the unbridled license of a Mongol envoy who stopped for lodgings at a village and demanded wine and a woman. According to Rashid al-Din, abuse had reached such dimensions that people purposely kept their houses in a shabby state in order to escape the obligation.

The rioters killed the official and rebellions subsequently broke out at a number of places. After they had ousted Mongol power from some towns and areas, the Sarbadars in 1337 set up their own state in Western Khorassan with its center in Sabzevar, which existed until 1381. The insurgents' ideology included equal rights to property and the abolition of all taxes that were contrary to the Sharia. Two directly opposing views have been expressed about the role of the Sarbadars: Petrushevsky considers them a social-revolutionary movement, while some others see them as a "robber state" (Nizami 1998b, 374–375).[115]

By the middle of the fourteenth century, the idea and the reality of the Mongol Empire had disappeared. The Pax Mongolica had disintegrated as a result of the demise of the Il-Khan regime in 1335; the definite end of Mongol rule in Khorassan, Persia, and Iraq in the early 1350s; the unrelated breakdown and partitioning of the Chagatay Khanate; and the collapse of the Empire of the Great Khan and fall of the Yuan dynasty to the native Chinese Ming in 1368. With the end of the Il-Khanate, the Middle Eastern branch of the SR (leading to the Eastern Mediterranean) closed, and European access was sharply curtailed. The other branch, via the Khanate of the Golden Horde (from China through CA, Saray, and Tana westward) remained open until the fall of the Great Khanate. As a result of this demise, Italian merchants' access to China all but collapsed (Gilomen 2014, 107–108). A long period of antagonism and conflict between the Middle Kingdom and the Eurasian nomads reopened (Masson-Smith 2003, 5).

Trade declined due to political and security reasons. The breaking up of territory, multiplication of customs duties and of tolls, (temporary) weakening of state power, brigandage, and robberies rendered trade dangerous, discouraged enterprise, and pushed prices of merchandise back up again to pre-Mongol levels. While traditional localized trade patterns between nomadic and sedentary people continued in various places, foreigners, including many merchants (notably C Asians and Europeans), were expelled from China.[116] There were massacres of Europeans in Persia and Turkestan (Findlay and O'Rourke 2007, 124). Various Genghisid and non-Genghisid princes started to plunder caravans for short-

---

[115] The Sarbadar rebellion against Mongol rule recalls a much earlier revolt in Persia: the Mazdakite insurrection (488–529) against the Sassanians (see Sect. 3.3.1.1). There are of course important differences: The Mazdakites included a peasant uprising against the land-owning aristocracy, while the Sarbadars rebelled against tax oppression and certain other practices of misrule. But parallels should not be overlooked: Both movements had religious aims and social-revolutionary goals of equal rights to property.

[116] For example, Northern Italian businessmen's trading colonies in the Far East were closed in the mid-fourteenth century (Feldbauer et al. 2010, 82).

term profits.[117] All this threatened to bring caravan trade to a total standstill (Masselos (ed) 2010, 43). However, with the Golden Horde still intact for some more decades after the Black Death and the end of the Yuan dynasty, at least some regional and even international trade recovered over the northern branch of the SR in the second half of the fourteenth century (Roux 1991, 290; see also below).

Box 3.4: Nomadism and Nomadic Statehood[118] at Its Mongol Apex

Regularities/recurrent patterns of nomadic statehood, empire formation, and decline in CA (according to Chaliand, Krieger, and Khazanov)

According to Chaliand, CA was the geographic pivot and the source of disruption ("foyer perturbateur") of the ancient and the medieval world (2003, 22). Krieger (2003, 253) detects detailed patterns of cyclical repetition or repetitive cycles: a powerful tribal community or confederation leaves its traditional territory (for whatever reason) in order to establish a new sovereign community elsewhere. In doing this, it often moves into a power vacuum left behind by another collapsing polity. The new community takes possession of the lands and subjugates tribes living in the area. After a relatively short period of political consolidation in the new homeland (possibly only lasting a few decades), a surprisingly swift expansion gets underway. A large realm or empire emerges, which is soon structured into a number of sub-empires (German: Teilreiche) following a tradition established by Turkic peoples in the sixth century. These sub-empires are frequently allocated to members of the ruling family as fiefs (but not in the precise sense of European feudalism), principalities, appanages, or domains. The allocation of territories is aimed at strengthening or

ensuring the ruling authorities' presence across an extended periphery. However, the subdivision in many instances sets the stage for particularism. At a certain point, the center gives up its claim to sovereignty. If a sovereign sub-empire or state becomes confronted with a superior adversary, or if hostilities erupt between two sub-empires, drawing in "external" allies, then definite disintegration or decline seems inevitable.

According to Khazanov (1983/1994, 166) in certain situations, nomadic polities can temporarily create very centralized systems of government in order to accomplish specific aims. Such an aim may be, e.g., defense against a military threat or a large construction project (a steppe capital, etc.). Sometimes, as these aims are fulfilled, the systems cease to exist. Such centralization or even statehood may be called dispositional. For instance, stronger and more influential Kazakh khans, such as Tauke at the turn of the seventeenth to the eighteenth century when the Kazakhs were at war with the Dzungars, emerged from time to time. Or strong Turkmen dispositional chiefdoms occasionally emerged in the Middle Ages and later when there was need for joint military action (1983/1994, 175–176, see also below).

Different types of nomadic control of sedentary cultures and the Mongols' use thereof (according to Khazanov)

Khazanov (1983/1994, 231–242, 299–302) postulates three possible types of nomadic states/nomadic rule over sedentary cultures, and provides examples for these types of states:

Nomadic states of the first type are those in which the subjugation and conquest of the settled indigenous populations result in vassal-tribute forms of collective dependence and exploitation. Thus, in these institutional conditions, external forms of rule predominate over internal ones (one might call it rule at arms' length): apart from possibly claiming and taking possession of territories at the borders of sedentary cultures for their exclusive use, nomads do not migrate in large numbers into (previously) settled areas. The subjugated sedentary state may continue to exist, as a vassal state, paying tribute, under nomadic suzerainty. Nomads, on the one hand, and farmers and townspeople, on the other, generally continue to live in two separate societies, inhabiting separate ecological zones. The two subsystems (or two sub-societies) are linked together mainly by political ties.

---

[117] In Olson's terms, the stationary bandit (prince) reverted back into a roving bandit.

[118] In the following, a state (or polity) – whether nomadic or sedentary – is assumed to perform *at least* two fundamental services to its inhabitants: provision of internal security (police and judicial functions) and of external security (military protection against attacks from the outside). In order to do this, the authorities must be able to tax inhabitants (in whichever way) and to call them up for security services (to uphold law and order). These basic elements of state power require at least a simple administrative apparatus, e.g., a ruler's court, to function adequately. A professional bureaucracy, consisting of various functional ministries and/or regional administrative structures, is not seen as a conditio sine qua non of statehood. Apart from organized power, statehood of course also requires a population and a territory (in German: Staatsmacht, Staatsvolk, Staatsgebiet).

(continued)

Box 3.4 (continued)

The nomadic authorities may nominate resident representatives and move some military detachments into dependent indigenous territories, but the settled areas are principally ruled from the outside, from the nomads' homeland, the (Eurasian) steppe. Given the nomadic armed forces' military superiority, any disturbances or unrest in indigenous areas can be effectively dealt with by punitive strikes and raids. This form of rule turned out to be relatively long term and stable, probably because the nomads, living separately from the settled people, were able to sustain their excellent military capabilities. The emergence of a nomadic state of the first type was, however, linked with at least limited sedentarization: the nomadic aristocracy could not do without towns on the steppe which became centers of political power, trade, and handicrafts. Sometimes the nobility or the ruler himself founded these towns.

The most prominent example of a nomadic state of the first type is the Khanate of the Golden Horde (1241—ca. 1440), which maintained a clear demarcation between the nomadic and the settled population (namely, the border between the Pontic and Kipchak steppes on the one hand and the Russian woodlands on the other). Other nomadic states of the first type were the Xiongnu Empire (209 BCE–93 CE), the Turk Khaganate (ca. 550 CE–765 CE), the Karakhitay Empire/Western Liao dynasty (1124–1211), and the Dzungar Empire (1640–1758, see below).

In nomadic states of the second type, nomads, peasants, and town dwellers were integrated into a single sociopolitical and partly even economic system. States of second type feature situations in which nomads, after conquering a sedentary state, moved on to the territory of the state and divided up the same ecological zones between themselves, farmers, traders, and craftsmen. In this framework, nomadic and settled people can also form two separate sub-societies. A second-type state as a whole may start to include and reflect interests of its sedentary inhabitants.[119] Thus, Khazanov concludes that states of the second type do not always remain nomadic even in the broad sense of the word.

The Empire of the Great Khan, ruled by the Mongol Yuan dynasty (ca. 1260–1368), was a developed state of the second type. With Kebek Khan's move to Transoxiana, and certainly with the split of the Chagatay Khanate in two parts (Mavarannahr and Moghulistan) in the middle of the fourteenth century, the region of Mavarannahr turned into a nomadic polity of the second type. Other states of this type were the Kushan Empire (ca. 50 BCE–230 CE), the Karakhanid state (942–1089/1210), the Seljuk Empire (1038–1194), and the Khanate of Bukhara (the Shaybanid state: 1510–late eighteenth century, see below).

Nomadic states of the <u>third type</u> were much less frequent. They are usually the outcome of a long historic development without fundamental ruptures. They feature a single socioeconomic and political system in which nomads, agriculturalists, and town dwellers are integrated. Social differences usually coincide with economic specialization and are often additionally linked to cultural or ethnic differences. At the basis of this nomadic state, there is division of labor, as a rule between pastoralists and agriculturalists. This process usually leads to the politically dominant nomadic nobility ceasing to be nomadic, although it may preserve some of its pastoral traditions as part of its cultural heritage and/or as criteria of social privileges.

Only in the most long-lived of the Seljuk states, the Sultanate of Rum and its successor, the Ottoman Empire, did the third type of nomadic state develop. If undisturbed, the nomadic state's evolution or piecemeal transformation can reach the stage of a polity like the Magyar Empire (from 1000 CE) and its eventual successor, modern Hungary. Other states of the third type are (Danube-)Bulgaria (from 681 CE),[120] the Mughal Empire (1526–1858), the Qing or Manchu Empire (1644–1912), and the Khanate of Bukhara as Russian protectorate (1868–1920). Lebedynsky's definition of "imperial nomadism" (see Box 2.1) can be seen to comprise all three of Khazanov's types of nomadic state. As Lebedynsky points out: "If the development is not interrupted, the nomads can end up by fully settling down and becoming a kind of aristocracy governing the indigenous population" (2007, 23).

(continued)

---

[119] This probably owes to the cumulative impact of increased contacts, interaction, and division of labor between both groups.

[120] At least in the case of Bulgaria, one has to add that the Turkic nomadic conquerors constituted a particularly thin stratum of the population (which was dominated by Southern Slavs) and were assimilated quickly.

Box 3.4 (continued)

Elements of typical evolution of taxation in the Mongol Empire

Mongol taxation in the broadest sense (exaction of resources) with respect to sedentary areas could—but by no means needed to—evolve in four successive stages:

(a) Irregular and uncontrolled pillage through raids. Once such military strikes and campaigns had inflicted enough damage and casualties on a sedentary state, and thus conditions were "appropriate," the conquered state hardly had a choice but to submit to Mongol rule and to accept a tributary relationship (examples: former Rus, Georgia, Korea).

(b) Organized tribute exaction had conquered groups give up part of the goods they produced and/or fulfill other duties for their conqueror, while at the same time preserving their economic and sociopolitical organization, although not always in an unchanged form (examples comprise states already mentioned under a) plus states that immediately surrendered: Uighur Kingdom, Karakhitay Empire/Western Liao dynasty).

(c) Direct predatory taxation: In contrast to tribute, this is a more "hands on" form of exploitation and is only possible in a situation in which nomads choose to directly take control of the fiscal apparatus themselves. As a rule, this apparatus is staffed by the bureaucracy of the sedentary population who go into the service of their new masters. In such cases extremely predatory forms of "tax farming" and "appanage policies" are often practiced first (examples: Northern China after ca. 1220; Transoxiana, Khorassan, Khwarazm, and Kashgaria after 1221; Persia and Mesopotamia after 1260).

(d) Direct regular taxation: Farsighted nomadic rulers or simply rulers oriented beyond the short or medium term (of one or a couple of years) such as Ögöday and Ghazan Khan, subsequently changed these methods by making tax collection more predictable, more systematic, and less confiscatory, thereby moving to fixed, more rule-based taxation in a framework of centralized fiscal control. But such cases were not too frequent under Mongol rule (e.g., Transoxiana after ca. 1235, Great Khanate and some other territories

from 1252 and the 1250s, respectively, Southern China from 1280, Il-Khanate from ca. 1295).

There were also relapses from (d) to (c) (for instance, Transoxiana, probably in the late 1200s—however, renewed reforms in 1320s; Il-Khanate, from ca. 1310; Great Khanate, likely in the second quarter of fourteenth century).

References

Abazov R (2008) The Palgrave concise historical atlas of CA. Palgrave MacMillan, New York

Abu-Lughod J (1989) Before European hegemony – the world system A.D. 1250–1350. Oxford University Press, New York

Agayanov S (1998) The states of the Oghuz, the Kimek and the Kipchak. In: UNESCO: History of civilizations in CA, vol IV

Akhmedov B (1998) CA under the rule of Genghis Khan's successors. In: UNESCO: History of civilizations in CA, vol IV

Allsen T (2009) Mongols as vectors for cultural transmission. In: Cosmo, Frank, Golden (eds) The Cambridge history of inner Asia. Cambridge University Press, New York

Amitai R (2001) Turko-Mongolian Nomads and the Iqta System in the Islamic Middle East (ca. 1000–1400 CE). In: Khazanov A, Wink A (eds) Nomads in the sedentary world. Routledge, London

Andrea A (2014) The silk road in world history: a review essay. Asian Rev World Hist 2(1):105–127

Anderle A et al (ed) (1973) Weltgeschichte in Daten. VEB Deutscher Verlag der Wissenschaften

Arp S (2007/2008) Die Straße der Globalisierung. In: Geo Spezial: Die Seidenstraße, No. 6, Dec/Jan, 133–135

Artykbaev Z (2007) Istoria Kazakhstana. Tsentralno-Aziatskoe knizhnoe izdatelstvo, Kostanay

Ashrafyan K (1998) CA under Timur from 1370 to the early 15th century. In: UNESCO: History of civilizations in CA, vol IV

Baipakov K, Kumekov B, Pischulina K (1997) Istoria Kazakhstana v srednie veka. Rauan, Almaty

Barfield T (1989) The perilous frontier – nomadic empires and China 221 BCE to 1757 CE. Blackwell, Cambridge, MA

Barfield T (2001) Steppe empires, China and the silk route: nomads as a force in international trade and politics. In: Khazanov A, Wink A (eds) Nomads in the sedentary world. Routledge, London

Baumer C (2014) The history of CA – the age of the silk roads. I.B. Tauris, London

Biarnes P (2008) La Route de la soie – Une histoire géopolitique. Ellipses, Paris

Bira S (1998) The Mongols and their state in the 12th and 13th century. In: UNESCO: History of civilizations in CA, vol IV

Black J (2006) Atlas der Weltgeschichte (World History Atlas). Weltbild (Dorling Kindersley), Starnberg

Bolshakov O (1998) CA under the early Abbasids. In: UNESCO: History of civilizations in CA, vol IV

Bonavia J, Baumer C (2002) The silk road—Xian to Kashgar. Odyssey, Hong Kong

Borgolte M (2015) Kommunikation – Handel, Kunst und Wissenstausch. In: Demel, W u.a. (eds) WBG Weltgeschichte – Eine globale Geschichte von den Anfängen bis ins 21. Band III

Bosworth C (1998) The Ghaznavids. In: UNESCO: History of civilizations in CA, vol IV

Boucheron P (2012a) Soie, épices et porcelaine: Les routes de l'Eurasie. In: Petitjean P (ed) Inventer le monde – Une histoire globale du 15e siècle, nov-déc

Boucheron P (2012) 1405: La mort de Tamerlan – Au centre effondré du monde. In: Petitjean P (ed) Inventer le monde – Une histoire globale du 15e siècle, nov-déc

Boulnois L (2009) Les Routes de la soie – Aux origines de la mondialisation, Entretien avec Grataloup. Sciences Humaines, Auxerre

Boyle J (ed) (1968) The Cambridge history of Iran, vol 5. Cambridge University Press, Cambridge

Brook K (2006) The Jews of Khazaria. Rowman and Littlefield, Lanham, MD

Burbank J, Cooper F (2010) Empires in world history – power and the politics of difference. Princeton University Press, Princeton, NJ

Burlot J (1995) La civilisation islamique. Hachette, Paris

Cameron R, Neal L (2003) A concise economic history of the world – from Paleolithic times to the present. Oxford University Press, New York

Chaliand G (1995) Les empires nomades—De la Mongolie au Danube (Ve-IVe siècles av. J.C., XVe-XVIe siècles ap. J.C.), Perrin

Chaliand G (2003) Atlas du nouvel ordre mondial. Robert Laffont, Paris

Chawla J (2006) India's overland trade with CA and Persia during the 13th and 14th centuries. Munshiram Manoharlal, Delhi

Chua A (2007) Day of empire – how hyperpowers rise to global dominance and why they fail. Random House, New York

Chvyr A (1996) Problema osedlo-kochevnicheskogo dialoga v drevney Sredney Azii. In: Rossiiskaya Akademia Nauk – Institut Vostokovedenia (ed) Azia – Dialog Tsivilizatsii, Giperion

Contamine P et al (1997) L'économie mediévale. Armand Colin, Paris

Cummings S (2012) Understanding CA – politics and contested transformations. Routledge, New York

Davidovich E (1998) The Karakhanids. In: UNESCO: History of Civilizations in CA, vol IV

Davidovich E, Dani A (1998) Coinage and the Monetary System. In: UNESCO: History of Civilizations in CA, vol IV

Dmitriev S (2009) Archéologie du Grand Jeu: Une brève histoire de l'Asie centrale. In: Piatigorsky J., Sapir J. (eds): Le Grand Jeu du XIX siècle – Les enjeux géopolitiques de l'Asie centrale, Autrement

Ducellier A et al (2012) Le Moyen Age en Orient – Byzance et l'Islam. Hachette, Paris

Emeliantseva E, Malz A, Ursprung D (2001) Einführung in die osteuropäische Geschichte. Orellifüssli, UTB, Zürich

Exenberger A (2009) Wellen im Wasser und in der Zeit: "Welt"-- Handel seit 1204. In: Feldbauer P, Hödl G, Lehners J-P (eds) Rhythmen der Globalisierung. Mandelbaum, Wien

Fang Ming (2014) Silk Road. Chinese Red, Beijing. Huangshan Publishing House

Fässler P (2007) Globalisierung – Ein historisches Kompendium. UTB Böhlau, Köln

Feldbauer P, Liedl G (2008) Die islamische Welt 1000 bis 1517 – Wirtschaft, Gesellschaft, Staat. Mandelbaum, Wien

Feldbauer P, Liedl G (2009) 1250–1620: Archaische Globalisierung? In: Feldbauer P, Hödl G, Lehners J-P (eds) Rhythmen der Globalisierung. Mandelbaum, Wien

Feldbauer P, Liedl G, Morrissey J (2010) Venedig 800–1600 – Die Serenissima als Weltmacht. Mandelbaum, Wien

Findlay R, O'Rourke K (2007) Power and plenty – trade, war and the world economy in the second millennium. Princeton University Press, Princeton, NJ

Fragner B (2008) Die "Khanate": Eine zentralasiatische Kulturlandschaft vom 15. bis zum 19. Jhdt. In: Nolte H.-H. (ed) Zeitschrift für Weltgeschichte – Interdispziplinaere Perspektiven, 9. Jg

Geiss I (1979) Geschichte griffbereit – Epochen – Die universale Dimension der Weltgeschichte. Rowohlt, Reinbek

Geng S (1998) The Uighur Kingdom of Qocho. In: UNESCO: History of civilizations in CA, vol IV

Gilomen H-J (2014) Wirtschaftsgeschichte des Mittelalters. C.H. Beck, München

Golden P (2011) CA in world history. Oxford University Press, Oxford

Gorod moy rodnoy Almaty–Tugan kalam Almaty (2004), Edelweis

Grataloup C (2007) Géohistoire de la mondialisation – Le temps long du monde. Armand Colin, Paris

Der Große Ploetz (2008) Die Enzyklopädie der Weltgeschichte, 35th edn. Vandenhoeck & Ruprecht, Göttingen

Grousset R (1946) Bilan de l'histoire. Desclee de Brower, Paris

Grousset R (1965) L'empire des steppes – Attila, Genghis-Khan, Tamerlan. Payot, Paris

von Gumppenberg M-C, Steinbach U (eds) (2004) Zentralasien: Geschichte – Politik – Wirtschaft – Ein Lexikon. C.H. Beck, München

Gunder Frank A (1992) The centrality of CA: Studies in history. VU University, Amsterdam

Guseinov R (2004) Istoria mirovoy ekonomiki – Zapad, vostok, Rossia. Sibirskoe universitetskoe izdatelstvo, Novosibirsk

Habib I (2003) Science and technology. In: UNESCO: History of civilizations of CA, vol V

Halperin C (1985) Russia and the golden horde – the mongol impact on medieval Russian history. Indiana University Press, Bloomington

Hambis L (ed) (1977) Asie centrale – Histoire et civilisation. Collège de France, Paris

Hambly G (ed) (1966) Fischer Weltgeschichte: Zentralasien (Band 16). Fischer Taschenbuch Verlag, Frankfurt, unaltered edition 1979

He X, Guo H (2008) A history of turks. China Intercontinental Press, Beijing

Höllmann T (2004) Die Seidenstraße. C.H. Beck, München

Hoffmann G (2011) Regionalisierung, Kontakte, Konflikte – Die islamische Welt. In: Schottenhammer A, Feldbauer P (eds) Die Welt 1000–1250. Mandelbaum, Wien

Jackson P (2005) The Mongols and the West 1221–1410. Pearson, Harlow

Jehel G (ed) (2007) Histoire du monde 500 – 1000 – 1500. Du temps, Nantes

Kaemmel E (1966) Finanzgeschichte – Sklavenhaltergesellschaft, Feudalismus, vormonopolistischer Kapitalismus. Die Wirtschaft, Berlin

Kappeler A (2000) Russische Geschichte. C.H. Beck, München

Kappeler A (2001) Russland als Vielvölkerreich – Entstehung, Geschichte, Zerfall. C.H. Beck, München

Kappeler A (2003) Vom Grenzland zur Eigenstaatlichkeit: Historische Voraussetzungen von Staat und Nation. In: Besters-Dilger J (ed) Die Ukraine in Europa. Böhlau, Wien

Karger A (ed) (1978) Fischer Länderkunde. Sowjetunion

Kasai N, Natsagdorj S (1998) Socio-economic development: food and clothing in Eastern Iran and CA. In: UNESCO: History of Civilizations in CA, vol IV

Kauz R (2009) Zerstörung, Eroberung, politische Umstrukturierung: Zentralasien. In: Ertl T, Limberger M (eds) Die Welt 1250–1500. Mandelbaum, Magnus, Wien

Kauz R (2011) Die Gründung des mongolischen Weltreiches – Zentralasien. In: Schottenhammer A, Feldbauer P (eds) Die Welt 1000–1250. Mandelbaum, Wien

Khazanov A (1983) Nomads and the outside world. University of Wisconsin, Madison

Kollmar-Paulenz K (2011) Die Mongolen – Von Dschingis Khan bis heute. C.H. Beck, München

Kozybaev M, Nurpeis K, Romanov Y et al (2010) Tom 1: Kazakhstan ot epokhi paleolita do pozdnego srednevekovia. In: Ministerstvo

Obrazovania i Nauki Respubliki Kazakhstan (ed): Istoria Kazakhstana s drevneishikh vremen do nashikh dney v piati tomakh, Atamura

Knobloch E (1999) Turkestan – Taschkent, Buchara, Samarkand – Reisen zu den Kulturstätten Mittelasiens (Beyond the Oxus). Prestel, München

Kocka J (2013) Geschichte des Kapitalismus. C.H. Beck, München

Kozak D (2007) La Marea delle popolazioni nelle steppe pontiche nel 1 millennio. In: Borona GL, Marzatico F (eds) Ori dei cavalieri delle steppe – Collezioni dai musei dell'Ucraina. SilvanaEditoriale, Cinisello Balsamo

Krieger M (2003) Geschichte Asiens – Eine Einführung. Böhlau, Köln

Laffer A (2004) The Laffer curve: past, present, and future. Heritage Foundation Backgrounder No. 1765

Laruelle M (2008) Kazakhstan – Enjeux identitaires et nomadisme. In: Le courrier des pays de l'Est: Symboles et mémoires à l'Est, 29 pays, 29 regards, mai-juin

Lebedynsky Y (2007) Les nomades – Les peuples nomades de la steppe des origines aux invasions mongoles (IXe siècle av. J.-C. – XIIIe siècle apr. J.-C.). Errance, Paris

Ledonne J (2008) Russia's eastern theater, 1650–1850: Springboard or strategic backyard? In: Cahiers du monde russe, janv-mars 2008 (EHESS)

Leipold H (2001) Islam, institutioneller Wandel und wirtschaftliche Entwicklung. Lucius & Lucius, Stuttgart

Lemercier-Quelquejay C (1970) La paix mongole – Joug tatar ou paix mongole? Flammarion, Paris

Linska M, Handel A, Rasuly-Paleczek G (2003) Einführung in die Ethnologie Zentralasiens (Vorlesungsskriptum). Universität Wien, Vienna

Litvinsky B (1996) India i tsentralnaya Azia. In: Rossiiskaya Akademia Nauk – Institut Vostokovedenia (ed) Azia – Dialog Tsivilizatsii, Giperion

Liu X (2005) Viticulture and viniculture in the Turfan region. Silk Road 3(1):23–27

Liu X (2010) The silk road in world history. Oxford University Press, Oxford

Lopez R (1987) The trade of medieval Europe: the South. In: Postan M, Miller E (eds) The Cambridge economic history of Europe, vol 2. Cambridge University Press, Cambridge

Ma D (2003) Tarim Basin. In: UNESCO: History of civilizations of CA, vol V

Maddison A (1998) L'économie chinoise – une perspective historique. OCDE, Paris

Man J (2014) The Mongol empire – Genghis Khan, his heirs and the founding of modern China. Bantam Press, London

Mankovskaya L (1982) Khiva – a museum in the open – a reserve of Khorezam architecture. Tashkent, Moscow

Marchand P (2014) Géopolitique de la Russie – Une nouvelle puissance en Eurasie. Presses universitaires de France, Paris

Marks R (2002/2006) Die Ursprünge der modernen Welt – Eine globale Weltgeschichte (The origins of the modern world – a global and ecological narrative), Theiss

Martinez A (2009) Institutional development, revenues and trade. In: Cosmo, Frank, Golden (eds) The Cambridge history of inner Asia – the Chinggisid age. Cambridge University Press, Cambridge

Masselos J (ed) (2010) Imperien Asiens – Von den alten Khmer bis zu den Meiji (The Great Empires of Asia), Theiss

Masson-Smith J (2003) The Mongols and the silk road. Silk Road Foundation

May T (2012) The Mongol conquests in world history. Reaktion Books, London

Mayhew B (2010) Central Asia highlights: history. In: Mayhew B, Bloom G, Clammer P, Kohn M, Noble J (ed) Lonely planet guide: Central Asia, 5th edn. Lonely Planet Publications, Melbourne, pp 34–61

Menzel U (2015) Die Ordnung der Welt – Imperium oder Hegemonie in der Hierachie der Staatenwelt. Suhrkamp, Berlin

Millward J, Perdue P (2004) Political and cultural history through the late 19th century. In: Starr F (ed) Xinjiang – China's muslim borderland. Sharpe, Armonk, NY

Mirow J (2009) Weltgeschichte. Piper, München

Mokyr J (2003) CA. In: Mokyr J (ed) The Oxford encyclopedia of economic history. Oxford University Press, Oxford

Morgan D (2007) The Mongols. Blackwell, New York

Mourre (ed) (2003) Le Petit Mourre – Dictionnaire de l'histoire. Bordas, Paris

Negmatov N (1998) The Samanid state. In: UNESCO: History of civilizations in CA, vol IV

Nizami K (1998a) The Ghurids. In: UNESCO: History of civilizations in CA, vol IV

Nizami K (1998b) Popular movements, religious trends and Sufi influence on the masses in the post-Abbasid period. In: UNESCO: History of civilizations in CA, vol IV

Nolte H-H (1991) Russland UdSSR – Geschichte, Politik, Wirtschaft. Fackelträger, Hannover

Nolte H-H (2005) Weltgeschichte – Imperien, Religionen und Systeme – 15. bis 19. Jahrhundert. Böhlau, Vienna

Norel P (2009) L'histoire économique globale. du Seuil, Paris

O'Brien P (ed) (2010) Atlas of world history, 2nd edn. Oxford University Press, Oxford

O'Rourke S (2007) The cossaks. Manchester University Press, Manchester

Oskolkov V, Oskolkova I (2004) Istoria Kazakhstana (Spravochnik). Oner Baspasy

Osterhammel J, Petersson N (2003) Geschichte der Globalisierung – Dimensionen, Prozesse, Epochen. C.H. Beck, München

Ott H, Schäfer H (eds) (1984) Wirtschaftsploetz—Wirtschaftsgeschichte zum Nachschlagen, Ploetz

Overseas Chinese Affairs Office (2006) Connaissances générales en histoire chinoise. Foreign Language Teaching and Research Press, Beijing

Overy R (ed) (2004) The times complete history of the world – the ultimate work of historical reference (6th edn)

Pander K (2005) Zentralasien – Usbekistan, Kirgistan, Tadschikistan, Turkmenistan, Kasachstan. DuMont, Ostfildern

Paul J (2012) Neue Fischer Weltgeschichte: Zentralasien (Band 10). S. Fischer Verlag, Frankfurt

Perdue P (2003) Silk road. In: Mokyr J (ed) The Oxford encyclopedia of economic history. Oxford University Press, Oxford

Perdue P (2005) China marches west – the Qing conquest of central Eurasia. Harvard University, Cambridge, MA

Pernau M (2011) Transnationale Geschichte. Vandenhoeck & Ruprecht, Göttingen

Petric B-M (2002) Pouvoir, don et réseaux en Ouzbékistan post-soviétique. Presses universitaires de France, Paris

Petrushevsky I (1968) The socio-economic condition of Iran under the Ilkhans. In: Boyle J (ed) The Cambridge history of Iran, vol 5. Cambridge University Press, Cambridge

Pickhan G (2009) Von der Kiever Rus zum Moskauer Reich – Osteuropa. In: Ertl T, Limberger M (eds) Die Welt 1250–1500. Mandelbaum, Magnus, Wien

P.M. History (2011) Von Europa nach China: Große Reiche und rätselhafte Kulturen an der Seidenstraße, no. 2

Ponting G (2001) World history – a new perspective. Pimlico, London

Poujol C (2000) Le Kazakhstan (Que sais-je?). Presses Universitaires de France, Paris

Poujol C (2001) Dictionnaire de l'Asie centrale. Ellipses, Paris

Poujol C (2008) Ouzbékistan – la croisée des chemins. Belin – La documentation française, Paris

Ptak R (2007) Die maritime Seidenstraße – Küstenräume, Seefahrt und Handel in vorkolonialer Zeit. C.H. Beck, München

Rashid al-Din (1971) The Successors of Genghis Khan (translated by John Boyle). Columbia University Press, New York

Rasuly-Paleczek G (2006) Von 'Wilden Reiterhorden' und 'Barbarischen Eroberern'. In: Steffelbauer I, Hakami K (eds) Vom Alten Orient zum Nahen Osten. Magnus, Essen

Reichert F (2015) Fernhandel und Entdeckungen. In: Demel W u.a. (ed) WBG Weltgeschichte – Eine globale Geschichte von den Anfängen bis ins 21. Jhdt. Band IV

Roberts J (2002) The new penguin history of the world. Penguin, London

Rodinson M (1966) Islam and capitalism (Islam et capitalisme). Saqi Essentials, London

Rossabi M (1990) The "Decline" of C Asian Caravan Trade. In: Tracy J (ed) The rise of merchant empires: long-distance trade in the early modern world 1350–1750. Cambridge University Press, Cambridge

Rossabi M (2012) The Mongols – a very short introduction. Oxford University Press, Oxford

Roudik P (2007) The history of the C Asian republics. Greenwood Press, Westport

Roux J-P (1991) Tamerlan. Fayard, Paris

Roux J-P (1993) Histoire de l'empire mongol. Fayard, Paris

Roux J-P (1997) L'Asie centrale – Histoire et civilisation. Fayard, Paris

Roux J-P (2000) Histoire des Turcs – Deux milles ans du Pacifique à la Mediterrannée. Fayard, Paris

Saidov A, Anarbaev A, Goriyacheva V (2011) Pre-colonial Legacy. In: Starr F (ed) Ferghana valley – the heart of CA. Sharpe, Armonk, NY

Scheck W (1977) Geschichte Russlands – Von der Frühgeschichte bis zur Sowjetunion. Heyne, München

Schmieder F (2013) Europa und das vormoderne Weltwirtschaftssystem. In: Ertl T (ed) Europas Aufstieg – Eine Spurensuche im späten Mittelalter. Mandelbaum, Wien

Schmieder F (2015) Nomaden zwischen Asien, Europa und dem Mittleren Osten. In: Demel, W u.a.(eds) WBG Weltgeschichte – Eine globale Geschichte von den Anfängen bis ins 21. Jhdt, Band III

Schottenhammer A (2015) Sino-arabische Beziehungen im 8. Jhdt – Eine frühe pan-asiatische Mächteallianz? In: Tremml-Werner B, Crailsheim E (eds) Audienzen und Allianzen – Interkulturelle Diplomatie in Asien und Europa vom 8. bis zum 18. Jhdt. Mandelbaum, Wien

Schwarz F (2004) Migration in vor-sowjetischer Zeit. In: von Gumppenberg M-C, Steinbach U (eds) Zentralasien: Geschichte—Politik—Wirtschaft—Ein Lexikon

Sellnow I et al (1977) Weltgeschichte bis zur Herausbildung des Feudalismus – Ein Abriss. Akademie Verlag Berlin

Sevim A, Bosworth C (1998) The Seljuks and the Kwarazm Shahs. In: UNESCO: History of civilizations in CA, vol IV

Shen F (2009) Cultural flow between China and the outside world throughout history. Foreign Language Press, Beijing

Shukow I et al (eds) (1955–68) Weltgeschichte in zehn Bänden (Vsemirnaya istoria v desiat tomakh), Bände 2–6 (Band 2 1956/

62, Band 3 1957/63, Band 4 1958/64, Band 5 1958/66, Band 6 1959/69). VEB Deutscher Verlag der Wissenschaften

Sinor D (1998) The Kitan and the Kara Khitay. In: UNESCO: History of civilizations in CA, vol IV

Soucek S (2000) A history of inner Asia. Cambridge University Press, Cambridge

Stanziani A (2012) Bâtisseurs d'empires – Russie, Chine et Inde à la croisée des mondes, XV-XIX siècles. Seuil

Starr F (2013) Lost enlightenment – CA's golden age from the Arab conquest to Tamerlane. Princeton University Press, Princeton

Starr F (ed) (2004) Xinjiang – China's muslim borderland. Sharpe, Armonk, NY

Stearns P (2009) Globalization in world history. Routledge, London

Stier H-E et al (eds) (1991) Großer Atlas zur Weltgeschichte. Orbis, Braunschweig

The Times (ed) (1982) The Times Concise Atlas of World History

Töpfer B et al (1985) Allgemeine Geschichte des Mittelalters. VEB Deutscher Verlag der Wissenschaften, Berlin

Tracy J (2011) Trade across Eurasia to about 1750. In: Bentley (ed) The Oxford handbook of world history. Oxford University Press, Oxford

Tröbst S (2009) Wirtschaft. In: Bohn T, Neutatz D (eds) Studienhandbuch Östliches Europa Band 2: Geschichte des Russischen Reiches und der Sowjetunion. Böhlau, Wien

Turnbull S (2008) Mongolen (The Mongols). Brandenburgisches Verlagshaus

de la Vaissière E (2004) Histoire des marchands sogdiens. Collège de France, Paris

de la Vaissière E (2013) Route de la soie: Un commerce mondial?. In: L'Histoire: Les Mongols – le plus grand empire du monde (dossier spécial), octobre

Vernadsky G (1953) Mongols and Russia. In: Vernadsky G, Karpovich M (eds) 1953: A history of Russia. Yale University Press, New Haven

Vogelsang K (2013) Geschichte Chinas. Reclam, Stuttgart

Walter R (2006) Geschichte der Weltwirtschaft – Eine Einführung. UTB Böhlau, Köln

Waugh D (2002) The Origins of the Silk Road. University of Washington Lecture Series

Waugh D (2007) Richthofen's "Silk Roads": toward the archaeology of a concept. In: The Silk Road, vol 5, no 1, summer

Waugh D (2008) The silk roads and Eurasian geography. University of Washington

Weiers M (2004) Geschichte der Mongolen. Kohlhammer, Stuttgart

Westermann (ed) (1997) Großer Atlas zur Weltgeschichte. Westermann, Braunschweig

Wild D (1992) The silk road. University of California, Irvine

Wink A (2001) India and the Turko-Mongol Frontier. In: Khazanov A, Wink A (eds) Nomads in the sedentary world. Routledge, London

Zhang Y (2005) Story of the silk road. China International Press, China

4.1 From Tamerlane to the Dzungar Empire: CA Moving from the Heart to the Periphery of the World Economy (ca. 1350–1750)

4.1.1 Fragile Recovery of CA and the SR (ca. 1350–Sixteenth Century)

For the following chapter, the author has primarily drawn from publications by M. Annanepesov, K.Z. Ashrafyan, Zhambyl Artykbaev, Elizabeth Bacon, Karl Baipakov, Thomas Barfield, E.A. Davidovich, Ronald Findlay, Paul Georg Geiss, Gavin Hambly, Andre Kamev, Andreas Kappeler, Anatoly Khazanov, Martin Krieger, James Millward, R.G. Mukminova, Kevin O'Rourke, Boris-Mathieu Petric, Peter Perdue, Catherine Poujol, Peter Roudik, Jean-Paul Roux, Florian Schwarz, I.M. Shukow, Svat Soucek, and Alessandro Stanziani.

Probably due to the differential Mongol impact on China, the Islamic Middle East and Europe—with Europe much less ravaged than the other two regions—by the second half of the fourteenth century, the West may have reached broad economic and technological parity with Middle Kingdom and the Muslim World (Darwin 2008, 31). Yet, the decline of Mongol power and the rise of the Mamluk Sultanate of Cairo and of the Ottoman Sultanate restrained European spatial scope for action and drove up prices for goods that Europe obtained from Asia (Wendt 2007, 28). The Sultans of Egypt, for instance, banned Italian merchants from traveling through their territory and rendered direct European-Indian trade contacts very difficult (Gilomen 2014, 108).

With the disintegration of the Mongol Empire, the revival of Islamic powers and the more inward-oriented policies of the Ming dynasty (compared to its predecessor)[1], the barriers rose up again on the land route across Eurasia. The breaking-up of territories multiplied customs tariffs, tolls, inspections, and made goods much more expensive. These partly disorderly changes were aggravated by two factors: the devastating impact of the spreading of the Black Death along the trade routes (see above) and increased road banditry and petty warfare, which rendered overland traffic dangerous and discouraged business (Roux 1991, 288).

However, despite or perhaps because of the colossal losses of life stemming from Mongol devastations and from the Great Plague, birth rates in many parts of CA soon surged so impressively that by the 1370s population levels had almost returned to what they had been in the early thirteenth century. Some Europeans continued to travel to the Middle East and India in the fourteenth and fifteenth centuries, and overland trade started to recover (Roux 1991, 305; Wendt 2007, 28). With the foundation of Timur's empire in the late fourteenth century, the southern SR branch leading from Persia to Anatolia or Syria received a boost. Soon trade linking Mavarannahr (Transoxiana) with India and China also revived. In the first half of the fifteenth century, all of the Eurasian civilizations were (re)connected by a network of long-distance trade routes that converged on the Middle East. The Khanate of the Golden Horde, Mongol successor states in CA, Iran, and Turkey, as well as China had generally reestablished or maintained peace and security along the trade routes (Feldbauer and Liedl 2009, 31; Haywood 2011, year 1400; Rossabi 1990).

In the fifteenth century, large-scale exportation of Chinese porcelain added to the recovery of Eurasian overland trade. Iran and the Near East, Korea, Japan, and the East Indies preceded Europe as important markets for the coveted product. The secrets of the production of china did not reach the West before the eighteenth century, at the same time as the first samples of kaolin. Notably under Emperor

---

[1] If Admiral Zheng He's exploration trips to the Indian Ocean, the Near East and East Africa had been successful, these ventures could have opened up a serious alternative to overland SR trade about a century earlier than it actually happened. But the great Ming explorer's voyages were soon terminated, partly due to C Asian factors (see below).

© Springer International Publishing AG 2017
S. Barisitz, *Central Asia and the Silk Road*, Studies in Economic History, DOI 10.1007/978-3-319-51213-6_4

Xuande (1426–1435) did the Ming dynasty and its civil service develop the porcelain industry; the imperial porcelain administration coordinated the work of about sixty furnaces producing ca. 100,000 pieces of china per year, including the highly valued "blue and white" vases (Boucheron 2012a, 50).[2]

Conflicts, while frequent, did not tend to seriously damage commerce between China, CA, India, Persia, Turkey, the city of Kaffa, Ukraine, Russia, and Poland-Lithuania (Stanziani 2012, 102). According to Ponting, important evidence shows that the SR continued to flourish well into the seventeenth century (2001, 531). But at least a relative decline—in relation to expanding maritime trade with India and China—must have already been perceptible at that time. Moreover, at least from the European viewpoint, the post-Mongol recovery of the SR must have been a fragile and instable one. This is because the Europeans (to name just Columbus and Vasco da Gama) would certainly not have stubbornly attempted to find new, seaborne routes to the Orient and would not have accepted such high risks that they eventually would even end up discovering America, if SR links to India and China had functioned that well. As "necessity is the mother of invention," frustrations and difficulties in reaching the post-Mongol Orient may have contributed to the inventions that would propel Europe's extremely successful seaborne expansion and substantially reduce the cost of maritime trade compared to overland trade.

The following factors contributed to driving the post-Mongol recovery:

- There was a base effect, namely, the low point of departure after the destructions of the Mongol era (notwithstanding the Genghisids' impressive accomplishments in forced trade integration), the collapse of Mongol authority, and the cataclysm of the Great Plague. In such circumstances, some recovery must be expected. The demographic "bounce back" in the second half of the fourteenth century supports this argument.
- The political stabilization and safeguarding of the trade routes in the post-Mongol era by successor states to the Mongol and Tamerlan Empires (in CA, Timurid/Shaybanid states; moreover, emergence of "Gunpowder Empires," Turkey, Ottomans; Iran, Safavids; India, Mughals; see below) (Findlay and O'Rourke 2007, 125).
- Despite the increasingly rigid and integral character of Muslim religious practices, the fact that Islam from the fifteenth century had finally encompassed all-but-entire CA (including Moghulistan) may have added to

economic cohesion and efficiency of doing business there. This is because of principles of common understanding, communication, and dispute resolution by Muslims: For one, relations between believers were easier in the commercial as well as diplomatic spheres; moreover, religious links permitted recourse to religious justice (Islamic courts, arbitration services, qadis) (Stanziani 2012, 103).

- After initial isolationist tendencies and a temporary turn toward the oceans, the Ming dynasty, ruling Eurasia's largest economy, became a dynamic force in international overland trade in the fifteenth century: China remained interested in the development and consolidation of trade relations with Central and Western Asia, e.g., to acquire large numbers of high-quality horses in order to stand up to the continuing or reemerging Mongol military menace (Kauz 2006, 128).

4.1.1.1 Empire of Tamerlane (ca. 1380–1405): A Model of "Oriental Despotism"?

Origins, Goals, Military Technology, Cruel Conquests, and Widespread Devastation

Like other regions of the former empire, CA was subject to mounting political instability after the collapse of Mongol rule. Major urban centers as well as nomadic lands were interested in supporting a capable leader who could bring back stability to Transoxiana (Mavarannahr) and adjacent regions. In 1370, Timur Leng or Tamerlane (1336–1405), member of a half-sedentarized Turko-Mongol tribe, born south of Samarkand and of Muslim faith, seized effective power in Transoxiana. He had found support among individuals from numerous nomadic and semi-nomadic tribes as well as from wealthy merchants and landlords of Samarkand and from Muslim clergymen; well-to-do notables underwrote his first military campaigns (Abazov 2008, Map 25).[3] As Timur was of non-Genghisid descent, he could not call himself khan and thus chose to rule as emir (prince). Given his talent as a commander and given very powerful armed forces at his disposal, Emir Timur may have regarded the waging of uninterrupted wars of conquest as the principal means of enhancing his power and rewarding his followers (Ashrafyan 1998, 325). Like a typical leader of a nomadic confederation, Tamerlane aimed at winning booty and gaining control of and revenue from major trade routes.

Tamerlane achieved his victories by using a new type of army that combined the traditional military system of the Mongols with tactical and technical innovations: The basic

---

[2] This recalls Chinese silk production, which also constituted a national monopoly for centuries.

[3] Timur is reported to have started out as the leader of a gang of four to five well-armed mounted roving freebooters (Ashrafyan 1998, 321).

striking force was an extremely nimble cavalry, recruited from the nomadic and semi-nomadic population; infantry units were recruited from settled peoples (e.g., Tajiks, Turks). Parts of the army seem to have consisted of well-paid professionals or ghulams, many of them Turkmens (which recall the highly effective Turkic slave soldiers that had served in earlier C Asian realms). Apart from crossbows, Timur's troops used oil slings, stone catapults, battering rams, and firearms, including canons (Shukow et al. 1957/ 1963, Band 3, 661). Special engineering units were set up to assist in the siege of cities. The command chain adopted the Mongol decimal system: The army was divided into tumens ("ten thousands") and into all lower decimal units.

Banking on his general military superiority, Timur adopted a stance toward his enemies that was quite similar to Genghis Khan's. For instance, in conquering cities, if surrender negotiations failed or if inhabitants rebelled after conquest, Tamerlane would resort to devastating military force and take ruthless punitive actions, showing urban dwellers little or no mercy (Roudik 2007, 44).

Tamerlane's conquests may be described in four concentric circles[4]:

- 1370s and 1380s: Mavarannahr (Bukhara 1372), Shash, Khwarazm (Urgench 1379), Ustyurt, Khorassan (Herat 1381), Northern Iran
- First half of 1390s: Otrar and other towns of the Syr Daria valley, Ferghana, Almalik, Semirechie, Kashgar, Kucha and other towns of the Tarim Basin (but of the latter only Kashgar remained under Timur's control), Transcaucasia, Southern Iran (Isfahan 1393), Mesopotamia (Baghdad 1393), Afghanistan, and Baluchistan
- Second half of 1390s: southern Desht-i-Kipchak and Pontic steppes (1395/1396: Saray Berke, Tana, Kaffa), Punjab (Multan 1398), Northwestern India (Delhi 1398), but of all these conquests only the Punjab remained under Timur's control
- 1400s: Syria (Aleppo, Damascus 1400), Anatolia, and Asia Minor (Ankara, Smyrna 1402), but of these conquests only Eastern Syria and Eastern Anatolia remained under Timur's control.

Urgench, Herat, Sarai-Berke, Multan, and Delhi are among the towns that were largely or utterly destroyed by Tamerlan. In 1379, Urgench, the capital of Khorezm, was attacked, plundered, and the local dynasty (under Golden Horde suzerainty) overthrown. When the capital of Khorezm rebelled in 1388, it was razed to the ground. Its inhabitants were deported to Samarkand and its site was sown with barley. In 1391 however, Timur ordered the reconstruction

of Urgench.[5] In 1381, Timur's forces encircled Herat and imposed a heavy tribute on it. Many leading citizens were displaced by force to Mavarannahr and such was the oppression that the population of Herat rose in insurrection. In 1383 the city was burnt down (Ashrafyan 1998, 329–330).

As Ashrafyan put it, the incursion into Punjab and Northern India reduced towns and fortresses there to "heaps of ashes and debris." Delhi was destroyed, its treasures looted, and almost all of its inhabitants either slaughtered or enslaved. Great stores of gold and silver that had accumulated through international trade were carted off, and large quantities of prisoners were hauled away to Samarkand. As a result, slave prices at C Asian markets slumped (Ashrafyan 1998, 333; see also Abu-Lughod 1989, 283; Paul 2012, 296). While preparing an invasion of China, Timur suddenly died.

Altogether, his campaigns are estimated to have resulted in the deaths of more than one million people. He became infamous for building pyramids or walls made from the cemented heads of a defeated army (Töpfer et al. 1985, 192). Timur's atrocities befell large parts of western CA, the region that had already suffered heavily from Genghis Khan's campaigns.[6] Moreover, the Khanate of the Golden Horde as well as the Sultanate of Delhi were decisively weakened, the Ottoman Empire's rise was set back, possibly by half a century, and thus indirectly, the—shrunk—Byzantine state's existence somewhat prolonged. Yet parts of CA, notably Timur's homeland Transoxiana and neighboring Shash (Tashkent), were spared destruction and experienced a totally different treatment (see below).

There was certainly an element of revenge and even punishment in Timur's campaigns against the leader of the Golden Horde Tokhtamish, whom the C Asian ruler had helped acquire the khanship in Saray and who had then apparently betrayed his protector by launching an invasion of Mavarannahr. But Timur's campaigns against the Golden Horde, starting with the seizure of Urgench and Khwarazm, probably also had strategic geoeconomic goals: Timur severely undermined economic activities and particularly transit trade via the lower Volga, the Pontic steppes and Crimea by partly or totally destroying all large cities lying on the western steppe route (Astrakhan, Sarai-Berke, Tana (Azov), Kaffa) (Fragner 2008, 54; Poujol 2000, 30). For instance, trade convoys in the Black Sea region were interrupted from 1400 to 1402 and again in 1405 (Gilomen 2014, 108).

---

[4] See also the resulting Empire of Timur depicted in Map 4.1.

[5] Despite its reconstruction, Urgench never fully recovered from its devastation at the hands of Tamerlane.

[6] Timur's military campaigns probably entailed greater cruelty than any undertakings of similar scale he previously had, including Genghis Khan's (Hambly (ed) 1966/1979, 164).

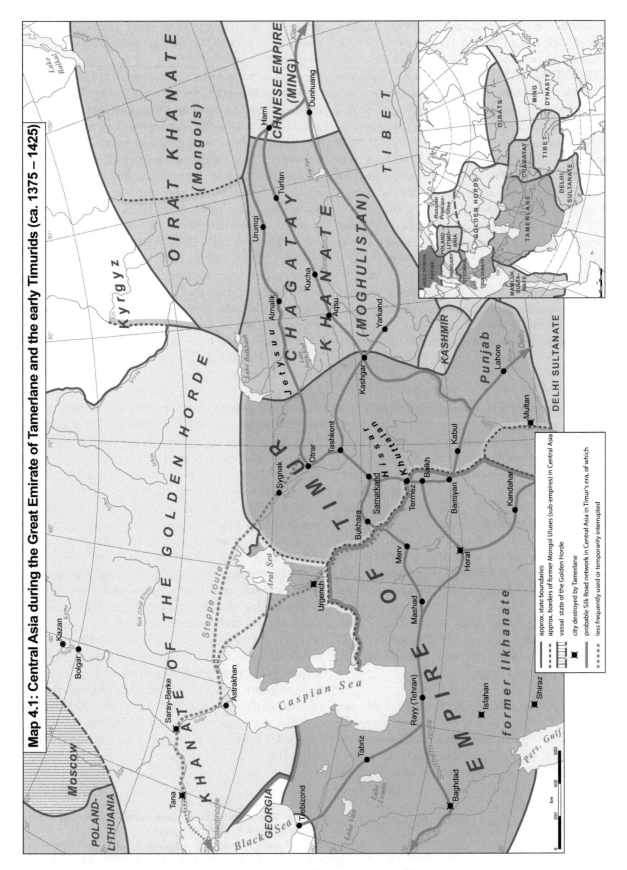

Map 4.1   CA during the Great Emirate of Tamerlane and the early Timurids (ca. 1375–1425)

The disruption of the caravan routes leading to the Black Sea had the consequence that for almost 30 years overland trade between Asia and the Mediterranean concentrated on SR branches linking CA, Iran, Mesopotamia, and Syria—routes largely controlled by Tamerlan and his successors. Through focused destruction as a calculated move, the emir may have effectively diverted trade from the steppe route to "his" southern route (Map 4.1). Accordingly, Timur's conquest of Aleppo from the Mamluks can be interpreted as securing a western terminus for this guarded trade corridor (Findlay and O'Rourke 2007, 124). However, the Crimean peninsula continued to be an outlet not only of exports of regional products but also of quantities of silk and spices that did not pass through the hands of the Mamluks of Cairo, who disputed Tamerlan's conquest of Syria and at least intermittently controlled the Eastern Mediterranean shoreline (Roux 1991, 292).[7] Thus Tamerlan may not have been entirely successful in securing the southern route and therefore possibly decided not to fully block the northern one.

Timur's Economic Policy: Forced and Costly Centralization of Resources in Flourishing Transoxiana, Control of Trade Routes

As Abazov points out, Tamerlan's capital Samarkand, with its population swelling to over 300,000, became one of the largest cities of the world at the time (2008, Map 25). Samarkand, in the middle reaches of the Zeravshan valley at the southwestern foothills of the Tienshan, was embellished at the orders of the C Asian ruler with grandiose architectural monuments. In lavish construction activity, large palaces and gardens were erected and splendid mosques and madrasas, magnificent mausoleums, and caravanserais emerged. The buildings put up under Timur and the Timurids feature among the most marvelous examples of Islamic architecture. From 1376, the great client had his capital transformed into the "Pearl of the Orient" (Soucek 2000, 123; Poujol 2008, 41). He became the patron of Iranian and C Asian art, literature, and science.

Timur also patronized trades and crafts and, as alluded to above, intervened in SR trade and helped to reintroduce and reorganize profitable regional and transcontinental trade networks. Samarkand also became the most important trade and industrial hub of Mavarannahr and thrived economically in the first half of the fifteenth century. In Timur's era, Samarkand's agricultural hinterland in Transoxiana seems to have flourished. As Clavijo reportedly put it, "This land is rich of all things: grain, fruit and various meats... bread is as cheap as it could possibly be, and there is no end to the rice available" (cited in Ashrafyan 1998, 339). Its hinterland was the city's source of supply not only of foodstuffs but also of industrial crops, especially cotton, which served as the raw material for weaving, the most important branch of urban handicrafts in Mavarannahr. The towns of the region manufactured a variety of metal articles: weapons, all kinds of implements, copper vessels, etc. They featured a wide range of production by woodworkers, leatherworkers, potters, jewelers, paper manufacturers, stone and alabaster carvers, carpet makers, bakers, cooks, confectioners, and other tradesmen (Ashrafyan 1998, 339). Tashkent (and Shash) likewise experienced an urban renaissance during the rule of Timur and his successors (Roudik 2007, 61).

However, the prosperity of the imperial center was overwhelmingly achieved by plundering, imposing heavy tributes and/or destroying hundreds of cities and towns in conquered territories. Vast quantities of resources, personal property of defeated rulers and princes, human capital, and labor, were confiscated or exacted by force and many goods and people were transferred to Transoxiana, particularly to Samarkand (Roux 1991, 304). More than a million people were enslaved (many of them Indians) and over 150,000 are estimated to have been deported with their families to Tamerlan's capital to carry out forced or slave labor (Boucheron 2012b, 25).

According to Roux, loot and confiscated goods were divided up between the imperial treasury, Emir Timur's governors, and soldiers. Enslavements and deportations from conquered big towns of the Near East and Persia had focused on tens of thousands of architects, builders, construction workers, craftsmen, engineers, businessmen, artists, and scholars (Roux 1991, 304). Similar to the Mongol model, many enslaved craftsmen, notably armorers, were organized in state workshops or manufacturers (karkhanas). These human resources were not only allocated to large-scale urban construction work in Tamerlan's homeland, they were also directed to farming exploitations and to laying out and repairing irrigation canals in Middle Eastern regions. For instance, extensive irrigation works were realized in the Mughan steppe (southern Azerbaijan) and in the Kabul valley (Ashrafyan 1998, 338).

Doubtlessly the artificially caused blossoming of trade and industry in Mavarannahr was the flipside of a very substantial brain drain, loss of labor, and of productive capacities in other regions, probably entailing decades of cultural and economic decline in peripheral lands of the empire (Abazov 2008, Map 25).[8] Thus regional economic

---

[7] This once again reminds of the bitter and in most cases unresolved clashes for control of the SR in approx. the same area—the Levant—between Romans and Parthians, Byzantines and Sassanians, Mamluks and Genghisids.

[8] This is reminiscent of some ways Tatar rule had exploited the Rus and its inhabitants, if to a lesser degree (see above).

disparities probably widened sharply in CA during Timur's reign. Disregarding the effects of the recovery of international trade, for all the splendor concentrated in Samarkand, Timur's era may have been less than a zero-sum game, for across entire CA there was probably no net value added, but at best value reallocated. In any case, most of the craftsmen and laborers that had originally been brought to Transoxiana as captives later became free tradesmen. They organized in guilds and worked in their own shops, with the help of apprentices and members of their families. Although the guilds took decisions in matters relating to production and some everyday social issues concerning their members, they possessed no political rights (Ashrafyan 1998, 340), which was nothing genuinely new in the region.

Emir Timur's state apparatus consisted of seven departments, headed by viziers (ministers) appointed by the ruler: the chancellery, military, state security, finance, court affairs, justice, and international relations. The viziers oversaw the allocation of resources and the collection of taxes, monitored the provinces and dependent states, conducted trade policy, and supervised the implementation of laws and the administration's activities. The chief cleric and the chief judges of the religious and civil courts were also members of the government. An official named arzbegi vested with authority similar to that of an ombudsman in present-day society was immediately subordinate to Tamerlane. The arzbegi was responsible for dealing with claims against officials submitted by citizens and military personnel. The state paid its numerous civil servants predominantly from taxes levied and goods confiscated (Roudik 2007, 43; Roux 1991, 303).

The authorities organized and financed public works—including the construction and maintenance of palaces, mosques, schools (madrasas), hospitals, caravanserais, irrigation canals, and last but not least, of trade routes—often quite cheaply, namely, through massive requisition of slave labor. Thus, Timur's empire, by embodying this kind of centralized exercise of (near) total political and economic power, might approach what Western scholars have sometimes called "Oriental despotism" (authoritarian and brutal type of government uninhibited by any effective constitutional or social control; see Wittfogel 1964/1977, 128–130), bearing in mind, of course, that political and economic dictatorship and extremely bloody totalitarianism are by no means alien to European history.

The Code of Timur, a major piece of medieval C Asian legislation, constituted a kind of synthesis between Mongol (nomadic) Yassa and the Islamic (sedentary) Sharia legislation. Various types of land ownership existed: The empire held the capacity of supreme proprietor of the lands. Apart from this very general title, the state and the ruler also possessed more concrete claims to so-called crown lands or imperial domains (khalisa)[9]. Some properties represented private holdings (mulk) of individuals. Muslim religious institutions possessed traditional inalienable titles to land of the waqf type. Finally, land of varying size could be bestowed as a soyurghal (land grant, in Mongol, "gift" or "enfeoffment") in exchange for service (in most cases of a military nature with a certain number of mounted warriors) to the state (Ashrafyan 1998, 335–336).

This latter practice became widespread in an empire that had been quickly conquered (in less than 30 years) and that constituted a sprawling conglomeration of states and tribal territories. Thus, soyurghals of regions or districts were bestowed on sons and grandsons of Timur, his military commanders, as well as on common soldiers who had shown particular bravery in campaigns. Under Tamerlane, soyurghals became hereditary. The owner of a soyurghal did not only have the right to receive taxes from people living or working on the land in question but also possessed independent judicial and immunity rights over respective inhabitants. This relatively strong authority of the owner of a soyurghal at least in the formal sense seems to be quite comparable to the position of a European lord of the manor or feudal lord.[10] At the same time, imperial officials supervised big landowners and their treatment of the peasants and sometimes also supplied peasants with farming tools they needed (Roux 1991, 304; Shukow et al. 1957/1963, Band 3, 661).[11]

The system of taxation in Timur's empire consisted of numerous levies, most of which were quite familiar and inherited from Mongol and Islamic fiscal traditions. There was the general land tax (kharaj or mal), levied from a part of the harvest mainly in kind, sometimes also in cash, at de-facto rates which apparently often exceeded the fixed norms of a quarter to one third. The tamgha (inherited from Mongol tradition) was the tax levied on handicrafts and urban business as well as on domestic and foreign trade. The headmen of the craft and trade guilds were responsible to the authorities for the collection of this tax from their members and the discharge of obligations. Quite similar to the situation under the Mongol Yam system, the Ulagh levy constituted a heavy burden. This concerned the obligation to provide government couriers with local relay horses and also to come up with logistical supplies for Timur's imperial mail and messenger system (Ashrafyan 1998, 337–338). It is easy to understand that just as it had been for the successors of

---

[9] This reminds of an institution going back to the Achaemenid Empire.

[10] In contrast, as described earlier, while iqta holders in many cases ended up wielding long-term power over their lands, at least formally the institution of iqta was revocable and not hereditary.

[11] Within limits, this may recall agricultural development policies of the Chinese bureaucracy.

Genghis Khan, for Tamerlane such a communication system was a key element of governance and power. Other levies included a tax on gardens, a tax on private (mulk) land, a capitation tax, and customs duties.

Probably bearing in mind their combat capabilities and value for the imperial army, Timur tended to exempt many nomads from liability to tax. On the other hand, as mentioned above, craftsmen, artisans, and farmers could be subject to mandatory project assignments and compulsory delivery obligations to the armed forces, which constituted in-kind taxation (Töpfer et al. 1985, 192). Here indeed Tamerlane seems to stick to the tradition of nomadic rulers who primarily laid the tax burden on their sedentary subjects. Individuals who had probably distinguished themselves by their valor or other feats and were designated as tarkhans also enjoyed tax exemptions. When the plunder from military campaigns was considerable though, taxation was simply suspended, sometimes even for a couple of years. For example, after the long but successful campaign against the Khanate of the Golden Horde, i.e., from 1395, no taxes were levied for 3 years (Roux 1991, 303). As to money circulation, around 1390, in Mavarannahr and Khorassan, Emir Timur began minting tangas[12] of about 6.0 g and 1/4 tangas (dirhams) weighing around 1.5 g. The latter were minted in large quantities. This is called the first stage of the Timurid monetary reform (Davidovich and Dani 1998, 408)[13].

Timur's Empire as Focus of Resuscitated Transcontinental SR Trade

If Ghiyath al-Din Ali[14] is to be believed, the trade routes, which had previously been obstructed by depredations of thieves and bandits, during Timur's rule were rendered safe and merchants took them freely. In a couple of years, security reigned extensively and crime had practically disappeared (Ashrafyan 1998, 340). Parallel to the security of the SR, Tamerlan provided for its maintenance and fitting out: military posts, bridges, signaling of fords, resting places, horse relay stations, and caravanserais. Tamerlan also assured, in a quasi-Mongol manner, the efficiency of the courier system: It only took 17 days (or an average of almost 150 km per day) for a Samarkand messenger to announce to the ruler, who happened to be in Shiraz

(or 2500 km away), the invasion of Transoxiana by Tokhtamish (Roux 1991, 289).

As mentioned above, Samarkand and some other Mavarannahr towns became major centers of international trade. Important trade arteries linking China and India with Europe and the Near East and leading through these towns were revived (Haywood 2011, 108) (see also Map 4.1). In Timur's era, large caravans (of about 800 camels loaded with merchandise) spent about 1 year on the SR traveling from Samarkand to Beijing (Burton 1998b, 37). This was clearly longer than such a trip had taken at the time of Genghis Khan or Ögöday Khan, which may have been due to the incipient political fragmentation of CA in the late fourteenth century (borders between the Empire of Timur and the Chagatay Khanate and between the latter and the Ming Empire) as well as to less political stability and less well-developed overland trade infrastructure in the latter two polities.

In any case, Clavijo was impressed in 1403: "The markets of Samarkand are amply stored with merchandise imported from distant lands. From Russia and Tartary [the Golden Horde] come leather and linens, from Cathay silk stuffs and satins that are the finest in the world. ... from India spiceries which are indeed the most valuable of the kind...." (Waugh 2002, 2). The development of external caravan trade involved not only merchants but also members of the Turko-Mongol nomadic and semi-nomadic tribal nobility and many representatives of the local landowning aristocracy, among them Muslim clergymen. Some merchants who were in difficulty or ruined were bailed out by Timur's state, who lent them money.[15] Writing to Charles VI of France, Tamerlane pointed out that merchants are the ones who make the world prosper. Apart from enrichment through confiscation, reallocation, and exploitation, the great fortunes made in Timur's empire do not seem to have been those of manufacturers or farmers, but those of merchants, businessmen, and moneylenders (Roux 1991, 303, 307).

Despite some abovementioned ambitious initiatives and some well-founded institutions and notwithstanding Tamerlane's military genius, this ruler—in contrast to Genghis Khan—did not possess a concept of rule able to hold the far-flung empire together on a sustained basis (Krieger 2003, 269).

---

[12] Note the similarity of "tanga" with "dengi" (Russian) or "tenge" (Kazakh).

[13] On the following states, see below.

[14] Ghiyath al-Din Ali was a fifteenth-century Persian physician and scientist from Isfahan.

[15] The subsidization of merchants by the Mongol authorities may be seen as a precursor to these activities.

4.1.1.2 Tamerlane's Successors: "Timurid Renaissance"

Shah Rukh and Ulugh Beg (First Half of Fifteenth Century): Political Stability and Economic Recovery, Cultural Florescence

Soon after Tamerlane's death, the empire started to shrink; it lost large territories to neighboring sedentary states and to nomads, particularly the Uzbeks in the north. What remained under Timurid control was essentially Mavarannahr, Shash, Ferghana, Khwarazm, Eastern Iran and Khorassan, and Afghanistan.[16] But the empire's successor state, the Timurid Emirates, achieved a degree of internal political and economic stability and cultural radiance unattained by their predecessor. This intellectual blossoming was called "Timurid renaissance" (Barrat et al. 2010, 54). The dominating figures in the emirates in the first half of the fifteenth century were Shah Rukh (1409–1447), the ruler, and Ulugh Beg (1411–1449), the grandson of Timur, who reigned as governor of Mavarannahr. The emirates consisted of a number of provinces ruled autonomously by governors or emirs (regional princes, commanders). While Shah Rukh resided in Herat, which became the Timurid capital (although it had been destroyed by Tamerlan in 1381), Ulugh Beg's residence was Samarkand. In a period of relative peace, both dignitaries patronized the development of trade, services, and industry; while Shah Rukh seems to have particularly supported culture and the arts, Ulugh Beg's passion was nurturing and contributing to scientific development.

Political and economic stability stimulated the rapid growth of Herat and Samarkand, as well as of towns linking the two centers, particularly Merv and Bukhara, and of other small and medium-sized trade centers on the SR. Shahrukh and his successors devoted much money and energy to promoting artists and writers, to the establishment of religious foundations, and to the building of saints' tombs, mosques, and madrasas (Timurid courtly patronage) (Hambly (ed) 1966/1979, 166). Many outstanding poets and painters, scholars, and historians lived and worked in Herat, whose appearance was improved by architectural monuments. Shah Rukh founded a library in the city on the Harirud (Tedzhen). This library was the workplace, e.g., of philologists, calligraphers, and bookbinders. Herat also became a renowned center for the production of Persian miniature paintings (Barfield 2010, 49).

After previous periods of cultural coexistence and synergy, it may have been with Shah Rukh that the remarkable

C Asian symbiosis of Perso-Islamic urbanized cultural traditions with the customs and methods of the still partly tribal and nomadic Turko-Mongols came to fruition (Soucek 2000, 126). Shah Rukh also had the city of Merv rebuilt and the irrigation system of the region (Margiana) and its embankments and dams reestablished or improved, which allowed the reanimation of local urban development. Despite this revival, the oasis town never fully regained the prosperity it had enjoyed prior to the Mongol onslaught (Kamev 2005, 79).

Monetary policy under Shah Rukh's reign was marked by an expansion of the number of mints, an increase in the money supply, and a piecemeal lowering of the weight standard. Thus the weight of the tanga coin that had been introduced by Tamerlane dropped to 4.72 g (under Timur it had been 6 g—see above) (Davidovich and Dani 1998, 408). This development, which lasted until the monetary reform of 1428/1429, could point to a phase of economic prosperity followed by inflationary tendencies.

Ulugh Beg was the most important builder of establishments of higher education in Samarkand as well as in Bukhara prior to modern times. Notably Samarkand became a center of mathematics and astronomy of world renown. The governor had a three-story observatory complete with a 55 m high sextant constructed in the Transoxianan capital in 1428/1429, which enabled him, under the guidance of Arab scholars, to prepare his famous astronomical tables, the Zij-i Sultan-i Gurkani (Astronomical Tables of the Gurkan Sultan) (Töpfer et al. 1985, 192; Habib 2003b, 464). Ulugh Beg's tables, i.e., represented the fixed stars and the orbits of seven planets; as Roudik emphasizes, the Transoxianan governor's measurements of the year's length in seconds were more precise than anyone else's before the invention of the computer. These tables featured among the salient astronomical works of the Middle Ages (Roudik 2007, 47).

Ulugh Beg moreover established an academy of sciences equipped with a large scientific library and successfully attracted some of the greatest astronomers of the time, like Ali Kushchi, Ghijas ad-Din Dzhamshid, and Qazi Zadeh Rumi, the latter called "a Plato of his time," to work at the institution in Samarkand. In this cosmopolitan intellectual climate, professors did not only teach theology but also medicine, mathematics, and (of course) astronomy.

Ulugh Beg put the exact sciences over religion and allowed women the right to education. The community could achieve brilliant scientific results that still matched or even excelled those of contemporary Europe, if it was stimulated by an inspired sponsor, like Ulugh Beg. Without such support, though, scientists had little institutional framework within which to develop and thrive (Soucek 2000, 129). The orthodox clergy supported the rebellious nobility, which brought about the downfall of Tamerlane's grandson.

---

[16] Thus important territorial losses included: the lower Syr Darya valley, Transcaucasia, Eastern Anatolia, Iraq, Western Iran, Baluchistan, Punjab, and Kashgar.

This happened against the backdrop of a rising tide of religious fervor that found its institutional base in the form of a new Sufi brotherhood, the Naqshbandia, founded in Bukhara in the fourteenth century.[17] The community demanded that piousness take precedence over erudition. And Sufis did not only start to set the intellectual tone in society. Subsequent generations of Naqshbandi khodzhas were able to claim hefty shares in the economic and political life of society, and over time they formed virtual dynasties of wealthy landowners, businessmen, political advisers, or even, on occasion, rulers (Töpfer et al. 1985, 193).

In CA, khodzhas (or khwajas) were understood to be religious people who claimed descent from the prophet or from one of the first four caliphs (Geiss 2003, 36). Khodzhas were charismatics, often Sufi mystics. In many cases they imposed themselves as leaders of Sufi orders and tended to exercise strong influence over the popular mind. This de-facto authority induced various rulers to keep the khodzhas and their orders satisfied with large grants of lands and other property (Adle et al. 2003b, 353).

According to the Timurid prince Babur (who later founded the Mughal dynasty in Northern India, see below), fifteenth-century Samarkand was a well-built town, with such handicrafts as weaving, garment making, dyeing, pottery, metal processing, and the production of high-quality paper. The most widespread use of peasants was made in metayage (sharecropping), and the typical peasant-leaseholder was a metayager who cultivated state, soyurghal, waqf, or mulk lands belonging to wealthy landowners. The cultivation of land on the base of metayage rent served many peasants as the main and, in some cases, the only source of income. Only a small part of the rural population of the Timurid Emirates constituted farmer-owners of mulk lands (Mukminova 1998, 356, 358).

In the first half of the fifteenth century, the economy probably took an upswing, and commodity-money relations (i.e., monetization) seem to have expanded and partly even spread to rural populations. After some apparent inflationary slippage, Ulugh Beg's monetary reform of 1428/1429 played a role in consolidating internal trade (Mukminova 1998, 349). As Davidovich and Dani explain, in what is seen as the second stage of Timurid monetary reform, all earlier issued copper coins of a low weight were banned and/or set for exchange into new, heavier coins, which were named "copper dinar." The main goal of the reform was to provide the market with a constant and stable copper coin for retail trading and, at the same time, to increase revenue

(seignorage) from the minting of such coinage (Davidovich and Dani 1998, 410).

The reform seems to have worked; after the completion of the exchange of old for new money, all mints, with the exception of that of Bukhara, were closed, and for a decade or two, copper money was only minted in Bukhara. Yet toward the end of Ulugh Beg's reign, the minting of coins started to become decentralized again, and a renewed trend toward lowering the weight of the reform coins apparently could not be resisted. After some time, the total amount of coins of the main denomination was far in excess of market demand, which started to boost prices anew (Mukminova 1998, 349; Davidovich and Dani 1998, 410).

Abu Said and Husain Baikara (Second Half of Fifteenth Century): Continuing Prosperity but Rising Political Instability

Relative peace and prosperity in the core of the former Timurid Empire continued under Sultan Abu Said (1451–1469). The sovereign took particular interest in improving agriculture in Mavarannahr and Khorassan, both through lower taxation of peasants and through irrigation projects (Soucek 2000, 137). Although inflation had been eliminated by the monetary reform of the late 1420s, a couple of decades later—around the beginning of Sultan Abu Said's reign—the rising price level had again become a serious problem. A new intervention therefore became necessary. This time the problem was solved by means of overstriking (third stage of Timurid monetary reform): The overstrike was a square cartouche with the inscription of the name of the mint (Samarkand, Bukhara, Karshi, Termez, Hissar, Khuttalan (Kulyab), Andijan, Shahrukhiyya, etc.) and the word "dangi"; the latter indicated that only coins with this overstrike possessed the basic face value; coins without overstrikes were not withdrawn, but served as the smallest fractions of the main denomination.[18] This reform supported a recovery of retail trading (Davidovich and Dani 1998, 410).

Under Abu Said the influence of Sufi khodzhas, sheikhs, and devishes (religious superiors or leaders) increased. In the fifteenth century, Alisher Navoy (1441–1501), a great Turkic poet and public administrator, whom some consider to be the founder of Uzbek literature, lived in Herat. Herat was also the home of Abd ar-Rakham Dzhami (1414–1492), an outstanding Persian and Tajik writer and philosopher (Shukow et al. 1957/1963, Band 3, 664). Toward and after the end of Abu Said's reign, rebellions

---

[17] Another such brotherhood was the Yasaviyya, founded in Yasy (Turkestan) in the twelfth century (see above). The Yasaviyya and later the Naqshbandia played an important role in the Islamization of C Asian nomadic tribesmen.

[18] Just like the method of withdrawing current coins and substituting some of them with specially minted new ones, the method of selective overstriking corresponded to a confiscatory reduction of the quantity of money.

and armed conflicts between rivaling factions for power became more frequent and weighed on the state's treasuries. Nomadic invasions of the Timurid Emirates occurred on repeated occasions throughout the fifteenth century, destroying towns, irrigation systems, and crops. Stored wealth was looted and thousands of people were enslaved by invaders (Roudik 2007, 48).

After some years of disturbances, Sultan Husain Baikara (1470–1506) reestablished stability and Herat, Bukhara, Samarkand, Balkh, Mashhad, and Nishapur recovered. Particularly Herat, which Husain Baikhara chose as residence, flourished. Recalling the economic and cultural prosperity of Shah Rukh's era, Herat once again became the focus of refined Timurid court culture and fashions, bearing an aura in the entire eastern Islamic world. The sultan was a patron of some of the best artists of his time, especially literary figures, architects, calligraphers, bookbinders, and painters (apex of miniature painting of the Herat school, of book arts, decorative arts, and illumination) (Hambly (ed) 1966/1979, 169; Fragner 2008, 57). Mukminova notes that the role of Tashkent as a northern outpost of the emirates had grown significantly by the end of the fifteenth century and that it produced metalware, earthenware, fabrics, and articles of leather. The development of many of these handicrafts was influenced by trade with the neighboring steppe nomads (Mukminova 1998, 358).

The large quantity of "old" moneys in circulation, issued in the 1420s, with or without overstriking, the persisting variations of the conversion rates, and the differing overstrikes marking various issues finally created enough confusion to unsettle money circulation in the emirates. In the last decade of the fifteenth century, the authorities proceeded to issue new moneys in central Mavarannahr and Ferghana (fourth stage of Timurid monetary reform): Copper coins were for the first time subjected to a definite weight standard with a very small tolerance. The regular minting in Samarkand, Bukhara, and other cities, starting in 1491–1492, of new coins with a fixed high weight, coupled with the withdrawal of coins of dissimilar weights struck earlier, cut and renewed the money supply. While again wiping out some pecuniary wealth, this intervention soon reestablished a degree of confidence (Davidovich and Dani 1998, 411).

Over the centuries, notably in relatively calmer periods like in the Timurid era, increasing tendencies of urbanization contributed to molding a new identity among the settled population of CA, whether living in towns or in rural areas. While these people still spoke Turkic or Iranian/Tajik or other languages (e.g., Mongol), many of them started to acquire an urbanized, social and Islamic identity in lieu of tribal identity. Lifestyles and customs became more alike. Such sedentary indigenous C Asians, typically city dwellers,

started to be called "Sarts,"[19] regardless of their language. Thus, tribal allegiance and division was partly replaced by the juxtaposition of the settled "Sart" population and neighboring nomadic or semi-nomadic inhabitants.

In the final decades of Timurid rule, the transfer of state (or crown) lands into hereditary soyurghals and the spread of the immunity of tarkhan holdings led to a loss of revenues of the treasury and to tendencies toward decentralization of the state.[20] Waqf lands, at least in theory, continued to be considered inviolable and hence, in comparison with other types of land ownership, maintained a more firm juridical basis. Political instability, internecine conflicts, and nomadic incursions from the Eurasian steppes gained momentum (Mukminova 1998, 355, 361; Soucek 2000, 141).

Timurid Emirates as a Turntable of SR Trade

Tamerlan's opposition to China was not continued by his successors; on the contrary, Shah Rukh and Ulugh Beg established friendly relations and close diplomatic, cultural, and economic contacts with the Middle Kingdom.[21] At the same time, mighty fleets commanded by the Chinese Muslim Admiral Zheng He reached Southeast Asia, India, the Persian Gulf, Aden, and the East African coast. Zheng He's expeditions also visited the key Iranian port of Hormuz and probably added to Chinese-C Asian trade and exchanges (Kauz 2006, 129). Timurid-Ming economic and trade relations were particularly intensive in the first half of the fifteenth century. Merchants of the Timurid Emirates bought silk fabrics, porcelain, silver, mirrors, and paper from China, despite the fact that in Samarkand paper of high quality was manufactured locally. Timurid merchants in turn sent locally made fabrics and luxuries, horses, and camels to the Ming Empire (Mukminova 1998, 360).

Trade connections to India were also strong, according to Babur: On the way from Khorassan to Hindustan, there were two trading towns: the commercial hub of Kabul and Kandahar (see Map 4.1). Up to 10,000 C Asian horses were brought to Kabul every year. From Hindustan slaves, white fabrics, sugar, dyestuffs, and medicine were delivered. It is as if Kabul were the entrepôt (overland trade outlet or portal) of Hindustan at the limits of CA. Given the high level of Indian-C Asian trade (or, for the most part trade between the Timurid Emirates and the Sultanate of Delhi) testified in contemporary documents, the largest towns of the emirates

---

[19] In Iranian languages (including Tajik), there is also a close resemblance between "Sart" and "Sogdian." The one may be derived from the other (Der Große Ploetz 1987, 30. A., 1068).

[20] Compare the trend toward feudal fragmentation in parts of Europe in the late Middle Ages.

[21] For instance, in 1421 an important Timurid diplomatic and trade mission hit the SR for Beijing.

had sarraf-khanas (houses for the exchange of foreign currency); the sarrafs (money changers) also issued cheques, whose origins go back to the time of Arab rule (the caliphate, see above). By means of a cheque issued in one town, a person could draw money in another. There also existed the practice of putting up capital for investment (mudaraba) that was legalized by an act made before the qadi. The Timurids themselves, e.g., Ulugh Beg, took part in such undertakings. He gave money to businessmen who, in turn, gave it back to him later with a share of their profit (Mukminova 1998, 360). Thus, Timur's grandson was not only a scientist at the cutting edge of astronomy, but also an active businessman.[22]

More generally, in order to encourage the development of handicrafts, domestic and foreign trade, the Timurids abolished or reduced the tamgha (sales tax or customs duty) on repeated occasions. However, the high returns from this levy did not allow them to renounce it wholly and its collection was always resumed (Mukminova 1998, 357). As the largest C Asian trading town in the fifteenth century, Samarkand played a major role in the circulation of goods between Eastern and Western Eurasia. Samarkand was not only famous for its paper (the production technology for which had been acquired from China more than half a millennium earlier and had since been improved) but also for its kermezi velvet; both products were exported internationally. Other export articles were fresh and dried fruit, with Samarkand apples enjoying particular fame (recalling the town's "golden peaches," highly appreciated in ancient times). As in earlier periods, Zandanachi fabric (a valuable cotton textile from Zand/Zandana near Bukhara) was exported as far as Novgorod (Rus, Muscovy); from this point, merchants of the Teutonic knights' order dispatched it to towns of Northwestern Europe (Mukminova 1998, 359). On the other hand, woollen stuffs from England took the opposite route to CA.

The importance that trade with the Orient had for Europe is signified by the dissatisfaction that the monopolization of pepper trade by the Timurid state in 1428 and other protectionist measures had provoked among Genoese and Venetian traders (Walter 2006, 83). The Timurid Emirates remained a key overland transit country for the spice trade, and maritime connections with spice producers were obviously yet far from satisfactory.

4.1.1.3 The Uzbek (Shaybanid) Khanate: Prosperity Weakened by Spreading Instability

Abul Khair Khan (r. 1428–1468) was a high-ranking tribal leader of a Genghisid-Jöchid line of the Khans of Sibir and originally ruled over parts of Western Siberia, his center was Tyumen. Probably in search of new lands to exploit, Abul Khair soon moved south with his tribes and occupied extensive areas in the Desht-i-Kipchak (from approx. the Mugodzhar range in the west, the Aral Sea and Lake Balkhash in the south, to the middle reaches of the Irtysh, and Tobol rivers in the north), apparently meeting little resistance. Thus the "Uzbek Khanate"[23] was established. The situation changed when he advanced further south, battled the Timurids, and in 1447 conquered towns on the middle and lower reaches of the Syr Daria (probably including Sygnak, Yasy, and Otrar) (Fragner 2008, 55; Petric 2002, 3).

Taking possession of these relatively rich towns meant taking possession of markets for trade between the nomads of the north and the settled population of the south as well as of transit trade centers on the east-west SR. The Uzbeks established winter encampments in the valleys of the Syr Daria (in proximity of these towns), at the foothills of the Karatau, and in the Priarale region (Baipakov et al. 1997, 113).

The Uzbek tribes were divided into subtribes and local clans that were governed by tribal nobles or chiefs, the begs. Between the begs and the khan, another group of steppe aristocrats emerged, the sultans (princes), who generally were descendants of Genghis Khan. According to the custom of the steppes, the khan had to allot to each sultan a yurt (in this case a kind of fief) comprising tribal terrains for summer and winter pastures. Frequent hostilities with the Timurids, tensions with other neighbors, and internal conflicts did not stabilize the polity. The two sultans Zhanibek and Kerey led a group of dissenting tribes that split away from Uzbek authority and migrated into the valleys of the Talas and Chu rivers, which at that time had been under the control of Chagatay Khanate. These tribes took the name of "Kazaks" or "Kazakhs" (fugitives, freebooters, roamers) and in 1465 formed an independent tribal confederation (Poujol 2000, 31).

The Khanate of Shaybani Khan and Successors: Replacing the Timurid State (1500–1533)

A new Uzbek offensive led by Muhammad Shaybani Khan (1451–1510, r. 1500–1510) crushed the crumbling Timurid

---

[22] This recalls the involvement of the Mongol nomadic aristocracy and even representatives of the highest echelons of power in creating and financing trading ventures.

[23] As explained earlier, the choice of the designation "Uzbek" probably goes back to the name of Khan Uzbek (1282–1342), one of the rulers of the Golden Horde (the former Mongol Ulus Jöchi).

state. Following a number of precedents going far back in history, we observe another successful north-south invasion coming from the Eurasian steppe and subjugating parts of the C Asian oasis belt.[24] In 1500, the Shaybanid Uzbeks or Shaybanids, as they were called, seized Bukhara, a year later Samarkand, and soon all of Transoxiana was in their hands. Then the Shaybanids invaded Ferghana, in 1506 they took Khwarazm, in 1507 they conquered Herat. Muhammed put an end to the Timurid dynasty and replaced it with his own, that of the Shaybanids (1500–1599). The Timurid prince Babur (1483–1530), who had ruled in Andijan (Ferghana), fled south to Afghanistan. The Shaybanids soon controlled a territory running from the southeastern shore of the Caspian Sea to the Pamir range and from the Aral Sea and the Syr Daria valley to Northern Afghanistan (Soucek 2000, 149; Poujol 2008, 43).

Once the conquered land was secured, migration of Uzbek tribal groups across the Syr Daria into Khwarazm, Mavarannahr, and beyond intensified. Mavarannahr and other territories were divided into appanages for powerful Shaybanid tribal princes (sultans): Regional governments were set up in Tashkent[25], Bukhara, Samarkand, Balkh, and many other cities (Hambly (ed) 1966/1979, 176). The old Timurid nobility was at least partly expropriated, but in many cases held on to property and managed to adapt to the new situation. The relationships of the appanage rulers with each other were unstable, and political tensions and even armed hostilities were frequent. While the Khan's authority included the customary prerogative to mint coinage, the regional rulers (sultans) all had vested claims to tax revenue gained from agriculture, trade, and business exercised on their appanages (von Gumppenberg and Steinbach 2004, 148; Fragner 2008, 65).[26]

The strong immigration of nomads to Western C Asian oases at least in the first decades of the sixteenth century raised the share of the nomadic pastoral population in Mavarannahr and adjacent areas. However, Iranian and Islamic sedentary cultural traditions soon started to influence Uzbek conquerors and migrants; through interaction with local settled populations, many of the newcomers began forming a new sedentary identity. Many Uzbeks moved to the oases, progressively abandoned their nomadic identity, and became farmers and even inhabitants of cities. Toward the end of the sixteenth century, most—but far from all—Uzbeks appear to have adjusted their general way of life to that of the Tajik (Iranian) and Turkic populations of these areas. Some Uzbeks, particularly those living in the north of the khanate, continued to be nomads.

Some of the already settled people, notably the Turkic elements, had themselves been nomads in the more distant past and had gone through a similar transformation as the majority of Uzbeks were going through. With time, many Uzbeks, like fellow sedentary and particularly town-dwelling C Asians, might have even started to feel as (non-tribal) "Sarts." In contrast to the Uzbeks though, Turkmens, Kazakhs, Kyrgyz, and Karakalpaks (a Kipchak-Turkic people of the Western Kazakh steppe, see below) continued to assert themselves as nomadic pastoralists and carried on their often symbiotic, but at times also dispute-ridden relations with oasis dwellers (Abazov 2008, Map 27; Hambly (ed) 1966/1979, 184).[27]

After his conquests, Shaybani Khan tried—largely in vain—to stabilize the political and economic situation in the Uzbeks' newly acquired extensive territories. He carried out a currency reform in 1507 and had a new silver tanga issued (the terms tanga, tangacha, and khani were all synonymous) in accordance with a new weight standard. Shaybani Khan's reforms created stable conditions for monetary transactions, if only for a brief period (Davidovich 2003, 431–434). To some degree following the example set by his Timurid predecessors, Muhammad Shaybani supported cultural activities and promoted poets, scholars, and theologists. Meanwhile, in 1504, the Timurid Babur, who counted both Genghis Khan and Tamerlane among his ancestors, established a state in Eastern Afghanistan, including Kabul, Peshawar (today in Pakistan), and Kandahar.

But a couple of years after taking power, Shaybani Khan was defeated and killed in a war against two enemies, the tribal confederation of Kazakhs led by Qasym Khan and the armed forces of the Safavids of Persia led by their new ruler Ismail Safavi (see below). Khorassan remained a chronic battleground between Uzbeks and Safavids and large parts of it, including Mashhad, Merv, and Herat, were lost to the Persian Empire (see Map 4.3). The Shaybanid-Safavid conflict also signaled the establishment of a longstanding religious antagonism between mostly Sunni CA and mostly Shiite Iran. Their common religious background (the Sunni school of Islam) as well as the common legitimacy of their rulers, who customarily traced their roots to the dynasty of

---

[24] To name some of the earlier nomadic invasions from a similar direction in about the same area: Massagetes and Sakas confronted the Achaemenid Empire and the Empire of Alexander in the sixth to the fourth century BCE, Yuezhi supplanted Greco-Bactria and established the Kushan Empire in the first century BCE, White Huns or Hephthalites evicted the Sassanian (Persian) Empire from parts of CA and set up their own confederation in the fifth century CE, Turkic conquerors extended their authority to the banks of the Oxus in 570 CE, and Karakhanids acquired Samanid territory and fixed the Amu Daria as their southern border in 999.

[25] "Tashkent" means stone settlement in Uzbek language.

[26] This reminds of initial Karakhanid treatment of their conquered former Samanid territories.

[27] In Eastern CA the piecemeal sedentarization of the Uighurs—as opposed to the Mongols—was a comparable process.

Genghis Khan, thus started to distinguish C Asian principalities and realms from some of their neighbors (Abazov 2008, Map 28). The Transoxianan economy suffered considerably as a result of the tensions and warfare, inflation accelerated, and numismatic data reflect the troubles: The silver and copper coinage issued under Muhammad Shaybani disappeared from circulation.[28] In 1511 and 1512, new copper coins with their standard weight reduced to 3.2 g began to be minted in large numbers as a replacement of Shaybani's copper coin weighing 5.2 g (Davidovich 2003, 432).

Meanwhile, unable to regain control of former Timurid territories of CA, Babur, after stabilizing his hold on Eastern Afghanistan, invaded India. In 1526 he captured Delhi and established the Mughal Empire of Hindustan (founded the dynasty of the Great Moghuls). This sweeping success was largely due to superior military technology and armament. Despite an inferiority in numbers, Babur won the Battle of Panipat in 1526 against the Sultan of Delhi due to his combination of effective use of cavalry and recourse to artillery (muskets and cannons) (Islam and Bosworth 1998, 291; Ali 1998, 300).

Under Shaybani Khan's successors, decentralizing tendencies gained momentum. At the same time, hostilities and insecurity calmed down somewhat, giving some breathing space to the economy even though economic stability was out of reach. The internal political situation of the khanate corresponded to a precarious equilibrium between increasingly strong appanage sultans. Some of the Shaybanid princes chose to pursue their own separate monetary policies. The standard weight for copper coins was further adjusted downward to 2.8 g and the coins were minted in abundance, which pushed prices higher (Davidovich 2003, 432). Ensuing attempts to stabilize the monetary situation were only temporarily successful and in the early 1530s yielded to new high inflation.

Mukminova elaborates on some aspects of the economy of the Uzbek Khanate in the first half of the sixteenth century: The Zeravshan valley was the main farming region of Mavarannahr. Corn, fruit, and vegetables were also grown in the fields of Ferghana, the Tashkent oasis, and the region of the Surkhandaria (a tributary of the Amu Daria, north of Termez). Khuttalan (Kulyab) and Hissar (the latter two: mountainous regions in the southwest of the Tienshan) were famed for their rich harvests of corn and melons. Melons from Bukhara and Khwarazm were also particularly appreciated. Across the oases of the khanate, wheat, barley, and millet were grown and vast areas were cultivated with lucerne. Special varieties of grapes, apples, and plums, exported to other regions (in continuation of Timurid traditions), were prized. The manufacture of various types of cotton cloth entailed the further spread of the cotton plant. Sheep breeding was, of course, strongly developed. There were many varieties of sheep; Hissar meat enjoyed particular renown. The Bukhara and Karshi regions specialized in the export of Karakul pelts. Horse breeding was highly developed across the khanate, which reflected the great number of horses needed for war. Camel breeding was also widespread, with some concentration in the Karshi region (Mukminova 1998, 353).

The Khanate of Bukhara of Ubaydullah Khan et al. (1533 to Mid-sixteenth Century)

Ubaydullah Khan (r. 1533–1539) was a strongly religiously oriented ruler. He scrupulously applied the tenets of Sharia to all matters of spirituality, the state, the army, and society. An amateur scholar and a famed warrior, Ubaydullah finally consolidated Uzbek rule in Transoxiana (Hambly (ed) 1966/1979, 176). Bukhara became the capital of the Shaybanid state, which came to be called "Khanate of Bukhara." His capital became the focus of a program of religious and secular construction. As could be expected, Ubaydullah's rule was fertile ground for the clergy, particularly Naqshbandi orders, to go on proselytizing Sufism. The khodzhas increased their wealth by becoming involved in commerce, manufacturing, and farming and sent their agents as far as Moscow on trade missions. Documents reveal the tax-exempt status of several of their properties (Soucek 2000, 155–156).

The clergy also strengthened its influence on education and culture. It seems to have been the time when activities in the worldly sciences in Bukhara were all but brought to a standstill. Theology, scholasticism, and studies of the Arab language and of Islamic law started to predominate. In contrast to earlier times, C Asian scholars in the sixteenth and seventeenth centuries hardly attained any new results of research in exact sciences, with the partial exception of medicine. Instead of astronomy, scholars increasingly occupied themselves with astrology (Roudik 2007, 54; Shukow et al. 1958/1964, Band 4, 659). Finally, as one could not expect otherwise, Naqshbandi sheikhs wielded power over rulers as their spiritual guides and continued to meddle in politics.

Notwithstanding mounting religious rigidity in the Shaybanid realm, some new ideas and creativity crossed the Amu Daria in the first half of sixteenth century: There was an influx to the Khanate of Bukhara of luminaries and highly qualified people fleeing Safavid persecution. Ubaydullah remained loyal to Timurid and Shaybanid traditions and promoted culture and the arts. The heyday of

---

[28] Possibly due to quickly rising prices, the nominal value of the circulating coins declined substantially (in relative terms) and thus may have fallen below the market value of the metal the coins consisted of, thereby making it profitable to melt the coins and sell the metal.

Timurid calligraphy, decorative arts, and architecture continued under Shaybanid auspices. Handwritten books were created in Bukhara with great mastery. The Bukhara school of miniatures may have reached its apex in the sixteenth century. Popular masters produced excellent works in wood carving, stone masonry, and in the decoration of buildings with colorful majolica. In the realm of applied arts, many Uzbeks and Tajiks specialized in wood and bone carving activities as well as in the jewelry trade.

Looking at the evolution of legal and economic structures: From the legal point of view, the khan was the head of state and owned the state or treasury lands (amlaka). Private property (mulk) was an important part of land relationships, yet was clearly defined only among sedentary agriculturalists. Nomadic pastoralist inhabitants of the Shaybanid polity (whether Kazakhs, Turkmens, Kyrgyz, or Uzbeks) generally identified their lands as communal. Communal lands were regulated by special legal norms in the Khanate of Bukhara (Roudik 2007, 55). In the sixteenth and seventeenth centuries, the older institution of iqta increasingly came to be used with the meaning of soyurghal (which points to a convergence of meanings in the direction of hereditary possession of land in exchange for service to the state) (Mukminova 1998, 354).

Linked to the intensity of exploitation, the structure of agricultural property in the Shaybanid oasis of Bukhara varied: Nearer to the center of town intensively irrigated land was parceled out in relatively small-sized properties, most of them in private (mulk) ownership. In the suburb areas to the east and the south of Bukhara, which some arms of the Zeravshan flowed through, there were extensive garden zones (cultivation of fruit trees, wine, and mulberry trees in mostly enclosed pieces of land of relatively high value). In these areas, there were only few owners of large estates. In contrast, in the western part of the oasis, directly bordering on the Kyzyl Kum, unparceled jointly cultivated land covered most of the area. Here one could also find unirrigated fields, larger state (amlaka) lands, and tracts of big landowners. Such properties in the hinterland might also comprise entire villages (Schwarz 2000, 52–56).

Usually smaller parcels prevailed in areas of intensive irrigation, while larger properties tended to be situated near the ends of canal networks (which were often fan or comb shaped). In the Bukhara oasis, the largest parts of canal networks were jointly operated. There were three systems of irrigation: the state or trunk canals (the main provider of irrigation was the state), middle-sized or communal canals, and small or private canals. A special tax was levied for the maintenance of the trunk canals (Schwarz 2000, 57; Roudik 2007, 55).

Under Ubaydullah Khan, monetary development stabilized. Following a temporary increase of the number of mints during and after Shaybani Khan's rule, policies were tightened. Over an extended period of time that went far beyond Ubaydullah's rule, the standard weight for the tanga was subjected to only marginal downward revisions (over a couple of decades starting in the early 1530s from 4.7 g to 4.55 g), and a high level of purity of the coin was upheld (Davidovich 2003, 434). Notwithstanding relative monetary stability, during the four decades starting about 1540, disputes and warfare between the Shaybanid sultans became more and more commonplace; regional potentates strived to turn their appanages into independent principalities.

From Khwarazm to the Khanate of Khiva

In 1511, the Yadigarids, another group of nomadic Shaybanid Uzbeks from the Desht-i-Kipchak, conquered the large oasis of Khorezm/Khwarazm and installed themselves as Khans of Urgench. Doing this, they also had to fight off Safavid attempts to subjugate the area. Control of large landed estates, along with the farmers living on them and partly also with the nomadic population of the vicinity, was concentrated in the hands of the ruling stratum of Uzbek clans and nobles. The latter did not entirely succeed in bringing the nomads of the vicinity—mostly Turkmens in the south—under their sway. The Uzbek clans' lands were cultivated not only by local peasants but also by Persian slaves, many of whom had been sold by nomadic Khorassanian Turkmens in Transoxianan markets, and by Russian slaves that had been captured by neighboring nomadic Kazakhs and Noghays. In the course of time, the slaves could become azad kerde (freed), once they had paid the master's price put on their freedom and so worked their way out of captivity (Annanepesov 2003a, 65).

In this period, urban life and handicrafts do not seem to have made much progress in Khwarazm. Resources obtained from military spoils in Khorassan, from incursions on Bukharan territory, and of course from agricultural exploitation sustained the Uzbek aristocracy of Khwarazm.[29] Mounting insecurity in the mid-sixteenth century, favored by the outbreak of military instability in the neighboring Khanate of Bukhara (see above), weighed on trade that was practiced by Khorezm or that passed through it, linking the SR network with the Pontic steppes and Russia (Soucek 2000, 181).

Instability in Khwarazm was topped by an incisive ecological change. As had happened centuries before, the lower Amu Daria modified its course; the flow of water that had gone via the Darialyk (the riverbed connecting today's Amu Daria with Lake Sarykamysh) and the Uzboy dried up in the middle of the sixteenth century, and the great C Asian river

---

[29] In this sense, robbery and slavery may have even taken precedence over earning income.

swerved its course back to the Aral Sea. As a consequence, the original Urgench, by then given the epithet Kunia ("old") and situated on the banks of the Darialyk, was soon deprived of water and after a few decades was a ruined site. The city's destruction had been started by Timur, but the spot was not abandoned until 1576, when New Urgench and Khiva (originally a fortress) had become the foremost urban agglomeration of Khorezm. Both latter towns were situated up the Amu Daria and were therefore no longer at the mercy of the river's ecological whims; given that the Khan had chosen Khiva as his new residence, the new Uzbek polity came to be called Khanate of Khiva (Barrat et al. 2010, 60; Soucek 2000, 181).

Sixteenth Century: Incipient Impact of Seaborne Competition on SR Trade

In the sixteenth century, SR trade within and through CA remained dynamic most of the time. It included transcontinental trade (from one end of Eurasia to the other), which often constituted transit trade (conveyance of goods across the respective region, in this case CA, without any processing, but possibly with re-selling). If not transcontinental, SR trade could be interregional or regional (depending on whether it was carried out between more than one or two regions or states or within a region or state). Whereas the above mentioned types of trade in most cases tended to run in an east-west direction, trans-ecological trade between nomadic and sedentary cultures and states often ran in a north-south direction (typically between the winter encampments of the nomads in the Eurasian grasslands and the markets of the C Asian oasis belt).

As Mukminova and Mukhtarov point out, much trade was done with the inhabitants of the Desht-i-Kipchak, who supplied local markets with livestock and livestock products, camels, and various distinctive craft items, such as sheepskin caftans dyed in various colors so that they resembled satin. The Karakalpaks (a Kipchak-Turkic people that originally nomadized in the area of the Turgay valley and then, possibly under pressure from the expanding Kazakh tribes, moved to the lower Syr Daria region in the sixteenth century) acted as intermediaries in the trade between the Uzbeks and the Kazakhs and brought livestock and furs, dyes, and wax to Bukhara. There was also substantial trade with the Turkmens who found a ready market in Bukhara for their woollen clothing, saddle bags, and horse cloth; moreover there was great demand for Turkmen carpets, which often adorned the floors of affluent households, and for special breeds of Turkmen horses (see below). In turn, these nomads and semi-nomads mainly purchased cotton fabrics from the Bukharan markets. Mavarannahr undoubtedly remained a producer and exporter of cotton fabrics and other cotton products; to a lesser degree, silk and writing paper were also exported (Mukminova and Mukhtarov 2003, 44).

In the sixteenth century, transcontinental overland trade, whose principal lines passed through Transoxiana and Xinjiang, acquired a European rival in the long-distance maritime route linking Europe, India, and China via the rounding of Africa and the Strait of Malacca (Vasco da Gama 1497–1499: Cape of Good Hope, Calicut/Southern India; D'Andrade 1516–1518: Canton or Guangzhou/Southern China). Uzbek rule in Mavarannahr and Khwarazm coincided with the beginning of the decline of the Eurasian caravan trade due to rising competition from the sea routes, but, as Soucek aptly notes, the decline happened unevenly, gradually, and later and was a protracted process (2000, 150). SR trade, particularly transit trade, generated the lion's share of the C Asian oasis towns' wealth (exceeding revenues from local farming or industrial activity) and in some cases may have even constituted their prime raison d'être. For the rulers of the khanates and polities whose territories harbored the overland silk routes, the eventual decrease of caravan trade through their lands implied the dwindling of (one of) their principal regular revenue sources, the customs duties and sales levies (often called tamgha) (Hambly (ed) 1966/1979, 184).

According to Hambly, erosion of wealth entailed piecemeal or sudden loss of power, as the khans were no longer capable of acquiring sufficient numbers of firearms to defend their states in a new world where guns and artillery were swiftly gaining importance. With less trade on "their" silk routes, and gradual loss of the region's previous mercantile centrality, C Asian rulers may have even lost interest in keeping these old routes open and upholding their security (Hambly (ed) 1966/1979, 184). These points to the non-excludability of a vicious circle, with less trade and revenue engendering less spending on security and transport infrastructure, which in turn triggered a further contraction of trade. This unfortunate development for the region may have contributed to the political instability and turmoil that plagued parts of CA from the seventeenth century (see below).

4.1.1.4 The Turkmens in the Fifteenth to Sixteenth Centuries: Living Under a Creative but Turbulent and Costly Anarchy

In the fifteenth and sixteenth centuries, the Turkmens occupied a large area that extended slightly northwest from where Turkmenistan lies today: Their habitat was bounded by the eastern coast of the Caspian Sea and included the Mangyshlak peninsula as well as the Ustyurt Plateau; it stretched east to the Aral Sea, Khwarazm, and the Amu Daria and south to the Balkhan and Kopet Dagh mountains. The Ustyurt Plateau was populated by a mosaic of mostly Turkmen but later also Kazakh nomadic tribes and served as a corridor of movement between the Desht-i-Kipchak and the Uzboy area. The plateau was used by the Turkmens in summer and the Kazakhs in winter.

The Turkmens consisted of a number of tribes, the most prominent of which were (from west to east) the Yomut (inhabiting the west of the above territory, including the Caspian littoral), the Teke (in the center of the habitat), and the Ersary (in the east, bordering on the Merv and Tedzhen oases). Most Turkmens were nomads or semi-nomads and lived of extensive animal husbandry, slave trading, craftsmanship, crop cultivation, and plunder. Turkmen auls or nomadic villages typically lay on the fringes of the sand desert Kara Kum. These fringes included the foothills of the Kopet Dagh and outlying areas of Khorezm and Margiana. Given its hostile nature, largely consisting of salt lakes and infertile sands, the Kara Kum was never permanently occupied. However, the Turkmens had developed practices of radial-circular migration, well adapted to the terrain (Annanepesov 2003b, 128–129; Khazanov 1983/1994, 52). Some of the Turkmen tribes repeatedly tried to break out of their habitat and to penetrate the fertile oases, where many Uzbeks had successfully adjusted to settled life as agriculturalists or urban dwellers and traders. Some Turkmens eventually settled in the foothills of the Kopet Dagh (Linska et al. 2003, 70; Kamev 2005, 82).

During most of the sixteenth century, the Turkmen tribes found themselves either under the temporary domination of the Khans of Urgench (Khiva) or of Bukhara, while in the south and west they were intermittently under the sway of the Persian Safavides (Kamev 2005, 82). Since these three sedentary states were often at war with each other, the Turkmen territory, particularly the disputed region of Khorassan (south of the Amu Daria), was not infrequently used as a battleground.

Moreover, internal political and military developments in Turkmenia were even more turbulent than the (above described) instability in Shaybanid territories because the Turkmen tribes (who were also superficially converted Muslims) never united to form a khanate or a centralized state of their own. Turkmens followed tribal customary law (Adat), but possessed no aristocracy nor a fixed order of administration. As Geiss explains, their acephalous (leaderless, without head) political community was strongly decentralized and lacked both rulers and staff of authority. Feuds and strife were widespread, since every tribesman would pursue his claims and not hesitate to enforce them on his own (Geiss 2003, 7). Thus the Turkmens often fought among themselves. A chief's prerogatives were strengthened only when the danger of war appeared or public works (construction of dams, canals, fortresses, etc.) became necessary (Annanepesov 2003b, 137).

Although the Turkmens typically supported the Uzbek khans of Khiva in their struggles with Bukhara, they often refused to pay them regular tribute. The opposition to this was especially strong from the Khorassan and Balkhan Turkmens (probably Teke and Yomut tribes). According to Annanepesov and Bababekov, in the first half of sixteenth century, there was a clash with the Balkhan Turkmens, who killed 40 of the khan's tax collectors; finally, it was agreed that the Turkmens should give 1000 rams for each tax collector killed. Later, the khans of Urgench exacted 40,000 rams annually and called the regularized levy a barat (authorized privilege); another 4000 rams were levied for the khan's qazan (cauldron, i.e., the ruler's kitchen). Taxes in the form of cattle and sheep were also exacted from other Turkmen clans and populations (Annanepesov and Bababekov 2003, 65). At least temporarily aligning with the Shaybanid rulers and raiding Persian territories to the south had religious merit (since Turkmens were of a heretical Shiite denomination) and produced material rewards in the form captives that could be marketed on the slave exchanges of Khiva and Bukhara (Soucek 2000, 182).

Turkmens boasted a multiskilled economic existence: As Annanepesov points out, in the steppe zone, notably the Ustyurt area, they combined livestock herding with crop cultivation, while in the oases they practiced crop cultivation together with livestock herding and the making of homecrafts and handicrafts. Along the Caspian Sea coast, the Turkmens fished and extracted oil, ozocerite (fossil paraffin), salt, and other resources. Thus, the same person could be both a farmer and a herder and was capable of changing from a settled way of life to a semi-nomadic or nomadic one and back again. Through centuries of selection, the Turkmens bred the famous Akhal-Teke horses, the Arwanas camels (C Asian dromedaries), and the big white Saracen sheep (Annanepesov 2003b, 129).

Annanepesov goes on to explain that cultivation was usually based on artificial irrigation. The Turkmens built hydraulic structures and water-lifting equipment (dams, waterwheels, and dykes) and dug canals and irrigation ditches. From the sixteenth to the nineteenth centuries, the main crops grown were grain, market-garden crops, oil-yielding plants, gourds, fruit, and some industrial crops (cotton and sesame). Cultivation and harvesting were carried out with simple tools made in domestic workshops. The Turkmens were essentially subsistence farmers, but they also enjoyed trading and would barter goods at many of CA's bazaars (Annanepesov 2003b, 129–130).

Turkmen-applied art and craftsmanship was outstanding, as highlighted by Perouse: Women-weaved carpets of artistic value and sophistication, notably those with "knotted points" (« à points noués »). These carpets were produced from sheep wool and served as yurts' principal pieces of furnishing and decoration. While the traditional patterns differed from tribe to tribe, the preferred colors were red and brown, but also yellow and blue. Specific geometric motifs (diamond- or cross-shaped decorations) and varying density of points were typical. As opposed to Persian carpets, Turkmen ones used little color play and few floral embellishments. Turkmen carpets were soon marketed in Bukhara, from where they received their name. Jewelry was another highly developed Turkmen handicraft. Jewelers of Mangyshlak made beautiful silver ornaments for women. Turkmen adornments mostly corresponded to precise geometric forms of great sobriety. They were made of silver, adorned by various precious stones, e.g., jasper and turquoise. Turkmen jewels could be headdresses, bracelets, necklaces, or earrings (Peyrouse 2007, 36–37).

4.1.1.5 The Chagatay Khanate in the Fifteenth to Sixteenth Centuries: Gradual Consolidation of an East-West Trade Turntable

Largely as a result of internal struggles, in the early fifteenth century the Chagatay Khanate split into distinct smaller state-like entities: into Moghulistan (north of the Tienshan), Altishahr (derived from "altae shaehaer" or "six cities," as the sources began to refer to Kashgar and most of the Tarim Basin), and the Turfan area. Altishahr (comprising the six towns of Kashgar, Yarkand, Khotan, Aqsu, Uch Turfan, and Korla) is often equated with Kashgaria (Millward 2007, 70).

In the course of the fifteenth century, almost all of the nomadic migrants from Moghulistan (particularly from Dzungaria) to the oases of the Tarim Basin adopted a sedentary way of life. And by the end of that century, most inhabitants of Xinjiang's oasis belt had converted to Islam. Turfan (the easternmost town in Chagatayid possession) had also turned from a largely Buddhist to an Islamic settlement, while continuing to harbor a strong Han-Chinese minority (Kauz 2006, 127). Buddhist stupas and temples were either destroyed, damaged, or left to crumble. Farther east, the oasis of Hami had the Ming emperor as suzerain and functioned as a Chinese military outpost (weisuo) on the SR (Soucek 2000, 132; Millward 2007, 74) (see also Map 4.1).

The Uighurs spread from the Turfan and Kucha area (that had been part of the former Kingdom of Qocho from the ninth to the thirteenth century) to other parts of the Tarim Basin and worked as settled farmers, skilled tradesmen, craftsmen, and clerical staff. Land in the khanate could roughly be divided into three types: state-owned land, mulk land (private land), and waqf land (owned by mosques, cemeteries, and other charitable institutions). In the Yarkand area, for example, the proportion of official land amounted to between a tenth and a fifth of the total arable land. This state land was cultivated by tenant farmers who worked under a system of crop division, paying half of their harvest to the khan or the state. This in-kind income was important for the khan's finances. Proceeds from privately owned land, which comprised more than three quarters of all tilled areas,

were divided up between farmers and land owners (Ma 2003, 187). Animal husbandry was also a major occupation in the khanate, which until the early sixteenth century included Semirechie or Zhetysu (approximately to the shores of Lake Balkhash) and southern Dzungaria (see also Map 4.1). Most of Zhetysu and large parts of Dzungaria, as well as all the river valley regions along the southern foothills of the Tienshan, provided good natural pasture.[30]

A familiar factor had contributed to the advance of Islam in East Turkestan: Just as they had done west of the Tienshan, the Sufis, or Islamic mystics undertook much to spread the religion among the settled and nomadic populations of Xinjiang. Some khodzhas (or khwajas), particularly Naqshbandi dervishes, migrated from Bukhara to Kashgar and, as they had done back in Transoxiana, also vied for increasing shares of worldly power in Kashgaria. In the oases of the Tarim Basin, among the khodzhas' major rivals was the Dughlat clan of rich landowners. Notwithstanding the regional split and distributional disputes, a relatively peaceful social environment seems to have emerged, the economy began to recover from instability in preceding times, and the population increased (Soucek 2000, 160; Ma 2003, 186).

Another reason why the regional economy did not fare badly was the revival of long-distance trade, notably with China (Millward and Perdue 2004, 47). As mentioned above, after Timur's death, the Timurids soon reanimated and strengthened trade relations with the Ming dynasty; connecting trade routes, of course, passed through East Turkestan. Moreover, the Islamized Turko-Mongol rulers of Turfan, geographically close to the border of the Ming Empire, were eager to trade their horses and camels for silk, metals, and other manufactures from China and dispatched numerous trade embassies to Nanjing and Beijing. Turfan sent no fewer than 54 such missions between 1407 and 1502. The Ming Yongle emperor (r. 1403–1424) sent a gift of silk in 1406 to Turfan's Eastern Chagatayid ruler, who reciprocated the following year; in 1408 the Ming court received a Turfani embassy and so forth (Findlay and O'Rourke 2007, 126; Millward 2007, 72).

Given its favorable location, Turfan had become a hub of trade with the Middle Kingdom: According to Millward, the cities of Altishahr as well as Samarkand and Herat (Timurid Emirates) sent envoys to and traded with the Ming via Turfan (2007, 72). By the fifteenth century, the salient components of Chinese-C Asian trade continued to be essentially the same as in the early stages of the SR: China delivered silk (which the C Asians could profitably sell in

---

[30] Zhetysu had reverted to a typical nomadic pastoral territory. In the aftermath of the Mongol invasion, former towns and farming oases had utterly fallen into ruins (Shukow et al. 1957/1963, Band 3, 657).

many markets along the trade routes) and received horses (which the Chinese military was in great need of for security reasons). From the 1430s, however, the powerful nomadic confederation of the Oirats, centered in Mongolia, started to put pressure on the trade routes from Xinjiang to Gansu, in the 1440s intermittently occupied Hami and thus took control or blocked a key part of the SR. But the Oirat Empire collapsed in the 1450s and the interference evaporated even more quickly than it had appeared (see below). In the following decades, though, Hami became the object of conflict between the Ming and the Eastern Chagatayids. Turfan and Beijing faced off over Hami, which was repeatedly conquered and pillaged. While this punctuated Sino-C Asian trade, embassies and missions continued (Millward 2007, 72–74). Both sides obviously needed each other's goods.

Trade was facilitated after 1514, when the Chagatayid ruler of Turfan and Moghulistan, Said Khan (r. 1514–1533), put a temporary end to political squabbling in Xinjiang and extended his sway to Kashgaria. Tarikh-I Rashidi characterized this rare episode of stability in the sixteenth century in the following way: "From this peace and reconciliation…. … resulted such security and prosperity for the people that anyone might travel alone between Kamul [Hami] or Khitay [China] and the country of Ferghana without provision for the journey and without fear of molestation" (Millward 2007, 74). After some hesitation on the Chinese side, permission was granted for larger and more frequent trade missions from CA and beyond; for instance, Ming annals list 150 "princes" from Samarkand, Turfan, Mecca, and elsewhere visiting the capital of the Middle Kingdom in 1536. In Millward's assessment, long-distance trade between CA and the Ming Empire had again become routine, if not exactly trouble-free (2007, 75).

4.1.1.6   The Disintegration of the Khanate of the Golden Horde and the Rise of Muscovy: From East-West to North-South Trade

From Limited Revival of SR Trade to Demise of the Golden Horde (Mid-fourteenth to Mid-fifteenth Centuries)

The disruption caused by the Black Death weakened the Tatar authorities' control over their East European vassals. As referred to above, in the second half of the fourteenth century Lithuania had brought large parts of the former Rus, including the old capital Kiev, under its rule. The Khanate of the Golden Horde, which until then had probably been the most stable of the former Mongol uluses, was dealt a blow by the defeat at the battle of Kulikovo pole in 1380 against Russian forces and a much heavier blow by the war with Tamerlan (in the late 1380s and the first half of the 1390s).

Still during most of the second half of the fourteenth century, some regional and even international trade continued or reappeared on the steppe route, notwithstanding the collapse of the Yuan dynasty and difficulties in the Chagatay Khanate. Crimea, at the end of the steppe route, continued to export not only regional products, e.g., wool, hemp, leather, flax, linen, caviar of the Caspian[31], wheat from the coastal areas of the Black Sea, and from the Volga-Kama Basin (the granary of the khanate), furs and slaves, but also silk, spices, and other exotic luxury goods (Roux 1991, 292; Karpov 2009). Tana (Azov), Kerch (the former Bosporus), Kaffa, and Soldaya (Sudak) remained or were reestablished as Genoese ports. The volume of overall deliveries from these ports was, however, more modest than in the past (Engel (ed) 1979/1995, 49).

Transcontinental silk and spice trade via the steppe route is likely to have continued even after Tamerlane had conquered Khwarazm in 1379 because the C Asian ruler does not seem to have been able to subjugate the Mamluk Sultanate or gain permanent access for "his" southern trade route (via Baghdad) to the Mediterranean coast. Thus, the steppe route may have continued to function as a substitute for the intermittently blocked southern branch of the SR.

As mentioned above, during the centuries of Mongol domination, the Russians and other Eastern Slavs had the opportunity to familiarize themselves with the tactics, equipment, and strategy of Tatar warfare. In what was the first major Russian victory over the Mongols, the Muscovite prince Dmitry Donskoy in 1380 defeated Emir Mamai's troops at Kulikovo pole (south of Tula). However, this victory did not quickly have a decisive effect, given that 2 years later the new Khan Tokhtamish smashed the Russian forces and in a campaign in 1383 put Moscow to the torch and sacked other Russian towns. The "Tatar yoke" went on and Dmitry and other Russian princes were forced to resume paying tribute to and accepting the overlordship of the rulers on the lower Volga (Chaliand 1995, 176).

But the Golden Horde did not have much time to recover from the shock. In his military campaigns against the former Ulus Jöchi, Timur first captured Urgench and Khorezm and then in the late 1380s and the first half of the 1390s ravaged the key Tatar power centers and trade settlements (New Saray, Tana, Kaffa). The Tatar state finally fell apart in the first half of the fifteenth century. In its place there emerged, i.e., the Khanate of Crimea (from 1438, comprising the Crimean peninsula and the adjacent Pontic grasslands including the lower reaches of the Don and Dnepr and the plains of the Kuban), the Khanate of Kazan (from 1445, in the Volga-Kama Basin, occupying and exceeding the territory of former Volga Bulgaria), the Khanate of Astrakhan

---

[31] Sales are attested in 1392 and 1399 (Roux 1991, 292).

(from 1466, comprising the lower course of the Volga and the Caspian Lowlands between Volga and Yaik/Ural rivers), as well as the Khanate of Sibir (from the first half of the fifteenth century, encompassing a core region between the Tobol and middle Irtysh, and beyond this, large parts of Western Siberia).

In the two most important khanates to emerge from the decaying Golden Horde, Crimea and Kazan, major decisions were made at the khan's council (divan), or if necessary, at a larger gathering (kurultay or kuriltay), which included nobles, clergy, and the "best" people (highly esteemed notables). The ruling strata of Tatar society, mostly former nomads, preferred to settle down in towns. Both khanates, in which for ecological or other reasons, nomadic pastoralists had become a minority, inherited the Golden Horde's regional administrative apparatus and maintained it to control and collect taxes from the farming communities on their territories (Khodarkovsky 2002, 11–12; Dmitriev 2009, 24).

At the time of the disintegration of the Golden Horde, transcontinental trade on the steppe route seems to have dwindled and to have been largely replaced by regional or interregional trade, which remained profitable for Italian trading towns, notably Genoa. For example, the following trading posts and entrepôts on the Crimean shore became or remained Genoese in the fourteenth and fifteenth centuries: Balaclava (Cembalo, from 1365 to 1434 Genoese), Yalta (1365–1434), Sudak (the former Sogdaya or Soldaya, 1358–1475)[32], and, of course, Kaffa (1266–1475) (Westermann (ed) 1997, Map: Anfänge des Osmanischen Reiches und Balkanraum um 1335, p. 70). Among the principal attractions of the Pontic region were its own products: grain (particularly wheat and millet), cattle and horse hides from the steppe nomads, fish (particularly sturgeon) from the Sea of Azov and the Caspian Sea, dried fruits, and slaves.[33] The slave dealing at Kaffa probably peaked around 1410–1420. The plains of Southern Ukraine may have even served as a lifeline—an irregular and vulnerable one admittedly—for parts of Northern Italy: In 1384 and 1406, for instance, Kaffa alone furnished Genoa with 36% of its known purchases of grain (Jackson 2005, 309).

The development of the Dnepr as a direct trading link between the Italian Black Sea ports and Lithuania, which had become the Khanate of Crimea's immediate neighbor to the north, contributed to the reorientation of trade from the east-west steppe route to north-south riverine and sea routes (Gilomen 2014, 108). Poland and Lithuania, which had

pushed back the Mongol frontier and had also fought against Muscovy, were keen to benefit from their newly acquired lands in Eastern Europe. This closer trade integration of Crimea and the Pontic zone with Europe also served to maintain the florescence of Kaffa and other ports—all the way to their Ottoman conquest in the late fifteenth century (Jackson 2005, 309). For once, intra-European trade gained the upper hand at the outer bounds of the Eurasian steppe. Further to the east, the Volga continued to function as a north-south trade axis along which the Russian principalities could ship their exports, including furs and leather—under Tatar oversight—to Persia (Nolte 2005, 39).

The Rise of Muscovy: Moving Beyond the Mongol Legacy (Late Fourteenth to Mid-sixteenth Centuries)

As Nolte points out, in the first half of the fifteenth century, the Russian principalities were able to compensate demographic losses as well as losses of good-quality land in areas adjacent to the Mongol-dominated steppe by more intensive cultivation of arable tracts in the mixed-woodland areas and by the exploitation of vast domains of coniferous forests (1991, 33).

It appears difficult to describe Moscow's seizure of its topographical and geopolitical advantages more eloquently than Ledonne does it: "The patient and determined efforts of the Muscovite grand princes to build a solid and homogeneous core around a hydrographic network of rivers forming so many spokes in a wheel, with Moscow as the hub[34], slowly created a seemingly irreversible momentum" (2008, 18). Ivan III "the Great" of Moscow (1462–1505) consolidated or "gathered" Russian lands, which had until then been divided between other principalities and republics, under Muscovite sovereignty (Yaroslavl, Perm, Novgorod, Tver, Viatka). The conquest and annexation of the important trading republic of Novgorod in 1478 most notably enhanced Muscovy's power and wealth, as Novgorod controlled vast tracts of land in Northeastern Europe from which it exacted furs and forest products that it sold to the Hanseatic League and other Western traders. In 1480 Grand Prince Ivan III terminated the vassal and tributary relationships that had still existed with two successors of the Golden Horde, the Khanates of Kazan and Astrakhan (Stanziani 2012, 96; Findlay and O'Rourke 2007, 126).

According to Finlay and O'Rourke, these considerable achievements were largely the result of Ivan's fiscal and military restructuring of the Muscovite state (2007, 127). A new statute book, the Sudebnik of 1497, limited the peasants' freedom of movement and took first steps to

---

[32] Sudak had already been a Genoese port from 1266 to 1322.

[33] For instance, a large number of adolescent Kipchak/Polovtsy males were reportedly shipped through the straits to Egypt, to be bought by the Sultan and his emirs, reared as Muslims, and trained as Mamluk servicemen (Jackson 2005, 308).

[34] It is not without reason that Moscow has been called the "capital of five seas": Moscow is not far away from rivers which drain into the Baltic, White, Black, Azov, and Caspian Seas.

introduce serfdom. A new "service nobility" was created and received estates and control over serfs in return for loyalty and service to the state. Apart from the discharge of duties in the grand prince's civil administration, this service first and foremost pertained to the provision of a mobile and disciplined cavalry force capable of standing up both to European powers' armies and to Tatar mounted warriors of the steppe. As a result, the Muscovite state became more centralized and the power of the traditional high aristocracy, the Boyars, was circumscribed (Donnert et al. 1981, 363).

Vassily III (1505–1533) managed to hold on to his father's gains and enlarged them by conquering another prosperous trading republic, Pskov (1510), by pushing forward the penetration of Lithuania on Russia's western border through the seizure of Smolensk (1514) and by annexing the principality of Riazan (1521) on the southeastern steppe frontier (Findlay and O'Rourke 2007, 127; Stanziani 2012, 98).

In contrast to Novgorod and Pskov (before they were conquered), urban oligarchies equipped with special rights or class privileges comparable to those of Western municipalities did not emerge in towns ruled by Moscow. In Muscovy, there was no salient distinction between the legal status of town dwellers and rural inhabitants. In this respect, similarities rather show up between conditions in Russia and CA. Distinct groups of, e.g., long-distance traders, called "gosti," were certainly perceptible in Russian towns. The same goes for craftsmen and artisans who, like the merchants, tended to live in distinct quarters (posady) outside the urban centers and who had certain economic and organizational self-management rights. But they were subjects of the grand prince like everybody else and possessed no autonomy before criminal law.[35] Most Russian cities did not have walls—only the Kremlins (citadels) were fortified—which again recall descriptions of C Asian towns (Karger (ed) 1978, 72). However, the Christian Orthodox Church (which possessed substantial property, a hierarchy reaching across the country, its own jurisdiction, and whose rights had been confirmed by the Tatar authorities), the Boyars, and big businessmen participated (de facto) in the exercise of power (Nolte 1991, 35, 38, 48).

With the aim of bolstering its army, Muscovy in the course of the sixteenth century purchased large quantities of horses from the Eurasian steppe nomads, notably from the Noghays. Specialized forces like the Cossacks were originally created or soon emerged as institutions linked to Muscovy or Poland-Lithuania. They proved quite

successful, and where the circumstances and the terrain allowed, their practices were copied in cavalry detachments of Western countries (Nolte 2005, 40).

In Moscow's and Russia's relationship with the nomads of the Eurasian grasslands, the Cossacks soon played a key role as guardians of the steppe frontier. The Western word "Cossack" derives from the Russian word "Kazak," itself a practically identical rendition of the Turkic term "Kazak" or "Qazaq," reflecting a cluster of meanings in the Turko-Mongol context: freebooter, vagabond, freeman, adventurer, and steppe brigand. Kazaki had existed from the time of the Mongol invasions and the disruption that these had brought to the traditional social order in occupied areas (O'Rourke 2007, 27–29) [36]. The great conqueror Tamerlane is thought to have begun his career as a Kazak (see above). The separation of the dissenting tribes of "Kazakhs" or "Kazaks" under their two sultans, Zhanibek and Kerey, from the strictures of the Shaybanid Uzbek tribal confederation, can be seen in comparable light. These dissenters seem to have preferred "free" life in the expanses of the Eurasian steppe to taking control and possibly administering relatively small settled oases. Thus, as Kappeler points out (and as already mentioned above), the terms "Cossack" and "Kazakh" effectively have the same origin (2013, 12).

Another point observed by Kappeler, Cossacks started out as independent and mobile river dwellers. Eastern European freebooters originally settled in the river forests along the middle and lower reaches of the Dnepr and the Don and later of the Volga and Yaik (Ural) rivers. In the deeply cut and meandering valleys, they erected fortified camps which provided some protection from Turko-Mongol riders. The Cossacks caught fish and beavers, hunted, and kept bees. Later on, they also reared livestock. Plunder attacks constituted an important source of income. At the outset, the Cossacks' prime means of transportation was not the horse (although they quickly learned to ride), but the boat, given that their primary habitat was not the steppe but the steppe river. Fords, where the nomads needed to cross the rivers with their horses, offered good occasions for assaults. The Cossacks were quick and adroit navigators not only on the rivers but also on the Black, Azov, and Caspian Seas. They got acquainted with the grasslands intimately, became superb warriors and often familiar with Tatar society (Kappeler 2013, 12).

O'Rourke explains how interests met: On the lookout for prospective employers, the fortresses of Muscovy's southeastern frontier were an option worth considering for the Kazaki. And to the often hard-pressed Russian fortress

---

[35] As mentioned earlier, C Asian towns also had their "corporations" of traders and artisans, but they too did not constitute independent political bodies.

[36] There appears to be a Mongol root of this word, namely, "ghasaghan" (obstinacy, refractoriness) or "ghazighu" (deviant, non-conform) (Martinez 2009, 96).

commanders, the skills that these men offered for hire were precious commodities (O'Rourke 2007, 33). On the steppe boundary between Christians and Muslims in Eastern Europe and CA, a Cossack was regarded as a lightly armed and mobile frontiersman who led a life free of subservience to aristocrats, however was paid for his armed services to the grand prince, later the czar. Many Cossacks were adventurers of Russian or Ukrainian origin that had fled feudal oppression and the spread of serfdom in Russia. Once in the grasslands, they were not easily accessible for the authorities (Kappeler 2013, 13).[37]

The Tatars, meanwhile, continued to dominate the elevated flat lands as riders and livestock breeders and used these plains as runways for their slave and cattle-capturing raids and razzias into Russia and Poland-Lithuania. The Cossacks, in turn, regularly raided Tatar's and other steppe nomads' encampments and occasionally also merchant caravans. The Tatars, of course, reciprocated, contributing to quasi-permanent low-level warfare along the steppe frontier (Nolte 1991, 48; Kappeler 2001, 51).

The Tatar Khanates of Kazan, Astrakhan, Crimea, and Sibir: Mostly Sedentarized Trading States

The Kazan Khanate (on the middle Volga, 1445–1552) was a focus of north-south trade and a traditional granary of Eastern Europe. Pastoral nomadism only played a secondary role, given that large parts of the khanate, including extensive woodlands, were unsuitable for such activities. The Turko-Mongol or Tatar conquerors had installed themselves as the ruling Islamized class of the state. The former nomads had settled, become urban traders, merchants and artisans, clergymen and scholars, or had taken control of agricultural activities of indigenous, often Finno-Ugric, populations, or in some cases, had become farmers themselves. The Turkic-speaking Kazan-Tatars carried out service in the khanate's cavalry army or in its public administration and were offered land as a quid pro quo, which corresponds to their hereditary soyurghal system.[38] In the eyes of the Austrian diplomat Sigismund von Herberstein in the first half of the sixteenth century: "The Tatars there are more humane than the others of their kind, they live in houses, cultivate fields, engage in trade, rarely wage wars" (Kappeler 2001, 29).

In the early sixteenth century, the state capital Kazan had about 20,000 inhabitants and functioned as the center and major entrepôt of the Volga trade. Muslim merchants controlled the main river routes, but Russians gained increasing influence. Commerce between Moscow and Kazan flourished. In agriculture, the chiefs of Tatar clans oversaw peasant communes headed by elders, and these groups were collectively called the "land" (Russian: Zemlia). The majority of the rural population were non-Tatars and farmed, fished, and kept bees. The khan of Kazan, a descendant of Genghisid Jöchi, collected revenues from personal landholdings, levies from the Tatar nobility, taxes on trade, and an in-kind levy or tribute, the Yasak, from indigenous inhabitants and from ordinary Tatars (Kappeler 2001, 29; Perdue 2005, 79).

Given the Khanate of Astrakhan's (1466–1556) geographical location and ecological conditions, it is not difficult to understand that in the fifteenth and sixteenth centuries most of this state's inhabitants were non-sedentary. Notwithstanding its key location harboring the center of the former Golden Horde and constituting a major junction between north-south trade along the Volga and through the Caspian Sea and east-west trade along the steppe route, this khanate was smaller and weaker than its other two Eastern European namesakes. This probably was because the Khanate of Astrakhan, while ruled by Tatars, who mostly lived in the capital at the mouth of the Volga and in other urban settlements, was dependent on Turkic-speaking steppe dwellers, the Noghays. The Islamized Noghays nomadized in the area between the Volga and the Aral Sea (Kappeler 2001, 30, 45). A second reason may have been the (temporary) loss of importance of the steppe route, while the Volga route continued to be used intensively, e.g., for fur trade. In any case, the khans of Astrakhan appear to have derived most of their income from trade, since there was little farming on the lower Volga steppe, and the khanate authorities do not seem to have been able to impose substantial levies on the Noghays (Khodarkovsky 2002, 12).

As mentioned above, the Crimean Khanate was established in 1438 and comprised the peninsula as well as an important share of the Pontic steppes north and east of it. The Turkic-speaking Muslim Crimean Tatars held sway. Settled activities (apart from trade, mostly farming, including the cultivation of wine) soon predominated on the relatively small Crimean peninsula, while the grasslands to the north and the east accommodated agriculture as well as nomadic pastoralism. Apart from shipments of livestock and luxury goods, exports of slaves remained especially lucrative and may well have constituted the mainstay of the Crimean economy. Slaves were procured as booty from Tatar raids on Muscovy and other Russian principalities, Lithuania and Poland, and were subsequently sold on regional and international markets (Khazanov 1983/1994, 244). Regular forays appear to have been carried out into the settlement areas of Eastern Slavic peasants living not far from the steppe boundary. Villages and sometimes towns were plundered and many Russians and Ukrainians captured.

---

[37] In any case, the Cossacks were unreliable allies for the ruler in Moscow. They participated in the large popular uprisings of the seventeenth and eighteenth centuries (Kappeler 2001, 51).

[38] This might also recall Muscovy's "service nobility" created at about that time.

Their belongings were robbed, their farms ravaged, and thousands of enslaved people were transferred to marketplaces further south where they tended to be the objects of profitable business deals (Kappeler 2001, 47–48).

About two decades after the Ottomans under Sultan Mehmed II had conquered Constantinople (1453), the Turkic fleet, aided by its artillery, seized Kaffa (Turkic: Kefe) from the Genoese in 1475 and took possession of the entire southern fringe of the Crimea.[39] Three years later the Turks extended their suzerainty over the rest of the khanate. The Ottoman authorities were certainly interested in Kaffa's, Azov's (Tana's), and other ports' strategic location and the revenue that came from controlling international trade flows (Stanziani 2012, 104). The southern coastal strip of Crimea with Kaffa as its center was turned into an Ottoman military-administrative district (Sandjak) under the direct control of the Sultan in Constantinople. Kaffa was the residence of a Turkic Pasha equipped with strong armed forces. The sultan left the Crimean Khan Mengli Girei, henceforth as an Ottoman vassal, in control of the northern part of the peninsula and the grasslands beyond. After the Turkic conquest of Crimea, the khanate's raids and slave hunts in Eastern Europe were facilitated by the backing that the khan received from the Sublime Porte. This in turn may have accelerated the arrangement of Cossack (Kazak) paramilitary structures on Muscovy's steppe frontier.

The Khanate of Sibir likely existed from some time in the 1420s to the end of the sixteenth century. As mentioned above, this state filled out most of Western Siberia and also included small parts of present-day Northern Kazakhstan. Rule of the khanate appears to have been contested on repeated occasions between members of the Shaybanid and Taibugid dynasties, both descendants of Genghis Khan. There are indications that the Shaybanids were more linked to the Turkic steppe nomads of the south, while the Taibugids had stronger links to the Khanty, the Mansi, and other forest peoples of the north and the east. In 1428 the Shaybanid Abul-Khair was chosen Khan of Sibir and established his capital in Tyumen, but he soon led his followers south in search of better pastures or of a better life (as explained in detail earlier). In the following decades, the remaining Shaybanids must have struggled with the Taibugids for control of the state.

The Noghay Confederation (Early Fifteenth Century to Late Sixteenth Century): Muscovy's Prime Supplier of Horses

The Noghay Horde, a purely nomadic confederation, was established in the early fifteenth century in the western parts of the Kazakh steppe, between the lower Volga and the Turgay valley. While it originally had no fixed capital, the confederation achieved a degree of centralization under Khan Nuraddin (r. 1426–1440) (Poujol 2000, 32). Its capital, Saraichyk, was eventually erected at the mouth of the Yaik (Ural) river and acquired some importance as a trading post on the steppe route of the SR.[40] During this period (the second quarter of the fifteenth century), the Noghays must have also made contact with the Shaybanid Uzbeks that were gradually moving south under Abul-Khair Khan (see above). The two nomadic polities probably temporarily shared pastures north of the Aral Sea or around the Mugodzhar mountains and may have had territorial disputes, which in turn may contribute to explaining the abovementioned centralization of Noghay politics that otherwise often tended to revolve around inter-tribal rivalry.

The traditional north-south migrational routes of the Noghay cattle breeders went from their winter encampments on the mouth of Volga and the northeastern shore of the Caspian Sea to the summer pastures of the middle reaches of the Volga and Yaik (Ural) rivers. The Noghay steppe aristocracy possessed significant wealth, including huge herds of horses and camels, flocks of sheep, and herds of cattle (Baipakov et al. 1997, 112, 113).

The Noghay confederation wielded considerable political influence in the Khanate of Astrakhan, which was established practically on the Horde's territory a quarter of century after Nuraddin's death. Since the end of the fifteenth century, Muscovy entertained close diplomatic and commercial relations with the Noghays. Above all, there were the yearly convoys of Noghay tribesmen taking thousands of horses to Moscow. According to Perdue, during the heyday of horse drives in the sixteenth century, as many as 30,000–40,000 horses were brought to the capital annually. This was a multiple of what the Ming usually obtained yearly from their steppe neighbors, the Chagatayids and the Oirats. Thus, for Muscovy, the Noghays were the most important source of horses for riding, just as Moscow was the Noghays' main source of income and of some coveted products (Perdue 2005, 79)[41]. In the 1520s and 1530s,

---

[39] Genoa's definite loss of Kaffa and thus of its direct access to the SR system after more than two centuries of presence probably contributed to the maritime trading nation's decision to reorient its commercial ambitions toward the Western Mediterranean and the Atlantic. Seventeen years later, the Genoese navigator Chistopher Columbus, sailing in Spanish services and searching a sea route to India unencumbered by Muslim middlemen, discovered the West Indies, and thus opened a new era in history.

[40] This steppe route (from the Black Sea to Transoxiana or China), however, at the time was on the decline.

[41] Khazanov points to even higher numbers of Noghay horses "exported" to Russia: While in the fall of 1527, 20,000 horses were driven into Muscovy "from the Nogai," in 1529/1530 it was 80,000, and in 1532/1533 it was 50,000 (1983/1994, 205).

Kazakh tribes, coming from the southeast, conquered territory east of the Yaik and pushed the Noghays further west. But the latter's profitable horse trade with Russia continued.

Like the Chinese (see below), the Russian authorities in the sixteenth and seventeenth centuries sought to strictly control the horse trade with the nomads. This business took place at a designated place near Moscow or in several towns along the Volga. As Khodarkovsky explains, items allowed for trade were, e.g., various types of woolens and other cloth, but objects of any military significance were banned: copper, tin, lead, iron, saltpeter[42], sulfur, gunpowder, bullets, firearms, spears, sabers, and other ironware. The horses were brought by Noghay merchant parties known as ordobazarnaya stanitsa (literally, the travelling bazaar of the horde), which could be quite large. One merchant party dispatched to Moscow in 1555 included 1000 merchants and 20,000 horses. The Noghays sought to obtain from Moscow a wide variety of products, including furs, hats, paper, dyes, tin pots, nails, saddles, falcons, gold, and silver in thin sheets (Khodarkovsky 2002, 26–27). Although they must also have been banned, even such items as light armor, saddles, bridles, and quivers seem to have been appreciated more by the nomads if these items were made in Moscow—which may point to some know-how acquired by Muscovite craftsmen in the production of instruments of traditional steppe warfare.

The Kazakhs: Emergence of a New Extensive C Asian Steppe State

– *Origins in Zhetysu/Semirechie (second half of fifteenth century)*

As mentioned above, in the 1450s and 1460s, some of the tribes of the Shaybanid Uzbek polity split off and moved to the valleys of Chu and Talas, where they were offered pastures by the khan of Moghulstan (Chagatay Khanate). Altogether, the sultans Zhanibek and Kerey had fled with about 200,000 followers to Western Zhetysu/Semirechie (Millward 2007, 71). These dissenting tribes called themselves or were soon called "Kazaks" or "Kazakhs" (freebooters, roamers, adventurers). In 1465/1466 the first Kazakh nomadic confederation was created under the rule of Khan Zhanibek (r. 1466–1480). Zhanibek—a vassal of the ruler of Moghulistan—expanded the borders of the confederation, which was facilitated by the Shaybanids' continuing southward migration and conquest of territories in the C Asian oasis belt. Indeed, the Uzbeks' migration to Mavarannahr and Khorassan left a large power vaccuum in the grasslands north of the Syr Daria, where the Kazakhs quickly gained the upperhand. In the last quarter of the fifteenth century, the Kazakh state stretched from the lower Ili valley via Chu and Talas and the Hunger steppe to the Sarysu valley (Krieger 2003, 269; Breghel 2003, 44, 50).

The Kazakhs in the fifteenth and sixteenth centuries asserted themselves as a distinct group of Turko-Mongol nomadic tribes living in the Desht-i-Kipchak and speaking a Kipchak Turkic idiom. Like under the Uzbeks, sultans (princes, steppe aristocrats) claiming Gengisid descent were entitled to become the khan, who was elected. The ruler of the lands, the khan, divided them up between the sultans as supreme managers of grazing grounds. The administrative system was based on customary law (Adat); moreover, Muslim norms were also valid (Baipakov et al. 1997, 127, 129).

– *The expanding Kazakh confederation: holding sway over southern settled areas and trade*

Artykbaev outlines that in the fifteenth and sixteenth centuries, the great majority of Kazakhs led a nomadic and semi-nomadic life of animal husbandry in accordance with the climatic conditions of dry steppes and semideserts (2007, 160). Toward the end of the fifteenth century, the Kazakhs expanded their territories of nomadization further west, crossed the Turgay valley and probably reached the Mugodzhar mountains. They also moved south, following and at times combating the Shaybanids in the Syr Daria valley, the lower and middle reaches of which the Kazakhs claimed for themselves. For Kazakh pastoralists (the sharua), sheep were the most important stock, followed by horses, goats, cattle, and camels. Cattle were raised in relatively small numbers, mostly in settled areas. Modest farming was concentrated in Southern Kazakhstan along the Syr Daria, but some small pockets also existed in the Saryarka (Kazakh Uplands), the Turgay valley, and in Semirechie.[43] The sharua had to pay taxes in sheep and, following old nomadic traditions, were obliged to contribute fully equipped warriors (with two horses, weapons, and provisions) to military campaigns (Baipakov and Kumekov 2003, 100).

Agriculture and handicrafts were not yet clearly separated from animal husbandry. Kazakhs tended to cultivate the soil with archaic farming tools, including hoes, wooden hook plows, and even gnarled tree stumps or bundles of twigs (instead of harrows). Crop yields were low. Crops were irrigated using primitive water-lifting engines (chigir), which had already been known for at

---

[42] Saltpeter—a naturally occurring potassium nitrate used in making fireworks, gunpowder, etc.

[43] This would imply that after the wiping out of agriculture in Zhetysu in the second half of the thirteenth century as a result of the Mongol invasion, (non-sedentary) farming made a humble reappearance in the region toward the end of the fifteenth or the early sixteenth century.

least half a millennium (see above). Kazakh agriculture hardly produced any surpluses; very little grain was exchanged for livestock. Poor Kazakhs (dzhataki), who were not able to work as pastoralists, had no choice but to resort to farming. The trades exercised on the grasslands included felt milling, leather and wood processing, simple weaving, and smithery. Tradesmen of the steppe produced wooden parts for yurts, strings for tying up yurt frames, saddles, and similar items and sold their goods to or bartered them with livestock breeders. Applied steppe arts included felt ornaments to decorate yurts or splendid leather caftans that were even on sale in the cities (Shukow et al. 1958/1964, Band 4, 655–656; Baipakov 2003, 387).

Some Kazakhs settled down in urban settlements, almost all of which were situated in the Syr Daria valley. Yet many towns were still recovering from past destruction or coping with persisting difficult circumstances: Otrar and some other Syr Daria towns (Sygnak, Dzhend, Tashkent) had been razed by Genghis Khan in one of his first devastating assaults and punitive campaigns in CA; over two centuries later there were still traces of the impact. Furthermore, upon the collapse of the Mongol Empire, the lower and middle Syr Daria had turned into a borderland in dispute, first between the Empire of Timur and the Golden Horde, then between the Timurids and the Uzbeks, and then between the Shaybanids and the Kazakhs. Finally, transcontinental SR trade over the route running along the Syr Daria, which was part of the "northern route" connecting China and Europe, was relatively weak in the fifteenth and sixteenth centuries. Notwithstanding the challenging factors described above, Otrar had again become an important trade and handicraft center. The same goes for Suzak, Yasy, and Sairam. Most of the trade and a lot of the handicraft production of the Syr Daria cities were oriented toward the needs of the steppe, which means that trans-ecological north-south trade prevailed at the time (Baipakov et al. 1997, 131–133).

Baipakov et al. take a closer look at Otrar in the fifteenth and sixteenth centuries (1997, 150–155): The total territory of the town equaled about 20 ha (200,000 m^2), the entire population came to between 4500 and 6300 inhabitants. The central part of the town, enclosed by a wall, was called khisar—a densely populated fortified part in which government buildings, barracks, the mosque, the main markets and craftsmens' workshops, and dwellings were situated. The territory beyond the khisar was the suburb, the rural zone. The street network of the town was complicated. Otrar consisted of about 100 small residential quarters (probably corresponding to mahallas), each of which had 6–12

houses. Streets inside quarters were not wider than 2 m. The side streets had "pockets" ("karmany")—widenings that served as enclosures for livestock. In Otrar only one quarter was identified by archeologists as the "potters' quarter." Generally there was no specialization of quarters by the activity of its inhabitants.

The Kazakh economy remained largely one of barter: Surplus production was bartered/exchanged for goods produced by urban dwellers and agriculturalists. Nomadic pastoralists drove livestock and took leather, wool, knives, wood articles, and other items to the markets of the south; in exchange the breeders received many goods: cotton and silk cloth, articles of pottery and ironware, attire and leather wares (dressing gowns, shawls, head attire, footwear), parts of horse equipment, various domestic items, weapons, decorative items made of precious metals, mirrors, etc. Sygnak had turned into the major economic and political center of the Eastern Desht-i-Kipchak and was the capital of the first Kazakh rulers (Baipakov et al. 1997, 130, 134).

In southern regions of Kazakhstan, stable forms of quasi-feudal land ownership of nomads or former nomads emerged, building on a mixture of Mongol and Islamic institutions: appanage, soyurghal, iqta, mulk, and waqf-type properties. The soyurghal corresponded to a widespread form of supremacy exercised by the nomadic aristocracy over the—often subjugated—sedentary population. A settlement and its agricultural surroundings, or the urban indigenous people (including Sarts) and the peasants living on large tracts of cultivated land on the periphery, were subordinated to the power of a specific local ruler—the owner of the soyurghal. The latter, a Kazakh nobleman, received these properties as a grant and had the right to collect taxes from tradesmen, merchants, and farmers for his own benefit, under conditions of military or civil service to the khan/the authorities (Baipakov et al. 1997, 127). This type of, one could argue, microeconomic control exercised over settled areas would point to a relatively high degree of nomadic-sedentary economic integration in the framework of the Kazakh Khanate, which therefore might be characterized as a "nomadic state of the second type" (according to Khazanov, see above).

In the farming belt of Southern Kazakhstan, Islam became the dominant religion. While its influence was spread by both Sufi orders, that of "Yasaviya" and that of "Naqshbandia," the latter gradually gained the upperhand. The Yasaviya had been founded in the twelfth century by Sheikh Yasavi, born in Yasy (Syr Daria valley). The Naqshbandia's origins can be attributed to Sheikh Naqshband (1318–1389), born near Bukhara. Open for everyone, simple, adaptable, and proposing to its adherents to "advance toward God while remaining on earth," the Naqshbandia brotherhood became the most popular across CA (Kamev 2005, 85).

- *Centralization and dissipation of sprawling statehood: from the Kazakh Khanate of the early sixteenth century to the three hordes (zhuz)*

In the early sixteenth century, Kasym Khan (r. 1511–1523) strengthened the Kazakh state and extended its borders once more. Kasym succeeded in shaking off Moghul/Chagatayid suzerainty in Semirechie and oversaw the extension of the khanate's territories west to the river Yaik (border with the Tatar Khanate of Astrakhan) (Oskolkov and Oskolkova 2004, 23; Poujol 2000, 35). As mentioned above, this westward expansion partly displaced the Noghay Horde. In the 1520s, the confederation enjoyed a period of relative peace and prosperity. Its population numbered about a million people; the nomadic aristocracy possessed huge herds, sometimes counting up to hundreds of thousands of animals (Artykbaev 2007, 162).

The unity of this confederacy remained fragile, however. After Kasym Khan's death, centrifugal tendencies made themselves felt and the khanate split into three hordes.[44] Each horde had its own geographic zone of nomadization, a zone that was economically relatively autonomous. Thus, the Junior Horde (Kishi Zhuz) emerged in the steppe north of the Aral Sea and south of the Ural mountains, the Middle Horde (Orta Zhuz) occupied the lower reaches of the Syr Daria and the Central and Northeastern Kazakh grasslands, and the Senior Horde (Ulu Zhuz) controled most of Zhetysu, the valleys of Chu and Talas, and the middle reaches of the Syr Daria (Geiss 2003, 113).

The nomads of all three hordes regularly moved between northern summer pastures (zhailau) in the steppe belt and southern winter encampments (qystau) and back again. As Masanov explains, a salient feature of life was the closed cycle of migration along strictly regulated routes, with permanent places for wintering, some of which could be near Syr Daria river oases and a system of wandering in the summer around the same sources of water. On average, the north-south distance of the migrations did not exceed 100 km, although it could on occasion reach up to 1000 km or even more (2003, 374). Grazing territories and nomadization routes tended to be stable for extended periods. When these territories and routes were broken up, in most cases for external political

reasons, the nomadic economy was often badly affected (Khazanov 1983/1994, 177; see also below).

4.1.1.7 The Kyrgyz: Mountain Nomads Practicing Transhumance in the Tienshan

The Kyrgyz formed a tribal community in the Tienshan in the 1480s, about the same time that the Kazakhs had installed themselves in Western Semirechie. Initially, both were under Moghul/Chagatayid overlordship. At the beginning of the sixteenth century, the Kyrgyz of Eastern Ferghana became subjects of the Shaybanids, whereas the Kyrgyz living around the Issyk-koel allied themselves with the Kazakhs and joined the latter in throwing off Moghul suzereinty in Jetisuu and Kyrgyzstan (Tchoroev (Chorotegin) 2003, 111). The Kyrgyz were mountain nomads exclusively: In the Tienshan, they practiced seasonal migration of the vertical type between the foothills and valleys (wintering grounds) on the one hand and the high mountain pastures (summer grazing grounds) on the other. Sheep were the principal item of Kyrgyz nomads' wealth (Tchoroev (Chorotegin) 2003, 112). These mountain dwellers were relatively little influenced by the farming and urban cultures of adjacent states and regions (the Uzbek Khanate, East Turkestan, the settled areas of Southern Kazakhstan).

4.1.1.8 The Safavid Empire Until the Late Sixteenth Century

After the fall of Il-Khan power (1335), for about half a century, two nomadic states followed each other on Persian territory, the state of the Chobanids (1340–1357) and that of the Jalayrids (1358–1390), before Iran was incorporated into Tamerlane's empire. When the latter fell apart, the eastern part of Iran, particularly Khorassan, remained with the Timurid Emirates, while the western part was conquered by the nomadic confederation of the Kara Koyunlu (Black Sheep Turk, 1410–1468), which preceded the Aq-Koyunlu (White Sheep Turk, 1468–1501). As Khazanov put it, with regard to the largest class of Iranian society, the peasantry (rayyats), the policies of the nomadic rulers fluctuated between, on the one hand, the situation in the aftermath of the Seljuk conquest and under the first Hülegüs and, on the other hand, that which existed during the heyday of the Seljuk Sultanate and under the Il-Khans after the reforms of Ghazan Khan. In other words, the first tendency involved excessive plunder of the peasantry; the second one comprised reformed nomadic rule (Khazanov 1983/1994, 268).

In 1501, the same year in which Muhammad Shaybani replaced the Timurids, another conqueror from the steppe, the Turkmen Ismail Safavi, who originated in a militant Sufi order on the southern shore of the Caspian Sea, founded a new Persian dynasty, the Safavids, who ruled until 1722 (Soucek 2000, 150). Shah Ismail I (1501–1524), like most

---

[44] In this connection, a "horde" (Russian—orda) or "zhuz" (Kazakh—hundred) corresponds to something like a "tribal union" (Russian—rodovoe obedinenie) led by sultans that sometimes proclaimed themselves as khans (Oskolkov and Oskolkova 2004, 25).

rulers of Iran since the Seljukids, and like many Muslim rulers in CA since the Samanids, based his military strength on Turkic tribal elites and manpower—in this case nomads of mostly Turkmen origin, the Kyzylbash. With the help of the Kyzylbash and probably also thanks to the establishment of "Twelver Shiism" (his own religion and that of his adherents) as a unifying official faith, Ismail was able to create a new Persian state based on centralized power. He achieved this although he himself was not of Persian origin.

Thus, in the early sixteenth century, Shah Ismail initiated a major schism in Eastern Islam and thus distinguished Iran from its Sunni neighbors to the west (the Ottoman Empire) and the north (the Shaybanid state). The oppressive religious policy of the Safavids (intolerance toward other faiths than the new state religion) gave rise to the emigration of a number of Persian intellectuals to the Uzbek Khanate and to India, including literary figures and religious scholars (Eshraghi 2003, 251). War quickly broke out with the Shaybanids and, as mentioned above, led to the defeat and death of Shaybani Khan. In 1510 the Persians conquered large parts of Khorassan including Mashhad—which became one of the holiest shrines of Shiism, Merv, and Herat (Map 4.3).

While using a military apparatus dominated by Turkic warriors, the Safavid ruler also based his authority on the Persian administrative structure, which was a tried and tested combination. The main form of land holdings was the soyurghal (Guseinov 2004, 81). These land holdings were often granted to the Kyzylbash who provided soldiers for the shah's army and collected revenues to pay for war. The oppression of the rayyats by the nomadic elite continued. The new rulers of Iran inherited a coinage from the preceding Turkic dynasties that lacked a uniform standard and had been considerably debased during the fifteenth century. In order to restabilize the monetary system and create confidence, under Shah Ismail I, the kingdom minted three silver coins, or tangas, of different weights and values. Over time, the weight of the tangas was reduced (Moosvi 2003a, 451).

Shah Tahmasp I (1524–1576) was very fond of culture and the arts. From the time he became ruler until the year 1555, when he underwent his celebrated tauba (repentance), the head of state was a generous patron of painters, calligraphers, and others in the fine arts. Many artistic masterpieces of the Safavid era, including miniatures, were created in this period.[45] The repentence of the shah and the subsequent tightening of the purse strings led to a dwindling of financial support for painters and calligraphers and

eventually prompted many of them to emigrate to the Mughal Empire in search of patronage, which added to the loss of human capital triggered by the previous tightening of the religious regime (Eshraghi 2003, 251). On the other hand, in 1561 a successful mission under Anthony Jenkinson on behalf of the English Muscovy Company came to the Safavid court and opened up important trade relations with England through Russia, as described below. While Shah Tahmasp began to rein in the privileges of the nomadic aristocracy, the latter continued to occupy predominant positions in the state. Shah Tahmasp gave the name shahi to a coin which from 1540 had a weight of 6.4 g; this coin was renamed more than once, and, like the tangas, its weight was successively decreased. In the seventeenth century, it weighed 4.7 g (Moosvi 2003a, 451).

The relative political stability and security regained in Safavid Persia after long-lasting turmoil may have contributed to a demographic recovery and a growth spurt for farming in the course of the sixteenth century. Harvests are reported to have become so stable that in agricultural core regions the absorption of up to 25% of the yield through taxation was possible for extended periods of time. That supported the development of an increasingly urbanized agro-bureaucratic state (Feldbauer and Liedl 2008, 22–23). While overall economic conditions in Persia stabilized, overland SR trade from China via Persia to Europe lost some of its dynamic from the early sixteenth century due to incipient competition from sea traffic.

4.1.1.9 The Oirat Empire of the Mid-fifteenth Century: Yet Again a Vast Steppe State Exacting Tribute from China

After the collapse of Mongol rule in China (1368) and the retreat of the Mongols back to their homeland, instability reigned for a couple of decades. In the early fifteenth century, two rival non-Genghisid Khanates emerged in Mongolia, that of the Western Mongols or Oirats (also called Kalmyks or Dzungars) and that of the Eastern Mongols, where the Khalkhas formed the most important group. The Oirats were the first to attain regional supremacy (Le Petit Mourre 2003, 786). Once the Oirats had incorporated all or almost all Mongol tribes into their confederation and consolidated its military structures, pressure was quickly put on the Ming. China's northern and northwestern borders were repeatedly threatened. Given the persisting balance of power on the C Asian borders of China (and across most of Eurasia) in the fifteenth century, the militarily superior Oirats started to exact tribute and subsidy payments from the Ming authorities. The Oirat or Kalmyk Empire reached its peak under Khan Esen Taiji (r. 1439–1453).

As is to be expected, Ming frontier trade with the Oirats tended to be unequal exchange highly beneficial to the nomads (Perdue 2005, 400). As Barfield explains, in Esen

---

[45] This, of course, recalls the Shaybanids' similar and practically simultaneous patronage policies, which probably were in competition with those of the Safavids.

Taiji's first year as ruler more than a thousand Oirats appeared as members of a tribute and trade mission in China, and in 1444 an embassy of more than 2000 arrived. The Chinese protested at this tremendous increase in visitors, whom they had to feed and treat. Tributary visits provided sought-after valuable goods (including still highly coveted silk) that could be redistributed among the nomads or traded elsewhere. Muslim traders often accompanied the embassies to take commercial advantage of the situation. The 1446 mission brought 800 horses, 130,000 squirrel pelts, 16,000 ermine pelts, and 200 sable pelts, which were exchanged for a variety of Chinese goods, most of them luxuries that the Oirats might not have been able to acquire by raiding (Barfield 1989/1992, 239).

Meanwhile, after attacks on the Chinese protectorate of Hami in 1443, 1445, and 1448, the Oirats forced the Ming out of their bridgehead in CA. The goal of these campaigns was first pillage and then a new peace treaty that would provide permanent subsidies and trade. In 1448–1449 (i.e., after the victorious confrontation over Hami) an embassy of 3500 Oirats arrived at the border. While the embassies increased in size, the intervals between them tended to shrink. The Chinese vigorously objected, but eventually acquiesced. Later an Oirat embassy, which brought horses to the border, took 90,000 bolts of cloth (Barfield 1989/1992, 238–41; Höllmann 2004, 84).

According to Perdue, apart from accepting embassies, the Ming organized officially supervised border trade in the form of horse and tea markets. Their aim was to exchange goods from the Chinese interior for the one necessary product the Middle Kingdom could still not produce in sufficient quality itself: militarily capable horses (Perdue 2005, 52). However the Ming frequently had to put up with poor quality animals for exorbitant prices. Esen's empire was at its height in 1450, and in a risky military campaign he even invaded Beijing and captured the Ming emperor. But his failure to collect ransom for the emperors' return disappointed his followers and contributed to the subsequent decline and demise of his state (Barfield 1989/1992, 241). This demise also brought about the discontinuation or severe curtailment of the abovementioned embassies and markets. In reaction to the Mongols' raid of Beijing, the Ming authorities decided to renew or reconstruct the Great Wall. In the following decades, the Eastern Mongols recovered and pushed the Kalmyks west; in a perhaps typical nomadic "domino effect," the latter took possession of entire Dzungaria.

Once the reparation of the Great Wall was completed, in the sixteenth century the Ming dynasty was more successful in controlling frontier contact with the Mongols, now represented by the Eastern Mongol Khanate. And the nomads for the time being were unable to reestablish a system of regular trade and subsidy flows from China (Barfield 1989/1992, 15). The Eastern Mongol Khanate

was probably weaker overall than its predecessor on account of the Eastern Khanate's inability to check internal instability and to contain lingering danger from the Oirats.

4.1.2 Aspects of the C Asian Oasis and Steppe Economies from the Fifteenth to the Eighteenth Centuries

4.1.2.1 The Oasis Economy
– *Traditional agriculture, water management, and oasis dwellings*

Although it was not the most lucrative source of earnings for the oases, the principal occupation of the settled people of CA was farming irrigated land. To support the dense population inhabiting the oases, a lot of time and attention had to be devoted to the irrigation system. Over the centuries, a sophisticated regime of water management had developed. Although a hierarchically organized control system had emerged, most of the responsibility remained at the local level. According to Islamic law, water is a social good. Inhabitants received user rights from local authorities who in turn were supervised from above. In the oases, water rights were often more important than land rights.

Even minor upland valleys were typically equipped with small channels leading water from mountain streams into the fields on either side. As mentioned above, sophisticated qanat or karez irrigation technologies (which had originated in Iran) spread across CA over the centuries. Underground channels were drawn from streams in snow-fed mountains; the channels sloped downward, ultimately to emerge in the open on the lower ground, where the water—all the way protected from evaporation—was used. Like in ancient times, the maintenance of the karez system as well as of the irrigation canals (aryks) along the large rivers required many workers and a major work effort. Taxes had to be paid for the irrigation water and peasants/local residents were obliged to take part in necessary works (mirab). The aryks were repeatedly soiled, silted, and even blocked every year by mud and sediments emanating from floods of the Syr Daria, the Amu Daria, the Ili, the Tarim, and other rivers. This called for regular cleaning up operations (von Gumppenberg and Steinbach 2004, 309; Bacon 1966/1980, 57).

Many traditional agricultural tools remained almost unchanged for centuries. Thus the C Asian farmer tended to use a relatively primitive plow (the omach) and a wooden harrow (mala), and he winnowed the grain with a wooden shovel. Earthwork was often carried out with a universal tool, a peculiar kind of hoe (ketmen) (Shukow et al. 1958/1964, Band 4, 648–649). In some oases a simple type of water-lifting device (chigir) remained in use for up to a millennium. Peasants' tools in parts of East Turkestan also included implements of iron and iron-steel alloy, for instance, the type of plow they used had an iron share and a wooden shaft.

As Elizabeth Bacon illustrates in detail, traditional C Asian oasis farming comprised the cultivation of wheat, barley, rice, and cotton; furthermore, sorghum, corn, millet, opium poppy, beans, various oilseeds (e.g., sesame), alfalfa (a forage crop), flax, hemp, and tobacco were grown. Silkworm breeding, vegetable growing (carrots, onions, radishes, cucumbers, red pepper), the cultivation of fruit (melons, peaches, grapes, pomegranates), and viniculture were important. Several types of gourds were cultivated, some for eating and others dried and turned into containers. Mulberry trees grew widely in the oases; their fruit was dried and pounded into a meal used for sweetening food, and the leaves were fed to silkworms. Dried fruit (particularly apricots and grapes) were not only sold on regional markets but also exported (Bacon 1966/1980, 57).

The most widespread form of exploitation of the peasants was metayage (sharecropping), and the typical peasant-leaseholder was a metayager who cultivated state, soyurghal, waqf, or mulk lands belonging to wealthy landowners (Mukminova 1998, 356). Prosperous urban inhabitants often maintained summer dwellings and gardens outside the town, where they spent the warm months of the year living on the produce of their gardens. Wherever space allowed, grape arbors provided shade in the dwellings' courtyards. Poplars planted along streams and canals served as windbreaks and as a source of lumber for woodwork and construction (Bacon 1966/1980; see also above).

Stockbreeding played a secondary role in the oasis economy. All men who could afford it rode horses and although some of these were bred in oases, most were purchased from nomads and semi-nomads. Both horses and oxen were used to draw plows and arbas, the high two-wheeled carts that were the normal conveyance for women, family parties, and farm produce. The poor man's beast of burden was the donkey. Camels for the caravan trade were obtained from nomads. In rural areas surrounding the oasis, town villagers often kept some sheep and goats and sent the village flock out to graze under a shepherd. Much of the mutton and wool used in the settlements and towns came from semi-nomads and nomads on the fringes of the oases or further at large (Bacon 1966/1980, 58).

According to Bacon, in areas where wood was precious and stone difficult to come by except in mountain regions, the most plentiful building material was mud—often the very loess soil which gave the oases their fertility. A typical urban dwelling and its outbuildings were surrounded by a thick wall built up of chunks of loess mud. The house (inside the wall) had itself thinner walls of tamped earth or sun-dried brick. Reed mats were laid on mud floors, and over these were spread felt or woven rugs. Uzbek families who had not forgotten their nomadic traditions often put up a yurt in the courtyard for living quarters and used the house for storage and the entertainment of guests (1966/1980: C Asians..., 60–62).

– *Elementary education, multifaceted trades, and crafts*
The level of literacy among most C Asians, particularly the nomads, was low. A religious education for boys, and partly for girls, from rich sedentary families was in most cases the only form of education. The latter aimed, i.e., at the transmission of basic literacy and proper models of behavior. As a rule, rigorous discipline was based on corporal punishment. Practical knowledge and skills were acquired in the context of work. Artisans were trained in risalas or craft guilds (not that much different from traditional practices in Europe). The master usually accepted an apprentice at age 12 and taught him the secrets of the trade over the following years (Roudik 2007, 62–64; see also below).

Tradesmen were to a large extent dependent on regional or local feudal rulers (often stemming from the nomadic aristocracy) and faced in-kind or monetized tax liabilities (trade and workshop levies). Tradesmen mostly sold their products themselves. They would typically produce the merchandise directly in their stores and display it in front of their doors, or they brought the goods to the nearest bazaar where business took place in the tradesmen's own selling stands or stalls (Conermann 2006, 103). Products (e.g., cotton and silk cloth, textile fabrics, leather goods) were still domestically produced and exported, but predominantly in neighborhood trade (to an adjacent foreign country), less in transcontinental long-distance trade (at least from the eighteenth century). Some urban workshops, like armorers, military equipment manufacturers, and jewelry makers focused on domestic demand. The latter was possibly because respective products started to lose competitiveness abroad or because there was less money available for the importation of firearms (see below).

Among major C Asian handicraft centers of the sixteenth century were Herat, Merv, Bukhara, Samarkand, Khiva, Tashkent, Otrar, and Kashgar. Later, towns like Khoqand, Andijan, Shahrukhia, Shimkent, Turkestan (Yasy), and Sauran (see Map 4.7) gained renown. As Baipakov carefully surveys, written sources bear information on blacksmiths, turners, locksmiths, coppersmiths, cutlers, jewelers, tanners, mat makers, armorers, papermakers, weavers, dyers, shoemakers, carpet makers, tailors, potters, builders, brick makers, charcoal burners, furriers, bakers, and grocers; further degrees of specialization may be observed within these crafts. Craftsmen of the leading professions often inhabited specialized quarters or places: Jewelers and goldsmiths lived near the urban center, whereas potters, tanners, and mat makers were located in the suburbs, close to running water; blacksmiths settled near the entrance to the city; and papermakers and charcoal burners beyond its limits (Baipakov 2003, 380).

As Baipakov further elaborates, a master craftsman (ustad) would have assistants and one or more apprentices. There might also be hired workers, who carried out particular tasks for payment. Each craft guild was headed by a specific ustad, the guild master, whose appointment was approved by the authorities. The guildmaster supervised the quality of the goods made by the craftsmen of his guild, ensured compliance with accepted standards, laid down prices, and was responsible for the apportioning and discharging of taxes. The guild masters sometimes also bought up goods, supplied raw materials, and lent money to other craftsmen.[46] Thus C Asian guild masters could wield substantial legal as well as economic power over their guild members, while themselves being under the sway of the local ruler. In some cases though, well-to-do merchants or moneylenders would buy up workshops and lease them out. Apart from privately owned workshops (associated in guilds), there were also public workshops in the large cities and at the courts of the khans and the Emir of Bukhara, producing goods for court use (Baipakov 2003, 381–384).[47]

The majority of craftswomen were engaged in the processing of raw materials and the preparation of component parts. In textiles, the cleaning cotton off seeds and the spinning of cotton yarn were the work of women, as was the raising of silk worms. But unwinding the silk from cocoons was the work of master craftsmen, as was the dyeing of yarns and cloth and the weaving of cotton, silk and cotton, satins, and velvets. Most craftspeople belonged to the middle and poor strata of the urban population. Jewelers, armorers, metal workers, and weavers were typically better off, while mat makers tended to be among the poorest (Baipakov 2003, 381; Bacon 1966/1980, 67).

- *Aspects of SR trade, urbanization, and currency reform-inflation cycles*

Trade (regional and long distance) was traditionally the most lucrative economic activity in the oases. As in material production, apart from private trade there was also publicly organized trade "for the needs of the khan." This trade was often carried out as barter, which in some cases included large business transactions in which many merchants and envoys of the khan would be involved as intermediaries. As far as international business was concerned, currencies were not widely used, although from the second half of the sixteenth century silver—as coins or bullion—once again started to play an important role. The slave trade continued to flourish, with supplies coming in after battles, raids or razzias, or when parents sold their children at times of severe famine. According to Audrey Burton, the greatest slave purveyors were the Khwarazmians, the Turkmens, the Dzungars, and the Kazakhs. The well-stocked slave markets in Mavarannahr functioned until the nineteenth century. In the first half of the eighteenth century, large numbers of Persian captives had been taken there and to Khiva, from where Nadir Shah (after his successful conquest) liberated tens of thousands. Horse trade remained strategically important and a significant business (Burton 2003, 410; Golden 2011, 116).

Looking at societal changes in the oases since the late Middle Ages, many people that had installed themselves in towns or settled in the countryside apparently started to detach themselves from their preceding ancestral references and to progressively lose their tribal affiliation to that of "sart" (see also above): C Asian urbanization and sedentarization favored an acculturation process which translated into the emergence of a new original group of inhabitants, bearing more socio-professional-religious attributes of identity than tribal or ethnic traits. Sarts included Turkic-speaking Uzbeks and Iranian-speaking Tajiks as well as people of other origin. Sarts came to represent a settled indigenous element vis-à-vis neighboring semi-nomadic and nomadic populations (Petric 2002, 11–12; Annanepesov 2003a, 63).

As opposed to nomadic civilizations, most sedentary states in CA did use coin money, even if their economies were far from fully monetized. As repeatedly described above, C Asian monetary policies tended to be quite active and monetary "regime changes" may have been almost as frequent as political ones. A recurrent pattern was that a new ruler carried out a (urgently needed) currency reform to provide a more stable framework for the economy. Then, over time either the weight of a coin was gradually reduced, or the precious metal content of the coin was decreased, or the number of mints authorized to issue the coin was increased, in each case typically combined with an expansion in the circulation

---

[46] This would invite comparison with early capitalist manufacturers and bankers in Europe.

[47] This, in turn, could recall tiraz factories in the caliphate or karkhanas in the Mongol Empire.

of the coin as well as of seignorage. This sustained expansion of money circulation triggered growing inflation and, sooner or later, a debasement of the currency loomed. Once the population had lost trust in the currency and the situation had become unsustainable, the cycle would start anew.

Such C Asian currency reform-inflation cycles have ancient roots (the Seleucid Empire had in the third century BCE already suffered from an inflationary crisis –see above) and could last from a few years to a couple of decades. In most cases, the basic coins for domestic retail market transactions were copper coins. It was silver coins, and more rarely, gold coins that were used for SR transactions, particularly from the late sixteenth century. Since no country-issued coins that constituted internationally accepted legal tender, only the weight and purity of silver (and gold) coins, and not any official inscription, was relevant for international traders. Thus, SR trade was somewhat protected from monetary instability in individual countries along the route.

4.1.2.2 The Steppe Economy

– *Specialization and sophistication of nomadic economic management: the Kazakh example*

Among the main nomadic populations of CA from the sixteenth to the eighteenth century feature: the Kazakhs, Kyrgyz, Turkmens, Karakalpaks, Mongols/Kalmyks, and some Uzbeks. Concerning the largest group, according to Masanov it may be assumed that the number of nomadic Kazakhs did not exceed 2–3 million, since that figure seems to be the highest possible size of pastoral population in the given territory of nomadization (the Desht-i-Kipchak or Kazakh steppe) sustainable by the environmental resources, notably grazing land (Masanov 2003, 374).

The Kazakh winter pastures and encampments were located mainly in the middle and lower valley of the Syr Daria, on the foothills of the Karatau, and in Southwestern Zhetysu, whereas their summer pastures lay in the extensive plains to the north. According to Masanov, a constituent feature of Kazakh nomadic life was the closed cycle of migration along strictly regulated routes, with permanent winter encampments in the south and a system of organized wandering in the summer around the same sources of water in the north. As mentioned above, on the average, the length of seasonal Kazakh migrations was up to 100 km, although it could occasionally exceed 1000 km (Masanov 2003, 374).

As Masanov underlines, the nature of the environment and economic needs determined the composition of the Kazakh herds and flocks: On average more than half of all

animals were sheep, the rest consisted of horses, goats, cattle, and camels. The extreme continental climate determined the selection of species that possessed a winter grazing reflex, as found in horses, sheep, and goats, while the need for efficient grazing necessitated a herding instinct, also found in horses, sheep, and goats. Apart from the main food product, namely, meat, sheep breeding also yielded leather, hides, pelts, and wool—used for making clothes, carpets/rugs, felt articles, etc. Animals of different species generally grazed separately in the steppe. Particular breeds of cattle were developed, the distinguishing features of which were a high level of adaptation to the sparse fodder resources, limited water supplies, climatic variations, and rhythmic adjustments of nomadic life in the grasslands. In a nutshell, the extensive stockbreeding economy of the Kazakh nomads may be characterized as diversified, quite sophisticated, and geared to the satisfaction of the consumer interests of the mobile population (Masanov 2003, 375–376).

– *Geographic types of nomadization, auxiliary farming, and nomadic handicrafts in CA*

Agricultural activity in the C Asian grasslands—apart from the northern fringes which benefited from more precipitation—was dependent on the scope for establishment of irrigation systems. The latter were created in river valleys or near lakes, which were not very numerous in the steppe. Therefore farming activity was of a subsidiary and secondary nature. Hunting and fishing had become even less important. The main source of water for animal husbandry in the grasslands and other arid regions was groundwater, to which access was normally secured through wells. A consistently spaced network of wells had to be laid out, preferably no more than 10 km apart and to a maximum of 20 km (daily watering of livestock) (Masanov 2003, 376).

Different geographic types of regular nomadization emerged: meridional (north-south), vertical or altitudinal (between mountain pastures and valley encampments), radial (circle-like), and less frequently, latitudinal (east-west). These various strategies allowed the nomads to secure water supplies, enabled the regeneration of pastures, and provided better climatic conditions which spared livestock the harshest conditions. Routes were customarily fixed and tended to be stable; as far as possible, nomads avoided moving to unknown, remote, or other stockbreeders' places. Water was the main priority in the summer, fodder in the remaining seasons. Meridional nomadization was practiced in the Desht-i-Kipchak and in Dzungaria by Kazakhs, Noghays, Kalmyks, and Mongols. The Kyrgyz and a minority of Uzbeks carried out vertical migration in the Tienshan and Pamir ranges. The Kara Kum desert was the prime location of the radial-circular wanderings which were practiced by the Turkmens and in which the availability of water was a permanent concern (Khazanov 1983/1994, 50).

The relatively long distances of Kazakhs' meridional migrations have already been mentioned. Among the Krygyz, the length of vertical nomadization routes varied between a few dozen and 150–200 km; the actual vertical difference in altitude between winter abodes and summer pastures could reach 1000–2000 m. The extent of the Turkmens' radial-circular migrations ranged from 20–30 to 150–200 km (Artykbaev 2007, 208; Khazanov 1983/1994, 52).

Nomadic handicrafts that processed materials from animal husbandry remained pivotal for satisfying tribes' immediate needs as regards clothes and everyday life, horse harnesses, some military equipment/outfits, and yurt accessories. More particularly, domestic craftspeople continued to process animal products (making felt from sheep wool, coarse woolen material from camel hair, leather shoes and saddlery for riders). There were also expert makers of caftans, evidently of the sheepskin-coat type, among the C Asian nomads. Specialists had emerged for the production of metallic objects (steppe smiths, armorers, and jewelers). Wood was the raw material out of which yurt bars, saddles, receptacles, and many other objects were made. Men predominantly occupied themselves with leather, wood, and metal working, while women usually attended to weaving and felt making. The domestic economies of the C Asian nomads continued to be predominantly of a barter type (Shukow et al. 1958/ 1964, Band 4, 656; Baipakov 2003, 387).

Box 4.1: Traditional CA: Stationary Societies and Economies?

The dual political heritage of the C Asian Khanates

As of 1750, basic structural and technological components of the C Asian economy and statehood had not essentially changed over the last two millennia; yet, just one or two centuries later, things would have evolved almost beyond recognition.

Over the centuries there was a tendency toward the sedentarization of nomadic peoples and the Turkization of settled peoples in CA. As Petric points out, the Genghisid state order, underpinned by the nomads' traditional military superiority over sedentary cultures, marked the political supremacy of nomadic (or formerly nomadic) tribes over sedentary populations. In the settled areas, the Muslim religion embodied social order and its perpetuation. Thus, a dichotomy developed between the more recently arrived holders of political power and indigenous representatives of spiritual and legal authority, including muftis, qadis and khodzhas. The reference to Islam constituted the second condition for the khan to be able to legitimize his political power (2002, 4).

Geiss confirms this view: Eventually, most khans based their authority not only on their status as ruler of the nomadic conquering people (in line with Yasa), but also on the conquered indigenous population and notably on its religious dignitaries and officials (who represented Sharia). Genghisid khans therefore usually also referred to Islamic concepts of just and pious rulers, who obeyed the laws of Allah.[48] The political heritage of the C Asian Khanates was thus molded by these two traditions (Geiss 2003, 126–127). A new dual socio-political order had emerged: The "ruling class" was the nomadic (or formerly nomadic) aristocracy; privileges were also enjoyed by the Muslim clergy, hereditary local landowners, and civil servants/bureaucrats. Over time, in the sixteenth and seventeenth centuries, a "Yasa-Sharia synthesis" emerged, in which Yasa covered court ceremonial, succession and authorization issues deriving from the Genghisid dynastic principle, and Sharia pertained to most of the rest of everyday life, at least in settled areas. With the decline of the Genghisid principle in the eighteenth century, references to Yasa became rarer and Sharia gained even more importance (Paul 2012, 318). The established order essentially lasted until the Chinese and Russian conquests of CA in the eighteenth and nineteenth centuries, and partly even survived these breaks.

(Central) Asian mode of production?

For various reasons, there can be little doubt that, compared with Europe's development of technology prior to its Industrial Revolution, the pace of change in CA was rather slow. As Habib puts it, Chardins's judgment about Iranians (in the second half of the seventeenth century) could perhaps apply to all peoples of CA: "They are not desirous of new

(continued)

---

[48] For instance, Shaybani Khan's (1500–1510) formal submission also to Muslim justice and his insistence on his role as a supporter and promoter of Sharia were typical of such Islamic precepts of a just ruler. Later on, despite the increasing identification of Uzbek elites with the sedentary regions they inhabited at the end of the seventeenth century, Genghisid rule remained intrinsic to legitimate leadership (Geiss 2003, 127).

inventions and discoveries,—choosing rather to buy goods from strangers, than to learn the art of making them." Chardin gives the example of watches, which were bought but not made; of printing and of guns (Habib 2003b, 473).[49] This fits in with the Marxist notion of Asiatic mode of production (certainly a controversial and Euro-centric term). In the framework of the Asiatic mode of production, a state can, i.e., emerge owing to two reasons: either due to functional necessity—a "hydraulic state" is established as a means to organize and coordinate large-scale irrigation systems or projects, which are (allegedly) necessary for agriculture under certain conditions; or due to a campaign of conquest—a people assumes power over another people, which is now exploited through tribute payments (Hindess and Hirst 1975/1981, 159). Karl Marx appeared to accept the idea that the fundamental social and economic structures of the Orient (up to his time) were static and immutable. The turbulent "history" of the East –political conflicts and wars, the rise and decline of states or the swift flourishing and vanishing of steppe empires (as also retraced and analyzed here)—only served to conceal the fundamental lack of development or change of economic structures. Only this solid basis of existing productive forces and production relations made possible the repetitive character of political events. Marx thus explained the "secret" of these eternal repetitions on the political level (the "superstructure") by the Orient's characteristic essential continuity on the economic level ("base") (Hindess and Hirst 1975/1981, 162). In this respect one can of course also hold with Bairoch that it was Europe and its unique capitalist take-off, not (Central) Asia that was the exception to the rule of economic development on a global scale from the sixteenth century (Bairoch 1985/1996, 469–470).

4.1.3   Gradual Loss of Prominence and Move to the Sidelines of the Increasingly European-Dominated World Economy (Sixteenth Century–1750)

Publications by the following authors feature among the primary sources of this chapter: Rafis Abazov, M. Annanepesov,

Zhambyl Artykbaev, Karl Baipakov, Yuri Bregel, Audrey Burton, Stephen Dale, E.A. Davidovich, E. Eshraghi, Ronald Findlay, Gavin Hambly, Andre Kamev, Andreas Kappeler, Michael Khodarkovsky, Ralph Kauz, Anatoly Khazanov, Martin Krieger, Ma Dazheng, Peter Golden, James Millward, A. Mukhtarov, R.G. Mukminova, Hans-Heinrich Nolte, Kevin O'Rourke, Juergen Paul, Peter Perdue, Sebastien Peyrouse, Catherine Poujol, Gabriele Rasuly-Paleczek, Morris Rossabi, Peter Roudik, Jean-Paul Roux, Florian Schwarz, I.M. Shukow, Svat Soucek, Alessandro Stanziani.

4.1.3.1 From Uzbek Rule to the "C Asian Khanates" (Bukhara, Khiva, Later: Khoqand)

From Khan Abdullah II to the Astrakhanids: Economic Revival of the C Asian Hub of SR Trade

In the mid-sixteenth century, the Shaybanid state had become subject to internecine struggles and instability. The English merchant and explorer Anthony Jenkinson arrived in Bukhara in 1558, having traveled down the Volga and the steppe route on behalf of the Muscovy Company, an English trading company chartered in 1555 that later was granted a monopoly in Anglo-Russian trade.[50] He was looking for trading opportunities and routes to China and India. But given the insecurity ruling at the time and the indifference of the authorities, his party was forced to retrace its steps.[51] Abdullah Khan (r. 1583–1598), the last ruler of the Shaybanids, was a great warrior and a strict sovereign. Abdullah reconquered a large part of the territories that the Uzbek Khanate had lost since Shaybani Khan's death, including some cities on the Syr Daria that had been under Kazakh rule (Hambly (ed) 1966/1979, 180).

Abdullah also made big efforts to remedy the consequences of unrest and civil wars and improve the

---

[49] There are, of course, counterexamples, like Genghis Khan's and Tamerlane's keen interest in innovations and new technologies of warfare, or the Dzungars' strenuous efforts to set up their own firearms and cannons industry.

[50] According to Stanziani, the Muscovy Company was the first trading company that was given a legal status (incorporated). In this respect other firms that were founded later (e.g., European trading companies of the East Indies or the West Indies) took the Muscovy Company as a model (Stanziani 2012, 106).

[51] In his official report, Jenkinson gave a very sober description of business conditions in the Shaybanid domains of the mid-sixteenth century. In his view, trade was hampered by a multitude of factors: military and political instability, lack of rule of law, and monetary insecurity due to arbitrary acts of the regime. The English businessman particularly criticized unfavorable regulations like the ruler's right of preemption and the high frequency of monetary reforms and confiscations. However, as Schwarz points out, there appears to have been a degree of ambiguity in Jenkinson's stance vis-à-vis business conditions in the Uzbek Khanate, if one consults a letter that he wrote upon his return to Moscow to the agent of the Muscovy Compony in Vologda (Northern Russia). This letter actually recommends trading English cotton cloth, even if it duly warns of risks (Schwarz 2000, 13). Jenkinson was more successful in Persia (see below).

conditions for domestic and foreign trade. In his struggle to strengthen central state power, he counted on the support of the higher Muslim clergy, defeated rivals, acquired their appanages, and installed a reign of merciless cruelty. However, the resulting political stabilization and order in the Khanate of Bukhara helped produce a period of economic recovery (Shukow et al. 1958/1964, Band 4, 652). Khan Abdullah was solicitous of the economy, regularized coinage, ordered the construction of many public buildings, bridges, fords, caravanserais, irrigation canals (aryks), covered water reservoirs (sardabas), and thus made efforts to lift farming productivity and output. Some parts of agriculture, notably irrigated farming, as well as handicrafts, trade, and construction expanded dynamically under Abdullah's rule (Soucek 2000, 150; Mukminova and Mukhtarov 2003, 42). While the oasis of Bukhara expanded and flourished again, the surface of its arable land did not reach the extent it had attained in pre-Mongol times again (Paul 2012, 291).

The construction boom of palaces, mosques, madrasas, and the arrangement of parks and water basins also reflected the fact that Bukhara had become the cultural center of Mavarannahr in the second half of the sixteenth century. Abdullah was a generous financier of architects and painters, a flourishing school of miniature painting developed (Mukminova and Mukhtarov 2003, 42). Abdullah's monetary reform provided for the reduction of the number of mints to issue Shaybanid silver tangas and for a good quality of the latter (Davidovich 2003, 437).

Mukminova and Mukhtarov aptly describe the various facilities for trade—apart from caravanserais—that existed or were set up in this period. Thus, goods were on display in tims (merchants' rows) and taqs (domed markets). One could visit the hat sellers' dome, the fletchers' dome, the goldsmiths' dome, the drapers' row (a covered row of warehouses for the sale of cloth and fabrics), the ironmongers' crossroads, the pomegranate sellers' crossroads, and the mulberry leaf market. Banking institutions also grew in importance in Bukhara in the second half of the sixteenth century, and sarrafs (money changers) and sarraf-khanas (money changers' marts) continued to have key roles in the economy of the city and its social life (Mukminova and Mukhtarov 2003, 42).

The city of Bukhara focused on the manufacture of jewelry, weaponry, alacha (striped cotton and silk fabric), and wines of which it was said that "there were none stronger in all Transoxiana." Bukharan knives and swords, inlaid with jewels, boasted particular renown. Samarkand became known for its artistic stone work, for various types of fabrics, and after centuries was still famous for its high-quality paper (Mukminova and Mukhtarov 2003, 41).

Caravan routes linked the cities of the Shaybanid polity to centers in Afghanistan, India, Persia, Russia, Europe, Turkey, Egypt, and China. Via the towns along the Syr Daria river, there were also connections to nomadic encampments in the Kazakh steppe and to Siberia (Mukminova and Mukhtarov 2003, 43) (see also Maps 4.2 and 4.3). Trade with neighboring regions of the khanate seems to have gathered momentum in the second half of the sixteenth and the first half of the seventeenth century. Commerce was highly valued by the khans as a source of income, i.e., through the taxes paid by local and foreign merchants, and as a result of the ruler's own trading activities. Increased demand for cotton and silk fabrics and leather goods in the sixteenth and seventeenth centuries in Muscovite Russia, as well as other markets, triggered a remarkable upswing of C Asian textile and leather production. The bulk of the khanate's stock-in-trade consisted of cotton goods of every type (Burton 1998a, 445).

Just as in the Timurid era, trade with the major marts of India remained intensive under the Shaybanids, particularly in the late sixteenth century. Documents refer to various types of cloth, woven fabric and other textiles, dyes, indigo, sugar, spices, and special medicinal herbs that were imported from India (Mukminova and Mukhtarov 2003, 43). The Mughal Empire's overland trade with CA and Iran, like that of the Delhi Sultanate, principally passed through Afghanistan (Kabul and Kandahar). India's—like China's –import demand from CA continued to concentrate on high-quality horses which both countries needed for transportation and military reasons but were still not able to produce in sufficient numbers at home.

According to Mukminova and Mukhtarov, Indian merchants were frequent visitors to the C Asian markets. Bukhara as well as Tashkent featured caravanserais for Indians. Moreover, in Bukhara there was an Indian quarter housing merchants, moneylenders, and userers, mostly from Punjab and Rajputana (see also Map 4.2). Merchants from Mavarannahr had their own caravanserais in Isfahan, Astrakhan, Baku, and other cities, probably also in South Asia. In the second half of the sixteenth century (after Muscovy's annexation of the Khanates of Kazan and Astrakhan, see below), commercial agents of the Stroganov brothers contributed to strengthening Shaybanid trade links with Russia; commercial relations with the Ottoman Empire also grew stronger (Mukminova and Mukhtarov 2003, 43). Bukharan-Chinese trade gathered momentum in the sixteenth century, before declining again somewhat toward the end of the century, probably due to intensifying nomadic raids on the SR in Xinjiang.

Overall, this seems to point to a tendency toward regionalization of SR trade—at least partly replacing the previous transcontinental dimensions. Rising maritime trade between Europe, China, and India (since Vasco da Gama's and others' discoveries) may contribute to explaining this phenomenon of declining overland transit trade across Eurasia in favor of—relatively—expanding regional and neighborhood trade, in the framework of overall SR trade. Given that

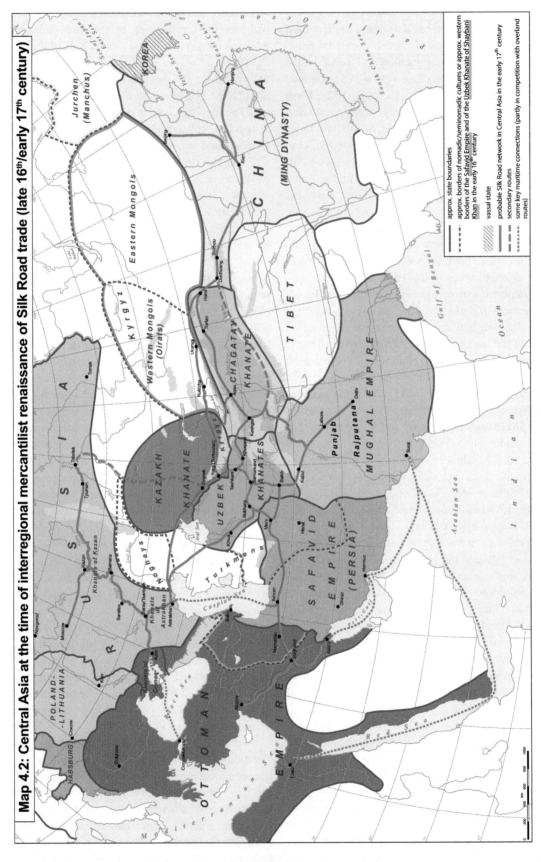

Map 4.2: Central Asia at the time of interregional mercantilist renaissance of Silk Road trade (late 16th/early 17th century)

Legend:
- approx. state boundaries
- approx. borders of nomadic/seminomadic cultures or approx. western borders of the Safavid Empire and of the Uzbek Khanate of Shaybani Khan in the early 16th century
- vassal state
- probable Silk Road network in Central Asia in the early 17th century
- secondary routes
- some key maritime connections (partly in competition with overland routes)

Map 4.2 CA at the time of interregional mercantilist renaissance of SR trade (late sixteenth/early seventeenth century)

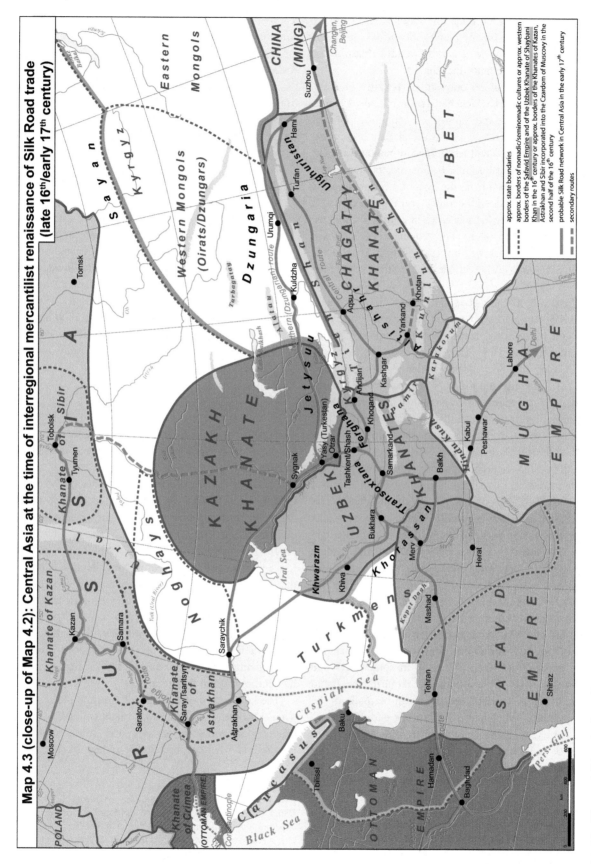

Map 4.3   (Close-up) CA at the time of interregional mercantilist renaissance of SR trade (late sixteenth/early seventeenth century)

seaborne links between the west and east of Eurasia were soon cheaper than overland trade, the latter would keep its cost advantages only for deliveries of goods between directly neighboring or at least nearby regions that did not have a quick, alternative maritime link.

Thus, SR trade remained buoyant or became buoyant again between countries which had (re-)established stable political regimes and adopted pro-trade economic policies (including mercantilist strategies) in the sixteenth century, but this tended to be less and less transcontinental trade. In any case, the peacemeal loss of customs receipts and other taxes and revenues due to the decline of overland transit trade from the early sixteenth century seems to have had a palpable impact. Despite his successes in political stabilization and economic recovery, the Khanate of Bukhara appears to have been less wealthy under Khan Abdullah II than about a century earlier under the Timurids (see also below).

After the death of Khan Abdallah II in 1598, his brother-in-law, Jani Muhammad, whose father had taken refuge with the Shaybanids after the conquest of the Khanate of Astrakhan by the Russians in 1556, took over the reins of Bukhara. Under the rule of the Janids or Astrakhanids (1599–1747)[52], the city and Khanate of Bukhara, as Soucek eloquently put it, crystallized into an almost classical pattern of a Muslim polity of its time, enhancing traditional values, while rejecting the vertiginous adjustments initiated by the Europeans and meanwhile reaching other parts of the world (Soucek 2000, 177). A preoccupation with theology at the cost of other fields of knowledge and science characterized Bukhara, called "Pillar of Islam" (Qutb ul-Islam). The clergy, whose wealth was secured by extended possessions of waqf properties and water rights, wielded major influence on politics. In the eighteenth century, Naqshbandi orders may have been omnipresent. Gradually, intellectual life in the khanate seems to have ground to a halt (Hambly (ed) 1966/1979, 182).

The Astrakhanids continued and deepened the appanage system. Their rule was characterized by a return of internal disputes, of political instability, and by wars against the nomads (Linska et al. 2003, 68). Still, in some ways one can speak of a Janid silver age of the Timurid-Shaybanid cultural tradition. A similar assessment can be made of the economy (see next subchapter). Toward the end of the seventeenth century, the Khanate of Bukhara disintegrated into a number of autonomous or de-facto independent small and local polities which often rivalled with each other.[53]

Political fragmentation favored inward-looking strategies. Yet continued armed tussles and neighborhood rivalries could not but also attract external forces. For instance, during the sixteenth to the eighteenth centuries, Uzbeks, Kazakhs, Persians, Mongols, and Kyrgyz all clashed for possession of Tashkent and its surroundings (Roudik 2007, 61).

Eventually, three independent jurisdictions emerged (there was little difference in their political systems) (see also Maps 4.2 and 4.4):

(a) The—remaining—<u>Khanate (or later Emirate) of Bukhara</u>, which ruled large parts of present day Central and Southern Uzbekistan as well as Tajikistan, Eastern Turkmenistan, and Northern Afghanistan

(b) The <u>Khanate of Khiva (the former Khanate of Urgench or Khwarazm)</u>, which comprised the lower reaches of the Amu Daria or most of present day Northwestern Uzbekistan and Northern Turkmenistan

(c) The <u>Khanate of Khoqand</u>, which occupied territories on both sides of the upper reaches of the Syr Daria, notably the Ferghana Basin, i.e., in present day Northeastern Uzbekistan, Southern Kyrgyzstan, and Northern Tajikistan

Khanate of Bukhara, from Mid-18th Century: Emirate of Bukhara—Gradual Decline of a Classic Muslim Polity

Under the greatest ruler of the Astrakhanid dynasty, Imam Quli Khan (1608–1640), the Khanate of Bukhara experienced another period of prosperity, in which the erection of buildings like the Shir Dar Madrasa of Samarkand (1619–1636) and the embellishment of the city bore witness to the still generous promotion of architecture and to the fact that the superb craftsmanship of the past was not yet lost. Under this khan, the engaged support of art and of Muslim erudition conserved a reflection of the gone Timurid Emirates (Hambly (ed) 1966/1979, 187; Krieger 2003, 273). Medicine still lived up to expectations. In the seventeenth century, a medical library, two medical schools, and a hospital existed in Bukhara.

The cultivation of cotton took a prime place in farming. The khanate's vegetables, melons, and horticultural products, particularly grapes and musk melons, were famous. The leather and textile industries, the production

---

[52] The new dynasty was called "Janid" because of its founder or "Astrakhanid" because it originated in Astrakhan on the Volga.

[53] For instance, the mountainous principality of Badakhshan (Bactria, Northern Afghanistan) began to assume independent ways and Mir Yar

Beg (the local prince) withheld the payment of taxes from the Badakhshan ruby mines. This led the Janid authorities to mount an expedition against him in 1691–1692. Mir Yar Beg was compelled to pay 2 years' taxes, but managed to retain control of his region. Moreover, he built the city of Faizabad, henceforth regarded as the capital of Badakhshan (Pirumshoev and Dani 2003, 232).

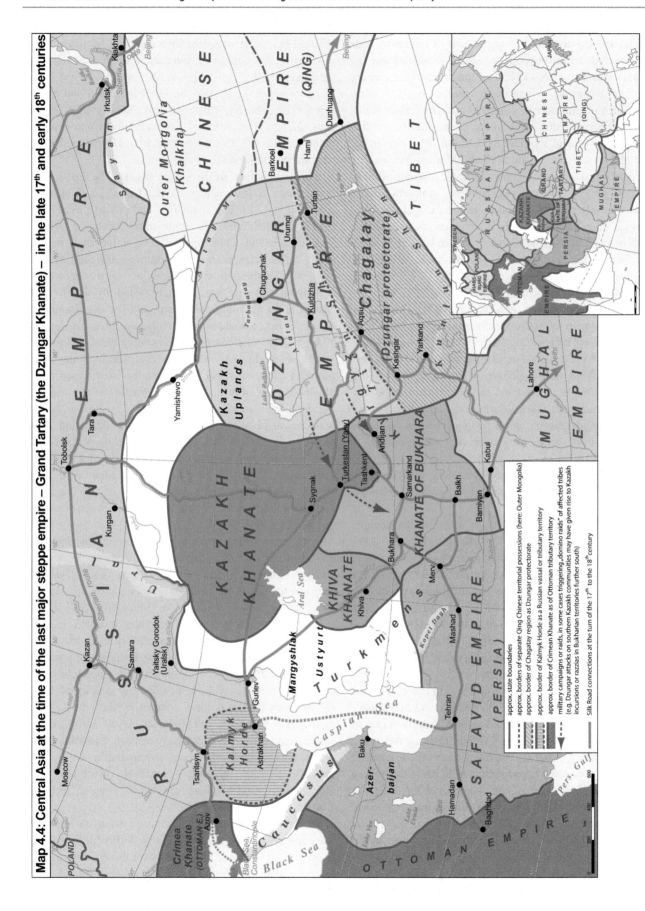

Map 4.4 CA at the time of the last major steppe empire—Grand Tartary (the Dzungar Khanate)—in the late seventeenth and early eighteenth centuries

of light, heat-permeable clothing, of bronze and copper vessels, and the making of carpets and of ceramic goods were developed. Writing paper produced in Samarkand and Bukhara still in the second half of the seventeenth century was regarded as very high-quality paper and was much appreciated in a number of European countries. Meanwhile, Bukhara's urban trades seem to have specialized even further. In the works of the poet Said Nesefi, who died in the early eighteenth century, more than 200 urban professions are mentioned, to cite some examples, confectioners, weavers, potters, tailors, soap boilers, armorers, dyers, musicians, tellers of fairy tales, bakers, carpet weavers, jewelers, water carriers, saddlers, stonemasons, and furriers (Shukow et al. 1958/1964, Band 4, 263–264). And Bukhara continued to be an important hub of trade, which was conducted with Afghanistan, India, Iran, Turkey, Russia, and, to a lesser degree, with China (Roudik 2007, 58).

During the seventeenth century and under the Janids, the share of copper in the (official) silver tanga (inherited from the Shaybanids) increased in three stages. As Davidovich explains, in the first stage, tangas were still minted from very pure silver. These were high-purity Shaybanid tangas. Then mixed hoards of Shaybanid and early Janid coins appeared. The tangas that were minted during this second stage were less pure, but their silver content remained no less than 60%. During the third stage, the silver content descended to 22.5–35% (Davidovich 2003, 441).

From around the mid-seventeenth century, the Khanate of Bukhara became engulfed in increasing internal rivalry and internecine warfare between regional princes as well as subject to rising attacks from the exterior, particularly nomadic incursions and wars with Iran (Krieger 2003, 273). The renewed flare-up of military hostilities between Safavids and Uzbeks in the seventeenth century reduced parts of Khorassan to ruins. Because of the key position of Merv on an important section of the SR (linking the Near East and Iran with Transoxiana and China), Bukhara, Khiva, and Persia often clashed for control of this oasis (Breghel 2003, 68). Intermittent raids by the Khivans from the 1660s to the 1680s contributed to the decline of the Janids. Disruptions of economic life seemed to have no end. Displaced by Dzungar attacks, the Kazakhs in turn pounced on the Khanate of Bukhara, which suffered 7 years of razzias (see Map 4.4). In 1681, the Kazakhs ravaged the entire Zeravshan valley. After a temporary recovery, a series of new Kazakh incursions happened in the 1720s (Chuvin et al. 2008, 65; von Gumppenberg and Steinbach 2004, 149).

In these unfortunate conditions, the khanate entered a period of prolonged decline. Tax pressure was high. State revenues fell, and the government tried to compensate for the losses by repeated debasements of the currency. However, the latter negatively affected already weakened trade and eventually only aggravated fiscal difficulties (Breghel

2003, 56). Furthermore, during Abaidullah-Khan's rule (1702–1711), currency debasement reportedly triggered an uprising in the capital of Bukhara. During this period of weakness in the early eighteenth century, Uzbek tribes from the steppe conquered the Ferghana Basin and created a new ruling Shaybanid dynasty there. This dynasty, the Min (just like the Yadigarids of Urgench almost two centuries before) split off from the common Uzbek polity and established the Khanate of Khoqand.

Finally, another major shock struck: The invasion by Nadir Shah of Iran, who subjugated Bukhara, Khiva, and Khoqand in 1740. The campaigns and punitive expeditions of Nadir Shah and his commanders strongly affected Transoxiana and Khorezm and accelerated their decline. Many cities were destroyed anew and agricultural oases ravaged. Inhabitants either fled or were deported to Khorassan (at that time entirely ruled by Iran). Nadir Shah's reign was only ephemeral, and Persia's domination of the Uzbek Khanates soon collapsed after his death in 1747. Still his rule contributed to ending the dynasty of the Astrakhanids. In 1747, Muhammad Rahim from the Uzbek Manghit tribe, who had been installed in Bukhara as the plenipotentiary of Nadir Shah, took the throne after murdering the Genghisid Khan (Roudik 2007, 57). He was the first non-Genghisid ruler in Bukhara for over three and a half centuries (since Tamerlane) and therefore took the title of emir—instead of khan—as ruler. Muhammad Rahim thus established the Manghit dynasty of the Emirate of Bukhara (which ruled until the Russian conquest of 1868 and then continued to hold some formal power until its dissolution by the Soviets in 1920).

Apart from increasing religious traditionalism, one of the reasons for or one of the aspects of the backwardness of the Bukhara Emirate in the mid-eighteenth century was the semiliteracy or illiteracy of most officials of the Manghit state, senior and less senior alike (Mukhtarov 2003, 62). A tragically familiar sad state that had installed itself in Mavarannahr in the seventeenth century (see above) and that endured throughout most of the Manghit era was stubborn political instability combined with ceaseless armed hostilities. Both town dwellers and rural inhabitants began to flee from the areas most infested by the unrest. While earthquake damage reportedly also played a role, during some decades of the eighteenth century Samarkand was almost entirely depopulated and abandoned, and in Bukhara only two city quarters remained inhabited (von Gumppenberg and Steinbach 2004, 149; Breghel 2003, 58; Chuvin et al. 2008, 61).

Areas of cultivation shrank sharply; extensive territories were reoccupied by nomads and transformed into pastures. Soon the emirate could no longer cover its cereal needs from its own production (Shukow et al. 1958/1966, Band 5, 264). No wonder that Bukhara could not resist pressure from a newly emerging state in the south, Afghanistan. This state was established on the ruins of Nadir Shah's empire in the Hindu Kush by Ahmad Shah Durrani (from 1747, see below). Soon after the creation of Afghanistan, the Emirate of Bukhara lost its possessions south of the upper Amu Daria, including the fertile areas surrounding Balkh. The Amu Daria border that emerged in the mid-eighteenth century essentially still exists today.

Khanate of Khiva: A Major SR Trading Post Affected by Increasing Instability

During Janid rule in Bukhara, a branch of Shaybanids—the Yadigarids—continued to hold the reins of power in Khwarazm (Khiva), despite repeated attempts by the khans of Bukhara to dethrone them. In 1592 Khiva became the capital of the state, which came to be called Khanate of Khiva. The late sixteenth and early seventeenth century saw a temporary stabilization of the oasis' political situation as well as of its economy (Map 4.3).

Besides Samarkand, Khiva became one of the most important slave markets of CA (Linska et al. 2003, 69). Mostly Turkmen nomadic slave hunters carried out forays into Southern Russia, Transoxiana, and Persia and provided sizable supplies to the regional slave markets, on which lucrative deals were struck. On the other hand, farming was less "competitive" in Khiva than in Bukhara. The growing of cereals, melons, mulberry tree cultures, and horticultural activities remained important around the lower reaches of the Amu Daria. In the seventeenth century, Bukharan businessmen purchased and traded with silk from the Khanate of Khiva. The eighteenth century reportedly saw the cultivation of tobacco in Khiva.

With the abovementioned and some other exceptions, Khivans tended to deal mainly in goods produced elsewhere, as Burton explains.[54] This goes for cotton, a favorite item of trade in various forms, including Bukharan-produced raw cotton, zandanichi (a sturdy and valuable cotton fabric woven in various colors), and karbas (finer cotton used for clothes or even maps). It is also valid for ready-made caftans and indigo that came from Bukhara and that Khivans took to Muscovy. Moreover, Khivans did their best to prevent others from trading directly with Russia. Merchants passing through without authorization were likely to be seriously delayed, taxed, or even thrown into jail in Khwarazm, while their goods would be confiscated (Burton 2003, 410–13).

Khivan farmers (predominantly Uzbeks) were taxed a tenth of their harvest. The tax (ushur) was most often paid in grain. The Turkmen nomads under the khanate's control paid one fortieth of their livestock (zyaket) as levy. The zakat, or cauldron tax (thousands of sheep to be provided annually for the "khan's cauldron"), remained an obligation imposed on the pastoral communities (subjects) of the khan. Some Turkmen tribes also raised warriors (nuker)[55] as bodyguards for the khan. Notwithstanding stepped-up efforts to integrate the Turkmens into the political and economic life of the state, nomadic unrest continued and insurgencies against the ruler and his representatives happened repeatedly.

On assuming the throne, Abul Ghazi Khan (1643–1663) found Khiva culturally very backward and assessed that none of his subjects was able to produce a historical work on his own race and dynasty. The khan therefore resolved to undertake the task himself (Annanepesov 2003a, 67). This points to the likelihood of illiteracy among the Khorezmian bureaucracy and inhabitants—recalling a comparable regrettable phenomenon in Bukhara. The minting of coins in the Khiva Khanate (that had been launched in the early seventeenth century) witnessed a worsening in the quality of silver coins under Abul Ghazi Khan (Davidovich 2003, 448).

In the seventeenth century, Khwarazm went through a period of internal strife and political instability. As could be expected, the khanate's military campaigns to expand its territory collided with its closest neighbors, the Turkmen tribes and the Bukhara Khanate. The raids that the khan of Khiva carried out in the 1680s against Bukhara as well as his defensive campaigns against the latter's attacks exhausted Khwarazm's financial and military resources and damaged trade and the economy. The additional taxation and other restrictions connected to the militarization of the state caused heavy suffering for the population (Annanepesov 2003a, 66; Abazov 2008, Map 28).

In 1717–1718 Khan Shir Ghazi (1715–1728) withstood what may have been the first official onslaught of European colonialism into the heart of CA. Peter the Great (1682–1725) sent to Khiva an expedition of 5000 troops with cannons under the command of Prince Alexander Bekovich-Cherkassky, a Muslim by birth and a military expert (Annanepesov 2003a, 68). The goal of the expedition was to investigate stories of Khorezmian gold and fabulous wealth and rumors of a waterway to India along the former Oxus riverbed. Peter also considered that the possession of Khiva, located midway between Russia and India, could provide a staging point in the region, a strategic location to control trade caravans plying CA (Roudik 2007, 59). But apparently despite an initial military success, the expedition was soon defeated. Many soldiers were enslaved and all

---

[54] This underlines the overall comparative weakness of the economic structure of the geographically rather isolated oasis of Khwarazm.

[55] "Nuker" of course relates to the Mongol "nöker" (free man and warrior under Genghis Khan).

officers as well as the commander himself massacred (Khivan disaster).[56]

Despite this victory over the Russian expedition, Khiva's economic decline continued in the first half of the eighteenth century, which was reflected in the decreasing quality of the coinage (Davidovich 2003, 448). Like Bukhara, Khiva in 1740 had to swallow another painful blow—its conquest, occupation, and plundering by the armies of Nadir Shah. He is reported to have found and liberated up to 20,000 Khorassanian slaves in the khanate. But this apparently did not stop Khorezm from continuing to function as a key slave market in the region. Nadir installed a subordinate khan in Khiva and levied a special lump sum tax on the population called mal-i aman (protection fee) (Annanepesov 2003a, 68; Paul 2012, 297).

While soon after Nadir's death in 1747, Persian pretensions to supremacy over Khiva collapsed; the khanate in the 1750s became the scene of attacks or clashes between different ethnic groups and of great turmoil: Incursions by nomadic Oirats or Dzungars that had already started in the seventeenth century intensified. Pushed south probably by Kazakhs and Dzungars, the Karakalpaks in the eighteenth century spread from the lower reaches of the Syr Daria to the lower reaches of the Amu Daria, i.e., migrated into the territory of the Khanate of Khiva in crisis. In their new environment, the Karakalpaks were able to guard a degree of autonomy.

Given all this unrest and instability in a pivotal section of caravan routes, SR trade suffered: The eighteenth century brought major losses. CA definitely forfeited its preponderant role in Eurasian trade (Linska et al. 2003, 68).

Khanate of Khoqand (Ferghana Basin, from 1710)

After establishing the Kingdom of Ferghana (also called "Dayuan" by its Han dynasty overlords in the second–first centuries BCE, see above), it was not before the eighteenth century CE that the Ferghana Basin again rose to form a distinct political unit of its own. The region accommodated a mix of peoples: descendants of Indo-Iranian Sogdians,

Sakas, and Turkic people, including Uzbeks and Kyrgyz, Mongols, and nomadic and settled inhabitants. In the seventeenth century, khodzhas or khwajas held sway in Ferghana, like they also did in Xinjiang and Shash (Tashkent) (Soucek 2000, 188). Many khwajas possessed extensive landed estates and had accumulated considerable wealth. Toward the end of the seventeenth century, some of these charismatic leaders, Sufi sheikhs and dervishes, even set up their own theocratically ruled domains (municipalities) in Ferghana.

Yet, in 1710 the khwajas of Ferghana had to yield to Shahrukh Biy[57], a chieftain of the Min, an Uzbek nomadic tribe that had moved into Ferghana and adjacent areas from the north (the Kipchak steppe). The Min founded their own Uzbek Khanate in the Ferghana Basin and established their capital in the small settlement of Khoqand, which was rebuilt into a fortress (1740) and which quickly expanded. Khoqand is situated in the western part of the valley with a direct connection to Tashkent (over the Kuraminsky mountains) and to Samarkand (via the Syr Daria valley). Khoqand soon became an important economic and cultural center with a caravanserai, four schools, and 20,000 families residing in town. Khoqand may have been chosen instead of a traditional capital like Andijan partly because it was farther from the inner Tienshan mountains, and thus less exposed to incursions by the Kyrgyz or the Oirats (Soucek 2000, 189; Roudik 2007, 60).

Given its strategic location on a SR branch directly linking East and West Turkestan, and, a fortiori East Asia with Europe, this new principality was deeply involved in regional as well as international trade and traffic (Bogdan 1993, 147; Khan 2003, 333). In a long-standing and fine tradition, horses continued to be exported to China.[58] Farming, particularly cotton cultivation, was rather highly developed in Ferghana. Gold was extracted from the Tienshan mountains surrounding the basin (Burton 1998b, 41).

Although the rule of the Min was subsequently shaken by the Dzungars, Khoqand gained strength at least in relative terms in the course of the eighteenth century, compared to its Uzbek rivals, Bukhara and Khiva; the latter had been much more ravaged by Nadir Shah's invasion and rule in the 1740s. As a result, a flood of refugees and resettlers from Khiva and Bukhara poured into Ferghana (Shukow et al. 1958/1966, Band 5, 273).

---

[56] This result may have partly been due to a military ruse of the khan, who thus overcame the significant advantage the Russians had possessed, thanks to their firearms (cannons). According to a few surviving members of Bekovich-Cherkassky's contingent, they advanced to within 120 km of Khiva, when the khan attacked them with a 24,000 strong army. After 3 days of bloody fighting, the Khivans were routed. Seeing that the enemy was very numerous, Bekovich-Cherkassky concluded that diplomacy would have a better chance of success. The khan welcomed the commander warmly, pretended to surrender to his proposed terms, and persuaded him to divide up the Russian army to dwell in separate towns in order to facilitate provisioning and the supply of forage. The Khivans then attacked the five towns one by one, slaughtering most Russians, selling the others as slaves, and executed all Russian officers including the prince (Allworth 1994, 9).

---

[57] "Biy" is the local form of the Pan-Turkic title "beg."

[58] This, of course, recalls the deliveries of "heavenly horses" by Dayuan to the Middle Kingdom almost two millennia before, which accompanied the official "launching" of the SR (see above).

4.1.3.2 The Turkmens: Incessant Nongovernmental Struggle for Resources

After Muscovy had seized the Khanates of Kazan and Astrakhan in the 1550s, and had thus obtained direct access to CA (see below), the commercial importance of the Turkmens of the peninsula of Mangyshlak grew considerably, as Annanepesov remarks. Russian merchants and envoys visited the area more frequently, exchanging goods and looking for routes to the Orient. The Turkmens were experienced caravan guides (caravanbashis) (2003b, 132).

According to Schwarz, ecological reasons appear to have set off the migration and the partial sedentarization of Turkmen tribes which started in the sixteenth century and lasted until the eighteenth. Continual dryness and increasing salinity of pastures in the north of their nomadization areas, e.g., of the Mangyshlak and Ustyurt territories, the drying up of the Uzboy, as well as pressure from migrating Kazakh and Kalmyk nomads likely pushed the Turkmen tribes in southeastern direction toward the border zones of the oases and the areas banking the big rivers. In the second half of the sixteenth century, the Turkmens increased their presence at the outskirts of the oases of present-day Southern Turkmenistan. In the seventeenth century, they spread from their already existing habitats in and near Khorezm to the middle reaches of the Amu Daria, the Tedzhen, and the Murgab. Within the oasis of Merv, a permanent presence of Turkmens can be attested in the eighteenth century (Schwarz 2004, 189). As could be expected, confrontations and conflicts of the newly arriving tribes with other tribes and oasis populations for the possession and sharing of water, irrigated lands, and other resources marked the seventeenth and eighteenth centuries.

During all of this time, as Peyrouse emphasizes, the Turkmen tribes continued to be divided and to lack a state of their own. The Turkmens became subject to different temporary rules or tutelages, but these alliances remained in flux and sometimes even coincidental. As already referred to above, a number of tribes specialized in capturing foreigners, Shiite pilgrims visiting Mashhad or Russian merchants arriving from the north were enslaved and sold on the markets of Khiva and Bukhara. No doubt, in this respect the Uzbek authorities cooperated in a frictionless manner with the Turkmen slave dealers. The Turkmens also regularly organized razzias in large urban centers and served as military guards for local rulers and potentates. The Turkmens contributed to undo alliances, to stir up political about-faces, and to prepare the ground for overthrows (Peyrouse 2007, 36).

The Turkmens remained torn apart between juxtaposed or competing claims to power over them on the part of their neighbors. Tribes situated in the south, including some of the Yomut, found themselves under Persian jurisdiction, although that allegiance was frequently called into question

by revolts.[59] Other tribes like the Ersary were ruled by the Khanate of Bukhara, which controlled the middle reaches of the Amu Daria. The Yomuts of the north were attached to the Khanate of Khiva. And in 1745, Turkmen tribes that had remained in the region of Mangyshlak demanded Russian protection. In any case, Turkmen relations with neighboring powers remained ambiguous, conflict prone, and dependent on conditions of access to water, pastures, urban products, and suchlike (Peyrouse 2007, 36–37).

4.1.3.3 The Chagatay Khanate: SR Trade Flourishes in the Sixteenth and Comes Under Pressure in the Seventeenth Century

The greater unity in the Tarim Basin that had been achieved under the reign of Said Khan (r. 1514–1533) brought a period of cultural and economic revival for the region. Yet almost simultaneously, the Chagatay Khanate lost its hold on Moghulistan: Zhetysu and Southern Dzungaria were increasingly overrun by Kazakhs and Kalmyks (Dzungars). Thus only Altishahr (or Kashgaria around Kashgar, Yarkand, and Aqsu) and Uighuristan (around Turfan) continued to be in Chagatayid possession (Soucek 2000, 165) (see Maps 4.2 and 4.3).

As Ma Dazheng describes, the crops cultivated in the oases of the Tarim Basin remained numerous, including wheat, paddy (rice), millet, sorghum, peas, beans, cotton, and hemp. Watermelons and muskmelons were also grown. Apart from seedless green grapes, there were pomegranates, apples, papayas, Chinese pears, cherries, apricots, walnuts, plums, and peaches. The type of plow used by peasants of the Tarim Basin had an iron share with a wooden shaft and was pulled by rope by two oxen. Farmers of the region already extensively employed implements made of iron and iron-steel alloy. There was much rotation cropping including fallow periods in order to retain the soil's fertility (Ma 2003, 189).

Crafts were fairly numerous, comprising textiles (including cotton, silk, and wool), leatherwork, metalwork, toolmaking, and carpentry. Among textile goods, silk floss and woven woolen products were of the finest quality. The area around Khotan was particularly abundant in silkworms, and the silk cloth woven was most valuable, which points to the continuity of ancient regional traditions.[60] Moreover, jade

---

[59] Given that the Turkmens of the Kopet Dagh area and of Khorassan connected Persia and the Uzbek Khanates economically—through slave and other trades and regional markets—the Safavid border to Sunni CA may in fact not have been as impermeable as sometimes thought.

[60] Silk has been produced in Xinjiang since antiquity (more precisely, since the fifth century, when the technology of silk production escaped the Middle Kingdom and arrived in the Kingdom of Khotan—see above).

remained (after as much as three millennia!) one of the Tarim Basin's leading exports (see above). But mining jade was not easy. Merchants purchased the mining rights from the khan at comparatively high prices. The miners hired went in groups to remote areas in the Karakorum or the Kun Lun, where the deposits were situated. The miners often took a year's dry food provisions. Furthermore, iron, copper, and gold were extracted and forged. Tools like axes, files, drills, saws, sickles, shovels, hoes, other farming implements, and weapons such as knives, arrows, and shields were made. Distilling spirits, preferably from wheat and millet, was also a traditional craft. Fruit wines were produced from the abundant local peaches, mulberries, and grapes (Ma 2003, 190–94).

Drawing on impeccable traditions going back a millennium, the Uighurs were renowned traders. Ma Dazheng further points out that most towns of Kashgaria and Uighuristan had a market, or bazaar, where "everything one needs in terms of clothes and food is traded." Yarkand was the prime trading center. Apart from the local markets, the Uighur trading caravans also maintained close links with other parts of CA and with the Middle Kingdom. Caravans frequently brought goods to Khoqand and Andijan for sale, and merchants from Afghanistan, Kashmir, and India came to Yarkand, Kashgar, and Aqsu to "sell items like pearls, skins etc." For commerce, the Uighurs had their own copper-based currency called pul (Persian for copper coin) (Ma 2003, 194–95).

During most of the sixteenth century, Ming China, supported by increasing maritime trade and exchanges with the West, also prospered, which had positive (trade creation) and negative (trade diversion) effects for Eurasian overland trade. A new Chinese urban mercantile society developed. Inflows of silver contributed to increasing monetization of trade and tax payments (silver currency). Production and trade in staples (e.g., rice, salt, cereals, cloth) grew dynamically. Yet, following an ancient Chinese tradition, the richest businessmen owed their wealth primarily to their involvement in a state-supervised economy and played an important part as suppliers to the civil service and the army (Gernet 1972/1985, vol. 2, 47, 173; Der Große Ploetz 2008, 35.A., 1208).

Trade across East Turkestan soon became subject to political interference again. Ahmad Razi, writing in 1593–1594, had gathered the information that whereas previously trade between Khotan and China had been so brisk that people could travel from one to the other in two weeks without needing to join a caravan, now owing to interference by the "armed tribes of the Kalmuks (Oirats)," the route was virtually closed (Ma 2003, 186). Ming documentation of "tribute trade" provides a good deal of evidence that large caravans plied various routes across Xinjiang between Mavarannahr and Northern China until the late

sixteenth century. Thereafter, missions were less frequently reported (Millward 2007, 77). Between 1600 and 1630, only two missions were sent to China from Kashgaria, and missions from Turfan, so frequent in the sixteenth century, had also become much fewer in number (Findlay and O'Rourke 2007, 295). At Khotan itself, a barter system gained the upper hand, with payments effected in cotton, silk, and wheat. Given the above observations, the declining frequency of trade caravans was obviously due to nomadic raids and upheavals, which affected China too (see below), but may also have been influenced by rising seaborne competition. [61]

Since the end of the sixteenth century, the west and the south of the Tarim Basin (or mostly Altishahr) were not only economically but in part also politically dominated by khodzhas of the prevailing religious order of the Naqshbandis. Given their social prestige, their capacities of persuasion and their accumulated economic wealth (as big landowners, merchants), these religious people (e.g., sheikhs, dervishes) often rose to politically powerful positions (Kauz 2006, 130). Whether this political "takeover" by the khwajas was somehow linked to the rising instability and the setbacks in SR trade and business is a question worth posing. The rise of religious power in Chagatayid society may have been accelerated by the weakness of traditional political leaders faced with increasing insecurity and economic decline.

In the late sixteenth century, not only East Turkestan but also Ming China had again come under nomadic pressure. Incursions of the Eastern Mongols (under Altan Khan) occurred, yet China was better protected than about a century ago, thanks to its repaired Great Wall. Still, a combination of factors destabilized the country and weakened its participation in international trade. In the 1590s and early 1600s, some Mongol tribes under Chinese suzerainty rebelled and seceded, ethnic minorities in Southern China revolted and the Japanese attempted an invasion of Korea, at that time a Chinese tributary state (Gernet 1972/1985, vol. 2, 174). While the Ming dynasty was able to put down the rebellions and fend off the attacks, subsequent tax increases by the authorities, rising corruption, natural disasters, and epidemics seem to have triggered famines and violent peasant uprisings which contributed to the ultimate downfall of the Ming in the 1640s (Findlay and O'Rourke 2007, 296; Der Große Ploetz 2008, 35.A., 1208). Exploiting the chaos, the Manchus (a semi-nomadic people ruling Manchuria and

---

[61] Due to reasons of proximity, this last factor was of course not valid for trade between China and Xinjiang, but it may well have had some validity for transit trade via Xinjiang between China and regions further afield (like Transoxiana, Khwarazm, Persia, and others), as the latter could have had recourse to alternate maritime routes.

neighboring regions, descendants of the Jurchen, a Tunguz people, see above) invaded China and conquered almost the entire former Ming Empire by the mid-seventeenth century.

Notwithstanding the momentous changes to its east, the Chagatay Khanate seems to have once again experienced a recovery under Abdullah Khan (1636–1667). As described by Ma Dazheng, Abdullah resisted the encroachment of the expanding power of the Oirats (Kalmyks) of Dzungaria, beating back threatening Oirat inroads into the Khotan and Aqsu regions (2003, 184). Apparently, trade with China under its new Manchu dynasty, the Qing, quickly resumed. Matteo Ricci observed that a community of C Asian Muslims had established itself in Suzhou (Gansu) by the mid-seventeenth century to broker trade between Kashgaria and the new Qing (Manchu) rulers (Millward 2007, 76). Francois Bernier confirmed in 1664 that Yarkand was the capital of what outsiders at that time called the Kashgar Khanate and pointed out that the region's chief exports were musk, jade, crystal, fine wool, and slave girls and boys. An annual caravan was dispatched to the Middle Kingdom (Ma 2003, 184). Eventually, however, Chagatayid resistance to Oirat pressure drew to a close. In 1680, the nomadic ruler Galdan led 100,000 Dzungar cavalry into the Tarim Basin, which was entirely occupied and incorporated into the Dzungar Empire (Ma 2003, 184).

4.1.3.4 Muscovy and Its "Collection" of Territories of the Former Golden Horde

Conquest of the Khanates of Kazan, Astrakhan, and Sibir (1552–1595): A Major Step Toward CA

The progress achieved by European nations in the fifteenth century in the construction of fortresses and the development of artillery was also appropriated by Muscovite Russia but was only insufficiently made use of by the Tatar Khanates. In order to improve his state's military capabilities, Czar Ivan IV "the Terrible" (r. 1547–1584) invited foreign, including English, military technicians to help modernize the artillery. Army reforms included the establishment of special troops, the "streltsy," about 12,000 soldiers equipped with firearms (Scheck 1977, 87). Russia's military superiority over the Tatars of the Volga Khanates in the sixteenth century was not only based on the possession of better firearms and artillery. It also had to do with division and continuous rivalry among the Tatars. Moreover, many Tatars had given up nomadism, which led to less regular training and less military preparedness of the male population (a preparedness that could have counterbalanced the lack of firearms) (Hambly (ed) 1966/1979, 138). Finally, the Volga-Kama Basin, where Kazan is located, is not part of the steppe belt, where nomads would have had clear advantages at that time.

Muscovy's conquest of Kazan in 1552 occurred with the use of streltsy and of 150 cannons and the carrying out of numerous blastings. The Tatars defended themselves with what they had: a few cannons, some rifles, bows and arrows, and projectiles of wood and stone (Scheck 1977, 91). Given the scale of the Russian assault, the defense was not very effective. Although largely situated in the steppe belt, the Khanate of Astrakhan was smaller and weaker than that of Kazan and dependent on the Noghay Horde, a major supplier, trading partner, and ally of Muscovite Russia. Astrakhan was conquered in 1556.

Henceforth the entire Volga from its source in the Valday Hills to its mouth on the shore of the Caspian Sea was in Russian hands. In 1560, Perm was founded and in 1574, Ufa. Both settlements lie in the borderlands of conquered territories, on the foothills of the Ural mountains, and on routes to Western Siberia. In 1586 Samara was established, in 1589 Tsaritsyn (near the ruins of Sarai-Berke), and in 1590 Saratov. With the conquest of Kazan and Astrakhan and thus the acquisition of the Volga route, which had borne major significance for traditional Eurasian steppe empires (starting with the Khazars), the Russian ruler—as Kappeler emphasizes—assumed the heritage of the empire of the Golden Horde (2006, 139).

For the Golden Horde, the Volga route had been the central north-south axis of its principally east-west-oriented state. Russia's southeastern expansion did not only provide access to the Caspian and thus to the markets of Iran and Azerbaijan but also created the possibility to block the steppe route from Crimea to CA (and further to India and China), which can be seen in Maps 4.2 and 4.3. Russia for the first time took up direct diplomatic and commercial relations with the Uzbek Khanates. Trade relations were also established with the Kazakhs (Kappeler 2001, 30, 2006, 141).

Thus, from the middle of the sixteenth century, the process of Muscovite Russia's "gathering of Russian lands" was complemented by the "collection of lands of the Golden Horde," as Kappeler expresses it; both endeavors were important in a global historic sense. For more than two centuries, the czardom's conquests would remain focused on more or less vast forest areas spanning Eurasia, while the open grasslands (with the exception of the just conquered Khanate of Astrakhan, the Don, and Northern Caucasus regions) continued to be controlled by the mounted nomads, who were militarily at least equally powerful here (Kappeler 2006, 140).

The Taibugids, that in the mid-sixteenth century were in control of the Khanate of Sibir, the eastern neighbor of the Kazan Khanate, congratulated Ivan the Terrible on his conquest of Kazan and soon paid limited tribute to Russia. In 1563, however, the Shaybanid prince Kuchum seized the throne of Sibir and, following the Russo-Crimean war (1571), discontinued tribute payments to Moscow and conducted raids on territory around the settlement of Perm. This may have been partly in response to Russian settlers crossing the Ural mountains and moving into Western Siberia from around 1570. The Stroganovs, a wealthy Russian family of merchants, industrialists, and landowners, probably of Tatar origin, had been granted large tax-exempt estates near Perm by Ivan the Terrible. With the help of private paramilitaries ("druzhinas"), these entrepreneurs seized lands from the local indigenous population, colonized them with incoming Russian peasants, and developed farming, hunting, fishing, saltworks, and ore mining at the border between Europe and Asia (Donnert et al. 1981, 365).

In 1579, the Stroganovs hired the Don Cossack ataman (headman) Yermak Timofeevich to protect their possessions from Khan Kuchum's forays. With Ivan the Terrible's implicit permission, Yermak launched a Cossack expedition, largely financed by the Stroganovs, against the Khanate of Sibir. Commercial interests in subjugating territories and cheaply acquiring valuable furs certainly weighed heavily. After Yermak's victory over Kuchum in 1582 and another one and a half decades of war, the taiga of Western Siberia was conquered and opened up for Russian settlement. As Perdue points out, this form of "contract colonialism" appears to have much in common with Western European colonial practices: European powers often delegated the initial conquest, by default or explicitly, to missionaries, adventurers, and trading companies.[62] Under Boris Godunov (regent 1584–1598, czar 1598–1605, also probably of Tatar descent), the Russians set up their first major fortresses (ostrogy) at Tyumen (1586), Tobolsk (1587), and Tara (1594). These places later gained importance as key staging posts for Russian trade with CA. Abundant furs started to be exacted from indigenous tribes of the region (Perdue 2005, 86–88, 92).

Box 4.2: Radical Technological Change and the "Gunpowder Revolution": Eurasian Steppe Nomadism and Empires on the Defensive Against Sedentary Civilizations

The heterogeneous boundaries of traditional lifestyles and their pattern of movement

In contrast to the nomads of the Eurasian steppe belt (i.e., of Northern CA), the nomads of the oasis belt (i.e., of Southern CA) were traditionally in closer, more permanent, and more day-to-day contact with the settled populations and states of the region (Khazanov 1983/1994, 184). The borders of sedentary civilization in the north and west toward the grasslands

became clearly delimited, e.g., in Russia these borders were first called Cossack barrier lines and then simply "linia" and guarded by fortresses at certain intervals; they may have to some degree resembled the US "frontier" of the late eighteenth and the first half of the nineteenth centuries. Areas of nomadic and settled economic activities in the southern oases were much more intertwined, producing complicated or fuzzy borders. There were "fingers" or "outposts" of settled activity along irrigation canals at the edge of oases, surrounded by extensive areas of nomadization and "pockets" of nomadic activity that could stretch from the limits to near the core of sedentary areas. Obviously, while at least into the eighteenth century there were hardly any permanent settlements in the Eurasian grasslands, the interdependence and division of labor between nomads, and the sedentary world were greater in the south.

After the Mongol invasion of CA, a number of Mongol and Turkic nomadic groups moved to the oasis belt. At first this led to a disruptive decline in farming and a partial transformation of areas of agriculture into territories of nomadic pastoralism. However, gradually the majority of the new arrivals in this ecological zone began to move from pure nomadism to semisedentary pastoralism and even to fully settled activities (Khazanov 1983/1994, 201). The exception was the region of Zhetysu, which had become entirely nomadic in the aftermath of the Mongol conquest, and overwhelmingly remained so for the time being. As shown earlier, similar processes occurred on a number of occasions in CA in the pre- and post-Mongol periods, probably already starting with the Scythian incursions and migrations into the Middle East (eighth to sixth century BCE), or with the movement of the Yuezhi to Bactria and Northern India (second to first century BCE); the last to follow this path were the Uzbeks accompanying and following Shaybani Khan's conquest of the Timurid Emirates in the early sixteenth century.

Essentially, after descending south in the wake of the Mongol conquest, in the following centuries the border between nomadic and sedentary lifestyles slowly moved north again. And in the eighteenth century it was nomadic conquerors, namely, the Dzungars or Oirats, who encouraged agriculture and industry north of the Tienshan (forced resettlement of Taranchi (see below) in the Ili region and in parts of Dzungaria).

(continued)

Box 4.2 (continued)

Confirmation of the unperturbed power of mounted archery in the fifteenth century: The abandonment of Zheng-He's naval expeditions

The key factor that decisively strengthened the position of sedentary versus nomadic cultures and economies in CA was the mastery and use of firearms/artillery, which started to transform the region in the sixteenth century. The "gunpowder revolution" allowed settled people to defeat the steppe horsemen in an open battle for the first time. For over two millennia before that, nomadic mounted archery had generally been superior (Hambly (ed) 1966/1979, 26; Barfield 2011, 172). Apart from numerous battles, successful raids, razzias, and tributary treaties, this supremacy can be vividly demonstrated by the indirect effect nomadic military pressure had on one of mankind's greatest ventures of discovery. As outlined earlier, under the Ming dynasty the admiral Zheng He led a number of large maritime expeditions far from China's coasts. The first expedition by the largest navy the world had seen until then was launched in 1405 and is reported to have consisted of 62 ships, including oceangoing junks—Nine Masters, some of which boasted a length of up to 160 m, a breadth of 60 m, and a crew of 500 men. In altogether seven expeditions, which lasted until 1431, Zheng He plied the South China Sea and the Indian Ocean and reached Southeast Asia, India, the Persian Gulf, Arabia, the Red Sea, and the East African coast. The admiral thus demonstrated China's claim to naval supremacy (Höllmann 2004, 25; Darwin 2008, 44; Szczepanski 2017: Zheng He's Treasure Ships).

However, naval might could not protect the Middle Kingdom from the nomadic military threat. Apart from the high cost of the expeditions, the persistent—and at that time rising—terrestrial threat probably was the most important reason for the eventual decision to abandon the Ming's maritime undertakings (Fässler 2007, 55; Perdue 2011, 405). It seems that the Ming dynasty's resources were simply not sufficient to strengthen northwestern defenses and complete the Great Wall and at the same time to continue its enormous naval expeditions.[63]

The tables turn: "Gunpowder revolution" in CA, technological determinism, and settled societies' advantages

Yet the balance of military power was soon shifting. According to Golden, in the mid-1600s, there may still have been parity between the nomad's composite bow and the matchlock musket; a century later, the flintlock rifle became the superior weapon (2011, 105). Thus one can invoke the technological factor and settled societies' greater capacity to generate innovations, including in the technology of warfare, once economic competition had intensified and institutions had evolved. In this way, the spread of gunpowder weaponry and artillery rendered obsolete the mounted cavalry warrior (Ponting 2001, 151)[64].

Moreover, the construction of firearms was much easier with factories, infrastructures, and economies of urban centers and sedentary societies at one's disposal and proved to be rather impractical for nomadic peoples. Whereas the best war horses were bred in the pastoral lands of the steppe dwellers, the best guns and cannons were manufactured in the workshops of settled societies (Adle et al. 2003a, 28). Gunpowder and firearms may have also contributed to a common pattern of political consolidation and centralization of sedentary monarchies across Eurasia, including the "Gunpowder Empires" (Turkey, Iran, and India, see below), but also Muscovite Russia and Ming China, as well as rising European powers (Millward 2013, 85–86).

As soon as global capitalist industrial development had started to gather momentum under the impact of European sedentary powers' breakthroughs and discoveries, there was no doubt that settled cultures were gaining the upper hand. Generally speaking, those sedentary states in or near CA that were not solely dependent on overland trade but that also had access to maritime trade or that were nearer to Western Europe also tended to be at an advantage in the trial of strength with the nomads.

(continued)

---

[63] The danger of nomadic conquests and campaigns that China (and other countries) faced in the early 1400s was real. The Ming dynasty was lucky that Tamerlane died (in 1405) immediately before his planned invasion of the Middle Kingdom. In this sense, Zheng He's expeditions may not have been well timed indeed.

[64] As Grousset appropriately put it: « L'antique supériorité tactique des nomades, due à l'extraordinaire mobilité, à l'ubiquité de l'archer à cheval, supériorité qui durait depuis le commencement des temps historiques, ceda devant la supériorité artificielle que l'usage de l'artillerie conféra d'un seul coup aux civilisations sédentaires » (1965/2008, 554). ("The ancient tactical superiority of the nomads, due to extraordinary mobility, to the ubiquity of the mounted archer, this superiority had persisted since the beginning of historical times. It yielded to the artificial superiority that the use of artillery had suddenly conferred on sedentary civilizations.")

Box 4.2 (continued)

Some nomads rejected the new technology as not suited to their traditional modes of warfare. Other nomads were willing to use it, but largely lacked the industrial capacity to produce the new weapons or the money to buy them, or were impeded by sedentary states' bans on selling weapons. The Dzungars of Grand Tartary (seventeenth to eighteenth century) did not lack funds to buy weapons, but were subject to Chinese and Russian bans on selling firearms, which proved relatively effective and could only be circumvented at the margins. The Dzungar Khanate made determined and strenuous efforts to establish an armaments industry and modernize artillery, but the settled areas available to set up the factories, workshops, and infrastructure may have simply been too small or too few to develop a productive capacity that could have matched China's (or Russia's).

The nomads were ill prepared to meet the challenges of rapid technological change and in the best case could try to copy new developments coming from neighboring civilizations as swiftly as possible. Overall, the nomads fell behind in the arms race (Golden 2011, 105, 116). As a consequence, beginning in the sixteenth century, the settled powers gradually began to encroach upon and conquer CA; nomads' domains began to shrink. As far as nomadic power also depended on overland (transit) trade revenues and as far as these latter were dwindling, the decline of SR trade and of CA's prosperity contributed to eroding nomadic power (including its capability to procure firearms).[65]

From encroachment to conquest and colonization of CA by technologically superior sedentary powers

The conquest of the Khanates of Kazan in 1552 and Astrakhan in 1556 by the czardom of Muscovy constituted a first major defeat of states founded by nomads/Tatars at the hands of sedentary foreign powers. The incorporation of the territories of the Volga Khanates into Russia constituted a first major encroachment on the western periphery of nomadic CA and put an end to C Asians' traditional control of the steppe route to the Black Sea. The Russians were probably successful because they combined nomadic military technology (mobility through cavalry) with

well-trained troops equipped with firearms (streltsy). Then Russia slowly and steadily advanced its own borders and areas of peasant settlement from Eastern Europe and Siberia into the C Asian grasslands, particularly the fringes of the Kazakh steppes (shrinkage of nomadic territory in the north).

Former nomadic conquerors themselves partly contributed to sedentarization. As mentioned above, this goes for the gradual process of the Shaybanid Uzbeks becoming settled in the oases of Western CA as well as for the forced resettlement of people under Oirat oversight in areas north of the Tienshan in Eastern CA (shrinkage of nomadic territory in the center). In a major battle in 1696, Qing China conquered (outer) Mongolia. The oases of Barkoel, Hami, and Turfan followed in the late seventeenth and early eighteenth centuries. The enlargement and modernization of C Asian oases under Manchu control ensued (shrinkage of nomadic territory in the east). The tragic and spectacular collapse of the Dzungar Empire (1755–1757), struck by disease as much as by Chinese artillery, sealed the fate of imperial nomadism in CA. One by one and definitely, the remaining independent nomadic hordes and polities moved from the formal status of political equals to that of colonial subjects of the victorious sedentary civilizations. Thus, large sedentary neighbors of CA, particularly China and Russia, took possession of lands and habitats previously controlled by khanates and made territories available to their growing peasant and urban populations (Barfield, 172; Abazov 2008, Map 29).

Kazan, Astrakhan, and Western Siberia Under Russian Rule

– *Oppression and pragmatic change in the former Tatar Khanates*

The conquest of Kazan was accompanied by massacres and followed by policies aimed at swiftly establishing control of the former khanate and its Muslim population. The first step of the "de-Tatarization" of the middle reaches of the Volga was the expulsion of the Tatars from important towns, particularly from Kazan, and the expropriation and reallocation of the fertile land and fishing grounds to the Russian aristocracy, primarily the service nobility, to Orthodox monasteries, and to free peasants. The Tatars were thus deprived of their economic and cultural center and pushed off into the more marginal countryside. A "flood" of Russian peasants covered the former khanate. The Muslim clergy's rights were restricted, the waqfs (inalienable property of religious institutions according to Islamic law) were seized, and mosques and madrasas torn down or closed. The Tatar

---

[65] But in this latter respect, of course, there is no difference between nomadic and sedentary C Asian states straddling the weakening Eurasian trade routes.

nobility was stripped of some of its privileges unless it converted to Christianity (Hambly (ed) 1966/1979, 197–198).

As regards taxation, Moscow continued the Tatar practice of collecting the Yasak, an in-kind levy; collection was made from the subjugated as well as the Russian population. The voevoda (the Muscovite governor) of Astrakhan, for instance, demanded Yasak "in grain from those who farm and in fish from those who fish" (Khodarkovsky 2002, 61). Peasants sometimes also fulfilled their tax liability in money. Nomadic pastoralists paid Yasak in terms of livestock and Siberian tribes in most cases had the obligation to deliver furs (Nolte 1991, 42).

The Tatars responded with desperate uprisings which lasted until the early seventeenth century and were all bloodily crushed. However, already starting a couple of years after the conquest, Moscow carried out a pragmatic change in its treatment of the Tatars. Forced proselytizations were practically banned for more than a century and the Muscovite authorities officially acknowledged and respected Islam. The state cooperated with loyal non-Russian elites, and the status quo was largely guaranteed. The property, farming land, and hunting grounds of the Muslim Tatar aristocracy and of Tatar peasants that had survived as well as their traditional rights were confirmed. The landowning nobility was co-opted into the traditional high aristocracy of the czardom. Tatar mounted battalions now served in the Russian armies instead of the khanates' forces (Kappeler 2001, 30–33).

Notwithstanding the more pragmatic treatment of the Tatars, many of the latter joined peasants and poor people mostly in the south of the country who rebelled against increasing feudal oppression and exploitation, which had been exacerbated by the czar's wars with Poland and Sweden in the mid-seventeenth century. Under the leadership of the Don Cossack chief, brigand and adventurer Stepan (Stenka) Razin (1630–1671), an insurgent Cossack territory established its headquarters in Astrakhan in 1670 and captured other towns of Southern Russia, particularly in the Don and Volga areas (e.g., Tsaritsyn, Saratov, and Samara). After killing all those in Astrakhan that were opposed to the insurgent leader, the rich bazaars of the town were looted and the population was divided up in groups of thousands, hundreds, and tens, supervised by their own officers.[66] Popular assemblies (veches) declared Stepan Razin their ruler (gosudar). Eventually,

the indisciplined and badly organized insurgents (most of whom consisted of poor Cossacks and fugitive peasants) succumbed to the blows of the regular army, and Razin was captured, transferred to Moscow, and executed on the Red Square. The insurrection was put down and massive reprisals were carried out.

In the course of the seventeenth century, as Hambly points out, the Tatar people experienced a partial transformation of its social structure. Having been expelled from the cities, aristocrats and tradesmen moved to small towns and rural areas and started to form a new merchant class, which slowly advanced eastward toward Russia's Siberian and C Asian frontiers and founded flourishing business communities in many places. Thus, save the peasantry, the Tatars partly became a diaspora people, dominated by a merchant bourgeoisie (Hambly (ed) 1966/1979, 199).

Peter the Great's (1682–1725) Westernization policies for Russia modified the government's relationship with Islam, indigenous minorities, the Tatars, and the nomads of the grasslands. The military balance of power with the steppe was changing fundamentally; Russia became a European and Asian great power, and the government adopted Western ideologies of progress and, as Kappeler puts it, of a "civilizational mission" of Europe in the world. A degree of estrangement and a feeling of cultural superiority vis-à-vis Russia's steppe neighbors and the country's Islamic subjects set in. In the early eighteenth century, the Muslim Tatars were no longer accepted as members of Russia's imperial nobility with equal rights. In 1731 a new campaign of forced conversion of the Tatars was launched (Kappeler 2006, 140; Hambly (ed) 1966, 198).

– *Gradual subjugation and integration of the Bashkirs (mid-seventeenth to mid-eighteenth centuries)*

In the second half of the seventeenth and the beginning of the eighteenth century, the Russian state gradually started to collect Yasak and other obligations from the Bashkirs (still living in the Southern Ural range and its western foothills between Kama and Yaik) in a more systematic way. At the same time, increasing numbers of Tatars, Turkic, and Finno-Ugric people as well as Russians migrated to the Central and Southern Urals and their foothills and settled down as farmers on Bashkir pastures, so that the Bashkirs in the eighteenth century became a minority on their ancestral territories of nomadization and settlement. This—together with rising fiscal demands of the state—constituted the background for Bashkir armed uprisings in 1662–1664, 1676–1682, and 1705–1710, which were often aimed at Russian settlers (Kappeler 2001, 43–44).

Later, new restrictions gave rise to new Bashkir revolts: The fortified barrier line against nomadic raids,

---

[66] This kind of behavior bears some—limited—resemblance to former Mongol procedures in taking possession of new territories (massacres, pillages, subdivision of the population according to the decimal system).

which was erected in 1735 to 1740 between Samara (on the Volga) and the newly founded Orenburg (on the Yaik river/Ural) cut the Bashkirs off from the steppe. The semi-nomadic people reacted with a number of well-organized uprisings which it took a 5-year-long war to quell. Further pacification and integration followed proven, if modified, patterns: The Bashkir elite that had not fallen victim to the wars with Moscow was acknowledged in its possessions and privileges—although it was barred from membership in the imperial high aristocracy; Bashkir mounted warriors were incorporated into the czardom's cavalry. The lower strata of the population had to continue to pay the Yasak, which however was differentiated between the Bashkirs who were saddled with lighter dues than migrants of other ethnic groups including Russian peasants. Although property rights were guaranteed in principle, the conflict surrounding the Bashkir land and pastures was not resolved (Kappeler 2001, 44).

- *Focus on Astrakhan and its development as Russia's mercantile trading hub at the doorstep of CA (mid-sixteenth–eighteenth centuries)*

In Dale's terms, the annexation of the Astrakhan Khanate gave the expanding Muscovite state a vital "Window on the East." For more than 150 years, the port of Astrakhan constituted one of the country's two most important links with the outside world; the other was Arkhangelsk. From Astrakhan Russian merchants gained influence on the C Asian caravan trade. The authorities sought to augment the state's customs revenue and to acquire silver for its currency. They tried to achieve these goals by inviting Indians and other Asian businessmen to settle and trade in the city (Dale 1994, 78).

In fact, Astrakhan soon became a center of international trade and boasted Indian, Armenian, and Bukharan, in addition to Tatar and Russian, quarters. Probably in the second half of the sixteenth century, it was trade with the Muslim states in the south that connected Muscovite Russia to world markets. Merchants from the C Asian Khanates, the Khanate of Crimea, the Ottoman, Safavid, and Mughal Empires brought goods highly appreciated in Moscow—lavish silk brocades, cottons, spices, horses, herbs, and musk—and in return purchased different kinds of furs, leather, walrus tusks, falcons, armor, wooden and metal utensils, and apparel. Russian merchants travelled to Persia, the Black Sea coast, and Turkey (Nolte 1991, 41; Stanziani 2012, 101; Khodarkovsky 2002, 27).

After meeting limited success in its ventures in Bukhara, the Muscovy Company (which soon had a monopoly for English-Russian trade), led by Anthony Jenkinson, was more successful in establishing profitable commerce in spices and silk between Persia, Muscovite

Russia, and England.[67] In exchange, the English sold wool and firearms to the Shah. The silk trade prospered, to the point where commercial deliveries of raw silk between Persia and Russia oscillated between 20,000 and 100,000 kg per year at the turn of the sixteenth to the seventeenth century, and increased in the following decades. But Persian silk was also delivered north in finished form, and both types of silk were partly consumed in Russia, partly reexported to England and other Western European countries.

The Armenians were well placed to conduct this trade since members of their community were active in Russia as well as in Iran. The Armenians were granted a privileged status as silk traders by Shah Abbas (1587–1629, see below) which was also recognized by the czar. Toward the middle of the eighteenth century, about a third of the raw silk produced in the Safavid Empire was shipped to the Russian Empire—to the detriment, particularly, of traditional Mediterranean trade links. In 1667, Armenian merchants also obtained the exclusive right of taking Persian cotton (both as raw material and fabric) to Russia and reexporting it from there to Europe (Stanziani 2012, 106; Findlay and O'Rourke 2007, 304; Burton 2003, 412).

After the intermezzo of the Razin insurrection (1670–1671, see above) as well as another local uprising in 1705–1706, Astrakhan continued as a busy trading center in the first half of the eighteenth century. For the early decades of this period, a Russian official, Ivan Kirilov, described brisk commerce, whose structure, though, had not changed substantially from the past: Foreign and Russian woolens, furs, leather, and linens exchanged hands to be taken to Persia, and Persian silks, brocades, and carpets went to Russia. While selling Persian and C Asian goods, Indians purchased Russian hides, furs, honey, and walrus tusks for export to Persia and other countries. "Bukharans" or merchants from the Khanate of Bukhara sold a variety of materials, sheepskins, and dried fruit from Mavarannahr in the 1750s. Meanwhile, the Kalmyks brought their horses, lambskins, camel hair, and special felt boots to Astrakhan. Kirilov noted that most of the merchants in the city at the mouth of the Volga were not Russians, but Indians,

---

[67] The Volga Route and Arkhangelsk seemed more promising than the southern maritime route as a link between England and Iran because the Portuguese had in the early sixteenth century established bases in the Persian Gulf (Bahrein 1507, Hormuz 1508) and in the Arabian Sea (Muscat 1508), which made seaborne access via the Indian Ocean to Persia more difficult for competitors. Moreover, the Levant and Egypt were ruled by the Ottoman Empire since the latter's incorporation of the Mamluk Sultanate of Cairo (1517), and in the mid-sixteenth century the Sublime Porte had also taken control of Mesopotamia, the Red Sea, the Bab-el Mandeb, and Aden, which probably rendered passage via the Near East and the Mediterranean more expensive.

Armenians, Bukharans, Khivans, and Persians (Khodarkovsky 2002, 28; Burton 2003, 412–415).

The czar's administration in Astrakhan apparently did make an effort to enforce merchants' contractual rights (in contrast to what could be observed in some other parts of CA). Merchants undoubtedly welcomed attempts to uphold the rule of law, but they were less pleased to have to accept strongly centralized monitoring and control of their own commercial affairs. According to Dale, mercantilism was the hallmark of Muscovite Russia's economic policy (1994, 13).

– *Economic apex and decline of the Noghay Horde (mid-sixteenth to early seventeenth century)*

The conquest of the Volga Khanates had made the Noghay Horde a direct neighbor of the Muscovite state; the Noghays' economic dependence on Moscow increased. Horse trade, already quite active, gained further momentum: 1551 to 1564 was the time of the most active trade between the Noghays and Muscovy; the nomads brought for sale to Russia up to 40,000 horses a year. In return, they received furs, wool, and apparently—despite the illicit character of this trade—arms. In 1557—a year after the conquest of Astrakhan—Prince Ismail accepted the czar's overlordship. Not unlike the Tatars, Noghay warriors were incorporated into the Russian armed forces and a number of noblemen entered the czar's service, among them the founding fathers of the Yusupov dynasty of princes. The Yusupovs received extensive estates with thousands of peasants in the upper Volga region (Kappeler 2001, 45). However, Moscow's relationship with the Noghays remained unstable. As mentioned earlier, the Noghay Horde had been substantially weakened and pushed west in the 1520s by the Kazakhs. Not really benefiting from Russian protection, the Noghay Horde probably received the finishing stroke from incoming Kalmyks who took possession of grasslands north of the Caspian Sea more than a century later.

– *Heightened feudal oppression in Russia's interior contributes to colonization of C Asian and Siberian borderlands*

The Russian colonization of Siberia and parts of CA was certainly due to the "pull factor" of the attraction of new vast lands and opportunities of enrichment, but it also owed to the "push factor" of increasing oppression and exploitation at home. As mentioned earlier, social tensions were manifest in the seventeenth century and they further increased in the eighteenth. In signs of the spread of market relationships, many of Russia's agricultural manors and estates became increasingly involved in trade and competition (Stanziani 2015, 96–97, 120–121). In order to keep abreast of competitive pressures, improvements in the productivity and/or cost reductions

of farming were necessary or at least helpful. These adjustments were often brought about by the ratcheting up of work duties and the conversion of further categories of peasants into surfs (Donnert et al. 1981, 365–366). These changes were supported by a new law, the Sobornoe ulozhenie, which came into effect in 1649, worsened the legal position of peasants and formally fixed their attachment to the farms they worked on (krepostnoe pravo). As new estate owners or pomeschiks, the nobility played an important role in this system. The greater the state's demands became on its servant class, the more the latter had recourse to its serfs and the more feudal landownership was expanded (Karger (ed) 1978, 72).

The peasants reacted to the worsening of their socio-economic situation and the curtailment of their rights with two classic responses, namely, contradiction (revolt) and migration (flight), both of whom were available in Russia—in contrast to Western Europe. A number of big insurgencies shook Russia throughout the seventeenth and eighteenth centuries, e.g., the Bolotnikov uprising (1606–1607) in Central Russia; the Razin insurrection (1670–1671) in the south of the country and the middle and lower reaches of the Volga (see above); the Bulavin insurgency (1707–1708) in the lower Don, Donets, and Dnepr regions; and the Pugachev rebellion (1773–1775) in the middle and lower reaches of the Volga and the Southern Ural areas (see below).

The farmers' second response eventually contributed to a major expansion of the territory of Russian settlement: Peasants fled into more difficult to control frontier regions of the Muscovite state and there took up agricultural activities anew or possibly joined Cossack freebooters. What is more, peasants were even encouraged to emigrate to the newly conquered farming lands, notwithstanding their employers' protests (Karger (ed) 1978, 72; Stanziani 2012, 135). From the end of the sixteenth century, more and more flights and migrations into the eastern peripheral regions of the country, bordering on CA, happened. Indeed, a colonization movement by fugitive farmers emerged which occupied terrain beyond the Ural mountains and engaged in agriculture, handicrafts, and trade and also started to influence the culture of indigenous people.

– *Russia's conquest of Siberia—largely in pursuit of furs ("soft gold")*

Once the Khanate of Sibir had been conquered, as Perdue observed, the process of Russia's second Asiatic expansion differed strongly from the first. No major nomadic khan blocked the way. The Russians faced only minimal resistance as they moved east, so they could easily control huge expanses with scattered forts and small garrisons up to the mid-seventeenth century.

Merchant entrepreneurs (promyshlenniki), following the example of the Stroganovs, and Cossack frontiersmen, probably modeling themselves on Yermak—in other words, semi-independent representatives of the state under the incomplete supervision of governors (voevody) and even less oversight of the ruler in Moscow—pushed the limits of Russian power forward, took recourse to violence and conducted negotiations with local tribes (Perdue 2005, 84, 86–88, 92). The Cossacks' traditional mastery of river navigation came in useful for the conquest of Siberia. This is because their eastward advance largely followed rivers and tributaries, and in less than half a century the Cossacks had covered over 6000 km and reached the Pacific (Kappeler 2013, 24).

The northern forest peoples of Siberia, e.g., the Yakuts and the Tunguz, were pastoral nomads[68], but the big difference to the steppe tribes was that they did not primarily breed or use horses, but reindeer—for obvious ecological reasons. Regarding the forest peoples, the main goal of the Russian conquerors was the exaction of wealth, not security; as with the subjugation of the Khanate of Sibir, furs or "soft gold" were the primary focus of interest (Millward and Perdue 2004, 49).

The exhaustion of nearer territories drove the Russians to pursue sable, otter, mink, and other fur-bearing animals farther eastward. With its furs—particularly sable—Siberia offered luxury that was much sought after on the world market (Uray-Köhalmi 2002, 143). Regional ecology decisively influenced Sibirian expansion, as the exhaustion of furs in one area of the north "pushed" the traders and Cossacks farther east. Like slash-and-burn agriculturalists or Canadian and American trappers, bison hunters and pioneers, Russian tribute collectors drained a region of its surpluses and then moved on to exhaust new regions. Step by step the fortresses marched eastward—to Narym (on the Ob) in 1596, Yeniseisk in 1619, Yakutsk in 1632, and Okhotsk (on the Pacific coast) in 1649 (Perdue 2005, 84–85, 87). In the course of these expeditions, around 1645, the Russians reached the Amur river and the borders of China.

The Cossacks reached the Pacific at about the same time that the Manchus (the Qing) expanded from Manchuria to the Pacific (or confirmed their hold on the Pacific coast of Sikhote Alin), into Mongolia, and took over China. The Amur river, along its whole length, for the time being became the border between the two empires. As furs provided generous revenues[69], the Russians by the mid-seventeenth century were strongly interested in developing the profitable fur trade, and Beijing offered by far the largest market for them.

The treaties of Nerchinsk (1689) and Kiakhta (1727) resulted from the rapprochement between the two powers, regularized trade relations, and fixed their mutual border: Russia in 1689 ceded the Amur province (the territory north of the Amur and south of the Stanovoy range) to China, the border was demarcated and populations on both sides were taken under control. The Treaty of Kiakhta established the town of Kiakhta, on the Selenga river (Southern Siberia, at the Mongolian border, which at that time was the boundary between the Qing state and Russia), as the border trading center of the two empires. According to Perdue, the Russians knew very little in detail about the Chinese Empire, but saw it as a major profitable trading opportunity from the beginning (2005: China marches west..., 164).[70]

Thus the Siberian Road (Moscow-Tobolsk-Irkutsk-Kiakhta-Beijing) was opened as a direct commercial connection between the two countries; after the maritime route, the Siberian route corresponded to a second, if less important, circumvention of CA on the way from Europe to the Orient. For most of the second half of the seventeenth century and the first half of the eighteenth century, disturbances and warfare in CA were rampant and often involved Grand Tartary (see below). The Siberian route therefore also functioned as an alternate route for Russia and China to contact and trade with each other, when this, as often, was not possible or was difficult through Dzungar transit. In the early eighteenth century, fur had clearly become the dominant merchandise in Sino-Russian trade, exchanged in Beijing mainly for silk, other textiles, and tea (Gunder Frank 1992, 39; Perdue 2005, 164–165).

Over time, Russian demand for tea increased; samovars were installed in many homes. Tea was mostly cultivated in Southern China and processed into bricks appropriate for a lengthy journey on camelback to Russia (brick tea). The Siberian Road also came to be called Tea Road (Lary 2012, 80–81; Odyssey Maps 2007/2011).

Russia and Its Early Expansion into CA

Since the first Cossack barrier lines (entanglements) of the sixteenth century, Russian settlement was successively pushed forward into the Pontic and Kazakh steppes. As

---

[68] This is valid for all North Asian forest peoples, except for Paleo-Siberians like the Chukchy and the Koriaks, who lived in the extreme northeast of the continent and were hunter-gatherers (Haywood 2011, 116–130).

[69] In 1644, 10% of the czar's revenues came from the taxation or sale of furs (Reinhard 2008, 184).

[70] This may remind of the Western (e.g., British) view of China about a century later or the US view of Japan in the mid-nineteenth century. In both cases one of the elements that probably attracted outside powers to the big East Asian nations was the opportunity for immense trading profits.

Kappeler notes, many Cossacks who lived in the areas of the Yaik (Ural), the lower Volga, Don, and Dnepr stemmed from Russian or Ukrainian peasants who had fled the intensification of serfdom, the tightening constraints, and the aggravation of tax pressure by moving to the relative "freedom" of frontier territories (2001, 51).

Upon conquest of Western Siberia (i.e., from about 1590), the Muscovite Russian state itself began to encourage peasant settlement. The main areas of initial organized settlement were between the lower Tobol and the lower Ishim rivers (between Tyumen and Tara) and in the upper Ob region (around Tomsk, founded in 1605). As Bregel explains, peasants gradually began to occupy the grasslands that served as northern summer pastures for the Kazakhs, who began to raid these settlements. To protect them, the Russian government began to build forts manned by military garrisons (no longer using mobile semi-independent Cossack colonies as the sole counterweight to the nomads). The first line (Russian "linia") of such forts extended from the Middle Tobol, near Kurgan (founded in 1670), through the Ishim grasslands to the lower Irtysh, south of Tara. Henceforth, the lines of these forts formed the empire's frontier with the Kazakh steppe (Breghel 2003, 56). In the seventeenth century, Russia acquired remaining territories not yet under its rule west and north of the Yaik river (foundation of Yaitsky Gorodok (Uralsk) 1620, of Guriev 1645). Fortresses were erected as cores of future cities.

The modernization of Russia in the middle of the seventeenth century and particularly under Peter the Great (1682–1725) entailed stepped-up exploitation of the peasant serfs. In the mercantilist tradition of economic reforms, the state viewed direct support measures for the country's economic development as one of its prime tasks (Hildermeier 2013, 620). Given that there was not enough free labor for the dozens of new metallurgical and metal processing plants established by the authorities in the Moscow-Tula and Ural regions, peasants were forcefully drafted to work in these government factories, many of which were later privatized (Nolte 1991, 60; Dale 1994, 84).

In any case, mining and manufacturing in the Urals took an important upswing. The state also acted as a key provider of infrastructure (e.g., construction of new roads and canals to facilitate national and international trade). Thus, while the peasants continued to be severely suppressed (in European Russia, but not in Siberia and in frontier areas to CA, see above), merchants were de-facto subsidized, and where entrepreneur-industrialists (like the Stroganovs) had not yet appeared, the state acted as a (temporary) surrogate businessman. While domestic tariffs were abolished, the authorities gradually succeeded in more strictly controlling and taxing activities at the empire's borders (Donnert et al., 366, 368) (see also Map 4.4).

The shifting of the military balance of power in the Eurasian steppe thanks to Russia's modernized army and to

the insufficient adaptation of the nomadic empires and states to the extremely effective weapons of firearms and artillery bore consequences, if only gradually. While Peter the Great vigorously promoted international trade and was looking for a trans-Eurasian direct link between his country and the Mughal Empire[71], which would have brought about an upswing or a recovery of SR trade across CA, he failed in this undertaking, i.e., for military reasons. As mentioned above, the Bekovich-Cherkassky expedition to Khiva (1717–1718) ended in a disaster. Almost at the same time (1716), another Russian expedition to CA was routed, namely, that of Ivan Bukholts (Buchholz) to Lake Yamysh (actually a cluster of salt lakes) east of the middle reaches of the Irtysh river, near later Pavlodar.[72] Like for the Khivan undertaking, one of the unsuccessfully aimed-for goals of the expedition up the Irtysh was to find gold, in the latter case suspected somewhere near Yarkand (Perdue 2005, 306; Paul 2012, 362–363; Ledonne 2008, 23) (see also Map 4.4).

While Russia in the first half of the eighteenth century may not yet have been prepared for or militarily capable of conquering the Desht-i-Kipchak or CA outright, the country was successful in incorporating steppe regions in Southern Siberia and at the border of present-day Northern Kazakhstan. Thus were founded (originally as frontier fortresses which later became towns featuring administrative, trade, and communication functions): Omsk (1716), Semipalatinsk (1718), Ust-Kamenogorsk (1720), Barnaul (1734), Orsk (1735), Orenburg (1743), Troitsk (1745), and Petropavlovsk (1752). Accordingly, between 1715 and 1757 several lines of fortifications were built, forming a continuous fortified boundary that was to protect Russian settlers both from Kazakh assaults and from the possible Dzungar threat and that served as a base for further advances into the steppe (Breghel 2003, 58).

These lengthy guarded "linii" altogether stretched about 2000 km through the Eurasian grasslands; from the 1740s until the 1820s, the "linii" constituted a largely stable frontier between sedentary Russia and nomadic CA: From the northern shore of the Caspian Sea, the border ran alongside the western and northern banks of the Ural (Yaik) river (except for Orenburg, where it crossed the river and made a small loop south) and then cut across the Tobol and Ishim

---

[71] Perhaps Peter was striving to duplicate on an Indian route the success Ivan the Terrible had achieved in commissioning booming and enduring trade with Persia, in which Muscovite Russia had also served as a turntable of trade with Western Europe (in the second half of the sixteenth century) (see also Bouvard 1985, 35).

[72] Although they were equipped with firearms, the participants of this expedition succumbed to Dzungar attacks and a winter-long siege that the far more numerous armies of these steppe nomads had laid to the fortress the expedition had built beforehand. After many participants had died of hunger and the Dzungars had taken a number of prisoners, what remained of the expeditionary corps was allowed to leave the site on a boat down the Irytsh to Russia.

rivers to reach the eastern banks of the Irtysh near Omsk and passed along that side of the river all the way to the Altai mountains (Breghel 2003, 63).

The authorities aimed at and were partly successful in establishing an important international commercial center in Orenburg, which offered trade facilities and low interest rates and charges for C Asian merchants. As Burton describes in detail, in 1744 the governor of Orenburg province, Neplyuev, had a huge building constructed which served as a covered central market and caravanserai; this building included a mosque, a church, lodgings, customs offices, hundreds of shops and stores, and dozens of warehouses; this market was the place where in the mid-eighteenth century Bukharan businessmen, including Jews, imported and sold Transoxianan and Indian cotton fabrics, raw cotton and cotton thread, caftans, lambskin, saltpeter, precious stones, and dried fruit. The launching of an annual fair in Orenburg favored the latter's rise too (Burton 1998b, 47–48).

From the Russian side, Tatar business elites (originating from the Volga) now experienced something like an economic renaissance: Tatar merchants spread out to CA and also represented Russian commercial interests there. The government, eager to protect the latter, perceived these Muslim subjects as convenient proxies and trade flourished. In the course of the eighteenth century, Orenburg probably eclipsed Astrakhan as Russia's most important trading town with CA and became, as it was said, the "gateway and key to the Orient" (Soucek 2000, 197; Poujol 2000, 40).

Orenburg's ascent happened despite the rise to prominence in the eighteenth century of another, secondary, trade route leading through Astrakhan: the route over the Caspian Sea, not to Iran but via the Mangyshlak peninsula into CA. In the Mangyshlak area, some Turkmens (the Salors) still retained their nomadic encampments and intermediated Russian, Central and Western European products (furs, leather, canvas, receptacles, metal objects) to CA; the Turkmen traders moreover contributed to C Asian exports of cotton, silk cloth, of light, heat-permeable clothing, and of spices to Russia and beyond (Shukow et al. 1958/1966, Band 5, 274).

The Khanate of Crimea (Under Ottoman Suzerainty Until Late Eighteenth Century)

As mentioned above, the Khanate of Crimea was indirectly ruled by the Ottomans since 1475. Being protected by such a large empire, the khanate remained outside of Moscow's reach for the time being. The Tatars of Crimea certainly exploited this sheltered position by launching large-scale lucrative slave-hunting incursions into Muscovite Russia and Poland-Lithuania. These violent and devastating expeditions were usually carried out once annually. In 1571 the Tatars made their ultimate appearance before Moscow and burnt down the city (Karger (ed) 1978, 66). On some of their incursions, they captured groups of more than 50,000 people in less than two weeks and shipped them south. Some men, women, and child slaves remained in Crimea; others were slated for Constantinople, still others for Anatolia. The main slave trading center was Kaffa. Poland also suffered badly from Tatar incursions and mass enslavements (O'Rourke 2007, 30; Chaliand 1995, 178).

Under Peter the Great, there were still raids in the region of Kharkov (1710–1718).[73] In Ukraine and Southern Russia, the danger remained pervasive throughout the first half of the eighteenth century. In those decades, though, the Russian Empire started to gain the military upper hand over the Sublime Porte in the Pontic steppes. The Ottomans had already been weakened by the long-lasting war against Habsburg Austria and the Turkic military defeat in the battle on the Kahlenberg, near Vienna in 1683. In 1736 and again in the next 2 years, Russian troops invaded and ravaged the Crimean peninsula, which was definitely occupied in 1771 and annexed to the czardom in 1783.

With no more razzias possible in Eastern Europe, the Tatars' revenues shrank, and Tatar income from agriculture also dwindled due to Russian confiscations of farming land in the framework of "de-Tatarization" campaigns. High-quality lands were often transferred to Russian noblemen, domestic, and foreign farmers (Ukrainians, Germans, Balts, Greek, Bulgarians); pauperized Tatar peasants were relocated to less fertile lands in the Crimean interior. Waqf land was also partly expropriated. Many Tatars chose to emigrate, preferably to Turkey. They were replaced by foreign and czarist immigrants and settlers (Hambly (ed) 1966, 202–204; Krieger 2003, 272). Thus in the late eighteenth century, the Pontic grasslands that from the times of the Scyths, the Sarmatians, and the Huns had constituted the domain of nomadic civilizations found themselves entirely in the hands of a major sedentary power. Now the possibility opened up of turning the fertile Chernozem soil of the Ukrainian steppes into a market-oriented granary.

4.1.3.5 The Kazakh Khanate from Overall Recovery to Trial (Sixteenth to Eighteenth Century)

Consolidation of the State in a Period of Economic Recovery Punctuated by External Pressures

Centrifugal tendencies that had developed after Kasym Khan's death (1523) were soon reined in by Kasym's son, Khan Aknazar (1538–1580), who reinstated the unity of the three hordes. Restabilization of political conditions in the mid-sixteenth century enabled the recovery of the economy, particularly urban development and trade, which were also favored by the politico-economic stablization of neighboring

---

[73] The territories east of the Dnepr plus Smolensk and Kiev had been acquired by the Russian Empire from Poland in 1667.

states in or at the borders of CA (Russia under Ivan the Terrible, the "Gunpowder Empires" (the Ottoman, Safavid, and Mughal states), the Chagatay Khanate under Said Khan and his successors, and Ming China) (see also Maps 4.2 and 4.3). Kazakh trade and transit trade with the C Asian oasis belt, India, China, and Muscovite Russia were lively. A network of caravan routes plied Kazakh territories (Baipakov et al. 1997, 134).

According to Baipakov and Kumekov, Sygnak remained the "trade harbor" and an important political center of the eastern Desht-i-Kipchak. Stockbreeders came to Sygnak, driving their beasts before them ("fat sheep, horses, and camels") and bringing the products of animal husbandry (meat, skins, hides, wool, and woolen goods) and furs. Such valuable goods as "fur coats of .... sable and squirrel, taut bows, arrows of white birch, silk cloth and other costly wares" also arrived in Sygnak to be sold (Baipakov, Kumekov: The Kazakhs, 101). The precious furs mentioned here probably point to increasing trade with Russian Siberia and with Muscovite Russia in general. After Astrakhan, the czardom's conquest of Western Siberia opened up new trade connections between CA and Russia. Kazakh and other C Asian embassies and merchants often entered Russia via Tobolsk; thus the importance of the trade route from Mavarannahr via Central Kazakhstan to Western Siberia gained momentum. Kazakh trade with Russia expanded in the late sixteenth and early seventeenth centuries.

Somewhat further south from Sygnak, Yasy (Turkestan) at the turn of the seventeenth century became the capital of the khanate, hosting the khan's headquarters. Yasy was also a prominent religious town. (It had been the birthplace of the brotherhood of Yasaviyya in the twelfth century, as mentioned above.) Apart from the two mentioned towns, Otrar (see also above), Sauran, Sairam, and Suzak (see Map 4.7) feature among the large Southern Kazakh trade and economic centers of the time. Tashkent (Shash) was temporarily under Kazakh rule (and was reconquered by the Khanate of Bukhara in the 1570s). Turkestan and Tashkent constituted urban centers of large farming areas. As Artykbaev describes, Kazakh towns, not unlike other C Asian towns, were typically surrounded by gardens and kitchen gardens (ogorody), watermelon plantations/pumpkin fields (bakhchy), vineyards, fields, and pastures (2007, 161).[74] In the sixteenth and the early seventeenth centuries, artificial irrigation developed on a larger scale than in the past.

In this period, the Kazakhs practiced many urban trades, prominent among which were blacksmithing, woodworking, jewelry making, leatherwork, carpet and rug producing, tailoring, and shoemaking. Blacksmiths made armor and weapons, such as bows, quivers, shields, knives, swords, spears and arrows, and the usual assortment of metal tools for farming and everyday domestic use. Woodworkers carved beautifully shaped, richly decorated wooden bowls for the drinking of kumys (fermented mare's milk). Leather artisans and saddlers made horse trappings, harnesses, and other implements for carriages and pack horses. The production of clothes, felt, carpets, and furnishings for yurts was mainly the task of women. Like in other parts of CA, Kazakh urban craftsmen were members of guilds (risalas) and lived by their rules (Baipakov and Kumekov 2003, 102).

The khans Tevekkel (or Tauekal, 1586–1598) and Esim (1598–1628) continued to fight against the Uzbeks and intermittently retook the Tashkent oasis and even the Ferghana Basin. The seventeenth century was generally characterized by intensifying internal and external tribal rivalries (Poujol 2000, 36). Decentralizing tendencies made themselves felt and the Kazakh polity was in danger of splitting up again. The migration of some dissenting Kalmyk tribes (also called Torguts) that rejected the authority of the new Oirat (Kalmyk) state created in neighboring Dzungaria in the first half of the seventeenth century proceeded across the Desht-i-Kipchak from east to west.[75] This migration from Dzungaria all the way to the plains of the lower Volga took a couple of decades and featured frequent raids, plundering, destruction, and casualties on the part of the migrating Torguts as well as of the Kazakhs whose territories the Torguts crossed. As Hambly put it, the long migration of the Kalmyks across the Kazakh steppes left a "bloody trail" without entailing permanent conquest (1966 (ed), 156) (see also below).

Another external shock that this time cost the Kazakhs an important chunk of their territory was the Dzungar or Oirat invasion of 1643–1644. Soon after the Oirats (Western Mongols, see above) had established their new nomadic state northeast of the Tienshan in 1635–1640, they embarked on expansion and attacked their immediate nomadic neighbors and rivals, the Kazakhs. Suffering a heavy defeat in battle, the Kazakhs lost most of Semirechie (Zhetysu) and lands in the Eastern Desht-i-Kipchak (Hambly (ed) 1966, 156). The Dzungars incorporated the entire territory surrounding Lake Balkhash (including the Saryarka, the upper Chu Valley, and the Ili Valley) into their khanate. Later Dzungar raids (in the 1680s and 1690s) were staged from Zhetysu and at first focused on the theft of livestock in the Kazakh steppe. Then Kazakh-ruled Syr Daria farming

---

[74] Compare also with the above description of the spatial arrangement of agricultural activities in Bukhara under the Shaybanids in the sixteenth century (Schwarz 2000).

[75] This dissent and separation of the Torguts somewhat resembles the dissent and separation of the Kazakhs under Zhanibek and Kerey almost 200 years earlier—with the difference that the Torguts chose to leave their region, Dzungaria, where their former fellow tribes were about the create a strong Oirat state, whereas the Kazakhs chose to discontinue their migration and not to participate in the creation of the Uzbek Khanate in newly conquered lands by their former fellow tribes.

areas and towns were ravaged and partly destroyed. Losses of life were considerable. These towns, e.g., Turkestan, Otrar, Sairam, Andijan, and Osh (the latter two in the Ferghana Basin), went into decline, and trade activity also took a heavy blow (Breghel 2003, 56–57; Oskolkov and Oskolkova 2004, 25). As depicted in Map 4.4, pushed by the Dzungar expansion, displaced Kazakh nomads invaded Transoxiana on repeated occasions, disrupted the region, and carried out razzias (as mentioned earlier).

Partly in reaction to this shock and severe pressure coming from a formidable enemy, Khan Tauke (1680–1718), the last ruler of a unified Kazakh Khanate, managed to recentralize the state and even carry out some important structural reforms.[76] Residing in Turkestan (Yasy), Khan Tauke was a key administrator and lawmaker whose codex, called "Zhety zhargy" (seven verdicts), gave Kazakh nomadic customary law (adat) the power of a written statute book.[77] Thus, at the end of the seventeenth century the social and political structure of Kazakh society received a definite codification (Hambly (ed) 1966, 155; Soucek 2000, 196). Somewhat in the manner of the Mongol Yassa, the Zhety zhargy includes norms of administrative, criminal, and civil law, regulations/provisions regarding taxes, and various dues for the benefit of the khan or sultans, religious issues, etc. Thus, for instance, nomadic pastoralists were liable to pay the zyaket (a twentieth of a herd), while agriculturalists were charged the ushur (a tenth of the harvest).[78] Moreover, an extraordinary tax was earmarked for equipping warriors for military campaigns.

Notwithstanding the persisting external threat, after Khan Tauke's death, Kazakh tribal particularism regained the upper hand and the far-flung khanate again split into three distinct and independent hordes which bore the same names, consisted of largely identical tribes and occupied mostly the same territories—except for the loss of Semirechie to the Dzungars and for some enlargements in the south and the west—as their predecessors had less than a century before: the Junior or Little Horde (Kishi Zhuz) in the West of the Kazakh steppe, the Middle Horde (Orta Zhuz) in the center, and the—spatially squeezed—Senior or Great Horde (Ulu Zhuz) in the

east. More precisely, in about 1725, the territories of the Kazakh Hordes were (Abazov 2008, Map 30):

(a) Senior Horde: Eastern Kazakh steppe, lower reaches of Chu and Talas rivers, fierce competition for control over Shash (Tashkent)
(b) Middle Horde: Central Kazakh steppe, lower Syr Daria, up to middle reaches of Ishim and Irtysh rivers;
(c) Junior Horde: Western Kazakh steppe, from the mouth of the Syr Daria, north and west of Aral Sea up to Ural and Tobol rivers.

Kazakhs Suffer from Devastating Dzungar Blows: Beginnings of Integration with Russia (Early Until Mid-eighteenth Century)

At the end of Khan Tauke's reign, the war with the Dzungar Empire intensified. In 1717–1718, after once again wiping out Kazakh forces on the battlefield, the Dzungars reinvaded the towns of the Syr Daria, particularly Yasy/Turkestan. Then a larger invasion was launched in 1723–1725, which struck the region of Turkestan a third time, but also ravaged Tashkent and parts of Ferghana. The crushing attacks and the accompanying massacres of thousands of people are remembered in Kazakh history as the "Great Calamity" or "Aktaban Shubyryndy" (in Russian, Velikoe bedstvie), literally the "barefooted forced migration," which refers to a mass flight exacerbated by harsh weather and famine in which as many as two thirds died. Parts of the population of the plundered Syr Daria towns were deported to Dzungaria (Artykbaev 2007, 312; Golden 2011, 120)[79]. In turn, chased away Kazakhs burst into and disrupted Astrakhanid Mavarannahr anew.[80]

Driven away from Lake Balkhash and the Syr Daria by the Dzungars, many Kazakhs in the first half of the eighteenth century moved westward and northward in the Desht-i-Kipchak and approached Russia's borders. For the time being outside of Dzungar reach, these Kazakhs soon controlled important trade routes linking the czardom and CA. In increasing numbers, Kazakhs guided caravans across the steppes and traded in the fortresses/towns of the frontier lines of the Irtysh, the Tobol, and the Ural rivers (in Semipalatinsk, Yamishevsk, Troitsk, and particularly in Orenburg) (Burton 2003, 414;

---

[76] This can be seen as a typical example of dispositional centralization and statehood as defined by Khazanov (1983/1994, 176, see also above). Geiss points out that powerful khans like Tauke were rare and owed their influence to the military threat caused by the Dzungars and the need for centralized defense (2003, 115).

[77] Despite the Kazakh capital's status as a religious center (and birthplace of the Yasaviyya) and despite the fact that at least parts of the Kazakh elite were of Muslim faith, the Zhety zhargy hardly incorporates elements of the Sharia. This is probably because most Kazakhs remained steppe nomads and as such were at best superficially Islamized.

[78] Zyaket and ushur were also collected in the Khanate of Khiva in the seventeenth century (see above).

---

[79] As Poujol points out, Dzungar historiography also deplores Kazakh depredations against Oirats as recurrent aggression (2000, 37).

[80] This once more demonstrates the "billard principle" explained above. At least in the case of the invasions of 1717–1718 and 1723–1725 it can be argued that there was a third "billard ball" involved: In the late seventeenth and the early eighteenth century, the Dzungars themselves had come under military pressure from the expanding Qing Empire (China), which produced a powerful push factor in the east, resulting in the "billard chain" Qing-Dzungars-Kazakhs-Uzbeks (compare also Maps 4.2 and 4.4, and see below).

Artykbaev 2007, 184). Being nomads, what the Kazakhs could not sufficiently acquire through animal husbandry, trade, and other services, they attempted to gain by attacking caravans traveling to and from Orenburg (Burton 1998b, 44). Thus, Kazakhs protected and Kazakhs looted caravans on the Orenburg route; it is difficult to imagine that they would not take protection fees from merchants—a classic way of earning money for steppe dwellers.

Given the Kazakhs' overall extremely precarious situation, in 1730 the khan of the Junior Zhuz, Abilay (Abulkhair) turned to the czar of Russia and requested protection for his people; moreover, Abilay declared his preparedness to acknowledge the Russian ruler as his suzerain (overlord). The czar approved his request the following year (Soucek 2000, 196; Chuvin et al. 2008, 65). In 1740, the Middle Zhuz demanded Russian protection and in 1742 part of the Senior Zhuz also did. The czardom at first contented itself with accepting these offers of vassaldom from Kazakh leaders, without actually acquiring military or administrative control over their territory beyond the erection of fortified posts gradually infringing on it, and therefore also without effectively granting much security to the empire's new subjects. Still, this was the formal beginning of Russia's annexation of Kazakhstan (Oskolkov and Oskolkova 2004, 31–32).

Possibly provoked by these actions, in 1741–1742 the Dzungars launched new campaigns into Kazakh lands and this time far to the west and deep into the steppe territories of the Middle and the Junior Hordes, which temporarily disrupted trade connections with Russia (Breghel 2003, 59, 69). The Senior as well as the Middle Horde (that had just sworn allegiance to the ruler in St. Petersburg) became subordinates of the Oirat Empire.[81] The newly acquired territories, i.e., paid the kibitka tax to the Dzungar authorities (Oskolkov and Oskolkova 2004, 32).

This new partition of lands in the Eurasian steppe only lasted about one and a half decades, though, and did not prevent Russia from strengthening its trade and economic ties with the Kazakhs of the Junior Horde, who, as mentioned above, had become subjects of the czar (as of 1731), and with Kazakh territories that remained unoccupied by the Dzungars. Artykbaev even identifies the late 1730s as the starting point of a tendency of continuous growth of Russian-Kazakh and Russian-C Asian trade (2007, 184). Yet given the extremely unequal size and differing interests of the Russian sedentary modernizing empire and the Kazakh nomadic traditionalist hordes, a first sign of conflict in Russian-Kazakh economic relations could not but show up soon: In 1756, the czarist authorities banned Kazakhs from driving livestock to the rich pastures west of the Ural river and thus limited the nomads' territory of (possible) pastoral migration.

In the 1750s, the tenuous politico-military equilibrium in the Eurasian steppe collapsed: As explained in more detail below, the Chinese military, for a long time at war with the Dzungar forces, in 1758 crushed Grand Tartary and in punitive operations, wiped out a major part of its Dzungar (Western Mongol) nomadic population. The territory of the former Dzungar state (or most of it, including Semirechie) was incorporated into the Qing Empire. This also goes for the Kazakh Senior Zhuz. The Middle Zhuz became a temporary vassal of the emperor in Beijing (Oskolkov and Oskolkova 2004, 32; Duby 2011, 189). Chinese fortresses were erected at the borders of conquered territories in the Kazakh steppe (e.g., near Lake Balkhash) and in the upper Irtysh region. However, the Manchu authorities soon displayed limited interest toward outlying regions at the far western limits of the empire—in contrast to the czarist authorities that continued to show vivid interest in the vast grasslands adjoining Western Siberia. In the late 1750s, Kazakhs were also banned from nomadizing across the Irtysh river into Russia. In 1762, the khan of the Middle Horde for a second time swore allegiance to St. Petersburg (Oskolkov and Oskolkova 2004, 33). Map 4.5 depicts some of these sweeping changes in Northern CA.

4.1.3.6 The Kyrgyz (Seventeenth to Mid-eighteenth Centuries): Second Wave of Migration to Tienshan, Marginal Sedentarization

In the early seventeenth century, Kyrgyz tribes essentially still lived in two separate mountainous regions, where they nomadized vertically: the Altai and Sayan ranges (including the uppermost Yenisey river) in Southern Siberia and the central part of the Tienshan range (around Lake Issyk Koel, and in Eastern Ferghana). With the approximately simultaneous Russian conquest of Central Siberia and the establishment of the Dzungar Empire (also ruling parts of the Altai), rivalry for collection of tribute from the Northern Kyrgyz emerged between the two powers. As Perdue explains, in 1641 the Oirat ruler Batur Khongtaiji claimed the right to exact tribute (mostly in furs), rejecting the competing claim of the voevoda (governor) of Tobolsk. War was avoided by an ingenious device, the establishment of dual sovereignty, obliging the unfortunate Kyrgyz to pay Yasak (in-kind levy) to both the Russians and the Dzungars (Perdue 2005, 105). In the early eighteenth century, Russian settlers began to move upstream along the Ob and Yenisey rivers, provoking attacks by Dzungar troops, which probably made life even more difficult for the Northern Kyrgyz, who eventually left the area and joined their ethnic kin in the Tienshan (Chuvin et al. 2008, 56).[82]

---

[81] Dzungar rule was formalized by the Middle and Senior Hordes' signing of a treaty of union with Dzungaria in 1743 (Artykbaev 2007, 313).

[82] This corresponds to the second wave of Krygyz migration to the Tienshan, about 800 years after the Kyrgyz had been expelled from Mongolia by the Khitan-Liao (see above).

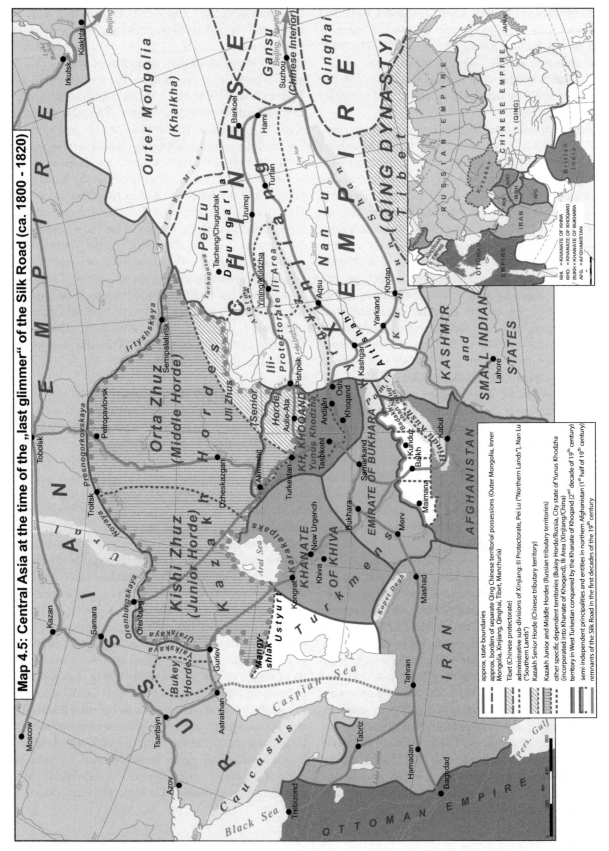

Map 4.5   CA at the time of the "last glimmer" of the SR (ca. 1800–1820)

In the first half of the eighteenth century, the Kyrgyz of the Tienshan were divided between two states, a nomadic and a semisedentary or sedentary one: the Oirat Empire (to which most of the Tienshan range, including the area surrounding Lake Issyk Koel, belonged) and the Uzbek Khanate of Khoqand (which ruled the Ferghana Basin and the upper Syr Daria Valley). The Kyrgyz economy essentially remained a nomadic one. Transhumance between valleys and mountain pastures was customarily fixed and movements toward little known or remote places were avoided.[83] Their livestock consisted of sheep, yaks, and goats (Tchoroev (Chorotegin) 2003, 120; Chuvin et al. 2008, 55).

The Kyrgyz needed to be herdsmen, warriors, and hunters at the same time. Blacksmiths made pastoral and farming tools in addition to warriors' weapons, which reflects even less specialization than among the Kazakhs. Even more than among the Kazakhs, local trade continued to be carried out on a barter basis. Kyrgyz society was dominated by the most senior members of clans and tribes (biys, corresponding to clan chiefs or tribal leaders or begs in some other Turkic societies). According to Chinese sources, in the eighteenth century biys followed the custom of passing on their authority to younger family members. Yet the Krygyz in the eighteenth century did not succeed in establishing a united tribal confederation featuring dynastic power of ruling khans or sultans, and there was no aristocracy deriving its origins from Genghis Khan.[84] Conversion to Islam was largely limited to the elites (Linska et al. 2003, 72).

Already in earlier periods, but particularly in the eighteenth century, some Kyrgyz moved down from the Tienshan to the plains of Ferghana and the foothills of Zhetysu and Kashgaria. Their biys began to rule agricultural areas and towns, and a minority of Kyrgyz became semisedentary or sedentary (Khazanov 1983/1994, 176). The first half of the eighteenth century was the period of Dzungar expansion and near-omnipresence, as far as the Kyrgyz were concerned. Still, the Khanate of Khoqand (that ruled the Ferghana Basin and the upper Syr Daria Valley from about 1710) made an effort to accommodate and protect the Kyrgyz of the region of Osh and Uzgend (towns at the edge of the basin) (see Map 4.7). Fortresses were built, which created a minimum degree of security for the local inhabitants, who increasingly developed a settled culture. They erected permanent homes and religious and educational buildings (mosques and madrasas). These migrational and societal changes notwithstanding, the majority of Kyrgyz continued to be mountain dwellers; on various occasions they remained unassailable in their elevated redoubts.

4.1.3.7 Safavid Empire from the Late Sixteenth Century, Nadir Shah, and Post-Nadir Shah Persia

From Heyday of State-Promoted Economic Development Under Shah Abbas I (Late Sixteenth to Early Seventeenth Century) to Instability and Decline

Upon taking power, Shah Abbas I the Great (1587–1629) soon tightened the reins and became an absolute despot. Politics and the military were centralized. A permanent imperial army was created. Changes were introduced in fiscal administration in order to provide for the expenses involved in the military reforms. Gradually, the various types of state-owned land were transformed into centrally administered royal demesnes (royal estates, domains); as a consequence, revenues from these lands went straight into the imperial treasury. Previously, governors and owners of soyurghals themselves had been responsible for the maintenance and expenses of the armed forces under their command. From now on, the Persian soldiers' wages were paid in cash from the treasury (Eshraghi 2003, 255).

As Eshraghi notes, the shah reinforced the equipment of the armed forces with artillery (tup) and muskets (tufangs).[85] The ruler met the English brothers, Anthony and Robert Shirley, who subsequently entered the Shah's service and by helping to establish workshops for casting cannons and upgrading the production of muskets played a role in strengthening the firepower of the Safavid army (Eshraghi 2003, 255–257).

Overall, Findlay and O'Rourke argue that the contemporary Iranian economy constituted an interesting mixture of market forces, reflecting the activities of a sophisticated merchant class of native Persians, Indians, and most prominently Armenians, and of vigorous and extensive state intervention motivated by revenue needs, institutional modernization aims, and a strong mercantilist desire for the enhancement of national wealth and power. What we would today call "import substitution" projects were undertaken by the shah's authorities for the production of indigo, cotton, and rice. The making of silk, a prime export product, as well as of textiles, was expanded through the establishment of royal factories in major towns (Findlay and O'Rourke 2007, 130).

Under Shah Abbas, efforts to improve industrial know-how were important and focused on a number of areas. Two

---

[83] In this respect, vertical (or altitudinal) nomadism resembles horizontal nomadism in that seasonal route and locations of pastures and encampments are usually clearly defined.

[84] The non-emergence of a state is parallel to the development of Turkmen society.

[85] Under his predecessor, Shah Tahmasp, Persia had already purchased firearms from England via the Muscovy Company (see above).

examples of this kind of "industrial policy"and new methods for the manufacture of glass were introduced from Italy. Three hundred Chinese potters were invited to Persia in order to instruct local artisans, which proved successful (Bairoch 1997, 967). Furthermore, measures were carried out to upgrade the national transportation and communications infrastructure. Rising revenues, urbanization tendencies, and Shah Abbas' enthusiasm for commercial development provided a new impetus for progress in architecture, craftsmanship, and in various arts (Eshraghi 2003, 257).

At the beginning of Shah Abbas I's reign, when the abbasi (coin) was introduced, its weight came to 12.8 g. Six years into his reign (in 1593), the abbasi was 5 g lighter (Moosvi 2003a, 451). The energetic ruler's reforms substantially cut back the predominance of the nomadic aristocracy in the Iranian society and state: The establishment of the permanent army lessened the significance of tribal corps. Moreover the tax burden on the nomads was raised and the most rebellious tribes were physically liquidated. These bloody actions may cast a light on the nomads' at least relative loss of military power at the turn of the seventeenth century. Although in the sixteenth and seventeenth centuries the socioeconomic position of ordinary nomads (iliyyats) was still better than that of peasants (raiyyats), the gap was gradually narrowing (Khazanov 1983/1994, 270).

Shah Abbas II (1642–1666) continued mercantilist-protectionist policies. For instance, the Persian ruler banned the import of lapis lazuli from Badakhshan (Khanate of Bukhara) for some years in order to stimulate sales of that precious stone from a domestic source near Taebriz (southern Azerbaijan) (Burton 1998b, 40). In the course of the seventeenth century, though, internal and external instability appears to have increasingly befallen the Safavid Empire. Armed conflicts with the Khanates of Bukhara and Khiva flared up again toward the middle of the century; and a "long period of decline" or of "political and economic crisis" or of "unfavorable economic development" reportedly set in (Eshraghi 2003, 258; Breghel 2003, 58; Bairoch 1997, 968). Some breakdown of Iranian roads was apparent in the latter part of the seventeenth century. To counter the spread of insecurity, rahdars (highway police) patrolled roads across the country to protect travelers and traders and to arrest robbers (Dale 1994, 39).

While profitable business in silk continued, European accounts of Iran's trade in the late Safavid times also remark the significance of pastoral products. John Fryer's late seventeenth century list of products which bore value for the British East India Company prominently features "Carmania wool" (i.e., cashmere, from goats), sheep's wool (kneaded into felts), sheepskins, lambskins, etc. (Bradburd 2001, 139). This, of course, points to maritime trade also of some animal husbandry products—likely another indicator of the progressing loss of competitiveness of the overland

SR. One should add, however, that (as mentioned earlier) Armenian merchants received the exclusive right in 1667 of exporting Persian cotton to Russia and reexporting it from there to Europe—on shipping routes that did not add to ocean-going competition.

Under Shah Abbas II, a gold abbasi of 144 grains was struck; its weight was later reduced to 120 grains. Under his successors, the Shahs Sulayman and Husayn, the later weight was further adjusted to 114 and 84 grains (Moosvi 2003a, 454)—a typical example of gradual debasement of a currency. Shah Husayn doubled the nomads' taxes in the early seventeenth century. The majority of the iliyyats soon came to form one of the dependent classes in the state (Khazanov 1983/1994, 270). The intermittent and continuing armed clashes in Khorassan (at the disputed boundaries between Iran and the C Asian Khanates) also triggered involuntary migration and displacement of labor: Peasants and urban dwellers living in Northeastern Iranian oases who had become prisoners of war were often sold as slaves in the markets of Bukhara or Khiva (Schwarz 2004, 190).

Quick Far-Flung Conquests, Concentration of Resources in Khorassan, and Collapse: Nadir Shah's Ephemeral Empire (1732–1747)

After the fall of the Safavids, the rule of the Ghilzais and Abdalis (in the 1720s) featured elements of anarchy. Some have called their successor, Nadir Shah, the last great Asian conqueror (Eshraghi 2003, 259, 261). Like Ismail Safavi, Nadir was the chief of a Turkmen tribe in Iran (although of Sunni faith) and a brilliant soldier and commander. In only a few years (in the 1730s and early 1740s), Nadir conquered an empire that was almost as large as Tamerlane's, but Nadir's power was even more ephemeral than his conqueror-predecessor's. After securing Persian possessions in the Caucasus and subduing Afghan tribes, Nadir's troops in 1739 invaded India and sacked Delhi.[86] In 1740 the Khanates of Khiva, Bukhara, and Khoqand were occupied and became Persian vassals (Breghel 2003, 58–59).

Notwithstanding awesome armed forces and territorial greatness, the numerous campaigns and wars had disrupted and damaged the economy. Also, Nadir did not manage to set up a stable civil administration for his state. The ruler's extreme authoritarianism, his oppression of the population through onerous taxation, and the death and misery he inflicted on subjugated people through punitive actions had repeatedly triggered unrest and uprisings, which ended in his assassination. While he himself had nomadic ancestors, he tried to further weaken the nomadic nobility and broke up and scattered tribes that were hostile to him. Upon his death,

---

[86] This may be interpreted as a dramatic sign of the decline of the Mughal Empire (Haywood 2011, 134).

his vast empire quickly fell apart despite the extensive military apparatus that had been put in place (Eshraghi 2003, 261, 263).

One region that probably had less reason than others to regret his rule was the long-disputed and ravaged border region of Khorassan (between Persia and the Uzbek Khanates). Under Nadir's rule, Khorassan (or "land of the rising sun," comprising territories from Nishapur to the Amu Daria) was fully incorporated into Iran and therefore—somewhat paradoxically and in contrast to other regions—was no longer as unstable and insecure as before. Also, as pointed out by Eshraghi, Nadir Shah made Mashhad his capital and did much to add to its architectural splendor. His campaigns in Transoxiana not only freed about 20,000 Khorassanian slaves, who had been captured and sold on the markets of Bukhara and Khiva, but also provided a temporary respite for the sedentary population from such enslavement (Eshraghi 2003, 263). Moreover, Nadir had Merv restored and the dams and embankments of the Murgab repaired (apparently the first such in-depth repair since the one ordered by Shah Rukh in the first half of the fifteenth century). Based on these focused improvements, the ruler resettled (by force) about 3000 families from Western Khorassan in the oasis of Merv (former Margiana) (Kamev 2005, 86; Peyrouse 2007, 35).

Following the collapse of Nadir Shah's empire, Karim Khan Zand (1750–1779) reestablished calm after the storm. The Persian fiscal system was reorganized and the taxation of agriculture reduced. Trade and the economy recovered and a modest degree of prosperity made itself felt (Bairoch 1997, 969).

4.1.3.8 Afghanistan: A Pivotal Mountain Redoubt Straddling Trade and Strategic Routes

Over many centuries, Afghans were predominantly nomadic pastoralists, and most of their pastures and encampments were situated in the Sulayman Ranges and the adjoining mountainous plateau between Ghazni (Ghazna), Kandahar and Quetta, an extensive elevated region straddling today's border between Pakistan and Afghanistan. From the sixteenth century, many Afghan tribes gradually became settled and took up farming. For a long time, Afghanistan and particularly its most important city, Kabul, and the Khyber Pass played the key role in trade between CA and India. Political and military links had also been strong, in most instances featuring the conquest and domination of parts of Northern India—most often the Punjab—by militarily well-trained Afghan tribes. The major sixteenth century invasion of South Asia by Babur (battle of Panipat, 1526) was not carried out by Afghans, but by Turko-Mongol Timurids; the latter had, however, conquered Kabul and ruled parts of Afghanistan some decades before the invasion was launched from Afghan territory.

Overall, the territory of Afghanistan (in its present-day borders) had been part of Timur's empire, and then of the Timurid Emirates in the fifteenth century. In the first half of the sixteenth century, Afghanistan was divided up between Safavid Persia, the (Uzbek) Khanate of Bukhara, and the just established Mughal Empire. As documented by Breghel, the borders of this division remained remarkably stable for about 200 years (until the first half of the eighteenth century) and more or less corresponded to the following (see also Map 4.4): The regions south of the upper Amu Daria (Balkh, Badakhshan, or former Southern Bactria) remained part of the Khanate of Bukhara or became independent; the areas south of the upper Murgab river and west of the middle reaches of the Hilmand river (including Herat and all of Sistan) were attached to the Safavid Empire; and the territories south of the Hindu Kush and east of the Hilmand (the rest of Afghanistan, including Kabul, the Khyber Pass, Ghazni, and Kandahar) belonged to the Mughal Empire (Breghel 2003, 52–58).

In the sixteenth century, the Mughal Empire received the lion's share of horses it needed to uphold its rule in India from the C Asian steppes via Kabul: 7000–10,000 horses passed through this strategic trading center to Delhi annually.[87] In return, India sent slaves, calico[88], sugar, and aromatic roots north (Hussain Shah 2003, 274, 278). In the late seventeenth century, Bernier wrote of yearly deliveries of about 25,000 C Asian horses to India. In the eighteenth century, in some years of Khan Aurangzeb's rule (1658–1707), the Mughal Empire apparently had an annual intake of up to 100,000 horses from Bukhara and Afghanistan (Golden 2011, 116; Paul 2012, 305). Kabul understandably enjoyed considerable prosperity under Mughal rule. To a lesser degree, prosperity may have also touched Kandahar, through which some trade with Iran was conducted.

The Durranis, a Pashtoon tribe (speaking Pashto, an Eastern Iranian language, like Tajik), formed one of the leading tribes of the Kandahar region. Upon subduing them, Nadir Shah soon realized their value as soldiers and enlisted large numbers of Durranis in his army. After Nadir's assassination in 1747, one of his regional commanders, Ahmad Khan, conquered Kabul and founded the Afghan state. The Durrani dynasty first ruled from Kandahar and then moved to Kabul (Hussain Shah 2003, 285–286; Chuvin et al. 2008, 68). Benefitting from the power vacuum after the sudden collapse of Persia, the accelerated decline of the Mughal polity (now

---

[87] The essential reason for the Mughal Empire's dependence on horse imports reportedly was the difficulty in breeding horses in South Asia's relatively humid climate (Wink 2001, 228–229; Pernau 2011, 114).

[88] Calico—a plain woven cotton cloth printed with a figured pattern, usually on one side (Random House Websters' Concise College Dictionary 1999, see also Glossary: some SR textiles, p. 266).

also under pressure from British seaborne colonial expansion) and the weakening and increasingly unstable Khanate of Bukhara, the founder of the Afghan state, who became Ahmad Shah Durrani (1747–1773), swiftly expanded his power and created the Afghan Empire.[89] Ahmad conquered large areas in Eastern Khorassan, Sistan, Beluchistan, Sind, Kashmir, and Punjab, although he was later ousted from Punjab by the Sikhs. Shah Durrani also projected his power north of the Hindu Kush to the banks of the Amu Daria, where territories were either directly incorporated (e.g., Balkh) or became vassal principalities (e.g., Badakhshan).

The Durrani tribes and clans, among whom nomads had become a minority, occupied the privileged positions in the new state, which continued to use parts of the administrative structures inherited from the Safavids and the Mughals. The percentage of nomads in tribes in the west of the empire was relatively high and the most important demand the Shah had on this population was the provision of warriors. The majority of Afghan tribes were relieved of liability to tax or if they did have tax obligations, the latter were low, sometimes purely symbolic. Ahmad Shah's successful campaigns enabled him to lay the basic burden of taxation on the non-Afghan inhabitants of the territories that had been conquered (regular tax on "hamsanyas"/dependent agriculturalists, "infidel tax" on the Hindus, customs levies collected on merchandise passing through the country/Kabul) (Khazanov 1983/1994, 273).

4.1.3.9 The Dzungar Empire/Grand Tartary (1635–1758) and the Middle Kingdom

Rise of a New Powerful State on the Mongol Steppe, Emigration of Dissenters to the Volga

Altan Khan (r. 1552–1582) suppressed internecine warfare and stabilized the Eastern Mongol state. Notwithstanding the Ming dynasty's construction of additional fortifications, producing the Great Wall in the form in which it is known today, Altan Khan's recurrent attacks and raids were successful and even reached the suburbs of Beijing. In 1571, a new Chinese-Mongol peace treaty was signed that provided for the resumption of regular trade including lucrative deals on horses in exchange for silk and tea, which strengthened the khanate economically. In 1578 a historic meeting

between the third Dalai Lama and Altan Khan was held in Koko Nur (Qinghai, Northeastern China). Thereafter, the various Mongol tribes converted to Buddhism, which thus spread across Mongolia and Dzungaria (Northern Xinjiang) (Adle et al. 2003a, 29).

In 1635 a new Oirat state was established in Dzungaria: the Dzungar Khanate, sometimes also called Grand Tartary (1635–1758); this was to be the last great nomadic empire in Eurasian and world history. Expanding from a core area (encampment) south of the Tarbagatay mountains—probably Chuguchak (Tacheng)—the confederation, tightly led by Khongtaiji[90] Batur, soon controlled Dzungaria and laid claim to a large area north of the Tienshan. As Perdue notes, Khongtaiji Batur (1635–1653), i.e., became known as the "sheep raising king" because of his efforts to build up his herds. Since the khanate's eastern neighbor, the Middle Kingdom, also needed sheep, the Oirats or Dzungars[91] were able to sell them profitably at border markets regulated by the Chinese authorities (Perdue 2005, 36, 39). Of course this trade remained extremely vulnerable to changes in the underlying political constellation.

Already in the early seventeenth century, the Oirats had started trading with Muscovite Russia, which Oirat merchants accessed via the Irtysh and Ob river valleys, reaching the fortresses of Tara and Tomsk. Thus, the Oirats had brought 550 horses to Tara in 1607 in exchange for money, writing paper, and cloth. Batur also reportedly agreed to Russian salt mining activities and the departure of regular salt caravans from Lake Yamysh (east of the middle reaches of the Irtysh river)[92], in exchange for increased trade. Soon, a separate quarter of Tobolsk emerged, called the Tatar settlement. The Dzungars traded their horses, livestock, sheepskins, and furs for handicrafts, leather, silk, silver, walrus ivory, and metals. While the Dzungars may have succeeded in acquiring some firearms, Russia generally refused to supply these weapons and avoided the promotion of arms flows to Dzungaria (Hambly (ed) 1966/1979, 303; Perdue 2005, 98, 106–107).

As mentioned above, initial rivalry and clashes on the exaction of tribute from Southern Siberian, including Northern Kyrgyz, tribes were resolved by the "creation" of dual sovereignty over the peoples concerned. This cumbersome rule contributed to eventually prompting the Kyrgyz to leave the area. Doubtlessly, in the first half of the seventeenth century (before the whole of Siberia had been conquered and the Cossacks had reached the Pacific), a trade route linked Russia and China via Dzungar territory (probably

---

[89] There are some parallels between Ahmad Khan and another very capable provincial military commander and founder of an empire in Afghanistan in the tenth century: As a Samanid regional commander, Sebüktegin held authority in the town of Ghazna (Afghanistan) within the rapidly declining Samanid Empire. Benefiting from weakening central power due to escalating hostilities with the Karakhanids (nomadic conquerors coming from the Eurasian grasslands), Sebüktegin usurped autonomy and independence as the ruler of a new Ghaznavid state in Eastern Afghanistan. He remodeled fiscal structures within his territory in favor of his followers, expanded his empire, and undertook numerous raids into India to exact booty (see above).

---

[90] The Oirat nomadic state was led by rulers bearing the title "khongtaiji," which more or less corresponds to "khan."

[91] The terms "Oirats" and "Dzungars" are here used as synonyms.

[92] Lake Yamysh (near later Pavlodar) was already mentioned above, in connection with the Bukholts expedition (1716).

running along the Irtysh and then to Chuguchak/Southern Tarbagatay, Kuldzha or Urumqi, and Suzhou/Gansu). Batur carried out numerous raids and incursions into the Kazakh steppe and in a major campaign in 1643 conquered Western Zhetysu (the part of Zhetysu the Oirats had not yet ruled) as well as territories in the Kazakh Uplands north of Lake Balkhash (as referred to earlier) (see Map 4.4).

The pastures in the areas of Semirechie and Dzungaria (including those of the rivers Ili, Manas (flowing from the Northern Tienshan west of Urumqi), and Emin (flowing from the Tarbagatay west to Lake Alakoel), and that of the oasis of Urumqi) reportedly provided an ample supply of good grass and water so that the size of herds was on the increase (Miyawaki et al. 2003, 162). Yet this economic factor was not sufficient to persuade all Oirats to stay in the region, once the new ruler had taken power. Several Oirat tribes, also called Torguts, rejected Batur's authority and broke away from the Dzungar state; as partly alluded to above, some 200,000 to 250,000 Torguts in the first half of the seventeenth century migrated in an east-west direction from Dzungaria through the Saryarka and the Desht-i-Kipchak to the lower Volga and the Caspian Lowlands, where they arrived in the middle of the century; from there, most Torguts, also called Kalmyks, moved on to the plains north of the Caucasus (Breghel 2003, 59).

Although Muscovite Russia had conquered Astrakhan in 1556, more than a century later the Russian state had not yet established a strong grip on the lower Volga region, as witnessed by the peasant and Cossack rebellion under Stenka Razin (1670–1671) and by uprisings in Astrakhan in the early eighteenth century. The Kalmyks drove off some nomadic Noghays (former allies and preferred horse suppliers of Muscovy, see above) in the mid-seventeenth century and established themselves as new masters of the Northern Caspian grasslands. The Torguts, who retained their belief in Tibetan Buddhism, were welcomed by the czar, i.e., because they appeared as valuable allies who could join Russian forces in putting pressure on the (Muslim) Crimean Tatars. In their new homeland mostly to the west of the Volga, the migrants established their own Kalmyk Horde, whose taiji (khan) in 1655 swore allegiance to the Russian ruler (on the territory of the new tributary polity, see Map 4.4). The horde originally benefited from a large degree of autonomy, including tax exemptions and trade privileges (Krieger 2003, 270; Perdue 2005, 293; Kappeler 2001, 46).

Under their greatest leader, Khan Ayuki (1669–1724), the Kalmyk Horde expanded its control over a huge swathe of territory of possibly up to one million km² in the steppes north of the Caspian Sea. The Kalmyks apparently took over the role of primary horse suppliers to Moscow from the Noghays: In 1688 Khan Ayuki dispatched more than 9000 horses to be sold in the Russian capital (Khodarkovsky 2002, 26)—which was much less, though, than the number of horses that had reportedly changed hands in Moscow during the heydays of Noghay horse drives in the mid-sixteenth century (see above). In the late seventeenth century, the Kalmyks increasingly sold their horses for cash in order to buy many sought after items on Russian markets. And Moscow—at variance with its principle ban on selling firearms to nomads—provided gunpowder weapons, which raised the military effectiveness of Ayuki's cavalry in battling the Crimean Tatars and their Ottoman suzerains, as well as other steppe foes (Golden 2011, 117).

Over the seventeenth and eighteenth centuries, the Russian authorities gradually encroached on Kalmyk autonomy: As Kappeler points out, increasing demands for military service were coupled with efforts to intervene in local affairs. Moreover, settlers (mostly Russians and Ukrainians) continued to move onto and occupy pasturelands and migration routes of the horde. Interference intensified after Khan Ayuki's death: To assume their positions, his successors needed St. Petersburg's ascent, and more and more internal affairs of the khanate were effectively decided or influenced by the voevoda (governor) of Astrakhan. As a result of these cumulative encroachments, the functioning of the khanate's nomadic economy suffered (Kappeler 2001, 46; Adle et al. 2003b, 345).

Conquest and Exploitation of Chagatay Khanate (from ca. 1680)

Khongtaiji Galdan (1670–1697), one of Batur's successors, further strengthened the Dzungar state's military power. He attracted European and Chinese technicians and obtained the technology to produce cannons from Russia. Galdan promoted mining in Dzungaria and Semirechie, which are rich in mineral resources: The focus was on the search for and the extraction of iron ore and saltpeter to produce gunpowder from domestic sources. Copper, silver, and gold mines were also opened. Iron smelting was done on quite a large scale. Galdan promoted the import of the technology of fine steel making from Xinjiang businessmen in contact with Persia. A weapons industry was established producing spears, shields, gunpowder, firearms, cannons, armor, bullets, hand weapons, and iron tools. Under the khongtaiji's orders, the army was expanded to reach the size of 100,000 well-disciplined and well-trained warriors. More importantly, the formidable cavalry was equipped with firearms. Plus, Dzungar mobile field artillery, i.e., consisted of cannons transported on camelback, along with advancing infantry forces (Miyawaki et al. 2003, 150, 164; Perdue 2005, 51, 305).

With such awesome armed forces, Galdan in 1678–1680 invaded and easily conquered the Tarim Basin, Turfan, Hami, and Barkoel. The last Chagatayid rulers were dethroned, Kashgaria (or Altishahr[93]) as well as Uighuristan

---

[93] The "six towns" of Kashgar, Yarkand, Khotan, Aqsu, Uch Turfan, and Korla—see also above.

(and its trading towns bordering on China) became a Dzungar protectorate (Map 4.4). All of Xinjiang, and more, was in Oirat hands; the Dzungars moved their capital south to Kuldzha on the Ili river (adjoining Semirechie, north of the Tienshan). In the seventeenth century, people living south of the Tienshan, whether in Kashgaria or Uighuristan, were mainly Muslims and speakers of the Uighur language. Galdan did not profoundly change the administration of the conquered territory. He installed an Oirat governor in Yarkand and kharaghans (special officials) in a number of cities, whose task was to assess sources of tribute exaction and make sure that the khanate's new, mostly sedentary subjects paid their taxes and fulfilled the obligations imposed on them (Hambly (ed) 1966/1979, 303; Ma 2003, 195). While the Khwajas and local notables had already accumulated and wielded considerable de-facto powers under the last Chagatayids, they now replaced them as indigenous rulers of the population of Kashgaria (Soucek 2000, 160).

The Dzungars did not post permanent troops to the south of the Tienshan, and their rule over the protectorate was mainly effected by their Khodzha proxies, under the watchful eye of the governor in Yarkand. Members of any group commanding local authority in Altishahr were held captive in Kuldzha. The hostage system was part of a policy to indirectly control local rulers, collect taxes, and exact services—at low costs (Ma 2003, 193). Grand Tartary's rule ("at arms' length") over Kashgaria and Uighuristan thus constituted a "nomadic state of the first type" (according to Khazanov).

As alluded to above, Galdan carried out repeated pillaging wars against the Kazakhs and continued making destructive inroads into the Syr Daria Basin, Shash (Tashkent), and Ferghana in the 1680s and 1690s. In the meantime (in 1644–1650, see also below), the Manchus, themselves a semi-nomadic people, had conquered most of China as well as what was later called Inner Mongolia. The Manchus established the Qing dynasty, which—in contrast to the Ming—was offensive in its pursuit of Chinese interests in the steppe. Although the khongtaiji sent tribute missions to Beijing twice a year to exchange furs and horses for silk, cotton textiles and money, and although the trade volume rose with successive missions, military tensions with China became more frequent (Perdue 2005, 257).

To support his campaigns, the khongtaiji forced the oasis inhabitants to deliver taxes (or tribute) in cash, in kind, and in labor. Heavy burdens were placed on the sedentary people. As Ma Dazheng explains, the collection of tribute obligations from each household relied primarily on the register drawn up by the kharaghan and by local khodzhas.[94]

Apart from the main tribute tax levied on households, there seem to have been many other types of taxes: the poll tax, the land tax, the fruit tax, levies on merchants and herdsmen, levies on distilling and milling, the gold and silver tax, the draught-animal tax, trade tax, the tree and grass levy (!), water conservancy tax, etc. (Ma 2003, 195, 196).

According to Perdue, one third of the settled population was asked to carry out compulsory labor each year in rotation. The Dzungars built up an urban center at Kuldzha and for this purpose forcefully resettled Uighur or East Turkestani oasis dwellers and peasants who knew the special skills of high yielding, irrigated agriculture—subsequently known as Taranchi or Tariachin (farmer, tiller of the land)—to cultivate fields and grow food in the Ili region. Skilled agriculturalists were also deported to the upper reaches of the Irtysh and to the Urumqi oasis (Perdue 2005, 306)[95]. Most of the Taranchi or Tariachin came from Uch-Turfan, Aqsu, Kashgar, and Yarkand (see Maps 4.4 and 4.7); they typically worked as slaves or laborers for Dzungar chiefs. Altogether, 20,000–30,000 people were taken to Northern Xinjiang. Nomadic frontier tribes of the region were supervised by a traveling inspector who exacted payments of horses, oxen, and sheep. With the Oirat takeover of the Tarim Basin, the pul (the local Uighur copper-based currency) had the name of the ruling khongtaiji cast in Dzungar on the obverse and in Uighur on the reverse side of the coin. With every change of ruler in Kuldzha, new pieces were issued (Perdue 2005, 305, 351; Ma 2003, 195, 197).[96]

The economic foundations of the Dzungar Khanate lay in the animal husbandry of its nomads, mostly living north of the Tienshan; in the profits gained from SR transit trade primarily between Russia and China, moreover between China and the Khanate of Bukhara, and, to a smaller degree, between China and India (Map 4.4);[97] in the tributes, taxes, and compulsory services provided by people (e.g., Uighurs) the Dzungars had brought under their control; and in the booty and slave labor exacted by raids beyond the state's borders (particularly in West Turkestan). Grand Tartary employed Muslim merchants from the Tarim Basin and Transoxiana to conduct its sizeable trade with China, Russia, and other neighbors. In some cases, these merchants were (originally) war captives from Turkestan. Whether they were locals of Mavarannahr, Kashgaria, or Turfan, they

---

[94] The Dzungar register recalls the Mongol census of taxpayers, their activities and wealth, carried out in all newly conquered territories of the Mongol Empire.

[95] Since the Ili Valley is at least partly located in Semirechie, one could argue that—after the disappearance of the region's sedentary civilization as a consequence of the Mongol onslaught of the thirteenth century—the Dzungar forced transfers of East Turkestani farmers to the Ili valley in the late seventeenth and early eighteenth centuries constituted first steps toward the resettlement of the wider region.

[96] This corresponds to old C Asian numismatic traditions, going back at least as far as the Kushanas (first century BCE).

[97] For instance, high-value satins and tea were trans-shipped west and sold at a profit (Millward 2007, 93).

came to be called "Bukharans," probably because some of their predecessors had stemmed from the Khanate of Bukhara and had later successfully spread their trading and business activities across CA.[98]

Tribute Trade and Eventual Fatal Hostilities with the Qing Empire

The late seventeenth and the early eighteenth centuries were tumultuous times for the Dzungars. Shortly after the mentioned incursions in West Turkestan, confrontation with the Qing dynasty came to a head. Khalkha Mongols, living in what came to be called Outer Mongolia (separated from Grand Tartary by the Altai mountains), asked for Chinese protection against the expanding Dzungars (Reinhard 2008, 195). After hostilities had broken out in Khalkha territory, the Chinese authorities cut off all trade with the Dzungars. In 1696, a massive Qing army of 400,000 delivered a crushing blow to the Oirats at the battle of Urga (the later Ulan-Bator, capital of Outer Mongolia/Independent Mongolia from 1912). This defeat was incurred because the Chinese military was even better equipped with artillery than the Dzungars and, possibly more importantly, because of the vast numerical superiority of the Manchu army (Perdue 2005, 184, 257; Golden 2011, 119). A year later (1697), Galdan died and the territory of the Khalkha Mongols (Outer Mongolia) was annexed by China. A strategic border section of the SR also changed owners: The Qing empire occupied Barkoel and Hami in 1698 (Breghel 2003, 59).

Increasing pressure from the East may have contributed to Khongtaiji Tsewang Rabtan's (1697–1727) resumption of large-scale Dzungar incursions in the other direction (Poujol 2000, 36). As mentioned above, these incursions by Galdan's successor into Kazakh and Uzbek territories took place in 1717–1718 and 1723–1725. In 1717–1720 succession disputes in Tibet (ruled by Dalai-Lamas since 1642) led to intervention by the (Buddhist) Dzungars. This, in turn, triggered another intervention, in which Qing armies drove the Dzungars out of Tibet. The same year Tibet passed under Chinese suzerainty.[99] A year later (1721), the Manchus took control of the oasis of Turfan (Golden 2011, 119; Breghel 2003, 59).

To the northwest of the empire, while the Dzungars had successfully repelled the Russian Bukholts expedition to Lake Yamysh (near the Irtysh) in 1716, in the following two to three decades Russia was successful in bringing large areas east of the Irtysh and around the upper Ob under its control (foundation of Semipalatinsk, Barnaul—see above), which indicates a weakening of Dzungar sway in these areas that used to be subject to "dual sovereignty."

After the painful clashes and some territorial losses, the Dzungar Khanate experienced a period of temporary stability at its eastern borders, which aided economic recovery (Miyawaki et al. 2003, 157). Tsewang Rabtan and his successor, Galdan Tseren (1727–1745), stepped up the development of agriculture, horticulture, and crafts as well as industrial activity and the production of arms in the oases of Dzungaria and of the Ili region. For doing this, the rulers continued to draw on captives, particularly Uighur farmers and craftsmen, but also, where possible, on professionals or experts of other nationalities, e.g., Russians, Swedes, Manchus, and Chinese (Perdue 2005, 184, 307).

Accordingly, in the second quarter of the eighteenth century, under nomadic rule, farming and settlement received a strong impetus north of the Tienshan. With the Taranchi settlers, many agricultural skills such as seasonal planting, building ditches, and digging irrigation channels took hold in Dzungaria and the Ili region. Apparently, even some Dzungars themselves started to engage in farming for their livelihood and to supplement herding with agricultural activities; farming was also collectively organized in military colonies, imitating Qing practice (see below) (Miyawaki et al. 2003, 163; Perdue 2005, 306).

As Miyawaki, Bai, and Kyzlasov point out, when the Russian explorer Unkovsky visited the capital of the big steppe state in 1723, he recorded in his work "Embassy to Dzungaria" that "farmers were widespread" in the Ili region and that "special attention was paid to dividing the land into fields." He added that "wheat, barley, millet, pumpkins, melons, grapes, apricots, and apples" were grown. In the region of Urumqi and along the Irtysh agriculture was also quite developed: The tilled land was extended and techniques of cultivation spread (Miyawaki et al. 2003, 163).

The Oirats moreover attempted to refine their knowledge of firearms and cannons. During their siege of the Russian Bukholts expedition in 1716 (see above), Dzungar forces had captured a highly skilled Swedish artillery officer, Johan Gustaf Renat, who spent the following 17 years in Oirat captivity.[100] In Dzungaria, Renat helped the rulers Tsewang Rabtan and Galdan Tseren organize an artillery regiment and develop military production of heavy

---

[98] This phenomenon is nothing new and recalls the long-standing profitable intermediary role of the Sogdians for the Kushan state, the Hephthalites, and the Turk Kaghanate in relation to the Middle Kingdom (see above). As far as the "Bukharans" were Uighurs from East Turkestan, they may be linked to Uighur commercial and trading traditions going back all the way to the Tang era (seventh to ninth centuries).

[99] In 1751 Tibet became a Chinese protectorate.

---

[100] During the Great Northern War (1700–1721) between Sweden and Russia, Renat (1682–1744) had served in the Swedish army as a warrant officer in the artillery. He was taken prisoner after the battle of Poltava in 1709. In 1711 Renat was sent to Tobolsk where many Swedish officers were kept as prisoners of war. He entered the czar's service, helped produce maps of Siberia for the Russian authorities, and participated in Bukholts' unsuccessful expedition up the Irtysh river (Wikipedia: en.wikipedia.org/wiki/Johan_Gustaf_Renat).

weaponry. According to Perdue, Renat supervised and instructed local forced laborers in the manufacturing of at least 15 cannons and 20 mortars. The Swede also assisted in the drawing up of the first maps of Dzungaria and taught the Oirats how to print books. Having carried out this technology transfer, the Swede was allowed to leave the steppe empire and return home. Captured foreigners also built factories to produce velvet, cloth, and paper (Perdue 2005, 305–307).

In the early 1740s, the Dzungars expanded their authority into the heart of the Desht-i-Kipchak by extensive raids (see above) that even reached the Kazakh Junior Horde and that led to the temporary vassalage of the Senior and Middle Hordes as well as the installation of a tributary relationship and a Dzungar tax regime in the Kazakh steppe. However, this turned out to be a rather unstable and short-term arrangement, dependent on the geopolitical balance of power of the moment.

While Dzungar caravans continued to travel frequently to Semipalatinsk and Tobolsk and boasted a significant presence in Siberian markets, it was in Dzungar trade with China that a "breakthrough" was achieved in the late 1730s and the 1740s. In 1739, a truce was agreed upon and regular trade relations were officially established between the Dzungar and the Qing Empires (Hambly (ed) 1966/1979, 305). In the next 15 years, economic integration between the two large states increased. As Perdue explains, officially regulated and closely supervised trade, from the Chinese perspective, allowed three types of missions: (a) embassies to the capital (Beijing), (b) border trade at Suzhou in Western Gansu, and (c) "presentation of boiled tea" (aocha) to lamas in Tibet (under Qing overlordship)[101] (2005, 257). According to a high-ranking Chinese official, Governor-General Qingfu, the goal of trade was to "transform" (xianghua) the fierce barbarian warriors into peaceful peoples by offering them goods from the Chinese interior. The Dzungars were authorized to send missions to Beijing every 4 years, in 1738, 1742, 1746, 1750, and so on and to trade at the Dzungar-Chinese border in 1740, 1744, 1748, 1752, etc. (Perdue 2005, 259).

As Perdue further sets out, the main goods offered by the Dzungars for sale were animals (horses, sheep, cattle, and camels), hides, furs, certain medicinal products (sal ammoniac and antelope horn), and dried grapes from Kashgaria. In exchange, the Qing provided brocades, silk, tea, rhubarb, pottery, and silver. The size of embassies was limited to 100 men for border trade and 200–300 men for missions to the capital. Exports to the nomads of gunpowder, metals, and weaponry were generally prohibited by the Chinese authorities—comparable to Russia's ban. Yet the Suzhou

border trade quickly grew beyond expectations, straining official capacities. From a value of 10,000 taels in 1738, trade expanded to 105,000 taels[102] (corresponding to almost 4000 kg of silver) in 1741. Moreover, these figures disregard a substantial amount of unregistered private trade going on alongside the publicly administered trade. Border officials were apparently caught by surprise when huge herds of animals and numerous herders and traders turned up at their posts, straining available local pastures. Rather than being held responsible for keeping these people at the border, the officials agreed to allow trade even in off years. Notwithstanding restrictions, trade actually occurred almost every year from 1738 to 1754. When Dzungars asked that markets be opened at Hami (Uighuristan) to relieve the pressure, officials reluctantly agreed (Perdue 2005, 260–261).

The Oirat traders—often "Bukharans" (from Kashgaria or Transoxiana, see above)—typically requested very high prices for their animals, causing officials to engage in weeks of haggling. As a result, amusing negotiations seem to have developed between exasperated Chinese civil servants and disingenuous C Asian traders (Perdue 2005, 262–263). "Bukharans" in many cases headed Dzungar trading missions to the Chinese capital and also moved bulk goods and currency in various directions along the tracks of the SR. Overall, as Map 4.4 shows, there were three major trade links connecting the Oirat economy (including the Tarim Basin protectorate) with its immediate neighbors: in the northwest; the Irtysh and Semipalatinsk with Russia, in the southwest; Tashkent or Ferghana with the Khanate of Bukhara, in the east; and Turfan, Hami, and Suzhou (Gansu) with China.

The apex of Dzungar-Chinese trade was probably reached in 1748–1750. While these peaceful exchanges certainly contributed to shoring up the Oirats' pastoral economy, they also appeared to have softened up Grand Tartary's support. Though at times exasperating for the Qing authorities, trade with the Dzungars promised longer term and larger political gains for China—thus vindicating Qingfu's stance—in as far as the exhibited wealth of the Chinese interior combined with the Qings' military might undermined loyalty of the nomadic state's subject peoples to their imperial leadership.[103]

Galdan Tseren's death (1745) triggered a succession dispute among his sons, which in turn gave rise to a political

---

[101] This third type of mission was of course also linked to the Dzungars' (Mongols') and Tibetans' common Buddhist faith.

[102] A tael is a Chinese measure of (mostly silver) currency weight of 34–38 g (depending on the region).

[103] This may bear—remote—similarity to the (eventually successful) policy of "change through rapprochement" (German: Wandel durch Annäherung) followed by Western powers in the Cold War of the 1970s and 1980s vis-à-vis the USSR and the Eastern bloc. This policy promoted increased trade and human contacts while upholding military deterrence.

crisis and internecine struggles. This destabilization of central power may have facilitated acts of resistance of Uighurs who resented the onerous tax burden and oppressive regime the Dzungars had imposed on them. Unrest soon started to hurt commerce (Ma 2003, 199; Perdue 2005, 265). When the Qing were drawn into the Dzungar conflict by the surrender of one of the warring parties to China, the Qianlong emperor (1736–1795) seized the chance to defeat and conquer Grand Tartary once and for all.

In 1755–1758 Chinese and Khalkha Mongol troops attacked and conquered Kuldzha, the Ili region, Semirechie, and the rest of the empire, including the Tarim Basin protectorate. The Qing armies penetrated the mountain pastures of the Kyrgyz and the Ferghana Valley beyond. One detachment reached the city of Talas—the first presence of the Chinese military there since the famous battle against the caliphate a thousand years earlier—and another camped outside Tashkent (Millward 2007, 96). The military factor—that the Manchu forces were familiar with the nomadic Oirat ways of waging war—combined with the major imbalance of human and material resources between the two adversaries played an important role.

Still, the elimination of the Dzungar Khanate would not have proceeded so swiftly had the Oirats not been hit at about the same time by smallpox, a totally unknown and deadly disease for them. The Oirats had apparently contracted this epidemic when coming into contact with Chinese settlers.[104] The last rebel against Qing domination, the young prince Amursana, also succumbed to smallpox at the age of 35. The total population of Oirats in the middle of the eighteenth century has been gauged between 600,000 and 1 million. According to estimates of the Chinese scholar Wei Yuan, about 40% of Dzungar households were killed by smallpox, 30% were gunned down by the Qing military, and 20% had fled to Russia or the Kazakh Hordes (Perdue 2005, 47–48, 285).

As a result, extensive territories in Dzungaria and Zhetysu were depopulated. Based on the above account, Chu Wen-Djang wrote that more than 80% of Oirats ended up dead by disease and Qing and Kazakh attacks (1966, 1), which Michael Clarke described as "the complete destruction of not only the Dzungar state but of the Dzungars as a people" (2004, 37). The Qing administration filled in the empty area with immigrants, mainly Turkic settlers and a small number of Han Chinese settlers (see also http://en.wikipedia.org/wiki/Zunghar_Khanate). Nomadic Kalmyks (originally Oirat tribes that had migrated to the lower Volga and Northern Caucasus plains over a century before,

but whose pastoral existence was increasingly hemmed in by Russian regulations and settlers) were also welcomed by the Chinese authorities in Semirechie and Dzungaria.

The Qing Dynasty: Incipient Colonization of Eastern CA (First Half of Eighteenth Century)

As mentioned earlier, the Manchus were not entirely pastoral nomads; their original economic system was based on a combination of livestock breeding, hunting, and farming in Manchuria on the Northeastern borderlands of China. Although not genuine steppe dwellers, the Manchus were influenced by C Asian political traditions; their ancestors, the Jurchen, had ruled the north of the Middle Kingdom as the Jin dynasty from 1125 to 1234, before falling to the Mongols (Findlay and O'Rourke 2007, 135, see also above).

As Findlay and O'Rourke point out, in the first half of the seventeenth century, the Manchus created a powerful military machine partly financed by the lucrative trade in furs and in the medicinal root ginseng that their location at the southern fringes of the Far East/Siberia gave them access to (2007, 135). From their homeland, the Manchus first conquered Inner Mongolia (1635). The conquerors adapted the Sogdo-Uighur-Mongol script to fit their own language (Millward 2013, 18). After invading China in 1644 and installing their own Qing dynasty on the throne in Beijing, the Manchus took control of the entire country (all Chinese territory south of the Great Wall) in the mid-seventeenth century.

The Qing state had three capable emperors until the end of the eighteenth century: They ruled under the devices of Kangxi (r. 1662–1722), Yongzheng (r. 1722–1736), and Qianlong (r. 1736–1795). Like earlier nomadic dynasties, the Qing established a dual administrative structure (one administration for nomadic territories, like Mongolia, the other for sedentary lands, possibly comparable to the institutional division of the Khitan-Liao Empire of 946–1125, see above). According to Barfield, this arrangement contributed to preventing the political unification of the steppe by coopting Mongol leaders and dividing their tribes into smaller autonomous units under Manchu oversight (1989, 16). But the Qing did not rule from the steppe (or from their territory of origin, Manchuria), but from Beijing. From the outset, the Qing began to assimilate themselves to Chinese society and statesmanship while retaining their own distinctive ethnicity and prohibiting intermarriage between the Manchus and Chinese. The Qing thus adopted traditional Chinese institutions inherited from the Ming era in the governance of their empire, which was largely staffed by Han civil servants (Haywood 2011, 126; Findlay and O'Rourke 2007, 135).

For the Manchus, the Dzungar Empire in the second half of the seventeenth century became a geopolitically dangerous neighbor, given its successful expansion into the Tarim Basin; its annexation of the trading and strategic cities of Turfan, Hami, and Barkoel at the doorstep of China; and its cultural/

---

[104] This recalls the tragedies that beset Native Americans and Oceanic populations, many of whom died not on the battlefields of European conquests but through contagion of illnesses alien to them. It also recalls the ravaging effect of the bubonic plague, "spread" by the Mongols, on Europeans (see above).

religious links to Mongolia and Tibet. After the treaties of Nerchinsk (1689) and Kiakhta (1727), Russia, induced by Chinese trading concessions, kept its distance from the Dzungars and in any case did not support them in periods of armed confrontation with the Qing (Kauz: China und Zentralasien, in: Fragner and Kappeler 2006: Zentralasien 13.–20. Jhdt, 129–130).

China's "March to the West" in the seventeenth and eighteenth centuries, organized by a semi-nomadic ruling dynasty, was seen as an offensive response to the persistent danger of destructive raids from the steppe, which replaced the Ming's defensive strategy of further fortifying the Great Wall and essentially retreating behind it (Abazov 2008, Map 29). Thus, the conquest of Outer Mongolia (1697) was followed by the reannexation of Hami and Barkoel at the end of the seventeenth century and of Turfan in 1720. The Qing colonization of CA in fact began half a century earlier than the final conquest of the region, in the early 1700s. According to Perdue, the two primary motives of this colonization were to raise grain production in the oasis settlements so as to provide reliable supplies for the troops stationed there and to relieve demographic pressure in the poorest regions of China's northwest (adjacent to CA) and thus to ward off social unrest. A third motive was to ensure permanent imperial control of the western region by establishing a new settler society there (Perdue 2005, 342).

In the first half of the eighteenth century, including the peaceful period from the late 1730s, the Qing army substantially strengthened supply routes, commerce, and access from China proper to CA. Apparently in a few years, the Chinese military grew thoroughly familiar with the transportation of vital grain supplies to far-flung garrisons (Perdue 2005, 230). As Perdue further explains, Qing garrisons, containing from 200 to 1000 servicemen, now became focal points of settlement in pastoral lands. The commanders searched for strategic sights near ample sources of water, grass, and wood. The settlements became stations for grain and weapons storage. Construction workers sent from the Chinese interior stayed for at least 1 year to build the settlements; considerable numbers of exiled criminals were also relocated (Perdue 2005, 232–233). The first state farms were founded in Eastern Xinjiang in the early 1700s (Millward 2007, 82).

Colonization was thus launched primarily under military auspices, and settled soldiers were among the first new farmers to clear land and prisoners helped them. But civil settlers, mostly Han peasants from the northwest, soon followed. Little by little, the camps evolved from military and penal colonies into sites of civilian settlement.[105] The

Han peasants worked under various forms of agrarian institutions, spanning from near-serfdom to independent ownership (Perdue 2005, 342).

Barkoel became the main Chinese military base. With its relatively small number of inhabitants—in contrast to Hami and Turfan—Barkoel could produce enough grain to support both the local population and a substantial garrison. Whereas the agricultural development of Turfan (the westernmost of the three towns) was less promising as long as it was at the very limit of Qing power and directly exposed to Dzungar incursions, the beg of Hami promoted land clearance after Qing troops had driven off raiders from that oasis in 1718 and had helped dig irrigation canals. In the 1730s, with 400–500 new settlers, the beg presided over good harvests and was able to provide the Qing garrison with substantial agricultural supplies. In 1742, subsidies for military land development were discontinued and settlements were converted into civilian colonies which had to pay 40% of their produce as an in-kind duty to the state (Perdue 2005, 351). This seems to imply that development measures considerably raised agricultural settlements' productivity in the first decades of the eighteenth century in Qing CA.

The Chinese economic system remained regulated and supervised by the imperial bureaucracy. Urban merchants, bankers, craftsmen, and industrialists possessed their guilds and professional associations to further their economic interests, but remained dependent on the goodwill of the renowned and powerful civil service. As Maddison notes, the impact of the bureaucracy was generally quite positive in the agricultural sector. Under central bureaucratic oversight, infrastructural works were carried out (e.g., irrigation canals dug in CA), new seeds and cultures were popularized, technical advice was provided, agricultural manuals were distributed, and farmers moved to new promising regions (e.g., parts of CA). A network of public granaries and storehouses was put in place to assure food supply and combat famines (Maddison 1998, 24–25).

Yet Maddison cautions that the effect of the bureaucracy was probably less positive in other branches of the economy. Like in past centuries and even millennia (see Box 2.3), entrepreneurial activity and private capital accumulation remained relatively weakly protected by the law. Businesses that promised or proved to be lucrative often attracted official attention and were liable to become subject to heavy taxation or to other kinds of "pressure" by the authorities. Large enterprises in the Qing Empire in most cases were either public monopolies or monopolies approved by the state. Power and prestige continued to lie in the imperial hierarchy (Maddison 1998, 25).

Once the truce had been agreed upon and regular trade relations had been officially established with the Dzungar Khanate in the late 1730s, the quantities of goods the Oirats brought to the border soon exceeded what local Chinese markets could bear. As Perdue vividly describes, dried

---

[105] Compare the foundation of British colonial establishments in Australia as convict settlements about half a century later (Anderle et al. (ed) 1973, 421). Of course the Qing settlements in Xinjiang also recall the ancient Han dynasty military-agricultural colonies/garrisons (tuntian system) in CA.

grapes and rare medicinal products like sal ammoniac and antelope horn piled up in warehouses from which it was difficult to arrange distribution, at least at the elevated prices that had been paid to the suppliers. Livestock and sheep served local interests better because they could be used to support garrisons, but even these herds seem to have surpassed local demand. Moreover, the Dzungars most of the time insisted on being paid in silver (instead of in tea, silk, or cloth offered by the officials), thus threatening to cause a substantial drain of Chinese bullion.[106] Apparently there was a real danger that Qing treasuries could approach exhaustion if all the goods that were on offer were actually purchased in silver (Perdue 2005, 263). Needless to say, any meaningful adjustment of purchase prices to prevailing market conditions seems to have been politically out of the question (at the time).

In order to unblock the marketing of Dzungar merchandise and, as far as possible, safeguard Chinese stocks of silver and thus maintain the stability of the currency, the Qianlong emperor turned to the initiative of private merchants and businessmen. But for whatever reasons (state overregulation of merchants or insufficient commercial viability) this recourse was only of limited avail. As Perdue explains, the government had to continue providing inducements to draw traders from the Chinese interior. It paid many of their transportation costs and furnished them with carts formerly used for military supplies. When the merchants complained that the amount of goods to be bought from the Dzungars was unpredictable or staggering, officials agreed to lend them funds to make up the difference. When the glut of medicinal goods could only be disposed of at low resale prices, causing businessmen to lose money, the authorities stepped in to bridge the difference. The governor of the province of Gansu, Huang Tinggui, argued that it was vital to accommodate market pressures, because this trade was a "national security" affair, in which all parts of the empire had their stakes. Due to the provision of sizable trade subsidies, the Qing treasury typically lost funds after the trading season had ended (Perdue 2005, 264).

After the utter defeat of Dzungar forces, the elimination of Grand Tartary and the incorporation of its territories into the Chinese Empire, the above type of subsidized trade was definitely terminated, and Qing colonization and development policies were spread to entire East Turkestan, which was henceforth officially called "Xinjiang" (New Lands or New Frontier) (Kauz 2006, 121; Millward 2007, 97).

4.1.4 Long-Term Factors Explaining CA's Economic and Political Decline from the Sixteenth Century

For assessing CA's (at least relative) economic decline from the early modern times, it appears important to distinguish from each other:

- The relationship between settled and nomadic civilizations (treated in Sect. 4.1.2)
- The relationship between CA and the rest of the world (treated in the present section)
- The relationship between SR trade and maritime trade (treated in Sect. 4.1.5)

Of course these factors can overlap (like nomadic empires and CA or the heyday of C Asian trading states and that of the SR business) and this is taken into account where necessary, but for the sake of the clarity and plausibility of the argument, they should be separated as far as possible.

4.1.4.1 Legacy of Weakened Production Potential (Mongol and Tamerlane Devastations, Thirteenth to Fifteenth Centuries)

Genghis Khan, his successors, and Tamerlane bear responsibility for immense destruction of physical and human capital, including millions of deaths during their wars of conquest and oppression. The long-term impact of these horrific acts on the most stricken region was quite sobering: As Kauz succinctly put it, CA would no longer play an outstanding role in world (economic) history (2009, 321)[107]. However, some of CA's regions, e.g., Transoxiana, Shash, Khorassan, or the Ili area were built up and even embellished by massive reallocation of human capital and material resources that had been forcefully withdrawn from other regions in and outside CA. Some towns, particularly those vital as capitals and overland trade centers (like Saray, New Saray, and Almalik/Kuldzha under the Mongols, Samarkand, Bukhara, and Urgench under Timur)[108] were constructed or rebuilt, while others were left to decay. Remarkably, after the Mongol devastations and the Great Plague of the mid-fourteenth century, birth rates soon recovered and apparently rose so much that around 1370 (i.e., before Tamerlane's reign), the demographic situation had

---

[106] This even corresponded to a—comparatively modest—reversal of the direction of the silver flow from China. After centuries of west-east flow from Europe to the Middle Kingdom, mostly along the maritime route, now there was a limited east-west flow along overland Eurasian routes. How much of the silver acquired by the Dzungars eventually reached Europe is unclear.

---

[107] Since these nomadic or semi-nomadic conquerors originated in or were closely attached to CA itself, with hindsight one might also call their behavior "self destructive."

[108] Here one should add the Mongol imperial capital of Karakorum, although it lies outside CA as defined in this study.

almost returned to its ex ante level of the early thirteenth century (Roux, 305).

4.1.4.2 Impact of European Discoveries

Discovery and Increasing Use of Sea Route from Europe to India and China, Circumventing CA (from the Sixteenth Century)

The reversion to the status quo ante of trade relations with the Orient following the collapse of the Mongol Empire certainly did not satisfy European merchants and statesmen, who attempted to find new routes to India and China, preferably bypassing Muslim middlemen. Yet this relapse after a trans-Eurasian trade boom was nothing genuinely new; such relapses had already happened at least twice: after the collapse of the Roman Empire and after the demise of the Tang dynasty (see above). Europeans seem to have resented having to buy Eastern spices and Chinese silk through powerful (Islamic) middlemen, apparently at great cost.[109] European voyages of exploration may have been the product of a sense of vulnerability and exclusion (Haywood 2011, 110).

But this time the Europeans had made a number of promising inventions and innovations, notably in the area of nautical technology: the use of the compass (inherited from China) was improved, cartography was developed, and caravels (broad-beamed ships which could carry ample supplies of water and provisions) were equipped with triangular sails (in addition to traditional square ones), which enabled navigation against the wind (Suret-Canale 1996, 236–237). European navigation in the late Middle Ages thus rendered possible in 1492 Columbus' voyage across the Atlantic and discovery of America, as well as in 1498 Vasco da Gama's opening up of the Cape route to India. In 1517, Portuguese caravels landed in Guangzhou (Canton) for the first time. Regular maritime trade relations were established and quickly grew between Portugal (later Spain and other Western European nations), India, and China. In a couple of decades, the Europeans became the world's leading merchants. As intended, the new naval routes freed European traders from exclusive reliance on Islamic middlemen and overland connections for access to coveted Asian goods (Roux 1997, 382; Haywood 2011, 138).

Mostly thanks to European inventions, advances, and discoveries, maritime transportation to and from Asia soon became cheaper than the overland alternative. As Roux

notes, already in 1505 spices are reported to have been less expensive in Lisbon than in Venice, where most goods from the Orient arrived via the land route across CA (1997, 382). The economies at both ends of Eurasia appear to have been stimulated by the new interaction; in Europe as well as the Near East, Chinese silk was once again in great demand, and porcelain (china), new to the Old World, became craved for. In this sense, according to Jacques Pirenne, « La caravelle a vaincu le chameau » ("The caravel beat the camel"), and the importance of CA as a transit region and of the SR as an international trade network started to decrease, at least in relative terms. Maritime east-west trade began to (partially) replace overland east-west trade (Boulnois 2008, 20, 2009, 54; Mokyr 2003, 371). Doubtlessly, C Asian transit in the early modern times lost some Chinese goods to seaborne delivery (Nolte 2005, 179).

The importance of trading towns along the SR, and later the size of their population, started to erode. Given the importance of trade for their economies, landlocked C Asian regions and states entered a period of—first relative, then absolute—economic decline. While seaborne trade was also saddled with pitfalls, like capricious weather and proliferous pirates, the costs of maritime connections eventually dropped to only half of those of the caravan trade. Thus gradually major international trade routes shifted away from the overland caravans, separating CA from the mainstream of world commerce (Wild 1992, 9; Kamev 2005, 81; Nolte 2005, 178).

However, this transition was a drawn-out process that happened unevenly and lasted for at least a quarter of a millennium. The changing importance of east-west trade routes was also influenced by other factors, like domestic political (in)stability and evolving geoeconomics (see below). And in many instances, the migration of trade from the overland to the seaborne variant essentially referred to transit trade, i.e., shipments going from one end of Eurasia to the other or at least over long hauls and did not pertain to regional, local, or neighborhood trade, which in most cases was not subject to maritime competition and remained quite active and competitive (Lary 2012, 80).

But the lion's share of tolls and levies could not be procured from the taxation of regional or local trade. In all likelihood, transcontinental caravan trade was the prime source of wealth of the SR oasis towns and even their principal raison d'être (Hambly (ed) 1966, 184; Mokyr 2003, 371). Once long-distance overland trade was on the wane, C Asian rulers (whether sedentary or nomadic) were left with less revenues to finance their administrations; purchase firearms and shore up their defenses; sustain security on the trade routes and in the bazaars; repair irrigation canals, karez, and other infrastructure; and subsidize culture and the arts. Loss of revenue from trade and less expenditure to support agriculture was one of the reasons for the decline

---

[109] One should add that after the demise of the Mongol Empire there were a number of Muslim middlemen, some of whom were in competition (and sometimes even at war) with each other, so that Westerners did not face an Islamic transit monopoly. For instance, there were the Golden Horde and its successor khanates (until the mid-sixteenth century), the Ottoman Empire, and the Mamluk Sultanate in Egypt (until the latter was incorporated into the Ottoman Empire in 1517).

of C Asian farming regions in the seventeenth century. Less prosperity reduced C Asian rulers' power to keep open and assure safety of trade routes and possibly also diminished their incentives and interest in doing so (Shukow et al. 1958/1966, Band 5, 648; Hambly (ed) 1966/1979, 184). Weaker security made overland routes even less attractive for long-distance traders, which could trigger a vicious circle of contracting SR trade and deteriorating trading conditions.

Fragner infers that CA was eventually exposed to the danger of marginalization and isolation (2008, 65). Soucek vividly concurs: At its most extreme, the effect of this changed environment could be viewed as one that transformed a once busy crossroads of world trade into a landlocked backwater (2000, 150). By the first half of the eighteenth century, what remained of the SR through CA was suffering from severe competition, to which the development of routes across Russian Siberia had added. What the Western Europeans had attained by their command over the sea routes and their East India companies, the Russians achieved by transcontinental expansion spearheaded by the Cossacks (Ponting 2001, 531; Krieger 2003, 271).

As mentioned above, the Russians were very interested in conducting trade with China and offered their precious furs in exchange for silk, tea, and other goods. Diplomatic relations were opened, leading to the landmark treaties of Nerchinsk in 1689 and Kiakhta in 1728, which, i.e., provided a framework for growing bilateral trade. Thus, from the end of the seventeenth century, the C Asian economies—or essentially the Khanates of Bukhara and Khiva, the Kazakh Hordes, and the Dzungar Empire—found themselves bypassed to the south by shipping lanes, as well as to the north by the Siberian Road (Roux 1997, 383).[110] While the Siberian route was relatively safe, did not pass through intermediaries (transit countries) and possessed only one toll station—in Kiakhta, from the eighteenth century onward—it also featured some logistical drawbacks: Sino-Russian trade had to be conducted through the forests of Northern Asia. This route was longer and more encumbered with snow (a winter problem) than alternative connections through CA (see Map 4.4). Moreover, the Siberian Road was often interrupted by rivers which flowed at right angles to the route to China (summer problem) (Nolte 2005, 179).

Conquest of America and Immense Silver Finds Strengthen Atlantic Europe, Indirectly Weaken CA

Thanks to its conquest of America and immense silver finds there, Atlantic Europe grew richer and much more important globally. The increased economic and political strength of

Portugal, Spain, France, the Netherlands, and England, which all, for obvious reasons, had easier seaborne access to India and China, indirectly confirmed the sidelining of CA.

In the 1520s, the Spanish conquistador Cortez conquered Mexico and the Aztec Empire; in the 1530s, his counterparts Pizarro and Almagro invaded Peru and what later became Bolivia and wiped out the Inca Empire. The conquests brought Spain large quantities of gold and more importantly, the world's richest silver mines were acquired in the 1540s (Potosi/Bolivia, Zacatecas/Mexico, and later Guanajuato/Mexico). The appropriation of huge amounts of silver and other resources from the New World contributed to vesting Spain, Portugal, and other countries of Atlantic Europe that had become colonial powers with important positions in global trade (Ott, Schäfer (eds.) 1984: Wirtschaftsploetz, 73–74, 79; Adle et al. 2003a, 28).

Europeans, particularly the nobility, remained strongly attracted by Oriental products, primarily Chinese ones (tea, silk, china, lacquer, etc.). While there was limited demand for European products in India, China, and the East Indies, there was considerable demand for silver as a means of exchange. This greatly expanded the credit available for financing European mercantile ventures. Spaniards, Portuguese, and others were now able to buy Eastern craft products and erstwhile luxuries by using their large stocks of bullion (Gernet 1972/1985, volume 2, 47; Haywood 2011, 138). As Ponting put it, European domination of the Atlantic and access to silver and other riches in previously undreamt-of quantities enabled the Europeans to buy their way into the Asian trading system (2001, 519).[111] A global increase and redistribution of purchasing power in favor of the Old World and a shift of demand from the previous European center of gravity, the Mediterranean, to the Atlantic seaboard, had major repercussions for CA.

Most of the American silver reportedly made its way across the Atlantic to Western Europe and from there around Africa to India and China or—once the Pacific had come under European control and the Philippines had become Spanish in the 1560s—directly across the Pacific Ocean to the Middle Kingdom (Gernet 1972/1985, vol. 2, 47). Flows of silver from America further boosted economic expansion in Europe as well as Asia and thus the emerging global economy. Given the influx of silver, the precious metal was increasingly used for monetary purposes in China as well as India; silver contributed to monetization and, to some degree, to commercialization of these two large economies (Findlay and O'Rourke 2007, 128). The entire output of the Spanish American mines from the mid-sixteenth to the early

---

[110] Of course the volumes of trade via the maritime routes dwarfed those of the Northern Asian route.

[111] Less well-financed and equipped Arab and other Muslim traders in the Indian Ocean and beyond were successively put out of business.

nineteenth century was at least 75,000 tons of silver, more than half of which was reportedly used for the purchase of Chinese staple and luxury goods that were desired literally around the world. Thus eventually the Middle Kingdom became the largest silver depot of the planet, which is not surprising given that the size of the Chinese market easily dwarfed all others (Perdue 2005, 380; Gernet 1972/1985, vol. 2, 47; Gunder Frank 2005, 52)[112].

Given its medium of exchange function, at least a marginal share of the large amount of silver flowing from America via Western Europe to Asia took the traditional overland SR. Therefore, in absolute terms, silver from America probably provided a (limited) impulse for Eurasian overland trade (Findlay and O'Rourke 2007, 132). However, in relative terms, overland trade was soon vastly losing ground. The overwhelming majority of American silver was shipped on the sea routes, which points to a substantial loss of importance of the SR in world trade from the sixteenth century.

Given the transfer of European purchasing power and economic activity from the Mediterranean to the Atlantic and the expansion of mercantile activity of Dutch, French, and English East India companies, there was a clear spatial shift of demand from Central and Eastern Europe and the Eastern Mediterranean to the Atlantic seaboard (Feldbauer and Liedl 2008, 31). Once the maritime route to the East had been discovered and secured, it was geographically obvious that this route was more favorable for merchants coming from Europe's western rim than the comparatively remote SR—which had strong links to traditional European trading powers like Genoa, Venice, the southern German cities, or the Hanse. This geographical obviousness is unconnected to the issue of whether an "Islamic bolt" hindered trade from the Eastern Mediterranean or not. Therefore, apart from the discovery and use of the sea route to the East itself, the geographic shift of demand/markets to the Atlantic seaboard constituted another reason for CA's loss of its strategic position as a prosperous turntable of trade between the Orient and the Occident (Adle et al. 2003a, 28).

Summing up, thanks to new navigation technology and the discovery of the maritime route (in the early sixteenth century), new European trade connections were created with the Orient and transit trade was deviated away from overland C Asian routes. CA thus lost its mercantile centrality in trade between East and West. Then the appropriation of American silver (second half of sixteenth century) brought about a market shift and new seaborne trade creation effects, which also led to some trade spillover to overland C Asian routes. But this spillover character was only a by-product of swiftly expanding trade elsewhere, which underlines that CA was in the process of losing an important share of global commerce. What probably started as a relative loss of importance of SR trade through CA eventually turned into a major decline affecting the entire region.

4.1.4.3 Impact of European Industrial Advancement

C Asian states (whether sedentary or nomadic) were soon outstripped by superior modern technologies of warfare and peaceful production:

As mentioned earlier in connection with the impact of the "gunpowder revolution" on steppe nomadism, Western advancements in military technology in terms of muskets and cannons soon cancelled out the relative advantage traditionally held by CA's mobile cavalry. More generally, from the seventeenth century, the level of manufacturing across the region failed to keep pace with that of Europe. With respect to guns and artillery, large-scale iron casting and the use of blast furnaces made a big difference. As Habib explains, cast-iron European firearms established their advantage with regard to cheapness; moreover, superior drilling techniques and the attainment of greater precision and standardization also counted (2003b, 475–476). The sedentary C Asian states like the Khanates of Bukhara and Khiva knew firearms, but they lacked expertise and had less experience with their use (notably of artillery) than the Safavid, Mughal, or Ottoman empires (the three so-called Gunpowder Empires), not to speak of Russia or China (Chuvin et al. 2008, 60).

Three factors (partly already mentioned) may explain this lack of expertise: First, as mentioned earlier, with the strong expansion of seaborne international trade, landlocked CA was put at a disadvantage vis-à-vis the "Gunpowder" Empires (that had access to the Indian Ocean and/or the Mediterranean Sea), when it came to absorbing European influences. Secondly, there was a loss of tolls and transit duties as a result of the weakening of overland trade in the wake of the establishment of the maritime route to the Orient. This undercut C Asian princes' capacity to buy firearms in sufficient numbers and quality. Thirdly, religiously influenced confrontation between the Khanate of Bukhara (which was mostly Sunni) and the Safavid Empire (whose official faith was Shiism) contributed to isolating CA further from outside influences, at least those coming from the Near and Middle East. All in all, the Uzbeks, whose khanate combined sedentary zones with nomadic territories, might have failed to build an empire because, while their military no longer possessed a formidable "cavalry arm,"

---

[112] The dimension of this flood also had consequences for the institutional organization of the Chinese monetary and fiscal system: Uncoined silver gained importance as an alternative monetary medium to the traditional bronze coin (the "qian," after all, dating back to the Han dynasty, see above). The Ming dynasty eventually became an active proponent of the silver economy when it converted most tax collection to silver in the "Single Whip" reforms (1580). Under Qing officials, silver flows were important for interregional transfers of tax proceeds between local treasuries (Perdue 2005, 380, 386).

they had not yet adequately developed a "gunpowder arm" (Adle et al. 2003a, 28).[113]

European technological advances, manufacturing productivity, and efficiency gains concerned a large range of industrial goods beyond weapons. In most of these fields, Western goods became cheaper and attained higher quality than products of C Asian provenance. Europe thus began to "outperform" CA in economic terms in more and more fields. At the same time, international demand for some C Asian export items that had been highly valued for centuries or even millennia—primarily horses—lost some momentum. The region's traditional and inherited technological profile, strength, and economic specialization started to be challenged by accelerating capitalist growth, structural change, and competition from the West. In this sense, CA's terms of trade, which had been favorable for a very long period of time, took a sharp turn for the worse.

4.1.4.4 Religious and Political Factors

Religious rigidity of regionally dominant Islam was on the increase: By the mid-fifteenth century practically the whole of Turkestan (except for parts of Dzungaria) had become Muslim. From the early sixteenth century, strong Shiite-Sunni antagonism (represented by the confrontation of the Safavid state and the Khanate of Bukhara) reduced religious and cultural relations and partly also hampered commerce between Iran and Turan. After a wave of refugees from Persia, including luminaries fleeing Safavid persecution, had contributed to a cultural blossoming of Shaybanid CA, religious rigidity of Islam, conventionalism, and even fanaticism seem to have gained the upper hand and to have produced a negative impact on C Asian economic development (Kamev 2005, 80; Adle et al. 2003a, 30).

These two spiritual factors—rigidity and isolation—probably soon entered into a kind of fateful convergence with each other. The newly created ideological enmity between CA and Persia isolated Turan from Iran, the Middle East, and the Indian Ocean. According to Soucek, the Sunni-Shiite divide gradually contributed to the landlocked region's (CA's) cultural provincialism and atrophy (2000, 150). A spirit of conventionalism pervaded C Asian thought and theology. A peculiar kind of skepticism toward science became typical for Transoxianan society and was partly responsible for CA's falling behind in economic development vis-à-vis Europe and other regions. Any break with tradition was deemed an offense to fundamental religious

values. This situation hardly changed with the passing of the Shaybanid and Astrakhanid dynasties. Thus the persistent spiritual isolation of the Emirate of Bukhara and the Khanates of Khiva and Khoqand, if anything, exacerbated religious rigidity and economic marginalization (Fragner 2008, 67; Roudik 2007, 55; Golden 2011, 115).

As regards political stability in CA (including the domestic situation within countries and their external relations), the overall development appears to have been toward increasing political instability and regional conflicts, albeit not without intermittent periods of restabilization: Following the manifold changes brought about by Genghis Khan and his successors as well as by Tamerlane, the fifteenth century saw a degree of political restabilization across Eurasia ("Timurid renaissance," recovery and consolidation of the Chagatay Khanate, stabilization of Volga Khanates, etc.). A number of authors, particularly Rossabi (1990, 351), consider the political disruption and instability that broke out along the SR from the sixteenth century onward, a salient factor for the long-term decline of the C Asian economy. A rising number of borders and tolls as such was nothing new and had also existed in the pre-Mongol era. Rossabi mentions the driving force that could have triggered the political destabilization: Probably the above-referred-to loss of trade revenues to seaborne competition from the early sixteenth century led to a situation where the overland route no longer carried sufficient traffic to support administrations strong enough to protect it and uphold stability in the region (Adle et al. 2003a, 28).

As mentioned above, from the early 1500s frequent wars between Safavid Shiites on the one hand and Shaybanid and Ottoman Sunnis on the other obstructed SR trade. The repeated outbreaks of internecine struggles among C Asian princes did not facilitate matters. In the seventeenth century, the Chagatay Khanate as well as the Kazakh Hordes became subject to devastating Dzungar blows and conquests. Rising internal and external instability contributed to an extended period of decline in Persia (mid-seventeenth to first half of eighteenth century), followed by an onerous upheaval. On-and-off Sino-Dzungar warfare was equally not conducive to long-distance Eurasian caravan trade, which suffered major losses.

Perhaps in a typical statement that could have easily been made 50 years earlier or later, the ambassador of Peter the Great, Florio Beneventi, in the early eighteenth century characterized the political situation in the Khanates of Bukhara and Khiva very succinctly: "All are usually at loggerheads with each other" (Shukow et al. 1958/1966, Band 5, 267). Having less revenues from the taxation of SR merchants at their disposal (due to the partial shift of trade from the overland to the maritime routes), the khans looked elsewhere for possibilities to replace lost proceeds and some employed and eventually wasted significant means in numerous wars to grab territory and assets from their

---

[113] Yet even Gunpowder Empires' military might in the eighteenth century became insufficient to resist European expansion: European military technology had given superiority to the English and French East India Companies' troops over strong Asian armies as shown in the Carnatic wars (1747–1763), which established British dominance over large territories on the Indian subcontinent and contributed to the downfall of the Mughal Empire (Habib 2003a, 337).

neighbors/rivals. The unstable budgetary situation and the deterioration of public order affected the C Asian Khanates' agriculture and industry, which also went into decline (Abazov 2008, Map 28). In this environment of economic recession, the warring parties were competing for shares of swiftly decreasing resources (or, so to say, of a rapidly shrinking economic pie).[114]

But there were also intermittent periods of political restabilization: the Khanate of Bukhara under Abdallah II (1557–1598) and the early Astrakhanids (first half of seventeenth century), the Chagatay Khanate under Said Khan and successors (1514–end of sixteenth century), the Mughal Empire under Akbar (1556–1605), the Safavid Empire under Shah Abbas I (1587–1629), the Kazakh nomadic confederacy under Kasym Khan and successors (sixteenth to early seventeenth century), and others. These periods of temporary restabilization will be dealt with in more detail below in the framework of the analysis of SR development from the early sixteenth century.

Box 4.3: Main SR Merchandise Exported in Sixteenth to Eighteenth Centuries (ca. 1500–1750)

Overall, in these centuries the importance of overland trade in luxury products further declined (compared to the past), although particularly silk and porcelain still constituted prominent merchandise. Interregional or neighborhood trade was made up of a multitude of products.

Main articles of SR export (according to various surveyed publications, and possibly including reexports):

China:

Tea, silk, silk fabric, porcelain, cotton fabric, textiles, silver, rhubarb, lacquer, precious handicraft, fashion accessories, brocades, grain, rice, metalware, precious stones, pottery, spices, tobacco, gold, medicinal plants

Dzungars/Dzungar Empire (excl. Tarim Basin, largely tribute trade with China):

Horses, sheep, camels, draught animals (oxen), hides, sheepskin, furs, wool, salt, certain medicinal products (sal ammoniac, antelope horn), special felt boots

Chagatay Khanate/Tarim Basin, Hami, Turfan:

Jade, musk, fine wool, cotton, cotton fabrics and clothes, dried grapes, slaves, dishes, fruit, carpets/rugs, arms, rice, bread, silk

Uzbek Khanates/Bukhara, Khiva, Khoqand:

Cotton, cotton cloth and apparel, chintz (printed cotton cloth), Bukharan lambskins (of karakul sheep), slaves (kuli), horses, dried fruit (apricots, raisins), high-quality paper, medicinal plants, camels, silk, silk fabrics and textiles, leather products, carpets/rugs, arms, rice, bread, precious metals, lapis lazuli, mirrors, pottery

Persia/Safavid Empire/Empire of Nadir Shah:

Silk, silk textiles (both in raw and finished form), carpets/rugs, silk brocades, cotton, cotton textiles, wool textiles, horses, precious metals

India/Mughal Empire:

Cotton cloth and textiles; chintz; batistes (fine fabrics); silk and other textiles; dyes; indigo; precious stones including pearls, gold; spices; sugar; medicinal herbs; slaves; calico (plain woven cotton cloth with figured pattern); opium; aromatic roots; corals

Kazakhs/Kazakh Khanate:

Sheep, horses, camels, rams, goats, wool and woolen goods, hides and leather, slaves, craft items, such as sheepskin caftans, furs and furcoats of sable and squirrel

Turkmens:

Horses, particularly famous Akhal-Teke horses, rams, slaves, carpets, woolen clothing, horse cloths, saddlebags

Russia:

Furs (i.e., precious sables, ermines), walrus tusks and ivory, processed and unprocessed leather, various types of woolens and other cloths, lumber, manufactured goods, grain, tobacco, bridles, saddles, metals, amber, honey, sugar, wooden and metal utensils, armor, glass

Western Europe (particularly Italy, Germany, Netherlands):

Silver, fine cloth, apparel, manufactured products, high-quality brocade

---

[114] Once a major source of regular revenue—SR trade—had started to diminish, one could argue with Olson that the stationary bandit at least partly reverted to a roving bandit. Or in other words, a model of largely predictable taxation more or less based on the respect of rules and rights changed back to a model of plundering and arbitrary exploitation of the economy. Or put even more crudely, some regional rulers may have readopted the logic: "If you can't get wealth from traders, rob your neighbors." Of course this was a vicious circle similar to but more general than the one mentioned in the text above dealing with the increasing use of the sea route: Declining political stability drove down tax proceeds which further compromised stability, etc.

4.1.5 From Dynamic Transcontinental Trade to Declining SR Due to Numerous Factors

4.1.5.1 SR Trade Comes Under Pressure from Maritime Competition (Early Sixteenth Century)

In the first half of the sixteenth century, the maritime route became a cheaper as well as quicker way to reach China from the Mediterranean and vice versa. At this time, a SR merchant might take 18 months to cross Eurasia overland from one end to the other, which was a little slower than if he/she had opted for the ocean route (Ponting 2001, 531). However, these 18 months were still (almost) twice as long as it had taken in the Mongol era.[115] Uzbek rule in Mavarannahr (1500–1599) coincided with the gradual decline of transcontinental caravan trade, which—more than farming or industrial activity—was the oasis towns' main source of wealth and their basis of livelihood (Hambly (ed) 1966/1979, 184).

There may be disputes about exactly when and why trans-C Asian trade declined in the sixteenth and seventeenth centuries, which factors were at work first and which intervened later, and, since we do not possess sufficient quantitative data, whether the decline was absolute or only relative to increasing trade elsewhere (Gunder Frank 1992, 39). Yet at the dawn of the era of capitalist economic expansion, a pertinent question appears to be "Supposing there was further absolute trade and economic growth on the SR, was this growth as dynamic as that of seaborne trade with East Asia after 1500?" Eurasian caravan trade could continue to be "brisk" and "of significance" and yet eventually succumb to marginalization in world trade (Golden 2011, 115; Fragner 2008, 65).

Of course, much depends on what one means by "Silk Road": Whether one considers only goods that went from one coast of Eurasia (more precisely from the shores of the Black Sea or the Eastern Mediterranean) to the other (more precisely the East or South China Sea) or if one also includes purely regional segments of the Eurasian trade web (e.g., the Chinese, C Asian, Russian, Indian, or Middle Eastern markets) in one's conception. A particular focus would pertain to trans-ecological trade between nomadic and sedentary cultures, which often ran in a north-south direction across the Eurasian steppe belt (typically between the winter encampments of the nomads at the edge of the grasslands and the markets of the C Asian oasis belt) (Millward 2007, 77). Some, but not necessarily all, of the regional segments may also be linked—as neighbors or adjacent regions more or less intensively trading with each other. Given the balance of power up to approximately the second half of the eighteenth century, trade between nomadic powers and sedentary cultures could be either based on tributary relations or on straight market exchange.

Thus, looking at the spatial dimension of SR trade, one can distinguish between:

(a) Transcontinental trade, which in almost all cases is transit trade[116]
(b) Interregional or neighborhood trade
(c) Regional and local trade

Regarding the power relationship between nomadic rulers and sedentary polities, there are:

(a) Tributary trade relations
(b) Non-tributary trade relations

Some examples of post-Mongol era tribute trade:

– Trade between the Golden Horde, respectively, its successor khanates (of Kazan and Astrakhan) and the Russian principalities (fourteenth to sixteenth centuries)
– Trade between the Kazakh confederacy/Kazakh Hordes and towns along the Syr Daria under its/their rule (late fifteenth to eighteenth centuries)
– Trade between Oirat Khanate and the Ming dynasty (sixteenth century), later between Grand Tartary and the Ming, respectively, Qing dynasties (seventeenth to eighteenth centuries)
– Trade between the Dzungar Empire (more precisely Dzungaria and Zhetysu) and its Tarim Basin protectorate (1680–1758)

4.1.5.2 Interregional Mercantilist Renaissance of Trade (Late Sixteenth to Early Seventeenth Centuries)

As alluded to above, from the sixteenth century there were important technological, economic, and political forces exerting a disadvantageous impact on SR trade: advances in navigation, competition from the maritime route, less resources for upholding security, and/or political destabilization. Yet these tendencies seem to have been temporarily counteracted or offset by factors that stabilized and even strengthened CA and the SR network (Table 3.1). These factors pertain to political authority, economic policy, and business development.

Simultaneous Rule of Strong Political Leaders Who Carried Out Important Economic Reforms in "Gunpowder Empires"

While transcontinental trade was no longer as competitive as before, interregional or neighborhood trade (between one state and the next, like between the Khanate of Bukhara and India or between Russia and Persia or between the Chagatay Khanate and China) did not immediately suffer

---

[115] This should not come as a surprise. As explained earlier, the Mongol rulers (who had governed practically the entire SR network) had eliminated almost all borders and customs duties and had set up a specific transcontinental infrastructure (the Yam system) geared to facilitating and accelerating overland communication and travel, and thus holding the giant empire together.

[116] Transit trade—conveyance of goods across a respective region (e.g., CA) without any processing, but possibly with reselling.

or was not necessarily affected (Nolte 2005, 178; Perdue 2005, 400). Given its nature and its relatively short distances, interregional or neighborhood trade continued to command cost advantages compared to maritime time between Europe and Asia. Against this background, a number of countries wielding power in CA and on the SR in the second half of the sixteenth century witnessed the:

- Simultaneous rule of strong political leaders
- Who carried out important economic reforms
- In an environment when the SR benefitted from some inflow of American silver

Given the weakening of the center of Eurasia after the fourteenth century and the strengthening of empires at its periphery that also had access to the sea (Muscovite Russia, Ming China, the "Gunpowder Empires," European colonial powers), over time SR trade became geographically "re-segmented" or "compartmentalized." Since nobody possessed the technology or capability to exert (or reestablish) control over the entire transcontinental trade network anymore[117] and since such control had become less attractive or profitable due to competing routes anyway[118], imperially oriented largely mercantilist trade schemes and policies of principally non-C Asian powers gained the upper hand (Osterhammel and Petersson 2003, 35–37).

Among the strong leaders who brought about political stabilization and centralization within their polities in the second half of the sixteenth century and partly later were:

In the Khanate of Bukhara: Khan Abdullah II (1583–1598), Imam Quli Khan (1608–1640)

In the Chagatay Khanate: Said Khan (1514–1533) and successors up to the late sixteenth century

In Mughal India: Khan Akbar (1556–1605), Khan Jahangir (1605–1627)

In the Kazakh Khanate: Kasym Khan (1511–1523) and his son Khan Aknazar (1538–1580)

In Muscovite Russia: Czar Ivan IV "Grozny" ("The Terrible") (1547–1584)

In Safavid Persia: Shah Abbas I "The Great" (1587–1629)

Political stabilization did away with insecurity, chaos, and uncertainty, which is a precondition for any meaningful expansion of economic activities. Fortunately, major lengthy wars were not typical for this period. Trade routes were

pacified. Rules were more strictly implemented and supervision of commerce stepped up. To take Russia as an example, while merchants certainly welcomed enforcement of their contractual and property rights, they were not that pleased about having to accept centralized monitoring of their business affairs (Dale 1994, 13).

The economic reforms carried out comprised fiscal reforms (in most cases centralization and strengthening of tax collection) which facilitated the financing of military reforms and various civilian expenditure policies. The latter often focused on infrastructural building programs (public edifices, irrigation canals (aryks), covered water reservoirs (sardabas), bridges, fords, caravanserais). In some cases, foreign (European or Chinese) technological assistance was accepted to modernize armies, but also civilian production (glass, pottery, etc.). The latter pertains to industrial policy, which also included the granting of large tax-exempt estates to wealthy merchants or tycoons (in Russia called "promyshlenniki") who developed agricultural, mining, or manufacturing activities.

On other occasions, import substitution and export promotion strategies were carried out, e.g., through the establishment of government factories, the increase of customs duties, and other vigorous state intervention. This included the promotion of infant industries. Silk and textile factories were set up by the Safavids and carpet workshops by the Mughals. Processing and exportation of imported unprocessed goods was also a strategy. Thus, the Muscovy Company's impressive but tightly regulated trade activities (e.g., Persian silk exports to Russia which were then processed and partly reexported) seem to have fit well into the mercantilist trade interests of the rulers concerned. The goal also was to acquire silver to buttress national currencies.

This leads to monetary reforms which flanked industrial policy and provided for the regularization of coinage, the increase or at least stabilization of the quality of the metallic currency, and if necessary, the reduction of the number of mints. Apart from avoiding instability and unrest, these policies were typically motivated by sovereign longer-term revenue needs and the desire for the enhancement of national wealth and power. The means as well as the goals of Eurasian powers' economic reforms resembled those of European mercantilism, which emerged at about the same time and may have—via the improved maritime communication routes—influenced Eurasian rulers' policy choices.

Attempts at creating regional/imperial trade spheres by military means—"gunpowder imperialism," as one might call it—did not always work in CA (see also above). Perhaps comparable to Moscow's successful quest to control the Volga trade route along its entire length and thus to hold sway over the Eurasian steppe route, the Mughals of India strived to reestablish authority over the trading routes north of the

---

[117] Tamerlane's and the Dzungars' attempts to regain control of trans-Eurasian trade routes failed. And the Manchu Empire (after 1758) was not willing or able to achieve such control either.

[118] These were from the early sixteenth century, the seaborne route (around Africa and through the Indian Ocean), and from the late seventeenth century its supplement, the Siberian route.

Hindu Kush and thus to regain[119] the possibility to regularly and directly recruit warriors and horses—an important asset for a ruling Muslim dynasty in South Asia. In the seventeenth century, the Mughals or Indian Timurids undertook their last attempt to reconquer their former possessions in CA; yet the capture of Balkh in 1646–1647 turned out to be a costly and catastrophic failure (Hambly (ed) 1966/1979, 173–174). The Russian Bekovich-Cherkassky expedition to Khwarazm in 1717–1718 to search for gold and open up trade routes to India likewise resulted in a spectacular failure.

Interregional Trade Boosted by Spillovers of Silver Flows from America

An early and clear-sighted witness of the transformation of transcontinental commerce was Anthony Jenkinson, the merchant of the English Muscovy Company (see above), who in 1558 observed in Transoxiana "The Indians bring top-quality batistes (a fine fabric)[120], which the Tatars wrap around their heads, and all other sorts of batistes which serve to make garments. But as far as gold, silver, precious stones, and spices are concerned, the Indians don't bring anything. I inquired and learned that all that commerce is carried out at sea, and that the ports where those things come from are in the hands of the Portuguese" (cited in Chuvin et al. 2008, 58). Thus one can infer that the SR was starting to lose precious international merchandise.

However, the following temporary recovery of overland trade was not only supported by restabilized political frameworks and wiser economic policies (as mentioned above).

Even if Niels Steensgaard may be somewhat too optimistic when he assesses that "at the end of the sixteenth century the transcontinental caravan trade reached dimensions which must presumably be regarded as its historical culmination" (cited in Millward 2007, 76), the increased availability of silver and its tendency to flow east in response to higher prices or larger markets offers one way to understand the late sixteenth century revival of overland trade between Asia and Europe, as Findlay and O'Rourke argue (2007, 132). Thus, with some delay, American silver mines' output found its way to India, where the amount of circulating silver is reported to have trebled and prices to have doubled between the early 1590s and the late 1630s (Rothermund 1985, 18–19). Indeed, Russia's, Iran's,

Turan's[121], India's and China's major SR means of exchange became silver, whether minted or in bullion form (Dale 1994, 29, 82). Obviously, a not inconsiderable share of the lavish amounts of the precious metal flowing from America via Western Europe to Asia took the traditional overland Silk Route. And the silver-induced upswing of trade and business had spillover effects on the C Asian economies.

"Bukharans" and Other Renowned C Asian Traders and Their Networks

The most important traders on the C Asian SR in the sixteenth to the eighteenth century were the "Bukharans," Armenians, and Indians (Schwarz 2000, 13; Breghel 2003, 68). Perhaps owing to traditions going back to Timur and the Timurids, merchants from the Khanate of Bukhara had apparently become quite versatile and well traveled. The long-lasting neighborhood with the Chagatay Khanate, unperturbed by major wars or bloodshed, as well as the fact that both polities occupied trunk parts of the SR, may have facilitated the spread of Bukharan merchants and their networks east and nearer to China. Soon the large country extending from Kashgar and Yarkand to Turfan and Hami also became known as "Little Bukharia" ("Petite Boukharie") and was distinguished from the lands of Bukhara and Samarkand or "Big Bukharia" ("Grande Boukharie") (Burton 1998b, 37; Paul 2012, 21).

Some "Bukharans" were from Turfan, Astrakhan, Nizhny Novgorod, and Tobolsk. Bukharans performed middleman services for Kazakh trade with the khanate, with Khwarazm, Muscovite Russia, or China. Thus, e.g., livestock, furs, and slaves were exchanged for ready-made clothes, silk, flour, cooking pots, items of adornment, and, sometimes, weapons. The Russian authorities from the mid-seventeenth century granted the "Bukharans" special protection and exempted them from some taxes (Burton 1998b, 50). Trade was effected for the most part along heavily traveled land routes, but also along waterways, notably the Amu Daria, for instance, "from the Kelif quayside at Termez, where the corn grows well and ripens early," boats left laden with corn for Khwarazm (Mukminova 2003, 51).

Bukharan traders were also active on the Siberian Route. As Burton explains, Chinese rhubarb, considered to be a universal cure and also regarded as a valuable dye, became a Bukharan monopoly in Persia and Russia from the early seventeenth century. The Bukharans' success was such that,

---

[119] As mentioned earlier, the Mughals' first ruler was Babur, a Timurid prince who had fled Transoxiana from the conquering Shaybanid Uzbeks. Thus, the Great Mughals ruling India were a Timurid dynasty and their attempts to invade CA corresponded to campaigns of reconquest.

[120] Batiste—a fine, often sheer, natural or synthetic fabric, constructed in either a plain or a figured weave (Random House Websters' Concise College Dictionary 1999, see also Glossary: some SR textiles, p. 266).

[121] "Turan" is here understood to correspond to the Khanates of Bukhara and Khiva.

according to a number of modern writers, in the seventeenth and eighteenth century any Turkestani merchant active in Russia or China was called "Bukharan"[122] (Burton 2003, 411–415, 1998b, 37–38). Armenians were particularly engaged in commerce between Iran and Russia, where they enjoyed privileged status as silk traders.

Indians' presence as merchants and moneylenders in CA was so strong that Bukhara boasted a caravanserai as well as a district for Indians (mostly coming from Punjab or Rajputana). Indian traders developed an extensive network stretching from Lahore and Multan to Kandahar, Isfahan, and Bukhara, linking Northern India with Afghanistan, Persia, CA, and Russia (Shukow et al. 1958/1966, Band 5, 265; Findlay and O'Rourke 2007, 304). Mukminova points to the fact that relations in the domain of handicraft production between Transoxiana and the Punjab were reflected in the attachments made to the patronymics of Indian master craftsmen, merchants, moneylenders, and usurers present in the Khanate of Bukhara. These attachments refer to the names of the towns they came from, e.g., Lahuri (from Lahore) or Multani (from Multan), which underlines the closeness of neighborhood contacts between the two regions (Mukminova 1996, 88).

Another example for the intensification of C Asian inter-regional trade and business relations under the impact of merchants' networks is highlighted by Dale: Before Muscovite Russia's conquest of Astrakhan, the Ottoman Empire had been Moscow's principal Asian trading partner, but after that date the focus appears to have shifted to Iran, Turan (the Khanates of Bukhara and Khiva), and, secondarily, India. Benefitting from the services of Indian, Bukharan, Armenian, Tatar, and Khivan traders, the czardom exported combinations of its own natural resource products and reexports of Western European industrial goods to Persia and the Khanate of Bukhara in the sixteenth and seventeenth century; from the mid-seventeenth century, this was complemented by small manufactured items produced in newly built Russian factories and workshops and shipped, often by C Asian traders, through Astrakhan. Iranian, Turanian, and Indian cotton and silk textiles as well as, intermittently, Iranian and Turanian horses constituted Russia's most important imports through Astrakhan (Dale 1994, 84).

4.1.5.3 Heavily Squeezed by Multiple Factors: SR Trade on the Decline (From Around Mid-seventeenth Century)

Political, Military, Economic, Technological, and Religious Factors Contribute to Renewed Loss of Importance

Following the rule of strong leaders and some able successors in a number of C Asian or adjacent countries, renewed political destabilization made itself felt in various places. Succession struggles or regional or social grievances could trigger domestic political instability, particularism, or internecine warfare (as it did in Astrakhanid Bukhara in the second half of the seventeenth century), which in turn could attract or at least facilitate outside intervention (whether of standing armies, like the Safavids', or of nomadic forces, like the Kazakh warriors). Religious or ideological differences or conflicts related to the dividing up of territories and resources gave rise to armed rivalries or wars between settled neighbors. Nomads were repeatedly interested in acquiring by force goods or assets that they (for whatever reasons) could not or did not wish to purchase on the market, and therefore launched plundering attacks and razzias. This was the case with many Dzungar raids into other nomadic (e.g., Kazakh) lands as well as into sedentary territories (e.g., Shash, Kashgaria). In some cases, nomads also retaliated against attempts to encroach on their pastures.

With renewed loss of political stability in CA, economic policies could not but go astray or experience neglect and thus further compromise the business climate. Typically, the erosion of revenues would be followed first by the ratcheting up of tax pressure, which in turn would chase away revenue sources or push them into the informal economy (and thus correspond to an "overoptimal" tax rate on the "Laffer curve"). Evaporation of revenue might subsequently trigger increased recourse to coin minting and boosting money circulation and seignorage, sooner or later followed by loss of confidence and debasements of currencies (e.g., in the Safavid state in the second half of the seventeenth century or in Khorezm in the first half of the eighteenth). In the background, technological, economic, and political factors (notably, further improvements and cost reductions of deep-sea shipping, extension of European control of maritime routes to the Orient and across the globe), which had all along been contributing to the marginalization of the SR, won further cumulative weight.

Moreover, toward the end of the seventeenth century, Russia and China had opened the Siberian Road (from Moscow via Tobolsk, Irkutsk, and Kiakhta to Beijing). Although its trade volume was dwarfed by that of the maritime route, the Siberian route also constituted a circumvention of CA (in this case to the north) and increased competition for the SR. Finally, with the unraveling of

---

[122] There even seems to have been a kind of division of labor: Merchants from "Grand Bukharia" were mostly active in trade with Russia and Russian Siberia, whereas "Little Bukharans" were more familiar with business with the Middle Kingdom.

political authority and stability and the erosion of economic reforms, the impact of religious rigidity and dogmatism, detachment from exact sciences and lack of curiosity gained weight again. While the emphasis on religious traditionalism may also have served to counter rampant instability (like in Kashgaria in the early seventeenth century), overall its influence on the business climate along the SR was probably unfavorable.

Thus, the multiple factors squeezing the SR from the seventeenth century essentially were:

- Political destabilization (anew) in important countries alongside the trade network
- Increasing intensity of conflicts, incursions, raids, and attendant destruction
- Unravelling of economic reforms and weakening of economic policies and of tax administration, more frequent debasements of currencies
- Maritime route to the Orient (bypassing the SR to the south) gains further competitiveness and is supplemented by the Siberian route (bypassing the SR to the north)
- Religious rigidity and dogmatism progress further or loom larger again

The Momentous Impact of Instability and Turmoil Across CA from the Seventeenth Century

Political and military conflicts appear to have gathered intensity, to have plagued various parts of CA from approximately the mid-seventeenth century, and therefore to have weighed particularly heavily in the decline of the SR after the temporary mercantilist renaissance of the late sixteenth century. Some dates and events:

- Seventeenth to eighteenth centuries: increasing political instability in Safavid Persia, the Khanates of Bukhara and Khiva, Mughal India, the Kazakh Khanate (Zhuz), and the Chagatay Khanate
- Seventeenth to eighteenth centuries: on-and-off warfare between Persia and the Khanate of Bukhara and among the Uzbek polities
- 1640–1643: Dzungar invasion and conquest of Western Zhetysu
- 1660s–1680s: Dzungar raids into the Kazakh steppe and on towns in the middle Syr Daria Valley (Sairam, Tashkent, etc.), Ferghana (Andijan), and the Tarim Basin (Kashgar, Yarkand, Aqsu, Turfan, Hami)
- 1670s: Kazakhs (displaced from middle Syr Daria by Dzungar raids) invade and carry out razzias in Mavarannahr
- 1690s–1720s: after Dzungar conquest of Chagatay Khanate intermittent warfare between Dzungars and Manchu China

- 1696–1697: Battle of Urga (later Ulan Bator), Qing conquest of (Outer) Mongolia
- 1717–1718: Bekovich-Cherkassky's unsuccessful expedition to Khwararzm
- 1717–1725: new Dzungar invasions of towns of middle and upper Syr Daria
- 1720s: renewed incursions by Kazakhs (displaced by Dzungars) in Transoxiana
- 1740–1745: Nadir Shah's campaigns of conquest—Eastern Caucasus, Afghanistan, Baluchistan, Khanates of Bukhara, Khiva, and Khoqand
- Eighteenth century: during some decades, Samarkand is totally and Bukhara partly depopulated
- 1741–1742: Dzungar raids in Kazakh Middle and Junior Hordes (Western Desht-i-Kipchak)
- 1755–1758: Dzungar-Qing wars, total destruction of Grand Tartary, major loss of life, Chinese (re)conquest of Dzungaria, Ili territory, Semirechie, and Tarim Basin

Even spillover effects of tributary trade on the SR could have fallen victim to the frequent hostilities afflicting various parts of CA from the seventeenth century. In keeping with very old traditions (going back to Xiongnu, Turkic, and Uighur economic exchange with China, see earlier), nomadic empires tended to exact large amounts of silk and other luxuries from the Middle Kingdom. These goods were typically paid for in horses or other livestock, whose market value was inferior to that of the provided (extorted) silk. After representative needs of the khan's court and the claims of the nomadic aristocracy or tribal leaders of the confederation had been taken care of, the rest of the exacted silk and luxuries could be resold along the SR for other goods in demand. This marketing of the surplus silk was often taken care of by specialized C Asian merchants or agents of the nomadic authorities (e.g., Sogdians for the Turks as well as the Uighurs).

In the case of Grand Tartary, which also exacted goods—primarily silk, tea, and silver—from China, in exchange for which livestock, medicinal products, and some other goods were offered, the trade agents were Bukharans. One could therefore ask why in the case of Dzungar tribute trade there is little information on any large-scale reselling of silk or tea further west on Eurasian overland routes, which would have given languishing SR trade a boost in the eighteenth century. One reason could be that during the heyday of Dzungar-Qing trade (from the late 1730s to the early 1750s), the political and military situation was very turbulent in Western CA (Nadir Shah's invasions, Dzungar warfare in Turkestan). Peaceful relations of Grand Tartary with its western neighbors may simply have been too scarce and the region too unruly to allow meaningful reexports of bulk tribute merchandise west. Secondly, silk in the first half of the eighteenth century was already produced in good quality by a number of Eurasian countries and potential competitors (e.g., Persia, the Khanate of Bukhara, India) as well as by Western European countries (Italy, France).

4.1.6 The Post-Mongol SR Trade Networks (Fourteenth to Eighteenth Centuries): Where Did They Run and Until When Were They Still Important?

The overland trade network that existed under the Mongols—with some minor reductions—still existed in the following centuries, yet the intensity and kind of use differed between regions. This corresponds to the above-mentioned weakening of transcontinental and the (partial) strengthening of interregional trade across Eurasia.

The westernmost part of the "steppe route" from Saray to Azov (Tana) and Kaffa remained an important revenue source for the Khanate of the Golden Horde until Tamerlane destroyed its capital and major trading towns in 1395/1396. Then trade was interrupted, but centers were rebuilt, the situation restabilized after Tamerlane's death, and trade resumed in more modest dimensions in the early fifteenth century (Map 4.1). In the Pontic and Volga regions, east-west transcontinental trade was, however, increasingly replaced by north-south neighborhood trade. These tendencies were confirmed after the Ottomans' conquest of the Khanate of Crimea and thus of Azov and Kaffa (1475). Muscovy's annexation of Astrakhan (1556) interrupted the steppe route and redirected some trade from China and CA toward the Volga route and the Baltics. Karakorum, on the eastern wing of the Mongol steppe route, lost importance. Following the demise of the Mongol Empire, the former capital was destroyed in around 1380 by the Ming dynasty. This accelerated the decline of the eastern stretches of the steppe route running through (Outer) Mongolia.

After Timur's defeat of the Golden Horde and the disruption of the trade connections via the Black Sea, the "southern route"—notably the one running from Samarkand via Nishapur, Teheran/Rayy, Baghdad, and Antioch, largely under the great ruler's control—took the lead in Eurasian overland trade with the West. However, the southern route was not permanently open, because the shore regions of the Eastern Mediterranean remained under the control of the Mamluk Sultanate of Cairo, which was often at loggerheads with its neighbors to the east. Imperial geopolitical power at the western end of the traditional SR network expanded with the Ottomans' conquest of the Mamluk Sultanate in 1517; as Map 4.2 illustrates, from this year until the late eighteenth century, the same power controlled the Eastern Mediterranean, the Red, and Black Seas, which contributes to explaining circumvention attempts (particularly via the maritime route circumnavigating Africa) (Findlay and O'Rourke 2007, 131).

The SR network east of Transoxiana, Shash, and Otrar was more or less the same as in Mongol times, yet over the centuries it came increasingly under the Dzungars' and partly the Kazakhs' nomadic sway, as can be seen in Maps 4.2 and 4.3. In the early sixteenth century, Oirats and Kazakhs took control of Semirechie and Southern Dzungaria. From then on, the "northern route"—the route just north of the Tienshan and running from Shash or Otrar via Balasagun, Almalik/Kuldzha, Urumqi, and Hami—was almost entirely under Oirat and Kazakh control. The "central route"—from Samarkand via Ferghana and then just south of the Tienshan: Kashgar, Aqsu, Kucha, Turfan, and Suzhou—remained important. With the conquest of the Chagatay Khanate, from 1680, the Dzungar Empire ruled over the whole of East Turkestan (Xinjiang) and thus controlled all sections of the SR linking China and Western Eurasia. As in the case of the Ottoman Empire, this gave rise to attempts to bypass it (i.e., via Northern Asia).

Occupying approximately the same territory as the Mongol Ulus Chagatay (of the times of Khan Kaidu in the late thirteenth and early fourteenth century), Grand Tartary thus effectively became a transasiatic north-south bolt controlling Eurasian east-west overland trade (compare Maps 3.7 and 4.4). However, Grand Tartary was a less effective and important bolt than the Ulus Chagatay because in the meantime more and better possibilities of circumvention had been found, and the SR's share in global trade had declined in the 400 years to the early eighteenth century. Dzungar-Chinese trade from the 1720s to the 1750s, including its intensive heyday in the 1740s, also constituted the last example of large-scale tribute trade between a nomadic and sedentary empire in the history of CA.

Some north-south routes or regional networks linked to Russia were increasingly used from the sixteenth century, for instance, the Volga route via Saray/Tsaritsyn to Astrakhan. From there, traffic continued either on the western shore of the Caspian Sea or across the Caspian to Iran (Rayy/Tehran). Or the sea was crossed from Astrakhan to the Mangyshlak peninsula, from where the trip went on to Khiva and the Amu Daria valley. Or the sea was bypassed via Guriev, from where the route also reached Khwarazm (part of the traditional steppe route)[123]. In the eighteenth century, a direct connection from Central Russia and the middle reaches of the Volga to CA was established: It ran from Samara (founded in 1586) via Orenburg (1743), across the Mugodzhar mountains to the lower Syr Daria (Sygnak) (Map 4.5). A branch of this route skirted the eastern shore of the Aral Sea to reach Khiva.

---

[123] In both of the latter two cases, caravan traffic from Astrakhan to Khiva in the sixteenth and seventeenth centuries took about 1½ to 2 months.

Another north-south route went from Tobolsk (Western Siberia) down the Ishim and Sarysu rivers (cutting through the Kazakh steppe) to the lower Syr Daria (Sygnak) (2½ to 3 months' travel in the seventeenth century). Then there was a route equally starting in Tobolsk, mounting the Irtysh upriver to Semipalatinsk (founded in 1718), then bending south, crossing the Tarbagatay and reaching Chuguchak (the original Dzungar capital) and eventually Kuldzha/Yining (the later Dzungar capital) (Map 4.4). The main route from CA to India continued to go from Transoxiana via Balkh through Bamian and Kabul to Lahore (2 months' travel from Balkh to Lahore in the seventeenth century). It was not passable for a couple of months a year because of snow in the mountain sections; otherwise the route was used intensively (Breghel 2003, 68–69).

Interregional or neighborhood trade, partially based on mercantilist initiatives and policies, often corresponded to interlocking trade areas[124]: There was busy trade between the following pairs of states or regions, which interlocked with each other: Russia-Persia, Persia-India, India-(Khanate of) Bukhara, Bukhara-Chagatay (Khanate), Chagatay-China, Chagatay-Dzungars, Dzungars-China, China (via Siberia)-Russia, Russia (via Khanate of Khiva)-Bukhara, Russia-Kazakhs, and Kazakhs-Bukhara. There were also trios of states or regions that witnessed active trade relations: Russia-Bukhara-India, Russia-Kazakhs-Bukhara, and China-Chagatay-Bukhara.

4.2 From Subject to Object: Twilight and Collapse of Nomadic and Khanate Power—CA Colonized by Its Big Neighbors (1750s–1880s)

While landlocked and mostly unstable C Asian states were increasingly bypassed by modern international trade, three great powers emerged on the borders of the region and accelerated their colonial expansions in the eighteenth and nineteenth centuries: Russia (that had gradually encroached on CA from the west and the north), the British Empire (which had defeated the Mughal Empire and conquered the rest of South Asia in the eighteenth and the first half of the nineteenth century, and thus extended its way to the borders of CA), and China (that had already conquered East Turkestan and Semirechie in the late 1750s).

Having definitely lost military superiority over their settled neighbors (due to the latters' large-scale use of guns and artillery), nomadic tribes and states also lost important sources of revenue in the form of tributes and other goods and services they had exacted for centuries or even millennia. This further tipped the balance in favor of the sedentary powers. Such states adjoining the Eurasian steppe now also began to acquire large territories inhabited by nomads—something unheard of in the past—and to distribute these lands among their growing peasant populations (Abazov 2008, Map 30).

While CA was finally about to be conquered by modern sedentary powers with their superior military know-how, paradoxically the contemporary advanced trade and shipment technologies (for the time being) favored maritime instead of land routes and transportation. This may have contributed to a lease of life for the traditional C Asian economies and their overland trade in the late eighteenth and the early nineteenth centuries. Given the spread of the Industrial Revolution in Europe and beyond, many goods that had traditionally been imported, such as textiles, began to be machine-produced in Europe. This undermined small-scale manufacturing in Asia and the Middle East; many formerly prosperous manufacturing centers across the Chinese, Mughal, Persian, and Ottoman Empires came under severe competitive pressure. European goods began to oust Chinese, Indian, and C Asian competition from the international markets.

Within CA however, the rearrangement of competitive forces was delayed. Landlocked as it was (and is), CA was more isolated from Western European influences and traders that mostly traveled and arrived via the sea routes. Having already lost a great deal of SR international transit trade to that sea route, C Asians had refocused on regional and neighborhood trade, as explained above. Despite the emergence in the eighteenth and nineteenth centuries of global productive, transport, and communication linkages (particularly maritime connections) of hitherto unknown density, CA remained a rather difficult to access region for advanced industrial powers, as Dubovitsky and Bababekov illustrate with respect to Britain (2011, 56).[125] What remained of SR and C Asian trade thus gained some economic reprieve (like an extensive area in which traditional business activities could temporarily preserve themselves) thanks to the region's relative isolation acquired through difficult accessibility for the new modern trade and shipping businesses, which were geared to maritime routes. In this sense, temporary protection through newly found isolation from the main routes of the modern world economy afforded C Asian traditional economies a "grace period."

---

[124] This is valid particularly from the sixteenth century onward. In the following only those interlocking trade areas are mentioned whose mutual trade and exchanges were most intensive or well-known.

[125] Partly, this is still the case today (see intermittent difficulties of Western military access to and control of Afghanistan and the tenuousness of Western presence in CA, moreover see stubborn obstacles to accessing the region's oil and gas via pipelines from the West).

Another unexpected benefit for CA was the decline in the number and intensity of wars since the Qing's defeat of the Dzungars and China's conquest of Xinjiang in 1758 and thus the de-facto establishment of a "Pax Sinica," at least for some decades. Moreover, possibly or not linked to this, a temporary political restabilization was registered across a number of SR countries in the late eighteenth and early nineteenth centuries. CA indeed experienced a remarkable trade and economic recovery—definitely the last one before the victory and takeover of a large part of the region by European colonialists (Chuvin et al. 2008, 83).

4.2.1 Following Chinese Conquest of Dzungar Empire: CA Witnesses Recovery and Temporary Stabilization (Mid-eighteenth to Second Quarter of Nineteenth Century)

For the following chapter, the author has primarily drawn from publications by M. Annanepesov, Zhambyl Artykbaev, Khaydarbek Bababekov, Paul Bairoch, Audrey Burton, Pierre Chuvin, Viktor Dubovitsky, Paul-Georg Geiss, Andreas Kappeler, Rene Letolle, Ma Dazheng, James Millward, V.S. Oskolkov, I.L. Oskolkova, Richard Overy, Peter Perdue, Sebastien Peyrouse, Gabriele Rasuly-Paleczek, Peter Roudik, E.V. Rtveladze, Florian Schwarz, and Svat Soucek.

4.2.1.1 West Turkestan and Russian Adjoining Areas: Some Political and Economic Developments

Restabilization: The Khanates En Route Toward Patrimonial States?

After numerous internal conflicts and outright warfare had devastated the economies of the Bukhara Emirate as well as the Khiva and the Khoqand Khanates[126], a degree of political restabilization made itself felt in the region. This was partly owed to the emergence of new dynasties—the Manghits in Bukhara, the Kungrats in Khiva, and the Min in Khoqand—which brought greater administrative centralization in respective polities. The enhancement of political cohesion facilitated the realization of some helpful infrastructural and irrigation projects, which in turn contributed to relaunching economic activity toward the end of the eighteenth century (Hambly (ed) 1966/1979, 186). Another contribution to economic recovery was furnished by the upswing of CA's trade and exchanges with Russia. Orenburg (on the Yaik/Ural river) became the most dynamic and largest market, outstripping Astrakhan (on the Volga) and other towns, like Troitsk, Petropavlovsk, and Omsk (Chuvin et al. 2008, 59; Burton 1998b, 47–48).

Political centralization and economic recovery in turn set the stage for important efforts to modernize governance and authority relations. While they remained technologically backward or antiquated (see below), the khanates' armies were restructured with varying degrees of success in the late eighteenth and early nineteenth centuries. The armies were directly subordinated to the rulers and separated (as far as possible) from tribal contingents. The infantry (though insufficiently equipped with firearms) gained importance in comparison to the cavalry.[127] The new armies included recruits from settled populations (Sarts), at times freed slaves, or slave soldiers. This more generally reflected a quest to move from a tribally or kinship-based political authority to a patrimonial state, with the latter featuring a standing army, a regular taxation system, and removable civil servants/bureaucratic staff. The emir of Bukhara proved more successful in establishing a centralized patrimonial administration than the khans of Khorezm and Khoqand (in direct vicinity to the Eurasian grasslands), whose security depended more on alliances with nomadic forces (von Gumppenberg and Steinbach 2004, 150; Geiss 2009, 297).

As Geiss emphasizes, the potential rift between the local inhabitants and the patrimonial administration was less pronounced where the administration committed itself more deeply to Sharia. The Islamization of authority relations facilitated the change from tribal following to patrimonially organized subservience. This type of adjustment was linked to the acculturation of tribesmen to the settled oases culture based on Islamic law (Geiss 2003, 161)[128].

Response to Oppression and Painful Economic Change: Torgut Migration (1771) and Pugachev Uprising (1773–1775)

With the czardom's settled civilization, laws and regulations slowly and relentlessly moving southeastward, the nomadic populations in Russia's way had two classic options left: either move away (escape) or object (resist). The Kalmyks/Torguts opted for the first response, the Kazakhs and Bashkirs joined others in choosing the second.

---

[126] When these three states (the Emirate of Bukhara, the Khanate of Khiva, and the Khanate of Khoqand) are dealt with together, they will henceforth be (somewhat imprecisely, but pragmatically) called "the khanates."

[127] This was possibly also in emulation of the British army (which however was well provided with artillery batteries) in India.

[128] The Islamization of authority relations, as described by Geiss, would appear to embody the further development of the dual socio-political order ("Yasa-Sharia") in CA, evoked by the same author and referred to above (Box 3.2).

As mentioned earlier, the Russian authorities gradually infringed on the autonomy of the Torguts (who had come to nomadize in pastures mostly to the west of the lower Volga/ in the western Caspian Lowlands) (Map 4.4). As Khodarkovsky put it, Russia's growing control of Kalmyk administrative affairs, its excessive demands for Kalmyk mounted battalions, and the loss of prime pasturelands to expanding farming colonies were among the critical factors contributing to the Kalmyks' decision to decamp for Dzungaria (1992, 230).

The majority of the Torgut population escaped these increasing difficulties by migration. This strategy greatly benefited from or even became possible due to a fortunate coincidence: While the Russian pressures were accumulating (push factor), the Chinese authorities, that had just wiped out the Dzungar state, invited the Torguts to return to their ancestral Dzungaria (pull factor). Warfare and disease had left the former Torgut homeland in old Moghulistan in a ruined and largely depopulated state. Led by Khan Ubashi, in 1771 more than two thirds of the Kalmyks (around 168,000 people, which made up over 30,000 tents) decided to follow the invitation. Yet after a 7-month trek over more than 2500 km back east, by the time the khan contacted officials in Ili, only some 66,000 people (about 40% of the initial number) were left; the migrants' numbers had been depleted by winter frosts, hunger, disease, and devastating raids by other nomadic peoples, particularly Kazakhs, on the way (Adle et al. 2003b, 345; Perdue 2005, 295; for continuation see Sect. 4.2.1.6).[129]

The Pugachev rebellion (1773–1775) in the Volga and Ural regions mobilized various population groups and minorities and was the expression of a number of grievances, including the rejection of accelerating changes and modernization policies. As Nolte explains, impoverished peasant serfs and bonded workers in the iron and steel works rose up against the worsening of their situation. They were joined by Yaik Cossacks, whose autonomy and privileges were increasingly under threat (e.g., through the introduction of duties on the salt extracted from the steppe and used to conserve caviar and fish). So did Tatars suffering from cultural oppression and religious intolerance, as well as Bashkirs and Kazakhs, whose habitats were increasingly under pressure from fortification lines (linii), or encroached upon by emerging state-supported factories or advancing farmer-settlers (Nolte 1991, 68–69).

In the case of the Kazakhs, the Russian authorities' bans on driving their livestock across the Ural and Irtysh rivers in the 1750s and the 1760s, respectively, added to the frustration. For the Younger Zhuz, the Ural river ban seems to have triggered severe distress, which probably gave a foretaste of what was awaiting other Kazakhs further east within the next century (Oskolkov and Oskolkova 2004, 33). A common aspect of the insurgent groups was that their way of life and well-being was endangered.

The Pugachev rebellion seized an extensive territory comprising the middle reaches of the Volga, including the cities of Tsaritsyn, Saratov, Samara and Kazan, and the Southern Ural range and its foothills as well as the Yaik river basin, taking in the towns of Cheliabinsk, Troitsk, Orenburg, and Guriev. Pugachev himself was a Don Cossack; a large part of his troops consisted of regional minorities (Tatars, Bashkirs, Kazakhs, and others). The insurgents were also assisted by some groups of bold Kazakh mounted warriors (Dzhigits) (Shukow et al. 1958/1966, Band 5, 269). The uprising was eventually bloodily suppressed and Pugachev was executed in Moscow in September 1774. One of the minor consequences of the quashing of the rebellion (albeit with topographical relevance for Russia and CA) was Catherine II's order to rename the Yaik river as Ural river (Frank 2009, 371).

Timid Czarist Economic and Social Reforms, Continuation of Trade Recovery

Czarina Catherine II (the Great, 1762–1796) changed Russian policy toward the Tatars and some other minorities. Wishing to avert any repetition of revolts like the Pugachev uprising and appreciating the advantages that the existence of Tatar trade communities in the C Asian border areas of the empire implied, the czarina ended religious persecution of Tatars and other Muslims. She granted Tatar nobles who had survived the insurgency the same rights as the Russian aristocracy possessed. Thus the Tatar nobility was—once again—coopted into the imperial hierarchy[130]. Catherine the Great, seeking to bring all religious institutions under state control, granted Muslims the status of a tolerated minority and established the Islamic spiritual assembly in 1788 to oversee their religious life (Hambly (ed) 1966/1979, 199; Golden 2011, 124).

Toward the end of the eighteenth century, Tatar commercial and religious communities were increasingly active in Russia's borderlands in West Siberian-Kazakh steppe territories. The Tatars constituted a vanguard of traders and merchants facilitating Russian commercial and industrial

---

[129] The remaining Kalmyk Khanate in the Caspian Lowlands was later abolished by the czar and the minority of Kalmyks that had not migrated east in 1771, as well as their pastures and habitat were brought under the full jurisdiction of the Governor of Astrakhan. Yet the Kalmyks managed to preserve their traditional socioeconomic order in the nineteenth century, even if increasingly hemmed in and restrained by settlers and the authorities (Kappeler 2001, 47).

---

[130] But this only corresponded to the reinstatement of a policy toward the Tatar elites that had by and large already been pursued from the late sixteenth century and that had been discontinued in the early eighteenth century by the reforms of Peter the Great.

access to CA. Thanks to Tatar commercial intermediation, Kazakhs became important buyers of Russian industrial products. Tatars also indirectly worked in favor of imperial interests by converting ordinary Kazakhs to Islam (at that point only ruling dignitaries and higher clan members and their families were Muslim) (Sellier, J. and A. 1993/2002, 157). This conversion was supported by the Russian authorities because it was considered to facilitate control of the steppe populations and favor their eventual sedentarization. In this way the Tatar bourgeoisie experienced unparalleled economic prosperity for more than a century (Hambly (ed) 1966/1979, 199).

The Bashkirs, who had not developed a comparable entrepreneurial class, were less lucky: In 1798, harsh military obligations were imposed on them. Later, more of their lands (than already) were seized, and in the first half of the nineteenth century, they faced by a "solid mass of resettled Russian peasants" in their homelands, the Southern Urals and its foothills (Habib 2003a, 340).

A decree by Czar Alexander I (1801–1825) permitted the purchase and sale of land in Russia (1803). The aristocracy lost its previous monopoly on land ownership. Lords of the manor were allowed to release serfs; thus (formally free) farmers emerged. However, the material situation of the peasantry hardly improved (Donnert et al. 1981, 370). Still, some human resources were effectively set free, which later contributed to the industrial development of the country and possibly to deepening the division of labor between Russia and CA, as will be argued below.

The Pugachev insurgency only interrupted the Eurasian overland trade recovery. In the 1780s, raw cotton, but also numerous value-added products made of cotton, like yarn, cotton fabrics (striped, plain color, or printed—vyboika bukharskaya), textiles (e.g., chintz, karbas/finer cotton cloth), curtains, and ready-made clothes, played an important role in Bukharan and/or Khivan exports to Russia.[131] By the late eighteenth century, Orenburg, the main entry gate for C Asian merchandise shipped to Russia, also registered large numbers of Kazakh horses and sheep being sold or imported (Burton 2003, 415, 1998b, 49).

In the late eighteenth and early nineteenth centuries, the Russian textile industry—already well linked with C Asian suppliers—expanded quickly. It was in cotton and silk processing that capitalist factories employing (legally) free workers first gained importance. However, most manufactures continued to employ serfs or bonded workers. With the mechanization of cotton processing, the spinning of threads (yarn) and cotton fabrics became much easier. Respective factories were located on the banks of the

Volga (e.g., in Samara). In the early nineteenth century, the Russian textile industry's output even surpassed that of the country's heavy industry (Göhrke 2010, 123). Production virtually exploded after 1825 once Britain had lifted the ban on exporting machine looms ("the Mule Jenny"). According to Chuvin et al., the reaction to this measure may be regarded as the beginning of Russia's industrialization (2008, 116)—difficult to imagine without inputs from CA.

French Revolutionary Wars and Continental Blockade (1799–1812) Indirectly Benefit C Asian Trade and Economies

During the wars of the French Revolution (notably from the Second Coalition War, 1799–1802, the czar participated in the coalition against France) and during the continental blockade (1806–1812) Russia increasingly depended on trade with CA and other Eurasian countries (Burton 1998b, 51). It was the continental blockade that closed the sea routes between Britain and Asia on the one hand and Continental Europe and Russia on the other. There were two types of reaction to this measure, which were both attempted or carried out. First, access some English goods through the "backdoor," i.e., overland from the British colonies in India via CA. Second, replace English goods with domestic production (as far as possible) and/or imports of Continental European, C Asian, Persian, or other goods accessible via the land route.

At the times of the hostilities with France, Russia's reliance on C Asian, particularly Bukharan, merchants grew. The "Bukharans" reportedly brought English merchandise to Russia that they had acquired in India. More generally, the czardom's imports from India, Iran, and CA increased. Among the most demanded goods apparently were cotton and cotton thread as inputs for the textile industry. Kashmir and Persian woolen shawls were also appreciated. The Russian authorities already in 1799 offered the "Bukharans" some concessions for their services: The merchants were allowed to export from Russia previously banned goods, including iron, tin, copper and steel objects (not destined for war), wheat, and rye. Moreover, for their highly valued assistance in circumventing the blockade, the Bukharans in 1808 were exempted from paying dues in Orenburg and Astrakhan, and they no longer had to declare and submit their goods to examination in Siberian trading towns (Burton 2003, 416).

Notwithstanding Encirclement by Big Powers: Inter-Khanate Warfare Takes Off Again (from 1820s)

Given their limited expertise of firearms, the use the khanates made particularly of artillery was even more circumscribed than in the "Gunpowder Empires" of Persia or Mughal India, which themselves were lagging behind European technologies (Chuvin et al. 2008, 60). As Roudik

---

[131] Apart from cotton and cotton products, Bukharan lambskins, caftans, furs, silk, and velvet also featured prominently in the khanates' deliveries to the czardom.

pointed out, even though copper cannons, cast-iron cannonballs, and lead rifles made their appearance in Bukhara and other C Asian capitals in the early nineteenth century, wars were still conducted primarily with bows, arrows, and swords (2007, 62).[132]

Mounting technological backwardness was no obstacle to the resurgence of bellicosity in CA in the second quarter of the nineteenth century. Intermittent warfare gained momentum again and affected the economic recovery. The war of 1825 between Khiva and Bukhara paralyzed commerce: Bukharan caravans bound for Russia or waiting to return were (temporarily) blocked. In the late 1820s, warfare involving the Qing authorities and Khoqand allies broke out in the western part of Xinjiang. Bukhara's war against Khoqand (1839–1842), preceded by years of hostilities, turned out to be inconclusive, but contributed to political strife, to the renewed destruction of productive forces, and to the hampering of trade and economic activities in the region. Further years and decades were spent in fruitless attempts to resolve differences between fighting neighboring khanates, worsened by increasingly menacing Russian incursions (Chuvin et al. 2008, 81; Fragner 2008, 71).

Altogether, as Soucek commented, the persisting squabbles among the three C Asian neighbors were characteristic of the incomprehension they showed of the historic changes that were about to close in on them (2000, 193). And Mayhew put forth a striking metaphor (which is probably only a slight exaggeration): The khans of Khiva and Khoqand and the emirs of Bukhara seemed able to will the outside world out of existence as they struck and clawed each other like a box of kittens (2010, 48).

4.2.1.2 Emirate of Bukhara: Emerging Patrimonial State and Increasing Cotton Trade with Russia

Hesitant Stabilization Under Early Manghits (from Mid-eighteenth Century)

Long-lasting instability, internecine conflicts, and maladministration in Bukhara were such that at least until the late eighteenth century every important public achievement in Mavarannahr, like the setting up of educational establishments, caravanserais, the construction of bridges, canals, and gardens dated back to Abdullah Khan, who had ruled centuries ago (the last ruler of the Shaybanids, 1583–1598) (Hambly (ed) 1966/1979, 180). And it was not until 1770 under the Manghits that Samarkand, the emirate's second city (which terrible internal disturbances, the

temporary breakdown of SR trade, looting, earthquakes, and famine had virtually emptied of its inhabitants) was repopulated and its houses, citadel, and town wall were repaired. The city of Bukhara had also lost a large part of its population during the turmoil and was finally recovering somewhat (Chuvin et al. 2008, 76; Roudik 2007, 53).

Yet, as Soucek points out, the Manghits succeeded better than their Genghisid predecessors in efforts to achieve centralized rule by curbing the power of (mostly Uzbek) tribal chieftains and increasingly relying on a (partly non-Uzbek) standing army[133]. As non-Genghisids, the Manghit rulers were emirs rather than khans and hence even more than the descendants of the great Mongol leader courted the support of the religious establishment to gain legitimacy. By assuming the image of devout Islamic rulers and sponsoring the religious class, they fostered internal stability and favored population growth and a certain economic revival. This, in turn, benefited from the decline of warfare in the region—against the backdrop of the "Pax Sinica"—and from increasing trade with Russia (Soucek 2000, 180; Golden 2011, 115).

Silver (tanga) and gold (tilla or ashrafi) coins of the emirate's mints were issued as early as under the reign of Muhammad Rahim (1750–1758). The tangas of this ruler were of low quality, consisting of 30% silver and about 70% copper. Their weight had initially been fixed at 4.8 g, but later varied between 2.4 and 3.9 g. The authorities also oversaw a transition to the "free minting of coins"—as Rtveladze explains, any private individual could take silver to the state mint and receive tangas in exchange.[134] Rtveladze also refers to Semyenov, who cites reports of such free mints, stating that gold and silver in the form of minted coins were of considerably greater value than in their raw state (seignorage). Accordingly, the illegal manufacture of coins was punished severely. Coins could be struck only at the government's mint, situated in Bukhara (Rtveladze 2003, 446–447).

Patrimonial Authority Under Shah Murad (1785–1800) and Successors

Shah Murad strengthened the emirate's government and its armed forces. As Geiss notes, he asserted that he did not acknowledge any other law than Sharia and that he wanted to collect only taxes that were prescribed by Islam (2003, 127). The authority of ulama (scholars) and qadi (judges of Islamic law) was enhanced. The new court system allowed everyone, even slaves, to come to court to resolve their claims (Roudik 2007, 58). The complicated tax system was

---

[132] Even in the mid-nineteenth century, foreigners reportedly observed that only one in five Bukharan infantry soldiers would have a rifle, usually an ancient flintlock or musket dating from the beginning of the century (Roudik 2007, 91).

[133] This Bukharan standing army, however, partly still depended on tribal nukers (warriors, probably derived from the Mongol term "noeker," see above).

[134] This practice was probably adopted from Mughal India.

streamlined, some duties (particularly those not legitimized by Islam) were abolished and some measures taken that facilitated the life of taxpayers. Shah Murad also carried out important administrative, monetary, and military reforms and ordered the restoration of numerous public buildings in Bukhara and Samarkand. During his and his successor's rule, large irrigation projects like those in the Zeravshan Valley were realized. All this helped to improve the economic situation and contributed to a short period of prosperity. On the other hand, the ruler's frequent wars with Iran and Afghanistan injected an element of uncertainty and led to the renewed destruction of the Merv oasis and the Murgab's irrigation system (see below).

Under Shah Murad, many Persian-speaking civil servants were recruited from the emir's slaves captured during his campaigns against Persia. To facilitate centralized bureaucratic control, the ruler divided the emirate into several districts (provinces, called bekliks in Uzbek or viloyats in Tajik), which were, in turn, subdivided into sections for tax collection. The administrative division was generally derived from the geography of land irrigation. Each district was ruled by a centrally appointed beg and each section by a bekcha (Roudik 2007, 58). In addition to imposing and collecting taxes in the provinces, the begs enforced the religious law (Sharia), maintained order, delivered troops for the emir during war time, supported the court of the visiting ruler, and customarily made large gifts to the latter. Outside the large towns, the begs assigned pastures and water rights to the nomads (mostly Uzbek tribesmen) of respective areas (Geiss 2003, 129, 131).

As Geiss continues, the mirob was Bukhara's supreme official to supervise the irrigation network. He was appointed by the emir and commanded full authority over the distribution of water and maintenance of the main canals. He was assisted by panj-begis, who arranged the distribution of water over a certain territory and sold surplus water at a fixed price. On the next-lower level, arbobs supervised irrigation in the villages. They could summon the villagers for help to repair common canals. The provincial qadi was the highest authority in regional judicial and notarial matters. Notwithstanding begs' provincial administrative powers, the amlokdor was the ruler's tax collector on the state land (amlok) formally owned by the emir, which comprised more than one half of the emirate's land. According to Istoria Uzbekistana, cited by Geiss, mulk (i.e., privately owned) properties accounted for about 25% of the emirate's irrigated land, vaqf property for 25%, and amlok land for 50% (2003, 131–132).

At the same time, Manghit administrative centralization was less than efficient. The qush-begi was the emir's chief minister, headed the begs in the provinces, was also the emirate's supreme military commander, and wielded supervisory power over the state's revenues and expenditure. The qush-begi, sometimes also called ataliq, was overburdened with various affairs of state, owing to the fact that there was no division of functions among separate departments and ministries (Mukhtarov 2003, 61). Another structural weakness was that a number of provinces were only nominally subordinate to the emir. Although Bukharan troops occupied these territories from time to time, the ruler was not effectively able to dismiss local elites who tended to enjoy support among the indigenous population and to form political alliances with neighboring bekliks. This happened on repeated occasions in some eastern mountainous provinces (e.g., Kuliab or Hissar in the Southwestern Tienshan or Karategin in the Pamir Highlands) (Geiss 2003, 135).

In such provinces, the beg was a local leader whose leadership emerged from his military success, from his wealth, or other factors. In provinces with a tribal background, customary law (Adat) remained pivotal in family matters, notwithstanding incumbent qadis. Central authority was often not fully able to control the provinces, especially the more peripheral ones, where senior district officials could get away with concealing or withholding information, reporting fiddled statistics, and keeping tax transfers (to the capital) as modest as possible (Geiss 2003, 132, 135).

In the military field, Shah Murad was largely successful in his campaigns against Qajar Persia: He conquered parts of Khorassan, particularly the oasis of Merv, which until then had been governed by a Persian prince. However, the hostilities led to the renewed destruction of the Merv oasis and the Murgab's irrigation system (see below). However, he was less successful in his struggle against the Durrani state in Afghanistan, which by and large defended its possessions south of the upper Amu Daria (Map 4.5).

Shah Murad repeatedly raided Khorassan and plundered its population. Thus, this region reverted to its state of ravaged border territory, a plight it had already suffered prior to Nadir Shah, who had (temporarily) protected and reconstructed "The Land of the Rising Sun." With the help of Uzbek and Turkmen tribesmen, Shah Murad destroyed the Merv oasis in 1789–1790. Merv, once a famous center of Iranian civilization (i.e., of the Sassanian, Samanid, and Safavid Empires), had already declined into a border town of lower status. After pillaging the town, the Bukharan troops penetrated further and destroyed the dam and the elaborate irrigation system on the river Murgab (a key piece of infrastructure that had been restored under Nadir Shah a couple of decades before). Consequently, the oasis became desolated. As Hambly put it, Merv and its vicinity now turned into the melancholic ruins as which they were described by European travelers in the nineteenth century (1966 (ed), 191–192).

The Bukharan authorities deported a large part of the Iranian population of Merv to Transoxiana. Iranians at the end of the eighteenth century swamped the slave market of Bukhara, where prices reportedly reached record lows. Khorassanian peasants were resettled in core provinces of the emirate in order to recultivate farming land. Persian slaves seem to have formed a significant element in the emirate's population still in 1831–1832. As alluded to above, many of them filled the ranks of patrimonial staff and proved to be capable bureaucrats. On the other hand, from the early nineteenth century, Turkmens had largely replaced the former Persian inhabitants of Northern Khorassan, including Merv (Schwarz 2004, 190; Hambly (ed) 1966/1979, 192). In the 1820s and 1830s, Bukhara successively lost control of the oasis of Merv to the rival warring Khanate of Khiva, which had allied itself with Turkmen tribes (see below).

Notwithstanding these losses, Emirs Haidar (1800–1826) and Nasrullah (1826–1860) continued Bukhara's military reforms and further reined in Uzbek tribal leaders' power by strengthening a regular army. In the 1830s infantry forces were established primarily consisting of farmers, craftsmen, other urban dwellers (Sarts), and slaves. These troops were trained with firearms and were personally loyal to the emir, but relatively modest in size at the outset. Eventually, Nasrullah was able to rule some provinces without tribal support, with the help of devoted servants (staff) and regular troops. The commitment of the non-tribal population became predominantly oriented toward Islamic law and patrimonialism (Geiss 2003, 129, 160).

While the Emirate of Bukhara in the first half of the nineteenth century in many respects resembled a patrimonial state, the authorities did not succeed everywhere in integrating the structurally diverse local tribal/nomadic and residential/sedentary populations. When strong and oriented rulers like Shah Murad promoted the settlement of tribesmen, they encouraged the transformation of tribal communal commitment toward residential communal commitment. As mentioned above, the process of change apparently occurred by way of Islamic acculturation to settled oasis life in CA. According to Geiss, only orthodox Islam was able to transform tribal commitment. Although Sufi khodzhas might have (superficially) Islamized Uzbek, Turkmen, or Kyrgyz nomads much earlier, only school Islam was able to take the place of tribal customary law (Geiss 2003, 161).

Bukhara, Still a Trade Gate to India, Becomes a Diversified Cotton Supplier to Russia

In the second half of the eighteenth century, Bukhara still or again functioned as a Eurasian trade turntable. India provided Bukharans with textiles, medicines, indigo, gold and jewels, luxurious silks and shawls came from Persia, and Kashgar (Xinjiang) supplied rhubarb, Chinese tea, porcelain, and medicinal herbs. In the late eighteenth and early nineteenth centuries, it was trade between Bukhara and Russia that started to soar. Cotton became the emirate's most important export staple to the czardom. While Bukhara purchased processed leather, furs, cloth, metal tools, and objects in

return, the emirate usually recorded a trade surplus with Russia (Burton 2003, 415; Mayhew 2010, 48).

Regular caravans between Russia and Bukhara typically numbered four to five thousand camels, arrived in Mavarannahr in the fall, and returned to Russia even before the end of the winter. An 1819 customs list from Orenburg shows that among Bukharan merchandise raw (275 tons) and spun cotton (300 tons) featured prominently, as did cotton materials (172,000 pieces), silk bolts and pieces, dried fruit, tea, rhubarb, and other goods. One camel carried up to 200 kg of cotton, which defined the weight of a bale of cotton. The annual average of cotton exports rose with time (Chuvin et al. 2008, 84, 116; Burton 2003, 418). Bukharans apparently soon came to dominate C Asian trade with Russia.

Despite increasing relational instability, Bukhara between 1827 and 1837 exported to Russia cotton and fabrics, silk, karakul fleece, dyes, and fruits at a much higher overall value than the imports of pottery, hardware, sugar, and manufactured goods it received in return. Notwithstanding imbalances, in the first half of the nineteenth century the scale of the emirate's trade with Russia became such that it could supply Russian articles to all its neighbors. Thus, as Burton states with reference to Nebolsin, copper, cauldrons, trunks, needles, knives, razors, gold thread, tinsel, and woolen cloth were supplied to Afghanistan. Moreover, Bukhara played a role of intermediary in (British) Indian exports of cotton materials (white cotton or printed calico) to Russia (Burton 2003, 423).

More generally, Bukharan trade with India remained important: Indian Muslin (plain-weave cotton fabric used especially for sheets), sugar, green tea, precious stones, and pearls were in demand by Bukharan traders, while the latter continued to sell furs, pelts, sheep, horses, lapis lazuli, gold, and slaves to their Indian partners. In the 1830s and 1840s, Turkmen businessmen (mostly subordinate to the Khanate of Khiva) continued to supply Persian slaves and carpets to Bukhara. In exchange, they probably bought Bukharan lambskins that they used to produce their tall hats, together with fabrics, sashes[135], ready-made garments and needles, tobacco, mercury, flour, trunks, iron, and cast-iron pots (the latter possibly procured from Russia) (Burton 1998b, 41; Burton 2003, 422).

The English traveler and explorer Alexander Burns (1834) noted that "the cotton plant is extensively cultivated" around Bukhara and that the emirate exported both raw cotton and cotton textiles. Sericulture was also practiced across the region. The same visitor found that "every stream was lined with mulberry plants" and that the slave bazaar

---

[135] Sash—a long band or scarf worn over one shoulder or around the waist.

(open on Saturday mornings) continued to function well (Adle et al. 2003c, 378–379). At Orenburg and Troitsk, the bulk of Bukharan goods declared in 1840–1849 consisted of raw cotton and yarn (over 2 mn roubles) and cotton materials (over 3 mn), followed by lambskins (830,000 roubles). This corresponded to smaller quantities of raw cotton and yarn that in 1819, but much larger quantities of byaz (woven fabric) and carpets (Burton 2003, 424). This, in turn, may point to a degree of progress reached in Bukhara's processing of cotton and thus in value-added activities, prior to the impact of Russian colonization.

As can be subsumed from the above outlined trade interlinkages, "Bukharan" merchants continued to constitute a functioning network of diaspora business communities active across large parts of Eurasia in the first half of the nineteenth century. "Indian" merchants, textile traders, and moneylenders also maintained a very important and well-studied trade diaspora in the emirate and later in the Russian Governorate-General of Turkestan.[136] These Indian communities held close contact with their "family firms" mostly located in northwest Indian regions (e.g., Multan, Shikarpur) (Schwarz 2004, 191). Bukharan Jews in the first half of the nineteenth century started to gain an enhanced role in trade with Russia (as well as with China) and thus received certain trade privileges from the czar (see Box 4.4).

Still, property rights do not seem to have been well protected in the emirate or the respect for rules may have degenerated since Shah Murad's times: Certain "Bukharan" merchants, such as Galibay Kushalov, even moved to Moscow (although Russia in the nineteenth century was certainly not a model of the rule of law). Having accumulated a capital of about one million roubles (according to estimates by Mihaleva cited by Burton), Kushalov apparently preferred to live abroad. Like other oriental rulers, the emir of Bukhara, if he deemed it necessary, did not hesitate to dip into the assets or resources of his subjects, as Burton vividly put it. This forced the latter—if they chose to remain in the emirate—to hide or conceal their fortune as well as possible (Burton 1998b, 51).

According to Davidovich, shortages of current coins frequently occurred in Bukhara in the first half of the nineteenth century. Commerce more often than in the past took place through barter and credit (Rtveladze 2003, 447). Troubles and turmoil were never far away. The strength achieved by the Emirate of Bukhara was lost in the course of the nineteenth century, when infighting and warfare against neighbors once again gained momentum—right up to the Russian invasion (Roudik 2007, 57, 58).

---

[136] Their total number has been estimated at 5000 to 10,000 (Schwarz 2004, 191).

4.2.1.3 Khanate of Khiva and the Turkmens: Stabilization and Decline of an Important Transit Center and Prime Slave Market

Extended Period of Instability in the Second Half of the Eighteenth Century

Political and social conditions took even longer to stabilize in Khiva than they did in Bukhara. Internal strife persisted in Khiva throughout the latter half of the eighteenth century. Distributional and power struggles between mostly sedentary Uzbeks and mostly nomadic Turkmens seem to have been at the center of the unrest. Protracted military tensions and wars with Bukhara, Iran, and at times, Russia did not contribute to hoped-for consolidation either. The population suffered from the high tax burden linked to the extensive military expenditures. Almost inevitably, the political and economic crisis had repercussions on the quality of coinage (Annanepesov 2003a, 68; Linska et al. 2003, 69; Shukow et al. 1958/1966, Band 5, 274).

A quick look at the khanate's population in the late eighteenth century: There were Uzbeks and Turkmens (both relatively large population groups) and Kazakhs and Karakalpaks (the latter two smaller groups). Uzbeks mostly led a settled urban life (as Sarts) in the center of the oasis at the head of the main irrigation channels. Semi-nomadic Turkmens in many cases occupied the tail ends of the main channels along the southwestern fringes of the oasis, the so-called old irrigated lands (probably called so because they were linked to Lake Sarykamysh and other remnants of the long dried-up Uzboy river). Other Turkmens nomadized in the Karakum desert north of the Kopet Dagh. Most Kazakhs of the khanate were mobile inhabitants of the northern border areas, and Karakalpaks lived on a stretch of land along the southeastern shores of the Aral Sea (including the lowest part of the Amu Daria delta).

Some descriptions of the khanate distinguished two component parts: the "water side" (the actual Khwarazm oasis) and the "land side" (the foothills of the Kopet Dagh) (Annanepesov 2003a, 68; Paul 2012, 382). Turkmens gradually replaced what was left of the old Iranian sedentary population of the "land side" oases (Breghel 2009a, 235–236).

Compromise and Renewed Tensions with Turkmens (First Half of the Nineteenth Century)

In 1804 an (Uzbek) dynasty of khans, the Kungrats, took power in Khiva. Muhammad Rahim Khan (1806–1825), one of the khanate's most capable nineteenth-century rulers, strengthened public administration and carried out military reforms. Under Muhammad Rahim, Turkmens' social position in the khanate was improved; many Turkmens were given land in Khorezm, some settled down, a large number received privileges in return for their military service.[137] The khan paid attention to irrigation work, set up customs offices, streamlined taxation, and organized the regular issue of gold, silver, and copper coins. According to Nikolay Muravev, who visited Khiva in 1819–1820, there were gold (tilla), silver (tanga), and copper (karapul) coins in circulation (Annanepesov 2003a, 68; Rtveladze 2003, 448; Breghel 2003, 62).

Khorezm remained a focus of transit trade, which remained an important pillar of the khanate's prosperity. Goods transited via Khwarazm between Russia (the lower Volga region) and Bukhara and between Russia and Iran/Afghanistan, respectively (Map 4.5). Trade was also conducted with the Kazakh Zhuz, especially with the Junior Zhuz. Benefiting from the participation or leadership of Turkmen, Karakalpak, and Kazakh nomads, Khivan slave hunting raids and razzias in neighboring countries, particularly in Persia and the czardom, constituted a second substantial source of the khanate's income. In contrast, craftsmanship, skilled trades, and urban life were less developed in Khiva than in Bukhara. Towns like New Urgench, Khazarasp, Kongrat, and Kunia Urgench featured communities of weavers, jewelers, potters, smiths, bakers, confectioners, and other craftspeople (Fragner 2008, 71; Annanepesov 2003a, 69).

Agriculture was also less developed than in Bukhara. Plowing in Khwarazm was still done with a wooden plow drawn by oxen, horses, and camels. The harvest was gathered by hand sickles. Use continued to be made of a particular type of water-lifting device—the chigir—like almost a thousand years before. The crops grown in addition to cereals (wheat, barley) included squashes (melons, water melons, pumpkins), vegetables (onions, carrots, red peppers), oil crops (sesame), cash crops (cotton, tobacco), and fruit, including grapes. The soil was manured and carefully tilled. Taxes were paid in kind as well as in money. As in other C Asian countries, there were obligations (servitudes) concerned with the cleaning of canals and irrigation ditches (Annanepesov 2003a, 69).

It was probably in the time of Muhammad Rahim's successor, Allah Quli Khan (1825–1840), that the city of Khiva flourished most, benefiting from generous reconstruction and renovation measures. As was almost usual for Khivan rulers, Muhammad Rahim and Allah Quli conducted frequent campaigns in Khorassan—in rivalry and war with Bukhara. In the 1820s, Merv became a bone of contention between Khiva and Bukhara and changed hands several times, but found itself for most of the nineteenth century under the sway of Khiva (Annanepesov 2003a, 70, b, 136;

Shukow et al. 1959/1969, Band 6, Map: Kasachstan und Mittelasien um 1873, 528).

In the nineteenth century, Khiva eclipsed Bukhara as CA's most important slave bazaar. Khivan forces in the first half of the century regularly attacked Shiite pilgrimage caravans in Northeastern Iran which were on the way to Mashhad. The Khivans (Muslim Sunnis) captured the pilgrims as "infidels" or "apostates" and had them sold on the Khwarazmian or Transoxianian slave markets. Similar campaigns were undertaken in a northwesterly direction over a much longer distance (around one thousand kms from Khiva) to the Caspian Lowlands, where Russian settlers living along the Ural river were kidnapped and also deported into slavery.[138] In most cases Turkmen tribal groups carried out the slave-hunting operations, raids and razzias, called "alaman" (Chuvin et al. 2008, 82; Fragner 2008, 71; Paul 2012, 383).

But the Turkmens also continued to be famous for their beautiful carpets and jewelry. No need to emphasize their carpet weavers' traditional skilfullness and sense for colors. Among Turkmen merchants who made a fortune, there were not only slave traders. Turkmen traders in the 1820s supplied Bukhara with slaves, fresh butter, horse blankets, woolen carpets, and warm materials of goat and camel hair, but their specialty was the remarkably speedy and handsome Akhal-Teke horse (in Russia also known as Argamak), for which local noblemen apparently paid as much as for a young and pretty female slave (Annanepesov 2003b, 139, Burton 2003, 418; Hambly (ed) 1966/1979, 195).

In general, slaves in CA were treated relatively humanely by their masters. Slaves could and did often redeem themselves.[139] Slaves' condition of life in the US cotton plantations in the mid-nineteenth century was probably much more painful than that of their C Asian counterparts. Iranian slaves, for instance, seem to have belonged to the same social world as their masters and could hope to fully integrate into that world (Chuvin et al. 2008, 82; Adle et al. 2003b, 355).

Harking back to the past (Bekovich-Cherkassky's expedition in the eighteenth century), but also reflecting pressures building up toward an eventually inevitable future conquest (given the unequal overall balance of forces), Russian General Perovsky's campaign against Khiva in the winter of 1839–1840 once again ended in failure. Perovsky, who was also the military governor of Orenburg, led an expedition of 5000 infantry and 10,000 camels, in the

---

[137] In any case, the majority of Turkmens remained nomads or seminomads throughout the nineteenth century. Islam exerted only a limited influence on their way of life.

[138] Some of the Russians sold in Khwarazm were apparently quite appreciated as builders of irrigation works (Osterhammel 2009/2013, 527).

[139] Compare abovementioned possibilities of slaves regaining freedom in the Golden Horde in the fourteenth century and in Khwarazm in the sixteenth.

name of freeing Russian slaves toiling in Khwarazm. Notwithstanding the Russians' superior military equipment, the defeat occurred due to insufficient preparation for desert warfare and ensuing logistical problems, given that the oasis is surrounded on most sides by inhospitable terrain. This left the Russian detachments at the mercy of sporadic and repeated deadly attacks by mostly Turkmen mounted warriors (Roudik 2007, 59; Soucek 2000, 197).

Muhammad Amin Khan (r. 1846–1855) reinforced central control of the khanate's irrigation system and seemed to favor settled farmers and town dwellers, who became his most reliable subjects. He also provided them with increased protection against nomadic covetousness and redistributional demands. His ban on visits to local bazaars could be used as a means of exerting pressure on recalcitrant Turkmen tribes—which points to the importance or possible preeminence the market economy had reached with respect to the subsistence economy for these mobile pastoralists.

Around the middle of the nineteenth century, popular unrest grew in Khiva, particularly among nomads, and the khanate went into decline again. Against the backdrop of tensions with Russia, a Turkmen uprising took place in 1855–1856. The irrigation system was disrupted and the farmlands were partly deserted. Continued political instability as well as relative military weakness left the khanate open to conquest by czarist forces, which happened in 1873 (see below) (Annanepesov 2003a, 70; Roudik 2007, 59).

4.2.1.4 Khanate of Khoqand and the Kyrgyz: Rising but Fragile Mini-Empire Controlling Trade and Tributes in the Heart of CA

Political Stabilization, Economic Recovery, and the Pax Sinica (Second Half of Eighteenth Century–Early Nineteenth Century)

The Khanate of Khoqand, whose core lay in the Ferghana Basin and along the upper reaches of the Syr Daria, appears to have gained political and economic strength throughout most of the long period from the 1760s to the 1840s. In the late 1750s, Khoqand had absorbed a temporary influx of refugees from Kashgaria fleeing the invading Qing troops. By 1760, Irdana (r.1751–1770), the Khoqand ruler of the (Uzbek) Min dynasty[140], formally submitted to the overlordship of the Qianlong emperor in Beijing (partly in gratitude for his defeat of the Dzungars).[141] Khoqand's strengthening was the result of (at least temporary) domestic stabilization as well as favorable external political conditions.

Presumably, in the final decades of the eighteenth and the first one or two decades of the nineteenth century, Chinese preeminence in the region, including the proximity of large armed forces in the Ili area[142], contributed to calming the overall situation (Pax Sinica).

In 1760 the Kyrgyz also nominally became Chinese subjects. Essentially however they remained quite independent and continued not to avail themselves of state structures. The Kyrgyz were ruled by their own tribal or clan leaders (called biys—corresponding to begs or beks of other Turkic or Turko-Mongol societies, as mentioned earlier). Islam had only superficially penetrated Kyrgyz society from the seventeenth century (see also above). In the course of the eighteenth century, the Kyrgyz became economically subdivided into two groups: (a) the Kyrgyz in the Ferghana Basin (the south of their habitat, including Osh, Dzhalal Abad, and Uzgend) gravitated toward a more settled way of life and were more influenced by Islam; (b) but in the main part, the Kyrgyz in the Tienshan (including the mountains surrounding Ferghana and the upper Talas, Chu, Naryn, and Issyk-Koel regions) undoubtedly remained transhumant (vertically nomadizing) pastoralists. The Kyrgyz economy (in any case that of the Tienshan dwellers) continued to be even more centered on subsistence and barter than that of the Kazakhs and Turkmens. Yet in the second half of the eighteenth century, trade with Ferghana as well as with Kashgaria intensified (Hambly (ed) 1966/1979, 160; Tchoroev (Chorotegin) 2003, 118).

Under Khan Narbuta (1774–1798), the Ferghana Basin registered a further period of relative economic prosperity. The settlement of Khoqand began to assume urban proportions. Local chroniclers reported a cheapening of products in the khanate and signaled favorable conditions for trade. The economic stabilization of the neighboring Emirate of Bukhara in this time certainly had positive repercussions. But, as Millward noted, it was trade in Chinese products that became especially lucrative for Khoqand from 1785 to 1792, when the Qing temporarily closed the market in Kiakhta on the Mongol-Russian border (and thus the Sibirian route); the C Asian Khanate could therefore

---

[140] No relationship with the Chinese Ming dynasty (1368–1644).

[141] Khoqand's recognition of Chinese suzerainty had two precursors in pre-Islamic times, when local rulers in Ferghana had a comparable relationship first with Han China, then with the Tang Empire.

[142] The "Ili area" or "Ili district" is a historically important and not always clearly defined territory that essentially comprises the upper reaches of the Ili river valley between the Tienshan and the Alatau ranges, including the city of Kuldzha (Yining) and at times also the town of Zharkent (Panfilov). The Ili area is not understood to include the surroundings of the city of Almaty (Alma Ata, Verny) further downstream. The "Ili protectorate" however, which existed for about half a century following the Qing conquest of the area in 1758, comprised the entire Ili valley and Semirechie south of Lake Balkhash as well as the area surrounding Lake Issyk Koel.

transship Chinese tea and rhubarb[143] to supply frustrated Russian buyers (Millward 2007, 110).

Expansion Creates East-West Trade Turntable and Tribute Collector at the Heart of CA (Early Nineteenth Century to 1840s)

Under Alim (1798–1811), Umar (1811–1822), and Muhammad Ali (or Madali) Khan (1822–1842), the Khanate of Khoqand came into its own as a vigorous and expanding polity. Some tribes voluntarily joined the khanate after they had been offered a beneficial tax regime, good and clearly demarcated pastures, and their leaders were awarded with honorable titles and positions at the khan's court. The spinning of cotton, carpet making, and weaving became domestic occupations of the Ferghana Kyrgyz (as well as of Uzbeks and other inhabitants of the basin). According to Tchoroev, Kyrgyz horses, furs, leather, wool, felt, and products of agriculture were sold in large bazaars, notably those of Andijan, Tashkent, Kashgar, and Turfan. The Kyrgyz, in turn, bought various goods, including adornments, fruit, dried apricots, sweets, rice, toys, etc. In the khanate, some mountain Kyrgyz began to have mobile schools. The hired teachers moved together with the tribe from one seasonal encampment to the other. The teachers may have been paid in horses and sheep instead of money (Tchoroev (Chorotegin) 2003, 120–121).

After bringing most Kyrgyz under its control, the khanate undertook expansion toward the north and northwest, where Alim Khan between 1803 and 1810 conquered the independent "city-state" of Tashkent and the towns of Sairam, Aulie Ata (the former Talas/Taraz), and Turkestan (Yasy) (Map 4.5). After the collapse of the Dzungar Empire, Tashkent had become an "aristocratic republic" and SR trade center (Breghel 2003, 60). In its heyday, the principality had been ruled by Yunus Khodzha (1784–1808) and had included Shimkent and collected levies (zyaket—a fraction of their herds) from parts of the Kazakh Senior Horde (Barrat et al. 2010, 60).

Umar Khan (1811–1822) was a highly educated man, patronized Islamic scholars (ulama) as well as poets and artists, and extended the reach of Islamic law in order to consolidate his administration. He had irrigated farming land distributed (as mulk or private land) under clerical legal supervision. Umar's Min (Uzbek) tribesmen ended up as major beneficiaries of the system, since the khan granted much land to them; this however, gave rise to tensions with those disadvantaged. Kyrgyz nomads who needed land for winter pastures were obliged to purchase this land (as mulk), which benefited the state treasury and in theory brought the tribes under firmer Muslim legal control.[144] Umar also carried out a monetary reform. Only under this khan was the minting of high-quality silver tangas undertaken in Khoqand, weighing 4.0–4.6 g; subsequently, however, their weight declined to between 2.9 and 3.2 g (Rtveladze 2003, 446). Thus, they had probably suffered some debasement.

In 1820, the Khoqandis founded the fortress and settlement of Akmeshit (Ak-Mechet, "White Mosque")[145] on the lower reaches of the Syr Daria, near the winter encampments of the Middle Horde (Map 4.5). A stronghold was further built in 1825 in Pishpek[146], in northern Kyrgyz-populated territory[147] (Soucek 2000, 190). While the Khoqandis imposed levies and servitudes on tribes of the Kazakh Senior Horde as well as on the northern Kyrgyz, neither the former nor the latter had become reconciled to a subordinate status, and some of these steppe and mountain dwellers repeatedly rose against the khanate and resisted taxation (Tchoroev (Chorotegin) 2003, 119). Notwithstanding occasional hostilities, trade between Kazakhs as well as Kyrgyz and the khanate continued. For example, Kazakhs often went to the Tashkent market, which opened twice weekly. In those days, the nomads brought their horses and sheep, and the settled people offered their corn, cotton, and silk fabrics, as well as various household articles (Dubovitsky and Bababekov 2011, 60).

While Khoqand's acquisitions and fortifications, garrisoned by troops, served a military purpose, some also had considerable economic importance: At Akmeshit, e.g., trade routes between CA and Russia converged. Pishpek lay on a route north of the Tienshan linking Tashkent with Yining (Kuldzha) and Xinjiang (China). Soon the Khanate of Khoqand became a prosperous trading center, competing with Khiva and Bukhara (Soucek 2000, 190; Roudik 2007, 61).

---

[143] Rhubarb, or more accurately, the dried yellow root of a strain of rhubarb that grows best in the highlands of Gansu and Qinghai, was much appreciated in early modern Europe as an effective astringent, purgative, and even an all-round "wonder drug," almost as important a commodity as tea (Millward 2007, 110).

[144] These practices recall Emir Shah Murad's endorsement of Islam to buttress his authority.

[145] Akmeshit was later renamed Perovsk by the Russian conquerors and Kyzyl-Orda by the Soviets.

[146] Pishpek was renamed Frunze in the Soviet era and is today's Bishkek, the capital of the Kyrgyz Republic.

[147] This territory was officially still part of the Qing Empire, but had around 1820 apparently been vacated by Chinese troops that no longer had sufficient means at their disposal for upholding military presence in Zhetysu/ Semirechie. Yet the Chinese military remained stationed in its regional headquarters in Yining/Kuldzha in the upper Ili valley. The reason why the troops abandoned Semirechie (apart from the Ili area) is probably connected to the declining quality of Qing rule in the Chinese interior, growing corruption, political instability, unrest, and therefore shrinking subsidies sent to military outposts at the periphery of the empire, such as Zhetysu (Overy 2004, Map: China 1644–1839, 192; see also below).

As in the past, one of the main taxes in Khoqand (and other khanates of the oasis belt), the kharaj, was levied on the product of land. For instance, from land planted with rice, wheat, sorghum, and other cereal crops, the government collected a fifth of the harvest. The tax on cattle, manufactures, and movable goods in general was known as the zakat[148] (Dubovitsky and Bababekov 2011, 63). While there were statutory levels for taxes, these were often exceeded in practice. In addition, there existed a multitude of special taxes, fees, duties, and levies on various tax bases from dairy cows to fodder for horses. Finally, the population was saddled with numerous other obligations and demands that left the labor force in quite a precarious state: As Dubovitsky and Bababekov point out, independent of the amount of taxes residents had paid, they were required to supply horses, wagons, and manpower for the construction or refurbishment of fortresses, irrigation canals, the cleaning up of stables, etc. (2011, 63). This state of affairs recalls the exploitative fiscal regime in the Dzungar-ruled Tarim Basin (until 1758).

Under Muhammad Ali (Madali, 1822–1841), the Khanate of Khoqand reached its greatest extension and probably, the height of its economic power. Khoqandi authority was also increasingly projected eastward (von Gumppenberg and Steinbach 2004, 151). The khanate started to exploit an environment where increasing internal unrest and disturbances in China (see below) triggered a rapid decline of Qing military and political power in Xinjiang and other peripheral regions of the empire in the first decades of the nineteenth century. Khoqand was well positioned to exploit the weaknesses, given the leverage it possessed in its dealings with the Qing. This was because influential Khoqandi khodzhas enjoyed a following on both sides of the border with Kashgaria/China.

It was only with difficulties that the Qing authorities managed to suppress a khodzha rebellion in Kashgar in the mid-1820s that had been supported by Khoqand. Given that the Chinese did not find it advisable to try to invade Khoqand in retaliation, they decided to impose a punitive boycott on Khoqandi trade (1827). This proved harmful for both sides, and turmoil in Kashgaria increased again (Millward 2007, 110). After a few years, the Qing backed down and reached an agreement with Khan Madali. At first sight, this agreement corresponded to a paradoxical and somewhat bizarre encroachment on Qing sovereignty in Xinjiang, as Soucek finds: According to the Khoqand-China treaty of 1832, the khan was vested with the right to send customs and tax collectors among the Muslim population of Kashgaria (Kashgar, Yarkand, Khotan, Aqsu, Uch Turfan and Korla) (2000, 190).

After the signing of the treaty, the situation stabilized again (temporarily). While certainly unwelcome in Chinese eyes, the Khanate of Khoqand had thus established a kind of "extractive link" between East and West Turkestan.[149] The tax intake from Kashgaria reportedly produced substantial revenues for the khanate (Dubovitsky and Bababekov 2011, 60). The ruler of Khoqand thus controlled the routes to the northwest, via Akmeshit toward Orenburg, to the northeast, via Pishpek toward Urumqi, and to the east, from Ferghana to Kashgar. He exerted "selective tax sovereignty" over western Xinjiang. Of course, there was also the important connection south (to Samarkand in the Emirate of Bukhara). Tashkent, at the center of these major routes, became the khanate's most important trading city (Chuvin et al. 2008, 84) (see also Map 4.5).

It is not difficult to infer that Khoqand had become the dominating C Asian SR trade link with China in the second quarter of the nineteenth century. But the khanate also—probably via Tashkent, Akmeshit, and the Kazakh Hordes—strengthened its trade links with Russia. According to Khanykov, cited by Burton, two main Khoqandi caravans arrived every year in Bukhara with Chinese goods. But many small groups of Bukharans traveled to Khoqand, taking raw cotton, English cheesecloth[150], and special plants used as dyes to be exchanged against tea, china cups, Chinese and local silk materials, and large quantities of Russian iron, cast-iron and steel goods. Khoqandis in turn transported Russian ironware, woolen cloth, hides, and cotton materials to Kashgar and returned with tea, porcelain dishes, silk, and silver ingots (Burton 2003, 423). In the 1820s, the Khoqandis (Tashkentis) apparently also gained the upperhand over or became prime competitors of the Bukharans in trade with Russian Siberia.

Increasing Focus on Cotton Production and on Trade with Russia

Khoqandi-Russian trade relations occupied an increasingly important place in the economic life of the khanate. Thus, according to Dubovitsky and Bababekov, from 1758 to 1853, the value of Khoqandian exports to Russia increased twentyfold, while the value of the khanate's imports from Russia grew more than tenfold, yet the latter in the mid-nineteenth century still clearly exceeded the former. Khoqand merchants mostly brought cotton, cotton fabrics,

---

[148] Compare the Bukharan zakot (tax on movable property, like livestock and merchandise), the Khivan zakat (cauldron tax), or the Turkmen or Kazakh zyaket (cattle levy) (see above).

[149] In fact, most Chinese and some other historians regard the Khoqand-China treaty of 1832 as the very first "unequal treaty" the country was compelled to sign with outside hostile powers (see also below).

[150] Cheesecloth = light weight cotton gauze (thin and often transparent fabric) (acc. to Random House Websters' Concise College Dictionary 1999).

silk, carpets, dried fruit, and rice to Russia, while they purchased iron, copper, steel factory products, faience dishes, mirrors, treated and finished leather, woven cotton, velvet, and sugar. With cotton already being Khoqand's main export to Russia, mutual interest in trade grew after the owners of Russian cotton mills had found out that the khanate could become an important market for their finished goods (Dubovitsky and Bababekov 2011, 61).

The construction of impressive irrigation canals contributed to an upswing in agricultural production and tax revenues for the khanate. As Soucek describes, the first major canal of the khanate, the Shahr-i-Khan Say ("The Stream of the Khan's City," so named after the new town whose establishment accompanied the project) was dug under the rule of Umar Khan to the west of Andijan. It was 120 km long and irrigated an area of about 77,700 ha. Similar projects emerged elsewhere, and not only in Ferghana but also in the annexed southernmost parts of the Kazakh Senior and Middle Hordes, which were administered by governors from Tashkent. In the area of the city itself, the Khan Ariq ("Royal Canal") was dug in 1835. Interestingly, canal-building reached its height in the 1850s—just on the eve of the Russian conquest—and covered an area north of the Tienshan from the city of Turkestan to the valley of the Chu (Soucek 2000, 191; Paul 2012, 379). Notwithstanding increasing regional political instability at the time, these investments should prove to be a viable use of available lands over the next decades.

Cotton, the cultivation of which was an old tradition in Ferghana (originating at the latest in the tenth century with the Samanids if not possibly already in the first or second century CE with the Kushans, see above), as well as silk supplied a local textile industry. Ferghana cotton exports to Russia were on the expansion in the first half of the nineteenth century and began to be commercialized already before the Russian conquest. This dynamic development came on top of the fact that, as mentioned above, Khoqand was already an east-west trade turntable and moreover enriched itself with tax income exacted from Western China. All this left visible traces. Urban architecture, both civic and religious, benefited from the new wealth. For example, the great mosque in Khoqand was built at the time. Arts and crafts flourished. There even seems to have been a minor renaissance in literature, above all poetry; women appeared in increasing numbers among poets (Soucek 2000, 191). The few contemporary travelers that visited the Khanate of Khoqand appear to have been impressed by its prosperity and commercial activity. These were impressions that visitors of Bukhara and Khiva in the nineteenth century did not share anymore (Hambly (ed) 1966/1979, 196).

Despite the expansion of its power and despite its economic successes, the khanate faced increasing domestic political strains over the decades. These were strains between the ruling elites and the exploited general populace and strains between sedentary people and nomadic inhabitants. Tensions flared up between the sedentarizing Min tribes who wielded power in the state and traditional settled citizens of Ferghana (Sarts). Intermittent clashes continued with the Kyrgyz nomads of the khanate's mountainous periphery and with Kazakhs nomadizing in its steppe periphery; both peoples wanted to take possession of some fertile plains. Moreover, growing corruption under Madali Khan and his successors against the background of persistent heavy tax pressure, added to overall dissatisfaction (Chuvin et al. 2008, 71; Soucek 2000, 192). In this situation, intensifying warfare with Bukhara (from 1840, even including the temporary Bukharan seizure of Khoqand and the killing of the khan in 1842) further heightened instability. This, however, does not seem to have seriously derailed or extensively obstructed the dynamics of cotton cultivation and the building of irrigation infrastructure.

4.2.1.5 The Kazakhs: Increasingly Under Russia's Political Sway and Economic Influence

Younger and Middle Hordes Adopt Russian Overlordship, Senior Horde Becomes Tributary to China (Eighteenth Century)

In their extremely difficult situation in the first half of the eighteenth century, being exposed to persistent Dzungar military pressure, the Kazakhs looked for strong allies and found one in the neighboring czardom; the Qing Empire's victory over the Dzungars in the late 1750s brought another powerful player into CA who started to exert authority over some Kazakhs. But the two big powers did not eventually clash in the Kazakh steppes because China did not exhibit any further-reaching imperial ambitions in the region (whereas Russia did).

In 1731, the Junior Zhuz declared its formal allegiance to the czar, who accepted the horde's "voluntary" submission to Russian protection. The Middle Zhuz made its declaration in 1740.[151] The two hordes had thus come under Russian suzerainty. After the Qing conquest of East Turkestan and Zhetysu, which included at least parts of the Senior Horde, the latter became a tributary to China. Some years after he had declared his allegiance to Russia, the ruler of the Middle Horde, Ablay Khan, in 1757 accepted becoming subject of the Qing emperor (Poujol 2000, 39–40). However, in 1762 he also renewed his oath to the czar.

---

[151] Respective khans signed deeds in which they approved to become Russian subjects/citizens (priniatie rossiiskogo poddanstva) (Oskolkov and Oskolkova 2004, 32).

In the following decades, according to Oskolkov and Oskolkova, the rulers of the Middle Zhuz continued to "maneuver" politically between Russia and China (2004, 31). Thus, Ablay's successor, Wali Khan—who was, however, only accepted by part of his horde—tried to found his authority also on Qing ascent; he received an official confirmation of his title of khan from the Qianlong emperor (Shukow et al. 1958/1966, Band 5, 270). On the other hand, he had been persuaded by the Russians to hold his accession ceremony in Petropavlovsk (in the far north of the zhuz, at the limits of Russian West Siberia) where the czarist authorities had built him a stone palace that was to serve as residence of the rulers of the Middle Horde (Frank 2009, 370) (see also division of tributary dependence of Kazakh Hordes as shown in Map 4.5).

While China successively relaxed its control of peripheral areas of its empire in Zhetysu and Eastern Kazakhstan, and entirely withdrew from these lands in the first decades of the nineteenth century (Paul 2012, 384; see also below), Russia under Catherine the Great (1762–1796) and her successors firmed its hold on Kazakh territories it had gained control of, although for the time being the czardom's control was exerted indirectly through the regional and tribal leaders and elites (Kappeler 2006, 143).

Russia Becomes the Kazakhs' Major Trading Partner (Late Eighteenth and Early Nineteenth Century)

As Kappeler emphasized, Russia's economic interest in the Kazakh steppe territories largely focused on the acquisition of livestock and livestock products like wool and leather; in return the nomads were provided with grain and finished goods (2006, 147). The czarist authorities had opened seasonal fairs (yarmarka) in 1743 at Orenburg for Kazakhs of the Junior Zhuz, and in the second half of the eighteenth century at the Troitsk fortress for the Middle Zhuz, and at the fortress of Semipalatinsk for the Middle and Senior Zhuz. The Kazakhs themselves saw important economic benefits from developing trade and exchange with their sedentary neighbors to the north. Reportedly, starting already in the late 1730s (a couple of years after the declaration of allegiance of the Junior Horde), a tendency of overall growth of Russo-Kazakh trade was observed (Khafizova 2007, 76; Artykbaev 2007, 184).

Yet, as far as they could, Kazakhs looked not only for political, but also for trade maneuverability. Particularly the Senior Horde maintained important—partly tributary—trade relations with Qing China. But these exchanges—centered on Kazakh horse deliveries—were overall quite strictly regulated and, after some decades, lost momentum (see below) (Perdue 2005, 402; Golden 2011, 124). In the eighteenth century, the Kazakhs appear to have taken the place of the Kalmyks and before them the Noghays as the czardom's primary horse suppliers. According to Levshin, cited by Artykbaev, in towns like Guriev, Uralsk, Petropavlovsk,

and Semipalatinsk, Russians purchased from Kazakhs about 100,000 horses and 1 million rams in the course of 1 year (Artykbaev 2007, 185). And Khazanov specifies that the Kazakhs of the Little Horde sold to Russia between 1798 and 1802, 10,900 horses and 650,000 rams; between 1803 and 1807, 4300 horses and 406,000 rams; and between 1808 and 1812, 282 horses and 318,000 rams (1983/1994, 205).

About 200,000 Kazakh sheep a year changed owners in Orenburg in the late 1780s, quite apart from the turnover of lambs, camels, goats, and furs from the steppes. From 1751 to 1762 in Orenburg, Kazakhs bought over 2000 tons of bread, in 1763–1766 almost 800 tons. From all of the goods sold in 30 years from 1745 to 1774 in Orenburg, 52% were provided by Russian merchants, 17% by Bukharan and Tashkenti merchants, and 31% by Kazakh salesmen. Kazakhs dealt in Bukharan chintzes and sold between 250 and 330 Bukharan curtains a year. C Asian and East Turkestani merchants supplied Kazakhs with big quantities of cotton fabrics/cloth, silks, dishes, fruit, carpets/rugs, arms, bread, and rice. The Kazakhs also functioned as intermediate traders (partly in cooperation with Khoqandians, Tashkentis, or Bukharans) between China and Russia, when direct Russian access to Chinese goods at Kiakhta was temporarily cut off in the late eighteenth century. Kazakhs definitely also supplied Bukhara and Khiva with Russian slaves captured in occasional regional raids in steppe border areas (Artykbaev 2007, 185; Burton 2003, 415).

More generally, Russia in the early 1800s in all likelihood became the steppe dwellers' number one trading partner.[152] On top of this, Russo-Kazakh trade further expanded during the continental blockade. Artykbaev notes that the intensification of trade in some cases led to the piecemeal (non-compulsory) settlement of nomads, the (further) increase in demand for bread, and to dependency on the Russian market (2007, 185, 207).

Kazakh Seasonal Migrations Increasingly Hemmed In

From the 1750s the Kazakhs were limited in their mobility of nomadization by Russian bans on driving their livestock across the Ural river to the west and across the Irtysh to the east (see above). Despite these—in some cases drastic—restrictions, at the turn of the eighteenth to the nineteenth century, Kazakhs continued their predominantly meridional (north-south) steppe migration practices in the Desht-i-Kipchak. Thus, to take two examples, in spring nomads moved from their winter quarters in Mangyshlak and Ustyurt up north to the valleys of the rivers Uila, Sagyza, and Emba (in the eastern Caspian Lowlands)[153] or groups of Kazakhs

---

[152] For the Senior Horde, this is probably only valid from the 1840s.

[153] This remarkably resembles the Polovtsy's nomadization routes of the twelfth century—see Sect. 3.3.4.5.

of the Middle Zhuz spent the winter in the valleys of the Syr Daria and the Chu and then they left for the rivers Esil (Ishim) and Nura in the northern grasslands (Artykbaev 2007, 209).

Sources from the beginning of the nineteenth century witness the presence of irrigation farming in the southern as well as in central regions of Kazakhstan (on the slopes of the Karatau, along the rivers Chu and Syr Daria, and pockets of irrigation agriculture in the central steppes). Levshin wrote of farming in Western Kazakhstan; he referred to Kazakh plowed fields that existed near the river Irgiz (a tributary of the Turgay). In Mangyshlak, eye witnesses pointed to the sowing of grain (cereals) and to the existence of watermelon and pumpkin fields (bakhchevye kultury) (Artykbaev 2007, 209–210).

The first major Kazakh revolt against Russian rule (if one does not include the Pugachev insurrection, which also featured Kazakh participants) took place in the years 1783–1797. It was an uprising of the Junior Zhuz triggered by the aggravation of the land issue stemming from limitation of use of pastures as a result of the Russian authorities' prohibition (1756) of Kazakhs crossing the Ural river (Oskolkov and Oskolkova 2004, 33). In order to somewhat defuse the tensions and grievances of the nomads of the Younger Zhuz, the czarist authorities in 1801 permitted Sultan Bukey, along with some 7500 families to cross the Ural river legally and reside permanently on the "Inner Side," as the western side of the river was known. Pasture-land between the lower Ural and Volga rivers, some of which had been vacated a couple of decades earlier by the Kalmyks/Torguts, was assigned to the Kazakh migrants. Thus the Bukey Horde (also called "Inner Horde") was set up under Russian supervision (Breghel 2003, 62).

Liquidation of Hordes, Establishment of Russian Administration (First Half of Nineteenth Century)

With increasing encroachment on and control of Kazakh territories, the Russian authorities in the early nineteenth century moved to centralize rule of the latter. First, the czar started to appoint khans himself. For example, in 1812 the Russian ruler named a new khan of the Younger Zhuz. Then the hordes were abolished. First in order was the Middle Horde: It is khan's powers that were liquidated in 1822. A reform of territorial government was carried out: The horde was replaced by a handful of okrugy (administrative districts), which more resembled the formal administrative structure in European Russia. The Junior Horde was eliminated in 1824, the Bukey Horde in 1845 (Oskolkov and Oskolkova 2004, 34–35).

The Senior Zhuz (or a large part of it), so to say, gradually moved from Chinese—via Khoqandian—to Russian oversight. From around 1810–1820, i.e., after the withdrawal of Qing officials and military, the southern part of the Senior Zhuz came under the rule of the Khanate of Khoqand (see above), which the Kazakhs resisted due to its practices of heavy taxation, cumbersome working duties, etc. The northern part, little by little, passed under Russian control.[154] In 1845, against the background of the weakening of Khoqand, most of the territory of the Senior Horde was annexed by Russia (and most of its population became subjects of the czar). Finally, after the crushing of the Kenesary insurrection (see below), the Senior Horde itself was liquidated in 1848 (La Decouverte 1993/2002, 157).

Following the abolition of the discrimination of Islam and the Tatars' rehabilitation by Catherine the Great, many of the latter moved to CA and particularly to the Desht-i-Kipchak. Tatar merchants and businessmen often represented Russian commercial interests there. As Soucek explains, the government, eager to protect these interests, saw in these Muslim subjects' convenient proxies and trade flourished, as explained above. Some commercial fortunes were earned on the Kazakh steppe. Moreover, the authorities deemed it expedient to consolidate control through the at first sight surprising device of tying the still only partially Muslim Kazakhs more firmly to Islam. The aim was, Soucek goes on, to entice the unruly and divided nomads to a more sedate and easier to control way of life, especially since it was the czar's subjects, the Tatar mullahs, who spread among the Kazakhs as preceptors and even had mosques and madrasas built in the grasslands. This policy of using Tatar elites, both mercantile and religious, as the czarist government's advanced infrastructure in the Kazakh steppes, devised in the late 1770s, largely proved successful and continued until the 1860s, i.e., until the definite completion of the conquest of Kazakhstan (Soucek 2000, 197; see also Linska et al. 2003, 71).

While the bulk of the Kazakh population was eventually converted to Islam, some members of the Kazakh tribal aristocracy received an excellent Russian education, which had considerable influence on their career perspectives. However, the social stratum of Russian acculturated Kazakhs who cooperated with the czarist authorities was thin (Linska et al. 2003, 71). At the same time, in principle all nomads of the Russian Empire were classified as belonging to the legal category of "inorodtsy," literally "people of different birth" or indigenous people. These subjects of the czar were not regarded as full Russian citizens and were also relieved of some of the latters' duties, e.g., inorodtsy were exempted from conscription (Kappeler 2006, 140, 146).

---

[154] For example, in 1831 Cossaks built the fortress of Sergiopol (Ayaguz) on the banks of the Ayaguz river at the northern border of Semirechie.

4.2.1.6 Qing Xinjiang: Strong State-Initiated Agricultural Development and Relative Colonial Prosperity (1758–1830)

Establishment of Indirect Rule of Peripheral Strategic Territory

In 1758 East Turkestan up to Lake Balkhash became Chinese. Before that Tibet (1720) and Qinghai (1724) had been conquered, and Tibet was turned into a Qing protectorate (1751). Before that, Outer Mongolia (Khalkha) had been attached to the Qing Empire (1697). Previously, far Eastern territories north of the Amur had been ceded by Russia in the Treaty of Nerchinsk (1689), and Taiwan (Formosa) had been annexed (1683). With all these conquests and incorporations, China by 1760 comprised a territory of about 11.5 million km^2, which corresponds to the country's largest extension in history.[155] Thus, measured in territory, the Qing Empire in the late eighteenth and the early nineteenth century was, after Russia, the second-largest country of the world. Meanwhile China remained economically and demographically by far number 1. Maddison estimates China's share in global GDP in 1820 at about one third (Maddison 2007, 125). Under the Qianlong emperor (1736–1796), the Middle Kingdom experienced an economic and cultural heyday. Farming, crafts, trades, notably the production of silk, and other branches of industry once again boomed.

East Turkestan or Xinjiang became a separate territorial possession of the Manchu dynasty, rather than being directly integrated into the Qing Empire as one more regular Chinese province. The region was indirectly ruled rather than being divided into prefectures and counties, each under a magistrate as in the provinces of China proper. As Soucek points out, indirect Qing rule had two important effects: Firstly, the native population of Xinjiang—mostly Muslims and Turkic speakers after the virtual wiping out of the Mongol population of Dzungaria—retained a considerable degree of self-rule at all but the highest levels; and, secondly, almost no immigration from China proper to the Tarim Basin was permitted, except for a limited number of Han merchants (Soucek 2000, 263).

The Manchus divided the administration of Xinjiang into three major geographic units: the Ili Protectorate (comprising Zhetysu, the Ili, and Issyk Koel regions), under the direct jurisdiction of a Qing military governor-general residing in Yining (Kuldzha); Pei Lu (the "Northern Lands," comprising the Urumqi region, Dzungaria, Turfan, Hami, and Barkoel), under the authority of a lieutenant-governor

(amban), residing in Urumqi; and Nan Lu (the "Southern Lands," essentially covering the Tarim Basin/Altishahr), ruled by an amban from Yarkand. The governor-general's residence in Yining was established by the Manchus near the remnants of the historic town of Almalik on the Ili river (the former capital of the Mongol Ulus Chagatay and of the Dzungar Empire). The Qianlong emperor ordered the construction of a new city—Yining—where soon nearly 100,000 Chinese military personnel and their dependents resided. Furthermore, many servicemen were stationed in Hami, Turfan, and Barkoel, while there was minimal military presence in the Nan Lu, where no permanent forces were stationed (Soucek 2000, 263; Perdue 2005, 340).

The beg system—the system of local governance through begs (chiefs, nobles, heads of district, deriving from Turkic traditions)—was quite common in the area inhabited by the Uighur people (predominantly Nan Lu) (Ma 2003, 203). In somewhat simplified terms, as Millward and Perdue explain, the Qing inserted themselves at the top of the traditional hierarchy, validated existing administrative titles in the Tarim Basin, added the word "beg" to them and ranked each position in the Chinese manner (Millward 2007, 79; Perdue 2005, 342). Thereby a relatively systematic bureaucracy emerged, consisting of autonomous local elites, who were supervised, appointed, and removed by the lieutenant-governors, in consultation with Beijing. The highest ranked beg officials, the "hakim begs," were typically old Qing allies, descendants of Turfan, and Hami ruling families allied with the Manchus during the conquest of the western frontier in the mid-eighteenth century. Lower-ranking begs could hold over 30 different offices dealing with the implementation of decrees, taxation, corvées, clerical work, irrigation, postal stations, police work, legal and penal matters, commercial affairs, and even some religious and educational duties (Millward 2007, 79).

Begs were on the Qing payroll, received modest salaries, and were granted lands and serfs to cultivate them in proportion to their ranks. Across Nan Lu, there were nearly 300 begs. Moreover, the Qing maintained relations with the ulama (Islamic clergy, learned community), who dealt with certain judiciary tasks involving Sharia law (e.g., marriages, inheritances) (Millward 2007, 79; Ma 2003, 205). Given the relative economic and political success of Qing rule over at least half a century (see below), the above described arrangement does appear to show a degree of sophistication with which the authorities in Beijing managed to interlink or dovetail two fundamentally different administrative and political systems at the local and regional level. The hybrid, multilayered and delicate Xinjiang governance structure of course also embodied fragility.

However, Chinese rule was not installed smoothly everywhere. In the first years after the conquest, some places apparently witnessed egregious misrule and exploitation by local officials. Hardly restrained by the new authorities, the

---

[155] This does not include tributary or vassal territories that were not possessions of the Qing dynasty, like Nepal, Burma, Siam, Laos, Tongking, Annam, Korea, the Khanate of Khoqand, and the Kazakh Senior Horde.

hakim beg of Uch Turfan (near Aqsu, on the foothills of the Tienshan) had installed oppressive corvée duties and other abuses. In 1765, Uch Turfan rebelled against the heightened exploitation. After some hesitation, the Qing commanders bloodily suppressed the revolt: Large parts of the town were destroyed, over 300 rebels were killed, and thousands deported to Ili. The authorities then rebuilt Uch Turfan almost from scratch. A reform of the beg system was undertaken, corvée duties were reduced, higher begs' privileges were reined in, and supervision was stepped up (Millward 2007, 108; Perdue 2005, 291–292).

Incorporation of (Eastern) Kazakhs and Torguts into the Qing Trading, Tax, and Political System (1760s–1770s)

After some hostilities and evictions of Kazakhs from Zhetysu by Qing forces, in 1767 the Manchu-Chinese authorities (ruling formerly Dzungar Zhetysu) reached an arrangement with the Kazakhs of the Senior Horde. The latter were allowed to migrate to the pastures of parts of Semirechie (e.g., the middle Ili valley and the northern foothills of the Alatau) which they had used prior to Oirat rule, during the winter months in exchange for compensations paid to the Qing authorities in the amount of 1% of the animals in their herds every time they crossed the Chinese border.[156] Moreover, Kazakh tribute missions presented special gift horses to the emperor. Thus, one can argue that the Senior Horde (under Qing overlordship) regained parts of Semirechie (or at least regained rights of nomadization there) (Roudik 2007, 50; Perdue 2005, 355).

Kazakhs soon participated in annual trade fairs at designated zones in Yining (Kuldzha), Tacheng (Chuguchak, Tarbagatay area), and Urumqi. In these places, relatively compliant Kazakh as well as Kyrgyz nomads traded with Qing or Chinese merchants, most of whom did business on behalf of the military. From the herders (at the source), the merchants obtained horses (3000–4000 per year), sheep, cattle, and other livestock necessary to support Qing garrisons, at only about half the prices paid in Kashgar markets.[157] The nomads in turn obtained silver ingots, metal utensils, cotton cloth, brocades, and apparel woven in Southern Xinjiang and valuable silks, satin, velvet, brick tea, and porcelain (typical goods of the SR) from China proper that they could sell further west (Millward and Perdue 2004, 60; Khafizova 2007, 70, 74–75).

Regarding the institutional aspect, it appears interesting to compare pre-1758 Qing-Dzungar trade with post-1767 Qing-Kazakh trade, as Perdue does: In the Dzungar trade, the main official goal was stability (security- or politically driven trade); the actual pecuniary gain or loss was of less concern to the Chinese authorities. In the Kazakh trade, both officials and traders responded swiftly to market demands so as to secure profits for both sides (profit- or economically driven trade—because there was no more serious nomadic threat) (Perdue 2005, 403–405). At the same time, given the changed overall balance of forces, Kazakh traders may have felt exploited in their deals.

Only after their arrival in Semirechie (mid-1771) did the Volga Torguts (Kalmyks) find out that there were not many pastures left for them, particularly after China had permitted the Kazakhs of the tributary Senior Zhuz to resume nomadization in parts of the region. The Torguts were temporarily settled near the Ili river, given relief supplies and later designated pastures. Notwithstanding initial difficulties, the help extended by the Qing authorities to the returning nomads was quite considerable, as Miyawaki, Bai, and Kyzlasov point out: Large quantities of supplies were promptly brought from Xinjiang itself, as well as from Gansu, Shanxi, Ningxia, and Inner Mongolia (including provisions of cattle, sheep, grain, tea, hides, cotton cloth, raw cotton, and felt) (2003, 161).

Subsequently, pastures were allocated to the Torguts, mostly in western Dzungaria and southern Zhetysu: the uppermost Irtysh region (of the Black Irtysh), the eastern and southern Tarbagatay region (around Tacheng/Chuguchak), the eastern Alatau region (near the Dzungarian Gate), the Urumqi oasis, the Manas river region (west of Urumqi), and finally the middle and upper reaches of the Ili valley. Yet, some of the designated habitats in the Ili valley and the Tarbagatay area were located very near to Kazakh encampments, so that tensions between the two nomadic peoples must have been inevitable. Moreover, the authorities forced some of the Torguts who had been resettled to oasis areas (notably the Urumqi and Ili areas) to take up farming (Miyawaki et al. 2003, 161–162; Millward 2007, 78; Perdue 2005, 298).

Major Government Agricultural and Infrastructure Investment, Sustained Subsidization, Peace, and Relative Prosperity (ca. 1760–1820)

According to Millward and Perdue, the Qing authorities' economic goals for Xinjiang were clear-cut but extremely ambitious: Once they had taken possession of East Turkestan, the Chinese authorities were concerned with reducing taxes and obligations from the very high levels inherited from their Dzungar predecessors; thereby they aimed to build legitimacy for Qing rule. At the same time, the new government intended to enhance the scope of

---

[156] Although a border levy, this bears some resemblance to a kibitka tax.

[157] From the beginning of the nineteenth century, more and more Russian businessmen accompanied Kazakh traders coming to the trading points established by the Chinese authorities and offered popular metallic articles and manufactured products (Khafizova 2007, 77).

imperial administration well beyond Dzungar levels. Furthermore—and actually in contradiction with the just mentioned aims—the Qing emperors expected Xinjiang to pay for itself, without substantial subsidies from the center to support the troops. This somewhat paradoxical goal was to be gradually achieved through extensive state-directed investment in farming, mining, manufacturing, infrastructure, and other areas of regional development (Millward and Perdue 2004, 58).

From the start of Qing rule of the western frontier region, large amounts of resources, notably annual silver stipends (regular government transfer payments from Beijing), were needed to support the Chinese military in Xinjiang. As Millward explains, in attempts to reduce the required stipends and consolidate Qing rule, officials launched a multitude of infrastructural projects, commercial ventures, and schemes to stimulate farming and handicrafts. They opened government farms to provide needed grain and managed state-owned stock-breeding units to supply meat (Millward 2007, 81).

Tax incentives were employed to encourage increased production of cotton cloth in Kashgaria that could be shipped north to supply the Torguts and trade with the Kazakhs for more needed livestock and horses. Iron and cooper mines were opened—or better, reopened, since many of these mines had probably already worked in the Dzungar era—and even gold was extracted. Civil servants also ran pawnshops, textile stores, lumber yards, and pharmacies, and they managed rental properties and commercial real estate to provide additional revenue. Finally, as Millward goes on to elaborate, officials joined in partnerships with private merchants to purvey tea and other products at a profit; they organized or relaunched jade mining from the mountains and rivers south of Khotan and had the precious stone shipped back to and sold in Beijing (Millward 2007, 81).

To come straight to the point, after a couple of decades of development and growth, the Xinjiang economy and tax base still failed to fully support the Qing military government and its troops stationed in the region. Self-sufficiency for Xinjiang was not achieved. Consequently, the need for annual silver stipends continued: Dozens or even hundreds of tons of silver had to be shipped every year from the provinces of China proper to Xinjiang. While the region eventually became self-sufficient in foodstuffs (certainly no modest feat), the regular silver payments were required to pay the salaries of soldiers and officials, as well as for clothing, military equipment, and construction costs (Millward 2007, 108, 116; Perdue 2005, 336).

Now to take a closer look at the authorities' development policies in the region, the Qing government's focus was on state-directed agricultural development following the resuscitated traditional model of the Chinese military-farming colony (tuntian).[158] A network of state agricultural colonies was created which vastly exceeded comparable structures that had been put in place in the past (Millward and Perdue 2004, 58; Hambly (ed) 1966/1979, 306). Beginning in 1760, Qing officials launched an extended campaign to promote immigration and—predominantly agricultural—settlement in Xinjiang. Except for Hami, Barkoel, and Turfan, that had been conquered earlier, very few Han settlers had entered the region before 1760. As Millward and Perdue point out, Chinese immigration in the eighteenth and early nineteenth centuries was channeled to the—at that time—sparsely populated east and north of Xinjiang (principally along the axis from Turfan via Urumqi to Yining). Before the 1830s, there reportedly were only a few hundred Chinese settled in the Tarim Basin, most of them merchants (Millward and Perdue 2004, 59).

According to Perdue, the first major Qing tuntian colonies were established in and around Urumqi. They expanded westward to comprise a total of 13,400 cultivator-servicemen (or soldier-farmers, consisting mostly of Han Chinese and of Manchus). Farther west, in the Ili valley, from 1761 to 1772 the number of colonies also multiplied. Soldiers were allotted fields in the vicinity of their garrisons in order to secure (most of) their own food supplies. The soldier-farmers initially did not have ownership rights to the land nor could they choose their crops. The authorities granted the colonists usage rights only and prescribed which crops would be grown (wheat, smaller amounts of barley, millet, and sesame). Cultivators paid a fixed harvested quota or quantity to the state (fixed rent system) and kept the rest for their families. Apart from Qing soldiers, some deported criminals were also settled. Ordinary convicts became bond-servants (de facto slaves) of garrisons at the frontier (Perdue 2005, 344–345).

Han civilian settlement began after 1761, as Perdue continues. The main focus of this state-sponsored program was the poor peasantry of Gansu. This SR province, adjacent to CA in the east, was often victim to inclement weather and suffered frequent droughts. Poor peasants were encouraged to migrate to Urumqi. They obtained generous official support for transport costs, animals, farming tools, seed, and housing. By 1781, nearly 20,000 households had moved. Organized official settlement ceased after that year, but numerous Chinese farmers continued to head out west toward the frontier on their own. Even in peripheral northern places, like Tarbagatay (Tacheng) settlers attempted to take

---

[158] As mentioned earlier, this model was first applied by the Han dynasty in around 100 BCE in China's "Western territories" (of the time) comprising the Tarim Basin. The Qing dynasty founded its first military farms in eastern Xinjiang (Hami and Turfan) early in the 1700s, while still at war with the Oirats (see above).

up agricultural activities. Merchants who brought large sums of capital could quickly invest in land and hire laborers to clear it, with official support. These "merchant colonists" (shanghu) constituted another important group of civilian migrants. Given the funds at their disposal, some of these businessmen controlled very large estates (Perdue 2005, 344–345, 350).

Furthermore, there were Muslim settlers from Southern Xinjiang. In 1761, Qing officials found some 2000–3000 Muslims in Ili that the former Dzungar authorities had brought from places in Altishahr (Yarkand, Kashgar, Aqsu, Uch-Turfan, etc.) and that were tilling the land in the fertile valley (Ma 2003, 197). Realizing that the agrarian conditions of the region favored special expertise, Qing administrators, like their Dzungar predecessors, continued recruiting Muslim Turkic-speaking inhabitants of Southern Xinjiang to move north to cultivate new land. Their know-how for the irrigation of arid lands was particularly appreciated. These recruits continued to be called Taranchis (or Tariachin) and were mostly resettled in the Ili area like in Oirat times (Perdue 2005, 341–342, 344–345).

Under Chinese rule, all Tariachin were state peasants, owing rents and labor dues to the authorities, with no freedom to leave the land.[159] As a result, in the Ili area the Taranchis became the largest group of agriculturalists. The area's production was more than enough to meet local demand for foodstuff (but not enough to finance all the stationed military's needs). Although the Tariachin were not allowed to leave and some were punished for fleeing, many other tenants from the south flocked to Ili to farm; as Perdue notes, these tenants preferred the Qing fixed rent system to the repeated exactions of smaller but more arbitrary amounts by the begs ruling in the Tarim Basin[160] (Perdue 2005: China marches west, 341, 351, 353).

To support the viability of Xinjiang's agricultural settlements, large investments were carried out in irrigation works, tools, seed, and livestock. For instance, the state invested heavily in the construction of irrigation canals (e.g., in the Ili valley). These projects raised the productivity of soil and expanded arable land at the expense of pasture land. The additional farming areas won and drew many new immigrants. Intensive agriculture increased demand for tools and implements. So, beginning in 1773, Ili administrators developed or reactivated iron mines, while other mines extracted lead and copper for currency, bullets, and weaponry. As with horses, it proved cheaper to procure replacements locally. Iron plows, hoes, sickles, and reapers

were produced in rising numbers at the western frontier. This boost of production largely came from craftsmen attracted from China proper, who received a generous remuneration for their scarce skills (Perdue 2005, 356, 357).

Notwithstanding priority given to agriculture, from 1760 the Qing officials established large stud farms in Xinjiang at Ili, Urumqi, Barkoel, and in the Tarbagatay region. Later, additional farms for sheep, cattle, and camels emerged. By the mid-1820s, the Ili area had 10,000 cows, several thousand camels, and about 42,000 sheep. The stud farms were under tight military control and had to fulfill a breeding plan providing for a new stock of horses equivalent to 1/3 of their total herd (of about 30,000 horses) every 3 years. In addition to breeding and purchases from other sources, Xinjiang officials could draw on a new source from the late 1760s, the extensive pastures controlled by Kazakhs (Senior Horde), who had tributary obligations to China. The large number of horses from the eastern Kazakh grasslands (in the immediate vicinity) sold in regional markets, particularly in Ili, drove horse prices down considerably. The Kazakh silk-horse exchange became a regular official business at the western border of the empire until the mid-nineteenth century (Perdue 2005, 355, 400, 404).

Denser trade routes tied the newly colonized regions more closely to the Chinese interior, but also to other parts of CA. Many of these routes were upgraded by the authorities, who installed roadside inns, water depots, and postal-horse stations on major interregional highways. Xinjiang officials kept in close contact with the court in Beijing through detailed written memos in Manchu and Chinese which were dispatched by fast horse over well-maintained and guarded highways. According to Millward, it was military necessity that kept key passes passable, but these improvements benefited businessmen as well. Chinese merchant firms engaged in long-distance trade via the central route along the Gansu corridor, either selling supplies to the military or opening branch stores in the western frontier region's larger cities. Also many smaller-scale merchants peddled goods or at times smuggled jade from Xinjiang, where it had been declared a controlled commodity, back to the Chinese interior, where it was a freely traded and coveted luxury item (Millward 2007, 79, 81). In the early nineteenth century, the new settlers comprised over 1/4 of the total population of the region (Xinjiang); but they remained concentrated in the Urumqi and Ili areas (Millward and Perdue 2004, 59).

When Wen Shou, a high-ranking Qing dignitary, toured oases of the new frontier in 1773, he enthusiastically related the sight of shops clustered "as closely as the teeth of a comb" along market streets, peddlers thronging the roads, and peasants busily toiling away on fertile lands (cited in Perdue 2005, 350). At this point it appeared that the tuntian system was functioning successfully. In the late eighteenth and early nineteenth century, average land yields were quite

---

[159] Thus, in practice there was probably no fundamental difference to the Dzungars' slave settlement policy in Ili.

[160] Apparently, Altishahr begs' taxation practices must have retained a degree of arbitrariness despite the Chinese authorities' clampdown and tightening of regulatory reins after the Uch-Turfan rebellion (of 1765).

high and stable, even if they did not eliminate the need for regular silver flows to finance requirements of the military (Perdue 2005, 361–362).

In Southern Xinjiang (the Tarim Basin), meanwhile, a well-established land system had already been in place long before the conquest, and the new rulers essentially left agrarian relations as they were. Local begs (key representatives of the Xinjiang administrative structure, see above) were often large hereditary landowners, who also wielded power over attached peasants (in near bondage-like conditions). Begs collected revenues from their subjects in grain, locally woven cotton cloth, and in copper coins, though often in a capricious or corrupt way. Like CA more generally, Xinjiang depended to a high degree on merchant and trade taxes which were often paid in silver[161], while Xinjiang land taxes tended to be collected in kind. Most settlers (in the north) also paid their taxes in kind (Perdue 2005, 341–342, 351; Millward and Perdue 2004, 60).

Looking at the pecuniary sphere in the late eighteenth century, the incorporation of East Turkestan into the Qing Empire led to the minting of copper coins on the Chinese model, with a square hole in the middle, which were known in Uighur as yarmaks, as Rtveladze explains. All old coins were withdrawn from circulation and smelted into or replaced by new, Chinese-style coins. Copper coins began to be minted on a regular basis in the city of Yarkand in 1760 in order to support local and cross-border trade, and later in the reign of the Qianlong emperor (1735–1796), mints were opened in Aqsu, Yining, Uch-Turfan, Khotan, and Kashgar (Rtveladze 2003, 444–445).

In 1804, the Xinjiang authorities privatized a considerable share of public holdings in the Ili area and other oases of the region. The argument was that making a landholding a private property would enhance incentives to work and raise productivity. Soldier-farmers' salaries were cut, while a system of special state granaries to buy up and, if necessary, redistribute surplus production was established.[162] The influx of civilian settlers had increased competition and driven down market prices, and the system soon functioned relatively well. According to Perdue, by the early nineteenth century, 200,000 civilians had cleared 1.8 million mou[163] (about 1200 km^2) of uncultivated land in Ili, and over 155,000 civilians had cleared 1.02 million mou (680 km^2) in Urumqi and Barkoel (2005, 346, 350). Private, commercialized land relations developed, including

mortgage loans. Average yields grew and remained satisfactory for decades. Thus the transformation of the western frontier from a military garrison zone toward a more civilianized economy dominated by private farmers seemed to proceed successfully (Perdue 2005, 346, 362).

Perdue points out that the effectiveness of the military colonies—compared to the civilian economy that had just taken root—declined during the first half of the nineteenth century (2005, 346). Civilian settlers soon became the majority of new migrants to Xinjiang. The most successful projects were based on a form of indentured servitude, much like the kind apparently often used to settle the New World:[164] Settlers received travel money, clothes, food, seeds, tools, animals, start-up loans, and 30 mou (about 2 ha) of land. For 5 years they had to cultivate the land, but paid no taxes; after 5 years, once they began paying taxes, the settlers received the title to their land. In these decades many people from the Chinese interior rushed to the western frontier eager to improve their lives (Perdue 2005, 349–350).

Overall Positive Economic Record of First Decades of Qing Rule

By and large, in the first decades of Chinese rule (until about 1820) East Turkestan was governed competently and efficiently. The region was relatively peaceful and prosperous, and many historians would speak of benign colonial rule (see, e.g., Hambly (ed) 1966/1979, 306; Soucek 2000, 263; Paul 2012, 371; Kauz 2006, 131). Yet, since Xinjiang never fully paid for itself, a continual flow of subsidies from China proper was required simply to hold the existing political, economic, and social balance in place (Perdue 2005, 357). From the time of the Qing conquest, besides agriculture, commerce had become an important part of the western frontier's economy. This was because peace through Chinese supremacy for a couple of decades in CA (Pax Sinica) allowed merchants of many backgrounds to restore Xinjiang's traditional position as commercial conduit between China on the one hand and India, the Middle East, and Russia on the other (Millward 2007, 154).

As Millward argues, given the relative calm, the expanding agriculture, thriving local and long-distance commerce, and growing populations of both Uighurs and Han Chinese, Qing governance in East Turkestan might even be called good (2007, 116). Demographic developments were indeed impressive: In 1766 there were around 262,000 Uighurs living north and south of the Tienshan; by 1777 the population of the region south of the mountain

---

[161] This silver was probably earned through transactions with soldier-farmers or through SR deals.

[162] This may recall an element of modern interventionist agricultural policy.

[163] "Mou" is a traditional Chinese unit of land measurement that varies with location, but commonly corresponds to 666.5 m^2 (Encyclopedia Britannica).

[164] An indentured servant (a dico) typically was an emigrant without means who was contractually obliged to render a couple of years of services to his lord of the manor in the New World who had paid his voyage.

chain—overwhelmingly Uighurs—had risen to about 320,000, and in the mid-1820s it reached about 650,000. This rate of population growth surpassed that of the rest of the Chinese Empire. In the second half of the eighteenth century, Yarkand was the biggest commercial center and the largest town of the Tarim Basin, containing about 66,000 people in 1766; Kashgar was the second-largest town, numbering 45,000 inhabitants (Ma 2003, 205–206).

It may not be surprising that in this favorable political and socioeconomic environment, the local (beg) and regional (Qing) authorities in Kashgaria were able to devote particular attention to the maintenance of the sophisticated karez irrigation system (of wells connected to downward sloping underground channels) of the region. According to an English observer of the early nineteenth century, the neighborhood of the three Altishahr cities Kashgar, Yangi Hisar (Yengisar), and Yarkand became known as the "Garden of Asia" (Ma 2003, 205).

Trade between Altishahr/China and its neighbors further west seems to have reached its apex in the late eighteenth century, before slightly declining, but remaining vigorous. In the 1820s, Khoqandis, Bukharans, Tashkentis, Russian Tatars, and Armenians all plied the route between Transoxiana, Ferghana, and Kashgar. They brought horses, livestock, leather, wool, woolen cloth, furs, felt, gold thread and braid, Russian iron, cast iron, steel, cotton materials, chintz, printed silks, gems, corals, and opium to Altishahr. In return, Kashgaria's main exported items were the region's products such as silk goods, woven cloth, jade ware, as well as merchandise acquired from the Chinese interior and reexported (green) tea, ceramics, china dishes, silk, rhubarb, and medicinal herbs. Silver ingots from Qing government coffers spread along the trade routes, often leaving Chinese territory altogether, and stimulating/animating what remained of the SR (Burton 2003, 419, 423; Millward 2007, 81; Millward and Perdue 2004, 60).

As Perdue underlines, managing the western frontier economy required a vast information gathering apparatus. The Qianlong emperor oversaw a system of empire-wide reporting on prices, harvests, and rainfall which generated voluminous data on agrarian conditions (organized across the largest and most populous economy of the world). The purpose of all these reports was to permit officials to intervene as needed with relief and adjustment measures. As alluded to above, the state mobilized its grain holdings to serve the civilian population in times of food scarcity or famine through an impressive system of granaries. Officials who ran the granaries set up in every district relied on incoming market reports for the timing of their coordinated interventions to stabilize quantities and prices. Perdue goes on to point out that the collection of standardized statistical data from localities is considered to be one of the hallmarks of a modern state. The most detailed harvest reports in the

empire were produced by the Xinjiang authorities (Perdue 2005, 358).

Finally, Perdue plausibly concludes that the Qing's economic management capacities were powerful enough that one might even call eighteenth- and early nineteenth-century China a "developmental agrarian state." The imperial authorities did not direct resources toward industrialization, but they did encourage the fullest possible exploitation of landed resources, including foodstuffs and minerals—within the given institutional and technological framework (Perdue 2005, 541).

Increasing Difficulties in China Proper, Instability Spreads to Xinjiang, Decline of Subsidies, and Evaporation of Growth (1820s–1830s)

Notwithstanding the Qing dynasty's undeniable success in building a strong and sprawling empire reaching far into CA, imperial might have started to erode in the nineteenth century. Having been in power for more than 150 years and having conquered eastern CA about half a century before, the Manchu authorities in the early 1800s were increasingly afflicted by practices of corruption and mismanagement. Worsening quality of government started to trigger unrest in the Chinese interior. The quickly expanding opium trade with Europe as well as rising opium consumption may also have played a role (Felber and Peters 1981, 206; Overy (ed) 2004, 192).

In increasingly straitened fiscal circumstances, the central authorities were less and less capable of transferring the annual silver stipends to the military in Xinjiang, which, consequently, started to lack resources. Moreover, spreading political instability in China proper made it necessary in the 1820s to withdraw and relocate some troops from Xinjiang to meet pressing needs elsewhere and to effectively evacuate the military from further outlying territories like Zhetysu (but not from the strategic Ili area). Tributary relationships with the Middle Kingdom's Asian neighbors (Khoqand, Senior Kazakh Horde), as far as they had still existed, evaporated.

The Qing authorities' weakening grip on Xinjiang facilitated the outbreak of unrest in Altishahr, where troop presence was very light anyway; local rebellions started in the mid-1820s and were often led or fomented by khwajas (or khodzhas—religious charismatics or leaders, often Sufi mystics, see above). These disturbances soon received some support from the Khanate of Khoqand, whose rulers, as mentioned above, possessed some leverage in dealings with Chinese Turkestan. This is because, due to centuries of close social relationships and religious links, khodzha clans had connections and followers on both sides of the border. The Manchus managed to suppress the uprisings, but only with increasing difficulties (Hambly (ed) 1966/1979, 307; Soucek 2000, 263).

The khan of Khoqand began demanding exemptions from customs duties for his trade with China, and when the Qing refused, Khoqandi troops supported an invasion in 1826 led by the khodzha Jahangir. The invaders slaughtered the Qing garrison and some Chinese merchants in Kashgar and destabilized a number of Tarim Basin cities. Kyrgyz forces carried out razzias. After an expensive campaign, Qing troops recaptured Altishahr a year later and took Jahangir as prisoner and executed him in Beijing (Millward and Perdue 2004, 61; Kauz 2006, 131).

Punitive measures were also undertaken or attempted against the khanate. However, a counter-invasion did not seem feasible, given the mounting troubles in the Chinese interior and the lack of troops and dwindling resources for the military in Xinjiang. Therefore, the authorities contented themselves with arresting some Khoqandi businessmen and notably with the imposition of a boycott of trade with the khanate (1827) (Kauz 2006, 131). While in some respects, this was helpful in that it facilitated combating opium purchases from Khoqand, it turned out to be a two-edged sword that did not only inflict pain on the Western neighbor's businesses but also damaged interests of Xinjiang merchants.[165] What presumably constituted a substantial, if temporary, blow to what remained of SR trade—the boycott—however proved far from sufficient to reestablish Qing political control of the situation. Interestingly, during the period of deteriorating political stability in the 1820s and later, money circulation in the region also fell into disorder due to a shortage of small copper coinage (Rtveladze 2003, 445).

In any case, using funds confiscated from Khoqandi merchants and local Jahangir supporters, the authorities partially rebuilt some cities of the western Tarim Basin and constructed stronger fortifications at some remove from the old Muslim quarters of the towns, as Millward explains. Chinese businessmen then located their shops and dwellings in between the old and new cities, on land the government now rented to them. The lingering effects of this pattern of separate Han and Uighur settlement are still present today in Kashgar (Millward 2007, 112).

4.2.1.7 At the Borders of CA: Iran, Afghanistan (Late Eighteenth–Nineteenth Centuries)

Iran: Repeated Attempts at Economic Modernization Only Partly Successful

After the political unrest that had followed the death of Nadir Shah (1747) and the collapse of his regime, a new Persian ruler, Karim Khan Zand (1750–1779) oversaw a degree of commercial and economic recovery. Apart from reorganizing the fiscal system and promoting science and the arts (see above), he also authorized the British East India Company to set up shop and even to establish two factories in Iran (Bairoch 1997, 969). This last measure of the ruler was a forerunner of important initiatives aimed at Iran's technological catching up and economic modernization. Understandably, the need to learn from the West was felt first of all from a military point of view. Remaining a traditional "Gunpowder Empire," Persia from the second half of the eighteenth century had come under increasing pressure from European imperialist powers (notably Britain and Russia) (Overy (ed) 2004, 188; Eshraghi 2003, 265).

From 1779, the leader of the Qajar Turkmens of Northeastern Iran, Agha Muhammad Khan, established his control over most of the country.[166] He then became shah of Iran (1794–1797) and founded the Qajar dynasty which ruled until 1924.[167] As in many cases of nomadic conquest before him, Agha Muhammad initially had difficulties in reining in his steppe army's depredations and exactions. Turkmens and other nomads kept privileges in the Persian society and economy until the second half of the nineteenth century. Even then, control of the tribes and collection of taxes from them remained a considerable problem (Khazanov 1983/1994, 271).

During Fath Ali Shah's reign (1797–1834), the first of two state-directed industrialization campaigns were made, as Bairoch explains. From 1812, Persian students were sent to England to acquire a technical education. From the 1820s, metallurgic as well as armaments industries were set up. Efforts were made to modernize agriculture. But these initiatives were not sustained and apparently petered out after the end of Fath Ali Shah's tenure (Bairoch 1997, 970–971). In any case, in the first decades of the nineteenth century the country was forced to cede claims to sovereignty in Transcaucasia to Russia (Treaty of Turkmenchay, 1828) (Overy (ed) 2004, 188).

The second industrialization drive was carried out a couple of decades later under Amir-Kabir's rule (1848–1851). After having stabilized the government's finances and reorganized the army (for the first time in a long period, soldiers effectively received pay and thus stopped requisitioning and pillaging), the ruler upgraded the education system: A high-ranking polytechnic school (with Austrian teachers and professors) was established in 1851. As one could expect, in the realm of industrial development,

---

[165] The interruption of the SR section linking China and Khoqand in the late 1820s should have indirectly boosted alternate connections, including the Siberian route (via Kiakhta).

[166] During the turbulent period of gaining control of Iran, however, the Qajars did not manage to gain control of the oasis of Merv. In other words, in 1790 Iran lost Merv to the invading Bukharans (see above).

[167] Agha Muhammad was not the first Turkmen nomadic chief to found a major Persian dynasty or become a famous imperial leader. Among his Turkmen predecessors were Ismail Safavi (Shah 1501–1524) and Nadir Shah (1732–1747).

arms production continued to claim priority, which, according to Bairoch, seems to have born some success: The armament industry became capable of producing about 16,000 guns of good quality annually. The textile industry also expanded due to the needs of the military. To these have to be added: sugar raffineries, paper mills, glassworks, and a factory for the production of sulfuric acid. The ousting of Amir Kabir entailed the termination of the second industrialization initiative. The second half of the nineteenth century did not witness any more serious industrialization attempts in Iran (Bairoch 1997, 972–973).

While the modernization attempts overall did not bring the hoped-for breakthrough to modernity and the town of Herat (Eastern Khorassan) was lost to Afghanistan in 1857, Iran under the Qajars did preserve its independence (Overy (ed) 2004, 188). Compared to the eighteenth century, that had been plagued by instability and warfare, the relative stabilization of the political situation in the nineteenth century probably contributed to increased population growth. Not only did Tehran (the new capital) expand, urbanization more generally made some progress and money penetrated larger parts of the economy (Bairoch 1997, 971; Anderle et al. (ed) 1973, 574).

On the other hand, pastoral nomadism maintained a strong position in the Iranian economy. According to Bradburd, one estimate for the beginning of the nineteenth century suggested that nomadic pastoralists comprised 50% of the country's population (2001, 138). One would therefore expect the contribution of these economic subjects to the country's output to have been substantial. This is all the more likely to be true when one considers that less than a fifth of Iran's land is suitable for settled farming[168], while vast expanses are available as seasonal pasture. The nomads' main contribution to the Iranian economy in the first half of the nineteenth century consisted of horses for sale, cattle, sheep, sheep milk, roghan (liquid butter produced from sheep milk), wool, woven rugs, and carpets (Bradburd 2001, 138–142).

Overall, among the most important branches of the Iranian economy around the mid-nineteenth century probably were animal husbandry and farming, textile industry (carpets, woolen cloth, chintz, shawls, silks), metallurgy, and armaments. The Persians also sold slaves to Khivan or Bukharan merchants,[169] or Persians themselves were captured and enslaved, often by Turkmen slave hunters and traders.

Afghanistan: While Still an Important Turntable of Eurasian Trade, Increasingly an Object of Imperialist Rivalry

After successfully battling the Persians, Ahmad Shah Durrani (1747–1772) in the 1760s sent an expedition to the north of the Hindu Kush that secured him the possession of Balkh, Maimana, Khanabad, and Faizabad (Badakhshan), thus establishing the Amu Daria border with the weakened Emirate of Bukhara (see Map 4.5). Upon the conquest of large territories in Northwestern India (following the collapse of the Mughal Empire in the wake of the Carnatic wars), Ahmad Shah set up his capital at Kandahar. Indian and Persian engineers were hired to design and construct buildings and fortifications. The ruler had rupees of the renowned Mughal standard issued in Lahore, Multan, Kabul, and other places (Rtveladze 2003, 459).[170] Timur Shah (1772–1793) moved the Afghan capital to Kabul. Lieutenant Vigne, a British officer who visited Afghanistan about half a century after Timur's death, commented that this ruler's reign was still remembered by the oldest inhabitants of Kabul as that in which the town had flourished most (Hussain Shah 2003, 292).

In the late eighteenth and the early nineteenth century, trade in and via Kabul was fairly brisk, often carried out by "Bukharans" (the network of merchants from the Emirate of Bukhara, Kashgaria, and other parts of CA) and "Indians" (mostly traders from northwestern Indian regions, e.g., Punjab). As Burton describes, Kashmir shawls,[171] Multani chintzes, turbans, indigo, and fine white cloth were taken to "Toorkistan"; in return, horses and gold and silver coins were brought over, together with Russian articles ranging from leather, tin, brass, cutlery, cast-iron pots, and needles to spectacles and mirrors. Finally, Kabul received a variety of goods from Xinjiang and China which included textiles (woolens, silks, satins, and raw silk), crystal, tea, porcelain, gold dust, and gold and silver ingots (Burton 2003, 416–417).

However, Afghanistan remained a fragile polity. As soon as the country's territorial expansion had stopped and the conquered or acquired wealth dwindled, quarrels between

---

[168] As mentioned earlier, lots of arable land in Persia had been destroyed by the Seljuks (eleventh century) and the Mongols (Hülegü Khan, second half of thirteenth century).

[169] The largest Iranian slave market was Mashhad, the largest C Asian markets were (as mentioned above) Khiva and Bukhara.

[170] Rupees of this standard constituted a highly valued and proven silver currency that had originally been launched in the mid-sixteenth century by the Afghan ruler Sher Shah and that had subsequently been adopted in Mughal India by Khan Akbar (1556–1605). Even after the demise of the empire, the Mughal rupee continued to serve as a model for coinages in the region (Rtveladze 2003, 459).

[171] In the early 1800s, the popularity of Kashmir shawls was at its peak. According to Meyendorff, 20,000 were taken to Kabul every year, of which 12,000 went to Persia and the Ottoman Empire, and 3000 to Bukhara. Two-thirds of the Kashmir shawls which reached Bukhara went on the Russian Empire, many to be sold at the Nizhny Novgorod fair (Burton 2003, 419).

the leading Pashtoon clans broke out again.[172] Soon after the rule of Timur Shah's successor, Zaman Shah (1793–1801), the country slid into political instability and chaos, which lasted for about a quarter of a century (La Decouverte 1993/2002, 135; Hussain Shah 2003, 292).

Upon reuniting most of Afghanistan, the new ruler, Emir Dost Muhammad (1826–1863), came under pressure from Britain, which by 1830 had conquered most of India, and for which Afghanistan, straddling the Hindu Kush and thus the link or barrier between South and C Asia, possessed strategic significance. The first Anglo-Afghan war (1839–1842) brought large casualties for both sides and effectively constituted a defeat for the British East India Company, which had to cease its activities in Afghanistan. The country then became the stage for British-Russian intrigues and mounting rivalry, which was part of the wider geopolitical "Great Game" between the imperialist powers in CA (see also Box 4.6). Anglo-Afghan relations subsequently improved and Dost Muhammad, with the help of British arms, reconquered the small semi-independent Uzbek and Tajik political entities between the Hindu Kush and Amu Daria (1855), including the regions of Maimana, Balkh, Kunduz, and the principality of Badakhshan. Another area and city incorporated into the Afghan state were Eastern Khorassan and Herat (1857) (Kircheisen 1981, 43).

– *A closer look at Badakhshan: A small, resource-rich mountain principality at the mercy of the geopolitical climate*
Badakhshan was an old mountain principality, a statelet that had been independent since the second half of seventeenth century[173]. It comprised the northeastern part of the Hindu Kush south of the upper reaches of the Piandzh river. At times the principality also included western parts of the Pamir Plateau (the Shugnan ranges). Badakhshan's capital was Faizabad (as it is today) (see Map 4.7). The Persian conqueror Nadir Shah (1736–1747) had brought the region under his authority. With the creation of the Afghan Empire, Badakhshan was subjugated by Shah Durrani in 1768. By the end of the century, the Afghan state had weakened substantially though, and the principality regained de facto independence once again (under Murad Beg, an Uzbek chief), before it was finally annexed by Dost Muhammad in the mid-1850s (see above).

Trade passing through Badakhshan in the first decades of the nineteenth century featured, amongst other things, Indian products, including Dacca muslins (plain-weave cotton fabric used especially for sheets), brocade, white cloth, and indigo, which were in great demand. Taxes on merchants and goods constituted an important source of the principality's revenue (Burton 2003, 420). In the realm of mining, Badakhshan remained famous for its rubies (see above), which were extracted in the Shugnan mountains; the mines were still working in the early nineteenth century, though the returns were no longer high. The equally famous lapis lazuli mines were situated in the Northeastern Hindu Kush; until the 1820s they yielded large quantities of this semiprecious stone which were exported partly to Persia, but predominantly to Russia (Moosvi 2003b, 407). When the English commercial agent Moorcroft visited Badakhshan in 1825, he found that the mines of both these precious stones had stopped working, which was attributed to the unsettled conditions in the area (Pirumshoev and Dani 2003, 234). As Pirumshoev and Dani note, ironware was produced at Faizabad for export to Mavarannahr. But at this time (1825), Russian cast iron was already being imported to Bukhara for the making of larger pans. It seems that more competitive Russian ironware was partly displacing traditional supplies from Badakhshan. Badakhshani farming was dependent on irrigation from snow-fed rivers since rainfall was low. Pastoralism was important. Horses, Bactrian camels, and sheep were prized products of the principality. Moorcroft also found sericulture being practiced in the region (Pirumshoev and Dani 2003, 234–235).

4.2.1.8 Trade and Economic Recovery in CA in Late Eighteenth and Early Nineteenth Centuries: "Last Glimmer" of the SR

– *"Pax Sinica," nomadic military superiority broken*
East as well as West Turkestan experienced a remarkable trade and economic recovery toward the end of the eighteenth and the beginning of the nineteenth century (Table 3.1). The number and intensity of wars in the region declined after the Qing's elimination of Grand Tartary and China's (re-)conquest of the Tarim Basin, Dzungaria, and Semirechie (1758). At least for a couple of decades from the late 1750s, a Pax Sinica can be assumed to have reigned also across part of Western CA. More generally, from the second half of the eighteenth century, nomads were militarily and politically weakened and on the defensive. Sedentary powers had definitely gained the upper hand over nomadic tribes and forces (due the formers' large-scale use of guns and artillery, which the latter were incapable of matching).

---

[172] This would imply that, at least in some respects, Afghanistan in the early nineteenth century remained a predatory or plunder economy (not fundamentally different from its predecessor of the eleventh century, the Ghazavid Empire).

[173] Today, Badakhshan is a province of Afghanistan.

Thus, nomadic tribute exaction, razzias, or pillaging campaigns became less and less frequent.

- *Strong government engagement in East Turkestan, political restabilization in West Turkestan, and increased trade with Russia*

In any case, the Xinjiang economy profited from major government agricultural and infrastructural investments and persistent subsidy flows to the military from Beijing. Western CA benefitted from a degree of domestic political stabilization, which was largely due to the emergence of new (capable) ruling dynasties, which combatted political fragmentation and enforced greater administrative centralization in respective polities. More political cohesion facilitated the realization of some helpful infrastructural and irrigation projects, which in turn contributed to relaunching and animating economic activity. The khanates, particularly Bukhara, became key suppliers of cotton to Russia's burgeoning textile industry, which in turn became a driving force of the czardom's industrialization (Hofmeister 2015, 125). The Napoleonic continental blockade (1806–1812) may have also indirectly benefitted C Asian traders and businesses as suppliers of Russia. Economic recovery was moreover reflected in less frequent debasements of currencies (than in preceding decades). In the late eighteenth and early nineteenth century, trade between Russia and the Kazakh Hordes (except perhaps for the Senior Horde which was a tributary to China) intensified and Russia became the Kazakhs' leading trading partner.

Accordingly, the economic heydays of C Asian Khanates, hordes, and Chinese dependencies in the region may have corresponded to the following periods:

- Emirate of Bukhara: ca. 1770–1830
- Khanate of Khiva: ca. 1805–1855
- Khanate of Khoqand: ca. 1760–1840/1860
- Kazakh Zhuz/sultan administrations: ca. 1790–1830
- Chinese Xinjiang: ca. 1760–1830

- *Landlocked and remote CA's difficult accessibility for modern European shipment technologies provides a respite for traditional economies and SR trade*

One final reason for CA's economic recovery in the abovementioned period was an indirect technological one. As explained earlier, big European sedentary powers' advanced trade and shipment technologies came to favor maritime as opposed to land routes and transportation. This may have given some respite to the traditional C Asian economies and their overland trade. Landlocked and comparatively remote as it was (and is), CA was more isolated from Western European influences and traders, who increasingly traveled and arrived via the sea routes. Having already lost a great deal of SR international transit trade to that sea route, C Asians had

refocused on regional and neighborhood trade, where they temporarily guarded logistical and comparative advantages. In this sense, given the region's—so to speak—newly acquired relative isolation thanks to difficult accessibility for the modern trade and shipping businesses of the times, what remained of SR and C Asian trade gained a "grace period" from the onslaught of advanced Western competition.

- *Renewed political destabilization and hostilities, followed by colonial conquest*

CA's economic recovery at the end of the eighteenth and the beginning of the nineteenth century was undoubtedly the last one before regional quarrels and unrest took over again across Turkestan and before Russia conquered the Kazakh steppes and the khanates, and thus the entire region became carved up between its two great Eurasian neighbors. After that, the C Asian colonies' economic ups and downs until World War I were more influenced by Russian and Chinese national and world market developments.

4.2.1.9 Increasingly Dual (Sino-Russian) Orientation of Remaining SR Network During Last Precolonial Recovery (ca. 1770–1830)

During the last economic and trade recovery in CA prior to the takeover of a large part of the region by European colonialists (see preceding subchapter), trade connections were increasingly oriented toward the two big neighbors to the northwest and to the east of the region—Russia and China. While the czardom largely exerted economic influence via import demand (notably cotton and livestock) and export supply (increasingly textiles, ironware, and other manufactured products), the Qing Empire had already politically incorporated a sizable part of CA (which it developed through substantial government investments and agricultural settlement). Clearly, in these conditions, C Asian routes of trade and communication were directed outward, namely, to the political and economic centers of their dominant neighbors.

The most important routes (remnants of the SR) in CA in the final decades of the eighteenth and the first decades of the nineteenth century were[174]:

---

[174] The routes listed below of course do not include the direct connection that had been established in the late seventeenth century between Russia and China—the Siberian route (Beijing-Kiakhta-Irkutsk-Tobolsk-Moscow).

(a) Toward Russia:
 Samarkand-Bukhara-Khiva-Guriev-Astrakhan-
 Tsaritsyn;
 Andijan-Khoqand-Tashkent-Akmeshit (Ak-Mechet)-
 Orenburg-Samara;
 Tashkent-Akmeshit-Dzheskazgan-Petropavlovsk-
 Tobolsk
(b) Toward China proper:
 Tashkent-Pishpek-Yining (Kuldzha)-Urumqi-Hami-
 Suzhou/Gansu;
 Andijan-Kashgar-Aqsu-Turfan-Hami-Suzhou;
 Kashgar-Khotan-Qiemo (Cherchen)-Suzhou
(c) Toward Iran:
 Samarkand-Bukhara-Merv (Mary)-Mashhad-Tehran
(d) Toward India:
 Samarkand/Bukhara-Balkh-Kabul-Peshawar-Lahore

4.2.2 West Turkestan: Russian Conquest Brings Upheavals and Incipient Inclusion into Modern Capitalist World Economy (Second Quarter till Late Nineteenth Century)

Among primary sources of the following chapter are the publications by Rafis Abazov, Zhambyl Artykbaev, Paul Bairoch, Yuri Bregel, Audrey Burton, Pierre Chuvin, Vincent Fourniau, Gavin Hambly, Andreas Kappeler, Anatoly Khazanov, Rene Letolle, V.S. Oskolkov, I.L. Oskolkova, Jürgen Osterhammel, Peter Perdue, Sebastien Peyrouse, Catherine Poujol, Wolfgang Reinhard, Peter Roudik, I.M. Shukow, and Svat Soucek.

While the range of goods traded on the SR could no longer be compared to what it had been in the past, C Asians adapted to ongoing changes and some made the most of the new possibilities. Thus, the C Asians in the 1840s took back and marketed large amounts of factory-made cotton materials from Russia (1/5 of Bukharan and over 1/3 of Khivan purchases from that country), together with substantial quantities of metal tools and goods (about 1/6 of respective Bukharan purchases) (Burton 2003, 424). As Burton emphasizes, the process had already begun whereby the raw cotton that they had provided was used by Russian manufacturers to industrially produce large quantities of cheap materials intended for Russian and C Asian consumers (2003, 424).[175]

4.2.2.1 Motives for the Russian Conquest of West Turkestan

Russia's conquest of Western CA bears many or all the hallmarks of nineteenth century Europe's and partly the US and Canada's colonial or territorial expansion, respectively. In a wide sense, the motives for the Russian Empire's conquest of the region can be subdivided into two groups: political and economic (Kappeler 2006, 142; Poujol and Fourniau 2005, 51).

First, political motives, including strategic and ideological arguments, as well as arguments aimed at defusing domestic political pressures

(a) The authorities repeatedly put forward the need to establish a secure, and preferably natural, border (which could correspond to the course of a river, e.g., the Amu Daria or to the crest of mountain ranges closing off the extensive plains of CA to the south, namely, the Tienshan, Hindu Kush, Kopet Dagh, etc.).
(b) This search for a reliable boundary was intensified by heightening diplomatic and military competition and fear of British expansion from India (which, including the Indus river valley and Kashmir, had already been conquered by the mid-nineteenth century, whereas Russian forces at that point only stood at the shores of the Aral Sea).
(c) After Russia's defeat in the Crimean War (1853–1856) and its loss of dominant position among Europe's continental powers, St. Petersburg stepped up its colonial expansion drive in the east (Asia) in order to compensate for the geopolitical setback in the west (Kappeler 2006, 142).[176]
(d) A specific geopolitical strategic aim focused on the northern part of the conquered territory—the Desht-i-Kipchak or the Kazakh steppe: This was the goal of expanding the contiguous Eurasian territory settled by Russians or Eastern Slavs or by Russian-speaking settlers.
(e) A colonialist ideological motive or justification consisted of subordinating the neighboring khanates to Russia's moral and civilizational influence, establishing peaceful and regulated trade relations with them, and eliminating raids, razzias, robberies, slave hunting, and other uncivilized behavior on the czar's territories (Roudik 2007, 78).

---

[175] Although not noticeable as yet, this process would eventually result in the full-scale elimination of C Asian textiles from the Russian market (ibid).

[176] This eastern expansion drive was not confined to CA; only few years after the end of the Crimean War the czardom acquired the Amur province (1858) and the Coastal province (Sikhote Alin 1860) in the Far East from China. Yet only a few years after that, Russia gave up its easternmost territories and sold Alaska (Russian America) to the USA (1867).

(f) A purely internal political argument in favor of the migration of European farmers east pertained to the aim of directing "free" peasant settlement out of serf-ridden and partly overpopulated territories of European Russia to new virgin lands in order to reduce possibly destabilizing political pressures.[177]

Second, economic motives, notably resource- and market acquisition-oriented arguments

(a) These include the motivation of acquiring abundant and cheap sources of raw materials such as cotton for the Russian textile industry[178], of gaining access to cheap labor, of expanding output in newly won territories, and of establishing a privileged position for the country's commerce. Given that Russia as the conquering power had the last say in the use of these resources, they can be considered "captive resources."

(b) The authorities aimed at opening up new markets for Russia's growing manufacturing and other industries; given the circumstances, these were effectively also "captive markets" for industrial products that may not have been that easy to sell in Western Europe (Soucek 2000, 199; Kappeler 2001, 162).

(c) A long-standing goal that possessed a political dimension too (and therefore could also have been mentioned above) was to strengthen Russian control of trade routes (former SR connections) to China, India, and Persia.

(d) The abovementioned Kazakh grasslands were gradually identified as a vast land reserve for expanding agricultural production, notably the cultivation of cereals, and for creating a new market of settlers (Kappeler 2006, 142).

Although the above economic arguments clearly bear weight and many aspects explained here relate to respective points, modern research accords prime importance to the (geo)political motives.

4.2.2.2 The Conquest (ca. 1820–1885)

The accumulated technological gap between the Russians and the C Asians (whether inhabitants of nomadic hordes or of sedentary khanates) may explain the swiftness of the Russian advance into CA. According to Soucek, the chief elements of this expansion were the ease and rapidity of military operations in which small numbers of well-armed

troops of a modern European power overcame often much larger indigenous forces[179], and the resulting pacification and organization of the conquered lands along pragmatic lines so as to suit primarily the conqueror/colonizer, but also, up to a point, to accommodate the colonized (2000, 200).

This conquest can be divided into two successive stages:

(a) In the first (until about 1860), Russia acquired the largest part of the Kazakh steppe and Semirechie (Zhetysu) (by and large, the territory of today's Kazakhstan).
(b) In the second (from about 1860 to 1885), Russia acquired the remaining areas of West Turkestan (by and large, the territories of today's Kyrgyzstan, Uzbekistan, Tajikistan, and Turkmenia).

First Stage: Occupation of Kazakh Steppe and Zhetysu (Until About 1860)

Similar to the previous conquests of the Khanates of Kazan, Astrakhan, and Crimea, Russia's annexation of the Kazakh Junior and Middle Hordes could be interpreted as part of the process of "collection of lands of the Golden Horde." But this stage was new in that the Eurasian steppe border was definitely eliminated (Kapeller 2001, 156). From the 1820s to the 1840s, St. Petersburg disbanded the four Kazakh Hordes or Zhuz (including the Bukey Horde); more precisely, the czar put an end to the offices of khan of the respective polities. Thus, the offices of khan of the Middle and Junior Hordes were abolished in 1822 and 1824. The Bukey Zhuz was done away within 1845 and the Senior Zhuz in 1848. During these decades, the Cossacks and the Russian army also advanced in a north-south direction on an extended front, leaving behind them the fortified barrier lines (linii) along the former border with the Kazakhs (Soucek 2000, 195).

New military strongholds (fortresses) were established in the Desht-i-Kipchak, such as Kokchetav (1824), Akmolinsk (1830), Sergiopol (Ayaguz) (1831), then—interrupted by the uprising in central Kazakhstan led by Sultan Kenesary Kasymov (see below)—Orenburgskoe

---

[177] This argument gained weight toward the end of the nineteenth century. For the czarist regime, the eastward migration of peasants probably became a political "safety valve" of considerable significance.

[178] Textile producers' demand for C Asian cotton temporarily skyrocketed when supplies from overseas dwindled during the US Civil War (1861–1865) (see also below).

[179] To give an example of the imbalance of military power reached between Europeans and C Asians in the second half of the nineteenth century: In 1864, General Cherniaev's troops stormed the city of Aulie-Ata (today's Taraz); victory cost them only three wounded servicemen, while the native garrison, which had consisted of about 1500 inadequately armed, weakly commanded, and undisciplined soldiers, incurred losses of 307 dead and 390 wounded. Thanks to artillery bombardment in the conquest of Khodzhent in 1865, the Russians lost five soldiers, while the defenders lost 2500 (Hambly (ed) 1966/1979, 219, 220; see also Marchand 2014, 14).

(Turgay) (1845). Moreover, the Cossacks established themselves south of the Kazakh steppes and set up fort Raim (later called Aralskoe) near the mouth of the Syr Daria and, much further east, Kopal (northern Semirechie, see Map 4.7). On the heels of the Russian advance, settlements and towns were built for military, administrative, trade, and communication purposes (Shukow et al. 1959/1969, Band 6, Map: Kasachstan und Mittelasien um 1873, 528; Roudik 2007, 65).

However, as mentioned above (in section "Compromise and Renewed Tensions with Turkmens (First Half of Nineteenth Century)"), another military undertaking, the expedition of General Perovsky to Khwarazm in 1839–1840, turned into a disaster. The troops met defeat at the hands of marauding Turkmen desert fighters (Roudik 2007, 59). Being well accustomed to the harsh climate and terrain, the nomads launched unexpected strikes and disappeared into the wasteland (which, of course, recalls tactical elements of steppe warfare).

In the early 1850s, there were first clashes between czarist and Khoqandi forces, triggered by attempts to take control of some southern Kazakh groups of the former Middle Zhuz that had rebelled against the khanate's rule. By 1853, the Russians, again led by General Perovsky, wrested Akmeshit (Ak-Mechet) from the Khoqandis. The general had thus regained his laurels, and Akmeshit was renamed Perovsk by the Russian authorities (today, Kyzyl-Orda, meaning "Red Army" in Kazakh). A year later the conquerors established the garrison town of Verny (the eventual Kazakh capital Almaty)[180]. They pushed on to Pishpek (a Khoqandi frontier post on the route to China, today Bishkek, the capital of Kyrgyzstan). Together with the north of the Kyrgyz-inhabited territory, Pishpek was taken in 1860. In the early 1860s, the whole of Semirechie (Zhetysu)[181] had become a Russian possession.[182]

Second Stage: Invasion of Southern Turkestan (from About 1860)

The assault on the south began with the invasion of the Khanate of Khoqand: In 1864 Shimkent and Aulie Ata (later called Dzhambul, now Taraz) fell, and in 1865 Tashkent was stormed and captured. This persuaded the khan of Khoqand, Khudayar (1845–1875) to give in: He swore allegiance to the czar, consented to the Russian conquests, allowed Russian citizens to carry out trade and commerce throughout the khanate, and paid an amount of compensation which should indemnify the conquerors for the cost of their victories. Thus Khudayar became the czar's vassal who ruled a substantially shrunk khanate (effectively cut to its original core, the Ferghana Basin), the rest of which was annexed by Russia. The khan, however, apparently went on leading a wasteful lifestyle; to compensate for the considerably shrunk tax base, he further raised levels of taxation of the oppressed population (Hambly (ed) 1966/1979, 221; Breghel 2009b, 410).

In 1867, Czar Alexander II (1855–1881) signed the decrees on the establishment of the Governorate-General of Turkestan (General-Gubernatorstvo Turkestan) and of the Governorate-General Steppe (General-Gubernatorstvo Step). Both new colonial territories were assigned to the defense ministry's area of responsibility. Tashkent and Omsk were chosen as the respective administrative capitals, as shown in Map 4.6 (for more details see also below).

What followed was a number of military campaigns between 1865 and 1885 that, in Soucek's words, stood squarely in the psychological context of Europe's competitive "scramble for the colonies" (2000, 195). Or one could speak of European powers' wish to acquire—and to deny to rivals—the few "white spaces" that were still left unruled by colonial powers toward the late nineteenth century. In 1868 czarist armies defeated the emir of Bukhara; in a treaty signed the same year, largely similar conditions were imposed as in the case of Khoqand: The emirate's territory was drastically reduced, part of it (including Samarkand) annexed by Russia, and incorporated into the Governorate-General of Turkestan (Map 4.6). Bukhara became a Russian protectorate, and Emir Muzaffar (1860–1885) accepted the czar as suzerain and a Russian garrison in the capital. The emirate was opened to Russian traders on an equal footing with native merchants; Russian goods were only weakly taxed. An indemnity was imposed to replace the conqueror's cost of conquest (Hambly (ed) 1966/1979, 212; Roudik 2007, 78).

The (temporary) collapse of Qing authority in East Turkestan (Yaqub Beg insurrection, 1865–1878) prompted Russia to occupy Kuldzha/Yining and the Ili area in 1871, which it held as "Kuldzha district" until 1883. As depicted in Map 4.6, Ili (save its westernmost part) was returned to China in accordance with the 1881 Treaty of St. Petersburg (Breghel 2003, 64; for more details see below).

In 1873, Russia subjugated the Khanate of Khiva without a blow being struck—quite a change after the miserable

---

[180] Verny (Almaty) was located near the ruins of an old Turkic settlement that had been wiped out by the Mongols (see above).

[181] At that point, Semirechie was inhabited by nomadic pastoralists—predominantly by Kazakhs in the northern steppe territories and by Kyrgyz in the foothill areas and mountain ranges. The upper Ili valley (part of China) also featured settled farmers and town dwellers (see above). Thus—disregarding the Ili area which was not part of Zhetysu anyway and had its own specific history strongly influenced by the Middle Kingdom—Zhetysu in the mid-nineteenth century was not a settled region, except for some auxiliary agriculture, mining activities, and trade settlements.

[182] The annexation of Semirechie was formally acknowledged by China in a border treaty of 1864 (Breghel 2003, 64).

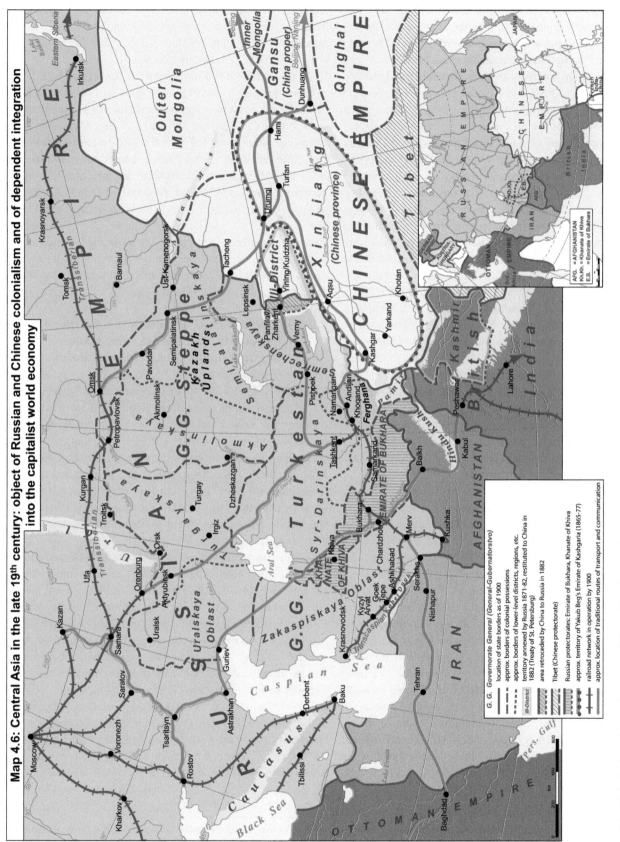

Map 4.6 CA in the late nineteenth century. Object of Russian and Chinese colonialism and of dependent integration into the capitalist world economy

failures of 1717–1718 and 1839–1840.[183] The khanate's entire territory north of the Amu Daria was annexed, the rest became as a protectorate, with the khan as the Russian ruler's vassal (Map 4.6) (Annanepesov 2003a, 71). The khan relinquished the right to entertain independent relations with outside powers and agreed to pay an indemnity. A garrison was stationed in Khiva, and Russian businessmen received the right to set up shop and trade free of taxes. Commercial and legal privileges for citizens of the czardom included the right to purchase and own real estate in the khanate, priority over Khivan creditors, and the transfer of all civil and criminal cases in which a Russian was involved to the jurisdiction of Russian courts. The czardom received control over navigation on the Amu Daria, which also gave rise to a corresponding change in the protectorate treaty with Bukhara (which was situated upstream). Russian trading posts were established along the river's banks, and the two vassal states' governments became responsible for the safety of the czar's subjects (Hambly (ed) 1966/1979, 225; Roudik 2007, 80).

The same year as Khwarazm was conquered, a series of rebellions broke out in the Khanate of Khoqand. Khan Khudayar was extremely unpopular due to his cruelty and his excessive tax claims. In 1875, the ruler fled the insurgents and sought refuge in the Russian mission. The disorders continued, and the following year the Russian army occupied the khanate's entire territory and put down the rebellion. In 1876, the authorities resolved to abolish the khanate and they incorporated its territory as the newly created province (oblast) of Ferghana into the Governorate-General of Turkestan (Hambly (ed) 1966/1979, 225–226; Soucek 2000, 193).

A final Russian military misfortune happened during the campaigns to conquer the remaining southernmost C Asian territories not yet under Russia's sway. The army suffered a serious setback and heavy casualties in 1879 when it attempted to take the Turkmen oasis and fortress of Goek-Tepe (on the northern foothills of the Kopet Dagh, in the vicinity of the present city of Ashgabat). After the Khiva disaster of 1839–1840, this was another rout at the hands of Turkmen warrior-nomads (in this case, people of the Akhal-Teke clan—breeders of the famous horse race of the same name, see above). The defeat was reportedly due to a militarily inappropriate attempt to storm prematurely a well-armed fortress, guarded by numerous fighters, and protected by earth walls. Yet the Russian army returned better prepared and with a larger force in 1881: General Mikhail Skobelev ordered an extended artillery bombardment of the fortress before attacking. Thus, a protracted siege of three

weeks followed by an offensive resulted in the death of about 15,000 Turkmens and "only" about 260 Russians. This massacre essentially crushed Turkmen and what remained of C Asian, resistance to Russian rule (Hambly (ed) 1966/1979, 226; Breghel 2003, 64).

At the end of 1881 Russia signed a convention with Iran establishing the boundaries between the two powers. In 1884, the czar's armies occupied the (mostly Turkmen controlled) oases of Tedzhen and Merv (today, Mary) and the following year proceeded further south to Kushka (today, Gushgi/Serhetabat) on the Afghan border (near Herat)[184]. With these conquests, the Russian Empire had not only become a direct neighbor of Afghanistan (which a couple of years before had become a British semiprotectorate) but had also reached proximity to British India. While this further southern thrust temporarily increased Anglo-Russian tensions, the Russo-Afghan border treaty of 1887 acknowledged the czardom's conquests (Map 4.6) (see also Box 4.6 on the "Great Game").

4.2.2.3 "Civilizational" Effects of the Russian Conquest: "Pax Russica," Separation of Populations, Urbanization, Painful Modernization

Remarkably for the C Asian countries that had to suffer intrusion and colonization from Russia and other outside powers, As Soucek underlines, it was actually relative peace and order that was installed by the conqueror in an area where internecine warfare and marauding had become endemic (2000, 202). As described above, insecurity across large parts of West Turkestan had even mounted in the decades preceding the Russian invasion. Once the region was pacified (in a way it had not been for centuries), the "Pax Russica" reigned in Western CA.

Under Russian rule, C Asia's nomads, but also its sedentary population, lived separately from European immigrants, settlers, and colonists. As mentioned earlier, nomads were called "inorodtsy" ("people of different birth"), while settled C Asians, like Sarts, were named "tuzemtsy" ("native people"). Inorodtsy and tuzemtsy were subjects of the czar, but did not have the same rights and obligations as the ruler's European subjects. Despite infringements, which were particularly serious in the case of nomads, C Asians' way of life and their religion were largely respected by the new authorities; the Russian Orthodox Church was prohibited from carrying out missionary work in the region (Hofmeister 2015, 127). C Asians were exempted from military service. Slavery was, however, abolished across West Turkestan, just

---

[183] The news of the conquest of Khiva was the first message sent to St. Petersburg from Tashkent through the newly constructed telegraph line (Roudik 2007, 79).

[184] Kushka was the southernmost location the czarist forces reached in CA and became the southernmost point of the Russian Empire and, later, of the Soviet Union.

as other European powers suppressed slavery in their colonies in the nineteenth century.

In some nomadic territories (e.g., in Kazakh or Turkmen populated areas), Russian colonization brought the first examples of urban life. Some of the present-day major C Asian cities, e.g., Almaty (former Verny), Astana (former Akmolinsk), Pavlodar, Tuerkmenbashi (former Krasnovodsk), and Ashgabat (former Ashkhabad)—while probably being situated near older villages, encampments or fortresses were essentially established as Russian settlements. Samarkand was partly converted into a new European-style city with radial streets. Parks were laid out; post offices and theaters were erected. Biannual trade fairs were organized in Tashkent, in which the telegraph made its arrival in 1873, and the first commercial bank of the region opened in 1875 (Roudik 2007, 85–86).

According to Kappeler, the legal, social, cultural, and religious order of the indigenous societies were by and large not interfered with,[185] yet the czardom's economic, transportation ,and settlement policies did trigger incisive changes (2006, 146). These changes in the south of Turkestan (the oasis belt) soon produced some impressive world market-oriented economic results, while the promising in-depth transformation of the north (the steppe belt) toward modernity came a couple of decades later. The transition of the north, however, entailed the marginalization or even the (partial) elimination of the hitherto predominant nomadic-pastoral economy, which had grave and long-lasting social consequences. The latter are one of the topics dealt with in the following chapters.

4.2.2.4 Oasis Belt: Swift, If Selective, Transformation into European Market Colonies

Low-Cost Administration of the Indigenous Population: The Governorate-General of Turkestan and the Protectorates of Bukhara and Khiva

As Roudik explains, Turkestan was governed by a temporary statute promulgated in 1867 and a permanent one in force from 1886. All military, civil, judicial, and political powers were concentrated in the governor-general's hands, a high-ranking military official who was appointed by the czar. The governor-general set and changed taxes, oversaw the expenditures of the Turkestani budget, and established privileges of Russian citizens in the designated territory (2007, 76–77). The Governorate-General of Turkestan (Turkestanskoe General-Gubernatorstvo) with its capital in Tashkent (centrally located in the territory and possessing

good transport links to European Russia via Orenburg) was subdivided into five oblasts (provinces), as can be seen in Map 4.6: Transcaspia (Zakaspiskaya Oblast), Syr Daria, Samarkand, Ferghana, and Semirechie. The total indigenous population of the governorate-general was about 5 million.

Tashkent quickly outstripped all other C Asian cities. Tashkent's population rose from around 70,000 inhabitants in 1865 to about 155,000 in 1897—in other words, it more than doubled in 30 years—and the city soon became CA's richest. As Soucek explains, much of this rise was, of course, due to the town's function as the first modern capital of the region and seat of the colonial administration and its bureaucracy. Moreover, Tashkent's entrepreneurship, it merchants, and its proximity to Russia, with which it had a long trading tradition, played a role. The Russians built their own quarter alongside the native city (but not within the existing urban area), establishing a pattern that they would adhere to in a number of other places: A new European city emerged through a system of urban planning, providing a sharp contrast to the traditional historic quarters (Soucek 2000, 203).[186]

The second governor-general of Turkestan was Konstantin von Kaufman, a general descended from a Russified German Baltic family who had commanded the czar's troops during the conquest of Bukhara. Von Kaufman was a competent officer and administrator, and his long tenure (1867–1882) did much to consolidate the colonial administration of CA (Soucek 2000, 203). Given the high density of the oasis population in Turkestan, where irrigation was pivotal to agriculture, particularly to cotton cultivation, and where little free land was available, Kaufman and his successors allowed Russian immigrants moving to the governorate-general to settle only in towns/on municipal land (Hambly (ed) 1966/1979, 228). In 1885, the Emirate of Bukhara (conquered in 1868) and the Khanate of Khiva (1873) joined Russia's customs territory. The upper Amu Daria, Kushka, and the Kopet Dagh—the czardom's southern boundary since 1885—finally also became its southern customs border 10 years later.

As Hambly explains, under Governor-General Kaufman the region was organized, approaching as far as was deemed feasible the model of civil administration of European Russia. Apart from the higher ranks, the Turkestani administration consisted almost exclusively of civil servants. Following a regional census, the oblasts were divided into uezdy (districts) which were subdivided into volosti (areas). Each volost comprised a number of nomadic Auls (encampments or patriarchal family groups or clans which consisted of up to 200 kibitkas or tents/households) and/or

---

[185] This bears resemblance to the post-1758 Qing treatment of Uighur society in Eastern CA.

[186] This practice seems comparable to how Chinese settlements were set up just beside native (Uighur) city centers, e.g., in Kashgar from the 1830s.

several kishlaks (villages with settled population).[187] Every aul and every kishlak elected its eldest as well as some other officials and representatives, who in turn appointed local judges. While decisions in principle were subject to review by the imperial Russian courts, the latter generally did not intervene and left local governance in the hands of the local authorities (Hambly (ed) 1966/1979, 221–222).

While the native Turkestanis were not full Russian citizens and could not be called up to military service, as mentioned earlier, they kept their own legal systems, which were based on the Muslim Sharia or on nomadic Adat (customary law). Only proceedings in which Russians were involved or larger criminal cases were heard in Russian courts (Hambly (ed) 1966/1979, 222). Islam, waqf, religious practices and education, and the general way of life were not interfered with unless in direct conflict with the state's interests (Soucek 2000, 204).

According to Kappeler, a land reform of 1873 nationalized properties belonging to chiefs and noblemen deprived of power (i.e., those begs and aristocrats living outside the remaining protectorates). Such irrigated land cultivated by peasants was then transferred to their hereditary ownership; in return they had to pay uniform property dues. The extensive landholdings of the Islamic religious institutions (waqf) were not encroached upon. The numerous Muslim schools (madrasas) were maintained. The traditional water rights and the legal regulation of irrigation were respected (Kappeler 2006, 145).[188]

An 1886 decree reestablished in principle the local inhabitants' right to own land. Dubovitsky and Bababekov have interesting findings on what impact this decree actually had in specific cases: Article 255 of the decree recognized that "the settled population is entitled to lands it has owned, used and disposed of on a permanent and hereditary basis and in accordance with local customs." Article 259 added that land could be used by a community or by households or neighborhoods, depending on local customs. Article 270 affirmed that "public lands occupied by nomadic groups are granted to nomads for their indefinite use[189], on the basis of custom and the provisions of this regulation." Yet this less firm legal title to nomadic pasturelands was often exploited by newly arrived inhabitants: European colonists sometimes arbitrarily seized native lands, particularly those used by nomads and semi-nomads. Thus, a contemporary document reports that as soon as the Kyrgyz shepherds made their

annual springtime trek to high country grazing land, the settlers "set out to build housing on the irrigated lands belonging to the indigenous Kyrgyz. In some places, they even seized the Kyrgyz winter huts, destroying the Kyrgyz structures and using the lumber for their own construction, and burning whatever was left as fuel for cooking" (Dubovitsky and Bababekov 2011, 78, 80).

Notwithstanding the just mentioned injustices and violations, one can certainly agree with Kappeler's general argument that indirect Russian colonial rule enabled political control and economic exploitation at modest cost (2006, 143). However, this also meant, as Soucek eloquently puts it, that the bulk of the subjugated population remained at least partly immune to the vertiginous intellectual and scientific progress in which the country had been taking part since the time of Peter the Great (2000, 204).

Substantial Investment in C Asian Cotton Production: Toward an Export-Oriented Monoculture Dependent on Food and Industrial Imports from Russia

– *Expanding Russian textile industry in growing need of cotton imports*

Among the crops of CA, Russian businessmen and politicians put a particular emphasis on cotton. Cotton was harvested in Turkestan since ancient times,[190] but its quality was relatively low, and cultivation, processing, and transport methods were far from the state of the art in the first half of the nineteenth century (Hambly (ed) 1966/1979, 229). In Russia (with some delay), as in other European countries, technical change more and more favored factories over workshops. Russian industrialization was initially strongly driven by the textile industry, notably the cotton branch. The country's cotton needs increased considerably, to the point where the C Asian Khanates (primarily Bukhara), that had been major traditional suppliers, could no longer fully cover them. Toward 1850, Russia commenced sizable purchases of the precious fiber from Egypt (Ottoman Empire) and then from the USA (Chuvin et al. 2008, 116).

Russia's defeat in the Crimean War (1853–1856) triggered an important drive to reform the country and eliminate or reduce its (economic) backwardness vis-a-vis the Western powers. Russia gradually opened itself to free trade. Important works were undertaken to develop a railroad network in the European part of the country including Orenburg, giving direct access to CA. Agrarian reforms were conducted in the late 1850s and early 1860s. A farming tax was introduced to produce funds to help finance

---

[187] This appears to imply a shift of meaning from the original Turko-Mongol "qishlaq" (nomadic winter camp, see above) to the Russian "kishlak" (C Asian village).

[188] The czardom's indirect military rule in Western CA (from the establishment of the Governorate-General in 1867 and the maintenance of the two protectorates) invites comparison with Qing indirect miliary rule in Eastern CA (notably in Nan Lu, from ca. 1760), which was not administered as a province of China proper.

[189] "Use," not ownership.

[190] As mentioned earlier, cotton originated in India and has been cultivated in CA since antiquity (the Kushan era, ca. 1–200 CE), especially in the Ferghana Basin (the most appreciated variety) and in Transoxiana (Chuvin et al. 2008, 116).

railroad construction. In 1861, Czar Alexander II abolished serfdom. However, the former serfs did not immediately gain freedom and mobility. They remained connected to the traditional village community (obschina) with its system of collective ownership and responsibility; moreover, the land parcels allotted to peasants were generally rather small, and the required redemption payments were high and often exceeded the property values (Ott, Schäfer (eds.) 1984: Wirtschaftsploetz, 380–381). Still, with some delay, many peasants started to move to more promising activities, such as work in the emerging industrial centers, e.g., Ivanovo, the focus of textile production northeast of Moscow.

– *Scarcity due to American Civil War (1861–1865) accelerates Russian quest for C Asian cotton*

The American Civil War (1861–1865) and the naval blockade imposed by the Union forces on the Confederate states temporarily stopped cotton exports from the South and triggered a cotton shortage in Europe and Russia. The expanding Russian textile industry, 90% of whose raw material imports came from the southern states of the USA, was destabilized and entered a crisis. From 1862, numerous factories had to close, namely, in Moscow and its surroundings. This upheaval raised concern in Russian industrial and political circles and indirectly increased the geopolitical importance of Bukhara and CA as a supplier of raw cotton and buyer of Russian manufactured goods. Textile industrialists partially readapted their factories to C Asian cotton and at the same time attempted to persuade local producers to try out and acclimatize seeds of American cotton, which promised to be more profitable (Burton 1998b, 53).[191]

Moreover, in the early 1860s military operations in CA were progressing and Russia's frontier of conquests was swiftly approaching Bukhara, Khoqand, and Khiva (see preceding chapter). The southern Turkestani oases, particularly Ferghana, appeared as a fertile ground for expanding cotton production, provided cultivation was technologically upgraded and spatially enlarged. There seem to have been many possibilities to raise the value added of C Asian cotton production in order to cater to Russian demand.

Soon after the capture of Tashkent (1865) and the subjugation of the Khanate of Khoqand, Russia sent engineers to Ferghana to improve the cotton cultures.

At the expense of the khan's budget, many irrigation canals were extended, numerous new canals were laid out, dams built, and the area under cultivation was expanded. In the late 1860s, the largest canal of the valley, the Ulugh Nahr ("large river") was dug under the sponsorship of the last Min khan, Khudayar, who acknowledged the czar's suzerainty. Upon the conquest of Samarkand (1868), cartographic work was undertaken and an irrigation cadaster compiled in Mavarannahr. At the end of the 1860s, Russian cotton imports from the khanates were about five times larger than they had been at the beginning of the decade (Chuvin et al. 2008, 73, 116–117; Soucek 2000, 191; Shukow et al. 1959/1969, Band 6, 532). This all happened notwithstanding the fact that after the end of the Civil War in 1865, the US authorities had lifted their embargo again.

– *From the introduction of American varieties of cotton to the prominence of "Bukharan Jews" in the C Asian cotton boom*

As Chuvin, Letolle, and Peyrouse explain, missions were dispatched to the USA to study the varieties of cotton that were most suitable and productive for CA. The indigenous farmers preferred their own variety, the Turkestan species (Gossypium herbaceum), which however gave modest yields, while it was easier to pick. It was necessary to compel the "tuzemtsy" to adopt the new species. Just after the annexation of Ferghana (and the abolition of the Khanate of Khoqand, 1876), the Russian authorities decided to encourage planting of more profitable American species of cotton, among which was Upland'a (Gossypium hirsutum). Farming schools and agronomical research institutes were set up (Chuvin et al. 2008, 117). The abovementioned measures of canal digging and enlarging irrigation areas were not only undertaken in the Ferghana Basin, but the majority of these initiatives were not as successful as in this case. For instance, an ambitious project providing for the construction of a network of canals was launched in the "Hunger steppe" (Betpak Dala), north of the Chu. There are hardly any traces of this latter project left today.

According to Poujol and Fourniau, booklets explaining how to cultivate the new cotton were printed in local languages, helping to accelerate the spread of modern know-how and raise productivity and competitiveness. St. Petersburg maintained a low freight rate on grain (mostly wheat) shipped on trains to Turkestan from the 1880s to provide more low-priced food to the local population. This was done with a view to encouraging the replacement of subsistence and local market-oriented grain cultivation with cotton production. The surfaces under cultivation of American cotton in Turkestan expanded

---

[191] This situation of being (temporarily) cut off from vital overseas deliveries by a trade embargo recalls the impact and the consequences of the continental blockade (1806–1812) on Russia's trade with CA: Necessity or distress can trigger the emergence of new business opportunities, activities, and links that may survive even after the original cause of the disruption (the trade restriction) no longer exists.

very quickly: from 300 desiatins in 1884 (1 desiyatin = 1.09 ha) to 12,000 in 1886, then 37,000 in 1887, 58,000 in 1890, etc. or, expressed in square kilometers, the American cotton cultivation grew from 3.3 to 632 km^2.[192] Russian-manufactured cotton goods and other industrial products and tools were soon flooding the C Asian markets (Poujol and Fourniau 2005, 58–59, 72).

Soon the processing of cotton was partially done in Turkestan itself. While cotton picking had been done manually, the first American cotton gins were imported and installed in the 1880s. Processing cotton led to the creation of dozens of small factories—cotton ginning mills—throughout the region. But this appears to have been the only or one of the few modern industrial activities that developed following CA's incorporation into the empire. Ferghana Oblast remained the most important cotton growing area in Russian CA. While the "white gold," as it was also called, already held a prime position in the Bukhara protectorate's range of products for sale, it likewise became the Khiva protectorate's leading export article (Hambly (ed) 1966/1979, 229; Poujol and Fourniau 2005, 58–59, 69, 70).

With respect to the unfolding "cotton boom," the role of oriental Jewish merchants appears worth highlighting: As a result of the conquest of Bukhara, Jews living in the emirate, called "Bukharan Jews," were treated by the Russian authorities in the same manner and received the same civil and economic rights as other subjects of the emir. This was in contrast to the discriminated-against state of Jews in other parts of the czardom. This de facto privileged treatment (vis-a-vis other people of Mosaic faith) made it possible for Bukharan Jews to seize the opportunity to become major entrepreneurs—notably exporters of cotton to European Russia. Indeed, even veritable dynasties of great businessmen emerged (e.g., the Davidovs and the Vodiaevs) that moreover came to dominate the Russian cotton business (Roudik 2007, 89; Burton 1998b, 52) (for more information see Box 4.4).

– *En route toward a mercantilist monoculture, with multiple drawbacks*

Russian CA's concentration on cotton production in the oasis belt intensified over the late decades of the nineteenth century, and in some areas—particularly the Ferghana Basin—monocultures emerged, supported by subsidized grain deliveries from Russia (see above) as well as by protective tariffs (Kappeler 2006, 147). The concomitant collapse of the cultivation of cereals rendered CA even more dependent on wheat purchases from outside the region. Often, hired workers for cotton plantations and gins were recruited from ruined traditional C Asian peasants. Apart from improvements in irrigation and transportation, credits to small cotton farmers in CA also helped the Russian textile industry reduce its dependence on cotton imports from the USA and Britain (India). Thus, given the governorate-general's and the protectorates' assigned role of large-scale cotton suppliers in the czarist government's plans, any possible new loss of access to foreign sources of the "white gold" should no longer find the czardom as vulnerable as in the past. The ultimate aim was the Russian textile industry's outright independence from cotton imports from (possibly hostile) foreign powers.[193] Most of the locals employed in Turkestani cotton and food industries worked 17 to 18 h a day, practically devoid of labor protection (Roudik 2007, 86).

Thus, in the Russian Empire's emerging geoeconomic division of labor, Turkestan soon fulfilled the role of a producer and supplier of raw and processed cotton and other commodities, and as a purchaser of food, textiles, clothes, metallurgical products and other value-added industrial goods and tools which mostly came from factories in European Russia. Cotton eventually accounted for over two thirds of all exports of the czardom's C Asian colonies to Russia proper. Many trades suffered or even vanished to the benefit of Russian competitors, e.g., pot making, shoemaking, domestic utensil making, etc. Many tuzemtsy became victims of the swift and forced specialization and modernization, bringing sudden, shock-like, and sometimes traumatic structural change (Poujol and Fourniau 2005, 68).

The disruption of the traditional economy and the increase in cotton cultivation to the extent of a near monoculture made the local population vulnerable to fluctuations in national and world market prices and dependent on credits. Traditional diversified food crop mixed farming, catering to the market while securing some subsistence, was replaced by increasingly standardized cotton plantations (Poujol and Fourniau 2005, 76; Roudik 2007, 84, 91; Soucek 2000, 203). Although most skilled workers were Russians, many indigenous people were included in largely up-to-date world market-oriented capitalist productive structures and started to come into contact with some cheap industrially produced consumer goods. Still, remuneration of the tuzemtsy was very modest and it was not clear to what

---

[192] While in 1877, 11,000 tons of Turkestani cotton were shipped to Russia, in 1915 it was more than 350,000 tons (more than 30 times as much) (Poujol and Fourniau 2005, 69).

[193] In other words, while the discontinuation of cotton imports from America in the early 1860s was a painful shock for Russia, one or two decades later this became an official policy goal—with far-reaching implications for CA (Beckert 2014, 346).

degree their material well-being had increased, compared to precolonial times.

Apart from cotton, the production of some other commodities also gained momentum in Russian CA's oasis belt. New commercial networks and trading outlets contributed to stepping up rice cultivation. In 1869 there were 11,000 ha of rice fields in the uezdy of Samarkand and Kattakorgan (both part of Samarkand Oblast), in 1875 there were 20,000 ha, and in 1900 in the uezd of Samarkand alone, this figure reached 43,000 ha. Silk production and silk trade constituted another significant branch of this colonial economy. Sizable quantities of silk cloth were exported from CA to Russia. Carpets were actively traded to Europe. The extraction of mineral resources also gathered momentum: In Turkestan, oil had already been discovered near Namangan (Ferghana Basin) prior to the colonial conquest. Industrial production of oil (the later "black gold") was launched at the beginning of the 1870s[194] (Poujol and Fourniau 2005, 59, 70, 72).

Early Expansion of the Railroad Network, Other Infrastructure, and Civic Activities

Soon after the conquest, but in some cases, accompanying it, the Russians built a modern transportation and communication system: Railroad and telegraph networks were set up. Both networks were important for the strategic safeguarding of Western CA and its economic integration into the empire (Kappeler 2006, 147). The construction of the first railroad line, the Transcaspian, from the eastern shores of the Caspian Sea, had immediate military goals: Work began in 1880 at the port of Krasnovodsk (originally set up as a fortress in 1869) and reached the Turkmen settlement of Kyzyl Arvat in 1881. This connection helped transport soldiers and military equipment from Astrakhan to near Goek Tepe in preparation of General Skobelev's offensive.

In 1886 the Transcaspian reached Merv and 2 years later the cities of Bukhara and Samarkand. The line thus cut through the emirate; a new treaty with the emir granted Russia sovereignty on the railroad and at all stations along it on Bukharan territory (Roudik 2007, 81). Once the Transcaspian had arrived in Chardzhou (at Bukhara's border on the middle reaches of the Amu Daria), the first train transporting cotton returned to Krasnovodsk (Chuvin et al. 2008, 117) (for the location of this line see Map 4.6). Bregel underlines the favorable impact the railroads had on cotton cultivation: The conveyance of the C Asian crop to the

textile centers in European Russia became much cheaper and faster; moreover, inexpensive Russian grain deliveries by rail to Turkestan supported increased regional focus on the production of the "white gold." Like elsewhere, the railroads also contributed to the development of industry in the towns they connected, as well as to greater mobility of the population. As mentioned above, most of the new industrial enterprises in Russian CA were cotton-ginning mills (Breghel 2003, 90)[195].

While the railroad doubtlessly carried the day in the late nineteenth century, river transport did not decline to a quantité négligeable. The Russian commercial fleet on the Amu Daria, created in the 1870s, was of some importance, although competition from trains soon became very strong. By far the most active river trade in the whole of Russian CA developed on the Irtysh. The reestablishment of a secure border with China at the beginning of the 1880s (return of Ili area, demarcation of state boundary, see below) led to an increase in river-borne trade with the Qing Empire (Poujol and Fourniau 2005, 64).

Immigrant colonists from Russia to Turkestan were mostly urban professionals and skilled workers[196]: They

---

[194] This was not the first time oil was extracted in the czarist empire. The first oil well was drilled in Baku (Azerbaijan) in 1846.

[195] In 1898, the Transcaspian line was extended to Tashkent, and in 1899 to Andijan (Ferghana). The same year another extension was laid to Kushka (on the Afghan border) (Map 4.6). The line Samarkand—Andijan served primarily economic interests, namely the transport of cotton. By 1906 the Trans-Aral railroad, a line linking Tashkent to Orenburg and thus to the rest of European Russia, e.g., on to Samara and Moscow, was completed. The resulting entire network (including a large C Asian "loop" leading from Orenburg via Tashkent and Merv to Krasnovodsk) had great strategic, economic and psychological significance in that it demonstrated the structural feasibility of CA's "seamless" incorporation into the compact landmass of the bicontinental empire. This kind of integration was impossible in the case of the overseas colonies of other European powers, but not impossible in the case of the US or Canada's transcontinental conquests and enlargements, in which the railroads also played a major role. Overall, shipments of cotton and other raw materials to European Russia, shipments of grain and finished goods in the other direction, and passenger transport in both directions (whether soldiers, merchants, businessmen, workers, civil servants, or tourists) were greatly facilitated and accelerated by trains, physically "binding" some of the czardom's sprawling regions together. The modern infrastructural rapprochement of CA to Russia was indirectly strengthened by the fact that projects that aimed at linking Turkestan to other adjacent regions, e.g., via Afghanistan to India, did not materialize (Kappeler 2006, 147; Duby 2011: Map: L'Asie investie 1850–1914, 251; Soucek 2000, 205). Interestingly, rail links to India failed to materialize partly because of British resistance. The British apparently feared a military and economic strengthening of Russian influence in their colonies as a result of such a connection (Hofmeister 2015, 127).

[196] Put differently, about 80% of skilled workers in Turkestan (and on the railroads practically all) were Russians (Breghel 2003).

were predominantly employed in civil administration, education, transportation, communications, and industry. A program of introduction to Russian culture was undertaken, as Roudik explains, the Directorate of Learning Institutions in Turkestan was established in 1870 to manage schools aimed at teaching indigenous people the Russian language, handicrafts, and farming without interfering in traditional educational affairs. Children were taught arithmetic, history, and geography. The Russians also brought European medical knowledge, built hospitals, medical offices, and pharmacies and gave treatment to local people (Roudik 2007, 85). In cultural life, the most important innovations introduced by the colonial power were the printing press, newspapers, and book publishing (Breghel 2003, 90).

According to Soucek, the Turkestani natives (whether Sarts, Uzbeks, Tajiks, Khoqandians, Khivans, or others), though essential to the base of the productive process, remained largely excluded on the executive and profit-taking level (2000, 204). In any case, as Roudik notes, popular resistance continued after the conquest because of Russian arbitrariness, exploitation, discrimination, and marginalization of the indigenous people. Protests against Russian domination occurred in the form of sporadic rural or urban riots as a response to the ongoing industrialization, disruption, and impoverishment of parts of the population. On frequent occasions, natives protested by refusing to pay taxes, ignoring local elections, attacking government officials, and burning government buildings. Around 200 antigovernment protest actions or incidents were registered in Ferghana from 1880 to 1890. Muslim mystical brotherhoods and Sufi orders continued to play a role in social upheavals (Roudik 2007, 81, 83). Yet the authorities did not encounter great difficulties in suppressing the unrest.

All in all, with production, trade, and exchanges swiftly growing in the second half of the nineteenth century, it appears that the C Asian oases had soon more than covered their expenses to the Russian treasury. Satisfaction on the part of the authorities and a number of influential merchants and businessmen was such that Turkestan came to be called "a jewel in the crown of the czar" (Roudik 2007, 86).

Box 4.4: The Bukharan Jews: Key Promoters of Russian-C Asian Trade in the Nineteenth Century
Jewish communities first moved to Persia after the destruction of the first temple of Jerusalem (in 587 BCE), then fled to Margiana and Transoxiana after

the Sassanians had taken power in Iran (in 226 CE). For almost two millennia, Jews lived in CA, surviving previous invasions (including the Mongol onslaught) and meeting Russian colonization. Because most of the Jews lived in and around the city of Bukhara, on the territory of present-day Uzbekistan and Tajikistan, the entire Jewish population of CA tended to be called "Bukharan Jews." They typically spoke Bukhrit, a combination of Hebrew and Farsi; according to other sources, their language was called "Judeo-Tajik." Most of them professed Sephardic Judaism (Poujol and Fourniau 2005, 66; Roudik 2007, 89).

In the Emirate of Bukhara in the early nineteenth century, like in many other places, Jews were discriminated. Unequal treatment included requirements such as living only in designated areas and bans on purchases of new houses and on the building of new synagogues (but not on the renovation of existing ones). Professional restrictions applied to posts in areas of administrative, fiscal, judicial, and military service. Moreover, all people of Mosaic faith as well as other "infidels" were subject to a special tax in the tradition of the jizya (nothing specific to Bukhara). Jews were often involved in trade, medicine, and translation. They worked as dyers, cobblers, and in other crafts (Roudik 2007, 69, 89). Some of them specialized in producing thin silk fabrics for kerchiefs and ornamented woman's attire and in dying silk fabrics with indigo. Around 1820, the Bukharan Jews reported only counted "two rich capitalists," but others were "merchants of unbleached silk and silk ware," and given that these articles were appreciated in Russia, it is quite probable that Russians were featured among the Jewish businessmen's clients (Burton 1998b, 52; Dmitriyev and Yakerson 2007, 20, 24).

In any case, according to Hagemeister, cited by Burton, the Bukharan Jews "were very active in trade and commerce" in 1836–1837, making frequent business trips to Chinese Turkestan. They reached Xinjiang via Balkh and Badakhshan in order to obtain European manufactured products doubtlessly arriving via British India, as well as to get gold or lapis lazuli. In the 1840s, Jews of Khiva, Khoqand, and Tashkent repeatedly went to the fairs

(continued)

Box 4.4 (continued)
of Nizhny Novgorod, Orenburg, and Astrakhan (Burton 1998b, 52).[197]

Roudik acquaints us with an astonishing legal state of affairs: The expansion of czarist territories to the borders of the Emirate of Bukhara and the latter's incorporation into the empire objectively improved the status of Bukharan Jews. Although discriminated against at home, Bukharan Jews received the same rights (including residence rights and access to property ownership) as other emirate subjects under treaties concluded between Bukhara and Russia in 1868 and 1873. They were free to move across the czardom, acquire assets, and join Russian professional and trade organizations, which remained closed for Russian Jews (mostly of Ashkenazi ethnic origin) (Roudik 2007, 89).[198] This situation, the colonization of Russian Turkestan, subsequent structural change, and economic expansion triggered major adjustments in the spatial pattern of Bukharan Jewish settlements, initiating a wave of migration from Bukhara mostly northeast to Samarkand, Tashkent, and the large centers of cotton cultivation in the Ferghana Basin. Within the emirate (in the restrained borders fixed by the treaty of 1868, which excluded Samarkand) various sources agree that the Jews numbered about 10,000 (Poujol and Fourniau 2005, 74).

Under czarist rule, the Bukharan Jews again proved their capabilities as traders and businessmen. Some became wealthy within a few years in Ferghana and Tashkent. What is more, a handful of Jewish C Asian businessmen eventually even managed to gain leading positions in cotton trade with European Russia (Roudik 2007, 90). As mentioned above, true dynasties of grand and very prosperous entrepreneurs emerged (like the Davidovs, the Vodiaevs, the Potilakhovs, the Simkhaevs). For instance, the Potilakhovs, settled in Khoqand, owned silk-spinning mills, karakul skin businesses, and railroad-car factories and at times monopolized cotton exports to Russia and Britain. The Vodiaev father and sons even called themselves the "Rothschilds of Turkestan" (Poujol and Fourniau 2005, 75).

4.2.2.5 The Kazakh Steppe: From Pastoral Nomadism and Social Turmoil to Large-Scale Settlement of European Farmers

Growing Adaptation of Kazakh Livestock Economy to Russian Market, Encroachment by European Settlers

After the abolishment of the Kazakh Zhuz their territory was divided into administrative units with mixed Russian and native administrations. Upon the liquidation of the respective khan's powers, the "regulations governing the Siberian Kazakhs" were introduced in 1822 and the "regulations governing the Orenburg Kazakhs" in 1824.[199] A three-tiered system was set up, consisting of Okrugy (administrative districts), nomadic tribal groups, and auls (encampments, patriarchal family groups, or clans). Okrug administrations were headed by a "sultan-governor" from the nomadic aristocracy, who became an official in Russian service.[200] The sultan-governor (or senior sultan) was elected by all the sultans (local steppe princes, often rulers of individual tribes) belonging to the respective district and confirmed by the czarist government. The sultan-governor's orders also required approval by the Russian authorities. Typically a Russian fort or Cossak settlement in the grasslands would be chosen as the administrative center of an okrug. On the aul level, councils of elders (aksakals or "white beards") wielded considerable power (Baipakov and Kumekov 2003, 99; Geiss 2003, 40; Frank 2009, 372).

A new judicial system was introduced which provided for a special Kazakh code that restrained the jurisdiction of the traditional bek courts (courts presided by local tribal or clan chiefs) and transferred all cases of murder, plunder, and other serious crimes as well as significant civil cases to the jurisdiction of the okrug administrations. The bek court continued to exist but resolved only secondary cases. Most rulings continued to be based on the norms of customary law (Roudik 2007, 50). The new system of government, which strengthened the authority of czarist officials, gave rise to dissatisfaction among the clan nobles, who had lost power, and among the people more generally (Baipakov and Kumekov 2003, 99).

The Kazakh pastureland was nationalized and the nomads had to pay the kibitka tax (Russian, kibitochnaya podat) for every tent or covered wagon to the new authorities.[201] For instance, this tax was collected (as a Russian levy) on the

---

[197] In some respect, therefore, Bukharan Jews may have upheld the traditional role of "Bukharans" (explained earlier) as intermediaries in trade between Russia, CA, China, and (British) India.

[198] The pattern of equal legal treatment for subjects of the Emir of Bukhara was preserved during the entire protectorate period and was inconsistent with domestic Russian legislation, which remained discriminatory toward Jews (Roudik 2007, 64).

---

[199] The "regulations governing the Siberian Kazakhs" essentially dealt with the former Middle Horde, the "regulations governing the Orenburg Kazakhs" with the Junior Horde. In the 1820s, the Senior Horde was not yet abolished and formally still under Chinese suzerainty.

[200] Up to a point, the sultan-governors were comparable to hakim begs as Qing Chinese officials, although the latter of course ruled sedentary, not nomadic populations.

[201] The kibitka levy was nothing new, of course. A similar levy was already collected, e.g., in the Senior Zhuz under Dzungar rule.

former territory of the Junior Horde in 1837; it equaled one and a half roubles of silver per kibitka. Apart from that, a number of other duties, obligations, and penalties existed. The fact that the Russian taxes in most cases had to be paid in silver or cash—not in-kind (e.g., in a fraction of a herd)— soon contributed to an increased role of money circulation on the steppes. Probably due to its proximity to European Russia, Western Kazakhstan (the former Younger Zhuz) experienced an intensive development of money-commodity relations (Artykbaev 2007, 207; Oskolkov and Oskolkova 2004, 35).

The penetration of European farmer settlement into the fertile chernozyem (black earth) areas in the north of the Kazakh steppe brought about a break in the centuries-old relations between sedentary Russian populations and their pastoral nomadic neighbors. However, in the first half of the nineteenth century, this was still a very gradual penetration and initially focused on the northwestern Kazakh pasturelands along the Ural river in the areas near Guriev (today, Atyrau), Uralsk, and Orenburg. With nomadic pastureland having been nationalized, as Paul explains, the authorities started to regulate land use by fixing spatial norms for nomadic production, which soon indicated "surplus areas" that could then be reallocated to European settlers (2012, 389).

Thus, the czarist authorities began distributing land among Cossack defensive peasants and Russian and Ukrainian farmers. The settlers often acquired the best and most fertile land, with the result that grazing territories were reduced and traditional migrations disturbed (Kappeler 2006, 147–148). In the first half of the nineteenth century, around 30,000 desyatins of land (or about 32,700 ha) of the Desht-i-Kipchak were worked on by European farmers; winter and spring wheat, oat, barley, peas, and buckwheat were sowed (Artykbaev 2007, 208).

Meanwhile, in the framework of their pastoral way of life, Kazakhs continued to carry out some auxiliary agriculture where the terrain permitted it (near watercourses, etc.). In traditional areas of settlement in the south (e.g., the oasis of Turkestan/former Yasy), the cultivation of millet, melons, and gourds occupied an important place. While a minority of Kazakhs traditionally carried out farming and while regulations and proclamations of the Russian government repeatedly pointed out that the Kazakhs needed to abandon their nomadic condition which prevented them from taking up agriculture, the same authorities banned the steppe dwellers from using land on the banks of the Ural, Irtysh, Tobol, and Ishim rivers, which deprived the agriculturalists of the possibility to irrigate their plowed fields with water from those rivers (Artykbaev 2007, 207–208).

What is more, Kazakh-plowed fields were often given to settlers. As Artykbaev explains, many of the European newcomers, not possessing sufficient experience in irrigated farming and lacking Kazakh know-how in tilling precarious steppe lands, spoilt/corrupted existing irrigation systems, collected one or two harvests from the fields, and then took

away new lands from the steppe dwellers. The czarist authorities thus actually contributed to impairing or destroying some existing farming structures. Yet, according to officials in Orenburg, in the mid-nineteenth century, despite the restrictions and infringements, there still existed some traditional agriculture along the rivers Ural, Khobda, Or[202], and Tobol (Artykbaev 2007, 208, 210).

Whatever the real intentions of the authorities, as Artykbaev argues, the growing Russian market for cattle and cattle products led to a piecemeal adaptation of the Kazakh cattle raising economy to this demand. Other branches of the Kazakh economy also took on more market- (and less subsistence-) oriented traits (Artykbaev 2007, 207). According to Burton, Hagemeister was told in 1837 that the quantities of cattle and horses that the Kazakhs sold to Russia equalled their combined sales to Khiva, Bukhara, Khoqand, and China (Burton 2003, 421). While the Kazakhs increasingly specialized in stockbreeding and animal products for the Russian market, their own role as a market for Russian grain, bread, cotton fabrics, and ironware gained importance. A typical market-oriented pattern of increased trade, specialization, and dependence emerged (Artykbaev 2007, 207–208; Shukow et al. 1959/1969, Band 6, 56).[203]

In Orenburg, Uralsk, Troitsk, Semipalatinsk, and other towns[204], Kazakh-Russian trade flourished. In the first half of the nineteenth century, livestock worth an annual average of 3–3.5 million roubles entered Russia from her Kazakh dependencies. Seasonal fairs (yarmarka), e.g., in the Irtysh valley, played a great role in the expansion of trade. Fairs generated stimuli for the marketing of cattle and cattle products and for the expansion of Kazakh trading firms. Wealthy urban Kazakh merchants appeared, which contributed to incipient tendencies toward sedentarization or semi-sedentarization of the nomads. Livestock tended to become concentrated among the richest Kazakhs, while poorer steppe dwellers found themselves more and more marginalized (Artykbaev 2007, 208, 211; Frank 2009, 375).

Nevertheless, this was an increasingly circumscribed and precarious boom. The shrinkage of pastures/the decrease of available pastureland eventually led to overgrazing and even desertification of some areas used by nomads. Moreover, epidemics coming from the outside claimed native victims.

---

[202] Khobda and Or are tributaries to the Ural.

[203] This could suggest that nomadic stockbreeding in low-precipitation grasslands (like a major part of the Desht-i-Kipchak) remained a relatively efficient and competitive activity even in the environment of a large emerging economy increasingly exposed to the nineteenth century world market (namely, Russia).

[204] These included smaller towns, like the strategically well-situated Alexandrov Gay and Novouzensk (on the northern border of the Bukey Zhuz, about 150–200 km from the central Russian market of Saratov (on the Volga).

Effectively, the crisis of the Kazakh nomadic economy had begun (Abazov 2008, Map 30; Khazanov 1983/1994, 51).

The Kenesary Rebellion (1837–1847) Against Czarist Oppression and Confiscation of Pasturelands

A series of anti-Russian movements already started in the late eighteenth century.[205] As Roudik notes, they usually took the form of intermittent raids and expeditions into Russian territories, the burning down of Cossack settlements, the plundering of trade outposts, and the killing of military guards (2007, 65). In the late 1820s, the Bukey Horde, situated in the area between the Volga and Ural rivers, became a focus of popular unrest, although its political structure had not yet been dissolved (in contrast to the fate of the Junior Horde). This unrest in the 1830s turned into a large-scale insurgency; the causes of the latter, according to Oskolkov and Oskolkova, included the high tax burden, the frequency, and arbitrariness of extortions and requisitions imposed on the population by local czarist officials, and most importantly, the multiplication of restrictions on the use of nomad pastoral land (2004, 39).

The Kazakh rebellions culminated in the second quarter of the nineteenth century, particularly in the period from 1837 to 1846, and were led by the charismatic sultan Kenesary Kasymov (1802–1847), the grandson of Ablay Khan of the Middle Horde. The aggravation occurred against the background of the worsening political and economic situation of most Kazakhs and the mounting dissatisfaction/discontent of the masses with czarist policies (ranging from the bans on crossing certain steppe rivers, via the elimination of the Kazakh Hordes and other administrative reforms, to the swelling encroachments on as well as occupation and appropriation of the best pasturelands). However, the Kenesary uprising was not purely anti-czarist; it was also directed against Khoqand's fiscal pressure and overall oppression of some of the southern Kazakh tribes (of the former Senior Horde) (Oskolkov and Oskolkova 2004, 34, 40). According to Khazanov (1983/94, 176), this insurgent merger of tribal forces corresponded to the last dispositional centralization of large Kazakh nomadic subdivisions. The rebel leader's aim was to resurrect a united and mighty Kazakh Khanate.

As Roudik explains, Sultan Kenesary fought his war by destroying or blocking trade along all of the caravan routes in Northern Kazakhstan and those leading to the oasis khanates in the south (2007, 66). In 1838, the Akmolinsk fortress (erected in 1830) was devastated. In 1840, Kenesary invaded Khoqand with the goal of liberating and uniting the Kazakhs. The success of his campaigns and the abundant booty he was able to distribute (for some time) boosted his popularity among fellow Kazakhs; in 1841 the sultan was proclaimed khan of the tribes of the former Middle Zhuz and

he also acquired some authority over parts of the former Junior and Senior Hordes. In 1844–1845, the insurrection held sway over many areas of present-day Kazakhstan (Oskolkov and Oskolkova 2004, 40). By 1846, however, his resistance movement had lost momentum as some of his rich associates had defected to the Russians, who apparently had made better offers. In 1847, Kenesary was captured and executed in Kyrgyz lands, and the great uprising that bore his name collapsed (Hambly (ed) 1966/1979, 208).

However, as the underlying grievances remained unaddressed, this was not the end of Kazakh revolts. Rebellions continued from time to time on a local scale. The last such uprisings took place and were put down by Russian troops in the western Kazakh steppe (Uralsk, Turgay) in the late 1860s and in Mangyshlak in 1870. As of the mid-1870s, it appeared that Kazakh lands were "pacified" (Hambly (ed) 1966/1979, 209). The steppe nomads seemed to have eventually and grudgingly accepted their impoverished and hemmed in, but still largely non-sedentary, existence. Unfortunately, things would soon get worse (see next sections).

Another tragedy that struck at about the same time was increasing numbers of dzhuty (mass deaths of livestock due to extreme weather conditions): According to Artykbaev, as a result of the severe winter of 1827, in the Bukey Horde, about 1200 heads of cattle died. In the winter of 1855–1856 during a period of black ice (gololed, gololeditsa) in Northern Kazakhstan, 771,000 sheep/rams and 228,000 horses perished (2007, 209). In the new colonial circumstances, consequences of dzhuty for the Kazakhs were aggravated: Prior to the Russian conquest, in comparable situations, in order to save their herds, the steppe dwellers would decide to move away far enough or to nomadize (migrate) longer distances. But the authorities' bans, regulations, and restrictions made such remedies more and more difficult or thwarted them altogether.

Establishment of the Governorate-General of the Steppe and Reorganization of Northern CA

As Soucek underlines, the distinctiveness of the Kazakh steppes, compared to Southern CA, resided, i.e., in their geographical and historical linkage with European Russia and Siberia (2000, 201). A year after the establishment of the Governorate-General of Turkestan, the Russian authorities in 1868 carried out an administrative reform of the C Asian steppe regions. Together with the transfer south of the customs border from the old Orenburg-Petropavlovsk-Irtysh line that had taken place in 1865, this reform marked the final annexation of the Kazakh steppe (Breghel 2003, 62–63).

Approximately where the Bukey and Junior Hordes had existed prior to their dissolution, the oblasts of Uralsk and Turgay were set up. The habitat of the former Middle Horde more or less corresponded to the two oblasts of Akmolinsk and Semipalatinsk. Finally, the territory of the former Senior Horde (mostly earlier Qing-ruled territory) was divided up between the easternmost part of the oblast of Semipalatinsk and smaller parts of the Semirechie and Syr Daria oblasts (the

---

[205] These uprisings may be seen to have had the Pugachev rebellion as a predecessor (in which Kazakhs also prominently took part).

latter two belonging to the Governorate-General of Turkestan) (see Map 4.6). The voevody (governors) of the Uralsk and Turgay Oblasts reported to the Minister of the Interior, while the oblasts of Akmolinsk and Semipalatinsk formed the Governorate-General of the Steppe (General-Gubernatorstvo Step), whose highest official resided just north of the regional border in Omsk (Western Siberia) and was subordinate to the Minister of Defense (Breghel 2003, 63, 90; Paul 2012, 386).

The new regional subdivision resembled that of the nomadic lands of the Governorate-General of Turkestan. Oblasts were composed of uezdy (districts), which were made up of volosti (areas), which in turn consisted of auly (nomadic encampments, often comprising patriarchal family groups or clans). The administrative structure was mixed, with members of the Russian military in the upper echelons and nomadic representatives at local levels. The governors of the oblasts and the "uezd commandants" were czarist officers, while the heads of the volosti and village elders (aksakals) were natives often elected by popular vote. Indigenous representatives were, i.e., responsible for tax collection. This system was called "military-popular administration" (voenno-narodnoe upravlenie) (Breghel 2003, 90; Kappeler 2006, 144). The colonizer identified the territory of Kazakh auls by the location of their winter encampments, which corresponded to their longest periodic stay, where property rights were most clearly defined and where buildings or fixed structures existed (houses built of clay bricks, enclosures and shelters for the livestock) (Ferret 2013, 41).

The Russian Empire attempted to integrate Kazakh elites into its system of government. This was done notably by education and schooling (Ohayon 2013, 237). Russian-Kazakh schools were founded, which aimed at the creation of a new European-style intelligentsia, open to Russian ideas of modernization and change of traditional Kazakh society. Hambly names three famous writers that featured among the high-ranking representatives of this new intelligentsia: Chokan Valikhanov (1835–1865 of Genghisid decent), an officer in the czarist army and specialist in Middle Eastern studies; Ibray Altynsaryn (1841–1889), an ethnographer and pedagogue; and Abay Kununbaev (1845–1904), a gifted philosopher oriented toward liberal ideas (1966, 58). However, these three men are just examples of a very thin elitist social stratum that turned out to be too weak to initiate a transformation of Kazakh society and mentality.

As mentioned above, since the abolition of the hordes, all nomadic lands were state lands that the nomadic communities therefore no longer possessed but only had a right to use. The reforms of the late 1860s in Northern CA provided for the standardization of taxes and their collection in cash. The kibitka tax (kibitochnaya podat) was sharply increased to 4.5 roubles[206] and later extended to all types of Kazakh housing.

Thus, a rising number of Kazakhs were forced to earn or obtain roubles by trading with Russia or carrying out other activities or to pay their taxes through intermediaries (Poujol and Fourniau 2005, 60–61). Additionally, Kazakhs were charged with the duty to convey mail and supply carriages for the Russian army. If local people wanted to become farmers, their land plots had to be apportioned by their communes (auls) (Roudik 2007, 77).

Russian mineral resource extraction activities in the Kazakh steppes already started in the late eighteenth and the first decades of the nineteenth century: The mining of lead and silver deposits in the Altai area near Ust-Kamenogorsk (today, Oeskemen) began in 1784. Lead and silver mines in the upper Ishim region (near Akmolinsk, today, Astana) operated from the 1830s. The commercial extraction of coal in the Nura river area (near later Karaganda, today, Qaraghandy) was launched in the 1850s; copper mining started in Spassky and Uspensky (see Map 4.7), somewhat further south, a couple of years later. Dzhezkazgan (in Central Kazakhstan, near the Sarysu valley) became one of the richest sites of copper extraction on earth. Commercial operations in Dzhezkazgan also started in the mid-nineteenth century (Hambly (ed) 1966/1979, 231).

Toward Large-Scale European Settlement and Drastic Expulsion of Nomads (from the 1880s)

While the abolition of serfdom eventually led many peasants to move to the emerging Russian industrial centers and look for work there, a large group of farmers took up the "traditional option" and searched for new virgin lands at the frontiers of the empire, including in the Kazakh steppes. Moreover, tendencies toward the rationalization of farming and the rise of commercial agriculture in European Russia implied that at least in some regions, fewer peasants were needed. In this situation, accelerating rural population growth and trends toward overpopulation in European Russia's countryside reinforced west-east migration pressure in the czardom (Dubovitsky and Bababekov 2011, 80). Thus, rural economic and demographic pressures in the last decades of the nineteenth century constituted a powerful "push factor" in favor of moving to the eastern prairies. And, as mentioned above, Kazakhstan had been largely "pacified" by Russian military actions up to the early 1870s. Its fertile, extensive, and largely virgin chernozem soils were henceforth under firm Russian control ("pull factor").

The agricultural development of the Kazakh steppes through massive European settlement only started in the 1890s (about two decades after the above-explained push and pull factors could have become effective). Prior to that, the authorities had made some occasional moves, for instance, in the late 1860s the government oversaw the settlement of some 12,000 Cossacks in the northern plains of the oblast of Semirechie (Turkestan). Nonirrigated farming was introduced in the Northern Kazakh steppes by first cohorts of Russian settlers in the 1870s (Hambly (ed) 1966/1979, 228; Artykbaev 2007, 210).

---

[206] As mentioned above, this tax had been introduced by the Russian administration on the former territory of the Younger Zhuz in 1837 at a level of one and a half roubles per tent/household.

After the issuance of provisional rules in 1881, the Steppe Statute of 1891 definitely regulated the resettlement of peasants from Russia to the Kazakh grasslands. The state provided resettlers from the European part of the country with up to 40 ha of land upon their arrival in the steppes; financial incentives (e.g., tax privileges) were added. Settlers' villages and settlements were generally arranged along the main routes of transportation (Oskolkov and Oskolkova 2004, 41). The czarist authorities "opened the gates" of the Eurasian grasslands beyond Europe to European agricultural settlement in the hope to attenuate the abovementioned economic and social problems. Aimed at flourishing farming communities in the Kazakh plains were expected to become new markets for Russia's products and to generate increased fiscal revenues. Finally, the imperial government favored the settlement of eastern Slavic peasants in the newly annexed territories in order to strengthen the Russian or Eastern Slav ethnic element in CA (Kappeler 2006, 148).

In the early 1890s, large waves of European immigrants reached the arable lands of the northwest, the north, and the northeast of Kazakhstan (Hofmeister 2015, 128). Mostly former Russian and Ukrainian serfs eager to till land of their own began to flood the czar's new territories, about a million new inhabitants on the Kazakh steppes alone (Mayhew 2010, 51). At the same time, the land used by (nomadic) Kazakhs was further drastically cut back. First the most fertile tracts, then second-rate lands, etc. were confiscated and handed to the settlers. The Steppe Statute principally restricted the land Kazakh "households" (families) could use to 16 ha per household. This rendered nomadic mobility exceedingly difficult (Kindler 2014, 35–36).

The pastoralists, of whom only few had turned to a settled life, were effectively pushed off to the southern "frontier" of European settlement and thereby separated from the more humid pasturelands, which were however indispensible during the summer drought periods within the annual cycle of meridional livestock migrations (Osterhammel 2009/2013, 527). The stock of cattle shrank precipitously and the impoverished native population continued to nomadize on ever more marginal soils and truncated trails. Disputes and fights between expanding settler communities and tribes literally living on the sidelines dragged on for years. Some of the most pauperized auls were eventually compelled to turn sedentary for lack of livestock that would justify continued mobility (Kappeler 2001, 159).

According to Breghel (2003, 90–91), the centers of European agricultural settlement in the grasslands between the lower Volga and the Altai and Northern Tienshan in the late nineteenth century were the middle and lower reaches of the Ural river (Orenburg, Uralsk, Guriev), the upper and middle reaches of the Ishim (Akmolinsk, Atbasar, Kokchetav, Petropavlovsk), Northern Semirechie (Kopal, today, Qapal; Lepsinsk, today, Lepsi), Southern Semirechie (Verny, today, Almaty) (see Maps 4.6 and

4.7).[207] As Hambly emphasizes, the Russian settlement and exclusive appropriation of large parts of the C Asian steppe certainly constituted the most disastrous aspect of the czarist conquest from the point of view of the nomads (1966, 229). In contrast to the traditional sedentary tuzemtsy of the governorate-general that continued their fragile existence and that were somewhat protected from Russian settlers outside the larger cities, the nomadic inorodtsy of the Kazakh steppes were not immediately, but eventually fully exposed to the juggernaut of European mass peasant settlement. One could argue that poverty was redistributed across Russia: from the czar's restive peasant subjects to his defeated nomadic subjects.[208]

---

[207] The resettlement of parts of Semirechie/Zhetysu under Russian rule came about six centuries after the de-sedentarization of this region under Mongol rule.

[208] One might ask why European mass colonization of the fertile Kazakh steppes only happened in the late nineteenth and the early twentieth century—why not immediately after the abolition of serfdom in 1861 or a couple of years later, in the 1870s, when the pacification of Kazakhstan was concluded? Given the above-described substantial economic and demographic pressure building up in European Russia (the push factor), why didn't the attractiveness of the newly won vast lands so apt for farming (the pull factor) play a role *a generation earlier*? Five reasons may explain why.

Reasons related to the push factor:

1. As mentioned earlier, the former serfs did not immediately (after 1861) gain freedom and mobility. Due to institutional constraints and shortcomings, incisive changes only came with a delay—of possibly about two decades.
2. The acceleration of demographic growth in Eastern Europe only happened toward the end of the nineteenth century.

Reasons related to the pull factor:

3. As also alluded to above, the specialization of nomadic stockbreeding in the low-precipitation grasslands for the Russian market turned out to be relatively efficient and profitable, at least for some time.
4. While the inorodtsy certainly did not benefit of the same rights as the European subjects of the czar, they had still formed part of the colonial administration set up in the steppes (the "voenno-narodnoe upravlenie"). The czarist authorities probably hesitated when they were confronted with the major social and political problems that the destruction of the nomadic Kazakhs' lifestyle by large-scale removal and deportation of millions from the grasslands would give rise to.

Infrastructural reason:

5. At the time, railroads were the quickest way to bring large numbers of immigrants to the steppe. In the 1870s, Russia was still in the early phase of building a network of rail connections in the central areas of the empire and had simply not yet reached the point when masses of European farmers could be swiftly transported east across Eurasia. The Transsiberian railroad only reached Omsk in 1894, and the Trans-Aral railroad (from Orenburg to Tashkent) was built even later (Kappeler 2006, 148). For comparison, the first transcontinental railroad of the USA was put into service and crossed the Great Plains in 1869, and Canada's first train went all the way out west in 1885. Before these years, no mass settlement of North America's West occurred.

Artykbaev points to the active penetration of Kazakhstan by Russian capital in the second half of the nineteenth century. The most important spheres of investment were the extraction and processing of natural resources, the processing of products of agriculture and animal husbandry, and trade. Fair trade (yarmarochnaya torgovlia) further developed in Kazakhstan. Very large fairs attained a turnover of 1 million roubles or more. However, trade often bore an "unequal" character from the viewpoint of Kazakh nomads: For instance, half a pound of tea and a pound of sugar were traded for a sheep, or a razor was offered for a sheep or a samovar—for 20–25 sheep (Artykbaev 2007, 210–211). This perceived or real exploitation recalls Qing trade practices with the Kazakhs soon after the conquest of East Turkestan and once the nomadic military danger was over and sedentary China had achieved definite superiority over the steppe dwellers (see above).

Overall (looking at entire Western CA) one can conclude that in the framework of enforced political stability (the "Pax Russica") and at high costs and human sacrifices (a) technology- and market-induced acceleration of cotton production in the south and (b) mass European settlement and farming in the north together initiated the truly capitalist phase of Russian colonialism in the 1880s and 1890s. One could argue that in this period Western CA's economic "take-off" à la Rostow was launched—although it was largely confined to colonial immigrants and settlers.

Box 4.5: Comparison: Settling the West by the USA and Canada/Colonizing the Eurasian Steppes by Russia/Developing the Western Borderlands (Xinjiang) by China

There appear to be many similarities and a few differences in the ways the settlement of newly won territories took place in the North American and Chinese "West" and the Russian "East."

Expansion of "civilization" and "progress" to ethnically different "frontier regions"

As Kang accurately observes, China's eighteenth and nineteenth century westward expansion features a number of striking similarities with the USA's (and one could argue, Canada's) nineteenth-century westward expansions. In both cases, (large and powerful) states with populous and urbanized east coasts or eastern core regions expanded into sparsely populated, ethnically different western "frontier areas." In both

cases, this was perceived as a natural and inevitable process of taming borderlands and bringing order and civilization to partly "wild" or "alien" areas (Kang 2010, 140). Russia's eighteenth and nineteenth century conquest of the Kazakh and West Siberian steppes featured a big power with a European core region expanding east into vast and culturally different expanses. Here too, the process was seen as a necessary advance of civilization and progress into new, virgin, territories. Like the North American societies of the New World, the Qing Chinese and the czarist Russian authorities generally viewed the replacement of grazing spaces with modern farming as an advance in social and economic development (Treue 1973, 667; Perdue 2005, 335).

According to Perdue, a glance at the agricultural colonization efforts in Xinjiang in the Qing era again evokes strong analogies to the settlement of the American Great Plains in the nineteenth century, where the arid region west of 100° longitude could not support large-scale farming settlement without heavy subsidies from the government back east (2005, 49). The Russian colonization of the Kazakh steppes also faced an important geographic aridity threshold. This limit (separating the grasslands from the desert steppe) displayed more of a north-south nature and, as explained above, possibly ran along 48° or 49° latitude.

If colonialism is identified as the establishment of rule over a territory through exploitation of developmental asymmetry (or technological superiority), then the conquest of the American as well as of the Chinese west, the Russian east, of Australia, Africa, and other lands can be subsumed under this term (Reinhard 2008, 177). In many cases, tribal societies' access to the land that they had hitherto used was cut off or severely restricted. As Marx would say, traditional producers were separated from their means of production or relegated to marginal spaces (Osterhammel 2009/2013, 537).

Of course, as Reinhard remarks, Chinese colonization and colonialism can boast of an age, a continuity, and a structural density that leave other colonial histories, e.g., European ones, far behind (2008, 193–194). After all, China conquered or reconquered Xinjiang at least three times (beginning with the Han dynasty in the first century BCE, followed by the Tang

(continued)

Box 4.5 (continued)

and the Qing dynasties; moreover East Turkestan was politically united with China in the Mongol era, although in this case of the Yuan dynasty it was a C Asian power that had subjugated the Middle Kingdom).

Can the US frontier thesis also be applied to the Russian conquest of eastern lands?

In recent decades, American scholars have made various attempts to apply Turner's[209] Frontier Thesis (1893) of American history in a modified form to the history of czarist expansion. A "frontier" is thus understood as a transitional region at the edge of a settled or cultivated area and differs from a fixed borderline between two states or polities (Tröbst 2009, 239). Or a "frontier" can be likened to a special kind of contact zone in which two collectives of different origin and cultural orientation interact with each other (whether in cooperative or noncooperative ways) (Osterhammel 2009/2013, 513).

As Troebst argues, in Russia's case, the western border of Muscovy could be seen as a clearly identified, if often revised, borderline between countries; yet the relatively fluid southern and eastern borders toward the Desht-i-Kipchak and Siberia would qualify as a frontier. Many US researchers have seen a link between the American "frontier" experience and the victory of the idea of liberty and individualism, while they have tended to interpret the Russian frontier experience in the opposite way. There are also researchers, including many Russian and Ukrainian historians, who point to the eastern Slavic capacity to rule and conquer vast lands and who perceive this as a pivotal unifying aspect of their history (Tröbst 2009, 239).

According to Turner's Frontier thesis, the challenges of the simple and harsh life at the edge of civilization helped create an efficient and competitive type of human being, whose congenial way of life is democracy, namely, the American (Reinhard 2008, 182).[210] In the czardom historical interpretations had emerged in the early nineteenth century that in some respects may have anticipated Turner's arguments. The Moscow historian Sergey Solovev (1820–1879) held the view that Russia's mission in Asia was to act as a champion of progressive European civilization (Osterhammel 2009/2013, 529).

North American Indians were never integrated into the society of the white man on the US or Canadian side of the frontier (as long as the latter existed), while white settlers never became part of the Indian societies and nations beyond the border. In this sense, the North American frontier was a socially excluding limit from the beginning. In the end, the indigenous population was moved to and territorially encapsulated in numerous small Indian reservations (Jacquin 2012, 58)[211]. In contrast, Russia's southern and eastern borders often witnessed the emergence of "frontier societies" with their own norms and practices, for instance, the Cossacks of the steppe rivers Dnepr, Don, Volga, Yaik (Ural), and of Siberia. Such "autonomized" social structures at the border never developed in North America (Tröbst 2009, 239; Osterhammel 2009/2013, 523).

According to Kappeler, the czardom featured traditions of polyethnic symbiosis going back to the Middle Ages (2001, 136). As also explained above, non-Russian peoples that were incorporated into the czarist state were not fully disarmed, and up to a certain point their elites were officially recognized and at times co-opted into the imperial nobility (Osterhammel 2009/2013, 523, 525). These populations in many cases did not encounter legal or psychological discrimination, as Hambly puts it (ed. 1966/1979, 231). Victims of czarist expansion were frequently afforded scopes of action that remained unattainable for native Americans (e.g.,

(continued)

---

[209] Frederick Jackson Turner, US historian (1861–1932), author of the influential scholarly paper "The Significance of the Frontier in American History" (1893).

[210] One could consider applying this thesis—in a modified form—to Cossacks, or even better, to Eurasian nomads: Thanks to excellent mounted archery in Ukraine, Southern Russia, and CA, horseback nomads enjoyed traditional military superiority for millennia. Displaying extreme mobility in a harsh environment, these competent human beings have typically also been more open-minded and religiously tolerant than their less dynamic sedentary neighbors.

[211] Indian populations inhabiting reservations in the USA today are recognized as "domestic-dependent nations" which possess autonomous tribal prerogatives (Rostkowski 2012, 79).

recognition of kishlaks and auls as official components of the czarist state hierarchy, ban on European settlement in the Governorate-General of Turkestan outside the large towns, retention of the Khanate of Khiva and the Emirate of Bukhara, even if as truncated vassal states).[212]

4.2.3 East Turkestan: Weakening Chinese Rule and Unrest Trigger Instability and Stagnation (Second Quarter till Late Nineteenth Century)

Publications by Yuri Bregel, Audrey Burton, Gavin Hambly, Ralph Kauz, Angus Maddison, Richard Overy, James Millward, Peter Perdue, and Svat Soucek feature among the primary sources of this chapter.

While Russia was expanding and consolidating its power in West Turkestan, China was slowly losing its grip on East Turkestan. As mentioned earlier, this was primarily due to cumulating internal disturbances, themselves triggered by worsening quality of government, swelling corruption, and mismanagement. Expanding opium imports from Britain, which had the drug produced in its Indian colonies, did not facilitate matters. Selling opium to the Chinese helped the British pay for their extensive purchases of tea[213], silk, china, sophisticated handicrafts, and other luxuries much coveted overseas. Chinese addiction to and demand for the drug soon got out of control. By the early 1830s opium imports had outgrown Chinese exports and a drain of silver out of the Middle Kingdom began. This had increasingly serious effects on the economy and further weakened state finances (Overy (ed) 2004, 193).

Chinese attempts to block the business, which was highly profitable for the British, triggered the First Opium War (1839–1842), which ended in the cession of Hong Kong and the forced opening of five southern Chinese ports to trade with Britain. As a result of the Second Opium War (1858–1860), in which Anglo-French attacks destroyed the summer palace of the emperor in Beijing, vast parts of the Chinese interior were opened up for Western businessmen who received extraterritorial privileges (Maddison 2007, 125). The non-Western states Russia and Japan also exacted trade and territorial concessions. For example, in 1858 in accordance with the Treaty of Aigun the czardom annexed the Amur province (north of the Amur, which it had already conquered in 1650 and then relinquished to the Qing Empire in the Treaty of Nerchinsk in 1689) and the Coastal province (east of Amur and Ussuri, Sikhote Alin, see above).

The grave domestic governance crisis, the spread of economic problems, and the painful humiliations at the hands of foreign powers contributed to further destabilizing the political situation. Gathering internal disorder triggered a succession of rebellions that culminated in the Taiping (Heavenly Kingdom) Uprising, which broke out in 1850. The Qing finally put down the insurgency in 1864, at the cost of around 20 million lives, but the dynasty's authority never fully recovered (Haywood 2011, 156).

China's decline from the early nineteenth century may have been linked—paradoxically, at first sight—to the Qing dynasty's own previous success. The Qing Empire had featured rapid and sustained preindustrial population growth.[214] With their country and economy remaining the world's biggest for a long time, the Qing elites and the Middle Kingdom's bureaucracy tended to be self-contented and guided by an education system and a mentality that remained largely indifferent to external influences, including intellectual or scientific developments in the West. This type of mindset lacked curiosity for innovations and was quite unconcerned about the domestic business climate (Maddison 2007, 125).

The continuously growing population had to be fed by evermore intensive and careful cultivation of a limited area. By the end of the eighteenth century, the area available for agriculture—based on given technologies—may have been fully exploited. It was the situation of intensive economic activity combined with the lack of possibility to further substantially raise productivity that the English sinologist Elvin, cited by Gernet, characterized as the "high level equilibrium trap" (1972/1985, vol. 2, 48). In other words, with China's given technologies and institutions—for want of important innovations and incentives that would have enabled a breakthrough toward industrialization—the country was unable to move to a

---

[212] After conquering Eastern CA in the mid-eighteenth century, the Qing authorities' approach to colonial rule left even more room to the indigenous peoples than Russia did in the nineteenth century: As explained above, indirect rule was established which rested on arrangements with the remaining traditional elites under the loose control of Chinese governors and garrisons. Notwithstanding continuous subliminal sinicization pressures on the defeated peoples, the Qing respected the culture of their new subjects and backed the integration of their upper strata into the hierarchy of the state (Reinhard 2008, 194, 197). Many of these rights were withdrawn, however, upon the incorporation of Xinjiang as a regular Chinese province (1884). But even then, some informal arrangements and de facto responsibilities survived (see below).

[213] As Vries underlines, until the 1840s, the Middle Kingdom was the only country in the world that cultivated and exported tea (2007, 5).

[214] Thus, in 1650, China had counted around 100 million inhabitants, in 1800 about 300 million, and in 1850 about 450 million (Overy (ed) 2004, 192).

new, higher level of productivity. In this sense, the Qing Empire probably experienced a "plateau phenomenon": An economic system that in the given circumstances had maximized its output and performance. Demographic pressures combined with economic stagnation and lack of new technological impulses probably facilitated the spread of corruption, mismanagement, and social tensions. Increasing difficulties and bottlenecks might only have been cured by large-scale innovation as well as radical and bold reorganization. Neither was imminent (Overy (ed.) 2004, 192).

4.2.3.1 From Dwindling Resources to Unrest, "Unequal Treaty" with Khoqand, and Temporary Stabilization (ca. 1830–1850)

Given the deepening political and economic crisis the Qing Empire was going through, China's trade embargo against the Khanate of Khoqand (imposed in 1827) did not endure. In 1830, Khan Muhammad Ali (1822–1841) exploited the Qing's weakness and launched a new military invasion of East Turkestan. The empire was soon compelled to accede to Khoqandi demands, which were judged to be cheaper than further emergency mobilizations in this peripheral region. In 1832 the Qing authorities granted Khoqandi merchants the right to trade tax-free in Xinjiang. Moreover, the khanate obtained special privileges in the western part of the region (Altishahr, comprising large trading towns like Kashgar, Yarkand, Khotan, and others, see above): Here the khan had the right to collect customs and tax revenue from the domestic Muslim population (Millward 2007, 110, 113; Kauz 2006, 131). In this way, Khoqandian businessmen and officials acquired some commercial and fiscal control over an important part of the Qing Empire's trade with its Western neighbors. According to Millward and Perdue, this agreement of 1832 with the "trading nation" of Khoqand—not the Treaty of Nanjing (1842) ending the First Opium War—probably constituted Beijing's first "unequal treaty" (2004, 61).

Having arrived at this surprising modus vivendi, both powers apparently shared an interest in border stability and the smooth functioning of commerce, and this showed in the region's relative calm over the next one and a half decades. After the hiatus of the late 1820s and early 1830s (the embargo), SR trade linking the Ferghana Basin, Tashkent, and regions further west with Xinjiang and China to the east "normalized" again. In order to stabilize money circulation in East Turkestan in the 1830s, a monetary reform was carried out: Copper coins were minted above the standard, and a new and heavier coin was launched with an increased face value (Rtveladze 2003, 445).

4.2.3.2 Heavy Losses Through Chinese Rebellions and Regional Insurgency (Yakub Beg), Followed by Fragile Qing Reconquest (ca. 1850–1885)

Pervasive Turmoil and Collapse of Financial Flows Trigger the Unraveling of Chinese Rule

The Taiping (Heavenly Kingdom) Uprising (1850–1864) was a major blow to the stability of the Qing dynasty. It affected more than half of China's provinces and did extensive damage to its richest areas, including the south and central Yangzi provinces, which were the country's "rice bowl" and the base of its silk industry (Maddison 2007, 125; Millward 2007, 116). At the same time the authorities needed more silver to pay for imports of opium, forced upon the country by Britain. Therefore, less silver was available for payments to the military in Xinjiang. Overall, economic distress, rampant misrule, the Taiping and other rebellions, the Opium Wars, and other tensions with European powers severely restricted the authorities' ability to maintain their garrisons in distant East Turkestan. In this situation, Muslim unrest broke out again and gathered momentum in Kashgaria in the early 1850s.

As Millward notes, by 1853 the Qing central treasury was depleted. From this year, silver stipends to Xinjiang fell into arrears, eventually stopping altogether. In response, the regional authorities first began to spend their savings, invest funds at interest with pawnbrokers, and requisition Uighur labor to mine for precious metals. Officials also imposed heavy new taxes on locals and allowed the hakim begs and the begs to do the same. Irrigation and other public works were more and more neglected. Offices started to be auctioned off to the highest bidders, who then pressured the populace under their jurisdiction to extract a return on their investment[215]. Hakim begs and their subordinates were given free rein in return for kickbacks to the Qing authorities. Many settlers fled (Millward 2007, 116; Perdue 2005, 353).

Millward adds that foreign merchants started to complain of the lack of Chinese goods in the bazaars and that military officials agonized over spreading grain shortages (2007, 116). According to Perdue, in the early 1850s, the stud farms shared in the general disorder of the region. Like other imperial institutions there, they quickly degenerated when official oversight slackened. Without the regular military inspections, herds rapidly shrank. By 1853, 40,000 of the 100,000 horses in Ili had died of disease (Perdue 2005, 353). Little by little, the Qing troops

---

[215] In this way, although they were originally probably intended as emergency fiscal procurement measures, corruption and blackmail gradually destroyed institutions.

stationed in Xinjiang fell into decrepitude and were depleted and demoralized by opium addiction and illnesses. Meanwhile, Russian merchants received the contractual right to sell goods duty-free and to set up shop in the Ili area and in Kashgaria. As Millward explains, this trade was regulated by the Sino-Russian treaty of Yining/Kuldzha of 1851 (also known as Yili-Tarbagatay commercial treaty). Due to the exemption from duties stipulated in the agreement, Chinese historians consider it too as an 'unequal' one (2007, 156).[216]

Yaqub Beg's Emirate of Kashgaria (1865–77): High Taxes, Low Trade with China, but Temporary Focus of "Great Game"

Chaos soon took hold of East Turkestan. In 1862, the Dungans of Gansu and Shanxi provinces rebelled against the Qing. The Dungans or Hui are Han Muslims; according to some scholars, they constitute an ethnic group of mixed Chinese-Turkic descendance. The rebellion lasted for some years and effectively set up a barrier between China proper and Xinjiang (Millward 2007, 117; Hambly (ed) 1966/1979, 307; Soucek 2000, 265). At least, the blocking of the Gansu corridor (or the "Jade Gate") made access to the western frontier region much more difficult. This improved the prospects for uprisings in East Turkestan itself.

In Yining (Kuldzha) and other towns of the Ili area, Taranchis successfully attacked the Qing authorities in 1864. In order to unite the East Turkestani rebels, a khwaja (a charismatic Sufi dignitary) from Khoqand arrived, accompanied by an experienced warlord. The warlord, Yaqub Beg, a native of Ferghana and Khoqandi general, soon took over the leadership of the uprising with dictatorial and brutal measures (Kauz 2006, 132).[217] In the mid-1860s, China lost control of the largest part of Kashgaria. According to Millward, Muhammad Yaqub Beg (1820–1877) was a C Asian strongman of the familiar type claiming descent from Tamerlane and patronizing the religious establishment—thus, like others before him, aspiring to dual legitimacy. Yet at the same time, he was well aware of CA's new geopolitical situation between expanding British and Russian Empires and its need of modern weapons and techniques (Millward 2007, 123).

While Yaqub Beg had in vain defended Akmeshit against the Russians in 1853, he did successfully organize the uprising in Kashgar and other cities against the Chinese more than

a decade later. In 1865 Kashgar was captured; Yaqub's forces massacred numerous Chinese merchants. In 1866–1867 the Tarim Basin was conquered, the khodzha was shoved aside, and the independent Emirate of Kashgaria was proclaimed. Thus Yaqub Beg established himself as the ruler of an Islamic state more or less comprising the Tarim Basin, but subsequently (1870–1871) expanding to Urumqi, Turfan, and Hami (see Map 4.6). The ruler also enjoyed some influence among the Torguts and other Mongols nomadizing in Dzungaria. The Ili district, however, had its own independent Tariachin government that endured until the Russian intervention of 1871.

As Millward aptly put it, Yaqub Beg, from his imposing court (orda) in Kashgar, appointed governors (hakims) and other officials to administer police and collect taxes in towns and rural areas throughout the emirate. Having positioned himself as a defender of the faith and holy warrior against the infidel Khitay (the Chinese), Yaqub strictly adhered to Islamic law in order to support his bid for legitimacy (Millward 2007, 120). Such visitors as Forsyth (a senior British diplomat) confirm the reality of this claim: The Sharia and religious precepts were being applied and rigorously enforced to the point where numerous local Uighurs grew uneasy about the changes, and growing parts of the Muslim population complained; some even started to feel nostalgia for the days of China's rule (Soucek 2000, 266).

Under the emirate, many suffered from a heavy burden of taxes and levies of various kinds and from an economy that was slow to recover from the preceding turmoil. Local officials usually received no salaries and lived off the population—a practice that did not differ much from that of Qing officials just before they had been ousted. The regime maintained an army of some 40,000 servicemen. Unlike the Manchu soldiers, who had been mainly stationed in Dzungaria and paid with silver from the Chinese interior, Yaqub Beg's forces had to be locally supported in Kashgaria, which contributed to the burden imposed on the population. Moreover, the disturbances further east as well as the conflict with Beijing apparently cut off the last trickle of trade with the Middle Kingdom and put an end to the important entrepôt business of reexporting Chinese tea, silk, silver, and other items. With dimming market prospects, even the jade mines worked at a slower pace or ground to a halt. As a witness, cited by Millward, put it "What you see on market day now … is nothing compared to the life and activity there was in the time of the Khitay. Next week's market day brings back our customers. In the Khitay time, people bought and sold every day" (Millward 2007, 121–122).

The Emirate of Kashgaria attracted considerable international attention, especially from Britain, Russia, and the Ottoman Empire. Constantinople sent weapons and military

---

[216] For the most part, the Russian merchants purchased Chinese brick tea, some silk, and cloth in return for which they sold livestock, hides, furs, and manufactured goods (ibid).

[217] Given Khoqand's militarily precarious situation just a year before the Russian invasion of Tashkent, (1865) one might have thought that the khanate was in need of all its capable military leaders to defend itself.

advisers to support the new Islamic state (Hambly (ed) 1966/ 1979, 308). By the 1860s, the so-called "Great Game"—the contest principally between Britain and Russia for the control of CA (see also Box 4.6)—was gaining momentum: In the mid-nineteenth century, the British had already conquered South Asia up to the Indus river, including most of Kashmir. The Russians took Tashkent in 1865 and Samarkand in 1868. Both big powers seemed to show "geopolitical appetite" for more. In this situation, the foundering of Qing rule in Xinjiang generated a power vacuum that further heightened the sparring of the two colonial empires (Soucek 2000, 265).

Russia invaded the Ili district in 1871 and put an end to the Taranchi government there. The czardom annexed the territory, claiming that the Chinese authorities were unable to keep order in Ili (Map 4.6). As Millward explains, the Russians seemed to have intended an extended stay in Kuldzha (Yining), for they restored major irrigation canals, built a hospital, established bilingual schools and other cultural institutions, including a Russian Orthodox Church (2007, 133). After the Muslim insurgency and warfare had brought all of East Turkestan's external trade to a temporary standstill, including trade with Russia, the latter gradually recovered. From 1870 to 1871, trade between the Emirate of Kashgaria and czardom doubled. The following year (1872), the Russian Empire concluded a commercial treaty with Yaqub Beg[218], and thereafter the trade volume almost doubled again—to a million roubles. Two years later (1874), the ruler of Kashgaria signed a corresponding treaty with Ambassador Forsyth, in the name of the government of British India. However, British and Indian businessmen, probably for geographic and technological reasons[219], were not as active as Russian merchants in Yaqub Beg's state (Hambly (ed) 1966/1979, 308, 311).

> **Box 4.6: The "Great Game" of the Nineteenth Century in an Economic and Geopolitical Perspective**
> The British intelligence officer, explorer, and writer Arthur Conolly (1807–1842) reportedly introduced the term "The Great Game" in the 1830s to describe the colonial rivalry between the British and Russian

Empires for supremacy in CA in the nineteenth century.[220] In this struggle, the British aimed at protecting and enlarging their colonial possessions in India/South Asia, preventing Russian expansion in their direction, and gaining new markets or client states in CA, while the Russians were interested in extending their influence and rule across CA, controlling the land routes to India, acquiring sources of raw materials for their industries (e.g., cotton) as well as cheap labor and new markets. Interestingly, both sides' actions oriented toward territorial gains were officially justified by the search for "defensive," "scientific borders" (Britain), or "secure," preferably "natural boundaries" (Russia).

Russia gained the upper hand in western CA economically

Burton describes a detailed report of 1830 to the British government (signed by the explorer Alexander Burnes), which listed requirements of the Emirate of Bukhara: good-quality broadcloth, cast-iron pots, glass bottles and mirrors, tea, indigo, sugar and paper, scissors, razors and penknives, etc. All of this, together with iron, steel, copper, and tin, it was argued, could be supplied at competitive prices by Britain and British India, "the freight of a load of 1 ton of iron" from England being "far less than the cost of [hiring] one camel from Orenburg to Bukhara." However, this seems to include only the sea freight from Britain to India and not also the land freight—probably via camelback—from the Indian seaport to Bukhara, which is also longer and topographically more difficult (mountain passes) than the flat land connection from Orenburg to Bukhara. The report went on to expound the much higher quality of tea, an item "of the greatest request among the Uzbeks," that could also be sent from Bombay to compete with the Kashgar variety available locally (both above citations in Burton 2003, 420). But in this case too, there appear to be logistical handicaps: Direct shipping on camels from

(continued)

---

[218] From a territorial viewpoint, this might be regarded a successor treaty to the Sino-Russian regional trade agreement concluded in the early 1850s (see above).

[219] For nineteenth century merchants from British India, trade links (over the high mountain passes) with East Turkestan or more generally with CA may have become—*relatively*—less attractive than in earlier periods, given the major improvements and enticements of international seaborne trade.

[220] Peter Hopkirk wrote a detailed account of this diplomatic struggle that lasted most of the century: "The Great Game: The Struggle for Empire in CA" (1990/1994).

Box 4.6 (continued)

Bombay to Bukhara corresponds to a route about three times as long as that from Kashgar to Bukhara.

It was probably due to these difficulties of physical accessibility and security of access to landlocked, remote, and partly mountainous CA from the sea[221] that the success claimed by Burnes in the 1830s for British goods appears to have been short-lived in the Emirate of Bukhara. Still, there can be no doubt that the above report pointed to the increasing availability at the borders of CA of competitive and modern products produced with superior Western technologies. In the first half of the nineteenth century, Russia, through its geographic proximity and its long-standing direct trade links seems to have gained the upper hand in the economic penetration of the region by outside powers (Dubovitsky and Bababekov 2011, 56). Many of the abovementioned goods, including popular English manufactured products (like broadcloth and other fine textiles) increasingly reached CA via Russia (Burton 2003, 420–421).[222]

… and the czardom acquired the lion's share of the region politically

If one judges by effective conquests in the direction of the three "khanates"[223] from the early nineteenth century, the British initially advanced more successfully: By 1848, Britain had conquered all of South Asia up to the Indus river and beyond including Kashmir, whereas at the time Russia had "only" reached the Mangyshlak peninsula, the Aral Sea and Lake Balkhash. Afghanistan, situated at the border between C and South Asia, was of particular interest to the British as a potential barrier to a possible Russian thrust southward. Moreover, as history taught, controlling the mountainous stronghold on the Hindu

Kush appeared pivotal to the security of the subcontinent, since almost all invasions of India had been launched from Afghanistan (see also above).

After Britain had failed to install a puppet regime in the first Anglo-Afghan war of 1838–1842, a peace treaty was concluded and relations improved. With the help of British arms, Emir Dost Mukhammed in 1855 reestablished his authority in Uzbek- and Tajik-speaking territories and principalities south of the Amu Daria (Maimana, Balkh, Kunduz, and Badakhshan) that had become semi-independent in the period of political instability in Afghanistan in the late eighteenth century (see also above). In the following years, Russia made some important acquisitions in CA (Tashkent 1865, Bukhara 1868, Khiva 1873) and even wooed the short-lived Emirate of Kashgaria (1865–1877) more successfully than did the British, before the statelet was reconquered by China. When in the late 1870s, the Afghan ruler showed some diplomatic inclinations toward the czar, this essentially triggered the second Anglo-Afghan war (1878–1881). As a result, the British established themselves in Peshawar and acquired the guardianship of the Khyber Pass. Britain provided some financial assistance and was conceded an important say in the country's foreign policy.

Imperial tensions continued with the czardom's move further south (1881 victory in the battle of Goek Tepe against the Turkmens, 1884 annexation of the Merv (Mary) oasis, 1885 of Kushka), but no hostilities broke out between the great powers. Finally, in 1895, the Afghan-Russian border was definitely fixed along the Amu Daria and in the Pamir (most of which was annexed by the czardom), and some years later the Russian Empire recognized that Afghanistan was outside of its "sphere of interests" (Der Große Ploetz 1987, 30. A., 1099).

---

[221] As mentioned above, from the eighteenth century advanced western trade and shipment technologies favored maritime instead of land routes and transportation, which contributed to CA's relative isolation from early modern international commerce. The advent of railroads in the second half of the nineteenth century changed the equation somewhat. However for topographic and geopolitical reasons land access to CA remained easier from Russia (practically no natural borders) than from India (across mountainous and unruly Afghanistan or sky-high Kashmir).

[222] The czardom also became the primary supplier of Chinese Turkestan with modern European industrial goods in the late nineteenth century (Millward 2007, 157; see also below).

[223] Namely, the Emirate of Bukhara and the Khanates of Khiva and Khoqand (in the first half of the nineteenth century).

China's Reconquest of East Turkestan (1876–1878)

In 1877 Yaqub Beg was defeated by the Chinese General Zuo Zongtang and East Turkestan was reclaimed by China. This surprising outcome against the background of the overall weakness of Qing authority was largely due to Zuo Zongtang's (1812–1885) own military and organizational capabilities, to his pertinent experience (he had successfully campaigned against the Taiping rebels and put down the Muslim revolts in Gansu and Shanxi), and to his personal perseverance in pursuit of the project of reconquest of the western frontier region. To top it off, this man was not only the chief proponent of the Xinjiang reconquest and the commander of the campaign, he was also the mastermind of the postwar political reintegration and economic reconstruction of the province (Millward 2007, 125–127). These remarkable deeds and events may provide an example of the weight the personal factor can assume in (economic) history.

As Millward explains, the general prepared the campaigns carefully, selecting an army of 60,000 soldiers and service personnel, well trained and armed with imported Western guns, and Chinese-made versions of new Western weapons. Partly benefiting from previously existing infrastructure, but also based on the important logistical apparatus Zuo had set up for the campaign, grain, and other provisions were secured. The court in Beijing even put at Zuo's disposal funds from imperial customs on maritime trade. The court also authorized the general to borrow from a foreign bank. From 1876, he spent annually an amount equivalent to one sixth of the yearly expenditure of the Chinese treasury (Millward 2007, 127, 130). The same year, the largest part of Dzungaria was reconquered. In 1877 Zuo defeated Yaqub Beg's army in two battles near Turfan and Urumqi, the Chinese military retook Kashgar, and the C Asian strongman died in Korla. In 1878 the reconquest of the region was completed.

The Qing reconquest of Xinjiang, let alone its speed, had not really been expected by Russia and other outside powers. In the Treaty of St. Petersburg (1881), China recovered Yining and the Ili district; however the Qing authorities paid a high indemnity (9 million roubles) to the Russians and retroceded a small part of the district (see Maps 4.5 and 4.6). Russia retained this slice of territory west of the Khorgos river (the area of Zharkent/Panfilov) apparently to resettle thousands of Tariachin (Kuldzha Uighur) and Hui refugees who feared Qing reprisals and who had appealed to the czar to accept them as subjects (Breghel 2003, 64–65; Millward 2007, 135). As Millward and Perdue put it in nutshell, the reconquest of Xinjiang had drained the dynasty's coffers, but it constituted one of the few Qing diplomatic and military triumphs in the nineteenth century (2004, 62).

Beijing's New Centralized Development Strategy for Xinjiang—Hampered by Resource Constraints

Zuo's proposal to confer upon East Turkestan, the status of a Chinese province was accepted in 1884 and Urumqi chosen as the governor's residence. The same year, an imperial decree declared Xinjiang ("New Lands," "New Territory," or "New Frontier," see above) a regular province of the Qing Empire. Chinese provincialization of Xinjiang included a sinicizing agenda, albeit an incompletely realized one (Kauz 2006, 132; Millward 2007, 124). The dynasty's new approach to ruling the Western frontier region embodied a fundamental shift in governing principles.

Millward and Perdue argue that the weakened Manchu ruling house, in a desperate search for cost-effective solutions to secure its fraying imperial borderlands, embraced a more "Chinese" way of running the empire (2004, 65). The late Qing state opted for an administrative model employed in the agrarian and Han Chinese core of its sprawling empire and applied it to the ecologically and culturally different regions of the periphery and the frontier. As Millward explains, the proponents of provincehood stressed the fiscal savings and reductions in troop numbers to be realized by a successful reform and integration of the region, and it was for these reasons that the court approved it. Underlying these claims, however, was the assumption that a Xinjiang that was demographically and culturally more like China proper would be both easier and cheaper to govern (2007, 138). Yet, such a major effort would of course require the settlement of large numbers of farmers and urban dwellers from the Chinese interior as well as a substantial initial allocation of funds and resources, which appeared at least improbable, given the overall very difficult economic conditions the empire was facing in the 1880s.[224]

With the shift to provincial status, Xinjiang was no longer under the jurisdiction of a Manchu military governor-general in Yining, but of a Han civilian governor-general in Urumqi. Four administrative segments (districts) were established in 1884, and their lieutenant governors (tao-tai) reported to the governor-general. The four districts were subdivided into more than 40 prefectures, themselves structured in counties. All administrative units across the province, in the north as well as the south, were headed by Confucian-trained Chinese officials. Although the new provincial regime represented a definitive departure from earlier Qing policy, which had left regional and local-level affairs in Muslim areas almost entirely to the hakim begs and the begs, still a degree of de facto local self-rule was retained by the Muslim population, especially in the Tarim Basin. The beg officials were downgraded, but still carried out essential tasks. Uighur elders and clerks continued to fulfill beg-like intermediary roles between the Chinese state and Turkic society (Millward and Perdue 2004, 65; Millward 2007, 132, 148; Soucek 2000, 267–268).

Reconstruction efforts proved difficult. As Millward and Perdue note, the Qing had reconquered a shattered land. Many settlements had been burnt down or flattened, bridges

---

[224] Interestingly, the concept of "cost-effective colonial administration" appears to correspond to opposite approaches in czarist West Turkestan and in Qing East Turkestan in the late nineteenth century. Whereas the Russian authorities practiced a kind of "hands-off" policy and at least in the first decades of rule over their part of CA seemed satisfied with its results, the Chinese authorities came to the conclusion that a "hands-on" strategy would save more resources—in the long run.

and roads ruined, and irrigation canals filled in. Devastations were most intense in the oases of the east (Hami, Turfan) and the north (Qitay, Urumqi, Jinghe, see Map 4.7), where the Qing military and Chinese agricultural presence had been the greatest. Even after Han refugees, new immigrants and Qing troops had resettled in Xinjiang, farming populations near Urumqi in the late 1870s amounted to only between a tenth and a quarter of what they had been before the uprisings. This limited the government's ability to provision servicemen and sustain an administrative apparatus in the territory (Millward and Perdue 2004, 64; Millward 2007, 131–132). Meanwhile, the Qing court's authority over the country as such was now largely supported by Western colonial powers. The latter had been granted various economic "concessions," extraterritorial privileges, and even a degree of control over the imperial customs system (Mourre 1996, 1114).

As Millward continues, the court authorized Zuo to take the first steps toward a Chinese-style administration in East Turkestan as part of his "post-pacification" reconstruction program in the region. The military began establishing for the first time the rudiments of a Chinese civil administration in Southern Xinjiang (the Tarim Basin). Specialized reconstruction agencies were established to collect taxes or to promote the production of grain or silk. More general tasks comprised the rebuilding of government offices, of bridges, roads and canals, the settling of land ownership issues, the minting of a new currency, and the opening of schools. In particular, reconstruction agencies established Confucian schools in both the Han and Turkic areas of Xinjiang, including some 50 schools in the Muslim cities of the Tarim Basin. Most of the work was carried out by Zuo's servicemen, many of whom came from the province of Hunan. These forces constituted by default the main governing body in postwar Xinjiang; they were supported and financed by the Chinese interior (Millward 2007, 132–133; Millward and Perdue 2004, 66).

To populate ravaged lands, expand arable territories and "consolidate control of the frontier" (shibian), exiles and homesteaders from the interior were enlisted in a civilian agricultural land reclamation program which provided Chinese settlers with land and loans of seed, tools, and draught animals. By their third year, homesteaders and other settlers and pioneers were expected to have reimbursed the loans and to start paying taxes. Yet reconstruction plans were not realized in a satisfactory manner due to budget constraints and organizational matters (Millward 2007, 133, 138–139).

After the establishment of Xinjiang province, the region's annual subsidy from the treasury was held more or less stable until the end of the nineteenth century. Still, as Millward and Perdue emphasize, in fiscal matters, the major problem was that the plan to reconstruct and repopulate East Turkestan depended on an initial investment from the court that never materialized. After regaining the Ili region in 1881, the fragile Qing dynasty soon turned from the Xinjiang crisis to growing troubles on the southern border, where hostilities with France over Vietnam (previously a Chinese tributary state) soon broke out (1884). The war in the south intensified the need for coastal defenses. After this new emergency, not only did Beijing fail to provide promised funds for the rebuilding of Xinjiang's infrastructure, but in some years it even missed the regular annual budget allocation (Millward 2007, 149; Millward and Perdue 2004, 66).

In any case, the results of the reconstruction and agricultural development programs in the last two decades of the nineteenth century were mixed and somewhat unexpected. While there was an initial rush of Han population into the western frontier province, as Millward points out, these migrants included many peasants temporarily fleeing the devastation of their homeland in Gansu (that had been ravaged by turmoil) and returning after some years. Furthermore, neither the demobilized soldiers from Hunan and Gansu nor exiled convicts made good farmers; many of the lands reclaimed in the 1880s were later abandoned. But this abandonment may not have lasted long: Attracted by the fertile soils in the north and east left unoccupied by the disturbances, wars, and fluctuating migrations, impoverished Uighurs began moving in the 1880s and 1890s from the Tarim Basin to the Ili region; the oases in the areas of Jinghe, Urumqi, and Qitay; and even to Tacheng (Chuguchak) in Northern Dzungaria (Millward 2007, 151–152). Thus, numerous Turkic farmers and merchants, in search for new arable lands and trading opportunities, left Kashgaria to install themselves permanently in the north and east of their province, a region that had hitherto been mostly populated by Mongols (Torguts) and Chinese.

Following the hiatus in Qing rule, commercial patterns changed: Certainly, after the low tide of trade during the era of Yaqub Beg, the markets of Kashgar became more lively again. In the region more generally, Chinese merchant groups gained importance beside Russian traders who had come to occupy a predominant position. The Treaty of St. Petersburg (1881) opened Xinjiang further to Russian businessmen (following respective agreements with the Qing in 1851 and with the Emirate of Kashgaria in 1872, see above): The czardom set up new consulates in Tacheng, Yining, Kashgar, and Urumqi. The treaty confirmed Russian goods' duty-free status[225] and extended exemptions to some other types of taxes. Therefore, not only did Russian subjects pay no or low taxes, but Chinese merchants who were not exempted consequently found themselves at a competitive

---

[225] This was valid for Xinjiang and Mongolia, but not for the Chinese interior.

disadvantage (Millward 2007, 154, 156–157)[226]. After the Qing reconquest, British and Indian businessmen also seem to have been in a less favorable situation than their Russian counterparts in East Turkestan, as Hambly points out: Apart from a brief experiment that the Central Asiatic Trading Company undertook in the 1880s, there was never a serious attempt in the Manchu era to invest British or western European capital in Xinjiang (1966, 311).

As explained above, by the 1880s, the czardom had consolidated its control of West Turkestan; more and more mass-produced modern products of industrialized societies started to enter East Turkestan from Russia and Russian CA. According to Millward, Russian and Western metal goods, fabrics, lamps, ceramics, watches, liquor, cigarettes, etc. were all much cheaper than their Chinese counterparts on Xinjiang markets—a fact reflected in the Russian-derived Uighur names for many modern Western products imported in the late nineteenth century: Millward furthermore denotes a number of these terms: lampa (oil lamp), sharpa (scarf), pilati (woman's Western-style dress), nefit (gasoline), and pechina (biscuit). The rouble apparently circulated freely in the bazaars of Kashgar. Also, Xinjiang exports (like previously, Mavarannahr exports) to Russia became more and more oriented toward Russian industrial demand. The large northwestern neighbor mainly imported raw materials from Xinjiang, including 60% of the cotton crop from Turfan, the largest cotton producing oasis in the Chinese frontier province. Some British and Indian goods competed with Russian-manufactured articles in southern Xinjiang, but Chinese manufactures do not seem to have been in the running (Millward 2007, 124, 157).

Glossary:	Some silk road textiles[a]
Batiste	A fine, often sheer fabric, constructed in either a plain or figured weave and made of any of various natural or synthetic fibers
Broadcloth	Closely woven fabric of cotton, silk, or a mixture of these, having a soft mercerized finish, used for shirts, dresses, etc.
Brocade	Fabric woven with an elaborate raised design, often using gold or silver thread
Calico	(a) A plain-woven cotton cloth printed with a figured pattern, usually on one side; (b) mottled or variegated in color; (c) having a variegated white, black, red, and cream coat
Carmania wool	Cashmere from goats
Cheese cloth	A lightweight cotton gauze of loose, open plain weave
Chintz	(a) A cotton fabric, usually glazed and often printed in bright patterns, used for apparel, draperies, slip covers, etc. (b) a painted or stained calico from India

(continued)

---

[226] "Unequal treaty" conditions, as the Chinese would argue, therefore continued with Russia.

Glossary:	Some silk road textiles[a]
Cochineal	A red dye prepared from dead bodies of female cochineal insects
Karbas	Finer cotton used for clothes or even maps
Indigo	Blue dye ($C_{16}H_{10}N_2O_2$), obtained from various plants, especially of the genus *Indigofera*, or manufactured synthetically
Mercerize	To treat (cotton yarns or fabric) with caustic alkali under tension, in order to increase strength, luster, and affinity for dye
Muslin	A plain-weave cotton fabric made in various degrees of fineness, used especially for sheets
Nasij	Golden brocade from the Middle East
Sash	A long band or scarf worn over one shoulder or around the waist, as a part of one's ensemble or uniform
Zandanichi	A sturdy and valuable cotton fabric woven in various colors (from Zand/Zandana near Bukhara)

[a]Source in most cases: Random House Websters' Concise College Dictionary (1999)

References

Abazov R (2008) The Palgrave concise historical atlas of CA. Palgrave MacMillan, New York

Abu-Lughod J (1989) Before European hegemony – the world system A.D. 1250–1350. Oxford University Press, New York

Adle C, Habib I, Baipakov K (eds) (2003a) UNESCO: History of civilizations of CA, vol V: Development in contrast: from the 16th to the mid-19th century

Adle C, Habib I, Baipakov K, Moosvi S, Tabyshalieva A (2003b) Social structure – nomadic societies. In: UNESCO: History of civilizations of CA, vol V

Adle C, Habib I, Baipakov K (2003c) Agriculture. In: UNESCO: history of civilizations of CA, vol 5

Ali A (1998) The Mughal Empire and its successors. In: UNESCO: History of civilizations of CA, vol V

Allworth E (ed) (1994) CA, 130 years of Russian dominance – a historical overview. Duke University Press, Durham, NC

Anderle A et al (ed) (1973) Weltgeschichte in Daten. VEB Deutscher Verlag der Wissenschaften

Annanepesov M (2003a) The Khanate of Khiva (Khwarazm). In: Adle C, Habib I, Baipakov K (eds) UNESCO: History of civilizations of CA, vol V

Annanepesov M (2003b) The Turkmens. In: UNESCO: History of civilizations of CA, vol V

Annanepesov M, Bababekov Kh (2003) The Khanates of Khiva and Khoqand. In: UNESCO: History of civilizations of CA, vol V

Artykbaev Z (2007) Istoria Kazakhstana. Tsentralno-Aziatskoe knizhnoe izdatelstvo, Kostanay

Ashrafyan K (1998) CA under Timur from 1370 to the early 15th century. In: UNESCO: History of civilizations in CA, vol IV

Bacon E (1966) C Asians under Russian rule – a study in culture change. Cornell University Press, Ithaca, NY

Baipakov K (2003) Handicrafts. In: The economy, production and trade. In: UNESCO: History of civilizations of CA, vol V

Baipakov K, Kumekov B (2003) The Kazakhs. In: UNESCO: History of civilizations of CA, vol V

Baipakov K, Kumekov B, Pischulina K (1997) Istoria Kazakhstana v srednie veka. Rauan, Almaty

Bairoch P (1985) De Jericho a Mexico – Villes et économie dans l'histoire. Gallimard, Paris

Bairoch P (1997) Victoires et déboires II – Histoire économique et sociale du monde du 16e siècle à nos jours. Gallimard, Paris

Barfield T (1989) The perilous frontier – nomadic empires and China 221 BCE to 1757 CE. Blackwell, Cambridge, MA

Barfield T (2010) Afghanistan – a cultural and political history. Princeton University Press, Princeton

Barfield T (2011) Nomadic pastoralism. In: Bentley (ed) The Oxford handbook of world history. Oxford University Press, Oxford

Barrat J, Ferro C, Wang C (2010) Géopolitique de l'Ouzbékistan. SPM, Paris

Beckert S (2014) Empire of cotton – a new history of global capitalism. Penguin Books, London

Bogdan H (1993) Histoire des peuples de l'ex-URSS – Du 9e siècle à nos jours. Perrin, Paris

Boucheron P (2012a) Soie, épices et porcelaine: Les routes de l'Eurasie. In: Petitjean P (ed) Inventer le monde – Une histoire globale du 15e siècle, nov-déc

Boucheron P (2012b) 1405: La mort de Tamerlan – Au centre effondré du monde. In: Petitjean P (ed) Inventer le monde – Une histoire globale du 15e siècle, nov-déc

Boulnois L (2008) Commerce et conquetes... sur les routes de la Soie. In: Testot L (ed) Histoire globale – Un nouveau regard sur le monde. Sciences Humaines, Auxerre

Boulnois L (2009) Les Routes de la soie – Aux origines de la mondialisation, Entretien avec Grataloup. Sciences Humaines, Auxerre

Bouvard G (1985) Au Kazakhstan soviétique – Chez les conquérants des Terres vierges et les pionniers de l'Espace. Editions du progrès, Moscou

Bradburd D (2001) The influence of pastoral nomad populations on the economy and society of post-Safavid Iran. In: Khazanov A, Wink A (eds) Nomads in the sedentary world. Routledge, London

Breghel Y (2003) An historical atlas of CA. In: di Cosmo N, Sinor D (eds) Handbook of oriental studies (Handbuch der Orientalistik), Section 8: Central Asian Studies. Brill, Leiden

Breghel Y (2009a) Uzbeks, Qazaqs and Turkmens. In: Di Cosmo, Frank, Golden (eds) The Cambridge history of inner Asia. Cambridge University Press, Cambridge

Breghel Y (2009b) The new Uzbek states: Bukhara, Khiva and Khoqand: c. 1750–1886. In: Di Cosmo, Frank, Golden (eds) The Cambridge history of inner Asia. Cambridge University Press, Cambridge

Burton A (1998a) The Bukharans – a dynastic, diplomatic and commercial history 1550–1702. St. Martin's Press, New York

Burton A (1998b) Marchands et négociants boukhares 1558–1920. In: Cahiers d'Asie centrale, no. 5–6

Burton A (2003) Trade. In: UNESCO: History of civilizations of CA, vol V

Chaliand G (1995) Les empires nomades—De la Mongolie au Danube (Ve-IVe siècles av. J.C., XVe-XVIe siècles ap. J.C.), Perrin

Chu Wen-Djang (1966) The Moslem rebellion in northwest China 1862–1878: a study of government minority policy. Mouton, The Hague

Chuvin P, Letolle R, Peyrouse S (2008) Histoire de l'Asie centrale contemporaine. Fayard, Paris

Clarke (2004) In the Eye of Power: China and Xinjiang from the Qing conquest to the 'New Great Game' for CA, 1759-2004. Doctoral theses, Griffith University, Brisbane

Conermann S (2006) Das Mogulreich – Geschichte und Kultur des muslimischen Indien. C.H. Beck, München

Dale S (1994) Indian merchants and Eurasian trade 1600–1750. Cambridge University Press, Cambridge

Darwin J (2008) After Tamerlane – the rise and fall of global empires 1400–2000. Penguin Books, London

Davidovich E (2003) Monetary policy and currency circulation under the Shaybanid and the Janid (Astarkhanid) dynasties. In: UNESCO: History of Civilizations of CA, vol V

Davidovich E, Dani A (1998) Coinage and the Monetary System. In: UNESCO: History of Civilizations in CA, vol IV

Dmitriev S (2009) Archéologie du Grand Jeu: Une brève histoire de l'Asie centrale. In: Piatigorsky J., Sapir J. (eds): Le Grand Jeu du XIX siècle – Les enjeux géopolitiques de l'Asie centrale, Autrement

Dmitriyev V, Yakerson S (2007) History and culture of Jewish people on the territory of Russia. Russian Ethnographic Museum, St. Petersburg

Donnert E, Anderle A, Gorski G (1981) UdSSR. In: Markov W et al (eds) Kleine Enzyklopädie Weltgeschichte, Band 2. VEB Bibliographisches Institut, Leipzig

Duby G (2011) Grand atlas historique – L'histoire du monde en 520 cartes. Larousse, Paris

Dubovitsky V, Bababekov K (2011) The Khoqand Khanate. In: Starr F (ed) Ferghana Valley – The Heart of CA. Sharpe, Armonk, NY

Engel J (ed) (1979) Großer Historischer Weltatlas – Zweiter Teil – Mittelalter. Bayerischer Schulbuch-Verlag, München

Eshraghi E (2003) Persia during the period of the Safavids, the Afshars and the early Qajars. In: UNESCO: History of Civilizations of CA, vol V

Fässler P (2007) Globalisierung – Ein historisches Kompendium. UTB Böhlau, Köln

Felber R, Peters H (1981) China. In: Markov W et al (eds) Kleine Enzyklopädie Weltgeschichte, Band 1. VEB Bibliographisches Institut, Leipzig

Feldbauer P, Liedl G (2008) Die islamische Welt 1000 bis 1517 – Wirtschaft, Gesellschaft, Staat. Mandelbaum, Wien

Feldbauer P, Liedl G (2009) 1250–1620: Archaische Globalisierung? In: Feldbauer P, Hödl G, Lehners J-P (eds) Rhythmen der Globalisierung. Mandelbaum, Wien

Ferret C (2013) Le pastoralisme nomade dans les steppes kazakhes. In: Stepanoff C, Ferret C, Lacaze G, Thorez J (eds) Nomadismes d'Asie centrale et septentrionale. Armand Colin, Paris

Findlay R, O'Rourke K (2007) Power and plenty – trade, war and the world economy in the second millennium. Princeton University Press, Princeton, NJ

Fragner B (2008) Die "Khanate": Eine zentralasiatische Kulturlandschaft vom 15. bis zum 19. Jhdt. In: Nolte H.-H. (ed) Zeitschrift für Weltgeschichte – Interdispziplinaere Perspektiven, 9. Jg

Fragner B, Kappeler A (eds) (2006) Zentralasien 13.-20. Jahrhundert – Geschichte und Gesellschaft. Promedia, Wien

Frank A (2009) The Qazaqs and Russia. In: Di Cosmo, Frank, Golden (eds) The Cambridge history of inner Asia. Cambridge University Press, Cambridge

Geiss PG (2003) Pre-tsarist and tsarist CA – communal commitment and political order in change. Routledge-Curzon, London

Geiss PG (2009) Mittelasien. In: Bohn T, Neutatz D (eds) Studienhandbuch Östliches Europa, Band 2: Geschichte des Russischen Reiches und der Sowjetunion. Böhlau, Wien

Gernet J (1972/1985) Le monde chinois – 3 volumes, Armand Colin. Volume 1: De l'âge de bronze au Moyen Age (2100 avant J.-C. – Xe siècle après J.-C.). Volume 2: L'époque moderne (Xe siècle – XIXe siècle)

Gilomen H-J (2014) Wirtschaftsgeschichte des Mittelalters. C.H. Beck, München

Göhrke C (2010) Russland: Eine Strukturgeschichte. Schoeningh, Paderborn

Golden P (2011) CA in world history. Oxford University Press, Oxford

Der Große Ploetz (2008) Die Enzyklopädie der Weltgeschichte, 35th edn. Vandenhoeck & Ruprecht, Göttingen

Grousset R (1965) L'empire des steppes – Attila, Genghis-Khan, Tamerlan. Payot, Paris von Gumppenberg M-C, Steinbach U (eds) (2004) Zentralasien: Geschichte – Politik – Wirtschaft – Ein Lexikon. C.H. Beck, München

Gunder Frank A (1992) The centrality of CA: Studies in history. VU University, Amsterdam

Gunder Frank A (2005) Von der Neuen Welt zum Reich der Mitte – Orientierung im Weltsystem. Promedia, Wien

Guseinov R (2004) Istoria mirovoy ekonomiki – Zapad, vostok, Rossia. Sibirskoe universitetskoe izdatelstvo, Novosibirsk

Habib I (2003a) Colonialism and CA. In: UNESCO: History of civilizations of CA, vol V

Habib I (2003b) Science and technology. In: UNESCO: History of civilizations of CA, vol V

Hambly G (ed) (1966) Fischer Weltgeschichte: Zentralasien (Band 16). Fischer Taschenbuch Verlag, Frankfurt, unaltered edition 1979

Haywood J (2011) The new atlas of world history – global events at a glance. Princeton University Press, Princeton

Hildermeier M (2013) Geschichte Russlands – Vom Mittelalter bis zur Oktoberrevolution. C.H. Beck, München

Hindess B, Hirst P (1975) Vorkapitalistische Produktionsweisen (Pre-capitalist modes of production). Ullstein, Frankfurt

Höllmann T (2004) Die Seidenstraße. C.H. Beck, München

Hofmeister U (2015) Zentralasien: Vom Zentrum der Seidenstrasse zum Hinterhof der Großmächte – und zurück? In: Grandner M, Sonderegger A (eds) Nord-Süd-Ost-West-Beziehungen – Eine Einführung in die Globalgeschichte. Mandelbaum, Wien

Hopkirk P (1990) The great game: the struggle for empire in CA. Kodansha America, Newport Beach, CA

Hussain Shah M (2003) Afghanistan. In: UNESCO: History of Civilizations of CA, vol V

Islam R, Bosworth C (1998) The Delhi Sultanate. In: UNESCO: History of civilizations in CA, vol IV

Jackson P (2005) The Mongols and the West 1221–1410. Pearson, Harlow

Jacquin P (2012) La politique indienne des Etats-Unis. In: L'Histoire (ed) L'aventure oubliée: Les indiens d'Amérique—Des Micmacs au Red Power, octobre

Kamev A (2005) Le Turkménistan. Karthala, Paris

Kang D (2010) East Asia before the west – five centuries of trade and tribute. Columbia University Press, New York, NY

Kappeler A (2001) Russland als Vielvölkerreich – Entstehung, Geschichte, Zerfall. C.H. Beck, München

Kappeler A (2006) Russlands zentralasiatische Kolonien bis 1917. In: Fragner B, Kappeler A (eds) Zentralasien 13.-20. Jhdt. Promedia, Wien

Kappeler A (2013) Die Kosaken. C.H. Beck, München

Karger A (ed) (1978) Fischer Länderkunde. Sowjetunion

Karpov S (2009) Economic and social effects of Italian trade in Tana/Azov 14th–15th centuries

Kauz R (2006) China und Zentralasien. In: Fragner B, Kappeler A (eds) Zentralasien 13.-20. Jahrhundert. Promedia, Wien

Kauz R (2009) Zerstörung, Eroberung, politische Umstrukturierung: Zentralasien. In: Ertl T, Limberger M (eds) Die Welt 1250–1500. Mandelbaum, Magnus, Wien

Khafizova K (2007) Kazakhskaya strategia Tsinskoy imperii. Institut ekonomicheskikh strategii – Tsentralnaya Azia

Khan I (2003) Inter-state relations (ca. 1500–1850). In: UNESCO: History of civilizations of CA, vol V

Khazanov A (1983) Nomads and the outside world. University of Wisconsin, Madison

Khodarkovsky M (1992) Where two worlds met: the Russian state and the Kalmyk nomads, 1600–1771. Cornell University Press, Ithaca, NY

Khodarkovsky M (2002) Russia's Steppe Frontier: the making of a Colonial empire 1500–1800. Indiana University Press, Bloomington

Kindler R (2014) Stalins Nomaden – Herrschaft und Hunger in Kasachstan. Hamburger Edition, Hamburg

Kircheisen I (1981) Afghanistan. In: Kleine Enzyklopädie Weltgeschichte, Band 1, VEB Bibliographisches Institut Leipzig

Krieger M (2003) Geschichte Asiens – Eine Einführung. Böhlau, Köln

Lary D (2012) Chinese migrations – the movement of people, goods and ideas over four millennia. Rowman & Littlefield, Lanham, MD

Ledonne J (2008) Russia's eastern theater, 1650–1850: Springboard or strategic backyard? In: Cahiers du monde russe, janv-mars 2008 (EHESS)

Linska M, Handel A, Rasuly-Paleczek G (2003) Einführung in die Ethnologie Zentralasiens (Vorlesungsskriptum). Universität Wien, Vienna

Ma D (2003) Tarim Basin. In: UNESCO: History of civilizations of CA, vol V

Maddison A (1998) L'économie chinoise – une perspective historique. OCDE, Paris

Maddison A (2007) Contours of the world economy 1–2030 A.D., Essays in macroeconomic history. OECD, Paris

Marchand P (2014) Géopolitique de la Russie – Une nouvelle puissance en Eurasie. Presses universitaires de France, Paris

Martinez A (2009) Institutional development, revenues and trade. In: Cosmo, Frank, Golden (eds) The Cambridge history of inner Asia – the Chinggisid age. Cambridge University Press, Cambridge

Masanov N (2003) Pastoral production. In: Production – Northern areas (Transoxania and the Steppes). In: UNESCO: History of civilizations of CA, vol V

Mayhew B (2010) Central Asia highlights: history. In: Mayhew B, Bloom G, Clammer P, Kohn M, Noble J (ed) Lonely planet guide: Central Asia, 5th edn. Lonely Planet Publications, Oakland, pp 34–61

Millward J (2007) Eurasian crossroads – a history of Xinjiang. Columbia University, New York

Millward J (2013) The silk road – a very short introduction. Oxford University Press, Oxford

Millward J, Perdue P (2004) Political and cultural history through the late 19th century. In: Starr F (ed) Xinjiang – China's muslim borderland. Sharpe, Armonk, NY

Miyawaki J, Cuigin B, Kyzlasov L (2003) The Dzungars and the Torguts (Kalmuks), and the peoples of southern Siberia. In: UNESCO: History of Civilizations of CA, vol V

Mokyr J (2003) CA. In: Mokyr J (ed) The Oxford encyclopedia of economic history. Oxford University Press, Oxford

Moosvi S (2003a) The Monetary System in Safavid Persia. In: UNESCO: History of civilizations of CA, vol V

Moosvi S (2003b) Southern CA. In: UNESCO: History of civilizations of CA, vol V

Mourre (1996) Dictionnaire encyclopédique d'histoire. Bordas, Paris

Mourre (ed) (2003) Le Petit Mourre – Dictionnaire de l'histoire. Bordas, Paris

Mukhtarov A (2003) The Manghits. In: UNESCO: History of civilizations of CA, vol V

Mukminova R (1996) Les routes caravanières entre villes de l'Inde et de l'Asie centrale: Déplacements des artisans et circulation des articles artisanaux. In: Cahiers d'Asie centrale

Mukminova R (1998) The Timurid states in the 15th and 16th centuries. In: UNESCO: History of civilizations of CA, vol IV

Mukminova R (2003) The Janids (Astarkhanids). In: UNESCO: History of civilizations of CA, vol V

Mukminova R, Mukhtarov A (2003) The Khanate (Emirate) of Bukhara. In: UNESCO: History of civilizations of CA, vol V

Nolte H-H (1991) Russland UdSSR – Geschichte, Politik, Wirtschaft. Fackelträger, Hannover

Nolte H-H (2005) Weltgeschichte – Imperien, Religionen und Systeme – 15. bis 19. Jahrhundert. Böhlau, Vienna

Odyssey Maps (2007/2011) The Ancient Silk Road – an illustrated map featuring the ancient network of routes between China and Europe

Ohayon I (2013) Temps coloniaux de la sédentarisation dans les steppes kazakhs. In: Stepanoff C, Ferret C, Lacaze G, Thorez J (eds) Nomadismes d'Asie centrale et septentrionale. Armand Colin, Paris

O'Rourke S (2007) The cossaks. Manchester University Press, Manchester

Oskolkov V, Oskolkova I (2004) Istoria Kazakhstana (Spravochnik). Oner Baspasy

Osterhammel J (2009) Die Verwandlung der Welt – Eine Geschichte des 19. Jhdts. C.H. Beck, München

Osterhammel J, Petersson N (2003) Geschichte der Globalisierung – Dimensionen, Prozesse, Epochen. C.H. Beck, München

Ott H, Schäfer H (eds) (1984) Wirtschaftsploetz—Wirtschaftsgeschichte zum Nachschlagen, Ploetz

Overy R (ed) (2004) The times complete history of the world – the ultimate work of historical reference (6th edn)

Paul J (2012) Neue Fischer Weltgeschichte: Zentralasien (Band 10), S. Fischer Verlag, Frankfurt

Perdue P (2005) China marches west – the Qing conquest of central Eurasia. Harvard University, Cambridge, MA

Perdue P (2011) East Asia and Central Eurasia. In: Bentley (ed) The Oxford handbook of world history. Oxford University Press, Oxford

Pernau M (2011) Transnationale Geschichte. Vandenhoeck & Ruprecht, Göttingen

Petric B-M (2002) Pouvoir, don et réseaux en Ouzbékistan post-soviétique. Presses universitaires de France, Paris

Peyrouse S (2007) Turkménistan – Un destin au carrefour des empires. Belin – La documentation française, Paris

Pirumshoev H, Dani A (2003) The Pamir, Badakhshan and the trans-Pamir states. In: UNESCO: History of civilizations of CA, vol V

Ponting G (2001) World history – a new perspective. Pimlico, London

Poujol C (2000) Le Kazakhstan (Que sais-je?). Presses Universitaires de France, Paris

Poujol C (2008) Ouzbékistan – la croisée des chemins. Belin – La documentation française, Paris

Poujol C, Fourniau V (2005) Trade and the economy (Second half of 19th century to early 20th century). In: UNESCO: History of civilizations of CA, vol 6

Random House (1999) Random house Webster's concise college dictionary. Random House Rey-Debove, New York

Reinhard W (2008) Kleine Geschichte des Kolonialismus. Kroener, Stuttgart

Rossabi M (1990) The "Decline" of C Asian Caravan Trade. In: Tracy J (ed) The rise of merchant empires: long-distance trade in the early modern world 1350–1750. Cambridge University Press, Cambridge

Rostkowski (2012) La longue marche des droits. In: L'Histoire (ed) L'aventure oubliée: Les indiens d'Amérique—Des Micmacs au Red Power, octobre

Rothermund D (1985) Indiens wirtschaftliche Entwicklung – Von der Kolonialherrschaft bis zur Gegenwart. UTB Schoeningh, Paderborn

Roudik P (2007) The history of the C Asian republics. Greenwood Press, Westport

Roux J-P (1991) Tamerlan. Fayard, Paris

Roux J-P (1997) L'Asie centrale – Histoire et civilisation. Fayard, Paris

Rtveladze E (2003) Eastern and Northern CA (1750 to 1850). In: UNESCO: History of civilizations in CA, vol V

Scheck W (1977) Geschichte Russlands – Von der Frühgeschichte bis zur Sowjetunion. Heyne, München

Schwarz F (2000) Unser Weg schließt tausend Wege ein. Klaus Schwarz Verlag, Berlin

Schwarz F (2004) Migration in vor-sowjetischer Zeit. In: von Gumppenberg M-C, Steinbach U (eds) Zentralasien: Geschichte – Politik – Wirtschaft – Ein Lexikon. C.H. Beck, Munich

Sellier J, Sellier A (1993/2002) Atlas des peuples d'orient—Moyen-orient, Caucase, Asie centrale, La découverte

Shukow I et al (eds) (1955-1968) Weltgeschichte in zehn Bänden (Vsemirnaya istoria v desiat tomakh), Bände 2 – 6 (Band 2 1956/62, Band 3 1957/63, Band 4 1958/64, Band 5 1958/66, Band 6 1959/69). VEB Deutscher Verlag der Wissenschaften

Soucek S (2000) A history of inner Asia. Cambridge University Press, Cambridge

Stanziani A (2012) Bâtisseurs d'empires – Russie, Chine et Inde à la croisée des mondes, XV-XIX siècles. Seuil

Stanziani A (2015) After oriental despotism – Eurasian growth in a global perspective. Bloomsbury, London

Suret-Canale J (1996) Panorama de l'histoire mondiale – De la conquête du feu à la révolution informatique. Marabout, Alleur

Szczepanski K (2017) Zheng He's Treasure Ships, Asian History

Tchoroev T (Chorotegin) (2003) The Kyrgyz. In: UNESCO: History of civilizations of CA, vol V

Töpfer B et al (1985) Allgemeine Geschichte des Mittelalters. VEB Deutscher Verlag der Wissenschaften, Berlin

Treue W (1973) Wirtschaftsgeschichte der Neuzeit, Band I: 18. und 19. Jhdt. Kroener, Stuttgart

Tröbst S (2009) Wirtschaft. In: Bohn T, Neutatz D (eds) Studienhandbuch Östliches Europa Band 2: Geschichte des Russischen Reiches und der Sowjetunion. Böhlau, Wien

Uray-Köhalmi K (2002) CA: Endspiel der großen Nomadenreiche. In: Edelmayer F, Feldbauer P, Wakounig M (eds) Globalgeschichte 1450–1620 – Anfänge und Perspektiven. Promedia, Wien

Vries P (2007) Rezension zu Nolte 2005: Weltgeschichte – Imperien, Religionen und Systeme – 15. bis 19. Jahrhundert (rez. für geschichte.transnational und H-Soz-Kult)

Walter R (2006) Geschichte der Weltwirtschaft – Eine Einführung. UTB Böhlau, Köln

Waugh D (2002) The Origins of the Silk Road. University of Washington Lecture Series

Wendt R (2007) Vom Kolonialismus zur Globalisierung – Europa und die Welt seit 1500. UTB Schoeningh, Paderborn

Westermann (ed) (1997) Großer Atlas zur Weltgeschichte. Westermann, Braunschweig

Wild D (1992) The silk road. University of California, Irvine

Wink A (2001) India and the Turko-Mongol Frontier. In: Khazanov A, Wink A (eds) Nomads in the sedentary world. Routledge, London

Wittfogel K (1964) Le despotisme oriental – Etude comparative du pouvoir total. Les Éditions de Minuit, Paris

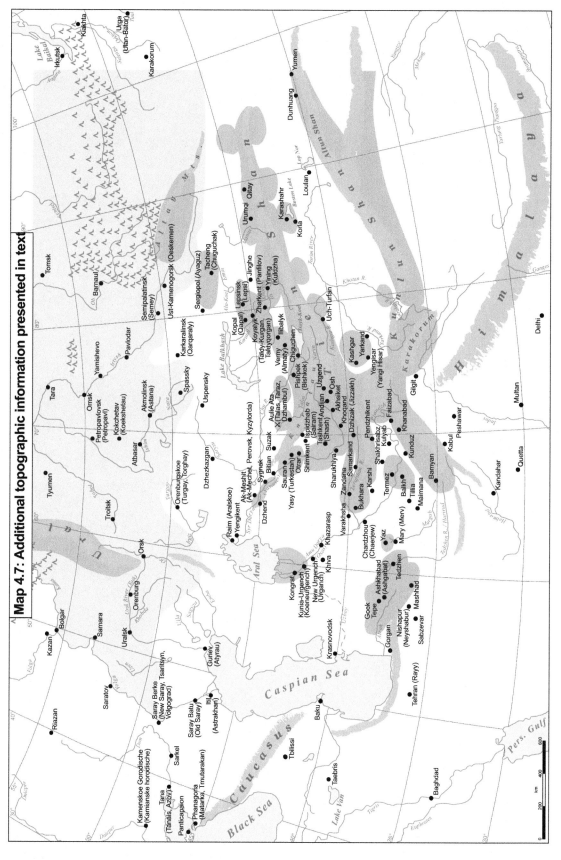

Map 4.7 Additional topographic information presented in text

In the following, the reader can find a concluding overview of some traits of the region, of its economic history that is subject of this work, and of the network of overland trade routes that are a key component of that economic history. This is a synthetic study covering existing historic literature from an economic perspective. The time span analyzed is lengthy and stretches back beyond the beginnings of antiquity, because the phenomenon of horseback nomadism and its decisive impact on C Asian, SR, and partly also European history up to the eighteenth century needs to be sufficiently captured. The wealth of material consulted and the several millennia of economic history surveyed enable the author to arrive at some new conclusions or interpretations regarding the causes and the periodization of the ups and downs of economic prosperity across CA and the SR.

5.1 CA: A Unique Global Region of Historic Nomadic-Sedentary Interaction

Borders and Location of CA: The Heart of the Eurasian Double-Continent

Among various definitions of CA, one can distinguish physico-geographic and politico-cultural definitions. The geographer Ferdinand von Richthofen toward the end of the nineteenth century defined the region as a vast intracontinental area lacking water drainage toward the oceans. This area also includes parts of Eastern Europe. The currently most often used politico-cultural definition limits itself to the joint territory of the five former Soviet republics of Kazakhstan, Kyrgyzstan (the Kyrgyz Republic), Tajikistan, Turkmenistan (Turkmenia), and Uzbekistan, which are independent countries today. They also tend to be jointly called the "Stans," or West Turkestan (an older definition). A somewhat larger, also frequently used, definition of CA

adds to the five "Stans" the Chinese autonomous province of Xinjiang, also called East Turkestan.

For the purposes of this study, this latter definition (Kazakhstan, Kyrgyzstan, Tajikistan, Turkmenistan, Uzbekistan, Xinjiang) is chosen. This is done for historico-economic reasons, as it is felt that too narrow a focus—e.g., only comprising the five former C Asian Soviet republics—would be too exclusively oriented toward the present and the most recent past and would not sufficiently take into account historical relationships as well as an open future. For instance, Silk Road connections were of eminent importance on both sides of the Tienshan and the Altai ranges (i.e., in West as well as East Turkestan) for many centuries.

Geographic Zones of CA: Steppe Belt, Deserts, Oasis Belt, Mountains

Given its scarcity of water and its intracontinental location cut off by mountainous barriers to the South from warm humid winds from the Indian Ocean, CA is characterized by an extreme continental climate as well as aridity that increases from north to south and from mountains to plains. Based on topography and vegetation, CA can be subdivided into four main regions running broadly in an east-west direction: the steppe belt (Eurasian grasslands, Kazakh steppe) in the north, followed by the desert zone further south, then the oasis belt, and the mountain region (Hindu Kush, Karakorum, a.o.) at the southern limits. There is, however, one succession of mountain chains that cuts through CA from the southwest to the northeast: the abovementioned Tienshan, Altai, and other ranges. The oasis zone stretches along the foot of the mountain ranges (featuring fertile loess lands) and along the riverbeds. Among the most important oases, one can cite Khorezm (Khwarazm), Mary (historic: Merv, Margiana), Bukhara-Samarkand (historic: Sogdiana or Transoxiana, Mavarannahr), Tashkent (historic: Shash), the Ferghana Basin, Yining (Kuldzha), Urumqi, Turfan, and Kashgar-Yarkand.

Some Natural Resources of the Region: Chernozem, Pasturelands, Fertile Oases, Oil, Gas, Metals

Depending on the amount of precipitation declining from north to south, the steppe zone can boast an abundance of both arable land and pastures. The northern grasslands with their fertile chernozem (black earth) are well suited to the cultivation of various cereals and sunflowers. Extensive pasturelands have provided an excellent ground for raising horses, sheep, camels, goats, and cows. Further south, beyond the deserts, the fertile oases have helped sustain flourishing cultivation of silk, cotton, tobacco, vegetables, peaches, melons, wine, and even rice. Large parts of West as well as East Turkestan bear oil and gas deposits. The Kazakh steppe stores large quantities of coal, copper, and iron ore. Extraction sites of precious metals, including gold, "sprinkle" the Tienshan. The highest ranges of CA (including the Karakorum) harbor deposits of jade stones.

The C Asian Steppe Belt: The Cradle of Horseback Nomadism, Far-Reaching Mobility, and Military Prowess

The invention of bronze (Bronze Age, from about 1800 BCE) facilitated the domestication of the horse on the Eurasian grasslands. The introduction of ferrous metallurgy (Iron Age, from around 900 BCE) contributed to a decisive breakthrough: the emergence of horseback nomadism. This multiplied steppe dwellers' mobility across large territories and qualitatively strengthened their military capabilities. Thus, the phenomenon of mounted warrior nomadism emerged, which had a major economic and political impact on developments in CA and far beyond for a long time.

CA as a Unique Terrain of Sedentary-Nomadic Interaction and of Related Economic and Political Dualism

Probably no other region's history was so much molded by interaction (cooperation, competition, and conflict) of sedentary and nomadic civilizations as CA's. The extent of this interaction is partly explained by the spatial size of the Eurasian steppe belt (extending from Eastern Europe to Mongolia and traditionally inhabited by pastoral nomads) and of the C Asian oasis belt (stretching from Persia to China and constituting a focus of traditional farming and urban settled cultures). Steppe dwellers' animal husbandry usually focused on sheep, horses, goats, cattle, and camels. Apart from the main product, meat, breeding yielded leather, hides, pelts, wool, and other products. Auxiliary crafts and agriculture played a role. Traditional oasis farmers cultivated wheat, barley, millet, cotton, and rice. Silkworm breeding, vegetable growing, the cultivation of fruit, and viniculture were important. Numerous different types of crafts were exercised, and highly developed commerce and quasi-banking activities were practiced in oases.

Therefore it is not difficult to identify a typical Eurasian type of economic and political dualism. Depending on various factors, including technological, social, and climatic ones, the "nomadic frontier" or nomadic-sedentary cultural and economic boundary moved north or south or at least was influenced in one way or the other. At the same time, this boundary was not a sharp demarcation line but most often embodied various transitional stages (seminomadic ways of life) between settled farming (and urban craft professions and trade) and mobile pastoralism.

Technologically Based Nomadic Military Supremacy Lasted Almost 2½ Millennia: Up to the Eighteenth Century

CA was the global region ruled by nomads most intensively and for the longest time—from around the seventh century BCE (when Scyths had carried out their first major incursions into the oases of CA, the Near and Middle East) to the mid-eighteenth century CE (when the last major steppe state, Grand Tartary or the Dzungar Empire, was wiped out by the Chinese military). This is almost two and a half millennia. Beyond CA, large parts of the Eurasian double continent were repeatedly ruled by or under military pressure from nomadic powers or empires. The establishment of nomadic hegemony was due to a technological breakthrough: the emergence of horseback nomadism and the invention and refinement of mounted archery (incl. the metallic stirrup, the saber and the composite bow). For a long stretch of time, sedentary cultures and states did not have the means to match nomads' military capacity—with far-reaching implications and consequences for economic history. This does not mean that well-organized sedentary powers could not defend themselves and even temporarily and at high costs gain the upper hand in some parts of CA (Persian Empire, Empire of Alexander, Han and Tang China, Samanids). The loss of nomadic hegemony equally owed to a technological breakthrough: the invention and adoption by settled cultures of firearms and artillery. The tables had definitely turned in the eighteenth century in favor of sedentary civilizations' military superiority.

Eurasian Steppe Civilization: Seamlessly Linking CA and Eastern Europe

Looking at the transcontinental stretch of the Eurasian grasslands, similar to the practice of including Mongolia in some definitions of CA, one could also argue on historic grounds that the eastern European steppes, including the whole of southern Ukraine, Crimea, and reaching all the way to the Carpathians, actually extended the C Asian geoeconomic and geopolitical sphere westward. The wide-open passage (between the southern Ural mountains and the Caspian Sea) provided a "peoples' gateway" (Hassinger) from Asia to Europe, through which Scyths, Alans, Huns,

Avars, Magyars, Pechenegs, Kipchaks, Mongols, Tamerlane and his mounted warriors, and others penetrated Europe. Arguably, the eastern European steppes, which in any case constitute the geographic prolongation of the C Asian grasslands beyond the Ural and Volga rivers, in pre-modern times belonged to CA in an institutional, in a cultural, and even in an ethnic sense—at least up to the sixteenth century, when the Czardom of Muscovy annexed the lower Volga lands and the Khanate of Astrakhan. This perspective has been carefully noted but not principally followed here, because it is felt that fundamental geographic conventions should take precedence.

No Other Region Can Call as Many Major Civilizations Its Neighbors: No Other Region Can Boast of as Complex a Political History as CA

No other region is surrounded by and situated at the crossroads of as many world civilizations as CA: Central and Eastern Europe/Russia, the Middle East/Iran, South Asia/India, and East Asia/China. Given the Eurasian grasslands' immense traditional nomadic habitat providing room for a multitude of quickly rising and declining polities (whose borders were usually in flux), and given the equally numerous and distinct settled civilizations that surrounded and interacted with the mobile cultures of the region, it is not difficult to infer that CA or the heart of Eurasia probably features the most complicated or complex political history of any region of the globe.

5.2   The SR: A Transcontinental Trade Network for Almost 2000 Years Featuring Three Heydays

Nomadic Powers Tended to be Materially Interested in the Good Functioning of International Trade Networks

Due to their traditional military edge and to the particular spatial dimension of their polities (given their mobile existence), the nomads often not only ruled over sedentary cultures but also controlled key overland trade and communication routes across Eurasia (sections of the SR). Rulers of these steppe states or empires levied taxes and tributes from inhabitants of settled areas and tolls from merchants traveling the SR. In case of resistance, if deemed necessary, booty was exacted through razzias (armed incursions, raids, pillaging campaigns). Since the Eurasian nomads themselves were not always adept at trading, they employed or cooperated with specialized traders and businessmen, e.g., Sogdians, Uighurs, and Bukharans (see below). Given their

revenue interest, nomads were generally interested in upholding peace, law and order, and in providing or safeguarding elementary infrastructure (functioning roads, bridges, fords, resting places, relay stations, caravanserais, security patrols) along the trade routes (parts of the SR) under their control.

The SR Was a Network of Overland Trade Routes Running Through CA that Provided Commercial and Cultural Exchange Between Europe, CA, India, and China

While there are disagreements on when exactly the Great Silk Road emerged and when it ended, most authors agree that it already existed in Roman times and that it still existed in the Mongol era. In the author's view, the (premodern) SR functioned from about 100 BCE to around 1850 CE. It was "inaugurated" through the official launching of Chinese commercial activities with the country's western Eurasian neighbors. The SR expired upon the European (Russian) conquest and colonization of large parts of CA and their inclusion as raw material suppliers into the capitalist industrial world economy.

The network of overland routes originally focused on the oasis belt and links to Mesopotamia and the Levant. Over the centuries, there was a tendency to integrate connections and areas lying further north—in the Eurasian steppe belt—into the network. This goes, e.g., for the "steppe route" leading from CA north of the Caspian to the shores of the Black Sea and Crimea. The political factor, i.e., whether political stability reigned in a territory crossed by the SR, turned out to be one of the most important determinants of the location of travel itineraries across Eurasia. The spatial extension of the SR network was largest during the Mongol era. Thereafter it partly receded and was partly bypassed by increasingly important maritime routes (Western seaborne competition) and land routes (Russian Siberian route) to China and/or India.

The SR Is Estimated to Have Existed for Almost Two Millennia—Up to the Nineteenth Century—and to Have Enjoyed at Least Three Heydays

(a) Han dynasty, Roman Empire (ca. 100 BCE–ca. 200 CE)
(b) Tang dynasty, Caliphate (ca. 675–875 CE)
(c) Mongol Empire (ca. 1245–1335)

Preceding the first heyday, there may have been an ancient precursor to the SR: The Xiongnu Empire had reexported Chinese luxury goods west. The first heyday of the SR was initiated by the Middle Kingdom for geopolitical, not primarily for economic, reasons. This period featured political stability and simultaneous flourishing of all four empires

Table 5.1 Heydays of the Silk Road and its predecessors (main points)

Period[a]	Overland trade development in CA
200–105 BCE	*"Ancient precursor" to the SR* Reexport of Chinese luxury goods through Xiongnu Empire (tribute trade)
105 BCE–200 CE	***First heyday of Silk Road*** Han dynasty, Kushan state, Parthian Empire, Roman Empire Transcontinental demand for Chinese silk
675–875 CE	***Second heyday of Silk Road*** Tang dynasty, Caliphate, Khazaria Political consolidation of new SR empires
925–1000	*Post-Caliphate temporary recovery of SR* Political re-stabilization, Samanid Empire as east-west trade hub, "Islamic renaissance"
1245–1345	***Third heyday of the Silk Road*** Mongol Empire (Yuan dynasty, Chagatay Khanate, Il-khanate, Golden Horde) SR security upheld (and trade initially subsidized) on a bicontinental politically integrated playing field; Pax Mongolica
1575–1625	*"Mercantilist" renaissance of SR trade* Simultaneous rule of strong political leaders who carried out economic reforms and largely maintained peace: Khanate of Bukhara, Chagatay Khanate, Mughal India, Kazakhs, Muscovite Russia, Safavid Persia
1775–1825	*"Last glimmer" of the SR* Lease of life for what remained of traditional trade in landlocked, newly isolated C Asian space difficult to access for modern European shipping technologies: Bukhara, Khiva, Khoqand, Kazakhs, parts of Russia and China; Pax Sinica

For the entire time span, also including downswings and more details, see Table 3.1
[a]Approximate indications

along the Eurasian trade network (Han China, Kushan state, Parthia, and Roman Empire). The second heyday was characterized by the political consolidation and economic stabilization of three new SR empires (Tang dynasty, Caliphate, Khazaria). During the third heyday, the Mongol Empire controlled practically the entire bicontinental network. SR security was upheld, and trade was initially even subsidized in a vast politically integrated playing field. Under the Pax Mongolica, it took around 8 to 10 months to reach Beijing from Crimea. This was somewhat quicker than the year it had approximately taken travelers to cross Eurasia in antiquity and the early Middle Ages.

Between the above peaks, there were periods of weakness, which included the outbreak of political instability along the SR, climate change, the resurgence of nomadic military pressure from the Eurasian steppe, Barbarian invasions, and the splintering of the Islamic polity (the Caliphate). The four centuries between the second and the third heyday included a post-Caliphate temporary recovery in the tenth century (political re-stabilization, Samanid Empire as an east-west trade hub), followed by a renewed receding of activities in the eleventh and twelfth centuries (repeated invasions by Turko-Mongol dynasties).

For more than 400 years, there was a period of post-Mongol decline of the SR (from the fifteenth to the mid-nineteenth centuries), accelerated by rising Western maritime competition, a tendency of increasing internecine warfare, and spreading religious dogmatism. This did not correspond to a continuous loss of importance, although there were some ups and downs here too: Two

relatively short-lived recoveries of SR trade and exchange interrupted the overall decline. These temporary recoveries were the mercantilist renaissance of overland trade (simultaneous rule of strong leaders who maintained peace and carried out economic reforms) in the late sixteenth and the early seventeenth centuries (in Bukhara, the Chagatay Khanate, India, the Kazakh Khanate, Russia, and Persia) and the "last glimmer" of the SR (as a relatively isolated and backward trading space and partly benefiting from the Pax Sinica) in the late eighteenth and early nineteenth centuries (i.a. "the Khanates"—Bukhara, Khiva, and Khoqand) (Table 5.1).

Transcontinental Political Stability May Have Been the Most Important Factor Favoring SR Activity

Factors supporting heydays of the SR:

– Political stability/simultaneous political stabilization in states straddling most or all of the Eurasian trade network.

– Successful economic reforms (e.g., fiscal, monetary, or structural reforms which, however, could not be effectively implemented without political stability).

– Investments in SR infrastructure (caravanserais, bazaars, bridges, relay stations, policing, etc.).

– In extreme cases, political unification of (large parts of the) SR network (e.g., Mongol Empire, Tamerlane) = (partial or total) economic unification (fewer border controls, fewer inspections and tolls, greater mobility of merchants, lower costs of trade).

– Climate change: warming up (may have facilitated, e.g., the second heyday of SR).
– Tendencies toward religious unification (spread of Islam and its social rules of behavior add to economic cohesion across CA).
– Spillovers of Western silver flows from America onto the SR in the second half of the sixteenth and the early seventeenth century; Europeans used a substantial share of these flows to pay for coveted Chinese goods (silk and silkware, tea, china, lacquer, etc.).
– Network of enterprising merchants prepared to take risks and get trade going (see below).

Spreading Political Instability and Warfare Most Often Caused Declines of SR Activity, and Rising Western Maritime Competition Relentlessly Eroded the Overland Network

Factors triggering downturns of the SR:
– Political instability/de-stabilization, turmoil, and warfare.
– Unraveling or lack of economic reforms, more frequent bouts of hyperinflation, and debasements of currencies.
– Possible vicious circle between political instability and loss of SR revenues: unrest/turmoil leads to decline of SR traffic, which leads to decline of revenues of SR tolls and taxes; this loss of funds available to rulers reduces money for policing the trade routes and/or triggers search for new funds, e.g., by extorting resources from neighbors which both gives rise to more instability, which in turn depresses SR revenues further; moreover, less revenue inflow can also directly reduce rulers' interest in upholding SR security.
– Climate change: increasing aridity (may have contributed, e.g., to the decline of SR after its first heyday and to setting the stage for the Mongol "breakout" from ancestral lands).
– Religious differences and conflict at borders of CA (Sunnis-Shiites), increasing religious dogmatism from the eleventh century, conventionalism, even fanaticism, and lack of curiosity.
– Diseases/pandemics spread by the SR, notably "Black Death"/bubonic plague (mid-fourteenth century).
– Rising Western maritime competition circumventing CA and the SR (Vasco da Gama reached India, D'Andrade reached China by sea) from the early sixteenth century.
– Emergence of Siberian route/Russia (from the late seventeenth century), equally bypassing the SR.
– Final point: conquest of most of CA and its trade network by Russia, termination of traditional SR exchanges and transformation of the region's economy by industrial capitalism to fulfilling role of specialized raw material supplier (cotton, livestock, grain).

Silk, Horses, and Other Goods Traded in Large Quantities, China, and Other Key Exporters on the SR
Exorbitant transport costs meant that only goods with very high value-to-weight ratios such as silk, horses, spices, glass, furs, gems, and slaves would be carried over long distances for profit. Over the centuries, regional markets for lower-cost bulkier goods like grain, olive oil, other preserved foodstuffs, livestock, ferrous metals and metalware, wax, and lumber expanded. During antiquity and well into the Middle Ages, silk (or bolts of silk, most often Chinese) was so popular as merchandise that it also served as a de facto means of payment. From the late sixteenth century, silver (whether minted or in bullion form) also attained importance as a medium of exchange. While silk, horses, spices, and slaves gradually lost importance in SR commerce over time (due to rising competition in product markets, via alternate trade routes, and on the technological front), they remained significant as commercial articles (almost) until the demise of the traditional Eurasian trade network.
Overview of principal exported products of key players/regions of the SR[1]:
East (China, India): silk and silk textiles, satin, brocades, dyes, ivory products, porcelain (china), lacquerware, tea, spices, rice, ceramics, precious handicrafts, pearls, corals, rhubarb, medicinal plants, and tobacco
CA (Transoxiana, Persia, Chagatay Khanate, Dzungars, Kazakhs, Uzbeks, a.o.): cavalry and race horses, camels, livestock, cotton, cotton cloth, sheepskin, slaves, carpets, rugs, archery weapons, saddlery, jade, glass, paper, dried fruit, silk, and caviar
West (Roman Empire, Western Europe, Russia): gold, silver, fine cloth, textiles, apparel, glass and glassware, furs, leather, grain, wood, amber, metalware, and manufactured products

From the Sogdians via the Uighurs to the Bukharans: On Some of the Renowned C Asian Traders and Their Networks
With CA located at the geographical center and constituting the traditional hub of the SR network, it is not surprising that various groups of C Asian merchants over time played pivotal roles in Eurasian trade and business. Practically all of these merchants were sedentary businessmen, not nomads. Given the logistical and strategic importance of the trade and communication network for many states and empires straddling the SR, it is also not surprising that respective authorities often invested in appropriate infrastructure and granted privileges to attract traders, while at the same time trying to benefit from taxing hoped for

---

[1] Given the long life of the SR, the importance of mentioned commercial articles for exporting regions of course varied much over time.

flourishing trade. (In contrast, relatively immobile peasants and other local social strata were typically at the fiscal mercy of rulers and tended to be heavily exploited.)

Depending on the times and places, Sogdians, Indians, Armenians, Khorezmians, Arabs, Turks, Uighurs, Persians, Chinese, Bukharans, Tatars, and less frequently, Italians (Genoese and Venetians), Jews, Greeks, and Russians traveled on the routes and traded in the markets of CA.

Three groups of C Asian traders are particularly often mentioned: Sogdians, Uighurs, and Bukharans. The Sogdians (sedentary eastern Iranians originating from the oases of Sogdiana/Transoxiana) played a pivotal role in SR trade from the first century BCE to the ninth century CE. They were active in the Kushan state, under the Han dynasty, in the Hephthalite confederacy, under Turkic oversight (as commercial agents of the Turkic Empire), and under the Tang dynasty. The Uighurs contributed to shaping trade from the ninth to the sixteenth centuries CE (Kingdom of Qocho, Uighur city-states and Mongol Empire, Chagatay Khanate). The "Bukharans" (originally from the Khanate of Bukhara, but soon spreading their networks to Altishahr/Kashgaria and other regions) were outstanding traders from the sixteenth to the nineteenth centuries (heads of Dzungar trading missions, Ming and Qing dynasties, Russia, India). In the second half of the nineteenth century, Bukharan Jews are reported to have at times monopolized C Asian cotton exports to Russia and Britain.

5.3   CA's Political/Mercantile Centrality in Eurasia up to the Fifteenth Century, Followed by Lengthy Decline

Nomadic Imperial "Law and Order" Was Not Generally Accompanied by "Rule of Law," Which Rendered Long-Term Investment Difficult

While the vast, quasi-borderless economic space under Mongol rule was generally well policed, sustainable capital accumulation based on SR trade and other market-oriented economic activities did not materialize within the multinational empire, but outside, e.g., in the Italian city-states of Genoa and Venice, which were prime participants in Eurasian trade. While "law and order" (i.e., elementary security) had been well achieved on Mongol territories, which facilitated or favored (short-term) trading activities, the imperial authorities—in contrast to the governing bodies of the Italian city-states—had not established a semblance of "rule of law" in a modern sense (i.e., a predictable framework of rules also respected by the authorities themselves), which would have accommodated (long-term) investment activities.

This supports the notion that "perfect safety" of the land route from Crimea to Beijing, as the Florentine businessman Pegolotti had perceived it in the 1330s, was not sufficient for creating an investment climate conducive to economic growth. Notwithstanding the huge size of the empire's market, product specialization and manufacturing innovations tended to gain more momentum outside than inside the sphere of Mongol control. This association of strict "law and order" with inadequate "rule of law" also held for other nomadic empires like that of Timur, the Turk Khaganate, and Grand Tartary/the Dzungar Empire. Probably for these rulers and authorities, in case of doubt, short-term unfettered access to and command over a large pool of resources primed a system which would have restrained rulers' immediate access but, over time, promoted the growth of earnings and assets which to tax.

CA as a Geopolitical or Geoeconomic Focal Region of Eurasia up to the Fifteenth Century, Followed by Prolonged Decline

At least during the three abovementioned heydays of international trade and up to the fifteenth century (Tamerlane, Timurid emirates), one can speak of CA's political and/or commercial centrality within the world known until then. CA, notably its historic regions Transoxiana/Mavarannahr (with the cities Samarkand and Bukhara), Shash (Tashkent), and Altishahr (Kashgar, Yarkand) obviously constituted something like the hub of the Eurasian SR network also beyond that time (see above Maps 2.4, 2.5, 3.1–3.7, and 4.1–4.5).

There were many reasons for CA's post-fifteenth-century (first relative, then absolute) decline, most of them overlapping with the abovementioned causes of the post-Mongol SR decline: the legacy of weakened production potential due to the previous destruction of physical and human capital by Genghis Khan, his successors, and Timur; the impact of European discoveries and conquests (America from the late fifteenth century; the sea route from Europe to the Orient, which circumvented CA and was increasingly used from the early sixteenth century); the impact of European industrial advancement (C Asian states and economies, whether sedentary or nomadic, were outstripped by more sophisticated technologies of warfare and peaceful production from the seventeenth century); and religious and political factors (rising rigidity of regionally dominant Islam, increasing tendency of political instability inside C Asian polities, internecine warfare, and regional conflicts, seventeenth to eighteenth centuries).

The mid-nineteenth century finally brought the colonial incorporation of what had remained of independent CA into the sphere of European rule and swiftly into the modern capitalist world economy: regional trade and economic activity were restructured. CA had definitely become a raw material appendage of an increasingly integrated and global economic system led by European industrial powers.

C Asian Versus European Medieval Experiences: Some Feudal Commonalities, Differential Exposure to Invasions, No Urban Bourgeoisie on the SR

Overall, CA's economic history appears to fit in with Clive Ponting's broad view of the emergence of feudalism across Europe and Asia. As noted above, he explains that in new empires, the initial rulers had to solve three linked problems—how to reward their followers, how to control the newly conquered territories, and how to maintain armed forces. Similar solutions were adopted in most cases: Conquered land was parceled out to individuals within the elite so that they could use it to support a given number of soldiers to be provided to the ruler when required. Ponting points out that this system is called "feudalism" in European history but that it is merely one expression of a phenomenon that was common across Eurasia for millennia.

Whether properties were initially distributed as Islamic iqta, Turkic appanages or Mongol soyurghals, land and rights to collect taxes from people living or working on this land were thus granted in exchange for service to the state (typically of a military nature, providing for a contingent of mounted warriors). In some cases, authorized members of the elite also possessed independent judicial and immunity rights over respective inhabitants. While original land assignments were usually revocable by the C Asian ruler, with time, they tended to become hereditary. This favored piecemeal political and economic decentralization and particularism. Moreover, former nomadic conquerors often settled down and gradually forfeited their outstanding military capabilities. All this increased exposure to potential invaders, who often came from the Eurasian steppe. Thus the C Asian geopolitical cycle of (predominantly nomadic) conquest and apportionment of land, gradual weakening of central authority, partial sedentarization, erosion of defensive capabilities, and invasions by superior forces started anew.

The fact that Europe had not been as frequently and deeply affected or afflicted by nomadic invasions as this had been the case for the C Asian oasis belt, Russia, Ukraine, Iran, India, or China certainly constitutes a factor that afforded Europe a relative advantage in its economic development in the late Middle Ages. Another difference between Europe and CA or other parts of Eurasia was that an urban bourgeoisie equipped with special rights or class privileges comparable to those of Western municipalities did not emerge in CA. There was no salient distinction between the legal status of town dwellers and rural inhabitants. The entire population of a khanate or a steppe empire was principally subject to the ruler's absolute powers.

Stylized Cycles of Monetary Reforms, Inflation, and Currency Crises in CA

Disregarding China, which was one of the first countries worldwide to introduce paper money (from around 650 CE), C Asian economies typically used coins, pieces of precious metal, bullion, and silk as money (general medium of exchange, unit of account, and store of value). As in other polities, the temptation for rulers was strong to monopolize the issue of specie because of the sovereign appropriation of seignorage (the difference between the value of money and the cost to produce and distribute it). Again and again, attempts were made to maximize seignorage through overissuing, at high (later) economic costs and political risks.

In this sense, C Asian monetary policies tended to be quite active and monetary "regime changes" may have been almost as frequent as political ones. A recurrent pattern was that a new ruler carried out an (urgently needed) currency reform to provide a more stable monetary framework for the economy. Then, over time either the weight of a coin (legal tender) was gradually reduced, or the precious metal content of the coin was decreased, or the number of mints authorized to issue the coin was raised, in each case typically combined with an expansion in the circulation of the coin as well as of seignorage. The sustained boost of money circulation (unmatched by a commensurate increase of goods supply on markets) triggered growing inflation and, sooner or later, a debasement of the currency loomed. Once the population had lost trust in the currency and the situation had become unsustainable, the cycle would start anew.

Coming back to the degree of newness that paper money still embodied in the medieval world outside the Middle Kingdom, the Mongols' attempted transfer of this innovation from their Chinese to their Iranian dependencies in the 1290s did not work: As mentioned above, for Persian merchants, not familiar with centuries of Chinese experience with paper script, it probably appeared as something bizarrely new, bearing the imperial stamp of authority, but devoid of any familiar material value like precious metals. Businessmen in the bazaars rejected the newly issued paper currency despite or probably because of the authorities' efforts to force its adoption by requiring merchants to turn in their precious metals in return for receiving new legal tender. Many did not trust the authorities and perceived this policy as a thinly veiled attempt to confiscate valuable gold and silver for what they saw as worthless paper. Contemporary European travelers like Wilhelm von Roebroeck and Marco Polo are also reported to have been profoundly amazed upon discovering the use of paper money in China. Examples of C Asian currency reforms abound, just to mention some: Möngke Khan (Mongol Empire, 1250s), Masud Beg (Ulus Chagatay/Mongol Empire, 1270s),

Kebek Khan (Chagatay Khanate/Mongol Empire, 1320s), Emir Timur (Tamerlane Empire, 1390), Ulugh Begh (Transoxiana/ Timurid Emirates, 1428/29), Sultan Husain Baikara (Mavarannahr, Ferghana/Timurid Emirates, 1491/92), Shaybani Khan (Uzbek Khanate, 1506), Khan Abdullah II (Uzbek Khanate, late sixteenth century), Shah Murad (Emirate of Bukhara, late eighteenth century), Umar Khan (Khanate of Khoqand, early nineteenth century), and Qing authorities (Chinese Turkestan, 1830s).

5.4   From Domestic Modernization Attempts to European Colonization

Premodern C Asian Statehood: En Route to Patrimonialism?

C Asian polities or states do seem to display a tendency to move from originally tribal or kinship-based political authority to (eventual) patrimonial statehood (generally consisting of a standing army, a system of regular taxation, and a corps of removable civil servants/bureaucratic staff). This goes for polities that are at the outset sedentary or nomadic. The earliest empire on C Asian territory that already developed elements of patrimonial statehood was Achaemenid Persia (550–330 BCE). Yet frequent attacks by or conflicts with horseback nomads up to about 1700 CE again and again disrupted, set back, or in any case substantially modified political evolutions in affected societies. Even once nomadic military superiority was dwindling, descendents of former conquerors continued to enjoy various political and economic privileges, which were often only hesitantly repealed. Maybe a final breakthrough toward patrimonialism in CA can be attested for the late eighteenth and early nineteenth centuries, e.g., in the Emirate of Bukhara—a couple of decades before the European invasion.

The Era of the Steppe Empires Was Not Over Before the Eighteenth Century

The institutional failure to create an investor-friendly climate and to accumulate capital on a sustained basis contributed to weakening nomadic polities (in relative terms) over time or in any case did not help strengthening them. The era of the steppe empires definitely drew to a close in the second half of the eighteenth century, when the Dzungar Empire, which had launched the last large-scale and initially successful imperial undertaking built around a core steppe region, and which had even acquired the know-how and assembled its own modest firearms industry (also producing cannons), succumbed to external military blows. Only with this break and with CA's subjugation under external empires did the formative impact of C Asian political

structures come to an end. The definite marginalization of the region was completed in the nineteenth century when sedentary powers—a European maritime empire (Britain) and, more importantly, two Eurasian land empires (China and Russia)—had divided up the heart of the double continent among themselves.

In the Nineteenth Century, Traditional CA and the SR Were Finally Overrun by Modernity

After the Russian expansion and conquest of the whole of western CA, the southern part of the new colonial sphere (the oasis belt) was turned into a principal supplier of cotton to the czardom and the capitalist world. In this sense, cotton was hailed as the "white gold" of the past, comparable to oil as the "black gold" of today. Many native Uzbeks, Tajiks, Sarts, and others had to abandon their traditional economic activities, which were no longer competitive, and became cheaply remunerated dependent laborers. Soon thereafter, northern CA (the Kazakh grasslands) was turned into a vast new homeland for European (mostly Russian and Ukrainian) farmer settlers. The indigenous Kazakh population was marginalized and/or expelled: While the steppe dwellers were not entirely disarmed nor encapsulated in reservations, they were frequently pushed off into precarious steppe zones. Many European settlers arrived by rail, and West Turkestan was opened up and connected to Europe by railroad networks.

While Qing Chinese rule in Xinjiang in the second half of the eighteenth century had embodied a "developmental agrarian state" (Perdue) and delivered some impressive economic results, the Middle Kingdom suffered political and economic decline from the early nineteenth century onwards. Although Beijing had lost control of East Turkestan to a Muslim rebellion in the mid-1860s, it unexpectedly reconquered its western frontier province in the late 1870s. Reversing its previous policy of decentralized rule, the still weak government opted for a modernizing strategy of centrally launched reconstruction, control, and development of the province—with mixed results.

5.5   China's Pivotal Importance

China Remained the Economically Predominant and Most Resourceful Power Along the SR

Throughout almost the entire premodern era, the Middle Kingdom stood out as the economically preeminent and most resourceful power along the SR. China inaugurated the transcontinental trade network. Chinese silk was the most coveted merchandise for centuries, so much so, that it temporarily functioned as a de facto currency along the trade routes of the same name. Generally, trans-Eurasian flows of information proved far more influential in the east-west direction than in the west-east direction. Thus, various kinds of Chinese know-how were transferred west, e.g., papermaking, the compass, engraving printing, paper money, use of coal as fuel, gunpowder production, the abacus, and playing cards.

Chinese colonization and colonialism can boast of an age, a continuity, and a structural density that leave other colonial histories, e.g., European ones, far behind (Reinhard). On repeated occasions, the Middle Kingdom managed to militarily subjugate its nomadic and oriental neighbors (in antiquity, the Middle Ages, and in the eighteenth and nineteenth centuries) and rule large parts of CA, even if it also repeatedly lost control later. This is in contrast to other big sedentary states, who either did not have the resources to project their power into CA for a sustained period or only achieved success later. For instance, Czarist Russia (for the first time in its history) subjugated West Turkestan only about a century after the Qing dynasty had already conquered East Turkestan. Even when it was incorporated with other powers into the giant Mongol Empire (thirteenth to fourteenth centuries), China became the centerpiece of the mightiest sub-empire, the Empire of the Great Khan, whose capital was eventually moved from Karakorum (Mongolia) to Khanbalik/Beijing. Within the Mongol imperial world, the Chinese Yuan dynasty became predominant economically and militarily, even if its powers were not sufficient or not sufficiently deployed to hold the entire bicontinental colossus together.

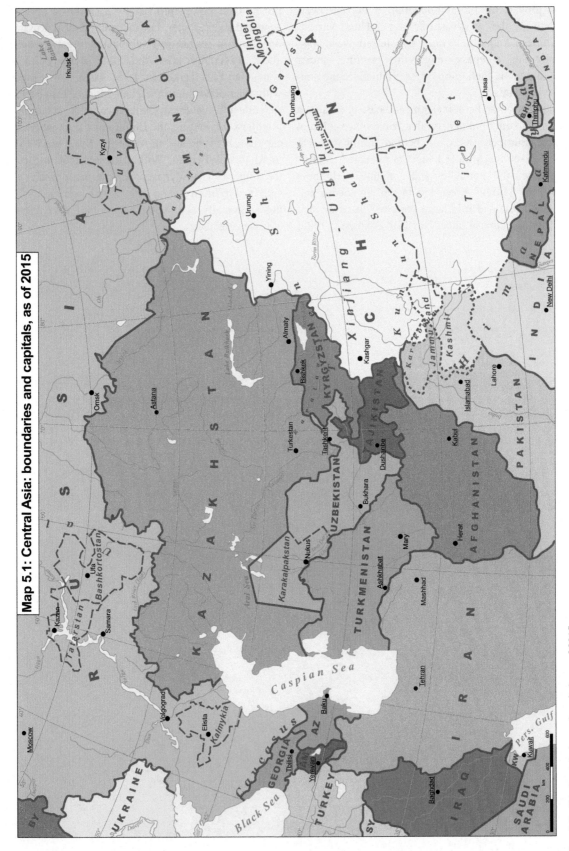

Map 5.1 CA: boundaries and capitals, as of 2015

Bibliography and Sources of Maps

Adle C, Palat M, Tabyshalieva A (eds) (2005) UNESCO: History of civilizations of CA, vol VI: Toward the contemporary period: from the mid-19th to the end of the 20th century

Asimov M, Bosworth C (eds) (1998) UNESCO: History of civilizations in CA – vol IV – The Age of Achievement A.D. 750 to the end of the 15th century

Barraclough G (ed) (2007) Atlas der Weltgeschichte (The Times Concise Atlas of World History)

Bertin J (ed) (1997) Atlas historique universel—Panorama de l'histoire du monde. Minerva, Genève

Besters-Dilger J (ed) (2003) Die Ukraine in Europa—Aktuelle Lage, Hintergründe und Perspektiven. Böhlau, Wien

Bohn T, Neutatz D (eds) (2009) Studienhandbuch Östliches Europa, Band 2: Geschichte des Russischen Reiches und der Sowjetunion. Böhlau, Wien

Borona G-L, Marzatico F (eds) (2007) Ori dei cavalieri delle steppe—Collezioni dai musei dell'Ucraina. Silvana Editoriale, Cinisello Balsamo

Chiao-Min Hsieh (1973) Atlas of China. McGraw-Hill, New York

di Cosmo N, Sinor D (eds) (1988) Handbook of oriental studies (Handbuch der Orientalistik), section 8: central Asian studies. Brill, Leiden

Edelmayer F, Feldbauer P, Wakounig M (eds) (2002) Globalgeschichte 1450–1620 – Anfänge und Perspektiven. Promedia, Wien

Engel J, Zeeden E-W (eds) (1981) Großer Historischer Weltatlas – Dritter Teil – Neuzeit. Bayerischer Schulbuch-Verlag, München

Ertl T (ed) (2013) Europas Aufstieg – Eine Spurensuche im späten Mittelalter. Mandelbaum, Wien

Ertl T, Limberger M (eds) (2009) Die Welt 1250–1500. Mandelbaum, Magnus, Wien

Farrington K (ed) (2002) Atlas der Weltreiche – Von 3000 v.Chr. bis zum 20. Jhdt. (Atlas of empires). Tosa, Wien

Federalnaya Sluzhba Geodesii i Kartografii Rossii (2002a) Atlas – Otechestvennaya istoria s drevneishikh vremen do kontsa XVIII veka. Roskartografia

Federalnaya Sluzhba Geodesii i Kartografii Rossii (2002b) Atlas – Otechestvennaya istoria XIX vek. Roskartografia

Feldbauer P, Hödl G, Lehners J-P (eds) (2009) Rhythmen der Globalisierung – Expansion und Kontraktion zwischen dem 13. und 20. Jahrhundert. Mandelbaum, Wien

Fischer Verlag (2016) Der Neue Fischer Weltalmanach 2017 – Zahlen, Daten, Fakten

Furtado P (ed) (2007) Der neue Atlas der Weltgeschichte – Von der Antike bis zur Gegenwart. Chronik, Gütersloh

Gauchon P (ed) (2006) Inde, Chine à l'assault du monde (Rapport Antheios). Presses Universitaires de France, Paris

Geo Spezial (ed) (2007/2008) Die Seidenstraße, No. 6, Dec/Jan

Gizi Map (2009a) China Northwest – Geographical Map

Gizi Map (2009b) Kazakhstan – Geographical Map

Gizi Map (2009c) Silk Road Countries – Geographical Map

Grandner M, Sonderegger A (eds) (2015) Nord-Süd-Ost-West-Beziehungen – Eine Einführung in die Globalgeschichte. Mandelbaum, Wien

L'Histoire (ed) (2013) Les Mongols – le plus grand empire du monde (dossier spécial), octobre

L'Histoire (ed) (2014) Inde, Chine – Atlas des mondes de l'Asie: Deux foyers de civilisation, La confrontation avec l'Europe, Une nouvelle aire de puissance, août

Jacquin P (2005) The Mongols and the West 1221–1410. Pearson, Harlow

Jackson P (2012) La politique indienne des Etats-Unis. In: L'Histoire (ed) L'aventure oubliée: Les indiens d'Amérique – Des Micmacs au Red Power

Khazanov A, Wink A (eds) (2001) Nomads in the sedentary world. Routledge, New York

Könemann L (ed) (2009) Historica – Der Große Atlas der Weltgeschichte mit über 1200 Karten. Parragon, Bath

Kruglikova O (2010a) Atlas po istorii Kazakhstana c dreveishikh vremen do XVIII veka. 8&8 Publishing House, Almaty

Kruglikova O (2010b) Istoria Kazakhstana XVII vek – nachalo XX veka. 8&8 Publishing House, Almaty

Kruglikova O (2010c) Atlas vsemirnaya istoria srednikh vekov. 8&8 Publishing House, Almaty

Marchand P (2012) Atlas géopolitique de la Russie – Puissance retrouvée. Autrement, Paris

Markov W et al (eds) (1981) Kleine Enzyklopaedie Weltgeschichte. VEB Bibliographisches Institut, Leipzig

McEvedy C (2002) The new penguin Atlas of ancient history. Penguin Books, London

Ministerstvo Obrazovania i Nauki Respubliki Kazakhstan (2010) Istoria Kazakhstana s drevneishikh vremen do nashikh dney v piati tomakh. Atamura

Le Monde (ed) (2009) Atlas des civilisations – 6000 ans d'histoire – 200 cartes

Mozja A (2007) Il principato Rus' di Kiev. In: Borona G-L, Marzatico F (eds) Ori dei cavalieri delle steppe – Collezioni dai musei dell'Ucraina. SilvanaEditoriale, Cinisello Balsamo

Neuer Konzenn-Atlas (Österreichischer Atlas für Höhere Schulen) (2009) Ed. Hölzel

Ott H, Schäfer H (eds) (1984) Wirtschaftsploetz 1984 – Wirtschaftsgeschichte zum Nachschlagen. Ploetz, Freiburg

Piatigorsky J, Sapir J (2009) Le Grand Jeu du 19e siècle – Les enjeux géopolitiques de l'Asie centrale. Autrement, Paris

Ponomarenko E, Dyck I (2007) Ancient Nomads of the Eurasian and North American Grasslands. Canadian Museum of Civilization, Samara Museum of History and Regional Studies

Postan M, Miller E (eds) (1987) The Cambridge economic history of Europe, vol 2. Cambridge University Press, Cambridge

Putzger (ed) (2011) Historischer Weltatlas. Cornelsen, Berlin

Rossiiskaya Akademia Nauk – Institut Vostokovedenia (1996) Azia – Dialog Tsivilizatsii. Giperion, St. Petersburg

Rudolf H-U, Oswalt V (eds) (2010) Taschenatlas Weltgeschichte. Ernst Klett, Gotha

Sapper M et al (eds) (2007) Machtmosaik Zentralasien – Traditionen, Restriktionen, Aspirationen. Osteuropa, September

Schottenhammer A, Feldbauer P (eds) (2011) Die Welt 1000–1250. Mandelbaum, Wien

Seidykhanova G (ed) (2011) Atlas po vsemirnoy istorii drevnego mira, Almaty

Sellier J, Sellier A (eds) (2002) Atlas des peuples d'Orient – Moyen Orient, Caucase, Asie centrale (La Découverte)

Serryn P (ed) (1994) Atlas Bordas géographique. Bordas, Paris

Sluglett P, Currie A (2014) Atlas of islamic history. Routledge, London

Stepanoff C, Ferret C, Lacaze G, Thorez J (2013) Nomadismes d'Asie centrale et septentrionale. Armand Colin, Paris

Starr F (ed) (2011) Ferghana valley – the heart of CA. Sharpe, Armonk, NY

Steffelbauer I, Hakami K (eds) (2006) Vom Alten Orient zum Nahen Osten. Magnus, Essen

Tasmagambetov I et al (eds) (2003) Atlas of Kazakhstan's geography. Globe, Almaty

Testot L (ed) (2008) Histoire globale – un nouveau regard sur le monde. Sciences Humaines, Auxerre

Testot L (ed) (2014/2015) La nouvelle histoire du monde—Un récit global. In: Histoire hors série no. 3, décembre-janvier

Tracy J (ed) (1990) The rise of merchant empires: long-distance trade in the early modern world 1350–1750. Cambridge University Press, Cambridge

Tremml-Werner B, Crailsheim E (eds) (2015) Audienzen und Allianzen – Interkulturelle Diplomatie in Asien und Europa vom 8. bis zum 18. Jhdt. Mandelbaum, Wien

UNESCO (1992) History of civilizations of CA, vols I–VI. UNESCO, Paris

VEB Hermann Haack (1981) Atlas zur Geschichte – Von den Anfängen der menschlichen Gesellschaft bis zum Vorabend der Oktoberrevolution 1917. Geographisch-Kartographische Anstalt, Gotha/Leipzig

Vernadsky G, Karpovich M (eds) (1953) A history of Russia. Yale University Press, New Haven

Wahlquist H (2004) Die Seidenstraße. In: Burenhult G (ed) Große Zivilisationen – Eine Kulturgeschichte der Menschheit von den Anfängen bis zur Gegenwart (Great civilizations – society and culture in the ancient world). Karl Müller, Köln

Whitfield S (ed) (2009) La Route de la soie – Un voyage à travers la vie et la mort. Fonds Mercator, Bruxelles

Zhumakanov E (2005) Atlas Istoria Kazakhstana XIX vek. 8&8 Publishing House, Almaty

Index

Printed by Printforce, the Netherlands